# THE DOCUMENTARY HISTORY OF THE RATIFICATION OF THE CONSTITUTION

## VOLUME XVII

### Commentaries on the Constitution
### Public and Private

Volume 5

# THE DOCUMENTARY HISTORY OF THE RATIFICATION OF THE CONSTITUTION

Volume XVII

# Commentaries on the Constitution

Public and Private

Volume 5
1 April to 9 May 1788

Editors

JOHN P. KAMINSKI     GASPARE J. SALADINO

Senior Associate Editor
RICHARD LEFFLER

Associate Editor
CHARLES H. SCHOENLEBER

Editorial Assistant
CHARLES D. HAGERMANN

MADISON
STATE HISTORICAL SOCIETY OF WISCONSIN
1 9 9 5

*The Documentary History of the Ratification of the Constitution* is sponsored by the National Historical Publications and Records Commission and the University of Wisconsin-Madison. Preparation of this volume was made possible by grants from the National Historical Publications and Records Commission; the National Endowment for the Humanities, an independent federal agency; the Lynde and Harry Bradley Foundation; the Evjue Foundation; the E. Gordon Fox Fund; the Oscar Rennebohm Foundation; and the Wisconsin Alumni Research Foundation. Publication was made possible in part by a grant from the National Historical Publications and Records Commission.

Manufactured in the United States of America

LIBRARY OF CONGRESS CATALOGING IN PUBLICATION DATA [REVISED]
Main entry under title:
The Documentary history of the ratification
    of the Constitution.
        Editors for v. 17: John P. Kaminski, Gaspare J. Saladino.
        Includes indexes.
        CONTENTS: v. 1. Constitutional documents and records,
1776–1787.—v. 2. Ratification of the Constitution by the States:
Pennsylvania.—v. 3. Ratification of the Constitution by the
States: Delaware, New Jersey, Georgia, Connecticut.—v. 8.
Ratification of the Constitution by the States: Virginia (1).—v. 9.
Ratification of the Constitution by the States: Virginia (2).—
v. 10. Ratification of the Constitution by the States: Virginia
(3).—v. 13. Commentaries on the Constitution, public and
private (1).—v. 14. Commentaries on the Constitution, public
and private (2).—v. 15. Commentaries on the Constitution,
public and private (3).—v. 16. Commentaries on the
Constitution, public and private (4).—v. 17. Commentaries on
the Constitution, public and private (5).
        1. United States—Constitutional history—Sources.
        I. Jensen, Merrill. II. Kaminski, John P. III. Saladino,
Gaspare J.
KF4502.D63        342'.73'029        75-14149
ISBN 0-87020-275-8        347.30229        AACR2

*To*
WILLIAM H. YOUNG

# Contents

# Acknowledgments

The editing of this volume was supported principally by grants from the National Historical Publications and Records Commission and the National Endowment for the Humanities. Substantial aid was provided by the Lynde and Harry Bradley Foundation, the Evjue Foundation, the E. Gordon Fox Fund, the Oscar Rennebohm Foundation, and the Wisconsin Alumni Research Foundation. Financial support has also been received from Frederick H. Campbell, Handy Bruce Fant, the Honorable Paul C. Gartzke, Mrs. Peter D. Humleker, Jr., and Jack McManus.

We extend our thanks to Gerald W. George, Roger A. Bruns, Nancy Sahli, and Richard N. Sheldon of the NHPRC; Margaret Scrymser and Douglas M. Arnold of the NEH; Michael S. Joyce and Hillel G. Fradkin of the Bradley Foundation; William H. Young of the Rennebohm Foundation; and Frederick W. Miller and David A. Zweifel of the Evjue Foundation.

A continuing debt of gratitude is owed to the administration, faculty, and staff of the University of Wisconsin-Madison, especially Chancellor David Ward; Dean John D. Wiley and Associate Dean W. Charles Read of the Graduate School; Dean Phillip R. Certain and former Acting Dean M. Crawford Young of the College of Letters and Science, and Margaret M. Sullivan and Donna C. Jahnke of the College's office of Personnel and Research Services; Arthur O. Hove of the office of the vice chancellor for academic affairs; Chair Kenneth S. Sacks, Vice Chair Jeanne Boydston, Sabrina L. Braaten, Sandra Heitzkey, Patricia L. Hepner, Mary L. Moffatt, Michelle Oddo-Marohn, and Kris Ann Ward of the Department of History; and Cheryl E. Gest, August P. Hackbart, Barbara M. Henn, Robert H. Perkl, Monya M. Schulenberg, and Mary Ann Stefonek of Research Administration. For aid in fund raising, we are indebted to these individuals from the University of Wisconsin Foundation: President Andrew A. Wilcox, Vice Presidents John W. Feldt and Martha A. Taylor, Director of Development Robert G. Lange, and Jennifer Kidon-DeKrey; and to Angela Lieurance formerly of the Foundation.

The staff of the State Historical Society of Wisconsin, our primary research library and our publisher, continues its invaluable support. In particular, we thank Director H. Nicholas Muller III, Associate Director Robert B. Thomasgard, Jr., James P. Danky, Michael Edmonds, James L. Hansen, Laura Hemming, Harold L. Miller, Sue Mueller, R. David Myers, and Geraldine E. Strey. The staffs of the Memorial and Law libraries of the University of Wisconsin-Madison have also been most helpful. At the Law Library, Mary Jo Koranda and Michael M. Morgalla were especially accommodating. Linda J. Pike, formerly of the Lafayette Papers, and Gail Walter helped in translating French-language documents, and Rick Hendricks of the Journals of don Diego de Vargas did the same for a Spanish-language document. Suzanne M. Desan and Laird Boswell of the University of Wisconsin's Department of History and Joan Leffler of its Department of German assisted in translating some difficult French- and Spanish-language passages. Others who have provided useful information or copies of documents are John Catanzariti and Eugene R. Sheridan of the Papers of Thomas Jefferson; Douglas E. Clanin of the Indiana Historical Society; Alice S. Creighton of the Special Collections Division, Nimitz Library, United States Naval Academy; Edward W. Hanson of the Papers of Robert Treat Paine; Mary Anne Hines of the Library Company of Philadelphia; Barbara B. Oberg of the Papers of Benjamin Franklin; Richard A. Ryerson of the Adams Papers; and Dorothy Twohig of the Papers of George Washington.

Several institutions have given permission to publish documents. We are grateful to them and to these staff members: Richard A. Ryerson, the Adams Papers, Massachusetts Historical Society; Jean Ashton and Bernard R. Crystal, Rare Book and Manuscript Library, Columbia University; and Daniel Meyer, Special Collections, University of Chicago Library.

Finally, we thank the project's former editorial assistants for their efforts: Marybeth Carlson, Ellen D. Goldlust, Cynthia L. Hecht, Cymbre G. Humphreys, and Daniel R. Modes.

# Organization

*The Documentary History of the Ratification of the Constitution* is divided into:

(1) *Constitutional Documents and Records, 1776–1787* (1 volume),

(2) *Ratification of the Constitution by the States* (13 volumes),

(3) *Commentaries on the Constitution: Public and Private* (6 volumes),

(4) *The Bill of Rights* (1 or 2 volumes).

*Constitutional Documents and Records, 1776–1787.*

This introductory volume, a companion to all of the other volumes, traces the constitutional development of the United States during its first twelve years. Cross-references to it appear frequently in other volumes when contemporaries refer to events and proposals from 1776 to 1787. The documents include: (1) the Declaration of Independence, (2) the Articles of Confederation, (3) ratification of the Articles, (4) proposed amendments to the Articles, proposed grants of power to Congress, and ordinances for the Western Territory, (5) the calling of the Constitutional Convention, (6) the appointment of Convention delegates, (7) the resolutions and draft constitutions of the Convention, (8) the report of the Convention, and (9) the Confederation Congress and the Constitution.

*Ratification of the Constitution by the States.*

The volumes are arranged in the order in which the states considered the Constitution. Although there are variations, the documents for each state are organized into the following groups: (1) commentaries from the adjournment of the Constitutional Convention to the meeting of the state legislature that called the state convention, (2) the proceedings of the legislature in calling the convention, (3) commentaries from the call of the convention until its meeting, (4) the election of convention delegates, (5) the proceedings of the convention, and (6) post-convention documents.

*Microfiche Supplements to Ratification of the Constitution by the States.*

Much of the material for each state is repetitious or peripheral but still valuable. Literal transcripts of this material are placed on microfiche supplements. Occasionally, photographic copies of significant manuscripts are also included.

The types of documents in the supplements are:

(1) newspaper items that repeat arguments, examples of which are printed in the state volumes,

(2) pamphlets that circulated primarily within one state and that are not printed in the state volumes or in *Commentaries,*

(3) letters that contain supplementary material about politics and social relationships,

(4) photographic copies of petitions with the names of signers,

(5) photographic copies of manuscripts such as notes of debates, and

(6) miscellaneous documents such as election certificates, attendance records, pay vouchers and other financial records, etc.

*Commentaries on the Constitution: Public and Private.*

This series contains newspaper items, pamphlets, and broadsides that circulated regionally or nationally. It also includes some private letters that give the writers' opinions of the Constitution in general or that report on the prospects for ratification in several states. Except for some grouped items, documents are arranged chronologically and are numbered consecutively throughout the six volumes. There are frequent cross-references between *Commentaries* and the state series.

*The Bill of Rights.*

The public and private debate on the Constitution continued in several states after ratification. It was centered on the issue of whether there should be amendments to the Constitution and the manner in which amendments should be proposed—by a second constitutional convention or by the new U.S. Congress. A bill of rights was proposed in the U.S. Congress on 8 June 1789. Twelve amendments were adopted on 25 September and were sent to the states on 2 October. This volume(s) will contain the documents related to the public and private debate over amendments, to the proposal of amendments by Congress, and to the ratification of the Bill of Rights by the states.

# Editorial Procedures

With a few exceptions all documents are transcribed literally. Obvious slips of the pen and errors in typesetting are silently corrected. When spelling or capitalization is unclear, modern usage is followed. Superscripts and interlineated material are lowered to the line. Crossed-out words are retained when significant.

Brackets are used for editorial insertions. Conjectural readings are enclosed in brackets with a question mark. Illegible and missing words are indicated by dashes enclosed in brackets. However, when the author's intent is obvious, illegible or missing material, up to five characters in length, has been silently provided.

All headings are supplied by the editors. Headings for letters contain the names of the writer and the recipient and the place and date of writing. Headings for newspapers contain the pseudonym, if any, and the name and date of the newspaper. Headings for broadsides and pamphlets contain the pseudonym and a shortened form of the title. Full titles of broadsides and pamphlets and information on authorship are given in editorial notes. Headings for public meetings contain the place and date of the meeting.

Salutations, closings of letters, addresses, endorsements, and docketings are deleted unless they provide important information, which is then either retained in the document or placed in editorial notes.

Contemporary footnotes and marginal notes are printed after the text of the document and immediately preceding editorial footnotes. Symbols, such as stars, asterisks, and daggers have been replaced by superscripts (a), (b), (c), etc.

Many documents, particularly letters, are excerpted when they contain material that is not directly relevant to ratification. When longer excerpts or entire documents have been printed elsewhere, or are included in the microfiche supplements, this fact is noted.

# Symbols

FOR MANUSCRIPTS, MANUSCRIPT DEPOSITORIES,
SHORT TITLES, AND CROSS-REFERENCES

## Manuscripts

| | |
|---|---|
| FC | File Copy |
| MS | Manuscript |
| RC | Recipient's Copy |
| Tr | Translation from Foreign Language |

## Manuscript Depositories

| | |
|---|---|
| CtHi | Connecticut Historical Society |
| CtY | Yale University |
| DeHi | Historical Society of Delaware |
| DLC | Library of Congress |
| DNA | National Archives |
| MB | Boston Public Library |
| MBNEH | New England Historic and Genealogical Society |
| MH | Harvard University |
| MHi | Massachusetts Historical Society |
| MWA | American Antiquarian Society |
| Nh-Ar | New Hampshire State Archives |
| NhHi | New Hampshire Historical Society |
| NHi | New-York Historical Society |
| NN | New York Public Library |
| NNC | Columbia University Libraries |
| NcD | Duke University |
| PHi | Historical Society of Pennsylvania |
| PPAmP | American Philosophical Society |
| PPL | Library Company of Philadelphia |
| ViHi | Virginia Historical Society |

## Short Titles

| | |
|---|---|
| Adams, *Defence of the Constitutions* | John Adams, *A Defence of the Constitutions of Government of the United States of America . . .* (3 vols., London, 1787–1788). |
| Blackstone, *Commentaries* | William Blackstone, *Commentaries on the Laws of England. In Four Books* (Re-printed from the British Copy, Page for Page with the Last Edition, 5 vols., Philadelphia, 1771–1772). Originally published in London from 1765 to 1769. |
| Boyd | Julian P. Boyd et al., eds., *The Papers of Thomas Jefferson* (Princeton, N.J., 1950–). |
| Burgh, *Political Disquisitions* | James Burgh, *Political Disquisitions: or, An Enquiry into Public Errors, Defects, and Abuses . . .* (3 vols., London, 1774–1775). |
| Butterfield, *Rush* | L. H. Butterfield, ed., *Letters of Benjamin Rush* (2 vols., Princeton, N.J., 1951). |
| DHFFE | Merrill Jensen, Robert A. Becker, and Gordon DenBoer, eds., *The Documentary History of the First Federal Elections, 1788–1790* (4 vols., Madison, Wis., 1976–1989). |
| Evans | Charles Evans, *American Bibliography* (12 vols., Chicago, 1903–1934). |
| Farrand | Max Farrand, ed., *The Records of the Federal Convention of 1787* (3rd ed., 3 vols., New Haven, Conn., 1927). |
| Fitzpatrick | John C. Fitzpatrick, ed., *The Writings of George Washington . . .* (39 vols., Washington, D.C., 1931–1944). |
| Ford, *Pamphlets* | Paul Leicester Ford, ed., *Pamphlets on the Constitution of the United States, Published during Its Discussion by the People 1787–1788* (Brooklyn, N.Y., 1888). |
| JCC | Worthington C. Ford et al., eds., *Journals of the Continental Congress, 1774–1789 . . .* (34 vols., Washington, D.C., 1904–1937). |
| Kline, *Burr* | Mary-Jo Kline, ed., *Political Correspondence and Public Papers of Aaron Burr* (2 vols., Princeton, N.J., 1983). |
| LMCC | Edmund C. Burnett, ed., *Letters of Members of the Continental Congress* (8 vols., Washington, D.C., 1921–1936). |

| | |
|---|---|
| McRee, *Iredell* | Griffith J. McRee, ed., *Life and Correspondence of James Iredell* . . . (2 vols., New York, 1857–1858). |
| Montesquieu, *Spirit of Laws* | Charles, Baron de Montesquieu, *The Spirit of Laws* (Translated from the French by Thomas Nugent, 5th ed., 2 vols., London, 1773). Originally published in Geneva in 1748. |
| PCC | Papers of the Continental Congress, 1774–1789 (Record Group 360, National Archives). |
| Rutland, *Madison* | Robert A. Rutland et al., eds., *The Papers of James Madison*, Volumes VIII– (Chicago, Ill., and Charlottesville, Va., 1973–). |
| Rutland, *Mason* | Robert A. Rutland, ed., *The Papers of George Mason, 1725–1792* (3 vols., Chapel Hill, N.C., 1970). |
| Shaw-Shoemaker | Ralph R. Shaw, Richard H. Shoemaker, and Frances P. Newton, *American Bibliography: A Preliminary Checklist, 1801 to 1819* (23 vols., New York and Metuchen, N.J., 1958–1983). |
| Smyth, *Franklin* | Albert Henry Smyth, ed., *The Writings of Benjamin Franklin* . . . (10 vols., New York, 1905–1907). |
| Syrett | Harold C. Syrett, ed., *The Papers of Alexander Hamilton* (27 vols., New York, 1961–1987). |
| Thorpe | Francis N. Thorpe, ed., *The Federal and State Constitutions* . . . (7 vols., Washington, D.C., 1909). |
| *Washington Diaries* | Donald Jackson and Dorothy Twohig, eds., *The Diaries of George Washington* (6 vols., Charlottesville, Va., 1976–1979). |

## Cross-references to Volumes of
### *The Documentary History of the Ratification of the Constitution*

| | |
|---|---|
| CC | References to *Commentaries on the Constitution* are cited as "CC" followed by the number of the document. For example: "CC:25." |
| CDR | References to the first volume, titled *Constitutional Documents and Records, 1776–1787*, are cited as "CDR" followed by the page number. For example: "CDR, 325." |
| RCS | References to the series of volumes titled *Ratification of the Constitution by the States* are cited as "RCS" followed by the abbreviation of the state and the page number. For example: "RCS:Pa., 325." |
| Mfm | References to the microform supplements to the "RCS" volumes are cited as "Mfm" followed by the abbreviation of the state and the number of the document. For example: "Mfm:Pa. 25." |

# Calendar for the Years
## 1787–1788

### 1787

|  | S M T W T F S<br>JANUARY | S M T W T F S<br>FEBRUARY | S M T W T F S<br>MARCH | S M T W T F S<br>APRIL |
|---|---|---|---|---|

**JANUARY**
```
S  M  T  W  T  F  S
      1  2  3  4  5  6
 7  8  9 10 11 12 13
14 15 16 17 18 19 20
21 22 23 24 25 26 27
28 29 30 31
```

**FEBRUARY**
```
S  M  T  W  T  F  S
               1  2  3
 4  5  6  7  8  9 10
11 12 13 14 15 16 17
18 19 20 21 22 23 24
25 26 27 28
```

**MARCH**
```
S  M  T  W  T  F  S
               1  2  3
 4  5  6  7  8  9 10
11 12 13 14 15 16 17
18 19 20 21 22 23 24
25 26 27 28 29 30 31
```

**APRIL**
```
S  M  T  W  T  F  S
 1  2  3  4  5  6  7
 8  9 10 11 12 13 14
15 16 17 18 19 20 21
22 23 24 25 26 27 28
29 30
```

**MAY**
```
S  M  T  W  T  F  S
         1  2  3  4  5
 6  7  8  9 10 11 12
13 14 15 16 17 18 19
20 21 22 23 24 25 26
27 28 29 30 31
```

**JUNE**
```
S  M  T  W  T  F  S
                  1  2
 3  4  5  6  7  8  9
10 11 12 13 14 15 16
17 18 19 20 21 22 23
24 25 26 27 28 29 30
```

**JULY**
```
S  M  T  W  T  F  S
 1  2  3  4  5  6  7
 8  9 10 11 12 13 14
15 16 17 18 19 20 21
22 23 24 25 26 27 28
29 30 31
```

**AUGUST**
```
S  M  T  W  T  F  S
            1  2  3  4
 5  6  7  8  9 10 11
12 13 14 15 16 17 18
19 20 21 22 23 24 25
26 27 28 29 30 31
```

**SEPTEMBER**
```
S  M  T  W  T  F  S
                     1
 2  3  4  5  6  7  8
 9 10 11 12 13 14 15
16 17 18 19 20 21 22
23 24 25 26 27 28 29
30
```

**OCTOBER**
```
S  M  T  W  T  F  S
    1  2  3  4  5  6
 7  8  9 10 11 12 13
14 15 16 17 18 19 20
21 22 23 24 25 26 27
28 29 30 31
```

**NOVEMBER**
```
S  M  T  W  T  F  S
            1  2  3
 4  5  6  7  8  9 10
11 12 13 14 15 16 17
18 19 20 21 22 23 24
25 26 27 28 29 30
```

**DECEMBER**
```
S  M  T  W  T  F  S
                     1
 2  3  4  5  6  7  8
 9 10 11 12 13 14 15
16 17 18 19 20 21 22
23 24 25 26 27 28 29
30 31
```

### 1788

**JANUARY**
```
S  M  T  W  T  F  S
      1  2  3  4  5
 6  7  8  9 10 11 12
13 14 15 16 17 18 19
20 21 22 23 24 25 26
27 28 29 30 31
```

**FEBRUARY**
```
S  M  T  W  T  F  S
                  1  2
 3  4  5  6  7  8  9
10 11 12 13 14 15 16
17 18 19 20 21 22 23
24 25 26 27 28 29
```

**MARCH**
```
S  M  T  W  T  F  S
                     1
 2  3  4  5  6  7  8
 9 10 11 12 13 14 15
16 17 18 19 20 21 22
23 24 25 26 27 28 29
30 31
```

**APRIL**
```
S  M  T  W  T  F  S
         1  2  3  4  5
 6  7  8  9 10 11 12
13 14 15 16 17 18 19
20 21 22 23 24 25 26
27 28 29 30
```

**MAY**
```
S  M  T  W  T  F  S
               1  2  3
 4  5  6  7  8  9 10
11 12 13 14 15 16 17
18 19 20 21 22 23 24
25 26 27 28 29 30 31
```

**JUNE**
```
S  M  T  W  T  F  S
 1  2  3  4  5  6  7
 8  9 10 11 12 13 14
15 16 17 18 19 20 21
22 23 24 25 26 27 28
29 30
```

**JULY**
```
S  M  T  W  T  F  S
         1  2  3  4  5
 6  7  8  9 10 11 12
13 14 15 16 17 18 19
20 21 22 23 24 25 26
27 28 29 30 31
```

**AUGUST**
```
S  M  T  W  T  F  S
                  1  2
 3  4  5  6  7  8  9
10 11 12 13 14 15 16
17 18 19 20 21 22 23
24 25 26 27 28 29 30
31
```

**SEPTEMBER**
```
S  M  T  W  T  F  S
    1  2  3  4  5  6
 7  8  9 10 11 12 13
14 15 16 17 18 19 20
21 22 23 24 25 26 27
28 29 30
```

**OCTOBER**
```
S  M  T  W  T  F  S
         1  2  3  4
 5  6  7  8  9 10 11
12 13 14 15 16 17 18
19 20 21 22 23 24 25
26 27 28 29 30 31
```

**NOVEMBER**
```
S  M  T  W  T  F  S
                     1
 2  3  4  5  6  7  8
 9 10 11 12 13 14 15
16 17 18 19 20 21 22
23 24 25 26 27 28 29
30
```

**DECEMBER**
```
S  M  T  W  T  F  S
       1  2  3  4  5  6
 7  8  9 10 11 12 13
14 15 16 17 18 19 20
21 22 23 24 25 26 27
28 29 30 31
```

# American Newspapers, 1787–1788

## SHORT TITLE LIST

The following short titles of selected newspapers and magazines are arranged alphabetically within each state. The full titles, the frequency of publication, the names of printers and publishers, and other information about all the newspapers of the period are contained in Clarence S. Brigham, *History and Bibliography of American Newspapers, 1690–1820* (2 vols., Worcester, Mass., 1947), and in his "*Additions and Corrections to* History and Bibliography of American Newspapers, 1690–1820," *Proceedings* of the American Antiquarian Society, LXXI, Part I (1961), 15–62. Similar data on magazines is in the first volume of Frank Luther Mott, *A History of American Magazines* (5 vols., New York and London, 1930–1968).

CONNECTICUT
*American Mercury*, Hartford
*Connecticut Courant*, Hartford
*Connecticut Gazette*, New London
*Connecticut Journal*, New Haven
*Fairfield Gazette*
*Middlesex Gazette*, Middletown
*New Haven Chronicle*
*New Haven Gazette*
*Norwich Packet*
*Weekly Monitor*, Litchfield

DELAWARE
*Delaware Courant*, Wilmington
*Delaware Gazette*, Wilmington

GEORGIA
*Gazette of the State of Georgia*, Savannah
*Georgia State Gazette*, Augusta

MARYLAND
*Maryland Chronicle*, Fredericktown
*Maryland Gazette*, Annapolis
*Maryland Gazette*, Baltimore
*Maryland Journal*, Baltimore
*Palladium of Freedom*, Baltimore

MASSACHUSETTS
*American Centinel*, Pittsfield
*American Herald*, Boston
*American Recorder*, Charlestown
*Berkshire Chronicle*, Pittsfield
*Boston Gazette*
*Continental Journal*, Boston
*Cumberland Gazette*, Portland, Maine
*Essex Journal*, Newburyport
*Hampshire Chronicle*, Springfield
*Hampshire Gazette*, Northampton
*Herald of Freedom*, Boston
*Independent Chronicle*, Boston
*Massachusetts Centinel*, Boston
*Massachusetts Gazette*, Boston
*Salem Mercury*
*Worcester Magazine/Massachusetts Spy*

NEW HAMPSHIRE
*Freeman's Oracle*, Exeter
*New Hampshire Gazette*, Portsmouth
*New Hampshire Mercury*, Portsmouth
*New Hampshire Recorder*, Keene
*New Hampshire Spy*, Portsmouth

NEW JERSEY
*Brunswick Gazette*, New Brunswick
*New Jersey Journal*, Elizabeth Town
*Trenton Mercury*

## NEW YORK

*Albany Gazette*
*Albany Journal*
*American Magazine*, New York
*Country Journal*, Poughkeepsie
*Daily Advertiser*, New York
*Federal Herald*, Albany
*Hudson Weekly Gazette*
*Impartial Gazetteer*, New York
*Independent Journal*, New York
*New York Gazetteer*
*New York Journal*
*New York Morning Post*
*New York Museum*
*New York Packet*
*Northern Centinel*, Lansingburgh

## PENNSYLVANIA

*American Museum*, Philadelphia
*Carlisle Gazette*
*Columbian Magazine*, Philadelphia
*Evening Chronicle*, Philadelphia
*Federal Gazette*, Philadelphia
*Freeman's Journal*, Philadelphia
*Germantauner Zeitung*
*Independent Gazetteer*, Philadelphia
*Lancaster Zeitung*
*Pennsylvania Chronicle*, York
*Pennsylvania Gazette*, Philadelphia
*Pennsylvania Herald*, Philadelphia
*Pennsylvania Journal*, Philadelphia
*Pennsylvania Mercury*, Philadelphia
*Pennsylvania Packet*, Philadelphia
*Philadelphische Correspondenz*
*Pittsburgh Gazette*

## NORTH CAROLINA

*North Carolina Gazette*, Edenton
*North Carolina Gazette*, New Bern
*State Gazette of North Carolina*, New Bern
*Wilmington Centinel*

## RHODE ISLAND

*Newport Herald*
*Newport Mercury*
*Providence Gazette*
*United States Chronicle*, Providence

## SOUTH CAROLINA

*Charleston Morning Post/City Gazette*
*Columbian Herald*, Charleston
*South Carolina Weekly Chronicle*, Charleston
*State Gazette of South Carolina*, Charleston

## VIRGINIA

*Kentucke Gazette*, Lexington
*Norfolk and Portsmouth Journal*, Norfolk
*Virginia Centinel*, Winchester
*Virginia Gazette*, Petersburg
*Virginia Gazette*, Winchester
*Virginia Gazette and Independent Chronicle*, Richmond
*Virginia Gazette and Weekly Advertiser*, Richmond
*Virginia Herald*, Fredericksburg
*Virginia Independent Chronicle*, Richmond
*Virginia Journal*, Alexandria

## VERMONT

*Vermont Gazette*, Bennington
*Vermont Journal*, Windsor

# Chronology, 1786–1791

## 1786

| | |
|---|---|
| 21 January | Virginia calls meeting to consider granting Congress power to regulate trade. |
| 11–14 September | Annapolis Convention. |
| 20 September | Congress receives Annapolis Convention report recommending that states elect delegates to a convention at Philadelphia in May 1787. |
| 11 October | Congress appoints committee to consider Annapolis Convention report. |
| 23 November | Virginia authorizes election of delegates to Convention at Philadelphia. |
| 23 November | New Jersey elects delegates. |
| 4 December | Virginia elects delegates. |
| 30 December | Pennsylvania elects delegates. |

## 1787

| | |
|---|---|
| 6 January | North Carolina elects delegates. |
| 17 January | New Hampshire elects delegates. |
| 3 February | Delaware elects delegates. |
| 10 February | Georgia elects delegates. |
| 21 February | Congress calls Constitutional Convention. |
| 22 February | Massachusetts authorizes election of delegates. |
| 28 February | New York authorizes election of delegates. |
| 3 March | Massachusetts elects delegates. |
| 6 March | New York elects delegates. |
| 8 March | South Carolina elects delegates. |
| 14 March | Rhode Island refuses to elect delegates. |
| 23 April–26 May | Maryland elects delegates. |
| 5 May | Rhode Island again refuses to elect delegates. |
| 14 May | Convention meets; quorum not present. |
| 14–17 May | Connecticut elects delegates. |
| 25 May | Convention begins with quorum of seven states. |
| 16 June | Rhode Island again refuses to elect delegates. |
| 27 June | New Hampshire renews election of delegates. |
| 13 July | Congress adopts Northwest Ordinance. |
| 6 August | Committee of Detail submits draft constitution to Convention. |
| 12 September | Committee of Style submits draft constitution to Convention. |
| 17 September | Constitution signed and Convention adjourns *sine die*. |
| 20 September | Congress reads Constitution. |
| 26–28 September | Congress debates Constitution. |
| 28 September | Congress transmits Constitution to the states. |
| 28–29 September | Pennsylvania calls state convention. |
| 17 October | Connecticut calls state convention. |
| 25 October | Massachusetts calls state convention. |
| 26 October | Georgia calls state convention. |
| 31 October | Virginia calls state convention. |
| 1 November | New Jersey calls state convention. |

| | |
|---|---|
| 6 November | Pennsylvania elects delegates to state convention. |
| 10 November | Delaware calls state convention. |
| 12 November | Connecticut elects delegates to state convention. |
| 19 November–<br>7 January 1788 | Massachusetts elects delegates to state convention. |
| 20 November–<br>15 December | Pennsylvania Convention. |
| 26 November | Delaware elects delegates to state convention. |
| 27 November–<br>1 December | Maryland calls state convention. |
| 27 November–<br>1 December | New Jersey elects delegates to state convention. |
| 3–7 December | Delaware Convention. |
| 4–5 December | Georgia elects delegates to state convention. |
| 6 December | North Carolina calls state convention. |
| 7 December | Delaware Convention ratifies Constitution, 30 to 0. |
| 11–20 December | New Jersey Convention. |
| 12 December | Pennsylvania Convention ratifies Constitution, 46 to 23. |
| 14 December | New Hampshire calls state convention. |
| 18 December | New Jersey Convention ratifies Constitution, 38 to 0. |
| 25 December–<br>5 January 1788 | Georgia Convention. |
| 31 December | Georgia Convention ratifies Constitution, 26 to 0. |
| 31 December–<br>12 February 1788 | New Hampshire elects delegates to state convention. |

## 1788

| | |
|---|---|
| 3–9 January | Connecticut Convention. |
| 9 January | Connecticut Convention ratifies Constitution, 128 to 40. |
| 9 January–<br>7 February | Massachusetts Convention. |
| 19 January | South Carolina calls state convention. |
| 1 February | New York calls state convention. |
| 6 February | Massachusetts Convention ratifies Constitution, 187 to 168, and proposes amendments. |
| 13–22 February | New Hampshire Convention: first session. |
| 1 March | Rhode Island calls statewide referendum on Constitution. |
| 3–27 March | Virginia elects delegates to state convention. |
| 24 March | Rhode Island referendum: voters reject Constitution, 2,711 to 239. |
| 28–29 March | North Carolina elects delegates to state convention. |
| 7 April | Maryland elects delegates to state convention. |
| 11–12 April | South Carolina elects delegates to state convention. |
| 21–29 April | Maryland Convention. |
| 26 April | Maryland Convention ratifies Constitution, 63 to 11. |
| 29 April–3 May | New York elects delegates to state convention. |
| 12–24 May | South Carolina Convention. |
| 23 May | South Carolina Convention ratifies Constitution, 149 to 73, and proposes amendments. |
| 2–27 June | Virginia Convention. |
| 17 June–26 July | New York Convention. |
| 18–21 June | New Hampshire Convention: second session. |

21 June          New Hampshire Convention ratifies Constitution, 57 to 47, and proposes amendments.
25 June          Virginia Convention ratifies Constitution, 89 to 79.
27 June          Virginia Convention proposes amendments.
2 July           New Hampshire ratification read in Congress; Congress appoints committee to report an act for putting the Constitution into operation.
21 July–4 August First North Carolina Convention.
26 July          New York Convention Circular Letter calls for second constitutional convention.
26 July          New York Convention ratifies Constitution, 30 to 27, and proposes amendments.
2 August         North Carolina Convention proposes amendments and refuses to ratify until amendments are submitted to Congress and to a second constitutional convention.
13 September     Congress sets dates for election of President and meeting of new government under the Constitution.
20 November      Virginia requests Congress under the Constitution to call a second constitutional convention.
30 November      North Carolina calls second state convention.

### 1789

7 February       New York requests Congress under the Constitution to call a second constitutional convention.
4 March          First Federal Congress convenes.
1 April          House of Representatives attains quorum.
6 April          Senate attains quorum.
30 April         George Washington inaugurated first President.
8 June           James Madison proposes Bill of Rights in Congress.
21–22 August     North Carolina elects delegates to second state convention.
25 September     Congress adopts twelve amendments to Constitution to be submitted to the states.
16–23 November   Second North Carolina Convention.
21 November      Second North Carolina Convention ratifies Constitution, 194 to 77, and proposes amendments.

### 1790

17 January       Rhode Island calls state convention.
8 February       Rhode Island elects delegates to state convention.
1–6 March        Rhode Island Convention: first session.
24–29 May        Rhode Island Convention: second session.
29 May           Rhode Island Convention ratifies Constitution, 34 to 32, and proposes amendments.

### 1791

15 December      Bill of Rights adopted.

*Commentaries on the Constitution*
*Public and Private*

## 655. St. John de Crevecoeur to William Short
### New York, 1 April (excerpt)[1]

... I am as Anxious to learn what is going on in Europe, & in particular in France as you are Impatient to know of the Progress that the new Constitution is making—6 States have already accepted it as you already doubtless know [from your Letters?], the adoption by Massachusetts was only by a Majority of 18. in the course of the Month we will know what Maryland will do.—here it is said that the most important People are all federalists; but that is not the case in Virginia, Mr. Maddisson left us almost a Month ago to return to Virginia,[2] where his Friends had a great desire to elect him a Member of the Convention for the County where he lives; the two parties are preparing themselves for the debates that I fear will be long & full of rancor—Until now the choice that was made appears to be favorable & in order to give you an Idea of it I am sending you the List of those who have already been elected[3]—Gl. Washington Always Wise & Modest, says Nothing, although his Name has a great Influence on the opinion of a great many People—they say that the greatest obstacle to the adoption of the new Constitution in Virginia, are debts & dignity; in effect, one can see that those who owe much look to put off the Establisht. of a Govt. that promises to all the most Impartial Justice—as for dignity, say those who know Virginia better than I, there are a great many People who fear to see their personal Importance eclipsed, by the brilliance of a truly Federal & Energetic Govt.—we have not yet had news of the Election of Mr. Maddisson it will not come until Saturday's Post[4]—in the most antifederalist Counties, the people have elected as delegates not those in whom they have had confidence up to now but several Sheriffs which appears a little Extraordinary, furthermore that happened in not a few Counties—One waits at this Moment of such great Importance for the choice that everyone is Interested in, & I, a great federalist, Judge as if I were right there—in effect, ⟨To be or not be a nation, what alternative,⟩[5] destruction or to plunge into anarchy, & divisions; if it forms two Confederations as P. Henry wishes,[6] goodbye to the Peace & the happiness of this Country; the convention of Maryland is to be held on the 31 of this Month, this state's 17. June, Virginia's the last week of the same Month, South Carolina's 12 May, North Carolina's July 4, & New Hampshire's the last week in June—you know, no doubt, what happened in the latter State. Federalists, fearing to lose the question, consented to adjourn at this Time in the hope of being able to Convert those men in the Minority;[7] are you afraid that in the 4 States of New England they are so weary of

3

this Government themselves that they long for Monarchy & that a very great number of people in some Counties would prefer to live once more under english administration—Lord Dorchester, Governor of Canada, has Spies everywhere; this City is full of them, as are the States to the East;[8] what would become of all these states if just once they were to disunite?—this Country Approaches a Time more Prickly, more dangerous than that of the War but I hope that the Stock of Reason & of good Sense for which this country is so distinguished that truly enlightened men will Turn the scale toward the Side of good; it remains to be seen how men who have been without check & without laws for so long a Time will submit to the Salutary check that is being readied for them. . . .

1. RC (Tr), Short Papers, DLC. The letter was endorsed: "Crevecoeur—April 1./June—14." The first portion of it (not printed here) is almost entirely in English, while the rest is in French.

2. James Madison left New York City (and Congress) for his home in Orange County on either 3 or 4 March (RCS:Va., 602).

3. Crevecoeur probably refers to a list of delegates reprinted in a New York City newspaper from Virginia newspapers. Such lists appeared in the *New York Journal* on 28 March and the *Daily Advertiser* on the 29th. (For Virginia Convention election returns as reported in Virginia newspapers, see Mfm:Va. 59, especially the *Virginia Independent Chronicle*, 19 March.)

4. On 24 March Madison and James Gordon, Jr., both supporters of the Constitution, were elected to represent Orange County in the Virginia Convention. (For the Orange County election, see RCS:Va., 595–606.)

5. The text in angle brackets is in English.

6. For Patrick Henry's alleged interest in establishing a separate confederacy, see CC:276, note 4; and RCS:Va.

7. For the adjournment of the New Hampshire Convention to 18 June, see CC:554.

8. For the American fear of British domination, see CC:5. See also *Massachusetts Centinel*, 12 April (Appendix I, below) and 2 July (CC:Vol. 6, Appendix I).

## 656. Publius: The Federalist 76
### New York Packet, 1 April

This essay, written by Alexander Hamilton, was reprinted in the New York *Independent Journal* on 2 April. It was number 76 in the M'Lean edition and number 75 in the newspapers.

For a general discussion of the authorship, circulation, and impact of *The Federalist*, see CC:201, 406, 639, and Editors' Note, 28 May.

The FŒDERALIST, No. 75.

*To the People of the State of New-York.*

The President is "to *nominate*[1] and by and with the advice and consent of the Senate to appoint Ambassadors, other public Ministers and Consuls, Judges of the Supreme Court, and all other officers of the

United States, whose appointments are not otherwise provided for in the Constitution.[2] But the Congress may by law vest the appointment of such inferior officers as they think proper in the President alone, or in the Courts of law, or in the heads of departments. The President shall have power to fill up *all vacancies* which may happen *during the recess of the Senate*, by granting commissions which shall *expire* at the end of their next session."

It has been observed in a former paper, "that the true test of a good government is its aptitude and tendency to produce a good administration."[3] If the justness of this observation be admitted, the mode of appointing the officers of the United States contained in the foregoing clauses, must when examined be allowed to be entitled to particular commendation. It is not easy to conceive a plan better calculated than this, to produce a judicious choice of men for filling the offices of the Union; and it will not need proof, that on this point must essentially depend the character of its administration.

It will be agreed on all hands, that the power of appointment in ordinary cases ought to be modified in one of three ways. It ought either to be vested in a single man—or in a *select* assembly of a moderate number—or in a single man with the concurrence of such an assembly. The exercise of it by the people at large, will be readily admitted to be impracticable; as, waving every other consideration it would leave them little time to do any thing else. When therefore mention is made in the subsequent reasonings of an assembly or body of men, what is said must be understood to relate to a select body or assembly of the description already given. The people collectively from their number and from their dispersed situation cannot be regulated in their movements by that systematic spirit of cabal and intrigue, which will be urged as the chief objections to reposing the power in question in a body of men.

Those who have themselves reflected upon the subject, or who have attended to the observations made in other parts of these papers, in relation to the appointment of the President, will I presume agree to the position that there would always be great probability of having the place supplied by a man of abilities, at least respectable. Premising this, I proceed to lay it down as a rule, that one man of discernment is better fitted to analise and estimate the peculiar qualities adapted to particular offices, than a body of men of equal, or perhaps even of superior discernment.

The sole and undivided responsibility of one man will naturally beget a livelier sense of duty and a more exact regard to reputation. He will on this account feel himself under stronger obligations, and more interested to investigate with care the qualities requisite to the stations to be filled, and to prefer with impartiality the persons who may have the fairest pretensions to them. He will have *fewer* personal attachments to gratify than a body of men, who may each be supposed to have an equal number, and will be so much the less liable to be misled by the sentiments of friendship and of affection. A single well directed man by a single understanding, cannot be distracted and warped by that diversity of views, feelings and interests, which frequently distract and warp the resolutions of a collective body.[4] There is nothing so apt to agitate the passions of mankind as personal considerations, whether they relate to ourselves or to others, who are to be the objects of our choice or preference. Hence, in every exercise of the power of appointing to offices by an assembly of men, we must expect to see a full display of all the private and party likings and dislikes, partialities and antipathies, attachments and animosities, which are felt by those who compose the assembly. The choice which may at any time happen to be made under such circumstances will of course be the result either of a victory gained by one party over the other, or of a compromise between the parties. In either case, the intrinsic merit of the candidate will be too often out of sight. In the first, the qualifications best adapted to uniting the suffrages of the party will be more considered than[5] those which fit the person for the station. In the last the coalition will commonly turn upon some interested equivalent—"Give us the man we wish for this office, and you shall have the one you wish for that." This will be the usual condition of the bargain. And it will rarely happen that the advancement of the public service will be the primary object either of party victories or of party negociations.

The truth of the principles here advanced seems to have been felt by the most intelligent of those who have found fault with the provision made in this respect by the Convention. They contend that the President ought solely to have been authorized to make the appointments under the Fœderal Government. But it is easy to shew that every advantage to be expected from such an arrangement would in substance be derived from the power of *nomination*, which is proposed to be conferred upon him; while several disadvantages which might attend the absolute power of appointment in the hands of that officer, would be avoided. In the act of nomination his judgment alone would be exercised; and as it would be his sole duty to point out the man, who with the approbation of the Senate should fill an office, his responsibility would be as complete as if he were to make the final appointment. There can in this view be no difference between nominating and appointing. The same motives which would influence a proper discharge of his duty in one case would exist in the other. And as no man could be appointed, but upon his previous nomination, every man who might be appointed would be in fact his choice.

⟨But might not his nomination be overruled?—I grant it might, yet this could⟩[6] only be to make place for another nomination by himself. The person ultimately appointed must be the object of his preference, though perhaps not in the first degree. It is also not very probable that his nomination would often be overruled. The Senate could not be tempted by the preference they might feel to another to reject the one proposed; because they could not assure themselves that the person they might wish would be brought forward by a second or by any subsequent nomination. They could not even be certain that a future nomination would present a candidate in any degree more acceptable to them: And as their dissent might cast a kind of stigma upon the individual rejected; and might have the appearance of a reflection upon the judgment of the chief magistrate; it is not likely that their sanction would often be refused, where there were not special and strong reasons for the refusal.

To what purpose then require the co-operation of the Senate? I answer that the necessity of their concurrence would have a powerful, though in general a silent operation. It would be an excellent check upon a spirit of favoritism in the President, and would tend greatly to preventing the appointment of unfit characters from State prejudice, from family connection, from personal attachment, or from a view to popularity. And, in addition to this, it would be an efficacious source of stability in the administration.

It will readily be comprehended, that a man, who had himself the sole disposition of offices, would be governed much more by his private inclinations and interests, than when he was bound to submit the propriety of his choice to the discussion and determination of a different and independent body; and that body an entire branch of the Legislature. The possibility of rejection would be a strong motive to care in proposing.—The danger to his own reputation, and, in the case of an elective magistrate, to his political existence, from betraying a spirit of favoritism, or an unbecoming pursuit of popularity, to the observation of a body, whose opinion would have great weight in forming that of the public, could not fail to operate as a barrier to the one and to the other. He would be both ashamed and afraid to bring forward for the most distinguished or lucrative stations, candidates who had no other merit, than that of coming from the same State to which he particularly belonged, or of being in some way or other personally allied to him, or of possessing the necessary insignificance and pliancy to render them the obsequious instruments of his pleasure.

To this reasoning, it has been objected, that the President by the influence of the power of nomination may secure the complaisance of the Senate to his views. The supposition of universal venality in human nature is little less an error in political reasoning than the supposition of universal rectitude. The institution of delegated power implies that there is a portion of virtue and honor among mankind, which may be a reasonable foundation of confidence. And experience justifies the theory: It has been found to exist in the most corrupt periods of the most corrupt governments. The venality of the British House of Commons has been long a topic of accusation against that body, in the country to which they belong, as well as in this; and it cannot be doubted that the charge is to a considerable extent well founded. But it is as little to be doubted that there is always a large proportion of the body, which consists of independent and public spirited men, who have an influential weight in the councils of the nation. Hence it is (the present reign not excepted) that the sense of that body is often seen to controul the inclinations of the monarch, both with regard to men and to measures. Though it might therefore be allowable to suppose, that the executive might occasionally influence some individuals in the Senate; yet the supposition that he could in general purchase the integrity of the whole body would be forced and improbable.—A man disposed to view human nature as it is, without either flattering its virtues or exaggerating its vices, will see sufficient ground of confidence in the probity of the Senate, to rest satisfied not only that it will be impracticable to the Executive to corrupt or seduce a majority of its members; but that the necessity of its co-operation in the business of appointments will be a considerable and salutary restraint upon the conduct of that magistrate. Nor is the integrity of the Senate the only reliance. The constitution has provided some important guards against the danger of executive influence upon the legislative body: It declares that "No Senator, or representative shall, during the time *for which he was elected*, be appointed to any civil office under the United States, which shall have been created, or the emoluments whereof shall have been encreased during such time; and no person holding any office under the United States shall be a member of either house during his continuance in office."

1. The italics in the passages quoted from the U.S. Constitution were inserted by "Publius."

2. In the Constitution, the passage "whose appointments are not otherwise provided for in the Constitution" actually reads "whose appointments are not herein otherwise provided for, and which shall be established by law."

3. See *The Federalist* 68 (CC:615).
4. This sentence was omitted in the M'Lean edition.
5. "Than" inserted in the M'Lean edition.
6. In the M'Lean edition the following was substituted for the text in angle brackets: "But his nomination may be overruled:—This it certainly may, yet it can."

## 657. Publius: The Federalist 77
## New York Independent Journal, 2 April

This essay, written by Alexander Hamilton, was reprinted in the *New York Packet* on 4 April. It was number 77 in the M'Lean edition and number 76 in the newspapers.

For a general discussion of the authorship, circulation, and impact of *The Federalist*, see CC:201, 406, 639, and Editors' Note, 28 May.

### The FEDERALIST. No. LXXVI.
### To the People of the State of New-York.

It has been mentioned as one of the advantages to be expected from the co-operation of the senate, in the business of appointments, that it would contribute to the stability of the administration. The consent of that body would be necessary to displace as well as to appoint.[1] A change of the chief magistrate therefore would not occasion so violent or so general a revolution in the officers of the government, as might be expected if he were the sole disposer of offices. Where a man in any station had given satisfactory evidence of his fitness for it, a new president would be restrained from attempting a change, in favour of a person more agreeable to him, by the apprehension that the discountenance of the senate might frustrate the attempt, and bring some degree of discredit upon himself. Those who can best estimate the value of a steady administration will be most disposed to prize a provision, which connects the official existence of public men with the approbation or disapprobation of that body, which from the greater permanency of its own composition, will in all probability be less subject to inconstancy, than any other member of the government.

To this union of the senate with the president, in the article of appointments, it has in some cases been suggested,[2] that it would serve to give the president an undue influence over the senate; and in others, that it would have an opposite tendency; a strong proof that neither suggestion is true.

To state the first in its proper form is to refute it. It amounts to this—The president would have an improper *influence over* the senate; because the senate would have the power of *restraining* him. This is an absurdity in terms. It cannot admit of a doubt that the intire power of appointment would enable him much more effectually to establish a dangerous empire over that body, than a mere power of nomination subject to their controul.

Let us take a view of the converse of the proposition—"The senate would influence the executive"—As I have had occasion to remark in several other instances,[3] the indistinctness of the objection forbids a precise answer. In what manner is this influence to be exerted? In relation to what objects? The power of influencing a person, in the sense in which it is here used, must imply a power of conferring a benefit upon him. How could the senate confer a benefit upon the president by the manner of employing their right of negative upon his nominations? If it be said they might sometimes gratify him[4] by an acquiescence in a favorite choice, when public motives might dictate a different conduct; I answer that the instances in which the president could be personally interested in the result, would be too few to admit of his being materially affected by the compliances of the senate.[5] The POWER which can *originate* the disposition of honors and emoluments, is more likely to attract than to be attracted by the POWER which can merely obstruct their course. If by influencing the president be meant *restraining* him, this is precisely what must have been intended. And it has been shewn that the restraint would be salutary, at the same time that it would not be such as to destroy a single advantage to be looked for from the uncontrouled agency of that magistrate. The right of nomination would produce all the good ⟨of that of appointment, and would in a great measure avoid its ills.⟩[6]

Upon a comparison of the plan for the appointment of the officers of the proposed government with that which is established by the constitution of this state a decided preference must be given to the former. In that plan the power of nomination is unequivocally vested in the executive. And as there would be a necessity for submitting each nomination to the judgement of an entire branch of the legislative, the circumstances attending an appointment, from the mode of conducting it, would naturally become matters of notoriety; and the public would[7] be at no loss to determine what part had been performed by the different actors. The blame of a bad nomination would fall upon the president singly and absolutely—The censure of rejecting a good one would lie entirely at the door of the senate; aggravated by the consideration of their having counteracted the good intentions of the executive. If an ill appointment should be made the executive for nominating and the senate for approving would participate though in different degrees in the opprobrium and disgrace.

The reverse of all this characterises the manner of appointment in this state. The council of appointment consists of from three to five persons, of whom the governor is always one. This small body, shut up in a private apartment, impenetrable to the public eye, proceed to the execution of the trust committed to them. It is known that the governor claims the right of nomination, upon the strength of some ambiguous expressions in the constitution; but it is not known to what extent, or in what manner he exercises it; nor upon what occasions he is contradicted or opposed. The censure of a bad appointment, on account of the uncertainty of its author, and for want of a determinate object, has neither pregnancy nor duration. And while an unbounded field for cabal and intrigue lies open, all idea of responsibility is lost. The most that the public can know is, that the governor claims the right of nomination: That *two* out of the considerable number of *four* men can too often be managed without much difficulty: That if some of the members of a particular council should happen to be of an uncomplying character, it is frequently not impossible to get rid of their opposition, by regulating the times of meeting in such a manner as to render their attendance inconvenient: And that, from whatever cause it may proceed, a great number of very improper appointments are from time to time made. Whether a governor of this state avails himself of the ascendant he must necessarily have, in this delicate and important part of the administration, to prefer to offices men who are best qualified for them: Or whether he prostitutes that advantage to the advancement of persons, whose chief merit is their implicit devotion to his will, and to the support of a despicable and dangerous system of personal influence, are questions which unfortunately for the community can only be the subjects of speculation and conjecture.[8]

Every mere council of appointment, however constituted, will be a conclave, in which cabal and intrigue will have their full scope. Their number, without an unwarrantable increase of expence, cannot be large enough to preclude a facility of combination. And as each member will have his friends and connections to provide for, the desire of mutual gratification will beget a scandalous bartering of votes and bargaining for places. The private attachments of one man might easily be satisfied; but to satisfy the private attachments of a dozen, or of twenty men, would occasion a monopoly of all the principal employments of the government, in a few families, and would lead more directly to an aristocracy or an oligarchy, than any measure that could be contrived. If to avoid an accumulation of offices, there was to be a frequent change in the persons, who were to compose the council, this would involve the mischiefs of a mutable administration in their full extent. Such a council would also be more liable to executive influence than the senate, because they would be fewer in number, and would act less immediately under the public inspection. Such a council in fine as a substitute for the plan of the convention, would be productive of an increase of expence, a multiplication of the evi[l]s which spring from favouritism and intrigue in the distribution of the public honors, a decrease of stability in the administration of the government, and a diminution of the security against an undue influence of the executive. And yet such a council has been warmly contended for as an essential amendment in the proposed constitution.

I could not with propriety conclude my observations on the subject of appointments, without taking notice of a scheme, for which there has appeared some, though but a few advocates; I mean that of uniting the house of representatives in the power of making them. I shall however do little more than mention it, as I cannot imagine that it is likely to gain the countenance of any considerable part of the community. A body so fluctuating, and at the same time so numerous, can never be deemed proper for the exercise of that power. Its unfitness will appear manifest to all, when it is recollected that in half a century it may consist of three or four hundred persons. All the advantages of the stability, both of the executive and of the senate, would be defeated by this union; and infinite delays and embarrassments would be occasioned. The example of most of the states in their local constitutions, encourages us to reprobate the idea.

The only remaining powers of the executive, are comprehended in giving information to congress of the state of the union; in recommending to their consideration such measures as he shall judge expedient; in convening them, or either branch, upon extraordinary occasions; in adjourning them when they cannot themselves agree upon the time of adjournment; in receiving ambassadors and other public ministers; in faithfully executing the laws; and in commissioning all the officers of the United States.

Except some cavils about the power of convening *either* house of the legislature and that of receiving ambassadors, no objection has been made to this class of authorities; nor could they possibly admit of any. It required indeed an insatiable avidity for censure to invent exceptions to the parts which have been excepted to. In regard to the power of convening either house of the legislature, I shall barely remark, that in respect to the senate at least, we can readily discover a good reason for it. As this body has a concurrent power with the executive in the article of treaties, it might often be necessary to call it together with a view to this object, when it would be unnecessary and improper to convene the house of representatives. As to the reception of ambassadors, what I have said in a former paper will furnish a sufficient answer.[9]

We have now compleated a survey of the structure and powers of the executive department, which, I have endeavoured to show, combines, as far as republican principles would admit, all the requisites to energy. The remaining enquiry is; does it also combine the requisites to safety in the republican sense—a due dependence on the people—a due responsibility? The answer to this question has been anticipated in the investigation of its other characteristics, and is satisfactorily deducible from these circumstances, from the election of the president once in four years by persons immediately chosen by the people for that purpose; and from his being at all times liable to impeachment, trial, dismission from office, incapacity to serve in any other; and to the forfeiture of life and estate by subsequent prosecution in the common course of law. But these precautions, great as they are, are not the only ones, which the plan of the convention has provided in favor of the public security. In the only instances in which the abuse of the executive authority was materially to be feared, the chief magistrate of the United States would by that plan be subjected to the controul of a branch of the legislative body. What more could be desired by an enlightened and reasonable people.[10]

1. In June and July 1789 the U.S. House of Representatives and the U.S. Senate agreed that the President, using his implied constitutional powers, could remove officers without the specific approval or without a general grant of authority from either the Senate or the Congress. This decision helped to set a precedent for the separation of powers under the Constitution. See Charlene Bangs Bickford and Kenneth R. Bowling, *Birth of the Nation: The First Federal Congress, 1789–1791* (Madison, Wis., 1989), 38–41; and Charles S. Hyneman and George W. Carey, eds., *A Second Federalist: Congress Creates a Government* (Columbia, S.C., 1967), 163–72.

2. "Objected" substituted in the M'Lean edition.

3. See *The Federalist* 67–76, which were published between 11 March and 1 April (CC:612, 615, 617, 619, 625, 628, 635, 644, 646, 656).

4. "Him" inserted in the M'Lean edition.

5. "Besides this, it is evident that" inserted before "The POWER" in the M'Lean edition.

6. In the M'Lean edition the text in angle brackets was deleted and replaced by "without the ill."

7. "Could" substituted in the M'Lean edition.

8. For the constitutional provisions concerning the New York Council of Appointment, see Thorpe, V, 2633–34. In 1789 and 1794 New York Federalists attacked Governor George Clinton's interpretation that the governor had the sole authority to make nominations in the Council. In 1794 a Federalist-controlled Council overruled Clinton's interpretation. A year later, however, Federalist Governor John Jay accepted Clinton's position and the Federalist councillors acquiesced. When Republicans regained control of the Council in 1801, they supported a broadened nomination. In October 1801 a special constitutional convention ruled that any councillor could nominate.

9. See *The Federalist* 69 (CC:617).

10. In the M'Lean edition this sentence was replaced by the following: "What more can an enlightened and reasonable people desire?"

## 658. Pennsylvania Gazette, 2 April[1]

The freedom of the human mind in its various operations is exemplified on no subject in a greater degree than in its reflexions and opinions on matters of government. The wise and good have been more dissentient on political topics, than on any other which have exercised their understandings, or excited their honest feelings. Hence the variety of opinion on the proposed constitution ought not to surprize us, nor, indeed, should we even regret a diversity of sentiment, that will ensure our safety, if regulated by reason, integrity and moderation. We see and feel the indispensible necessity of union among the states. We know, too, that our present articles of confederation are faulty on some important points, and do not extend to many others which are requisite to the existence and administration of government. Let not then a too excessive jealousy prevent *a trial* of the proposed plan. Amendments have been proposed in the way the constitution points out. The most jealous friends of liberty in America have acquiesced with a frank and noble spirit in the adoption of the government, when they found amendments were to be recommended to the first assembly of the states under the new constitution. They saw that the edifice contained many valuable materials, judiciously combined, and tho' they were of opinion that it was not perfect, yet they thought it more easy and more safe *to attempt to complete this*, than to overturn the whole, and attempt to build one anew. We know, without doubt, that this constitution is a well intended attempt of men, many of whom possessed our sincerest affections and highest esteem before the revolution, and who possessed them afterwards. If we were to form a list of characters to whom America owes in the most eminent degree her freedom and independence, omitting the worthies of whom Providence has been pleased to deprive us, we shall find a great proportion of them on the list of the Convention, and a great part of the others may be counted among the friends and supporters of the constitution. Let us not then suppose that these men could combine *to cheat* their country of Property—Liberty—and all Happiness. 'Tis too unkind, too harsh a suggestion. It cannot be agreeable to a just and grateful people, that the yet tender wounds of patriot valour should be excoriated by the *brand* of traiterous conspiracy.

'Tis said by the votaries of *the divinity of Kings*, that we have chosen forms of government which cannot be administered. Let us take care that we do not become melancholy examples, by which the *supposed* truth of their assertions may be apparently established. Republics, we trust in Heaven, can be energetic, wise and upright. Yet we must candidly acknowledge, that *it yet remains* for America to establish, by her example, the truth of this position. Hitherto our governments have wounded our best feelings, by their alternate want of efficiency, honesty and wisdom. Mark well, then, ye patriot members of the State Conventions, the present condition of things, and consider, before you throw away the opportunities of this your day, the future prospects of your country.

1. Reprints by 7 May (8): N.Y. (2), N.J. (1), Pa. (2), Md. (1), Va. (1), S.C. (1). In reprinting this item, the Winchester *Virginia Gazette*, 7 May, reversed the order of the paragraphs.

### 659. A Native of Virginia: Observations upon the Proposed Plan of Federal Government, Petersburg, 2 April

On 2, 9, and 16 April, the weekly *Virginia Independent Chronicle* of Richmond announced that Hunter and Prentis of the Petersburg *Virginia Gazette* had "Just Published" a pamphlet by "A Native of Virginia." This sixty-six-page work, entitled *Observations upon the Proposed Plan of Federal Government. With an Attempt to Answer Some of the Principal Objections that Have Been Made to It* (Evans 21264), was available at the *Chronicle* office for a shilling and a half. (No advertisements have been found in the Petersburg *Virginia Gazette* because only the issue of 13 March is extant for March and April.)

According to "A Native of Virginia," his pamphlet "was intended to counteract the misrepresentations of the proposed Federal Government, which the antifederalists have most industriously disseminated in the southern counties. The writer had no idea of publishing any thing upon the subject of the Constitution, till a visit he made to one of those counties, where at the desire of his friend, he was induced to write in haste the pamphlet now offered to the public. It was to have been published [in] time enough to be dispersed before the elections [3–27 March], but the Printer found it impossible to deliver it in time. The primary intention being thus defeated, it would not have been published at all, had it not been put into the press at the time stipulated. The writer had neither Mr. Mason's, Mr. Gerry's, nor Mr. Lee's objections by him: This it is hoped will be a sufficient apology for its inaccuracies, as far as their objections have been taken notice of. . . . He does not pretend to have gone fully into the objections which have been raised to the government: His design was to obviate only the most popular, and in a manner as popular as he was able."

The identity of "A Native of Virginia" has not been determined. James Madison's copy of the pamphlet, now in the Rare Book Room at the Library of Congress, has a faint pencilled annotation (perhaps by Madison) that could be read as "Mr. Fisher" or "Mr. Tyler" (Evans, VII, 238). Daniel Fisher, a planter-lawyer, was treasurer and the commonwealth's attorney for Greensville, a southern county. He was also a member of the Virginia House of

Delegates and the Virginia Convention, where he voted to ratify the Constitution in June 1788. Another copy of the pamphlet, located in the St. George Tucker pamphlets in the Virginia Historical Society, is annotated: "By Burwell Starke." Starke and Tucker attended the College of William and Mary in the early 1770s. Starke, a planter-lawyer from the southern county of Dinwiddie, never sat in the legislature or held an important county office. A last possible author is Edward Carrington, who toured three southern counties early in 1788 to determine the extent of their Antifederalism.

The pamphlet is divided into several parts. The first part (pages 3–10) examines the reasons for calling the Constitutional Convention, praises its work and members, traces the evolution of the bill of rights in England, and explains why a bill of rights was unnecessary in America. The main portion (pages 10–62) prints almost every clause of the Constitution (in italic type) and after each clause or group of clauses answers the objections raised to them. Sometimes, "A Native of Virginia" replies specifically to criticisms raised by George Mason, Elbridge Gerry, Edmund Randolph, and the "Dissent of the Minority of the Pennsylvania Convention" (CC:138, 227–A, 276, 353, 385). In the third part (pages 62–64), entitled "NOTE," "A Native of Virginia" explains why he has not answered the objections made by Richard Henry Lee (CC:325). The last two pages of the pamphlet, which are unnumbered, contain the author's reasons for writing the pamphlet and an errata.

[For the text of "A Native of Virginia," see RCS:Va., 655–98.]

### 660. Alexander Hamilton to James Madison
### New York, 3 April[1]

I have been very delinquent My Dear Sir in not thanking you sooner for your letter from Philadelphia. The remarks you make on a certain subject are important and will be attended to. There is ~~one~~ truly much embarrassment in the case; ~~but when impossibilities are to be reconciled, what but embarrassment can be expected~~?

I think however the principles we have talked of, in respect to the legislative authorities,[2] are not only just but will apply to the other departments. Nor will the consequences appear so disagreeable, as they may seem at first sight, when we attend to the true import of the rule established. The states *retain* all the authorities they were *before* possessed of not alienated in the three modes pointed out;[3] but this does not include cases which are the *creatures* of the New Constitution. For instance, the crime of treason against the United States *immediately*, is a crime known only to the New Constitution. There of course *was* no power in the state constitutions to pardon that crime—There will therefore be none under the new &c. This or something like it seems to me to afford the best solution of the difficulty.

I send you the Fœderalist from the beginning to the conclusion of the commentary on the Executive branch. If our suspicions of the author be right, he must be too much engaged to make a rapid progress in what remains.—The Court of Chancery & a Circuit Court are now sitting

We are told that your election has succeeded; with which we all felicitate ourselves. I will thank you for an account of the result generally.[4]

In this state our prospects are much as you left them—a moot point which side will prevail. Our friends to the Northward are active. I remain Yr. affectionate & obedt serv

1. RC, Madison Papers, DLC. In part, this letter responds to one (not located) that Madison wrote in Philadelphia en route from New York City to his home in Orange County. Since Madison left the city on either 3 or 4 March and arrived at Mount Vernon on 18 March (RCS:Va., 596n, 602), the letter was written some time between these dates. The editors of the *Madison Papers* believe that the letter was dated around 10 March (Rutland, *Madison*, XI, 2). Madison was in Philadelphia on the 11th because he received a letter of that date from James Wilson who wanted it delivered to George Washington (CC:661).

2. Possibly a reference to *The Federalist* 52–66, essays respecting the House of Representatives and the Senate that appeared between 8 February and 8 March. (See CC:Vol. 4.)

3. See *The Federalist* 32, 2 January (CC:405).

4. For the Virginia Convention elections, held between 3 and 27 March, see RCS:Va., 561–631, especially pp. 595–606 dealing with Madison's election from Orange County.

### 661. George Washington to James Wilson
### Mount Vernon, 4 April[1]

You will please to accept of my best thanks for the copy of the debates of your late convention[2] which you have been so polite as to send me—That, together with your favor of the 11 Ulto. was handed to me by Mr. Madison.

The violent proceedings of the enemies of the proposed constitution in your State are to be regreted as disturbing the peace of society; but in any other point of view they are not to be regarded; for their unimportance effectually precludes any fear of their having an extensive or lasting influence, and their activity holds up to view the general cast & character of them, which need only be seen to be disregarded.[3]—

It is impossible to say, with any degree of certainty, what will be the determination of the Convention in this State upon the proposed plan of Government. I have no opportunity of gaining information respecting the matter but what come through the medium of the news papers or from those Gentln. who visit me, as I have hardly been ten miles from my farms since my return from Philadelphia. Some judgement may be formed when the members chosen by the several Counties to serve in Convention, are known, as their sentiments will be decided, and their choice determined, by their Attachments or opposition to the proposed System.—A majority of those names I have yet seen are said to be friendly to the Constitution but these are from the Northern parts of the State from whence least opposition was to be expected. It is however certain that there will be a greater weight of abilities opposed to it here than in any other State.—

1. FC, Washington Papers, DLC.

2. See CC:511 for Thomas Lloyd's version of the debates of the Pennsylvania Convention, first offered for sale on 7 February. Lloyd's debates consist largely of the speeches of Wilson and Thomas McKean.

3. Washington refers to the continued opposition to the Constitution that manifested itself in a riot in Carlisle on 26 December, the publication of numerous newspaper articles, and in a barrage of petitions requesting that the Pennsylvania legislature not "confirm" the state's ratification of the Constitution (RCS:Pa., 642–725. See also CC:407, 665.).

## 662. Luther Martin: Address No. IV
## Maryland Journal, 4 April[1]

### To the CITIZENS of MARYLAND.

If those, my fellow-citizens, to whom the administration of our government was about to be committed, had sufficient wisdom never to err, and sufficient goodness always to consult the true interest of the governed,—and if we could have a proper security that their successors should to the end of time be possessed of the same qualifications, it would be impossible that power could be lavished upon them with too liberal a hand.

Power absolute and unlimited, united with unerring wisdom and unbounded goodness, is the government of the Deity over the universe!—But remember, my fellow-citizens, that the persons to whom you are about to delegate authority, are and will be weak, erring mortals, subject to the same passions, prejudices and infirmities with yourselves; and let it be deeply engraven on your hearts, that from the first history of government to the present time, if we begin with Nimrod, and trace down the rulers of nations to those who are *now* invested with supreme power, we shall find few, very few, who have made the beneficent Governor of the Universe the model of their conduct, while many are they who, on the contrary, have imitated the demons of darkness.

We have no right to expect that our rulers will be more wise, more virtuous, or more perfect than those of other nations have been, or that they will not be equally under the influence of ambition, avarice, and all that train of baleful passions, which have so generally proved the curse of our unhappy race.

We must consider mankind such as they really are,—such as experience has shewn them to be heretofore, and bids us expect to find them hereafter, and not suffer ourselves to be misled by interested deceivers or enthusiastick visionaries; and therefore in forming a system of government, to delegate no greater power than is *clearly* and *certainly necessary*, ought to be the first principle with every people, who are influenced by reason and a regard for their safety, and in doing this, they ought most solicitously to endeavour so to qualify even that power, by such checks and restraints, as to produce a perfect responsibility in those who are to exercise it, and prevent them from its abuse with a chance of impunity;—since such is the nature of man, that he has a propensity to abuse authority and to tyrannize over the rights of his fellow-men;—and to whomsoever power is given, not content with the actual deposite, they will ever strive to obtain an increase.

Those who would wish to excite and keep awake your jealousy and distrust, are your truest friends;—while they, who speak peace to you when there is no peace—who would lull you into security, and wish you to repose blind confidence in your future governors, are your most dangerous enemies.—Jealousy and distrust are the guardian angels who watch over liberty:—security and confidence are the forerunners of slavery.

But the advocates for the system tell you that we who oppose it, endeavour to terrify you with mere possibilities, which may never be realized, that all our objections consist in saying government *may* do this,—and government *may* do that.—

I will, for argument sake, admit the justice of this remark, and yet maintain that the objections are insurmountable.—I consider it an incontrovertible truth, that whatever by the constitution government even *may* do, if it relates to the *abuse* of power, by acts tyrannical and oppressive, it some time or other *will* do.—Such is the ambition of man, and his lust for domination, that no power less than that which fixed its bounds to the ocean, can say, to them, "thus far shall ye go and no farther."[2]—Ascertain the limits of the *may*, with ever so much precision, and let them be as extensive as you please, government will speedily reach their utmost verge; nor will it stop there, but soon will overleap those boundaries, and roam at large into the regions of the *may not*.—Those who tell you the government by this constitution *may* keep up a *standing army*,—abolish the trial by jury,—oppress the citizens of the states by its powers over the militia,—destroy the freedom of the press,—infringe the liberty of conscience, and do a number of other acts injurious to and destructive of your rights, yet that it *never will do so*; and that you safely may accept such a constitution, and be perfectly at ease and secure that your rulers will always be so good, so wise, and so virtuous—such emanations of the Deity, that they will never use their power but for your interest and your happiness—contradict the uniform experience of ages, and betray a total ignorance of human nature, or a total want of ingenuity.

Look back, my fellow-citizens, to your conduct but a few years past, and let that instruct you what ought to be your conduct at this time.

Great-Britain then claimed the right to pass laws to bind you in all cases whatever.[3]—You were then told in all the soft insinuating language of the present day, and with all the appearance of disinterested friendship now used, that those who insisted this claim of power might be abused, only wandered in the regions of fancy—that you need not be uneasy, but might safely acquiesce in the claim—that you might have the utmost possible confidence in your rulers, that they never would use that power to your injury;—but distrustful of government, and jealous of your liberty, you rejected such counsel with disdain;— the bare possibility that Britain might abuse it, if once conceded, kindled a flame from one end of this continent to the other, and roused you to arms—Weak and defenceless as you were, unused to military exertions, and unsupplied with warlike stores, you braved the strength of a nation the most powerful and best provided—you chose to risk your lives and property rather than to risque the possibility that the power claimed by the British government should be exercised to your injury—a possibility, which the minions of power at that time, with as much confidence as those of the present day, declared to be absolutely visionary.

Heaven wrought a miracle in your favour, and your efforts were crowned with success.

You are not now called upon to make an equal sacrifice—you are not now requested to beat your ploughshares into swords, or your pruning hooks into spears[4]—to leave your peaceful habitations, and exchange domestic tranquility for the horrors of war;—peaceably, quietly and orderly to give this system of slavery your negative, is all that is asked by the advocates of freedom—to pronounce the single monosyllable *no*, is all they entreat;—shall they entreat you in vain?—when by this it is to be determined, whether our independence, for obtaining which we have been accustomed to bow the knee with reverential gratitude to Heaven, shall be our greatest curse;—and when on this it depends whether we shall be subjected to a government, of which the little finger will be thicker than the loins of that of Great-Britain.

But there are also persons who pretend that your situation is at present so bad, that it cannot be worse, and urge that as an argument why we should embrace any remedy proposed, however desperate it may appear.

Thus do the poor erring children of mortality, suffering under the presence of real or imaginary evils, have recourse to a pistol or halter for relief, and rashly launch into the *untried* regions of eternity—nor wake from their delusion, until they wake in endless wo[e].—Should the citizens of America, in a fit of desperation, be induced to commit this fatal act of political *suicide*, to which by such arguments they are stimulated, the day will come when labouring under more than Egyptian bondage, compelled to furnish their quota of brick, though destitute of straw and of mortar;[5] galled with your chains, and worn down by oppression, you will, by sad experience, be convinced (when that conviction shall be too late) that there is a *difference* in evils, and that the buzzing of gnats is more supportable than the sting of a serpent.

From the wisdom of antiquity we might obtain excellent instruction, if we were not too proud to profit by it—Æsop has furnished us with the history of a nation of Frogs[6]—between which and our own there is a most striking resemblance.—Whether the catastrophe shall be the same, rests with ourselves.

Jupiter, out of pure good nature, wishing to do them as little injury as possible, on being asked for a King, had thrown down into their pond a Log to rule over them;—under whose government, had they been wise enough to know their own interest and to pursue it, they might, to this day, have remained happy and prosperous.—Terrified with the noise, and affrighted by the violent undulations of the water, they for some time kept an awful distance, and regarded their monarch with reverence; but the first impression being in some measure worn off, and perceiving him to be of a tame and peaceable disposition, they approached him with familiarity, and soon entertained for him the utmost contempt:—In a little time were seen the leaders of the Frogs croaking, to their respective circles, on the weakness and feebleness of the government at home, and of its want of dignity and respect abroad, till the sentiment being caught by their auditors, the whole pond resounded with "Oh Jupiter, good Jupiter, hear our prayers—take away from us this vile Log, and give us a ruler who shall know how to support the dignity and splendor of government!—give us any government you please, only let it be energetic and efficient."— The Thunderer, in his *wrath*, sent them a *Crane*. With what delight did they gaze on their Monarch, as he came majestically floating on the wings of the wind!—They admired his *uncommon* shape—it was *such* as they had *never before seen*—his deformities were, in their eyes, the greatest of beauties—and they were heard, like Aristides, to declare, that, were they on the verge of eternity, they would not wish a single alteration in his form[7]—His monstrous beak, his long neck, and his enormous poke—even these, the future means of their destruction, were subjects of their warm approbation.—He took possession of his new dominions, and instantly began to swallow down his subjects; and it is said, that those who had been the warmest zealots for Crane-administration, fared no better than the rest.—The poor wretches were now much more dissatisfied than before, and, with all possible humility, applied to Jupiter again for his aid, but in vain—he dismissed them with this reproof, "*that the evil of which they complained, they had foolishly brought upon themselves*, and that they had no other remedy now, but to submit with patience."—Thus forsaken by the God, and left to the mercy of the Crane, they sought to escape his cruelty by flight; but pursuing them to every place of retreat, and thrusting his long neck through the water to the bottom, he drew them out with his beak from their most secret hiding-places, and served them up as a regale for his ravenous appetite.

The *present* federal government is, my fellow-citizens, the *Log* of the fable—the *Crane* is the system now offered to your acceptance.—I wish you not to *remain* under the government of the *one*, nor to *become subjected* to the tyranny of the *other*.—If either of these events take place, it must arise from your being greatly deficient to yourselves, from your being, like the nation of Frogs, "a *discontented, variable* race, *weary of liberty*, and *fond of change*."—At the same time I have no hesitation in declaring, that if the one or the other must be our fate, I think the *harmless, inoffensive*, though *contemptible Log*, infinitely to be preferred to the *powerful*, the *efficient*, but *all-devouring* Crane.

*Baltimore, March* 29, 1788.

1. On 1 April the *Maryland Journal* announced that Martin's Address No. IV "will be inserted in our next." This address, the last in the series, was reprinted in the Philadelphia *Independent Gazetteer*, 14 April; *New York Journal*, 28 April; and Providence *United States Chronicle*, 8 May. For a general discussion of Martin's addresses, see CC:626; and for a spurious address number V, see CC:675.

2. Job 38:11. This passage was previously quoted by Antifederalists Mercy Warren as "A Columbian Patriot" and General Samuel Thompson in the Massachusetts Convention (CC:581, notes 11 and 15).

3. Martin refers to the Declaratory Act of 1766 which received the royal assent the same day (18 March) as the act repealing the hated Stamp Act of 1765. The Declaratory Act stated that the King, by and with the advice and consent of Parliament, "had, hath,

and of right ought to have, full power and authority to make laws and statutes of sufficient force and validity to bind the colonies and people of America, subjects of the Crown of Great Britain, in all cases whatsoever." The act also declared "utterly null and void" all colonial resolutions, votes, orders, and proceedings which denied this power and authority.

4. Joel 3:10.

5. Exodus 5:6–19.

6. "The Frogs Desiring a King."

7. Martin refers to a statement made by "Aristides" (Alexander Contee Hanson) in a pamphlet published in Annapolis, Md., on 31 January. See CC:490, p. 543, at note "o."

### 663. George Nicholas to James Madison
### Charlottesville, Va., 5 April[1]

I consider the present moment as so important to America, that I shall take the liberty of communicating to you my sentiments, as to the conduct that her real friends ought to pursue.

The adoption of the new constitution (on which I conceive her salvation to depend) in this state depends much on the conduct of the other states; from the list of members returned to the convention, I think a majority of them are federal; but that majority if it exists, will be but small, and I apprehend some of them will fear to give the last hand to the business,[2] unless the conduct of the other states will justify it. The adjournment of the New-Hampshire convention[3] puts an end to the hope that nine will adopt before the meeting of our convention, but it will be a great matter to have the sanction of eight states. Maryland and South-Carolina are the only ones which are now to meet, and I flatter myself will both be favorable to the plan; but I apprehend great efforts will be made to induce them to adjourn until after our meeting, and if this can be brought about, depend on it Sir, it will have great influence in this country; if you consider this matter in the same point of view that I do, may I hope that you will impress on your friends in those states, the importance of their sanction prior to the meeting of this state.[4] I have great expectations from the influence of Mr. Pendleton, and know that effort will be used to induce him to come into the proposition of demanding amendments before the adoption, you can prevent the danger from that quarter.[5] Not having been in the state for some time, perhaps you are a stranger to the real sentiments of some of the leaders of the opposition. You know better than I do what was the conduct of Mr. Mason at the convention, immediately after his return, he declared, that notwithstanding his objections to particular parts of the plan, he would take it as it was rather than lose it altogether;[6] since that I have reason to believe his sentiments are much changed which I attribute to two causes: first the irritation he feels from the hard things that have been said of him,[7] and secondly to a vain opinion he entertains (which has industriously been supported by some particular characters) that he has influence enough to dictate a constitution to Virginia, and through her to the rest of the union. Mr. Henry is now almost avowedly an enemy to the union, and therefore will oppose every plan that would cement it. His real sentiments will be industriously concealed, for so long as he talks only of amendments, such of the friends to the union, as object to particular parts of the constitution will adhere to him, which they would not do a moment, if they could be convinced of his real design. I hope to be possessed of sufficient information by the meeting of the convention to make that matter clear, and if I am it shall not be withheld.[8] The opposition except from that quarter will be feeble. Our friend E: R. talks of a compromise between the friends to the Union,[9] but I know of but one that can safely take place; and that is on the plan of the Massachussetts convention:[10] it appears to me impossible, that another continental convention assembled to deliberate on the whole subject, should ever agree on any general plan.

Let the decision of our convention be what it may, I think it will be of great consequence that an address to the people at large should go forth from such of the members as are friends to the constitution: if this had been done in Pennsylvania, it would have counteracted much of the poison contained in the *dissent of the minority*.[11] I consider the situation of the friends as very different, and requiring them to pursue a line of conduct, which would not be justifiable in the minority after the adoption of the government. Their only object could be to wish to foment a civil war to destroy a government, which they suppose not perfect; but if this government is rejected, America will be left without one, at least only in possession of one which all parties agree is insufficient; it will therefore be our duty to state to the people the necessity of a change and place in it's true point of view the one now offered. Nine tenths of the people are strong friends to the union, and such of them as are opposed to the proffered government, are so, upon suppositions not warranted by the thing itself. No person in the convention can so well prepare this address as yourself, and if it appears as important in your eyes as it does to me, I hope that you will undertake it. The greater part of the members of the convention will go to the meeting without information on the subject, it will be very important to give this as early as may be, and if possible before they go from home. *Publius of the fœderalist* if it is published in a pamphlet, would do it better than any other work; if it is published can I get the favor of you to procure me thirty or forty copies of it, that I may distribute them; if they were sent to Orange or Richmond I should soon get them.[12]

The only danger I apprehend is from the Kentucky members; and one consideration only has any weight with them: a fear that if the new government should take place, that their navigation would be given up.[13] If Mr. Brown could be satisfied on this subject, and would write to that country, and also have letters here for the members,[14] I am satisfied they would be right.

You will pardon this liberty and believe me to be with respect and esteem Dr. Sir, Yr. obdt. servt.

[P. S.] I wrote the above on a supposition that you had or would immediately return to New York but being informed yesterday that you did not intend it, one other consideration appears as important as any that I have yet mentioned. If the convention adopts the new government it will depend on the next assembly whether it shall be set in motion; if they reject it, no plan for a substitute can come from any other quarter: so that on either event it will be material to have a majority there federal. We laid the ground work of a reform in our courts of justice last fall, it requires the finishing hand; you know the number that are opposed to all reforms, and how formidable they will be with Henry at their head. If then as I suppose the truth is, that nothing very important can come before the present Congress, will it not be necessary for you to go into the assembly. At any rate none but federal men should be elected.

Has Congress determined on any thing as to the separation of Kentucky?[15] I am much interested in the welfare of that country as I expect to reside in it within twelve months.[16]

1. RC, Madison Papers, DLC. For Madison's 8 April reply, see CC:667.

2. For lists of delegates elected to the Virginia Convention, see RCS:Va., 626–31.

3. For the impact of the adjournment of the New Hampshire Convention to 18 June, see CC:554.

4. By 10 April, Madison had written to friends in both Maryland and South Carolina (RCS:Va., 705, note 2).

5. One such effort was made by Richard Henry Lee who wrote Edmund Pendleton on 26 May, to which Pendleton replied on 14 June (CC:755, 782).

6. Madison disagreed with Nicholas, believing that Mason had "returned to Virginia with a fixed disposition to prevent the adoption of the plan if possible" (to Thomas Jefferson, 24 October, CC:187). On 7 October Mason wrote George Washington that he had some "capital" objections to the Constitution, but that he would oppose any attempt to prevent the calling of a state Convention (CC:138–A). After reading Mason's letter, Washington concluded that Mason seemed intent on alarming the people by accompanying his objections with "the most tremendous apprehensions, and highest colouring" (to Madison, 10 October, CC:146). On 25 October Mason told the Virginia

House of Delegates, of which George Nicholas was also a member, that the Constitution was "repugnant to our highest interests,—and if with these sentiments I had subscribed to it, I might have been justly regarded as a traitor to my country. I would have lost this hand, before it should have marked my name to the new government" (Petersburg *Virginia Gazette*, 1 November, RCS:Va., 114. See also Philadelphia *Independent Gazetteer*, 27 October, RCS:Va., 125.).

7. For examples of attacks upon Mason, see "The Attack on the Non-Signers of the Constitution," 17 October (CC:171); and for criticism of his published objections, see the editorial note to CC:276.

8. For Patrick Henry's alleged interest in establishing a separate confederacy, see CC:276, note 4; and RCS:Va.

9. At about this time, items began to appear in the newspapers indicating that Governor Edmund Randolph, who had not signed the Constitution and whose objections to it were published in December 1787 (CC:385), had become a supporter of it. A Richmond gentleman noted that Randolph "now speaks in favour" of the Constitution; while another had "many reasons for believing that the constitution will have his firm support" (*Massachusetts Centinel*, 19 March, CC:627; and Philadelphia *Federal Gazette*, 12 April, RCS:Va., 737). A Marylander stated unequivocally that "*Randolph* is *uncommonly* federal" (*Maryland Journal*, 4 April. See also CC:666.). Charles Lee, however, was uncertain about Randolph's position (to George Washington, 11 April, RCS:Va., 735).

10. The Massachusetts Convention ratified the Constitution on 6 February, recommending nine amendments. They were not a condition of ratification; the state's representatives to the first Congress under the Constitution were enjoined "to exert all their influence, and use all reasonable and legal methods to obtain a ratification" of the amendments (CC:508).

11. For the "Dissent of the Minority of the Pennsylvania Convention," *Pennsylvania Packet*, 18 December, see CC:353. For its circulation in Virginia and the reaction to it, see RCS:Va., 401–8, 438–45.

12. Through Alexander Hamilton, whose assistance Madison sought out, more than fifty copies of each of Volumes I and II of *The Federalist* were sent to Virginia in May and June. See "The Circulation of the Book Version of The Federalist in Virginia," 2 April (RCS:Va., 652–54).

13. For the concern of Kentucky and much of western America that Congress might cede the navigation of the Mississippi River to Spain, see CC:46, 270, 523, 578.

14. On 9 and 21 April Madison wrote to John Brown of Kentucky, then serving as a Virginia delegate to Congress. In the 9 April letter, Madison noted that he had written to several Kentuckians, but he did not ask Brown to write to friends in Kentucky (RCS:Va., 711–12). Madison probably asked Brown to do so in his letter of 21 April (not located), to which Brown replied on 12 May (RCS:Va., 793–95). For Brown's view that Congress would not cede the navigation of the Mississippi River to Spain, see his 28 January letter to James Breckinridge (CC:480).

15. For the action of Congress on Kentucky statehood, see CC:480, note 2.

16. Nicholas moved to Danville, Ky., early in 1789.

### 664. The Governor of Rhode Island to the President of Congress Providence, 5 April

Rhode Island was the only state that refused to send delegates to the Constitutional Convention. On 15 September 1787 the state legislature wrote to the president of Congress explaining its actions (CDR, 225–27). At the

October session, the legislature formally received the Constitution from Congress. On 3 November it voted to print 1,000 copies for distribution to the state's thirty towns, but it rejected a motion to call a state convention.

When the legislature reconvened, it refused to call a state convention (29 February 1788) in favor of a statewide referendum on the Constitution to be held in each town on 24 March. In the referendum, the freemen overwhelmingly rejected the Constitution by a margin greater than eleven to one. This lopsided vote occurred largely because Federalists in Newport and Providence boycotted the referendum. Had all Federalists in these two towns voted, the Constitution still would have been defeated by a two-to-one margin.

Shortly after the referendum, the town clerks submitted their returns to the assembly. On 2 April the assembly again defeated an attempt to call a state convention and appointed three men to a joint committee (Jonathan J. Hazard, Thomas Joslin, and Rowse J. Helme) to draft a letter to Congress explaining the state's actions. On 4 April the upper house added Deputy Governor Daniel Owen to the committee. The committee submitted its draft letter to the assembly on Saturday, 5 April, on which day the assembly considered and approved the letter. The assembly requested that Governor John Collins "subscribe" the letter on behalf of the legislature and transmit it to the president of Congress. Later in the day, the upper house concurred and the legislature adjourned.

Congress received and read the letter on 2 May. The following day, Secretary Charles Thomson wrote Governor Collins that Congress had received his letter. Thomson also observed that Rhode Island had not been represented in Congress one day during the past year.

For commentary on the legislature's actions in drafting the letter to Congress, see the *Newport Herald*, 10 April; the Providence *United States Chronicle*, 10 April; and note 2 (below).

The letter printed here has been transcribed from the recipient's copy in PCC, Item 64, State Papers of New Hampshire and of Rhode Island and Providence Plantations, 1775–88, pp. 603–5, DNA.

State of Rhode-Island and Providence-Plantations.
In General Assembly.

April 5th. 1788

Sir, The Report of the Convention assembled in Philadelphia, being transmitted by the Secretary of Congress, was received by us at October Session last; & 1000 Copies thereof were ordered to be printed and sent into the respective Towns within this State, that the People at large might have a full Opportunity of considering and communing upon so important an Object; which was immediately done.—And at February Session last the Consideration thereof was submitted to the Freemen of this State by the inclosed Act: And, the Returns from each respective Town being delivered in, it appears that the Yeas for adopting the Constitution for the United States were Two Hundred and Thirty seven, and the Nays Two Thousand Seven Hundred and Eight, agreeably to the within Return.[1]

Altho this State hath been singular from her Sister States in the Mode of collecting the Sentiments of the People upon the Constitution, it was not done wth. the least Design to give any Offence to the respectable Body who composed the Convention, or a Disregard to the Recommendation of Congress, but upon pure Republican Principles, founded upon that Basis of all Governments originally deriving from the Body of the People at large.—And altho' the Majority hath been so great against adopting the Constitution, yet the People in general conceive that it may contain some necessary Articles which could well be added and adapted to the present Confederation. They are sensible that the present Powers invested with Congress are incompetent for the great national Government of the Union, and would heartily acquiesce in granting sufficient Authority to that Body to make exercise and enforce Laws throughout the States which would tend to regulate Commerce, impose Duties and Excise, whereby Congress might establish Funds for discharging the public Debt.[2]

We regret that any Dissensions should [be?] in this State, when the Good of the Community is our Wish, and it will ever be our Disposition to endeavor to promote whatever appears to us to be of public Utility, and to harmonize as much as possible.

In Behalf of the General Assembly I have the Honor to be, with every Sentiment of Esteem, Sir Your Excellency's Most humble and Most obedient Servant

1. Because of minor errors in addition by the town clerks, disagreement exists among historians as to the exact vote. The Providence *United States Chronicle*, 10 April, reported that 4,170 votes were cast in the previous general election.

2. After reading the legislature's letter, a writer in the *Providence Gazette*, 12 April, said that "A Doubt arose whether the General Assembly possessed Authority to make a Tender of Powers to Congress, so essentially diminishing the Privileges of their Constituents, without consulting them on that Subject also.—Several Members discovered an Inclination to adopt some Measures for reducing to a Certainty the Powers which the Freemen of this State were willing to devolve on Congress, but after some ineffectual Motions this Business was wa[i]ved."

Rhode Island's legislature had already approved both grants of power to Congress to regulate trade and the Impost of 1783. The first grant of power, proposed by Congress on 30 April 1784, was adopted by the legislature in March and October 1785. The second grant, proposed by Congress on 28 March 1785, and the Impost of 1783 were adopted by the legislature in March 1786. For the impost and the grants of power, see CDR, 146–48, 153–56.

### 665. Francis Hopkinson to Thomas Jefferson
### Philadelphia, 6 April (excerpt)[1]

. . . I have another Gathering of Magazines, Museums, & News Papers for you, waiting a suitable opportunity.—We are in a high political Fermentation about our new proposed federal Constitution. There are in every State People who have Debts to pay, Interests to support, or Fortunes to make—these wish for scrambling Times, paper Money Speculations, or partial Commercial advantages—An effective general Government will not suit their Views, & of Course there are great oppositions made to the new Constitution—but this opposition chiefly arises from a few leading Party Men in the Towns & Cities, who have been very industrious in holding it up as a political Monster to the Multitude who know nothing of Government, & have gained many Proselytes in the back Counties.—The Lees[2] & Mr. Mason have so exerted themselves in Virginia as to make the Determination of that State doubtful—Maryland is infected with a Mr Martin—but I am told the Constitution will be adopted there We shall know in a few Weeks— The Convention met in New Hampshire & adjourn'd to sometime in June—The City of New York is federal, but the ~~State~~ Country much opposed, under the Influence of Govr. Clinton.—Altho' Pennsylvania has long since adopted the proposed System, yet in no State have the People behaved so scandalously as here—George Bryan & his Party (formerly called the Constitutional Party) have been moving Heaven & Earth against the Establishment of a federal Government—Our Papers teem with the most opprob[r]ious Revilings against the System & against all who befriend it—These Scriblers began with Arguments against the proposed Plan, such Arguments as would stand with equal Force against every or any Government that can be devised—they were Arguments against Government in general, as an Infringement upon natural Liberty—they then poured forth a torrent of abuse against the Members of the late general Convention personally & individually— You will be surprized when I tell you that our public news Papers have anounced General Washington to be a Fool influenced & lead by that Knave Dr. Franklin, who is a public Defaulter for Millions of Dollars, that Mr. Morris has defrauded the Public out of as many Millions as you please & that they are to cover their frauds by this new Government[3]—What think you of this.—Some of the Authors of these inflamatory Publications have been traced, & found to be Men of desperate Circumstances—I had the Luck to discover & bring forward into public View on sufficient Testimony the Writer of a Series of abominable Abuse, under the Signature *Philadelphiensis*, he is an Irishman who came from Dublin about 3 Years ago & got admitted as a Tutor in Arithmetic in our University—I am now under the Lash for this Discovery, scarce a Day passes without my Appearance in the News Paper in every scandalous Garb that scribling Vengeance can furnish[4]— I wrote also a Piece stiled *The new Roof* which had a great Run—I would send you a Copy but for the Postage—you will probably see it in some of the Papers, as it was reprinted in, I believe, every State[5]—

I am sorry to tell you that our friend Mr. Rittenhouse[6] is anti federal—However, we never touch upon Politics Dr. Franklin is as well as usual. . . .

1. RC, Jefferson Papers, DLC. Printed: Boyd, XIII, 38–41.

2. Arthur and Richard Henry Lee.

3. "Centinel" I (CC:133) had charged that Washington had been duped into signing the Constitution. "Centinel" XVI (CC:565) accused Franklin and Morris of being public defaulters.

4. For the exchange between Hopkinson ("A.B.") and "Philadelphiensis" (Benjamin Workman), see the editorial note to CC:237.

5. By 28 April "The New Roof," *Pennsylvania Packet*, 29 December, was reprinted in fourteen newspapers in eight states and Vermont (CC:395).

6. David Rittenhouse—mathematician, astronomer, and treasurer of Pennsylvania—was on the unsuccessful Antifederalist ticket for state Convention delegates for the city of Philadelphia.

## 666. Observations on the Proposed Constitution
## New York, c. 6 April

For five days beginning on 29 April, voters in the state of New York elected delegates to their state ratifying convention—the last state to elect such delegates. (The Rhode Island legislature refused to call a convention and freemen overwhelmingly rejected the Constitution in town meetings on 24 March 1788 [CC:664].) Federalists and Antifederalists campaigned strenuously. The New York Antifederal Committee (composed largely of New York City Antifederalists) flooded the state with literature opposing unconditional ratification. One of these pieces was a 126-page anthology entitled *Observations on the Proposed Constitution for the United States of America, Clearly shewing it to be a complete System of Aristocracy and Tyranny, and Destructive of the Rights and Liberties of the People* (Evans 21344). No publisher's name appears in the colophon, but Thomas Greenleaf of the Antifederalist *New York Journal* probably published the pamphlet in either late March or early April. The pamphlet was not advertised in the newspapers perhaps because the committee intended it primarily—or maybe exclusively—for free statewide distribution.

The reprinted documents in the anthology were introduced by a single sentence: "Although the following pieces were addressed to the inhabitants of Pennsylvania, &c. they are (in almost every respect) as applicable to this state, and to every other state in the union." The anthology consists of: (1) the "Dissent of the Minority of the Pennsylvania Convention" (CC:353); (2) Governor Edmund Randolph's letter of 10 October to the speaker of the Virginia House of Delegates explaining why he had not signed the Constitution (CC:385); (3) the first nine essays by "Centinel" (CC:133, 190, 243, 311, 318, 379, 394, 410, 427); and (4) an appendix containing the Constitution and the 17 September 1787 resolutions of the Constitutional Convention (CC:76).

At about the time that the anthology appeared, Thomas Greenleaf reprinted

"A Columbian Patriot's" *Observations on the New Constitution* . . . . This twenty-two-page pamphlet, written by Mercy Warren of Massachusetts, had first been published in Boston in late February (CC:581). On 6 April the New York Antifederal Committee sent copies of "A Columbian Patriot" "under cover" to the county Antifederal committees throughout the state, asking them to help defray the printing costs (Lamb Papers, NHi). Two days later it forwarded copies of the anthology.

Charles Tillinghast, the committee's secretary, kept a list of the number of pamphlets transmitted to each county and to whom they were sent. Richmond and Clinton counties alone are not listed—perhaps they received copies of the pamphlets from neighboring counties. (Voters in newly created Clinton County were not represented in the state Convention as a county, but they voted in the Washington County election.) Tillinghast's list includes only the names of individuals in New York County who were to receive pamphlets but no reference is made to the actual number of pamphlets distributed there. Perhaps these individuals received the residue of the pamphlets not sent to other counties. In all, the New York Antifederal Committee distributed 1,700 copies of "A Columbian Patriot" and 225 copies of the anthology outside New York County. (See undated two-page document initialed "C.T." in Box 5 of the Lamb Papers at the New-York Historical Society.)

Albany Antifederalists wrote their brethren in New York City on 12 April, acknowledging the letters of 6 and 8 April and the copies of "A Columbian Patriot." They noted, however, that "The Pamphlets from Greenleaf [i.e., the anthologies] are not arrived—By this Stage we send a special Messenger to find out what is become of them and if found to bring them up, but they will at any rate arrive too late to be of any Service." In a postscript, the Albany committee added: "We shall also disperse the Residue of your Pamphlets in this County, but do not expect to pay for them, as we are but few in Number who manage the Business in this City and have already incurred a considerable Expence exclusive of throwing away the Money for Greenleafs Pamphlets" (Lamb Papers, NHi).

In Dutchess County, where the anthology had been "sent up in vast quantities from New-York," "A Federalist" attacked the "inflamatory" title page and noted that he detected "a gross imposition" in the publication of Governor Randolph's letter. (Fifty copies of the pamphlet had been earmarked for Dutchess County.) Governor Randolph, stated "A Federalist," "appears to surmount all the leading objections which have been so profusely raised against the Constitution—he advocates with great ingenuity and precision all its essential principles, and then (to the astonishment of his friends, and as a strong instance of the weakness of human reason) he appears to refuse his assent on some of the lesser and very immaterial parts of its structure. But in this pamphlet, the most interesting paragraph in the whole letter is wantonly suppressed to the great injustice of that liberal patriot, and with the most daring affrontery to the public."

"A Federalist" pointed to the omission of the next to the last paragraph that stated: "But as I affect neither mystery nor subtilty, in politics, I hesitate not to say, that the most fervent prayer of my soul is the establishment of a firm, energetic government; that the most inveterate curse, which can befal us, is a dissolution of the union; and that the present moment, if suffered to pass away unemployed, can never be recalled. These were my opinions, while I acted as a Delegate; they sway me, while I speak as a private citizen. I shall therefore cling to the union, as the rock of our salvation, and urge Virginia to finish the salutary work, which she has begun. And if after our best efforts for amendments they cannot be obtained, I scruple not to declare, (notwithstanding the advantage, which such a declaration may give to the enemies of my proposal,) that I will, as an individual citizen, accept the Constitution; because I would regulate myself by the spirit of America." (The quoted text is taken from "A Federalist," Poughkeepsie *Country Journal*, 22 April.)

"A Federalist" admired the spirit of "moderation" in the omitted paragraph and wished that such a spirit were present in New York, where the enemies of the Constitution "are for setting the whole continent at defiance." Moreover, he wanted to instruct the people about "the tricks which are practising to delude them." He concluded: "I would only observe, that if we can rely on the public accounts from Virginia, Governor Randolph has changed his mind since the ratification of the Constitution by Massachusetts. If this cannot be depended on, yet we have not only their own papers, but the very authentic evidence of General Washington's letter to induce a belief that Virginia will undoubtedly ratify the Constitution" (Poughkeepsie *Country Journal*, 22 April. For Washington's letter of 29 February to Caleb Gibbs which was reprinted six times in New York, see CC:638.).

### 667. James Madison to George Nicholas
### Orange County, Va., 8 April[1]

Your favor of the 5th. instant was duly handed to me last evening. The sentiments contained in it appear to me to be dictated by the most perfect propriety both as they regard the importance of the present moment, and the measures which it renders expedient. As I wish not to decline any cooperation that may tend to save America from anarchy and disunion, I shall cheerfully execute the task you suggest of urging on Gentlemen in Maryland & South Carolina[2] the mischievous influence here of such examples as N. Hampshire has set. I hope you will not omit the same precaution as to Maryland at least. I know that the opposition there, despairing of success in a direct attack on the Constitution, mean to contend for a postponement of the question.[3] It is extremely probable that the same policy will occur or be suggested to the opposition in S. Carolina. I will write to several Gentlemen in Kentucky also, with a view to counteract efforts which I understand are on foot, for turning their jealousy on the subject of the Mississippi, against the proposed change in the fœderal System. It is obvious to me that the obstacles to a sacrifice of that important object will be increased at the same time that the pretexts for it will be removed, by an establishment of the new Government; and that this event alone can promise in any short time such arrangements with Spain as Kentucky must wish for. No fœderal Government will in my opinion be able very long to procrastinate an effectual assertion of the right agst. the Spaniards. The chief question with Kentucky ought therefore to be whether the present or the proposed system be most likely to obtain a positive and speedy recognition of it. From the present she cannot possibly have any thing to hope. From neither do I believe she has any thing to fear.[4] You will do well I think to correspond also with Kentucky on this subject. I hope indeed that you have already done so. Your known purpose of becoming a resident must secure you an attention that no other could expect. The necessity or at least the nature of an address to the people from the friends of the Constitution may perhaps be best judged of, after the views of the adverse party are bro't forward in the Convention, and the event reduced to certainty. And I should suppose the preparation of it may be brought within the compass of time then attainable.

I think entirely with you on the subject of amendments. The plan of Massts. is unquestionably the Ultimatum of the fœderalists.[5] Conditional amendments or a second general Convention will be fatal. The delay only of such experiments is too serious to be hazarded. It is a fact, of which you though probably not a great number may be apprized, that the late Convention were in one stage of the business for several days under the strongest apprehensions of an abortive issue to their deliberations. There were moments during this period at which despair seemed with many to predominate. I can ascribe the final success to nothing but the temper with which the Members assembled, and their ignorance of the opinions & confidence in the liberality of their respective constituents. The circumstances under which a second Convention composed even of wiser individuals, would meet, must extinguish every hope of an equal spirit of accomodation; and if it should happen to contain men, who secretly aimed at disunion, (and such I believe would be found from more than one State) the game would be as easy as it would be obvious, to insist on points popular in some parts, but known to be inadmissible in others of the Union. Should it happen otherwise, and another plan be agreed on, it must now be evident from a view of the objections prevailing in the different States among the advocates for amendments, that the opponents in this State who are attached to the Union and sensible of the necessity of a nervous[6] Government for it, would be more dissatisfied with the result of the second than of the first experiment. From the account I have of Mr. Pendleton's opinions I have no great apprehensions of his falling into the scheme of preliminary alterations. I had some days ago an opportunity of conversing pretty fully with his colleague & particular friend Col. Taylor, and of stating such facts & remarks as appeared to combat that scheme. Should a convenient occasion offer, I may take the liberty of repeating them to the Chancellor.[7] When I write to [our?] friend in Richmond[8] I shall feel no restraint from giving him similar intimations. If report be not more than usually incorrect as to the conduct and language of Col. Mason, he has totally abandoned his moderation on this subject; and is pursuing his object by means which will neither add to the dignity of his character; nor I should hope, to the success of his cause. The manner in which you account for his intemperance is, I fancy, the true one.

Congress had come to no decision when I left N. York, on the proposed separation of Kentucky. Nine States had been but a few days only on the floor, and were then engaged on the subject. I waited as long as I possibly could in hopes of seeing something done, but was not gratified; and I learn by subsequent information that the Representation soon fell to seven States, which had suspended the consideration of the subject.[9] The opposition to the measure had not fully shewn itself when I came away. It will proceed chiefly from a scruple drawn from the peculiar State of our affairs, and from the defect of power under the existing Confederation. There are individuals who will throw obstacles in the way, till Vermont can be let in at the same time. And others, I suspect, who will do the same, with the covert view of irritating Kentucky into an opposition to the new Government. Being aware of the influence which the temper of Kentucky might have on the event in this State, I was anxious that Congress should at once accede to her wishes; without regarding scruples which otherwise could not be denied to have weight. I fear somewhat that Mr. Brown's anxiety to obtain a favorite point for his district, may expose him to impressions from the difficulties I have hinted, which will not be auspicious to the present conjuncture of things. This however is but conjecture. His judgment I have reason to believe is favorable to the New Government as it relates to the general interest of America; nor do I know that he views it in a different relation to that of Kentucky in particular. I know only that pains were taken with him on his way to Congress, if not also before he set out, to alarm his fears for the Miss-pi, and prepare him for unfavorable impressions. I will think of the hint you throw out, and will endeavor to give it effect, if I can devise any convenient means of success.

It is not in my power to obey the last of your suggestions. I have made declarations which do not now admit of my being a candidate for the assembly. If I have not mistaken the law a member of Congs.

is *ineligible* to a seat there;[10] and I do not know that I could resign that Character to any existing authority. But independently of these considerations, I am led to suppose that advocates for the requisite measures for setting the new machine at work may be needed as much in Congress as in this State. I do not understand that any opposition will be made here to Mr. Gordon & Mr. Burnley;[11] both of whom are declared and the former a proved federalist—The publication of which you wish a number of copies, is to come out in two parts.[12] The first is probably ready by this time. The other will be delayed a few weeks. I will take measures for obtaining as soon as possible the number you desire.—I have just recd. from Mr. Griffin[13] some of the late numbers which are herewith inclosed.

[P.S.] I find that Rhode Island has submitted the Constitution to the people to be decided by majority of voices *immediately* given.[14] This mode precludes every result but that of a total adoption or rejection; and as the latter was foreseen, shews a determination there to involve all things in Confusion. The question will be decided precisely by the same majority as have prevailed in every other instance of late; the paper money party being agst. & the other party for the Constitution.

1. RC, Reuben T. Durrett Collection, George Nicholas, Department of Special Collections, University of Chicago Library. Madison replies to Nicholas' letter of 5 April (CC:663).

2. By 10 April, Madison had written to friends in both Maryland and South Carolina (RCS:Va., 705, note 2).

3. Madison had cause for concern. See headnote to CC:695.

4. The next day, Madison wrote John Brown of Kentucky, then a Virginia delegate to Congress in New York City. Reviewing the returns of the Virginia Convention elections, Madison told Brown that "A good deal may depend on the vote of Kentucky in the question [of ratifying the Constitution]. I have taken the liberty of stating to several gentlemen in that quarter my opinion that the constitutional impediments to improper measures relating to the Missisṗpi will be greater as well as the pretexts for them be less under the new than the existing System; and that the former alone can promise any effectual measures either in favor of that object, or of a dispossession of the English of the posts, an object of still more immediate consequence perhaps to the district" (RCS:Va., 711–12). On 10 April Madison wrote Washington that "I have written several letters since my arrival, to correspondents in that district [Kentucky], with a view to counteract antifederal machinations. I have little expectation however that they will have much effect, unless the communications that may go from Mr. Brown in Congress, should happen to breathe the same spirit: and I am not without apprehensions that his mind may have taken an unlucky tincture from the difficulties thrown in the way of the separation of the district, as well as from some antecedent proceedings of Congress" (RCS:Va., 732). None of Madison's letters to Kentuckians has been found.

5. Madison refers to the recommendatory amendments of the Massachusetts Convention (CC:508).

6. At this time, "nervous" meant "strong, vigorous, robust."

7. Colonel James Taylor and Edmund Pendleton (the president of the High Court

of Chancery) represented Caroline County in the Virginia Convention, where they voted to ratify the Constitution in June.

8. Probably Governor Edmund Randolph to whom Madison wrote on 10 April (CC:673).

9. For the status of Kentucky statehood in Congress, see CC:480, note 2. The Articles of Confederation required the assent of nine states for the admission of any new state (except for Canada) to the Union (CDR, 93).

10. According to a 1783 Virginia law, delegates to Congress could not serve simultaneously in the state legislature (William Waller Hening, ed., *The Statutes at Large; Being a Collection of All the Laws of Virginia, from the First Session of the Legislature, in the Year 1619* [13 vols., Richmond and Philadelphia, 1809–1823], XI, 249–50).

11. Later in the month, James Gordon, Jr., and Hardin Burnley were elected to represent Orange County in the Virginia House of Delegates. Along with Madison, Gordon had already been elected a delegate to the Virginia Convention, where he voted to ratify the Constitution in June. Burnley opposed the Constitution. (For the state Convention election in Orange, see RCS:Va., 595–606.)

12. For the circulation of *The Federalist* in Virginia, see RCS:Va., 652–55.

13. Cyrus Griffin, a Virginia delegate and the President of Congress, regularly sent Madison New York City newspapers containing *The Federalist*. His letters of 17 and 24 March probably included essays 64–73, printed between 5 and 21 March (Rutland, *Madison*, XI, 3, 5. Madison had left New York on either 3 or 4 March.). Inadvertently, Griffin omitted essay 70 (Griffin to Madison, 28 April, RCS:Va., 764–65).

14. For the Rhode Island referendum on the Constitution, see CC:664.

## 668. "K"
### Philadelphia Federal Gazette, 8 April

"K" was written by Benjamin Franklin. A manuscript of this essay, in Franklin's handwriting, is in the Franklin Papers at the Library of Congress. Moreover, an annotation in that library's file of the Philadelphia *Federal Gazette*, where the essay first appeared on 8 April, identifies Franklin as "K"; and Franklin himself took credit for writing the article in several letters that he wrote in October 1788. (There are no significant differences between the newspaper and manuscript versions. The draft was docketed: "Law by Moses.")

"K" was reprinted in the *Pennsylvania Gazette*, 9 April; Baltimore *Maryland Gazette*, 11 April; *Carlisle Gazette*, 23 April (under the pseudonym "Z"); and *Virginia Independent Chronicle*, 23 April. On 15 October the *Federal Gazette* printed "K" again with this preface: "The following is copied from the Federal Gazette of the 8th of April last. It is republished by the particular desire of a large and respectable number of subscribers, who wish to have so valuable a performance effectually preserved." About two weeks later the Philadelphia *American Museum* reprinted "K" in its October issue preceded by this summary: "Impossibility of devising a form of government universally acceptable. Conduct of the Jews. Corah's conspiracy. Moses accused of peculation."

On 22 October Franklin sent a copy of "K" to John Wright, a Quaker and a London banker. Wright gave the essay to the editor of the London *Gentlemen's Magazine*, where it was printed in the February 1789 issue with the signature "B.F." (Franklin to Wright, 22 October, Franklin Papers, DLC;

and Wright to Franklin, 31 July 1789, Franklin Papers, PPAmP). The *Gentleman's Magazine* included a prefatory statement by "J.B.": "If the following address to the inhabitants of the United States of America, by the celebrated Dr. Benjamin Franklin, on the disaffection that has prevailed towards the new system of government introduced in that country, is thought worth a place in your useful Repository, the immediate insertion of it will oblige." (Franklin also sent a copy to Londoner Benjamin Vaughan [24 October, Smyth, *Franklin*, IX, 676].)

On 24 October Franklin transmitted copies of his article to two friends in France—Ferdinand Grand, a Paris banker, and Louis-Guillaume Le Veillard, the operator of mineral baths in Passy. Franklin described "K" as the only essay that he had written on the Constitution and stated that it "was said to have had some good Effect" (*ibid.*, 673–74, 678). It is possible that one of these two men showed "K" to the Abbé André Morellet, a writer and political economist, who published it in Paris in 1789 as a twelve-page pamphlet entitled: *Avis Aux Faiseurs de Constitutions par M. Benjamin Franklin.*

For an unpublished essay that Franklin wrote in late March 1788 which attacked the vitriolic nature of the debate on the Constitution, see Mfm:Pa. 588.

### To the Editor of the Federal Gazette.

Sir, A zealous advocate for the proposed Federal Constitution, in a certain public assembly, said, that *the repugnance of a great part of mankind to good government was such, that he believed, that if an angel from heaven was to bring down a constitution formed there for our use, it would nevertheless meet with violent opposition.* He was reproved for the supposed extravagance of the sentiment; and he did not justify it. Probably it might not have immediately occur[r]ed to him that the experiment had been tried, and that the event was recorded in the most faithful of all histories, the Holy Bible; otherwise he might, as it seems to me, have supported his opinion by that unexceptionable authority.

The Supreme Being had been pleased to nourish up a single family, by continued acts of his attentive providence, 'till it became a great people; and having rescued them from bondage by many miracles performed by his servant Moses, he personally delivered to that chosen servant, in presence of the whole nation, a *constitution* and code of laws for their observance, accompanied and sanctioned with promises of great rewards, and threats of severe punishments, as the consequence of their obedience or disobedience.

This constitution, though the Deity himself was to be at its head, and it is therefore called by political writers a *Theocracy*, could not be carried into execution but by the means of his ministers; Aaron and his sons were therefore commissioned to be, with Moses, the first established ministry of the new government.

One would have thought, that the appointment of men who had

distinguished themselves in procuring the liberty of their nation, and had hazarded their lives in openly opposing the will of a powerful monarch, who would have retained that nation in slavery, might have been an appointment acceptable to a grateful people; and that a constitution fram'd for them by the Deity himself, might, on that account, have been secure of an universal welcome reception; yet there were in every one of the *thirteen tribes*, some discontented restless spirits, who were continually exciting them to reject the proposed new government, and this from various motives.

Many still retained an affection for Egypt, the land of their nativity; and these, whenever they felt any inconvenience or hardship, though the natural and unavoidable effect of their change of situation, exclaimed against their leaders as the authors of their trouble, and were not only for returning into Egypt, but for stoning their deliverers.[a] Those inclined to idolatry were displeased that their *golden calf* was destroyed. Many of the chiefs thought the new constitution might be injurious to their particular interests, that the *profitable places* would be *engrossed by the families and friends of Moses and Aaron*, and others equally well-born excluded.[b] In Josephus, and the Talmud we learn some particulars, not so fully narrated in the scripture. We are there told, that Corah was ambitious of the priesthood, and offended that it was conferred on Aaron, and this, as he said, by the authority of Moses only, *without the consent of the people*. He accused Moses of having by various artifices fra[u]dulently obtained the government, and deprived the people of *their liberties*; and of CONSPIRING with Aaron to perpetuate the tyranny in their family. Thus though Corah's real motive was the supplanting of Aaron, he persuaded the people that he meant only the *public good*; and they, mov'd by his insinuations, began to cry out, "Let us maintain the *common liberty* of our *respective tribes*; we have freed ourselves from the slavery imposed upon us by the Egyptians, and shall we suffer ourselves to be made slaves by Moses? If we must have a master, it were better to return to Pharaoh, who at least fed us with bread and onions, than to serve this new tyrant, who by his operations has brought us into danger of famine." Then they called in question the reality of his conferences with God, and objected [to] the *privacy of the meetings*, and the *preventing any of the people from being present* at the colloquies, or even approaching the place, as grounds of great suspicion. They accused Moses also of *peculation*, as embezzling part of the golden spoons and the silver chargers, that the princes had offered at the dedication of the altar,[c] and the offerings of gold by the common people,[d] as well as most of the poll tax;[e] and Aaron they accused of pocketing much of the gold of which he pretended to have made a molten calf. Besides *peculation*, they charged Moses with *ambition*; to gratify which passion, he had, they said, deceived the people, by promising to bring them *to* a land flowing with milk and honey; instead of doing which, he had brought them *from* such a land; and that he thought light of all this mischief, provided he could make himself an *absolute prince*.[f] That to support the new dignity with splendor in his family, the partial poll-tax already levied and given to Aaron[g] was to be followed by a general one,[h] which would probably be augmented from time to time, if he were suffered to go on promulgating new laws, on pretence of new occasional revelations of the divine will, 'till their whole fortunes were devoured by that aristocracy.

Moses denied the charge of *peculation*; and his accusers were destitute of proofs to support it; though *facts*, if real, are in their nature capable of proof. "I have not," said he (with holy confidence in the presence of God,) "I have not taken from this people the value of an ass, nor done them any other injury." But his enemies had made the charge, and with some success among the populace, for *no kind of accusation is so readily made, or easily believed, by KNAVES, as the accusation of knavery.*

In fine, no less than two hundred and fifty of the principal men "famous in the congregation, men of renown,"[i] heading and exciting the mob, worked them up to such a pitch of phrensy, that they called out, Stone 'em, stone 'em, and thereby *secure our liberties*; and let us chuse other captains that may lead us back into Egypt, in case we do not succeed in reducing the Canaanites.

On the whole it appears, that the Israelites were a people jealous of their newly acquired liberty, which jealousy was in itself no fault; but, that when they suffered it to be worked upon by artful men, pretending public good, with nothing really in view but private interest, they were led to oppose the establishment of the *new constitution*, whereby they brought upon themselves much inconvenience and misfortune. It farther appears from the same inestimable history, that when, after many ages, that constitution was become old and much abused, and an amendment of it was proposed, the populace as they had accused Moses of the ambition of making himself a *prince*, and cryed out *stone him, stone him*; so excited by their high priests and SCRIBES, they exclaimed against the Messiah, that he aimed at becoming *king* of the Jews, and cryed out *crucify him, crucify him*. From all which we may gather, that popular opposition to a public measure is no proof of its impropriety, even though the opposition be excited and headed by men of distinction.

To conclude, I beg I may not be understood to infer, that our general convention was divinely inspired when it formed the new federal constitution, merely because that constitution has been unreasonably and vehemently opposed; yet I must own, I have so much faith in the general government of the world by PROVIDENCE, that I can hardly conceive a transaction of such momentous importance to the welfare of millions now existing, and to exist in the posterity of a great nation, should be suffered to pass without being in some degree influenced, guided, and governed by that omnipotent, omnipresent and beneficent Ruler, in whom all inferior spirits live and move and have their being.

(a) Numbers chap. xiv.

(b) Numbers chap. xvi. ver. 3. And they gathered themselves together against Moses and against Aaron, and said unto them, Ye take too much upon you, seeing all the congregation are holy, *every one of them,*—wherefore then lift ye up yourselves above the congregation?

(c) Numbers chap. vii.

(d) Exodus chapter xxxv. ver. 22.

(e) Numbers chap. iii. and Exodus chap. xxx.

(f) Numbers chap. xvi. ver. 13. Is it a small thing that thou hast brought us up *out of a land* flowing with milk and honey, to kill us in this wilderness, except thou make thyself *altogether a prince* over us?

(g) Numbers chap. iii.

(h) Exodus chap. xxx.

(i) Numbers chap. xvi.

### 669. Henry Knox to John Sullivan
### New York, 9 April[1]

I have hitherto deferred my dear Sir, answering your esteemed favor of the 27th of February[2] in hopes of being able to give you a satisfactory statement of public affairs. But the unfortunate check the new constitution received in New Hampshire has given new life and Spirits to the opponents of the proposed system, and damped the ardor of its friends

The Convention in South Carolina is to meet on the 12th of next month—The general tenor of the information is that it will be adopted there but not without considerable opposition—

North Carolina is not to meet untill July—The general opinion seems to be that they will follow the example of Virginia—The convention of which meets in June—The constitution in that state will meet with great opposition indeed, and the issue extremely doubtful—As far as information has been received of the elections which were finished in March, the complection is favorable.[3] The arguments against it there are mostly local although many ostensible ones will appear—Impositions by the eastern states on their commerce; & Treaties being the supreme law of the land thereby compelling the payment of the british debts will be the real objections of the greater part of the opposers— while some others apprehend a consolodation of the Union as a real evil

In Maryland it is highly probable according to the information received, that the constitution will be adopted there by a great majority their convention will meet the last of this month—

In the state of New York the interests pro and con are so divided that it is impossible for an impartial person to say on which side the scale will turn. Both sides appear confident of victory and both sides are pretty industrious in preparing for the elections which are to take place in about a fortnight—

The Rhode Island people are riveted to the works of paper money and darkness—They will reject the New Constitution

I am happy that you have such confidence in the future conduct of your convention—I hope in God you may not be disapointed

The business of electioneering runs high—We cannot judge who will be the president you or Mr Langdon[4] But in either case your friends who are the friends of the Union rest assured that you are both too good patriots, to be disgusted in such a manner as to suffer your ardor for the constitution to be abated—A Man possessing all the virtues of an angel may not have the majority of votes in states where the choice very frequently may depend on mere trifles not more important than the color of a mans hair, eyes—his size or carriage

I hope to have the pleasure to see you in the ensuing summer in New Hampshire—in the mean time I shall be happy to learn from you the fate of the constitution

I am with great respect and affection Your humble Servant

1. RC, New Hampshire Miscellany, 1782–1809 (Peter Force), DLC.
2. This letter has not been found, but, in a 10 March letter to George Washington, Knox stated that "I have received a letter from President Sullivan in which he says that the adjournment will be attended with the hapiest consequences, and that the convention in their next session will adopt the constitution by a majority of three to one" (CC:610). Sullivan probably also outlined the reasons for the adjournment of the New Hampshire Convention on 22 February without ratifying the Constitution (CC:554).
3. For a later and more precise estimate by Knox of the Federalist majority in the Virginia Convention, see his 27 April letter to Jeremiah Wadsworth (CC:712).

4. In March 1788 ballots were cast for the election of president of New Hampshire, but they were not officially counted until the new legislature met in June, when it was discovered that John Langdon had defeated John Sullivan, and several other candidates, thereby replacing Sullivan as president.

## 670. Consider Arms, Malachi Maynard, and Samuel Field: Dissent to the Massachusetts Convention, Northampton Hampshire Gazette, 9, 16 April

After a month of heated debates, the Massachusetts Convention narrowly ratified the Constitution on 6 February by a vote of 187 to 168. The opponents of the Constitution had held a majority, but the promise of recommendatory amendments led some of them to support the Constitution. Immediately after the vote, several delegates who had voted against ratification informed the Convention that they would accept the will of the majority and support the Constitution. They were joined by a few other Antifederalists the next day (CC:508). News of the acquiescence of these Antifederalists was disseminated rapidly throughout America and was applauded by numerous Federalists, among them George Washington whose published letter praising them was widely reprinted (CC:638).

Three Hampshire County delegates who had voted against ratification, however, continued to oppose the Constitution, and they decided to publish their reasons of dissent in the *Hampshire Gazette*, one of the county's two newspapers. These three delegates, who apparently did not speak in the Convention debates, were Samuel Field of Deerfield and Captain Consider Arms and Malachi Maynard of Conway, all of whom had been figures of controversy before. During the Revolution, Field and Arms were Loyalists; while Arms and Maynard were active in Shays's Rebellion, 1786–87. After the Shaysites were defeated, Arms and Maynard were among the 790 insurgents who took and subscribed the oath of allegiance to the state of Massachusetts. They were two of the twenty-nine insurgents in the Massachusetts Convention, all but one of whom voted against ratification.

Sensitive to their controversial pasts and their vote on ratification, Field, Arms, and Maynard concluded their reasons of dissent by promising not "to be disturbers of the peace," but "to be subject to 'the powers that be' " if the Constitution were adopted and put into effect. No newspapers reprinted their dissent.

Samuel Field (1743–1800), a graduate of Yale College (1762), was variously a divinity student, lawyer, merchant, farmer, and poet. A Sandemanian in religion, it was his Christian duty to be obedient to the King of England. Consequently, he opposed the Revolutionary War, but remained neutral during the fighting. Field represented Deerfield in the House of Representatives, 1773, 1774, 1791; he was also a town selectman, 1782, 1791, moderator, 1783–84, and clerk, 1791.

Captain Consider Arms (1736–1792), a farmer and large landholder, was Conway town clerk and treasurer, 1767–75; selectman, 1767, 1774; assessor, 1767, 1770–74; and representative, 1788. Arms was elected to the Massachusetts Provincial Congress in 1774, but he did not attend and afterwards became a Loyalist. Malachi Maynard (1746–1824), a farmer, was Conway town assessor, 1781–82, 1784, 1786–87, 1792, 1794–99, 1803; selectman, 1782–83, 1797–99; treasurer, 1784–96, 1800–11, 1816; and representative, 1799–1801. Maynard was on the patriot side during the American Revolution. Arms and Maynard were neighbors and good friends.

On 23 April "Philanthrop" answered Field, Arms, and Maynard in the *Hampshire Gazette*. He could not understand why they published their dissent because "Their objections have adorned the news papers for several months past, and often received answers, which to many persons appeared satisfactory." "Philanthrop" challenged their objections to the power of Congress to regulate federal elections, the power of Congress over the military and finances, the three-fifths clause, and, most particularly, the slave-trade clause. He also defended the Massachusetts Convention against charges that "unfair methods were practised" in order to produce a majority in favor of the Constitution and that the Convention supported the slave trade. (For a reply to "Philanthrop's" comments concerning the slave trade, see "Phileleutheros," *Hampshire Gazette*, 21 May.)

Mr. PRINTER, We the Subscribers being of the number, who did not assent to the ratification of the Federal Constitution, under consideration in the late State Convention, held at Boston, to which we were called by the suffrages of the corporations to which we respectively belong—beg leave, through the channel of your paper, to lay before the public in general, and our constituents in particular, the reasons of our dissent, and the principles which governed us in our decision of this important question.

Fully convinced, ever since the late revolution, of the necessity of a firm, energetic government, we should have rejoiced in an opportunity to have given our assent to such an one; and should in the present case, most cordially have done it, could we at the same time [have] been happy to have seen the liberties of the people and the rights of mankind properly guarded and secured. We conceive that the very notion of government carries along with it the idea of justice and equity, and that the whole design of instituting government in the world, was to preserve men's properties from rapine, and their bodies from violence and bloodshed.

These propositions being established, we conceive must of necessity produce the following consequence, viz. That every constitution or system, which does not quadrate with this original design, is not government, but in fact a subversion of it.

Having premised thus much, we proceed to mention some things in this constitution, to which we object, and to enter into an enquiry, whether, and how far they coincide with those simple and original notions of government beforementioned.

In the first place—as direct taxes are to be apportioned according to the numbers in each state, and as Massachusetts has none in it but what are declared freemen, so the whole, blacks as well as whites, must be numbered; this must therefore operate against us, as two fifths of the slaves in the southern states are to be left out of the numeration; consequently, three Massachusetts infants will increase the tax equal to five sturdy, full grown negroes of theirs, who work every day in the week for their masters, saving the Sabbath, upon which they are allowed to get something for their own support. We can see no justice in this way of apportioning taxes; neither can we see any good reason why this was consented to on the part of our delegates.

We suppose it next to impossible that every individual in this vast continental union, should have his wish with regard to every single article, composing a frame of government; and therefore, although we think it more agreeable to the principles of republicanism, that elections should be annual; yet as the elections in our own state government are so, we did not view it so dangerous to the liberties of the people, that we should have rejected the constitution merely on account of the biennial elections of the representatives, had we been sure that the people have any security, even of this; but this we could [not] find. For although it is said, that "the House of Representatives shall be chosen every second year, by the people of the several states," &c. and that "the times, places and manner of holding elections for senators and representatives, shall be prescribed in each state by the legislature thereof;" yet all this is wholly superseded by a subsequent provision, which empowers Congress at any time to enact a law, whereby such regulations may be altered, except as to the places of chusing senators. Here we conceive the people may be very materially injured, and in time reduced to a state of as abject vassallage, as any people were under the controul of the most mercenary despot, that ever *tarnished* the pages of history. The depravity of human nature, illustrated by examples from history, will warrant us to say, it may be possible, if not probable, that the Congress may be composed of men, who will wish to burthen and oppress the people. In such case, will not their inventions be fruitful enough to devise occasions for postponing the elections? And if they can do this once, they can twice— if they can twice they can thrice, so by degrees render themselves absolute and perpetual. Or, if they choose, they have another expedient; they can alter the place of holding elections. They can say, whatever the legislature of this state may order to the contrary, that all the elections of our representatives shall be made at Mechias, or at Williamstown; consequently, nine-tenths of the people will never vote. And if this should be thought a measure favourable to their re-election, or the election of some tool for their mercenary purposes, we doubt not it will be thus ordered. But says the advocates for the constitution, "it is not likely this will ever happen; we are not to expect our rulers will ever proceed to a wanton exercise of the powers given them." But what reason have we more than past ages, to expect that we shall be blessed with impeccable rulers? we think not any. Although it has been said that every generation grows wiser and wiser, yet we have no reason to think they grow better and better. And therefore the probability lies upon the dark side. Does not the experience of past ages teach, that men have generally exercised all the powers they had given them, and even have usurped upon them, in order to accomplish their own sinister and avaricious designs, whenever they thought they could do it with impunity? This we presume will not be denied. And it appeared to us that the arguments made use of by the favourers of the constitution, in the late Convention at Boston, proceeded upon the plan of righteousness in those who are to rule over us, by virtue of this new form of government. But these arguments, we confess, could have no weight with us, whilst we judged them to be founded altogether upon a slippery *perhaps*.

We are sensible, that in order to the due administration of government, it is necessary that certain powers should be delegated to the rulers, from the people. At the same time we think they ought carefully to guard against giving so much as will enable those rulers, by that means, at once, or even in process of time, to render themselves absolute and despotic. This we think is the case with the form of government lately submitted to our consideration. We could not, therefore, acting uprightly, consulting our own good and the good of our constituents, give our assent unto it. We could not then, we still cannot see, that because people are many times guilty of crimes, and deserving of punishment, that it from thence follows the authority ought to have power to punish them when they are not guilty, or to punish the innocent with the guilty without discrimination, which amounts to the same thing. But this we think in fact to be the case as to this federal constitution. For the Congress, whether they have provocation or not, can at any time order the elections in any or all the states, to be conducted in such manner as wholly to defeat and render entirely nugatory the intention of those elections, and convert that which was considered and intended to be the palladium of the liberties of the people—the grand bulwark against any invasion upon them, into a formidable engine, by which to overthrow them all, and thus involve them in the depth of misery and distress. But it was pled by some of the ablest advocates of the constitution, that if Congress should exercise such powers to the prejudice of the people (and they did not deny but they could if they should be disposed) they (the people) would not suffer it. They would have recourse to the *ultima ratio* the *dernier resort* of the oppressed—*the sword*.

But it appeared to us a piece of *superlative incongruity* indeed! that the people, whilst in the full and indefensible possession of their liberties and privileges, should be so very profuse, so very liberal in the disposal of them, as consequently to place themselves in a predicament miserable to an extreme—so wretched indeed, that they may at once be reduced to the sad alternative of yielding themselves vassals into the hands of a venal and corrupt administration, whose only wish may be to aggrandize themselves and families—to wallow in luxury and every species of discipation, and riot upon the spoils of the community; or take up the sword and involve their country in all the horrors of a civil war—the consequence of which, we think, we may venture to augur will more firmly rivet their shackles, and end in the entailment of vassallage to their posterity. We think this by no means can fall within the description of government beforementioned: Neither can we think these suggestions merely chimerical, or that they proceed from an over heated enthusiasm in favour of republicanism; neither yet from an ill-placed detestation of aristocracy; but from the apparent danger the people are in by establishing this constitution. When we take a forward view of the proposed Congress, seated in the federal city, ten miles square, fortified and replenished with all kinds of military stores, and every implement—with a navy at command on one side, and a land army on the other. We say, when we view them, thus possessed of the sword in one hand and the purse-strings of the people in the other, we can see no security left for them in the enjoyment of their liberties, but what may proceed from the bare possibility, that this supreme authority of the nation may be possessed of virtue and integrity sufficient to influence them in the administration of equal justice and equity among those whom they shall govern. But why should we voluntarily choose to trust our all upon so precarious a tenure as this? We confess it gives us pain to anticipate the future scene: a scene presenting to view miseries so complicated and extreme, that it may be part of the charms of eloquence to extenuate, or the power of art to remove.[1]

But we pass on to another thing, which (aside from every other consideration) was, and still is an insuperable objection in the way of our assent. This we find in the 9th section under the head of restrictions upon Congress, viz. "The migration or importation of such persons as any of the states now existing shall think proper to admit, shall not be prohibited by the Congress, prior to the year one thousand eight hundred and eight," &c. It was not controverted in the Convention, but owned that this provision was made purely that the southern states might not be deprived of their profits arising from that most *nefarious trade* of enslaving the Africans. The hon. Mr. King himself, who was an assistant in forming this constitution, in discoursing upon the slave trade, in the late Convention at Boston, was pleased to design it by this epithet, *nefarious*, which carries with it the idea of something peculiarly wicked and abominable: and indeed we think it deserving of this and every odious epithet which our language affords, descriptive of the iniquity of it. This being the case, we were naturally led to enquire why we should establish a constitution, which gives licence to a measure of this sort—How is it possible we could do it consistent with our ideas of government? consistent with the principles and documents we endeavour to inculcate upon others? It is a standing law in the kingdom of Heaven, "Do unto others as ye would have others do unto you."[2] This is the royal law—this we often hear inculcated upon others. But had we given our affirmative voice in this case, could we have claimed to ourselves that consistent line of conduct, which marks the path of every honest man? Should we not rather have been guilty of a contumelious repugnancy, to what we profess to believe is equitable and just? Let us for once bring the matter home to ourselves, and summons up our own feelings upon the occasion, and hear the simple sober verdict of our own hearts, were we in the place of those unhappy Africans—this is the test, the proper *touch-stone* by which to try the matter before us. Where is the man, who under the influence of sober dispassionate reasoning, and not void of natural affection, can lay his hand upon his heart and say, I am willing my sons and my daughters should be torn from me and doomed to perpetual slavery? We presume that man is not to be found amongst us: And yet we think the consequence is fairly drawn, that this is what every man ought to be able to say, who voted for this constitution. But we dare say this will never be the case here, so long as the country has power to repel force by force. Notwithstanding this we will practise this upon those who are destitute of the power of repulsion: from whence we conclude it is not the tincture of a skin, or any disparity of features that are necessarily connected with slavery, and possibly may therefore fall to the lot of some who voted it, to have the same measure measured unto them which they have measured unto others. If we could once make it our own case, we should soon discover what distress & anxiety, what poignant feelings it would produce in our own breasts, to have our infants torn from the bosoms of their tender mothers—indeed our

children of all ages, from infancy to manhood, arrested from us by a
banditti of lawless ruffians, in defiance of all the laws of humanity,
and carried to a country far distant, without any hopes of their return—
attended likewise with the cutting reflection, that they were likely to
undergo all those indignities, those miseries, which are the usual con-
comitants of slavery. Indeed when we consider the depredations committed in Africa, the cruelties exercised towards the poor captivated
inhabitants of that country on their passage to this—crowded by droves
into the holds of ships, suffering what might naturally be expected
would result from scanty provisions, and inelastic infectious air, and
after their arrival, drove like brutes from market to market, *branded*
on their naked *bodies* with *hot irons*, with the initial letters of their
masters names—fed upon the entrails of beasts like swine in the slaugh-
ter-yard of a butcher; and many other barbarities, of which we have
documents well authenticated: then put to the hardest of labour, and
to perform the vilest of drudges—their master (or rather *usurpers*) by
far less kind and benevolent to them, than to their horses and their
hounds. We say, when we consider these things (the recollection of
which gives us pain) conscience applauds the dicision we have made,
and we feel that satisfaction which arises from acting agreeable to its
dictates. When we hear those barbarities pled for—When we see them
voted for, (as in the late Convention at Boston) when we see them
practised by those who denominate themselves Christians, we are presented with something truely *heterogeneous*—something *monstrous* indeed! Can we suppose this line of conduct keeps pace with the rule
of right? Do such practices coincide with the plain and simple ideas
of government beforementioned? By no means. We could wish it might
be kept in mind, that the very notion of government is to protect men
in the enjoyment of those privileges to which the[y] have a natural,
therefore an indefeasible right; and not to be made an engine of
rapine, robbery and murder. This is but establishing inequity, by law
founded on usurpation. Establishing this constitution is, in our opinion[,] establishing the most ignominious kind of theft, man-stealing,
and so heinous and agrivated was this crime considered, by ONE who
cannot err, that under the Jewish theocracy it was punished with
death.[3] Indeed what can shew men scarcely more hardened, than being
guilty of this crime? for there is *nothing else* they will stick at in order
to perpetrate this.

The question therefore—Why should we vote for the establishment
of this system? recoils upon us armed with treple force—force which
sets at defiance, the whole power of sophistry, employed for the defence of those, who by a "cursed thirst for gold," are prompted on

to actions, which cast an indelible stain upon the character of the human species—actions at which certain quadrupeds, were they possessed of Organs for the purpose, would discover a BLUSH.

But we were told by an honourable gentleman who was one of the framers of this Constitution, that the two souther[n]most states, absolutely refused to confederate at all, except they might be gratified in this article. What then? Was this an argument sufficient to induce us to give energy to this article, thus fraught with iniquity? By no means. But we were informed by that gentleman, further that those two states pled, that they had lost much of their property during the late war. Their slaves being either taken from them by the British troops, or they themselves taking the liberty of absconding from them, and therefore they must import more, in order to make up their losses. To this we say they lost no property, because they never had any in them, however much money they might have paid for them. For we look upon it, every man is the sole proprietor of his own liberty, and no one but himself hath a right to convey it unless by some crime adequate to the punishment, it should be made forfeit, and so by that means becomes the property of government: But this is by no means the case in the present instance. And we cannot suppose a vendee, can acquire property in any thing, which at the time of purchase, he knew the vendor had no right to convey. This is an acknowledgment, we are constrained to make as a tribute due to justice and equity. But suppose they had lost real property; so have we; and indeed where is the man, but will tell us he has been a great looser by means of the war? And shall we from thence argue that we have a right to make inroads upon another nation, pilfer and rob them, in order to compensate ourselves for the losses we have sustained by means of a war, in which they had been utterly neutral? Truly upon this plan of reasoning it is lawful thus to do, and had we voted the constitution as it stands, we must have given countenance to conduct equally criminal, and more so, if possible. Such arguments as the above seem to be calculated and designed for idiotcy. We however acknowledge, we think them rather an affront, even upon that.

The hon. Gentleman above named, was asked the question—What would be the consequence, suppose one or two states, upon any principle, should refuse confederating? His answer was—"The consequence is plain and easy—they would be compelled to it; not by force of arms; but all commerce with them would be interdicted; their property would be seized in every port they should enter, and by law made forfeit: and this line of conduct would soon reduce them to order." This method of procedure perhaps no one would be disposed to reprehend;

and if eleven, or even nine states were agreed, could they not, ought they not to take this method, rather than to make a compact with them, by which they give countenance, nay even bind themselves (as the case may be) to aid and assist them in spor[t]ing with the liberties of others, and accumulating to themselves fortunes, by making thousands of their fellow creatures miserable. To animadvert upon the British manœvres at that time, would not fall within the compass of our present design. But that the Africans had a right to depart, we must assert, and are able to prove it from the highest authority perhaps that this Commonwealth does or ever did afford. In a printed pamphlet, published in Boston in the year 1772, said to be the report of a Committee, and unanimously voted by said town, and ordered to be sent to the several towns in the state for their consideration. In said pamphlet we find the following *axiom*, which we will quote verbatim,— page 2d—"All men have a right to remain in a state of nature as long as they please, and in case of intolerable oppression, civil or religious, to leave the society they belong to, and enter into another."[4] If it can by any kind of reasoning be made to appear, that this authority is not pertinently adduced in the case before us, then we think it can by the same reasoning be investigated, that black is white and white is black— that oppression and freedom are exactly similar, and benevolence and malignity synonymous terms.

The advocates for the constitution seemed to suppose, that this restriction being laid upon Congress only for a term of time, is the "fair dawning of liberty." That "it was a glorious acquisition towards the final abolition of slavery."[5] But how much more glorious would the acquisition have been, was such abolition to take place the first moment the constitution should be established. If we had said that after the expiration of a certain term the practice should cease, it would have appeared with a better grace; but this is not the case, for even after that, it is wholly optional with the Congress, whether they abolish it or not. And by that time we presume the enslaving the Africans will be accounted by far less an inconsiderable affair than it is at present: therefore conclude from good reasons, that the *"nefarious practice"* will be continued and increased as the inhabitants of the country shall be found to increase.

This practice of enslaving mankind is in direct opposition to a fundamental maxim of truth, on which our state constitution is founded, viz. "All men are born free and equal."[6] This is our motto. We have said it—we cannot go back. Indeed no man can justify himself in enslaving another, unless he can produce a commission under the broad seal of Heaven, purporting a licence therefor from him who created all men, and can therefore dispose of them at his pleasure.

We would not be thought to detract from the character of any person, but to us it is somewhat nearly paradoxical, that some of our leading characters in the law department (especially in the western counties) after having (to their honour be it spoken) exerted themselves to promote, and finally to effect the emancipation of slaves, should now turn directly about, and exhibit to the world principles diametrically opposite thereto: that they should now appear such strenuous advocates for the establishment of that diabolical trade of importing the Africans.[7] But said some, it is not we who do it—and compared it to entering into an alliance with another nation, for some particular purpose; but we think this by no means a parallel. We are one nation, forming a constitution for the whole, and suppose the states are under obligation, whenever this constitution shall be established, reciprocally to aid each other in defence and support of every thing to which they are entitled thereby, right or wrong. Perhaps we may never be called upon to take up arms for the defence of the southern states, in prosecuting this abominable traffick.

It is true at present there is not much danger to be apprehended, and for this plain reason are those innocent Africans (as to us) pitched upon to drag out their lives in misery and chains. Such is their local situation—their unpolished manners—their inexperience in the art of war, that those invaders of the rights of mankind know they can, at present, perpetrate those enormities with impunity. But let us suppose for once, a thing which is by no means impossible, viz. that those Africans should rise superior to all their local and other disadvantages, and attempt to avenge themselves for the wrongs done them? Or suppose some potent nation should interfere in their behalf, as France in the cause of America, must we not rise and resist them? Would not the Congress immediately call forth the whole force of the country, if needed, to oppose them, and so attempt more closely to rivet their manacles upon them, and in that way perpetuate the miseries of those unhappy people? This we think the natural consequence which will flow from the establishment of this constitution, and that it is not a forced, but a very liberal construction of it. It was said that "the adoption of this Constitution, would be ominous of much good, and betoken the smiles of Heaven upon the country." But we view the matter in a very different light; we think this lurch for unjust gains, this lust for slavery, portentous of much evil in America, for the cry of innocent blood, which hath been shed in carrying on this execrable commerce, hath undoubtedly reached to the Heavens, to which that cry is always directed, and will draw down upon them vengeance adequate to the enormity of the crime. To what other cause, than a full conviction, of the moral evil in this practice, together with some fearful forebodings of punishment therefor arising in the minds of the Congress in the year 1774, can it be imputed, that drew from them at that time, (at least an implied) confession of guilt, and a solemn, explicit promise of reformation? This is a fact, but lest it should be disputed, we think it most safe for ourselves to lay before our readers, an extract from a certain pamphlet, entitled "Extracts from the votes and proceedings of the American Continental Congress, held at Philadelphia, on the 5th of September, 1774, &c." In the 22d page of this same pamphlet, we find the following paragraph, viz. "Second. That we will neither import, nor purchase any slave imported, after the first day of December next; after which time we will wholly discontinue the slave-trade, and will neither be concerned in it ourselves, nor will we hire our vessels nor sell our commodities or manufactures to those who are concerned in it."[8] The inconsistency of opposing slavery, which they thought designed for themselves, and by clandestine means, procuring others to enslave at the same time—it is very natural to suppose would stare them in the face, and at all times guard them against breaking their resolution. Hence it appears to us unaccountable strange, that any person who signed the above resolve, should sign the federal constitution. For do they not hold up to view principles diametrically opposite? Can we suppose that what was morally evil in the year 1774, has become in the year 1788, morally good? Or shall we change evil into good and good into evil, as often as we find it will serve a turn? We cannot but say the conduct of those who associated in the year 1774 in the manner above, and now appear advocates for this new constitution, is highly inconsistent, although we find such conduct has the celebrated names of a *Washington* and an *Adams* to grace it. And this may serve as a reason why we could not be wrought upon by another argument, which was made use of in the Convention in favour of the constitution, viz. *the weight of names*—a solid argument with some people who belonged to the Convention, and would have induced them to comply with measures of almost any kind. It was urged that the gentlemen who composed the federal Convention, were men of the greatest abilities, integrity and erudition, and had been the greatest contenders for freedom. We suppose it to be true, and that they have exemplified it, by the manner, in which they have earnestly dogmatized for liberty—But notwithstanding we could not view this argument, as advancing any where towards infallibility—because long before we entered upon the business of the Convention, we were by some means or other possessed with a notion (and we think from good authority) that "*great men are not always wise.*"[9] And to be sure the weight of a name adduced to give efficacy to a measure where liberty is in dispute, cannot be so likely to have its intended effect, when the person designed by that name, at the same time he is brandishing his sword, in the behalf of freedom for himself—is likewise tyranizing over two or three hundred miserable Africans, as free born as himself.

In fine we view this constitution as a curious piece of political mechanism, fabricated in such manner as may finally despoil the people of all their privileges; and we are fully satisfied, that had the same system been offered to the people in the time of the contest with Great-Britain, the person offering the same would not have met the approbation of those who now appear the most strenuous advocates for it. We cannot slip this opportunity of manifesting our disgust at the unfair methods which were taken in order to obtain a vote in this state, which perhaps was the means of producing the *small* majority of *nineteen*, out of nearly three hundred and sixty members. What those methods were is well known. It is past dispute that the opposers of the constitution were, in sundry instances, treated in a manner utterly inconsistent with that respect which is due to every freeborn citizen of the commonwealth, especially when acting in the capacity of a representative.

Notwithstanding what has been said, we would not have it understood, that we mean to be disturbers of the peace, should the states receive the constitution; but on the contrary, declare it our intention, as we think it our duty, to be subject to "the powers that be," wherever our lot may be cast.

> CONSIDER ARMS, ⎫
> MALICHI MAYNARD, ⎬ Conway.
> SAMUEL FIELD, Deerfield.

1. At this point, the dissent is followed by the signatures of the three men and this statement: "*To be concluded in our next.*"

2. Matthew 7:12; and Luke 6:31.

3. Exodus 21:16

4. This pamphlet, probably written by Samuel Adams, was published by Edes and Gill and T. and J. Fleet of Boston and was entitled *The Votes and Proceedings of the Freeholders and Other Inhabitants of the Town of Boston, in Town Meeting Assembled, According to Law . . .* (Evans 12332). The quoted material is from the first part of the pamphlet: "a State of the *Rights* of the Colonists and of this Province in particular." The Boston town meeting approved the pamphlet, which was based upon a report of a committee of correspondence, and ordered 600 copies distributed throughout Massachusetts.

5. On 12 February the Reverend Jeremy Belknap wrote Benjamin Rush that Theophilus Parsons, a Newburyport delegate, "construed that article into a dawn of hope for the final abolition of the horrid Traffick & spoke of it as a great Point gained of the southern states." Parsons' remarks have not been preserved in any of the notes taken

of the debates, but on 16 February the *Massachusetts Centinel* reported the essence of the comments of several Federalist delegates: "that the step taken in this article, towards the abolition of slavery, was one of the beauties of the Constitution. They observed, that in the Confederation there was no provision whatever for its ever being abolished; but this Constitution provides, that Congress may, after 20 years, totally annihilate the slave trade; and that, as all the States, except two, have passed laws to this effect, it might reasonably be expected, that it would then be done—in the interim, all the States were at liberty to prohibit it" (CC:Vol. 2, pp. 529, 530n).

6. Article I of the Massachusetts Declaration of Rights (1780) states: "All men are born free and equal, and have certain natural, essential, and unalienable rights; among which may be reckoned the right of enjoying and defending their lives and liberties; that of acquiring, possessing, and protecting property; in fine, that of seeking and obtaining their safety and happiness" (Thorpe, III, 1889).

7. The reference is probably to Federalist Convention members Theodore Sedgwick of Stockbridge and Caleb Strong of Northampton. In 1781 Sedgwick represented and won the freedom of Elizabeth Freeman, a slave known as "Mumbet." Two years later Sedgwick was a member of a committee of the state House of Representatives which was asked to draw up a bill declaring that slavery had never been legal in Massachusetts. The bill passed the House, but failed in the Senate. Along with Levi Lincoln, Strong was involved in two of three cases regarding Quok Walker between 1781 and 1783. Walker had run away from his master and was hired as a servant by another man. Walker's master pursued, caught, and beat him badly. As a result of these cases, Walker was declared free and received damages for the beating. Chief Justice William Cushing, one of the judges in the third case, in which neither Lincoln nor Strong took part, declared in his charge to the jury that, under Article I of the state Declaration of Rights (note 6 above), slavery was unconstitutional.

8. This paragraph was part of the Articles of Association adopted by the First Continental Congress on 20 October 1774 (JCC, I, 75–80). The pamphlet (described by the three dissenters) was printed in Philadelphia and then reprinted in many other American towns and cities in 1774 (Evans 13713–36). Two Boston printers published the pamphlet.

9. Job 32:9.

## 671. Centinel XVIII
## Philadelphia Independent Gazetteer, 9 April

"Centinel" XVIII, the last in the series, was also printed in the Philadelphia *Freeman's Journal* on 9 April and it was reprinted in the *New York Journal* on 12 April. The series was revived with number XIX in the *Independent Gazetteer* on 7 October 1788.

For a general discussion of the authorship, circulation, and impact of "Centinel," see CC:133.

### To the PEOPLE of PENNSYLVANIA.

*Fellow-Citizens,* The measures that are pursuing to effect the establishment of the new constitution, are so repugnant to truth, honor, and the well-being of society, as would disgrace any cause. If the nature and tendency of this system were to be judged of by the conduct of its framers and patrons, what a picture of ambition and villainy would present itself to our view! From the specimens they have already given, anticipation may easily realise the consequences that would flow from the new constitution, if established; may bid adieu to all the blessings of liberty, to all the fruits of the late glorious assertion of the rights of human nature, made at the expence of so much blood and treasure. Yet such is the infatuation of many well meaning persons, that they view with indifference the attrocious villainy which characterises the proceedings of the advocates of the new system: The daring, and in most parts of the United States, the successful methods practised to shackle the press, and destroy the freedom of discussion; the silencing the Pennsylvania Herald, to prevent the publication of the invaluable debates of the late convention of this state;[1] the total suppression of real intelligence, and of the illuminations of patriotism through the medium of the post-office;[2] the systematic fraud and deception that pervade the union; the stigmatising, and by every art which ambition and malice can suggest, labouring to villify, intimidate and trample under foot every disinterested patriot, who preferring his country's good to every other consideration, has the courage to stand forth the champion of liberty and the people; and the intercepting of private confidential letters passing from man to man, violating the sacredness of a seal, and thus infringing one of the first privileges of freemen— that of communicating with each other:[3] I say all these are overlooked by the infatuated admirers of the new system, who, deluded by the *phantom* of wealth and prosperity, profit not by the admonitory lesson which such proceedings afford, are deaf to the calls of patriotism, and would rush blindly into the noose of ambition.

However, to the honor of Pennsylvania, a very large majority of her citizens view the subject in its true light, and spurn the shackles prepared for them. They will in due time convince the aspiring despots and avaricious office-hunters, that their dark intrigues, and deep concerted schemes of power and aggrandisement, are ineffectual, that they are neither to be duped nor dragooned out of their liberties. The conspirators, I know, insolently boast that their strength in the other states will enable them to crush the opposition in this; but let them not build upon that which is in its nature precarious and transient, which must fail them the moment the delusion is dispelled: Their success in the other states is the fruit of deceptions that cannot be long supported. Indeed the audacity and villainy of the conspirators on the one hand, and the frantic enthusiasm, and easy credulity of the people on the other, in some of the states, however well attested and recorded in the faithful page of history, will be treated by posterity as fabulous.

The great artifice that is played off on this occasion, is the persuading the people of one place, that the people every where else are nearly unanimous in favor of the new system, and thus endeavouring by the fa[s]cination of example and force of general opinion to prevail upon the people every where to acquiesce in what is represented to them as the general sentiment.

Thus as one means of deception has failed them, they have adopted another, always avoiding rational discussion. When the glare of great names, the dread of annihilation if the new system was rejected, or the adoption of it even delayed, were dissipated by the artillery of truth and reason; they have recurred to the one now practising, the intimidating and imposing influence of imaginary numbers and unanimity that are continually reverberated from every part of the union, by the tools and vehicles of the would-be despots; and in which they have had astonishing success. The people in the Eastern states have been taught to believe that it is all harmony to the Southward; and in the Southern states they are discouraged from opposition by the unanimity of the Eastern and Northern states; nay, what will appear incredible, considering the distance, a gentleman of veracity just returned from New-York, assures that the conspirators have had the address to inculcate an opinion there that all opposition had ceased in this state, notwithstanding the evidence of the contrary is so glaring here; this gentleman further informs, that so entirely devoted is the post-office, that not a single newspaper is received by the printers of that place from this city or elsewhere; and a Boston newspaper come by private hand, announces [to] the public, that for some months past, the printers there have received no newspapers to the Southward of New-Haven,[4] in Connecticut, where the press is muzzled,[5] and consequently, cannot injure the cause; that all intelligence of the occurrences in the other states is withheld from them; and that they know more of the state of Europe, than of their own country.

Notwithstanding many thousand copies of the Reasons of Dissent of the minority of the late convention of this state were printed and forwarded in every direction, and by various conveyances, scarcely any of these got beyond the limits of this state, and most of them not until a long time after their publication. The printer of these Reasons, by particular desire, addressed a copy of them to every printer in the union, which he sent to the Post-office to be conveyed in the mail as usual, long before the *new arrangement*, as it is called, took place; and yet we since find that none of them reached the place of their destination. This is a full demonstration of the subserviency of the Post Office, and a striking evidence of the vigilance that has been exerted to suppress information. It is greatly to be regretted that the opposition in Massachusetts were denied the benefits of our discussion, that the unanswerable dissent of our minority did not reach Boston in time to influence the decision of the great question by their convention, as it would in all probability have enabled patriotism to triumph;[6] not that I would derogate from the good sense and public spirit of that state, which I have no doubt would in common circumstances have shone with equal splendor, but this was far from being the case; the new constitution was viewed in Massachusetts through the medium of a SHAYS, the terrors of HIS insurrection had not subsided; a government that would have been execrated at another time was embraced by many as a refuge from anarchy, and thus liberty deformed by mad riot and dissention, lost her ablest advocates.

As the liberties of all the states in the union are struck at in common with those of Pennsylvania, by the conduct of the Post-Master General and deputies, I trust that the example which her Legislature[(a)] has set by instructing her delegates in Congress on this subject,[7] will be followed by the others, that with one accord they will hurl their vengeance on the venal instruments of ambition, who have presumed to prostrate one of the principal bulwarks of liberty. In a confederated government of such extent as the United States, the freest communication of sentiment and information should be maintained, as the liberties, happiness and welfare of the union depend upon a concert of counsels; the signals of alarm whenever ambition should rear its baneful head, ought to be uniform: without this communication between the members of the confederacy the freedom of the press, if it could be maintained in so severed a situation, would cease to be a security against the encroachments of tyranny. The truth of the foregoing position is strikingly illustrated on the present occasion; for want of this inter-community of sentiment and information, the liberties of this country are brought to an awful crisis; ambition has made a great stride towards dominion; has succeeded thro' the medium of muzzled presses to delude a great body of the people in the other states, and threatens to overwhelm the enlightened opposition in this by *external* force. Here, indeed, notwithstanding every nerve was strained, by the conspirators, to muzzle or demolish every newspaper that allowed free discussion, two printers have asserted the independency of the press,[8] whereby the arts of ambition have been detected, and the new system has been pourtrayed in its native villainy; its advocates have long since abandoned the field of argument, relinquished the unequal contest, and truth and patriotism reigns triumphant in this state; but the conspirators trust to their success in the other states for the attainment of their darling object, and therefore all their vigilance is exerted to prevent the infectious spirit of freedom and enlightened patriotism communicating to the rest of the union—all intercourse is as far as possible cut off.

To rectify the erroneous representation made in the other states of the sentiments of the people in this respecting the new constitution, I think it my duty to state the fact as it really is:—Those who favor this system of tyranny are most numerous in the city of Philadelphia, where, perhaps, they may be a considerable majority; in the most eastern counties they compose about one-fourth of the people, but in the middle, northern and western counties not above a twentieth part; so that upon the whole the friends to the new constitution in this state are about one-sixth of the people. The following circumstance is an evidence of the spirit and decision of the opposition:—An individual unadvisedly and without conceit, and contrary to the system of conduct generally agreed upon, went to the expence of printing and circulating an address to the Legislature, reprobating in the strongest terms the new constitution, and praying that the deputies of this state in the federal Convention, who in violation of their duty acceded to the new constitution, be called to account for their daring procedure; this address or petition was signed by upwards of four thousand citizens in only two counties, viz. Franklin and Cumberland, and if the time had admitted, prior to the adjournment of the Legislature, there is reason to believe that this high-toned application would have been subscribed by five-sixth of the freemen of this state.[9] The advocates of the new constitution, availing themselves of this partial measure of two counties, have asserted it to be the result of a general exertion, which is so evidently false that it can only deceive people at a distance from us, for the counties over the mountain are nearly unanimous in the opposition; in Fayette at a numerous county meeting, there appeared to be but two persons in favor of the constitution; in Bedford county in the mountains, there are not above twenty; in Huntingdon adjoining, about 30; in Dauphin, in the middle country, not 100; in Berks, a large eastern county that has near 5000 taxable inhabitants, not more than 50, and so of several others, and yet no petitions were circulated or signed in those counties.—The system of conduct alluded to is the forming societies in every county in the state, who have committees of correspondence; these are now engaged in planning a uniform exertion to emancipate this state from the thraldom of despotism; a convention of deputies from every district will in all probability be agreed upon, as the most eligible mode of combining the strength of the opposition, which is increasing daily both in numbers and spirit.[10]

The Centinel, supported by the dignity of the cause he advocates, and sensible that his well-meant endeavors have met the approbation of the community, views with ineffable contempt the impotent efforts of disappointed ambition to depreciate his merit and stigmatize his performances, and without pretending to the spirit of divination, he thinks he may predict that the period is not far distant when the authors and *wilful* abettors of the new constitution will be viewed with detestation by every good man, whilst the Centinels of the present day will be honored with the esteem and confidence of a grateful people.

Great pains have been taken to discover the author of these papers, with a view, no doubt, to villify his private character, and thereby lessen the usefulness of his writings, and many suppose they have made the discovery, but in this they are mistaken. The Centinel submits his performance to the public judgement, and challenges fair argumentation; the information he has given from time to time, has stood the test of the severest scrutiny, and thus his reputation as a writer, is established beyond the injury of his enemies. If it were in the least material to the argument, or answered any one good purpose, he would not hesitate a moment in using his own signature; as it would not, but on the contrary, point where the shafts of malice could be levelled with most effect, and thus divert the public attention from the proper object, to a personal altercation, he from the first determined that the prying eye of party or curiosity, should never be gratified with his real name, and to that end to be the sole depository of the secret. He has been thus explicit to prevent the repetition of the weakness of declaring off, when charged with being the author, and to put the matter upon its true footing; however, it may flatter his vanity, that these papers should be ascribed to an illustrious patriot,[11] whose public spirit and undaunted firmness of mind, eclipse the most shining ornaments of the Roman commonwealth, in its greatest purity and glory, whose persevering exertions for the public welfare, have endeared him to his country, whilst it has made every knave and aspiring despot, his inveterate enemy, and who has never condescended to deny any writings that have been ascribed to him, or to notice the railings of party.

Philadelphia, April 5th, 1788.

(a) *The application to Congress from our Legislature, was made upon the complaint of all the printers of newspapers in the city of Philadelphia.*

1. In January 1788 editor Alexander J. Dallas was dismissed for publishing the Pennsylvania Convention speeches of Antifederalists and for indicating that Antifederalists had sometimes bested Federalists in the debates (CC:Vol. 1, xxxix; and RCS:Pa., 38, 40).

2. For the post office's alleged suppression of newspapers, see "The Controversy over

the Post Office and the Circulation of Newspapers" (CC:Vol. 4, Appendix II). "Centinel" himself touched off this controversy on 8 January with the publication of his ninth essay (CC:427).

3. On 26 March the Federalist *Pennsylvania Gazette*, at the request of "X," published two intercepted letters purportedly written by George Bryan to John Ralston on 7 and 12 March (CC:647). Their publication precipitated a newspaper debate on the propriety of intercepting and publishing letters. An Antifederalist writer, who also signed himself "X," attacked the printing of the purported Bryan letters as "a violation of that confidence without which society cannot exist. A seal in all civilized nations has ever been deemed sacred, but especially in mercantile Communities" (Philadelphia *Freeman's Journal*, 9 April, Mfm:Pa. 617).

4. On 21 March the *Massachusetts Gazette* stated "that scarcely a news-paper has been received by the Printers in this town, southward of New-Haven, since the commencement of the present year." From 3 to 5 April, this item was reprinted in three Philadelphia newspapers (CC:Vol. 4, Appendix II).

5. For the partisan nature of the Connecticut press, see RCS:Conn., *passim*, but especially pp. 329–31, 492–94.

6. For the circulation of the "Dissent of the Minority of the Pennsylvania Convention," see CC:353.

7. On 29 March the Pennsylvania General Assembly instructed the state's delegates to Congress to inquire into the complaints of Philadelphia's newspaper publishers that the post office had refused to carry their newspapers free of charge. (See CC:Vol. 4, pp. 562–66.)

8. Probably Francis Bailey of the *Freeman's Journal* and Eleazer Oswald of the *Independent Gazetteer*. (See CC:Vol. 1, xxxiv–xxxvi.) Both men were also involved in the controversy over the post office. (See CC:Vol. 4, Appendix II.)

9. In late December 1787 or early January 1788 Antifederalist John Nicholson, the state comptroller general, coordinated a petition campaign requesting that the Pennsylvania legislature not "confirm" the state's ratification of the Constitution. Copies of the petition went to at least nine of the state's eighteen counties, and in March six counties submitted petitions signed by over 6,000 people to the state legislature. The number of signers from Franklin and Cumberland exceeded 4,200. The legislature tabled the petitions before it adjourned on 29 March. (See RCS:Pa., 709–25.)

10. On 3 July 1788 a circular letter was issued by Cumberland County Antifederalists calling for a convention to meet in Harrisburg to consider amendments to the Constitution and to nominate candidates for the first U.S. House of Representatives. The convention met from 3 to 6 September, agreed to "acquiesce" to the new government, proposed amendments, and discussed but made no nominations for members to the House (DHFFE, I, 240–41, 258–64).

11. The reference is to George Bryan who was still being accused of writing the "Centinel" essays. For example, on 26 March, in a preface to the two purported Bryan letters to John Ralston (note 3, above), "X" declared that the letters "*afford one proof amongst a thousand, that the indefatigable Monster, the CENTINEL, is endued with a zeal and activity in every work of mischief always commensurate with its extent*" (CC:647). On 9 April, the same day that "Centinel" XVIII appeared, Benjamin Rush wrote a friend that "I suppose you have seen Geo: Bryan's detested letters. They infallibly prove that he is the Author of the Centinel" (to [John Montgomery?], Mfm:Pa. 614).

## 672. Philadelphiensis XII
## Philadelphia Freeman's Journal, 9 April

"Philadelphiensis" XII, the last in a series of controversial essays probably written by Benjamin Workman, was reprinted in the Philadelphia *Independent Gazetteer* on 11 April. Since January, Workman had been one of the most harshly criticized Antifederalist essayists in Philadelphia and such criticism continued after the series ended. For a discussion of the authorship and reaction to "Philadelphiensis," see CC:237, and note 1, below.

"Philadelphiensis" XII agitated Philadelphia merchant John Vaughan. At this time, Vaughan was acting as intermediary for John Dickinson of Delaware, a former Constitutional Convention delegate, whose "Fabius" essays Vaughan was arranging to have published in the *Pennsylvania Mercury.* "Fabius" was not specifically intended to refute "Philadelphiensis," but in mid-April Vaughan told Dickinson that "Fabius" II, which would appear three days later (CC:684), "will form a Complete answer" to "Philadelphiensis" XII (to "Mr. Thomas" [i.e., John Dickinson], Dickinson Papers, PPL).

*My Fellow-Citizens,* The essays under the signature of Philadelphiensis are represented as without argument, and their prime object is said to be to involve this devoted country in a civil war.[1] But *time,* the discoverer of future events, will certainly shew that the calling another Federal Convention is the only rational way to prevent it. Heaven grant that these eyes may never behold that dreadful scene. The writer of these essays was actuated by the purest motives, namely, to defend the liberty and advance the happiness of his fellow-citizens. These he conceived insecure, or rather destroyed, if the proposed constitution should be established, and hence he laboured to procure another Convention. The expediency of this measure was demonstrated by illustrating the principal defects in the proposed system;—defects did I say—the expression is too soft—the ruin that must follow its adoption.

If pointing out the unlimited powers of the new Congress over the lives and property of their fellow-citizens, which may and certainly would be abused, be not an argument against it, there remains no fixed determinate idea to be annexed to the term argument; indeed, on such principles right and wrong, freedom and slavery have no essential difference, and the human mind is a mere chaos.

Some feeble attempts have been made by the advocates of this system of tyranny, to answer the objections made to the smallness of the number of representatives and senators, and the improper powers delegated to them; but, as far as I recollect, no one has been found bold enough to stand forth in defence of that dangerous and uncontrouled officer, the *President-General,* or more properly, our new KING.

A few pieces under the signature of *An American Citizen*[2] were published immediately after the Constitution broke the shell, and the hydra made its way from the *dark conclave* into the open light; in the first number of which the writer, in touching on the *President,* endeavoured to conceal his immense powers, by representing the King of Great Britain as possessed of many hereditary prerogatives, rights and powers that he was not possessed of; that is, he shews what he is not, but neglects to shew what he really is; but so flimsey a palliative could scarce escape the censure of the most ignorant advocate for such an officer; and since we hear of no further attempts to prove the necessity of a King being set over the freemen of America.

The writer of these essays has clearly proven, that the president is a King to all intents and purposes, and at the same time one of the most dangerous kind too—an *elective King*, the commander in chief of a standing army, &c.;[3] and to these add, that he has a negative over the proceedings of both branches of the legislature: and to complete his uncontrouled sway, he is neither restrained nor assisted by a *privy council*, which is a novelty in government. I challenge the politicians of the whole continent to find in any period of history a monarch more absolute.

Who is so base as not to burn with resentment against the conspirators, who have dared to establish such a tyrant over his life, his liberty and property? Is the flame of sacred liberty so entirely extinguished in the American breast as not to be kindled again? No; you mistaken despots, do not let such a preposterous thought madden you into perseverance, lest your persons fall sacrifices to the just resentment of an injured country. Stop at once, and join the rest of your fellow-citizens. Let another Convention be immediately called, and let a system of government fitted to the pure principles of the Revolution, be framed. Then a general amnesty among all ranks and degrees of your fellow-citizens must succeed, and America become the seat of liberty, peace, friendship and happiness; and her government have ample *energy* and *respectability* among the nations of the earth; yea, she will thereby be rendered the great arbiter of the world.

1. On 13 March a correspondent, who requested the publication of "Probus" (a critic of "Philadelphiensis"), had declared that "Justice to the American name and character demands that the calumniating assassin, who, under the signature of Philadelphiensis, has aspersed and vilified her most virtuous citizens, and who has practised every art to excite a civil war, should be known as a *renegade European*, who but a short time since fled from the injured laws of his own country" (Philadelphia *Federal Gazette*, Mfm:Pa. 519. See also "A Foe to Falshood," *Federal Gazette*, 24 April, Mfm:Pa. 654.). For defenses of "Philadelphiensis" and his supporters, see "Impartial," *Federal Gazette*, 18 March, and "Obediah Forceps," Philadelphia *Independent Gazetteer*, 22 March (Mfm:Pa. 536, 557). On two other occasions, Workman denied that he was trying to foment civil war ("W" and "Benjamin Workman," *Independent Gazetteer*, 21 March and 29 April, Mfm:Pa. 553–B, 663).

2. See Tench Coxe's "An American Citizen" I–IV, which were published in Philadelphia between 26 September and 21 October (CC:100–A, 109, 112, 183–A).

3. See "Philadelphiensis" IX–XI, *Freeman's Journal*, 6, 20 February, and *Independent Gazetteer*, 8 March (CC:507, 547, 609).

## 673. James Madison to Edmund Randolph
## Orange County, Va., 10 April[1]

My dear friend

Since I got home which was on the day preceding our election,[2] I have received your favor of the 29th. of Feby. which did not reach New York before I had left it.[3]

I view the amendments of Massachussetts pretty nearly in the same light that you do. They were meant for the people at large, not for the minority in the Convention. The latter were not affected by them, their objections being levelled against the very essence of the proposed Government. I do not see that the 2d. amendment, if I understand its scope, can be more exceptionable to the S. Sts. than the others. I take it to mean that the number of Reps. shall be limited to 200, who will be apportioned from time to time according to a census; not that the apportionment first made when the Reps. amount to that number shall be perpetual. The 9th. amendment I have understood was made a very serious point of by S. Adams.[4]

I do not know of any thing in the new Constitution that can change the obligations of the public with regard to the old money. The principle on which it is to be settled, seems to be equally in the power of that as of the existing one. The claim of the Indiana Company can not I should suppose be any more validated by the new System, than that of all the creditors and others who have been aggri[e]ved by unjust laws.[5] You do not mention what part of the Constitution, could give colour to such a doctrine. The condemnation of retrospective laws, if that be the part, does not appear to me, to admit on any principle of such a retrospective construction. As to the religious test, I should conceive that it can imply at most nothing more than that without that exception a power would have been given to impose an oath involving a religious test as a qualification for office. The constitution of necessary offices being given to the Congress, the proper qualifications seem to be evidently involved. I think too there are several other satisfactory points of view in which the exception might be placed.

I shall be extremely happy to see a coalition among all the real federalists. Recommendatory alterations are the only ground that occurs to me. A conditional ratification or a second convention appears to me utterly irreconcileable in the present state of things with the dictates of prudence and safety. I am confirmed, by a comparative view of the publications on the subject, and still more of the debates in the several conventions, that a second experiment would be either wholly abortive, or would end in something much more remote from your ideas and those of others who wish a salutary Government, than the plan now before the public. It is to be considered also that besides the local & personal pride that wd. stand in the way, it could not be a very easy matter to bring about a reconsideration and recision of what ~~has~~ will certainly have been done in six and probably eight States, and in several of those by unanimous votes. Add to all this the extreme facility with which those who secretly aim at disunion, (and there are probably some such in most if not all the States) will be able to carry on their schemes, under the mask of contending for alterations popular in some places and known to be inadmissible in others. Every danger of this sort might be justly dreaded from such men as this State & N. York only could furnish, playing for such a purpose, into each others hands. The declaration of H——y mentioned in your letter is a proof to me that desperate measures will be his game.[6] If Report does not more than usually exaggerate, M also is ripening fast for going every length. His licentiousness of animadversion, it is said, no longer spares even the *moderate opponents* of the Constitution.[7] Yrs. affecly

1. RC, Madison Papers, DLC. In this letter, marked *"Private"* by Madison on the address page, he answered Randolph's 29 February letter which had considered the recommendatory amendments of the Massachusetts Convention (RCS:Va., 436–37. For the amendments, see CC:508.). Randolph answered Madison on 17 April (RCS:Va., 741–42).

2. On 24 March Madison was elected one of Orange County's delegates to the Virginia Convention (RCS:Va., 595–606).

3. Madison left New York City on 3 or 4 March.

4. The ninth amendment reads: "Congress shall, at no time, consent, that any person, holding an office of trust or profit, under the United States, shall accept of a title of nobility, or any other title or office, from any king, prince, or foreign state." For Samuel Adams's antipathy to aristocracy, see his 3 December 1787 letter to Richard Henry Lee (CC:315).

5. For the land claims of the Indiana Company and for Randolph's support of them against a Virginia law, see Rutland, *Madison*, X, 543n–44n.

6. In his 29 February letter, Randolph reported that Patrick Henry allegedly expressed "his determination to oppose the constn. even if only 1/2 a state should oppose" (RCS:Va., 436).

7. On 22 April Madison informed Thomas Jefferson that George Mason "is growing every day more bitter, and outrageous in his efforts to carry his point; and will probably in the end be thrown by the violence of his passions into the politics of Mr. H——y" (RCS:Va., 745. See also Madison to George Nicholas, 8 April, CC:667.).

### 674. Brutus XVI
### New York Journal, 10 April

On 3 April the *New York Journal* announced that "Brutus" XVI had been received but that it "could not possibly be inserted this day." The *Journal* promised that "it will appear" next Thursday (10 April). Despite two refer-

ences in number XVI in which "Brutus" promised "a future number," this
essay concluded the series. "Brutus" XVI was reprinted in the Boston *American
Herald* on 8 May.

For a general discussion of the authorship, circulation, and impact of "Brutus," see CC:178.

When great and extraordinary powers are vested in any man, or
body of men, which in their exercise, may operate to the oppression
of the people, it is of high importance that powerful checks should
be formed to prevent the abuse of it.

Perhaps no restraints are more forcible, than such as arise from
responsibility to some superior power.—Hence it is that the true policy
of a republican government is, to frame it in such manner, that all
persons who are concerned in the government, are made accountable
to some superior for their conduct in office.—This responsibility should
ultimately rest with the People. To have a government well administered in all its parts, it is requisite the different departments of it
should be separated and lodged as much as may be in different hands.
The legislative power should be in one body, the executive in another,
and the judicial in one different from either—But still each of these
bodies should be accountable for their conduct. Hence it is impracticable, perhaps, to maintain a perfect distinction between these several
departments—For it is difficult, if not impossible, to call to account
the several officers in government, without in some degree mixing the
legislative and judicial. The legislature in a free republic[1] are chosen
by the people at stated periods, and their responsibility consists, in
their being amenable to the people. When the term, for which they
are chosen, shall expire, who will then have opportunity to displace
them if they disapprove of their conduct—but it would be improper
that the judicial should be elective, because their business requires that
they should possess a degree of law knowledge, which is acquired only
by a regular education, and besides it is fit that they should be placed,
in a certain degree in an independent situation, that they may maintain
firmness and steadiness in their decisions. As the people therefore
ought not to elect the judges, they cannot be amenable to them immediately, some other mode of amenability must therefore be devised
for these, as well as for all other officers which do not spring from
the immediate choice of the people: this is to be effected by making
one court subordinate to another, and by giving them cognizance of
the behaviour of all officers; but on this plan we at last arrive at some
supreme, over whom there is no power to controul but the people
themselves. This supreme controling power should be in the choice of
the people, or else you establish an authority independent, and not

amenable at all, which is repugnant to the principles of a free government. Agreeable to these principles I suppose the supreme judicial ought to be liable to be called to account, for any misconduct, by some body of men, who depend upon the people for their places; and so also should all other great officers in the State, who are not made amenable to some superior offic[er?]. This policy seems in some measure to have been in view of the framers of the new system, and to have given rise to the institution of a court of impeachments—How far this Court will be properly qualified to execute the trust which will be reposed in them, will be the business of a future paper to investigate. To prepare the way to do this, it shall be the business of this, to make some remarks upon the constitution and powers of the Senate, with whom the power of trying impeachments is lodged.

The following things may be observed with respect to the constitution of the Senate.

1st. They are to be elected by the legislatures of the States and not by the people, and each State is to be represented by an equal number.

2d. They are to serve for six years, except that one third of those first chosen are to go out of office at the expiration of two years, one third at the expiration of four years, and one third at the expiration of six years, after which this rotation is to be preserved, but still every member will serve for the term of six years.

3d. If vacancies happen by resignation or otherwise, during the recess of the legislature of any State, the executive is authorised to make temporary appointments until the next meeting of the legislature.

4. No person can be a senator who has not arrived to the age of thirty years, been nine years a citizen of the United States, and who is not at the time he is elected an inhabitant of the State for which he is elected.

The apportionment of members of [the] Senate among the States is not according to numbers, or the importance of the States; but is equal. This, on the plan of a consolidated government, is unequal and improper; but is proper on the system of confederation—on this principle I approve of it. It is indeed the only feature of any importance in the constitution of a confederated government. It was obtained after a vigorous struggle of that part of the Convention who were in favor of preserving the state governments. It is to be regret[t]ed, that they were not able to have infused other principles into the plan, to have secured the government of the respective states, and to have marked with sufficient precision the line between them and the general government.

The term for which the senate are to be chosen, is in my judgment too long, and no provision being made for a rotation will, I conceive, be of dangerous consequence.

It is difficult to fix the precise period for which the senate should be chosen. It is a matter of opinion, and our sentiments on the matter must be formed, by attending to certain principles. Some of the duties which are to be performed by the senate, seem evidently to point out the propriety of their term of service being extended beyond the period of that of the assembly. Besides as they are designed to represent the aristocracy of the country, it seems fit they should possess more stability, and so continue a longer period than that branch who represent the democracy. The business of making treaties and some other which it will be proper to commit to the senate, requires that they should have experience, and therefore that they should remain some time in office to acquire it.—But still it is of equal importance that they should not be so long in office as to be likely to forget the hand that formed them, or be insensible of their interests. Men long in office are very apt to feel themselves independent. To form and pursue interests separate from those who appointed them. And this is more likely to be the case with the senate, as they will for the most part of the time be absent from the state they represent, and associate with such company as will possess very little of the feelings of the middling class of people. For it is to be remembered that there is to be a *federal city*, and the inhabitants of it will be the great and the mighty of the earth. For these reasons I would shorten the term of their service to four years. Six years is a long period for a man to be absent from his home, it would have a tendency to wean him from his constituents.

A rotation in the senate, would also in my opinion be of great use. It is probable that senators once chosen for a state will, as the system now stands, continue in office for life. The office will be honorable if not lucrative. The persons who occupy it will probably wish to continue in it, and therefore use all their influence and that of their friends to continue in office.—Their friends will be numerous and powerful, for they will have it in their power to confer great favors; besides it will before long be considered as disgraceful not to be re-elected. It will therefore be considered as a matter of delicacy to the character of the senator not to return him again.—Every body acquainted with public affairs knows how difficult it is to remove from office a person who is long been in it. It is seldom done except in cases of gross misconduct. It is rare that want of competent ability procures it. To prevent this inconvenience I conceive it would be wise to determine, that a senator should not be eligible after he had served for the period assigned by the constitution for a certain number of years; perhaps three would be sufficient. A farther benefit would be derived from such an arrangement; it would give opportunity to bring forward a greater number of men to serve their country, and would return those, who had served, to their state, and afford them the advantage of becoming better acquainted with the condition and politics of their constituents. It farther appears to me proper, that the legislatures should retain the right which they now hold under the confederation, of recalling their members. It seems an evident dictate of reason, that when a person authorises another to do a piece of business for him, he should retain the power to displace him, when he does not conduct according to his pleasure. This power in the state legislatures, under confederation, has not been exercised to the injury of the government, nor do I see any danger of its being so exercised under the new system. It may operate much to the public benefit.

These brief remarks are all I shall make on the organization of the senate. The powers with which they are invested will require a more minute investigation.

This body will possess a strange mixture of legislative, executive and judicial powers, which in my opinion will in some cases clash with each other.

1. They are one branch of the legislature, and in this respect will possess equal powers in all cases with the house of representatives; for I consider the clause which gives the house of representatives the right of originating bills for raising a revenue as merely nominal, seeing the senate are authorised to propose or concur with amendments.

2. They are a branch of the executive in the appointment of ambassadors and public ministers, and in the appointment of all other officers, not otherwise provided for; whether the forming of treaties, in which they are joined with the president, appertains to the legislative or the executive part of the government, or to neither, is not material.

3. They are part of the judicial, for they form the court of impeachments.

It has been a long established maxim, that the legislative, executive and judicial departments in government should be kept distinct. It is said, I know, that this cannot be done. And therefore that this maxim is not just, or at least that it should only extend to certain leading features in a government. I admit that this distinction cannot be perfectly preserved. In a due ballanced government, it is perhaps absolutely necessary to give the executive qualified legislative powers, and the legislative or a branch of them judicial powers in the last resort. It may possibly also, in some special cases, be adviseable to associate the legislature, or a branch of it, with the executive, in the exercise of acts of great national importance. But still the maxim is a good one, and a separation of these powers should be sought as far as is practicable. I can scarcely imagine that any of the advocates of the system will pretend, that it was necessary to accumulate all these powers in the senate.

There is a propriety in the senate's possessing legislative powers; this is the principal end which should be held in view in their appointment. I need not here repeat what has so often and ably been advanced on the subject of a division of the legislative power into two branches— The arguments in favor of it I think conclusive. But I think it equally evident, that a branch of the legislature should not be invested with the power of appointing officers. This power in the senate is very improperly lodged for a number of reasons—These shall be detailed in a future number.

1. The original reads "The legislature in a free and republic. . . ." The reprint in the Boston *American Herald*, 8 May, corrected this error.

## 675. Spurious Luther Martin: Address No. V
## Philadelphia Federal Gazette, 10 April

In November and December 1787, the Connecticut "Landholder" IV, V, and VIII (Oliver Ellsworth) criticized Elbridge Gerry of Massachusetts for his role in the Constitutional Convention and his objections to the Constitution (*Connecticut Courant*, 26 November, and 3 and 24 December 1787, CC:295, 316, 371). Gerry responded in the *Massachusetts Centinel* on 5 January (CC:419), and Luther Martin, a Maryland delegate, defended Gerry in the *Maryland Journal* on 18 January (CC:460). (Gerry had refused to sign the Constitution, while Martin had left the Convention before the signing took place. For Gerry's published objections, see *Massachusetts Centinel*, 3 November, CC:227–A.) On 29 February "Landholder" X, who was apparently not Connecticut delegate Oliver Ellsworth but one of Martin's fellow Convention delegates from Maryland, replied to Martin in the *Maryland Journal* (CC:580).

In turn, Luther Martin answered the Maryland "Landholder" X in three essays printed in the *Maryland Journal* on 7, 18, and 21 March (CC:604, 626, 636). The last two replies were addresses to the citizens of Maryland, to which Martin added two more numbered addresses on 28 March and 4 April making a total of four (CC:650, 662). Among the newspapers that reprinted the Maryland "Landholder" X was the Philadelphia *Federal Gazette* which did so on 15 and 18 March, setting the stage for a spurious Address No. V from Martin (printed here). The identity of the author of this spurious address has not been determined, but it was apparently someone who, like the Maryland "Landholder," knew Martin's role in the Constitutional Convention.

*To the Editor of the Federal Gazette.*

Sir, I observe, that you have republished the Landholder, No. X. against me. Your publishing my fifth Number to the Citizens of Maryland, will be a proof of your impartiality, and will much oblige your humble servant,

L——R M——N.

Baltimore, 5th April 1788.

### NUMBER V.
### *To the Citizens of Maryland.*

To you, my fellow-citizens, I beg leave to address a few thoughts more upon that *villainous system of tyranny*, fals[e]ly called *a federal constitution*, formed by a band of conspiring traitors, in a secret conclave at Philadelphia last summer.

I, my fellow citizens, I was *the only honest man* in that *democratic* (not *aristocratic*) *junto*, for a considerable time. I was the only man who, with becoming firmness, decidedly opposed every measure of that body; because I knew them, *every man*, to be aspiring tyrants. Did "Mr. WASHINGTON or Mr. FRANKLIN" act thus nobly? No truly: they approved of several of the propositions of the conspiring committee; at least they tacitly acquiesced in some of their measures, and had not spirit nor patriotism enough to bellow out against all their doings whether right or wrong, as I did: nay more, they finally took an active part in the plot, and assisted in forming this damnable constitution.

Perhaps it may be asked, why I uniformly opposed every step taken by the convention? I answer briefly—*they were ALL wrong*. Does any one ask, Is it not more likely, that they were right and you wrong? Impossible! for I applied myself with all my might to the study of government from the first day I took my seat in convention, which was on Saturday, I forget the hour.[1] The next day (being Sunday, which still is the next day after Saturday, you know) notwithstanding my "religious scruples," I entirely spent in examining their journals. I then studied the science of government, beginning with the first principles, for the space of "*THIRTY days*." Consider this, my fellow-citizens, *THIRTY days* devoted to the study of government! with all the "histories" on politics both ancient and modern, to assist me; and a private tutor, the most intelligent that Philadelphia could afford, to throw light upon the most difficult parts of that abstruse science.

Having thus attained a superlative knowledge of government, I boldly ventured to open upon the members of convention, and not only proved them *aspiring traitors*, but also ignorant ones: that they were not polite enough to listen attentively to me (as that babbling rascal the Landholder has divulged) was not my fault; it must be attributed to their ill-breeding, and their aversion to the important doctrines I communicated to them, and which they had not sufficient understanding to comprehend.

But to come to the point—A greater part of the members were for proportioning the number of representatives in Congress, to the number of taxable inhabitants in the respective states. This met with my decided opposition. I did not wish that the smaller states (especially Rhode Island, where I have many friends) should be deprived of their equal suffrage in the federal government, *if we must have one*: besides, upon their plan, which was unfortunately carried by a large majority, the state of Maryland is to send to the federal house of representatives more than *one thirteenth*, which should be her part in that body; for the whole number of representatives is to be *sixty five*; of these Maryland is to send *six*, when her number ought to be no more than *five*. This kind of representation I opposed upon the principles of common honesty; for if Maryland be thus suffered to have an undue influence in the federal body, she may possibly exert it to the prejudice of the worthy little state of Rhode Island, and to her own aggrandisement.

But a still greater cause for my uniform opposition was, the mode by which the president and federal delegates are to be elected—not by the legislatures of the different states, as heretofore, but by the *mob*, the *rabble*, the *scum of the earth*, in short, to give them their worst name, by the *common people*. What do the *common herd* of mortals know of any thing, especially of government? What right have they to chuse legislators, &c. in all probability they will elect to this trust some low rascals, ignorant as themselves. For this reason, I say, I object to the new government; for what a mortifying thought would it be to *me*, or to any other *gentleman*, to be sent to congress with one, nay perhaps two or three such fellows for my colleagues! Oh ye powers! I sicken at the thought of serving in congress with a parcel of low bred ruffian farmers!

Suffer me, my fellow citizens, (I mean the better sort, for I would scorn to address the rabble) suffer me, I say, to mention another great cause of my opposition to this constitution:—The framers of it have inserted a clause prohibiting paper-money emissions, and legal tenders, in any of the states; now every one of you must know, that without these the courts of justice, and that valuable class of citizens called *lawyers*, would be deprived of more than two thirds of their employment; consequently many of those worthy gentlemen would be obliged to seek their bread in a foreign land. Should this be the case what is to become of the United States? Is it not well known that WE are the best arbitrators for settling any disputes which may arise between man and man? And are not WE the brightest ornaments of every state in the union? Pardon me if I request you for a moment to turn your eyes to *myself and to another worthy character* in your state, who were not concerned in the late rebellion against Great Britain; but on the present occasion we would not hesitate to sacrifice our *lives* (pardon the mistake, I mean WIVES) to procure the rejection of this constitution, which I look upon as little better than a Pandora's box to our profession. I trust it is unnecessary to mention the name of C——e;[2] you are well acquainted with his important services. Had *we* the power of deciding upon the federal constitution, which *we*, and not the *common people*, should certainly have, *we* would soon give it the *go by* in this state. This brings me to my concluding objection.

The mode which the convention have pointed out for the ratification of this constitution by *the people, the very common people too*, is intolerable. What! do they think that L——r M——n will live under a constitution the merits of which are to be determined by the *boors*, the *peasants*, the *farmers*, the *millers*, the very *off-scourings* of Maryland! Whoever thinks so is egregriously mistaken. I would inform such, that there is an asylum for me in Rhode Island, where the worthy friends to *legal tenders* long to receive me with open arms;[3] and thither I shall certainly repair so soon as this constitution shall have been adopted by the state of Maryland. Nor is this an empty threat; for by the profits of my Att——y-G——lship I swear, that I will put it in execution, and, in so doing, deprive you of a valuable officer. Attend to my declaration, ye stalls of asses! ye rabble of Maryland! reject this constitution immediately, unless you wish to lose me for ever.

In my next number I shall let you see something of my importance: at present it may suffice to remind you, that notwithstanding I "exhausted the politeness of the convention," and met with nothing but silent contempt from that body, in answer to all my long-winded speeches;[4] yet I was honoured with the *intimate friendship* of Mr. Mason, Mr. Gerry, and some other gentlemen, and held private meetings with them, as I mentioned before in my first number. And don't you all remember my vindication of Mr. Gerry's character, which would have been ruined but for me? These circumstances prove, beyond a doubt, that I am held in great esteem, as a politician, a lawyer, (I was going to say, a *man of honour*, and *a gentleman*; but curse on such empty names, I heartily despise them) and a *gentle* man.

L——R M——N.

Baltimore, 5th April 1788.

P. S. It may seem a little singular, that my objections to this constitution are widely different from those of every other man who has written on the subject; and that, when others are contending for greater powers to be lodged with the people, I am for curtailing those already granted them, viz. the election of the president and house of representatives; and the ratification or rejection of the proposed constitution. The truth is, that I wish to be singular; therefore while some are stickling for that *vile democracy* which they so blindly admire, I should wish to see an *aristocracy*, similar to that of Venice, established in the United States. This would effectually exclude the base born rabble from a share in the government—stupid fellows who, as I already told you in my fourth number, are not an atom better than the nation of frogs, in the fable.[5]

Oh my fellow-citizens! "I do not wish that you should beat your plow shares into swords, nor your pruning hooks into spears; nor do I ask you to perplex your minds in reasoning upon this new constitution: to give it your simple negative, to pronounce the single monosyllable NO, is all I ask of you."[6] Is this an unreasonable request? No surely; you have a right to obey the command of your Att—y G—l in this trifling instance.

1. Luther Martin first attended the Constitutional Convention on Saturday, 9 June.

2. Samuel Chase, Maryland's leading opponent of the Constitution and a supporter of conditional amendments, voted against ratification in the Maryland Convention on 26 April.

3. Several Maryland Antifederalist leaders, including Martin and Samuel Chase, advocated the emission of paper money and other measures to assist debtors.

4. See "The Landholder" X, *Maryland Journal*, 29 February (CC:580, pp. 266–67).

5. See "Luther Martin: Address No. IV," *Maryland Journal*, 4 April (CC:662, at note 6).

6. This quoted material is based upon comments made in "Luther Martin: Address No. IV," *Maryland Journal*, 4 April (CC:662, at note 4).

### 676. Charles Lee to George Washington
### Richmond, 11 April (excerpt)[1]

. . . What the result will be of retaining your public securities, is a thing of great uncertainty upon which opinions are very different: Unless there be a quiet and peaceable transition from the present american government, into another more powerful and independent of the people, the public debts and even private debts will in my opinion be extinguished by acts of the several Legislatures of the several states. The temper of the people in general, their habits, their interests all combine in producing such an event, and against these, natural justice will make but a feint opposition. If the proposed constitution be agreed to, and the administration be mild, just and wise, if it be so conducted as to engage the affections of the people, the public securities will appretiate and in a few years perhaps, be of considerable value.[2] . . .

1. RC, Washington Papers, DLC. For a longer excerpt, see RCS:Va., 734–35.

2. In his letter of 4 April, to which Lee is replying, Washington wrote: "In addition to the disappointment which I have met with from those who are indebted to me, I have in my hands a number of indents and other public securities which I have received from time to time as the interest of some Continental loan office certificates &c. which are in my possession; as I am so little conversant in publick securities of every kind as not to know the use or value of them, and hardly the difference of one species from another, I have kept them by me from year to year without having an idea that they would depreciate as they were drawn for interest, and never doubting but they would be received in payment of taxes at any time, till I have found by the Revenue Law of the last session, that only a particular description of them will pay the taxes of the year 1787—the others pay all arrearages of taxes and I am informed are not worth more than 2/6 in the pound, the injustice of this measure is too obvious and too glaring to pass unobserved; it is taxing the honest man for his punctuality, and rewarding the tardy or dishonest with the sum of 17/6 in every pound which is due from him for taxes. . . ." Washington reminded Lee that he had loaned the Continental government his money "in the day of its distress." "Strange indeed it seems," he continued, "that the Public Offices should take in the original Certificates.—Issue new, by a scale of their own—reducing the money as *they say*, to specie value—give warrents for interest accordingly—and then behold! these specie warrents are worth 2/6 in the pound.—To commit them to the flames, or suffer this is a matter of indifference to me.—there can be no Justice where there is such practices.—You will pardon me for dwelling so long upon this subject—It is a matter which does not concern me *alone* but must affect many others" (Fitzpatrick, XXIX, 460–61).

## 677. Fabius I
## Pennsylvania Mercury, 12 April

Between 12 April and 1 May, the triweekly *Pennsylvania Mercury* published nine essays of "Fabius" under the title "Observations on the Constitution Proposed by the Federal Convention." The essays were written by John Dickinson of Wilmington, Del., a wealthy lawyer and landowner. Dickinson (1732–1808) was born in Maryland but moved with his family to Delaware in 1740. A law student at Middle Temple in London from 1753 to 1757, he opened a law office in Philadelphia in the latter year. Dickinson sat in the Delaware Assembly, 1759–61, serving as its speaker the last two years, and in the Pennsylvania Assembly, 1762–65, 1770–71, and 1774–77. An opponent of British imperial policy, he represented Pennsylvania in the Stamp Act Congress in 1765 and was the principal author of that body's "Declaration of Rights and Grievances." In 1767–68, he published *Letters from a Farmer in Pennsylvania*, which, although critical of British policy, emphasized the need for reconciliation with Great Britain.

Dickinson served in the Continental Congress, representing Pennsylvania from 1774 to 1776 and Delaware in 1779. A leader of the forces seeking reconciliation with Great Britain, he voted against independence in 1776 and did not sign the Declaration of Independence. Dickinson was chairman of the committee that prepared the first draft of the Articles of Confederation in 1776 and in 1779 he signed the Articles as a Delaware delegate. He was President of Delaware, 1781–82, and President of the Supreme Executive Council of Pennsylvania, 1782–85.

In 1785 Dickinson moved to Wilmington. The next year he represented Delaware in the Annapolis Convention, serving as chairman of that body. As a delegate to the Constitutional Convention in 1787, he spoke often in support of the establishment of a strong central government; but as a delegate from a small state, he wanted the states to have a prominent role, too. Dickinson vigorously supported equality of suffrage in the Senate. He believed that money bills should originate in the House of Representatives but that the Senate should have the right to amend them. Dickinson feared a strong executive and recommended the creation of an executive council. He also favored a federal judiciary which, however, could not declare federal laws unconstitutional. Poor health forced Dickinson to leave the Convention around 15 September, but he authorized fellow Delawarean George Read to sign the Constitution for him.

Dickinson acknowledged that he was "Fabius" in private correspondence in 1796 and 1797 at the time when the essays were republished anonymously in a pamphlet, along with new numbers on Franco-American relations. The pamphlet, entitled *The Letters of Fabius, in 1788, on the Federal Constitution; and in 1797, on the Present Situation of Public Affairs* (Evans 32042), was published by W. C. Smyth of the Wilmington *Delaware Gazette*. (See Dickinson to Benjamin Rush, 29 December 1796, and 30 September 1797, Dickinson College, Carlisle, Pa.; Dickinson to Rush, 27 April 1797, Dickinson Papers, DeHi; Dickinson to Tench Coxe, 4 May 1797, Coxe Papers, Series II, Correspondence and General Papers, PHi; Joseph Priestley to Dickinson, 30 November 1797, Loudoun Papers, John Dickinson Section, PHi; and Samuel H. Smith to Dickinson, 9 November 1797, Dickinson Papers, PPL.) The term "letters," appearing in the title of the pamphlet edition, was not used in 1788 by the printer of the *Pennsylvania Mercury*, and, in fact, at that time Dickinson himself described his essays as addresses, not as letters. Occasionally, however, Philadelphia merchant John Vaughan, who had encouraged Dickinson to write the "Fabius" essays, employed the terms "letter" or "letters" in his correspondence with Dickinson.

Further evidence of Dickinson's authorship is in the R. R. Logan Collection at the Historical Society of Pennsylvania and in the Dickinson Papers at the Library Company of Philadelphia. The R. R. Logan Collection has drafts of the "Fabius" pieces in Dickinson's handwriting and what are apparently some research notes, entitled "Delaware Letters," that Dickinson probably used in writing the essays. The Dickinson Papers has several letters to Dickinson concerning the publication and distribution of "Fabius" that John Vaughan wrote to Dickinson in 1788. Vaughan acted as Dickinson's agent and forwarded the "Fabius" letters to the editor of the *Pennsylvania Mercury*. Three of Vaughan's letters concerning "Fabius," written in April 1788 while the "Fabius" pieces were being printed, were addressed to "Mr. Thomas," in order to protect Dickinson's identity. Vaughan dated only one of the three letters, and, to hide his own identity, he signed the first letter "N.W." and left the other two unsigned. Vaughan told Dickinson that "*much* enquiry is made after the author, but he cannot be discovered" (CC:694). (On the other hand, Vaughan's June and July letters about "Fabius" were signed and were addressed directly to Dickinson. In one of the letters [see below], he even asked Dickinson to lift the veil of anonymity. All of Vaughan's letters concerning "Fabius" are cited below and in subsequent numbers of "Fabius.") Vaughan was so successful in protecting Dickinson's anonymity that in 1797 Benjamin Rush, who had been a frequent contributor to the *Pennsylvania Mercury* in 1788, wrote Dickinson that "Never till now did I know you were the author of the letters under the signature of Fabius in defense of the general government" (11 October 1797, Butterfield, *Rush*, II, 792).

According to nineteenth-century historian Jared Sparks, John Vaughan told him in 1826 that Dickinson insisted upon anonymity, that it was a "condition" for his acceding to Vaughan's request to write the essays "that no person but Mr. Vaughan should know the author." Vaughan personally obtained the articles from Dickinson in Wilmington, twenty-eight miles southwest of Philadelphia, and had them "first published in an obscure paper in Philadelphia to insure secrecy. The editor supposed them to come from Lancaster" (Herbert B. Adams, *The Life and Writings of Jared Sparks* . . . [2 vols., Boston and New York, 1893], I, 482–83). Whether or not Daniel Humphreys, the editor of the *Pennsylvania Mercury*, knew that Dickinson was "Fabius" is not clear. On 31 May 1788 Humphreys wrote Dickinson and forwarded him newspapers containing the first three essays, without indicating that he knew Dickinson was "Fabius" (Dickinson Papers, PPL. The complete issues of the *Mercury* for the 12th, 15th, and 17th of April are filed with Humphreys' 31 May letter.).

It is unclear why, in 1788, Dickinson wanted his authorship of the "Fabius" essays to be kept secret, but in April 1797, he explained the reason for maintaining anonymity in publishing the pamphlet edition of "Fabius." "As to my Friends' advice of 'giving my name to the public,' I have great Reluctance. I feel a Respect for the public that represses a Compliance. In all probability, it will be known: as it is very difficult to conceal the Writer, when a party of violent Passions is determined to know him. That Consideration gives Me not the least Uneasiness. In such a Cause I fear no Consequences. To do Good is my sole aim: And if I can do the least Good upon the present momentous Occasion, I shall [be] wholly inattentive to what merely concerns Myself.

"If it is thy opinion, that an Intimation of my being the Writer may be of any service whatever, I shall leave it to thy Discretion, whether such an Intimation should be given or not in some very impartial Newspaper—as drawn from a similarity of Stile and Temper with former publications of mine" (to Benjamin Rush, 27 April 1797, Dickinson Papers, DeHi). To another correspondent, Dickinson noted in May 1797 that he used a pseudonym because he "did not wish to obtrude my Name in such momentous Business, tho perfectly easy as to any Discovery of my being the Writer, which I expected" (to Tench Coxe, 4 May 1797, Coxe Papers, Series II, Correspondence and General Papers, PHi).

In his second essay (CC:684), Dickinson asserted that he wrote the "Fabius" series to combat charges that the new Constitution "has such inherent vices, as must necessarily produce a bad administration, and at length the oppression of a monarchy or an aristocracy in the federal officers." Because such mistaken notions "may lead to the perdition of his country," Dickinson felt that it was "his indispensable duty, strenuously to contend, that—THE POWER OF THE PEO-

PLE prevading the proposed system, together with the STRONG CONFEDERATION OF THE STATES, forms an adequate security against *every* danger that has been apprehended." Consequently, Dickinson hoped that his series would remove "painful anxieties . . . from the minds of some citizens, who are truely devoted to the interests of *America*, and who have been thrown into afflictive perplexities, by the never-ending mazes of multiplied, intricate, and contrariant disquisitions."

The idea for writing the series, however, did not originate with Dickinson, but with John Vaughan. On 9 and 20 March 1788 a concerned Vaughan informed Dickinson about the adjournment of the New Hampshire Convention without ratifying the Constitution, an event which threatened to derail the entire process of ratification (Dickinson Papers, PPL. In a sense, Vaughan's concern was verified by the editor of the 1797 pamphlet edition who declared in the preface that "The first Nine Letters in this Collection, published in the beginning of the Year 1788, were occasioned by an alarming hesitation of some States to ratify the Constitution proposed by the Federal Convention in 1787."). In late March or early April 1788 Vaughan traveled to Wilmington to ask Dickinson to write a series of essays supporting the Constitution. After returning to Philadelphia, Vaughan wrote Dickinson "I hope this will find you in better health than when I left you & that you was not a Sufferer for the hour's conversation with which I was indulged notwithstanding your Indisposition" (6 April, Dickinson Papers, PPL). To assist Dickinson, Vaughan sent him copies of Volume I of *The Federalist*, Thomas Lloyd's *Debates* of the Pennsylvania Convention, and other writings on the Constitution. He also kept him informed about the progress of ratification.

Despite his poor health, Dickinson began to write the essays soon after Vaughan left Delaware. Vaughan personally picked up most of the articles, read them closely and critically, and occasionally made changes before submitting them for publication. He also distributed the newspapers containing "Fabius" to individuals in other states. On or soon after 12 April, the day that the first essay was published, Vaughan wrote Dickinson that "The first letter has given *much Satisfaction* & I can with pleasure assure you that means are taken to have it reprinted in *N York, Baltimore, Richmond & Charleston*" ("N.W." to "Mr. Thomas," n.d., Dickinson Papers, PPL. These were the principal cities in four of the seven states which had not yet ratified the Constitution and where ratifying conventions were scheduled to meet next.). On 17 and 21 April Vaughan sent the first four essays to George Washington in Virginia (Washington to Vaughan, 27 April, Fitzpatrick, XXIX, 468). Around 19 April, the day that "Fabius" IV was printed, Vaughan told Dickinson that numbers III and IV "are regularly forwarded as before mention'd," apparently meaning that they had been sent to the four cities already named. Vaughan also informed Dickinson that he had transmitted the first four essays to John Langdon, a member of the New Hampshire Convention which was scheduled to reconvene on 18 June (CC:694). He forwarded the last five numbers (V to IX) to Langdon on 25 April and 2 May, declaring on the 25th that "I have no doubt but you will find them applicable to the occasion—& as the republication of them may assist *our great cause*, should it even make but a few Converts, you may think proper to aim at putting them in the way of General Circulation" (Langdon/Elwyn Papers, NhHi).

On 9 June Vaughan told Dickinson that, "at particular request," he had sent a complete set of "Fabius" to New York to get them reprinted, but that "they have been kept back I imagine with a view of timing them" (Dickinson Papers, PPL). Two days later Vaughan, much concerned about the prospects of ratification in the New York Convention which was due to meet on 17 June, asked Dickinson for "the liberty of mentioning your name in that State—If you have a Set corrected I wish you would send them as early as possible, if not they will be published from the News Papers—Remember Sir this request is not the offspring of Indiscreet Zeal—but of high handed [i.e., high minded] necessity in a Cause we have all at heart; Render one more essential service to the Country which has received so many from You, & at a time when it is more necessary than at *any* period." To encourage Dickinson to reveal his authorship, Vaughan told him about a discussion that he had had the previous evening with Benjamin Franklin concerning a pamphlet that John Jay had published under the pseudonym "A Citizen of New-York." According to Franklin, "when Men of Weight, & ability at this Crisis wish to serve their Country by publishing their sentiments; they ought to give their names in order to call the Attention of the publick towards the sound Doctrine their publications contain but amidst the Numerous, & Voluminous anonymous publications which have appeard upon the Subject; they should not have their due Weight." Vaughan also told Dickinson that the prospects for ratification in Virginia were good (*ibid.* For Jay's pamphlet, see CC:683.).

Apparently, a corrected set of essays was sent to New York because on 26 July Vaughan wrote Dickinson that he had been "disappointed in the return of the Corrected papers from New York which I had [reason?] to expect long since having written for them instantly upon receipt of yours—The delay I find can in some measure be accounted for the Gentn having been at Poughepsie. I have again pressed him to send them & have No doubt I shall Soon receive them—They have had a Very extensive Circulation in that State by means of the Newspapers & have been quoted, but where men *will not* be persuaded, inspiration itself would lose its powers" (Dickinson Papers, PPL. Dickinson's "Fabius" essays have not been found in any extant New York newspaper. Poughkeepsie was the site of the New York Convention. The "Gentn" to whom Vaughan referred was possibly John Jay, a New York Convention delegate, with whom he corresponded.).

The complete "Fabius" series was reprinted in the Baltimore *Maryland Gazette*, 22 April to 24 June; the *Providence Gazette*, 3 May to 2 August; and the *New Hampshire Spy*, 17 May to 21 June. The first five essays appeared in the Richmond *Virginia Independent Chronicle*, 30 April to 28 May, and the *New Hampshire Gazette*, 22 May to 19 June. The first essay was also reprinted in the Philadelphia *Independent Gazetteer* on 15 April, and the Charleston *State Gazette of South Carolina* on 8 May; while the seventh number appeared in the New Jersey *Brunswick Gazette* on 6 May. The *New Hampshire Spy* introduced its republication of "Fabius" with this statement: "Having finished the 'Address to the Citizens of New York, on the subject of the new Constitution,' [CC:683] we now proceed to lay before our readers the following 'OBSERVATIONS,' on that very important subject. They were published in the Pennsylvania Mercury, in periodical numbers, under the signature of *Fabius*. In republishing these numbers, we shall unavoidably be obliged to postpone a variety of speculations on lesser subjects—and we presume our correspondents will not be displeased, when they are informed, that the sentiments which they contain, are congenial with the happiness and prosperity of the United States." (For a detailed discussion of the reprinting of "Fabius" I, see note 1, below.)

Even after ten states ratified the Constitution, John Vaughan continued to search for outlets in which to print the "Fabius" essays. On 26 July he informed Dickinson that "I have more than once Conversed with Mr Carey about the Insertion in his Museum & have lately Seen him—I find the whole will be inserted in this next Volume if nothing Interferes, but, he is not Steady" (Dickinson Papers, PPL). Mathew Carey reprinted all nine numbers in his Philadelphia *American Museum*. (Numbers I–III appeared in July, August, and September, respectively; IV–V in October; VI–VII in November; and VIII–IX in December.) Carey had evidently received a corrected set or a list of errata because substantial differences appear in some of the essays. (For these differences, see the footnotes to each essay.) From September to December 1788 Carey also reprinted Dickinson's *Letters from a Pennsylvania Farmer*.

The "Fabius" essays were generally well received. Just after the first three numbers appeared in the *Pennsylvania Mercury*, John Vaughan wrote John Dickinson that "I think they will be of Considerable Service, as they have commanded the publick attention, & being attended to leave useful impressions; They assist by divesting of party & leading to cool reflection—The Cause want nothing more to carry it thro!" (to "Mr. Thomas," 17 April, Dickinson Papers, PPL). When he sent Dickinson the newspapers containing numbers III–IV, Vaughan said "they are admired by all who wish to be *enjoind to do right* & Strongly approved of by men of weight & reflection" (CC:694). George Washington, commenting on the first four essays, declared that "The writer of the pieces signed Fabius, whoever he is appears to be master of his subject; he treats it with dignity, and at the same time expresses himself in such a manner as to render it intelligible to every capacity.—I have no doubt but an extensive republication of them would be of utility in removing those impressions which have been made upon the minds of many by an unfair or partial representation of the proposed Constitution, and would afford desireable information upon the subject to those who seek for it" (to John Vaughan, 27 April, Washington Papers, DLC). On 2 June Tobias Lear, Washington's secretary who was visiting his family in Portsmouth, N.H., informed Washington that "Fabius is now republishing in the papers of this town, and as the papers under this Signiture are written with perspicuity & candour I presume they will have a good effect" (*ibid.*).

John Vaughan was happy to learn that John Langdon thought that the "Fabius" essays "might be useful." Vaughan believed that the articles, although they conceded "the possibility of Defects" in the Constitution, showed how those defects "may be amended, that no danger can arise from them which is not provided against, & that if we do not adopt we cannot correct" (Vaughan to Langdon, 6 June, Langdon/Elwyn Papers, NhHi). Vaughan also wrote Dickinson that Henry Laurens of South Carolina "was much pleased with the letters" (26 July, Dickinson Papers, PPL). An anonymous Federalist asserted that the essays "are full of profound political wisdom" (*Pennsylvania Gazette*, 30 April, CC:719). Shortly after the publication of the 1797 pamphlet edition of "Fabius," Benjamin Rush wrote Dickinson that he had read the essays "with pleasure" in 1788 and that he had "often since spoken of them as the most practical and useful things published upon the controversy which then agitated the public mind" (11 October 1797, Butterfield, *Rush*, II, 792. In his autobiography, Rush stated that the "Fabius" essays "exceeded" anything that he had written in favor of the Constitution [Mfm:Pa. 704].). For two criticisms of "Fabius" I, see notes 2 and 4, below.

### OBSERVATIONS on the CONSTITUTION
### proposed by the FEDERAL CONVENTION.[1]

The Constitution proposed by the Federal Convention now engages the fixed attention of *America*.

Every person appears to be affected. Those who wish the adoption of the plan, consider its rejection as the source of endless contests, confusions, and misfortunes; and they also consider a resolution to alter, without previously adopting it, as a rejection.

Those who oppose the plan, are influenced by different views. Some of them are friends, others of them are enemies, to the United States. The latter are of two classes; either men without principles or fortunes, who think they may have a chance to mend their circumstances, *with impunity*, under a *weak government*, or in *public convulsions*, but cannot make them worse even by the last—or men who have been always averse to the revolution; and though at first confounded by that event, yet, their hopes reviving with the declension of our affairs, have since persuaded themselves, that at length the people, tired out with their continued distresses, will return to their former connection with *Great-Britain*. To argue with these opposers, would be vain—The other opposers of the plan deserve the highest respect.[2]

What concerns all, should be considered by all; and individuals may injure a whole society, by not declaring their sentiments. It is therefore not only their *right*, but their *duty*, to declare them. Weak advocates of a good cause or artful advocates of a bad one, may endeavour to stop such communications, or to discredit them by clamor and calumny. This, however, is not the age for such tricks of controversy. Men have suffered so severely by being deceived upon subjects of the highest import, those of religion and freedom, that *truth* becomes infinitely valuable to them, not as a matter of curious speculation, but of beneficial practice—A spirit of enquiry is excited, information diffused, judgment strengthened.

Before this tribunal, let every one freely speak, what he really thinks, but with so sincere a reverence for the cause he ventures to discuss as to use the utmost caution, lest he should lead into errors, upon a point of such sacred concern as *the public happiness.*

It is not the design of this address, to describe the present derangement of our affairs, the mischief that must ensue from its continuance, the horrors of a total dissolution of the union, or the division of it into partial confederacies. Nor is it intended to describe the evils that will result from pursuing the plan of another Federal Convention; as if a better temper of conciliation, or a more satisfactory harmony of decisions, could be expected from men, after their minds are agitated with disgust and disappointments, than before they were thus disturbed; though from an uncontradicted assertion it appears, that without such provocations, the difficulty of reconciling the interests of the[3] several states was so near to INSUPERABLE, in the late Convention, that after many weeks spent in the most faithful labors to promote concord, the members were upon the very point of dispersing in the utmost disorder, jealousy and resentment, and leaving the states exposed to all the tempests of passions, that have been so fatal to confederacies of democratical republics.[4]

All these things have been laid before the public in a much better manner, than the writer of this address is capable of, and to repeat what has been said, he means not. What he wishes, is to simplify the subject, so as to facilitate the enquiries of his fellow citizens.

Many are the objections made to the system proposed. They should be distinguished. Some may be called *local*, because they spring from the supposed interests of individual states. Thus, for instance, some inhabitants of large states may desire the system to be so[5] altered, that they may possess more authority in the decisions of the government; or some inhabitants of commercial states may desire it to be so altered, that the advantages of their trade may center almost wholly among themselves; and this predilection they may think compatible with the common welfare. Their judgment being thus warped at the beginning of their deliberation, objections are accumulated as very important, that, without this prepossession, would never have obtained their approbation. Certain it is, that strong understandings may be so influenced by this insulated patriotism, as to doubt, whether general benefits can be communicated by a general government.

Probably nothing would operate so much for the correction of these errors, as a perusal of the accounts transmitted to us by the ancients, of the calamities occasioned in *Greece* by a conduct founded on similar errors. They are expressly ascribed to this[6] cause—*that each city meditated apart on*[7] *its own profit and ends—insomuch that those who seemed to contend for union, could never relinquish their own interests and advancement, while they deliberated for the public.*

Heaven grant! that our countrymen may pause in time—duly estimate the present moment—and solemnly reflect—whether their measures may not tend to draw down the same distractions upon us, that desolated *Greece*.

They may now tolerably judge from the proceedings of the Federal Convention and of other Conventions, what are the sentiments of *America* upon her present and future prospects. Let the voice of her distress be venerated—and adhering to the generous *Virginian* declaration, let them resolve to CLING TO UNION AS THE POLITICAL ROCK OF OUR SALVATION.[8]

1. Reprinted: Philadelphia *Independent Gazetteer*, 15 April; Baltimore *Maryland Gazette*, 22 April (announced on 18 April); *Virginia Independent Chronicle*, 30 April; *Providence Gazette*, 3 May; *State Gazette of South Carolina*, 8 May; *New Hampshire Spy*, 17 May; *New Hampshire Gazette*, 22 May; Philadelphia *American Museum*, July. In reprinting "Fabius" I, the publisher of the Philadelphia *Independent Gazetteer* noted: "The following is copied, at the particular request of a number of our subscribers, from *Humphrey's* Mercury of Friday last."

On 26 April the *Pennsylvania Mercury* printed, immediately below "Fabius" VII (CC:710), an errata for "Fabius" I–II. For the changes made, see notes 3, 5–7, below. In reprinting "Fabius" I, the Philadelphia *American Museum* included all of the errata and removed all of the italics and the small capital letters. The *Museum* printing also added this dateline at the end: "Philadelphia, April 12, 1788." The 1797 pamphlet edition changed the dateline to April 10, 1788.

2. Commenting on "Fabius's" division of Antifederalists into three classes, a writer styling himself "No Conspirator, Tory, Plunderer, Dependant, or Office-Hunter" divided Federalists into three categories: "First, conspirators, base designing men, and generally of the well born too, who wish to crush liberty, and to reduce the poorer part of their fellow citizens to a state of dependance and slavery; second, their flatterers and dependants; third, a few *honest* but *mistaken men*, who were either surprised into acquiescence, or deceived through the fascination of names; the number of the last description, is however reduced almost to a cypher." "Fabius" was in either the first or second category. According to "No Conspirator . . .," "Fabius" wanted a commission in "the standing army" or a position in the federal judiciary. "No wonder then that the patriotic Fabius should tremble at the thoughts of another convention; now it's neck or nothing with him, there is no second chance of another *dark conclave*" (Philadelphia *Independent Gazetteer*, 17 April, Mfm:Pa. 636. See also "No Conspirator, &c.," *Independent Gazetteer*, 18 April, Mfm:Pa. 639.).

3. "The" inserted here in the *Mercury's* errata.

4. "Z" attacked "Fabius" for asserting "that another convention would be equally or more divided than the last." He called this "a palpable mistake; for if the last convention had not concealed themselves from the public, they dare not have advocated, or even mentioned many things in the constitution so dangerous to liberty, and so opposite to the principles of the revolution, which are now foisted into it" (Philadelphia *Independent Gazetteer*, 16 April, Mfm:Pa. 627).

5. "So" inserted here in the *Mercury's* errata.

6. "This" substituted for "the" in the *Mercury's* errata.

7. "On" substituted for "in" in the *Mercury's* errata.

8. Virginia Governor Edmund Randolph, in his 10 October 1787 letter to the speaker of the Virginia House of Delegates, stated in the next to the last paragraph: "I shall therefore cling to the union, as the rock of our salvation, and urge Virginia to finish the salutary work, which she has begun" (CC:385). For more on this paragraph, see CC:666.

## 678 A–D. Luther Martin: Pamphlet Edition of the Genuine Information, Philadelphia, 12 April (excerpts)

On 29 November 1787 Luther Martin and three of the other four Maryland delegates to the Constitutional Convention, upon the request of the Maryland House of Delegates, gave "information of the proceedings" of the Convention. After he left the House, Martin expanded and reorganized his speech which was published in the Baltimore *Maryland Gazette* between 28 December 1787 (CC:389) and 8 February 1788 (CC:516) in twelve unnumbered installments, as "*Mr.* MARTIN's *Information to the House of Assembly.*" One or more of these installments was reprinted in nine newspapers in five states. The Philadelphia *Independent Gazetteer* and the *New York Journal*, both Antifederalist newspapers, reprinted all twelve installments. (For the text of Martin's speech to the Maryland House of Delegates, see CC:304, and for a discussion of the circulation and impact of the published installments of the speech, see CC:389.)

Martin's "information" caused a sensation. In the next three or four months, Federalists charged that his account of the proceedings of the Constitutional Convention was filled with lies and distortions, while Antifederalists heaped extravagant and prolific praise on his assertions that the Convention had been far from unanimous and that the Constitution had serious flaws. In his fourteenth number "Centinel," a leading Antifederalist essayist, complimented Martin for "standing forth" as the "champion" of the people "at a crisis when most men would have shrunk from such a duty" (Philadelphia *Independent Gazetteer*, 5 February, CC:501).

As Martin emerged as a leading Antifederalist spokesman, the prospects for the ratification of the Constitution appeared to be less certain. On 6 February Massachusetts became the sixth state to ratify the Constitution, but the first to recommend amendments to it (CC:508). About two weeks later the New Hampshire Convention, which most people thought would ratify, adjourned without taking any action on the Constitution (CC:554). This setback was followed by the rejection of the Constitution by a statewide referendum in Rhode Island on 24 March (CC:664) and the refutation of a false report that North Carolina had adopted the Constitution. (For this false report, see CC:Vol. 4, pp. 507–9.) Between 21 April and 18 June five state conventions—Maryland, South Carolina, New Hampshire, Virginia, and New York—were scheduled to convene, and prospects for ratification were not favorable in the last two. Antifederalists believed that Martin's "Information" would be useful in these five states and that it could best be disseminated as a pamphlet—a view well expressed by the Albany Antifederal Committee during the campaign to elect New York state convention delegates: "The Publication of Luther Martins Speech in a Pamphlet would be of great Service, and tend to open the Eyes of our Country more than any Thing yet published" (to New York City Antifederal Committee, 12 April, Lamb Papers, NHi). According to Luther Martin, writing in 1804, his "Information" "was thought by a certain *sect* to be highly meritorious—Col Oswald was deputed by the Democratical Society of Philadelphia to obtain from me the original and the permission for its publication,—And I always understood that the present Governor Clinton [of New York] paid part of the Expence of Publication" (to Aaron Burr, 27 March 1804, Kline, *Burr*, II, 861).

On 12 April Eleazer Oswald, the printer of the Philadelphia *Independent Gazetteer*, announced that he had just published Luther Martin's "Genuine Information," and that it was available for two shillings and nine pence at his print shop and at his coffee house for merchants. After reproducing the title and epigram from the pamphlet's title page, the advertisement concluded with this editorial statement: "This excellent performance ought, for the solid and serious truths it contains, like the *Bible* and the letters of *Junius*, to be in the hands of every real friend to American liberty—In the language of the sacred law, 'Teach them diligently unto thy children—talk of them when thou sittest in thine house—and when thou walkest by the way' [Deuteronomy 6:7]. Impress it on their tender minds, as the first article of their political creed, *That there is no government safe with a standing army, and there is no government that is not safe without one.*"

The 101-page pamphlet is entitled *The Genuine Information, Delivered to the Legislature of the State of Maryland, Relative to the Proceedings of the General Convention, Lately Held at Philadelphia; By Luther Martin, Esquire, Attorney-General of Maryland, and One of the Delegates in the Said Convention. Together with a Letter to the Hon. Thomas C. Deye, Speaker of the House of Delegates, an Address to the Citizens of the United States, and some Remarks relative to a Standing Army, and a Bill of Rights.* The epigram from the Roman poet Horace reads: "Nullius addictus jurare in Verba Magistri" (Not pledged to swear to the words of any particular master).

As the title indicates, the pamphlet has several parts. Luther Martin's letter to Thomas Cockey Deye, dated 27 January 1788, includes an extract from the 21 December 1787 letter of Robert Yates and John Lansing, Jr., to New York Governor George Clinton (CC:447) supporting Martin's contention that they had left the Constitutional Convention early and had refused to return because they had despaired of obtaining "a proper" Constitution (CC:678–A). Martin's preface, dated 30 March, gives his reasons for publishing the "Information" and answers his many critics (CC:678–B). The third and longest part of the pamphlet consists of Martin's "Information." The pamphlet prints the installments as a single document with no breaks in the text and with no significant changes made from the original newspaper printings. In his pamphlet edition, Oswald retained Martin's extensive italics, even though he had deleted most of the italicization when he had reprinted the installments in his Philadelphia *Independent Gazetteer*. Martin's "Information," now called *The Genuine Information*, is followed by an article written by "A Citizen of the State of Maryland" attacking a standing army and another essay on the need for a bill of rights (CC:678–C, D).

The daily *Independent Gazetteer* carried its announcement of the sale of *Genuine Information* almost continuously between 12 April and 30 July. The weekly Antifederalist Philadelphia *Freeman's Journal* reprinted the *Gazetteer's* advertisement on 16, 23, and 30 April. The daily *New York Journal* reprinted the announcement on 24 April and ran it almost continuously until 26 July, when the New York Convention ratified the Constitution and a Federalist mob ransacked the *Journal's* office. The Charleston *State Gazette of South Carolina* advertised the sale of *Genuine Information* on 22 May, the day before the South Carolina Convention (meeting in Charleston) ratified the Constitution; while the North Carolina *Wilmington Centinel* advertised the pamphlet weekly from 11 June to at least 2 July—about three weeks before the North Carolina Convention was scheduled to meet. The *Centinel's* printers sold the pamphlet for six shillings. The Richmond *Virginia Gazette and Independent Chronicle* advertised the pamphlet on 28 June, three days after the Virginia Convention ratified the Constitution. On 9 October the Worcester *American Herald* announced the sale of the pamphlet for one shilling and six pence. The *Herald* repeated its advertisement on 5 and 19 March and on 2 April 1789.

Some Antifederalists complained that the pamphlet arrived too late to be helpful or that it did not reach them at all. Joshua Atherton, a New Hampshire Convention delegate, said that he received *Genuine Information* from "a Friend the Day I set out to Convention had not Time to possess myself but of a very small part of his Sentiments. Is it not surprising how these Pamphlets have been kept back?" (to John Lamb, 23 June, CC:750–L). William Williams, an opponent of the Constitution who nevertheless voted to ratify in the Connecticut Convention on 9 January, requested a copy of the pamphlet from a friend because it "is not to be obtained in this State. . . . You will be kind enou[gh] not to mention to any, this request &c for I suppose it is treason with the hot Constitutionalists as I am told He was an opposer of it" (to Benjamin Huntington, 21 October 1788, Thomas C. Bright Autograph Collection, Jervis Library, Rome, N.Y.).

The publication of the pamphlet aroused little Federalist commentary, although the editorial statement in Eleazer Oswald's advertisement caught the attention of some Federalists. A "gentleman" who recently had left Baltimore stated that Luther Martin's *Genuine Information* "have made no impressions on the minds of the people [of Maryland], tho' in the language of antifederalism, they are ranked with the Bible" (Philadelphia *Federal Gazette*, 17 April, Appendix I). Another Federalist noted sarcastically that Martin's *Genuine Information* and the *Letters of Junius* "are our unquestionable authority; and it is with very sensible regret, that I have lately read an advertisement, in the Independent Gazetteer, and Freeman's Journal, which only places the writings of those *immortal* men on a par with the ridiculous absurdities contained in the Bible. . . ." ("No Conspirator," Philadelphia *Federal Gazette*, 19 April, Mfm:Pa. 641). According to the New York *Daily Advertiser*, 20 May, one hundred copies of the pamphlet were sent to Baltimore, but only one copy was sold and that to a Virginian. Martin's opinion of the Constitution, declared the *Advertiser*, "seems to be but little valued" by the people of Maryland.

*678–A. Luther Martin to Thomas Cockey Deye*
*Baltimore, 27 January*[1]

*To the* HONORABLE THOMAS COCKEY DEYE,

SPEAKER *of the* HOUSE *of* DELEGATES *of* MARYLAND.

*Sir,* I flatter myself the subject of this letter will be a sufficient apology for thus publicly addressing it to you, and through you to the other members of the house of delegates. It cannot have escaped your or their recollection, that when called upon as the servant of a free State, to render an account of those transactions in which I had had a share, in consequence of the trust reposed in me by that State, among other things, I informed them, "that some time in July, the Honorable Mr. Yates and Mr. Lansing of New-York, left the convention; that they had uniformly opposed the system, and that I believe, despairing of getting a proper one brought forward, or of rendering any real service, they returned no more." You cannot, Sir, have forgot, for the incident was too remarkable not to have made some impression, that upon my giving this information, the zeal of one of my honorable colleagues, in favour of a system which I thought it my duty to oppose, impelled him to interrupt me, and in a manner which I am confident his zeal alone, prevented him from being convinced was not the most delicate, to insinuate pretty strongly, that the statement which I had given of the conduct of those gentlemen, and their motives for not returning were not candid.[2]

Those honorable members have officially given information on this subject, by a joint letter to his Excellency Governor Clinton—it is published.—Indulge me, Sir, in giving an extract from it, that it may stand contrasted in the same page with the information I gave, and may convict me of the want of candor of which I was charged, if the charge was just—if it will not do that, then let it silence my accusers.

"Thus circumstanced, under these impressions, to have hesitated would have been to be culpable;—we therefore gave the principles of the constitution, which has received the sanction of a majority of the convention, our decided and unreserved dissent. We were not present at the completion of the new constitution; but before we left the convention, its principles were so well established as to convince us, that no alteration was to be expected to conform it to our ideas of expediency and safety. A persuasion that our further attendance would be fruitless and unavailing rendered us less solicitous to return."[3]

These, Sir, are their words; on this I shall make no comment; I wish not to wound the feelings of any person, I only wish to convince.

*I have the honor to remain, With the utmost respect, Your very obedient servant,*

LUTHER MARTIN.

BALTIMORE, *January* 27, 1788.

### 678–B. *Luther Martin: To the Citizens of the United States*
*Baltimore, 30 March*

The following sheets contain the information given by me to the legislature of Maryland, when officially called before them for that purpose:—No friend to his country will think that they require an apology; I should have been unworthy the trust reposed in me, and guilty of the blackest ingratitude to a State, which has given me the most distinguishing marks of its confidence, had I not been explicit.— No *fact* has been intentionally mis[s]tated by me, I aimed to be perfectly correct; and, though in some measure obliged to depend on my memory, I believe I have in no instance, given malice an opportunity to charge me with misrepresentation. No writer, with his name, has denied the information to be just—I think they never will—though we differ in politics, should it be necessary, there are men of honor who were in the convention, who are ready to decide in my favour; and I can, with confidence, appeal to a *Washington*, a *Franklin*, and other respectable members of the convention, for the veracity of my information. Few, very few, even of the *anonymous* publications have *insinuated* the information to be in any respect uncandid; and those few have confined themselves to generals, without *daring* to descend to particulars.—The lowest *scurrility* in the form of *Extracts of letters*, coined at the mint of meanness and falsehood, I have experienced; it is what I expected; I know myself, and I am known by others, to be infinitely above them, and have read them with a smile of contempt.— Me they *cannot* injure;—but they disgrace their authors, and the cause in which they are engaged.—This is a trifling sacrifice—In the cause of freedom, were it necessary, I am ready to make a much greater.

As far as I have expressed my opinions of the views of the framers of the constitution, I have followed the fullest conviction of my mind, founded on my own observations made on their conduct while in convention, and confirmed by the conduct of the friends of the system since that time.—They were my sentiments while there; I at that time expressed them freely, and then found many who perfectly corresponded with me in sentiment, although some of them may not now choose to avow it, or, no doubt from a conviction of their error, may now advocate the system they there condemned and opposed. But as to myself, so far from having any reason to change the opinion I there formed, every circumstance which has since taken place has confirmed it.

The conduct adopted by the convention, rendered the dissemination of these sheets the more necessary: Could there possibly be a greater indignity and insult offered to the majesty of the free States, and the free citizens of America, than for the very men who were entrusted with powers for the preservation and security of their rights, and for the establishment of a permanent system to promote their happiness, to make use of that power to destroy both the one and the other?— For this purpose, in time of profound peace, to shut themselves up in mystery and darkness; to keep all their deliberations an absolute secret from their constituents, who were to be affected thereby; to prevent the publication of their journals; to deprive the free citizens of America of every means of information: to attempt to pass upon them, as meeting with their unanimous approbation, that which did not in reality meet with the perfect approbation of perhaps one individual in the convention; to give you no other alternative but to accept of it as proposed, without alteration, or to reject it entirely, while at the same time some of them were resounding, from one end of the continent to the other, the necessity of its acceptance, and that none but the enemies of their country would reject it—And to abuse your confidence in them, by endeavouring to hurry you into a hasty adoption, under that delusion, before you could obtain information, and be able to form a proper judgement for yourselves.

Such a conduct in any other country, or even in this, at any other time, would have drawn down upon them the indignation and resentment of those who were thus attempted to be abused and enslaved.

To counteract the views of ambition and interest has been my aim— To this I devoted every effort while in convention—The same motives have directed my conduct since—Should my exertions in the smallest degree assist in effecting the rejection of this detestable system of slavery, I shall enjoy the highest possible gratification, that of rendering my country an essential benefit.

But should the system be adopted, I shall even then enjoy the highest possible consolation which a good citizen can enjoy in the public calamity, that of having conscientiously discharged my duty to my country, by endeavouring to avert it.

BALTIMORE, *March* 30, 1788.

678–C. A Citizen of the State of Maryland
Remarks on a Standing Army

*The following* REMARKS *on a* STANDING ARMY, *were written by a Citizen of the State of Maryland, and we judge them well worthy the attention of the friends to liberty at this critical juncture.*

In *England*, by their bill of rights, a standing army is declared to be contrary to their constitution, and a militia the only natural and safe defence of a free people—This keeps the jealousy of the nation constantly awake, and has proved the foundation of all the other checks.

In the *American constitution* (now proposed) there is no such declaration, or check at all.

In *England*, the *military* are declared by their constitution, to be in *all* cases subordinate to the civil power; and consequently the civil officers have always been active in supporting this pre-eminence.

In the *American constitution*, there is no such declaration.

In *England*, the mutiny bill can only be passed from year to year, or on, its expiration every soldier is free, and the equal, by law, of the first general officer of the land.[4]

In *America*, the articles of war, which is the same thing, have been already considered as *perpetual* (as I am well informed) under even the present Congress,[5] although the constitutions of all the States positively forbid any standing troops at all, much less laws for them.

In *England*, the appropriation of money for the support of their army must be from year to year; in *America*, it may be for double the period.

How favourable is this contrast to Britain; that Britain which we lavished our blood and treasure to separate ourselves from, as a country of slavery; but we then held different sentiments from those now become so fashionable; for this I appeal to the constitutions of the several States.

In the declaration of rights of Massachusetts, sect. 17.—The people have a right to keep and to bear arms for the common defence. And as in time of peace, armies are dangerous to liberty, they ought not to be maintained without the consent of the legislature, and the military power shall always be held in exact subordination to the civil authority, and be governed by it.

Sect. 27. In time of peace, no soldier ought to be quartered in any house without the consent of the owner; and in time of war, such quarters ought not to be made but by the civil magistrate, in a manner ordained by the legislature.[6]

Declaration of rights of Pennsylvania, sect. 13—That the people have a right to bear arms for the defence of themselves, and the State; and as *standing armies*, in the time of peace, are dangerous to liberty, they ought not to be kept up; and that the military should be kept under strict subordination to, and governed by, the civil power.[7]

Declaration of rights of Maryland, sect. 25—That a well regulated militia is the proper and natural defence of a free government.

Sect. 26. That *standing armies* are dangerous to liberty, and ought not to be raised, or kept, without consent of the legislature.

Sect 27. That in all cases, and at all times, the military ought to be under strict subordination to, and controul of the civil power.

Sect. 28. That no soldier ought to be quartered in any house in time of peace, without the consent of the owner; and in time of war, in such manner only as the legislature shall direct.[8]

Declaration of the rights of Delaware, in the same words as Maryland.[9]

Declaration of rights of North-Carolina, Sect. 17—That the people have a right to bear arms for the defence of the State; and as standing armies in times of peace are dangerous to liberty, they ought not to be kept up; and that the military should be kept under strict subordination, and governed by the civil power.[10]

Constitution of South-Carolina, sect 42—That the military be subordinate to the civil power of the State.[11]

But some writers have told us, that our *poverty* is our best *security* against many standing troops; are we *then*, and *our posterity* always to be poor? This security would certainly cease with out poverty; but the truth is, our poverty instead of preventing, will be the first cause of the increase of a standing army; our poverty will render the people less able to pay the few troops, it is admitted we must keep. This expence, added to the immense public and private debts, which an efficient government seems to be requisite to enforce payment of, together with the onerous and complicated civil governments, both Continental and State, will be productive of future uneasiness and discontent. The most sanguine among us, must expect some turbulence and commotion; let the smallest appearance of commotion peep out again in any part of the continent, and there is not a rich man in the United States, who will think himself or his property safe, until *both* are surrounded by standing troops. This is the only public purpose for which these men ever did, or ever will, willingly contribute their money. But then, according to their laudable custom, they must have interest for their advances; this increases the public burthens; commotion is followed by commotion, until the spirit of the people is broken and sunk, by the halter, the scaffold, and a regular army of mercenaries.

My Countrymen! never forget this truth, which the sad experience of your fellow mortals, has witnessed with their blood! Remember it yourselves! Engrave it on the tender minds of your children, as the first article of their political creed: *That there is no government safe with a standing army,* and *there is none that is not safe without.* A people may frequently be so unfortunate as to lose their liberties. They may be so foolish as to give them away, as in *Denmark,* where not only the senators and representatives of the people, but also every man in the whole empire of the smallest note or consequence, signed a formal surrender of their liberties, on an instrument now kept in the archives of that kingdom;[12] an everlasting monument of—*how catching a thing this signing of names is,* or of what is now called—*a modest deference for the opinion of others:*[a] But whether they lose them or give them away, they will soon regain them, or resume them, unless they are prevented by *a standing army.*

> (a) The conduct of some people in Philadelphia, immediately after the general convention broke up, was equally foolish and absurd. They blindly followed the dictates and tenets of a few ambitious demagogues, who prepared petitions to the legislature, praying the adoption of the proposed government,[13] and, like the miserable Danes, would have readily *signed away* not only their own, but even the liberties of their children.

*678–D. A Citizen of the State of Maryland*
*Remarks Relative to a Bill of Rights*

### REMARKS *relative to a* BILL *of* RIGHTS.

It has been asserted by many, that a bill of rights was altogether useless, and in some respects a dangerous experiment; such an opinion is evidently calculated to mislead the people, and to take off the necessary checks from those who will be entrusted with the administration of government.

We are told by that able advocate for constitutional liberty, Lord *Abingdon,* that in every free government "there are found *three principal powers,* the first of these is the *power of the people*; the second, the *power of the constitution*; the third, the *power of the law.*—That the constitution ascertains the reciprocal duties, or several relations subsisting betwixt the *governors* and *governed*; that the law, or third power of the State, maintains the rights, and adjusts the differences arising between individuals, as parts of the same whole."[14]

Thus his Lordship makes a very evident distinction between the constitution and the law; he also calls *the rights of the people* the *substantial parts* of the constitution.

From a perusal of his letter to Mr. *Edward Burke*, it is evident, he considers the constitution, as that power which gives law, or restrains the conduct of the legislature; that as the laws of the land are the rule of action to the people; so the principles of the constitution direct the legislature in their several duties, for the rules of the one are to the other, what the law is to the Judges. In examining the constitution for the United States, as proposed by the late convention, I do not find any explicit declaration respecting the rights of the people, that can be considered as a sufficient guide on these points to the legislature, though they ought to to have been its SUBSTANTIAL parts.

It is true, the legislature may act according to their own principles of equity and reason; but these may differ from real constitutional principles, which should be so particularly expressed, that the constitution might have a controul over the legislature and the law. "My idea of government," says Lord Abingdon, "to speak as a lawyer would do, is, that the legislatures are the *trustees* of the people, the constitution the *deed of gift*, wherein they stood seized to *uses* only, and *those uses being named*, they cannot depart from them; but for their due performance are accountable to those by whose conveyance the trust was made. The *right* is therefore *fiduciary*, the power *limited*; or, as a mathematician would say, more in the road of demonstration; the *constitution* is a *circle*, the *laws* the *radii* of that circle, drawn on its surface with the pen of the legislature, and it is the known quality of a circle that its *radii* cannot exceed its *circumference*, whilst the people, like the *compasses*, are fixed in the center, and describe the circle."[15]

I do not perceive in the new constitution, *those uses named*, for which the administration of government is entrusted; no directing principles, sufficient for security of life, liberty, property, and freedom in trade; and therefore, as a supplement, a declaration or bill of rights is evidently wanting; otherwise, we shall have a legislature without check or controul; which if it should take place, it would open a door to every species of fraud and oppression.—Should the present system now proposed, pass without amendments, it would immediately constitute an aristocratic tyranny, a many-headed leviathan, an ungovernable monster, without constitutional checks, deplorable and to be deplored, dangerous and destructive, in proportion to the number of which it consists.

An eminent lawyer expressed an idea, which has been re-echoed, and become pretty general, "that what power was not expressly given, was retained by the people."[16]—Another civilian, of equal standing and professional abilities, has asserted the reverse of this proposition, and insisted that what power was not expressly declared, was relinquished and given up:—Since then, the sentiments of men, respectable for their talents, are so discordant on essential points surely, the common people may well be at a loss in a choice of their political guides,—and the safest way for them must be, to insist upon a *solemn declaration* of their rights and privileges, as the *substantial* and unalterable parts of the constitution: for such a *declaration* cannot be prejudicial; but may restrain the growth of despotism, the wantonness of power, and the base, licentious attempts of juvenile, daring ambition.

In fine, let me caution the supreme power, *the people*, to take care how they part with their birth-right; that they do not, like *Esau*, sell it for a *mess of pottage*;[17] and let them reflect, *seriously* reflect, on the inestimable value of the least atom of their liberty; she is more precious than rubies, and all the things that can be desired, are not to be compared unto her.

1. Deye (1728–1807), a Baltimore County planter, was speaker of the Maryland House of Delegates from 1781 to 1788, having been fairly regularly a member of that body since 1757.

2. For this incident which involved Martin and fellow Constitutional Convention delegate Daniel of St. Thomas Jenifer, see the Baltimore *Maryland Gazette*, 4 January 1788 (CC:414, note 7).

3. This letter from Robert Yates and John Lansing, Jr., dated 21 December 1787, was first published in the New York *Daily Advertiser* and *New York Journal* on 14 January (CC:447) and reprinted in the Baltimore *Maryland Journal* on 22 January—five days before Martin addressed his letter to Deye.

4. The first Mutiny Act was passed in 1689—the same year as the Bill of Rights. Mutiny acts, governing military discipline, were usually in force for one year.

5. The Articles of War, consisting of sixty-nine articles, were adopted by the Second Continental Congress on 30 June 1775, and on 7 November Congress made some alterations and additions to them. They were ordered printed on 13 November (JCC, II, 111–23; III, 331–34, 352). On 3 June 1784 the Confederation Congress created a force of 700 non-commissioned officers and privates "for taking possession of the western posts," and resolved "That the said troops when embodied, on their march, on duty, and in garrison, shall be liable to all the rules and regulations formed for the government of the late army of the United States, or such rules and regulations as Congress or a committee of the states may form" (JCC, XXVII, 538–40).

6. Thorpe, III, 1892.

7. Thorpe, V, 3083.

8. Thorpe, III, 1688.

9. See sections 18–21 of the Declaration in Mfm:Del. 1; and *The Constitutions of the Several Independent States of America* . . . (2nd ed., Boston, 1785), 93 (Evans 19306).

10. Thorpe, V, 2788.

11. Thorpe, VI, 3257.

12. For background to the 1661 signing of the "Instrument or Pragmatic Sanction Regarding the King's Hereditary Rights to the Kingdoms of Norway and Denmark" that gave the hereditary monarch absolute power, see RCS:Va., 1509n–10n.

13. In September 1787 these petitions were signed by more than 4,000 people in the city of Philadelphia and in the counties of Philadelphia and Montgomery (RCS:Pa., 62, 64, 64–65, 65, 67, 104, 130, 134, 137–38).

14. See the Earl of Abingdon, *Thoughts on the Letter of Edmund Burke, Esq; to the Sheriffs of Bristol, on the Affairs of America* (Lancaster, Pa., 1778), 13 (Evans 15740). This pamphlet was first printed in Oxford, Eng., in 1777. Willoughby Bertie (1740–1799), the fourth Earl of Abingdon, was an active member of the House of Lords and a frequent newspaper political essayist. He criticized Edmund Burke for softening his opposition to British policy toward the American colonies.

15. *Ibid.*, 21.

16. See James Wilson's 6 October 1787 speech before a Philadelphia public meeting (CC:134).

17. Genesis 25:29–34.

## 679. Ebenezer Hazard to Mathew Carey
## New York, 14 April[1]

Your Favor of 10th. Inst. with the Pamphlets & News Paper came duly to hand, & I am much obliged to you for your ready Compliance with my Request.—The Style of the Poetry needs no Apology:—I think it exactly suited to the Subject, & therefore a *better* one (if you will allow the Expression) would not have been *equally good.* That Style, at the same Time that it admits of a ludicrous Inflection of Words to serve practical Purposes, contains a kind of sarcastic Contempt which must greatly injure the delicate Feelings of such a man as your Hero:— and to despise such Folks is to destroy them.[2]—

I am sorry there is so much Reason to suppose that any among you at this Day "pant after the horrors of civil War":—may their hopes be blasted! & no doubt they will be, for such People will find but few any where who will co-operate with them:—there is very little of that Spirit to be found any where in the Union (as far as my Information extends) except in Pennsylvania: and I can hardly think any there seriously wish for Commotions which may involve themselves in Ruin:—their View, probably, is to lead the States which have not yet met in Convention, to think there is such Opposition to the new Constitution in others that it will not be expedient to adopt it:—even in that I think they will fail, for the Probability is that all the States will adopt it though they may propose Amendments. When this Event takes Place, we may hope for a Reformation of Manners, & that wholesome Laws will restrain the Passions of unprincipled & protect Reputation as well as Property.—

1. RC, Lea and Febiger Collection, PHi.

2. Carey's letter of 10 April has not been found. In "haste," Hazard wrote Carey on 7 April that "I have never had an Opportunity of seeing the Plagi-Scurrilliad til very lately, when a typographical friend, finding that the Hero of that Poem had *bejuniused*

me, put it into my hands. Whether the Introductory Remarks of Gulliverus, the Recommendation of Scribblerus Quartus, the Approbation of the Secretaries, or my own [Opinion?] Feelings prejudiced me in its Favor, I will not pretend to say, but I wish to own the Poem, & to add it to my Farrago of Pamphlets. Can you favor me with a Copy, under an Assurance that I will never let it be known from whence I recd. it; if you can you will much oblige" (Lea and Febiger Collection, PHi). The "Hero" was Eleazer Oswald, the publisher of the Philadelphia *Independent Gazetteer* and Carey's bitter enemy, and the pamphlet was *The Plagi-Scurriliad: A Hudibrastic Poem. Dedicated to Colonel Eleazer Oswald* (Philadelphia, 1786) (Evans 19540). Hazard, the U.S. postmaster general, had been charged by Oswald with stopping newspapers in the mails. The publication of the pamphlet so galled Oswald, that in January 1786 he challenged Carey to a duel in which Carey was shot through the thigh. His wound took more than a year to heal.

## 680. Benjamin Rush to David Ramsay
## Charleston Columbian Herald, 14 April

In late March or early April Dr. Benjamin Rush of Philadelphia wrote his good friend Dr. David Ramsay of Charleston a long letter requesting that Ramsay have it printed. Ramsay extracted the letter and took it "immediately" to the Charleston *Columbian Herald*, in which it appeared on 14 April. (The manuscript of Rush's letter has not been located.) "Agreeably" to Rush's request, Ramsay sent Rush some copies of the newspaper containing the letter (Ramsay to Rush, 21 April, Rush Papers, PPL). On 6 May Rush forwarded one of these copies to another friend, the Reverend Jeremy Belknap of Boston, stating that "As my opinions Upon the subject of the fœderal goverment have been often misrepresented, by our antifœderal Scriblers, I have to beg the favor of you to republish the enclosed extract of one of my letters to my friend Dr Ramsay of Charleston in some of your papers.—It contains my principles fairly stated. I beleive I gave *a part* of them in my last letter to you" (CC:733. Rush probably refers to his letter of 28 February, CC:573.). By the time that Belknap received Rush's request, two Boston newspapers had reprinted the letter. Belknap told Rush that the letter "was much approved" (22 June, Rush Papers, PPL).

The extract of Rush's letter to Ramsay, identifying Rush as the writer, was reprinted in the May issue of the Philadelphia *American Museum* and in eight newspapers by 24 June: Mass. (3), R.I. (1), N.J. (2), Pa. (1), Md. (1). In addition, the London *Gentleman's Magazine* reprinted Rush's letter in June 1788, dating it "*Philadelphia, April 10.*" Only the Philadelphia *American Museum* and the two New Jersey newspapers, which appeared after the *Museum*, identified Dr. David Ramsay as the recipient of the letter. Five of the newspaper reprints omitted the last sentence and closing of the extract. (See note 3, below.)

*Extract of a letter from Dr.* RUSH, *of Philadelphia, lately received by [a] gentleman of this city.*

DEAR SIR, "I presume before this time you have heard, and rejoiced in the auspicious events of the ratification of the federal government by *six* of the United States.

"The objections which have been urged against the federal constitution from its wanting a bill of rights, have been reasoned and ridiculed out of credit in every state that has adopted it. There can be only *two* sureties for liberty in any government, viz. *representation* and *checks*. By the first, the rights of the people, and by the second, the rights of representation are effectually secured. Every part of a free constitution hangs upon these two points, and *these* form the two capital features of the proposed constitution of the United States. Without them, a volume of rights would avail nothing, and with them a declaration of rights is absurd and unnecessary; for the PEOPLE where their liberties are committed to an equal representation, and to a compound legislature (such as we observe in the new government) will always be the sovereigns of their rulers, and hold all their rights in their own hands. To hold them at the mercy of their servants, is disgraceful to the dignity of freemen. Men who call for a bill of rights, have not recovered from the habits they acquired under the monarchical government of Great-Britian.

"I have the same opinion with the antifederalists of the danger of trusting arbitrary power to any single body of men; but no such power will be committed to our new rulers. Neither the house of representatives, the senate, or the president can perform a single legislative act by themselves. An hundred principles in man will lead them to watch, to check and to oppose each other, should an attempt be made by either of them upon the liberties of the people. If we may judge of their conduct, by what we have so often observed in all the state governments, the members of the federal legislature will much oftener injure their constituents by voting agreeably to their inclinations, than *against* them.

"But are we to consider men entrusted with power as the receptacles of *all* the depravity of human nature? By no means. The people do not part with their full proportions of it. Reason and revelation both deceive us, if they are all wise and virtuous. Is not history as full of the vices of the people, as it is of the crimes of the kings? what is the present *moral* character of the citizens of the United States? I need not discover it. It proves too plainly, that the people are as much disposed to vice as their rulers, and that nothing but a vigorous and efficient government can prevent their degenerating into savages, or devouring each other like beasts of prey.

"A simple democracy, has been very aptly compared by Mr. Ames of Massachusetts, to a volcano that contained within its bowels the fiery materials of its own destruction.[1] A citizen of one of the Cantons of Switzerland in the year 1776, refused to drink in my presence 'the commonwealth of America' as a toast, and gave as a reason for it, 'that a simple democracy was the devil's own government.'[2]—The experience of the American states under the present confederation has in too many instances justified these two accounts of a simple popular government.

"It would have been a truth, if Mr. Locke had not said it, that where there is no *law*, there can be no *liberty*, and nothing deserves the name of law but that which is certain, and universal in its operation upon all the members of the community.

"To look up to a government that establishes justice, insures order, cherishes virtue, secures property, and protects from every species of violence, affords a pleasure, that can only be exceeded by looking up in all circumstances to an over[r]uling providence.—Such a pleasure I hope is before us, and our posterity under the influence of the new government.

"The dimensions of the human mind, are apt to be regulated by the extent and objects of the government under which it is formed. Think then my friend, of the expansion and dignity the American mind will acquire, by having its powers transferred from the contracted objects of a state to the unbounded objects of a national government!— A citizen and a legislator of the free and UNITED STATES of America, will be one of the first characters in the world.

["]I would not have you suppose, after what I have written, that I believe the new government to be without faults. I can see them, but *not* in *any* of the writings or speeches of any of the persons who are opposed to it. But who ever saw any thing perfect come from the hands of man? It realises notwithstanding in a great degree, every wish I ever entertained in every stage of the revolution for the happiness of my country, for you know that I have acquired no new opinions or principles upon the subject of republics, by the sorrowful events we have lately witnessed in America.—In the year 1776, I lost the confidence of the people of Pennsylvania, by openly exposing the dangers of a simple democracy, and declaring myself an advocate for a government composed of three legislative branches.[3]

"Adieu—from dear sir, yours sincerely."

1. On 15 January 1788 Fisher Ames of Dedham noted in the Massachusetts Convention: "A democracy is a volcano, which conceals the fiery materials of its own destruction. These will produce an eruption, and carry desolation in their way" (Boston *Independent Chronicle*, 17 January).

2. Rush refers to John Joachim Zubly (1724–1781), a native of Switzerland and a Georgia delegate to the Second Continental Congress in 1775. Fellow delegate John Adams described Zubly as "a clergyman of the independent persuasion," "a learned man," and "a man of a warm and zealous spirit" (LMCC, I, 194–95). Zubly left Congress

late in 1775 and returned to Georgia because he opposed the drift of Congress toward independence. He refused to support any measure that would endanger the efforts to reconcile with Great Britain, even though he supported American rights. During a debate in Congress on the state of trade, Zubly said that "A republican government is little better than government of devils. I have been acquainted with it from six years old" (12 October 1775, JCC, III, 491). In his diary, Zubly wrote: "I made it a point in every company to contradict and oppose every hint of a desire of independence or of breaking our connection with Great Britain. . . . A separation from the Parent State I wd dread as one of the greatest evils and should it ever be proposed write pray and fight against it. . . . I have more than a little thought on this matter, and being borned and bred in a commonwealth should not be unacquainted with republican Govt. but wish never to see the day when the Q[uestio]n whether we ought to Separate shl. be agitated" (LMCC, I, 521n).

3. This sentence was omitted by the *Massachusetts Centinel*, 7 May; Boston *Independent Chronicle*, 8 May; *Pennsylvania Packet*, 16 May; Baltimore *Maryland Gazette*, 20 May; and Portland *Cumberland Gazette*, 22 May.

In September 1776 a state convention adopted a new constitution for Pennsylvania that placed most power in the hands of a single-house legislature. Laws could not be vetoed by the Supreme Executive Council which had replaced the colonial governor. In 1777 Benjamin Rush, under the pseudonym "Ludlow," published four essays attacking the constitution in the *Pennsylvania Journal* on 21, 28 May, and 4, 11 June, and then in a pamphlet entitled *Observations upon the Present Government of Pennsylvania. In Four Letters to the People of Pennsylvania* (Evans 15589). The pamphlet insisted upon a government of checks and balances and called for a new convention to revise the constitution (David Freeman Hawke, *Benjamin Rush: Revolutionary Gadfly* [Indianapolis and New York, 1971], 195–202). Because of his opposition to the constitution, the state assembly did not reappoint Rush to Congress.

## 681. Antoine de la Forest to Comte de la Luzerne
### New York, 15 April[1]

The *federalists'* cause has suffered a dangerous defeat since the account that I had the honor to give you on the 18th of last february[2] of the progress of the new constitution proposed for the United States. Its adoption by Massachusetts had swelled the hopes of all good patriots. There was no doubt whatever that the convention of the people of New Hampshire that was to be held soon after would follow the example set by those of the six other States. But too much confidence in the goodness of their cause, led New Hampshire *federalists* to neglect to enlighten the backcountry inhabitants. They were astonished to see that their delegates had received an explicit instruction from their respective Towns to vote against the new constitution; federalists saw that it was risking the question to press for a decision on it in the convention; they had no other recourse than to adjourn until the 18th of June.[3] This lack of success had the most unfortunate effect on the people of the States of Newyork, Maryland, Virginia and the two Carolinas. The opposition there has taken on new strength; *antifederalists* have insinuated themselves more easily into all the State [conventions] that have taken place since then; at this time the most favorable political [– – –] still maintain an uncertain balance.

The State of Rhode Island itself, in spite of its insignificance and the scorn in which the party that has directed affairs there for three years is held, serves to encourage, by its conduct, the obstinacy of the opposition in these states. Its legislature, which steadfastly refused to convene a convention of the people, was no longer able to avoid acknowledging the proposed constitution, and has referred it for consideration by each Town. It well knew that it would be easier to make this plan fail there than in a large assembly where discussion enlightens the mind and where the arguments of *antifederalists* cannot hold out against those of their adversaries; some of these Towns have in effect voted against the new Government. The others have [met?] in order to examine it, have protested against [the] resolution of the legislature, and have demanded the convocation of a convention like the other States. The legislature has rejected this [demand?] and, [in] what is the height of bad faith, informed Congress of the negative vote of the ill-disposed Towns as the decision of the entire State. It is however established that there are almost 7000 votes in [the state?] and that the negative votes amounted to only 2500.[4] *Federalists* can expect nothing more from Rhode [Island], and there is reason to believe that it will yield only to the unanimity of its sister States.

But we hear that several Towns in New Hampshire have revoked the explicit instructions given to their delegates to vote against the new constitution, and are giving them the freedom to follow their own Judgment. It is hoped that the convention in June, bringing together more unrestricted votes, will be able to vote according to its convictions, and *federalists* think they will have a majority of votes there. They count on the same advantage in Maryland and South Carolina, whose conventions are to convene soon and where the two parties already have reckoned their strength. They have fewer hopes for the States of Virginia, North Carolina, and Newyork.

If patriotism could suppress local views and individual interests, the state of national affairs alone would be enough to reconcile all votes in favor of the new Government. Each state acts as it pleases, without considering the general good; the union is without funds to meet its expenses; its most useful officers have not been paid; Congress meets every day and adjourns to the next, for want of a sufficient representation to proceed with business; one of the States, whose development has been the most rapid, Georgia, is harassed by the Savages and left to its own devices; Pennsylvania was on the brink of an insurrection like the one in Massachusetts, and the government preserved the peace only by pretending to ignore the insult;[5] a [kind?] of civil war has flared up in the district of Franklin between the partisans of the Government of North Carolina and those of independence.[6] No one can foresee what the limits of the [damage?] will be if the new constitution does not soon form a great nation out of all these weak parts.

1. RC (Tr), Affaires Étrangères, Correspondance Consulaires, BI 910, New York, ff. 37–38, Archives Nationales, Paris, France. This letter, dispatch number 227, was endorsed as received on 9 June 1788.

2. See CC:536.

3. For the adjournment of the New Hampshire Convention and its impact on the other states, see CC:554.

4. For the Rhode Island referendum on the Constitution, see CC:664.

5. For the Carlisle Riot and its aftermath, see CC:407; and RCS:Pa., 670–708.

6. The State of Franklin was created in 1785 out of the western counties of North Carolina. It collapsed in 1788 because of internal dissensions and the opposition of North Carolina, Virginia, and Congress.

### 682. From Thomas Rodney
### Poplar Grove, 15 April[1]

Our Government having apparrently lost all respect for its Officers and Magistrates, by Subjecting them to the rude insults of every petty passion, Seems attentive only to the exercise of those powers which Tend most to Oppress and distress the people, merely To Satisfy the mutual rage of Faction, or personal peak and resentment. When this is the case it does not require any Extraordinary degree of Presient Skill to decern that anarky and confusion must Shortly, follow.

The Fœderel Constitution is proposed as a cure for these evils, and such others as prevail at present; but I fear this will not answer the purpose. the resistance already made to it, forebodes a greater one Yet to come, or if adopted that it will not be so generally Supported as to give it the best opperation that its own principles would incline to: Yet it is favoured by verry powerful Influence. The people at large feel Some alteration in their Government Necessary; The wealthiest Citizens are for it because they know that the Government must naturally come into their hands; The Officers of the Army are for it, because, by the Sword being once more put in their hands, they may Obtain their wishes: for while they ware the golden medal of the Cincinnati, they will not be easy Untill Some Order of military Knighthood is established. Perhaps when one of these Interests Obtains the Government And the other the Sword they will agree, That the one Shall be Peers of the realm; and the other Knights of the Golden Eagle. This at first perhaps would not be relished by the people at large, but

I do not know that it would prejudice the common welfare. The republicks of Greece and Rome Had both their Knights And Nobles, and these Seem to have been necessary To that freedom and Splendor, of those celebra[ted] Republicks, which Still enlightens the World. Military Knighthood is an exciting reward to Young Soldiers; and pays them better than Money and after a Man has Served his country through the prime of life—He considers it as a full reward for all his Services to be raised to the highest Seat of Honour. Therefore a Country that is without Honors, lacks those rewards which are a far Stronger Excitment to publick Services than Money. The Article in the Constitution against confering any degree of Nobility, is an evidence that there is a Strong disposition in favour of it, otherwise Such an Article would have been unnecessary but this will be Too weak to Stand in the way when there comes an Opertunity of introducing it. For it is in vain to limmit The Sovereign Power; it cannot be controled but when the people rise up in a body to resist it, and this never will happen but when Some great and general calamity prevails from the Misusage of it. Indeed the rights and liberty of the people is far Safer In the hands of a legislature wherein their different interests are Seperately and distinctly established than in the hands of a convention Elected by themselves, for nothing is more likely than that a majority of Such a Convention would be Composed of one class of Citizens Only. in which case they would favour their Own interest to the disadvantage of the rest of the community.

1. FC, Brown Collection, DeHi. The letter was addressed only to "Dr. Sir" and may have been intended as a newspaper article. Rodney (1744–1811), owner of an estate called "Poplar Grove," in Kent County, Del., was a judge of the state admiralty court, 1778–85; register of wills for Kent County, 1778–88; delegate to Congress, 1781–82, 1786; and a Kent County delegate to the state House of Assembly, 1786–88, serving as speaker in 1787. He was a Whig in state politics and became a Republican in national politics. For his opposition to the Constitution, see his letters to Caesar A. Rodney, 14 June 1788, and to Alexander Hamilton, 10 February 1791 (Mfm:Del. 46, 50).

### 683. A Citizen of New-York: An Address to the People of the State of New York, 15 April

On 15 April Samuel and John Loudon, publishers of the *New York Packet*, advertised that they had "Just Published" a pamphlet written by "A Citizen of New-York." The nineteen-page pamphlet was entitled *An Address to the People of the State of New-York, on the Subject of the Constitution, Agreed upon at Philadelphia, the 17th of September, 1787* (Evans 21175). The Loudons asserted that "This Address is written with candor, and in a manner truly decent and respectful. It contains many serious truths; and is replete with observations worthy the attention of *every* Citizen of America, who is anxious for the welfare of *his country*, at this *important crisis*." The advertisement ran almost continuously in the triweekly *New York Packet* until 11 July 1788.

The pamphlet was written by John Jay—a New York City lawyer, the Confederation Secretary for Foreign Affairs, and the author of five numbers of *The Federalist* (CC:201). Jay essentially identified himself as "A Citizen of New-York" when he sent a copy of the pamphlet to George Washington on 20 April, five days after it was offered for sale (Washington Papers, DLC. Jay's draft of this letter was dated 12 April, three days before the Loudons' advertisement [John Jay Papers, NNC].). Jay was identified as the author by Samuel Blachley Webb, a New York City commercial agent; John Vaughan, a Philadelphia merchant; and by three newspapers (one as early as 30 April) and the Philadelphia *American Museum* (Webb to Joseph Barrell, 20 April, Webb Papers, CtY; and Vaughan to John Dickinson, 9 June, Dickinson Papers, PPL. For the newspapers and the *Museum*, see below.). Even though he received the pamphlet from Jay, Washington would only "conjecture but upon no certain ground" that Jay was "A Citizen of New-York" (to James Madison, 8 June, RCS:Va., 1586).

In mid-June, John Vaughan tried to get Jay to admit to his authorship, but Jay refused. Vaughan wrote that "I have perused with Singular pleasure some thoughts on the Constitution addressed to the State of N Yk & was expressing my Sentiments to our good friend Dr Franklin—who observed that if you was the Author (as Said) he thought it incumbent upon you to put your name to it—to give it additional Weight at this awful Crisis I call it awful because a rejection in your State will be productive of infinite mischief. . . . Let me request Sir that you will attend to the observation of our Venerable friend Could I presume I could with propriety intrude my own opinion upon the occasion—I would urge it from myself—being actuated not by intemperate Zeal—but by a Strong impression & persuasion that you will by it add one more to the many Signal Services you have rendred this Country" (n.d., John Jay Papers, NNC. On 11 June Vaughan had used this same conversation with Franklin to encourage John Dickinson to disclose his authorship of the "Fabius" essays. See CC:677, headnote.). On 27 June Jay, a delegate to the New York Convention, replied from Poughkeepsie: "I have considered the Hint suggested in your Letter . . . very long, and I may say habitual Respect for the Sentiments of Dr. Franklin, at first inclined me [to] adopt them relative to the Subject in Question. Further Consideration induced me to suspect that he has estimated the Influence of my opinions beyond their value. If the Reasoning in the Pamphlet you allude to is just, it will have its Effect on candid and discerning minds—if weak & inconclusive my name cannot render it otherwise" (Madeira-Vaughan Collection, PPAmP).

"A Citizen of New-York" appeared two weeks before the elections for delegates to the New York Convention (29 April–3 May) and was part of the campaign to elect Federalist delegates. In his letter of 20 April, in which he sent Washington a copy of the pamphlet, Jay appears to explain why he wrote the pamphlet: "The Constitution still continues to cause great party Zeal and Ferment, and the opposition is yet so formidable that the Issue appears problematical" (Washington Papers, DLC. In his retained draft of the letter, Jay described "the Issue" as "~~very~~ problematical" [John Jay Papers, NNC].). "A

Citizen of New-York" was a highpoint in the Federalist propaganda campaign to elect Convention delegates, which included the publication of pamphlets, broadsides, election handbills, newspaper articles, and nomination tickets. This campaign began intensely in early February, after the New York legislature called the Convention and set the dates for the elections.

Wherever "A Citizen of New-York" circulated in New York, it solidified Federalist support for the Constitution and converted some Antifederalists. Writing from New York City, Samuel Blachley Webb declared that the pamphlet "has had a most astonishing influence in converting Antifeoderalists, to a knowledge and belief that the New Constitution was their only political Salvation" (to Joseph Barrell, 27 April, Webb Family Collection, CtY). William Bingham, a Pennsylvania delegate to Congress in New York City, claimed that the pamphlet "has operated very forcibly on the Minds of the People here" (to Tench Coxe, 30 May, Coxe Papers, Series II, Correspondence and General Papers, PHi). A reviewer in the April issue of the New York *American Magazine*, probably editor Noah Webster, praised the pamphlet's "moderation of temper, and sound judgement." In particular, he believed that "the author's arguments against appointing a new general Convention for the purpose of altering and amending the constitution, are altogether unanswerable."

On 23 April New York state chancellor Robert R. Livingston wrote an unidentified correspondent from his Clermont estate in Columbia County, about 120 miles north of New York City: "I enclose you a number of copies of the address to the citizens of New York. Be pleased to distribute them as soon as possible" (John Heise, *Catalogue of Autograph Letters [and] Signatures* [Syracuse, N.Y., 1912], Catalogue no. 53, p. 22). Samuel Blachley Webb mailed a copy of the pamphlet to his fiancee's brother in Claverack, Columbia County (about 136 miles north of New York City), although it appears that it may have been lost in transit. Webb lamented that "the Mail is not altogether so sacred as it should be" (Webb to Catherine Hogeboom, 27 April and 4 May, Webb Papers, CtY). On 3 June a correspondent, commenting on the elections in Dutchess County, noted in the Poughkeepsie *Country Journal* that "at least one third" of the voters chose Federalist candidates, while at the beginning of the year only one-twentieth were "inclined to the federal side." "Had the pamphlet attributed to Mr. Jay made its appearance a little sooner, I am well persuaded there would have been a still more compleat Revolution in the minds of the people." And in Suffolk—Long Island's easternmost county—Antifederalist John Smith noted that "A Citizen of New-York" circulated before the elections and that people "are halting" between the opinions expressed in it and an Antifederalist pamphlet written by "A Plebeian" (Smith to David Gelston, n.d., John Smith of Mastic, L.I., Misc. Mss., NHi).

"A Citizen of New-York" also circulated widely outside the state of New York. It was reprinted in toto in the *New Hampshire Spy*, 2, 6, 10, and 13 May; *New Jersey Journal*, 7, 14 May; Exeter, N.H., *Freeman's Oracle*, 16, 23 May; *Carlisle Gazette*, 21, 28 May, and 4 June; Providence *United States Chronicle*, 22, 29 May, and 26 June; *Pennsylvania Packet*, 5, 9, and 10 June; and the June issue of the Philadelphia *American Museum*. It is also probable that the entire pamphlet was reprinted in no longer extant issues of the *State Gazette of North Carolina*. Federalist Hugh Williamson, a North Carolina delegate to

Congress, sent Governor Samuel Johnston an unidentified Federalist pamphlet, probably "A Citizen of New-York," in one of two letters dated 23 and 26 May. Johnston responded on 10 June that the entire pamphlet had already been reprinted in the *State Gazette of North Carolina*, and that it had been "very well received" (Governors' Papers, North Carolina Division of Archives and History).

The two New Hampshire reprintings of "A Citizen of New-York" probably occurred through the efforts of either John Langdon or John Sullivan—both members of the New Hampshire Convention. Langdon and Sullivan each received a copy of the pamphlet from Federalist Rufus King, who had recently taken up permanent residence in New York City. Like many other Federalists, King wanted to make certain that the second session of the New Hampshire Convention, scheduled to reconvene on 18 June, ratified the Constitution. On 16 April, the day after "A Citizen of New-York" was first advertised for sale, King wrote Langdon that the pamphlet "may be of use in New Hampshire—if you should judge it a publication of value, I think the public Happiness will be advanced by circulating it in your State—Be assured that you ought not on any consideration to omit every Exertion which prudence and Virtue will authorise in favor of the constitution; very much will depend on your Decision" (CC:686). On the same day, King wrote Sullivan that "I am ignorant of the Author but think the performance has merit—perhaps in your Judgment it may be worth republication in your State with such alterations as its locality and other circumstances may render proper" (King Family Papers, Cincinnati Historical Society). In reprinting the first part of the pamphlet on 2 May, the *New Hampshire Spy* noted that "By a gentleman from New-York, we have been favored with the following address to the citizens of that state, on the subject of the New Constitution. This address, supposed to have been written by one of the first characters in America, contains such a fund of reason, and is so well calculated to obliterate the prejudices, and remove the beam from off the eyes of the uninformed (the *candid* opposers of the New Constitution) that we feel a peculiar pleasure in laying it before our readers." (A similar prefatory statement also appeared in the Exeter, N.H., *Freeman's Oracle*, 16 May.)

In its reprinting of the first installment of "A Citizen of New-York" on 7 May, the *New Jersey Journal* identified John Jay as the author. (Jay was also identified by the *Massachusetts Centinel* on 30 April; the Providence *United States Chronicle* on 29 May; and by the Philadelphia *American Museum* in its June issue.) On 19 June Jay's wife Sarah wrote to him from Elizabethtown (where she was visiting) that the pamphlet "has been received in this State with great approbation, nor has the tribute of applause been with-held from the author that usually accompanies his writings; for tho' thro' modesty his name was conceal'd it seems the well-known style discovered him" (John Jay Papers, NNC).

When the Providence *United States Chronicle*, 22 May, reprinted its first installment of the pamphlet, it included this preface: "A Publication has lately appeared in New-York, on the Subject of the proposed Federal Constitution—fraught with useful Truths and Sound Argument, and said to be written by a Gentleman, who has been universally acknowledged a Patriot, and Friend to America.—Some Extracts, which we propose to make from it, we have no Doubt will be read with Pleasure, by every *real* Friend to this Country—by those who are *opposed* to the Constitution *from Principle*, as well as those who agree in Sentiment with the worthy Author." When it printed its third and final installment on 26 June, the *Chronicle* noted that "The Sentiments advanced in this Publication deserve the *serious Attention* of every Friend to the State of Rhode-Island." The *Chronicle's* reprinting contains much additional italicization.

In addition to the complete reprintings of "A Citizen of New-York," the first eleven paragraphs of the pamphlet appeared in the *Massachusetts Centinel* on 30 April, with the heading "A Gem of the first lustre" and with this concluding statement: "Our brethren of the type in New-Hampshire will, we doubt not, do the cause of federalism the justice to insert the forgoing elegant extract, in their papers.—The address is supposed to be written by Mr. Jay." The *Centinel* identified the pamphlet by its title and noted that it was reprinting an extract, but it did not indicate that the pamphlet was written by "A Citizen of New-York." The *Centinel's* extract, which outlined the problems of the Confederation, was reprinted in the Boston *American Herald,* 1 May; *New Hampshire Gazette,* 7 May; and *Massachusetts Spy,* 15 May. Only the *New Hampshire Gazette* reprinted the *Centinel's* heading, while no newspaper reprinted its concluding statement identifying Jay as the author. The printer of the *American Herald* also published this excerpt as a broadside.

The extract printed in the *Massachusetts Centinel* was inserted there by Boston merchant Joseph Barrell. He had received the pamphlet from Samuel Blachley Webb, who had identified Jay as the author. In his reply to Webb, Barrell described the pamphlet as "Excellent" and the excerpt printed in the *Centinel* as "a choice Morsel." (See Webb to Barrell, 20 and 27 April, Webb Papers, and Webb Family Collection, CtY, respectively; and Barrell to Webb, 4 May, Barrell Papers, CtY.) After reading part of the pamphlet in the 5 June issue of the *Pennsylvania Packet,* John Hubley of Lancaster, Pa., also described it as "excellent" (to Benjamin Rush, 8 June, Correspondence of Dr. Benjamin Rush, PPL).

A number of individuals received copies of "A Citizen of New-York" from Federalists in New York City. In addition to getting two copies from Jay, George Washington received other copies, one of which he forwarded on 8 June to James Madison who was attending the Virginia Convention in Richmond. Washington told Madison that "A Citizen of New-York" was "written with much good sense & moderation" (RCS:Va., 1586. For the second copy that Jay sent to Washington, upon request, see Jay to Washington, 29 May, John Jay Papers, NNC.). In thanking Jay on 15 May, Washington had been even more complimentary: "The good sense, forceable observations, temper and moderation with which it is written cannot fail, I should think, of making a serious impression even upon the anti-fœderal mind where it is not under the influence of such local views as will yield to no arguments—no proofs" (RCS:Va., 803). Asserting that "A Citizen of New-York" had "considerable Merit," William Bingham transmitted a copy to Tench Coxe in Philadelphia (30 May, Coxe Papers, Series II, Correspondence and General Papers, PHi). Edward Carrington, a Virginia delegate to Congress, sent the pamphlet to

William Short in Paris, expressing the hope that Short would also allow
Thomas Jefferson to peruse it (17 May, Short Papers, DLC. Short probably
turned the pamphlet over to Jefferson who had a copy of it in his library [E.
Millicent Sowerby, comp. and ed., *Catalogue of the Library of Thomas Jefferson*
(5 vols., Washington, D.C., 1952–1959), III, 226].). John Brown, another
Virginia delegate to Congress, forwarded what apparently was the pamphlet
to a correspondent in Williamsburg, stating that "the Banefull Consequences
of a rejection [of the Constitution] were painted [in the pamphlet] in Just &
Lively Colours" (to James Breckinridge, 21 June, RCS:Va., 1661–62).

For the most part, New York Antifederalists ignored "A Citizen of New-
York," despite the pamphlet's wide circulation. The only substantial criticism
of the pamphlet was made by "A Plebeian" (possibly New York Antifederalist
Melancton Smith), whose pamphlet was offered for sale on 17 April, two days
after "A Citizen of New-York" was first advertised. Since "A Plebeian's"
pamphlet was in press when "A Citizen of New-York" appeared, "A Plebeian"
appended a four-page postscript attacking "A Citizen of New-York" for overly
criticizing the government under the Confederation and for excessively praising the Constitution. "A Plebeian" was especially disturbed by "A Citizen of
New-York's" dismissal of the Antifederalist argument that a bill of rights was
necessary (CC:689).

*Friends and Fellow Citizens,* There are times and seasons when *general
evils* spread general alarm and uneasiness, and yet arise from causes
too complicated, and too little understood by many, to produce a
unanimity of opinions respecting their remedies. Hence it is, that on
such occasions, the conflict of arguments too often excites a conflict
of passions, and introduces a degree of discord and animosity, which,
by agitating the public mind, dispose it to precipitation and extravagance. They who on the ocean have been unexpectedly inveloped with
tempests, or suddenly entangled among rocks and shoals, know the
value of that serene, self-possession and presence of mind, to which
in such cases they owed their preservation: nor will the heroes who
have given us victory and peace, hesitate to acknowledge, that we are
as much indebted for those blessings to the calm prevision, and cool
intrepidity which planned and conducted our military measures, as to
the glowing animation with which they were executed.

While reason retains her rule, while men are as ready to receive as
to give advice, and as willing to be convinced themselves, as to convince
others, there are few political evils from which a free and enlightened
people cannot deliver themselves. It is unquestionably true, that the
great body of the people love their country, and wish it prosperity;
and this observation is particularly applicable to the people of a *free*
country, for they have more and stronger reasons for loving it than
others. It is not therefore to vicious motives that the unhappy divisions
which sometimes prevail among them are to be imputed; the people

at large always mean well, and although they may, on certain occasions, be misled by the counsels, or injured by the efforts of the few who expect more advantage from the wreck, than from the preservation of national prosperity, yet the motives of these few, are by no means to be confounded with those of the community in general.

That such seeds of discord and danger have been disseminated and begin to take root in America, as unless eradicated will soon poison our gardens and our fields, is a truth much to be lamented; and the more so, as their growth rapidly encreases, while we are wasting the season in honestly but imprudently disputing, not whether they shall be pulled up, but by whom, in what manner, and with what instruments the work shall be done.

When the King of Great-Britian, misguided by men who did not merit his confidence, asserted the unjust claim of binding us in all cases whatsoever, and prepared to obtain our submission by force, the object which engrossed our attention, however important, was nevertheless plain and simple. "What shall we do?" was the question—the people answered, let us unite our counsels and our arms. They sent Delegates to Congress, and soldiers to the field. Confiding in the probity and wisdom of Congress, they received their recommendations as if they had been laws; and that ready acquiescense in their advice enabled those patriots to save their country. Then there was little leisure or disposition for controversy respecting the expediency of measures—hostile fleets soon filled our ports, and hostile armies spread desolation on our shores. Union was then considered as the most essential of human means, and we almost worshipped it with as much fervor, as pagans in distress formerly implored the protection of their tutelar deities. That Union was the child of wisdom—Heaven blessed it, and it wrought out our political salvation.

That glorious war was succeded by an advantageous peace. When danger disappeared, ease, tranquility, and a sense of security loosened the bands of union; and Congress and soldiers and good faith depreciated with their apparent importance. Recommendations lost their influence, and requisitions were rendered nugatory, not by their want of propriety, but by their want of power. The spirit of private gain expelled the spirit of public good, and men became more intent on the means of enriching and aggrandizing themselves, than of enriching and aggrandizing their country. Hence the war-worn veteran, whose reward for toils and wounds existed in written promises, found Congress without the means, and too many of the States without the disposition to do him justice. Hard necessity compelled him, and others under similar circumstances, to sell their honest claims on the public for a little bread; and thus unmerited misfortunes and patriotic distresses became articles of speculation and commerce.

These and many other evils, too well known to require enumeration, imperceptibly stole in upon us, and acquired an unhappy influence on our public affairs. But such evils, like the worst of weeds, will naturally spring up in so rich a soil; and a good Government is as necessary to subdue the one, as an attentive gardener or husbandman is to destroy the other—Even the garden of Paradise required to be dressed, and while men continue to be constantly impelled to error and to wrong, by innumerable circumstances and temptations, so long will society experience the unceasing necessity of Government.

It is a pity that the expectations which actuated the authors of the existing Confederation, neither have nor can be realized:—accustomed to see and admire the glorious spirit which moved all ranks of people in the most gloomy moments of the war, observing their steadfast attachment to Union, and the wisdom they so often manifested both in choosing and confiding in their rulers, those gentlemen were led to flatter themselves that the people of America only required to know what ought to be done, to do it. This amiable mistake induced them to institute a national Government in such a manner, as though very fit to give advice, was yet destitute of power, and so constructed as to be very unfit to be trusted with it. They seem not to have been sensible that mere advice is a sad substitute for laws; nor to have recollected that the advice even of the all-wise and best of Beings, has been always disregarded by a great majority of all the men that ever lived.

Experience is a severe preceptor, but it teaches useful truths, and however harsh, is always honest—Be calm and dispassionate, and listen to what it tells us.

Prior to the revolution we had little occasion to enquire or know much about national affairs, for although they existed and were managed, yet they were managed *for* us, but not *by* us. Intent on our domestic concerns, our internal legislative business, our agriculture, and our buying and selling, we were seldom anxious about what passed or was doing in foreign Courts. As we had nothing to do with that department of policy, so the affairs of it were not detailed to us, and we took as little pains to inform ourselves, as others did to inform us of them. War, and peace, alliances, and treaties, and commerce, and navigation, were conducted and regulated without our advice or controul. While we had liberty and justice, and in security enjoyed the fruits of our "vine and fig tree,"[1] we were in general too content and too much occupied, to be at the trouble of investigating the various political combinations in this department, or to examine and perceive how exceedingly important they often were to the advancement and protection of our prosperity. This habit and turn of thinking affords one reason why so much more care was taken, and so much more wisdom displayed, in forming our State Governments, than in forming our fœderal or national one.

By the Confederation as it now stands, the direction of general and national affairs is committed to a single body of men, viz. the Congress. They may make war, but are not empowered to raise men or money to carry it on—They may make peace, but without power to see the terms of it observed—They may form alliances, but without ability to comply with the stipulations on their part—They may enter into treaties of commerce, but without power to inforce them at home or abroad—They may borrow money, but without having the means of repayment—They may partly regulate commerce, but without authority to execute their ordinances—They may appoint ministers and other officers of trust, but without power to try or punish them for misdemeanors—They may resolve, but cannot execute either with dispatch or with secrecy—In short, they may consult, and deliberate, and recommend, and make requisitions, and they who please may regard them.

From this new and wonderful system of Government, it has come to pass, that almost every national object of every kind, is at this day unprovided for; and other nations taking the advantage of its imbecility, are daily multiplying commercial restraints upon us. Our fur trade is gone to Canada, and British garrisons keep the keys of it. Our ship-yards have almost ceased to disturb the repose of the neighbourhood by the noise of the axe and hammer; and while foreign flags fly triumphantly above our highest houses, the American Stars seldom do more than shed a few feeble rays about the humbler masts of river sloops and coasting schooners. The greater part of our hardy seamen are plowing the ocean in foreign pay; and not a few of our ingenious shipwrights are now building vessels on alien shores. Although our increasing agriculture and industry extend and multiply our productions, yet they constantly diminish in value; and although we permit all nations to fill our country with their merchandizes, yet their best markets are shut against us. Is there an English, or a French, or a Spanish island or port in the West-Indies to which an American vessel can carry a cargo of flour for sale? Not one. The Algerines exclude us from the Mediterranean, and adjacent countries; and we are neither able to purchase, nor to command the free use of those seas. Can our little towns or larger cities consume the immense productions of our fertile country? or will they without trade be able to pay a good price for the proportion which they do consume? The last season gave a very unequivocal answer to those questions—What numbers of fine cattle have returned from this city to the country for want of buyers? What great quantities of salted and other provisions still lay useless in the stores? To how much below the former price, is our corn and wheat and flour and lumber rapidly falling? Our debts remain undiminished, and the interest on them accumulating—our credit abroad is nearly extinguished, and at home unrestored—they who had money have sent it beyond the reach of our laws, and scarcely any man can borrow of his neighbour. Nay, does not experience also tell us, that it is as difficult to pay as to borrow? That even our houses and lands cannot command money—that law suits and usurious contracts abound—that our farms sell on executions for less than half their value, and that distress in various forms, and in various ways, is approaching fast to the doors of our best citizens.

These things have been gradually coming upon us ever since the peace—they have been perceived and proclaimed, but the universal rage and pursuit of private gain conspired with other causes, to prevent any proper efforts being made to meliorate our condition by due attention to our national affairs, until the late Convention was convened for that purpose. From the result of their deliberations, the States expected to derive much good, and should they be disappointed, it will probably be not less their misfortune than their fault. That Convention was in general composed of excellent and tried men—men who had become conspicuous for their wisdom and public services, and whose names and characters will be venerated by posterity. Generous and candid minds cannot perceive without pain, the illiberal manner in which some have taken the liberty to treat them; nor forbear to impute it to impure and improper motives—zeal for public good, like zeal for religion, may sometimes carry men beyond the bounds of reason, but it is not conceivable, that on this occasion, it should find means so to enebriate any *candid* American, as to make him forget what he owed to truth and to decency, or induce him either to believe or to say, that the almost unanimous advice of the Convention, proceeded from a wicked combination and conspiracy against the liberties of their country. This is not the temper with which we should receive and consider their recommendations, nor the treatment that would be worthy either of us or of them. Let us continue careful therefore that facts do not warrant historians to tell future generations, that envy, malice and uncharitableness pursued our patriotic benefactors to their graves, and that not even pre-eminence in virtue, nor lives devoted to the public, could shield them from obloquy and detraction. On the contrary, let us bosoms always retain a sufficient degree of honest

indignation to disappoint and discourage those who expect our thanks
or applause for calumniating our most faithful and meritorious friends.

The Convention concurred in opinion with the people, that a national government *competent to every national object*, was indispensably
necessary; and it was as plain to them, as it now is to all America, that
the present confederation does not provide for such a government.
These points being agreed, they proceeded to consider how and in
what manner such a Government could be formed, as on the one hand
should be sufficiently energetic to raise us from our prostrate and
distressed situation, and on the other be perfectly consistent with the
liberties of the people of every State. Like men to whom the experience
of other ages and countries had taught wisdom, they not only determined that it should be erected by, and depend on the people; but
remembering the many instances in which Governments vested solely
in one man, or one body of men, had degenerated into tyrannies, they
judged it most prudent that the three great branches of power should
be committed to different hands, and therefore that the executive
should be separated from the legislative, and the judicial from both.
Thus far the propriety of their work is easily seen and understood,
and therefore is thus far *almost* universally approved—for no one man
or thing under the sun ever yet pleased every body.

The next question was, what particular powers should be given to
these three branches? Here the different views and interests of the
different States, as well as the different abstract opinions of their members on such points, interposed many difficulties. Here the business
became complicated, and presented a wide field for investigation; too
wide for every eye to take a quick and comprehensive view of it.

It is said that "in a multitude of counsellors there is safety,"[2] because
in the first place, there is greater security for probity; and in the next,
if every member casts in only his mite of information and argument,
their joint stock of both will thereby become greater than the stock
possessed by any one single man out of doors. Gentlemen out of doors
therefore should not be hasty in condemning a system, which probably
rests on more good reasons than they are aware of, especially when
formed under such advantages, and recommended by so many men
of distinguished worth and abilities.

The difficulties before mentioned occupied the Convention a long
time, and it was not without mutual concessions that they were at last
surmounted. These concessions serve to explain to us the reason why
some parts of the system please in some States, which displease in
others; and why many of the objections which have been made to it,
are so contradictory and inconsistent with one another. It does great

credit to the temper and talents of the Convention, that they were able so to reconcile the different views and interests of the different States, and the clashing opinions of their members, as to unite with such singular and almost perfect unanimity in any plan whatever, on a subject so intricate and perplexed. It shews that it must have been thoroughly discussed and understood; and probably if the community at large had the same lights and reasons before them, they would, if equally candid and uninfluenced, be equally unanimous.

It would be arduous, and indeed impossible to comprize within the limits of this address, a full discussion of every part of the plan. Such a task would require a volume, and few men have leisure or inclination to read volumes on any subject. The objections made to it are almost without number, and many of them without reason—some of them are real and honest, and others merely ostensible. There are friends to Union and a national Government who have serious doubts, who wish to be informed, and to be convinced; and there are others who, neither wishing for Union nor any national Government at all, will oppose and object to any plan that can be contrived.

We are told, among other strange things, that the liberty of the press is left insecure by the proposed Constitution, and yet that Constitution says neither more nor less about it, than the Constitution of the State of New-York does.[3] We are told that it deprives us of trial by jury, whereas the fact is, that it expresly secures it in certain cases, and takes it away in none—it is absurd to construe the silence of this, or of our own Constitution, relative to a great number of our rights, into a total extinction of them—silence and blank paper neither grant nor take away any thing. Complaints are also made that the proposed Constitution is not accompanied by a bill of rights; and yet they who make these complaints, know and are content that no bill of rights accompanied the Constitution of this State. In days and countries where Monarchs and their subjects were frequently disputing about prerogative and privileges, the latter often found it necessary, as it were to run out the line between them, and oblige the former to admit by solemn acts, called bills of rights, that certain enumerated rights belonged to the people, and were not comprehended in the royal prerogative. But thank God we have no such disputes—we have no Monarchs to contend with, or demand admissions from—the proposed Government is to be the government of the people—all its officers are to be their officers, and to exercise no rights but such as the people commit to them. The Constitution only serves to point out that part of the people's business, which they think proper by it to refer to the management of the persons therein designated—those persons are to receive that business to manage, not for themselves, and as their own, but as agents and overseers for the people to whom they are constantly responsible, and by whom only they are to be appointed.

But the design of this address is not to investigate the merits of the plan, nor of the objections made to it. They who seriously contemplate the present state of our affairs will be convinced that other considerations of at least equal importance demand their attention. Let it be admitted that this plan, like every thing else devised by man, has its imperfections: That it does not please every body is certain, and there is little reason to expect one that will. It is a question of great moment to you, whether the probability of our being able seasonably to obtain a better, is such as to render it prudent and advisable to reject this, and run the risque.—Candidly to consider this question is the design of this address.

As the importance of this question must be obvious to every man, whatever his private opinions respecting it may be, it becomes us all to treat it in that calm and temperate manner, which a subject so deeply interesting to the future welfare of our country and posterity requires. Let us therefore as much as possible repress and compose that irritation in our minds, which too warm disputes about it may have excited. Let us endeavor to forget that this or that man, is on this or that side; and that we ourselves, perhaps without sufficient reflection, have classed ourselves with one or the other party. Let us remember that this is not to be regarded as a matter that only touches our local parties, but as one so great, so general, and so extensive in its future consequences to America, that for our deciding upon it according to the best of our unbiassed judgment, we must be highly responsible both here and hereafter.

The question now before us naturally leads to *three* enquiries:
1. Whether it is probable that a better plan can be obtained?
2. Whether, if attainable, it is likely to be in season?
3. What would be our situation, if after rejecting this, all our efforts to obtain a better should prove fruitless?

The men who formed this plan are Americans, who had long deserved and enjoyed our confidence, and who are as much interested in having a good government as any of us are, or can be. They were appointed to that business at a time when the States had become very sensible of the derangement of our national affairs, and of the impossibility of retrieving them under the existing Confederation. Although well persuaded that nothing but a good national Government could oppose and divert the tide of evils that was flowing in upon us, yet those gentlemen met in Convention with minds perfectly unprejudiced in favor of any particular plan. The minds of their Constituents were at that time equally unbiassed, equally cool and dispassionate. All agreed in the necessity of doing something, but no one ventured to say decidedly what precisely ought to be done—opinions were then fluctuating and unfixed, and whatever might have been the wishes of a few individuals, yet while the Convention deliberated, the people remained in silent suspence. Neither wedded to favorite systems of their own, nor influenced by popular ones abroad, the members were more desirous to receive light from, than to impress their private sentiments on one another. These circumstances naturally opened the door to that spirit of candor, of calm enquiry, of mutual accommodation, and mutual respect, which entered into the Convention with them, and regulated their debates and proceedings.

The impossibility of agreeing upon any plan that would exactly quadrate with the local policy and objects of every State, soon became evident; and they wisely thought it better mutually to concede, and accommodate, and in that way to fashion their system as much as possible by the circumstances and wishes of the different States, than by pertinaciously adhering, each to his own ideas, oblige the Convention to rise without doing any thing. They were sensible that obstacles arising from local circumstances, would not cease while those circumstances continue to exist; and so far as those circumstances depended on differences of climate, productions, and commerce, that no change was to be expected. They were likewise sensible that on a subject so comprehensive, and involving such a variety of points and questions, the most able, the most candid, and the most honest men will differ in opinion. The same proposition seldom strikes many minds exactly in the same point or light: different habits of thinking, different degrees and modes of education, different prejudices and opinions early formed and long entertained, conspire with a multitude of other circumstances, to produce among men a diversity and contrariety of opinions on questions of difficulty. Liberality therefore as well as prudence, induced them to treat each other's opinions with tenderness, to argue without asperity, and to endeavor to convince the judgment without hurting the feelings of each other. Although many weeks were passed in these discussions, some points remained, on which a unison of opinions could not be effected. Here again that same happy disposition to unite and conciliate, induced them to meet each other; and enabled them by mutual concessions, finally to compleat and agree to the plan they have recommended, and that too with a degree of unanimity, which, considering the variety of discordant views and ideas they had to reconcile, is really astonishing.

They tell us very honestly that this plan is the result of accommodation—they do not hold it up as the best of all possible ones, but only as the best which they could unite in, and agree to. If such men, appointed and meeting under such auspicious circumstances, and so sincerely disposed to conciliation, could go no further in their endeavors to please every State and every body, what reason have we at present to expect any system that would give more general satisfaction?

Suppose this plan to be rejected, what measures would you propose for obtaining a better? Some will answer, let us appoint another Convention, and as every thing has been said and written, that can well be said and written on the subject, they will be better informed than the former one was, and consequently be better able to make and agree upon a more eligible one.

This reasoning is fair, and as far as it goes has weight; but it nevertheless takes one thing for granted, which appears very doubtful; for although the new Convention might have more information, and perhaps equal abilities, yet it does not from thence follow that they would be equally *disposed to agree*. The contrary of this position is the most probable. You must have observed that the same temper and equanimity which prevailed among the people on the former occasion, no longer exists. We have unhappily become divided into parties, and this important subject has been handled with such indiscreet and offensive acrimony, and with so many little unhandsome artifices and misrepresentations, that pernicious heats and animosities have been kindled, and spread their flames far and wide among us. When therefore it becomes a question who shall be deputed to the new Convention; we cannot flatter ourselves that the talents and integrity of the candidates will determine who shall be elected. Fœderal electors will vote for fœderal deputies, and anti-fœderal electors for anti-fœderal ones. Nor will either party prefer the most moderate of their adherents, for as the most staunch and active partizans will be the most popular, so the men most willing and able to carry points, to oppose, and divide, and embarrass their opponents will be chosen. A Convention formed at such a season, and of such men, would be but too exact an epitome of the great body that named them. The same party views, the same propensity to opposition, the same distrusts and jealousies, and the same unaccomodating spirit which prevail without, would be concentred and ferment with still greater violence within. Each deputy would recollect *who* sent him, and *why* he was sent; and be too apt to consider himself bound in honor, to contend and act vigorously under the standard of his party, and not hazard their displeasure by preferring compromise to victory. As vice does not sow the seeds of virtue, so neither does passion cultivate the fruits of reason. Suspicions and resentments create no disposition to conciliate, nor do they infuse a desire of making partial and personal objects bend to general union and the common good. The utmost efforts of that excellent disposition were necessary to enable the late Convention to perform their task; and although contrary causes sometimes operate similar effects, yet to expect that discord and animosity should produce the fruits of confidence and agreement, is to expect "grapes from thorns, and figs from thistles."[4]

The States of Georgia, Delaware, Jersey and Connecticut, have adopted the present plan with unexampled unanimity; they are content with it as it is, and consequently their deputies, being apprized of the sentiments of their Constituents, will be little inclined to make alterations, and cannot be otherwise than averse to changes which they have no reason to think would be agreeable to their people—some other States, tho' less unanimous, have nevertheless adopted it by very respectable majorities; and for reasons so evidently cogent, that even the minority in one of them, have nobly pledged themselves for its promotion and support. From these circumstances the new Convention would derive and experience difficulties unknown to the former. Nor are these the only additional difficulties they would have to encounter. Few are ignorant that there has lately sprung up a sect of politicians who teach and profess to believe, that the extent of our nation is too great for the superintendance of one national Government, and on that principle argue that it ought to be divided into two or three. This doctrine, however mischievous in its tendency and consequences, has its advocates, and should any of them be sent to the Convention, it will naturally be their policy rather to cherish than to prevent divisions: for well knowing that the institution of any good national Government, would blast their favorite system, no measures that lead to it can meet with their aid or approbation.

Nor can we be certain whether or not any and what foreign influence would, on such an occasion, be indirectly exerted, nor for what purposes—delicacy forbids an ample discussion of this question. Thus much may be said without error or offence, viz. That such foreign nations as desire the prosperity of America, and would rejoice to see her become great and powerful, under the auspices of a Government wisely calculated to extend her commerce, to encourage her navigation and marine, and to direct the whole weight of her power and resources as her interest and honor may require, will doubtless be friendly to the Union of the States, and to the establishment of a Government able to perpetuate, protect and dignify it.—Such other foreign nations, if any such there be, who, jealous of our growing importance, and fearful that our commerce and navigation should impair their own— who behold our rapid population with regret, and apprehend that the enterprizing spirit of our people, when seconded by power and probability of success, may be directed to objects not consistent with their policy or interest, cannot fail at least to wish that we may continue a weak and divided people.

These considerations merit much attention, and candid men will judge how far they render it probable that a new Convention would be able either to agree in a better plan, or with tolerable unanimity, in any plan at all. Any plan forcibly carried by a slender majority, must expect numerous opponents among the people, who, especially in their present temper, would be more inclined to reject than adopt any system so made and carried. We should in such a case again see the press teeming with publications for and against it; for as the minority would take pains to justify their dissent, so would the majority be industrious to display the wisdom of their proceedings. Hence new divisions, new parties, and new distractions would ensue, and no one can foresee or conjecture when or how they would terminate.

Let those who are sanguine in their expectations of a better plan from a new Convention, also reflect on the delays and risques to which it would expose us. Let them consider whether we ought, by continuing much longer in our present humiliated condition, to give other nations further time to perfect their restrictive systems of commerce, to reconcile their own people to them, and to fence and guard and strengthen them by all those regulations and contrivances in which a jealous policy is ever fruitful. Let them consider whether we ought to give further opportunities to discord to alienate the hearts of our citizens from one another, and thereby encourage new Cromwells to bold exploits. Are we certain that our foreign creditors will continue patient, and ready to proportion their forbearance to our delays? Are we sure that our distresses, dissentions and weakness will neither invite hostility nor insult? If they should, how ill prepared shall we be for defence! without Union, without Government, without money, and without credit!

It seems unnecessary to remind you, that some time must yet elapse, before all the States will have decided on the present plan. If they reject it, some time must also pass before the measure of a new Convention, can be brought about and generally agreed to. A further space of time will then be requisite to elect their deputies, and send them on to Convention. What time they may expend when met, cannot be divined, and it is equally uncertain how much time the several States may take to deliberate and decide on any plan they may recommend—if adopted, still a further space of time will be necessary to organize and set it in motion:—In the mean time our affairs are daily going on from bad to worse, and it is not rash to say that our distresses are accumulating like compound interest.

But if for the reasons already mentioned, and others that we cannot now perceive, the new Convention, instead of producing a better plan, should give us only a history of their disputes, or should offer us one still less pleasing than the present, where should we be then? The old Confederation has done its best, and cannot help us; and is now so relaxed and feeble, that in all probability it would not survive so violent a shock. Then "to your tents Oh Israel!"[5] would be the word. Then every band of Union would be severed. Then every State would be a little nation, jealous of its neighbours, and anxious to strengthen itself by foreign alliances, against its former friends. Then farewell to fraternal affection, unsuspecting intercourse, and mutual participation in commerce, navigation and citizenship. Then would arise mutual restrictions and fears, mutual garrisons,—and standing armies, and all those dreadful evils which for so many ages plagued England, Scotland, Wales and Ireland, while they continued disunited, and were played off against each other.

Consider my fellow citizens what you are about, before it is too late—consider what in such an event would be your particular case.—You know the geography of your State, and the consequences of your local position. Jersey and Connecticut, to whom your impost laws have been unkind—Jersey and Connecticut, who have adopted the present plan, and expect much good from it, will impute its miscarriage and all the consequent evils to you. They now consider your opposition as dictated more by your fondness for your impost, than for those rights to which they have never been behind you in attachment. They cannot, they will not love you—they border upon you, and are your neighbours, but you will soon cease to regard their neighbourhood as a blessing. You have but one port and outlet to your commerce, and how you are to keep that outlet free and uninterrupted, merits consideration.—What advantages Vermont in combination with others, might take of you, may easily be conjectured; nor will you be at a loss to perceive how much reason the people of Long-Island, whom you cannot protect, have to deprecate being constantly exposed to the depredations of every invader.

These are short hints—they ought not to be more developed—you can easily in your own minds dilate and trace them through all their relative circumstances and connections.—Pause then for a moment, and reflect whether the matters you are disputing about, are of sufficient moment to justify your running such extravagant risques. Reflect that the present plan comes recommended to you by men and fellow-citizens, who have given you the highest proofs that men can give, of their justice, their love for liberty and their country, of their prudence, of their application, and of their talents. They tell you it is the best that they could form; and that in their opinion, it is necessary to redeem you from those calamities which already begin to be heavy upon us all. You find that not only those men, but others of similar characters, and of whom you have also had very ample experience, advise you to adopt it. You find that whole States concur in the sentiment, and among them are your next neighbours; both of whom have shed much blood in the cause of liberty, and have manifested as strong and constant a predilection for a free Republican Government as any States in the Union, and perhaps in the world. They perceive not those latent mischiefs in it, with which some double-sighted politicians endeavor to alarm you. You cannot but be sensible that this plan or Constitution will always be in the hands and power of the people, and that if on experiment, it should be found defective or incompetent, they may either remedy its defects, or substitute another in its room. The objectionable parts of it are certainly very questionable, for otherwise there would not be such a contrariety of opinions about them. Experience will better determine such questions than theoretical arguments, and so far as the danger of abuses is urged against the institution of a Government, remember that a power to do good always involves a power to do harm. We must in the business of Government as well as in all other business, have some degree of confidence, as well as a great degree of caution. Who on a sick bed would refuse medicines from a physician, merely because it is as much in his power to administer deadly poisons, as salutary remedies.

You cannot be certain, that by rejecting the proposed plan you would not place yourselves in a very awkward situation. Suppose nine States should nevertheless adopt it, would you not in that case be obliged either to separate from the Union, or rescind your dissent? The first would not be eligible, nor could the latter be pleasant—A mere hint is sufficient on this topic—You cannot but be aware of the consequences.

Consider then, how weighty and how many considerations advise and persuade the People of America to remain in the safe and easy path of Union; to continue to move and act as they hitherto have done, as a *Band of Brothers*;[6] to have confidence in themselves and in one another; and since all cannot see with the same eyes, at least to give the proposed Constitution a fair trial, and to mend it as time, occasion and experience may dictate. It would little become us to verify the predictions of those who ventured to prophecy, that *Peace*, instead of blessing us with happiness and tranquility, would serve only as the signal for factions, discords and civil contentions to rage in our land, and overwhelm it with misery and distress.

Let us also be mindful that the cause of freedom greatly depends on the use we make of the singular opportunities we enjoy of governing ourselves wisely; for if the event should prove, that the people of this country either cannot or will not govern themselves, who will hereafter be advocates for systems, which however charming in theory and prospect, are not reducible to practice. If the people of our nation, instead of consenting to be governed by laws of their own making and rulers of their own choosing, should let licentiousness, disorder and confusion reign over them, the minds of men every where, will insensibly become alienated from republican forms, and prepared to prefer and acquiesce in Governments, which, though less friendly to liberty, afford more peace and security.

*Receive this Address with the same candor with which it is written; and may the spirit of wisdom and patriotism direct and distinguish your counsels and your conduct.*

1. 1 Kings 4:25; Haggai 2:19; Micah 4:4; and Zechariah 3:10.
2. Proverbs 11:14 and 24:6.
3. The New York constitution said nothing about the freedom of the press.
4. Matthew 7:16.
5. 2 Samuel 20:1; 1 Kings 12:16; and 2 Chronicles 10:16.
6. William Shakespeare, *King Henry V*, act IV, scene 3, line 60: "We few, we happy few, we band of brothers."

## 684. Fabius II
## Pennsylvania Mercury, 15 April

Soon after "Fabius" I was printed on 12 April (CC:677), John Vaughan wrote the author John Dickinson that "The Second is in the hands of the printer & cannot fail of giving great pleasure & what is more material *of being of great use.*—The Facts are Incontrovertible & the reasonings upon them easily & clearly deduced & conveyed in a manner that cannot fail of captivating the attention & insuring the Conviction of every honest, well meaning, & well principled man—& as I hope *Some Such* are to be found amongst those who are now opposers to the System, I have no doubt of its making Some Converts. . . . I have some doubts whether the 2d Can appear *at once If it cannot* I have directed the division to be made where *the Senate finishes* & the Continuation will contain *all that relates to the president* & will form a Complete answer to Philadelphiensis last piece—, & will be marked as continuation of No 2—you will I hope approve of this—It is not possible for me to correct the press but as the Printer is careful it is Scarcely necessary.—I send you No 1. . . ." ("N.W." to "Mr. Thomas," n.d., Dickinson Papers, PPL. For "Philadelphiensis" XII, see CC:672.).

On 17 April Vaughan informed Dickinson that "No. 2, 3, are published, No 4 is with the printer. I think they will be of Considerable Service, as they have commanded the publick attention, & being attended to leave useful impressions; They assist by divesting of party & leading to cool reflection— The Cause want nothing more to carry it thro!" (to "Mr. Thomas," Dickinson Papers, PPL).

"Fabius" II was reprinted in the Baltimore *Maryland Gazette*, 2 May (announced on 29 April); *Virginia Independent Chronicle*, 7 May; *Providence Gazette*, 17 May; *New Hampshire Spy*, 20 May; *New Hampshire Gazette*, 29 May; and in the August issue of the Philadelphia *American Museum*.

An errata for "Fabius" II was printed immediately below "Fabius" VII in the *Pennsylvania Mercury*, 26 April. See footnotes for the changes made. In reprinting "Fabius" II, the *American Museum* included all of the errata; removed all of the small capital letters and almost all of the italics; and changed some of the paragraphing.

## OBSERVATIONS on the Constitution
### proposed by the Federal Convention.

But besides the objections originating from the before mentioned cause, that have been called *local*, there are other objections that are supposed to arise from the maxims of liberty and policy.—

Hence it is inferred, that the proposed system has such inherent vices, as must necessarily produce a bad administration, and at length the oppression of a monarchy or an aristocracy in the federal officers.

The writer of this address being convinced by as exact an investigation as he could make, that such mistakes may lead to the perdition of his country, esteems it his indispensable duty, strenuously to contend, that—THE POWER OF THE PEOPLE pervading the proposed system, together with the STRONG CONFEDERATION OF THE STATES, forms an adequate security against *every* danger that has been apprehended.

If this single assertion can be supported by facts and arguments, there will be reason to hope, that painful anxieties will be removed from the minds of some citizens, who are truely devoted to the interests of *America*, and who have been thrown into afflictive perplexities, by the never-ending mazes of multiplied, intricate, and contrariant disquisitions. The objectors agree, that the *confederation of the states will be strong*, according to the system proposed, and *so strong*, that many of them loudly complain of that strength. On this part of the assertion, there is no dispute: But some of the objections that have been published, strike at another part of the principle assumed, and deny, that the system is sufficiently founded on *the power of the people*.

The course of regular enquiry demands, that *these* objections should be considered in the first place. If *they* are removed, then *all the rest* of the objections, concerning unnecessary taxations, standing armies, the abolishment of trials by jury, the liberty of the press, the freedom of commerce, the judicial, executive, and legislative authorities of the several states, & the rights of citizens, and the other abuses of federal government, must, of consequence, be rejected, if the principle contains the salutary, purifying, and preserving qualities attributed to it. The question then will be—*Not what may be done, when the government shall be turned into a tyranny; but, how the government can be so turned?*

Thus unembarrassed by subordinate discussions, we may come fairly to the contemplation of *that* superior point, and be better enabled to discover, whether our attention to it will afford any lights, whereby we may be conducted to *peace, liberty,* and *safety.*

The objections, denying that the system proposed is sufficiently founded[1] on *the power of the people,* state, that the *number* of the federal trustees or officers, is too *small,* and that they are to hold their *offices too long.*

One would really have supposed, that *smallness of number* could not be termed a cause of danger, as *influence* must encrease with *enlargement.* If this is a fault, it will soon be corrected, as an addition will be often made to the number of the *senators,* and, almost every year, to that of the *representatives*; and in all probability much sooner, than we shall be able and willing to bear the expence of the addition.

As to the *senate,* it never can be, and it never ought to be large, if it is to possess the powers, which almost all the objectors seem inclined to allot to it, as will be evident to every intelligent person, who considers those powers.

Tho' small, let it be remembered, that it is to be created by the *sovereignties* of the several states; that is, by the persons, whom the people of each state shall judge to be *most worthy,* and who, surely, will be religiously attentive to making a selection, in which the interest and honour of their state will be so extensively concerned. It should be remembered too, that this is *the same manner,* in which the members of Congress are *now* appointed;[2] and that *herein,* the *sovereignties* of the states are so intimately involved, that however a *renunciation* of part of these powers may be desired by *some of the states,* it NEVER will be obtained from *the rest* of them. Peaceable, fraternal,[3] and benevolent as these are, they think, the concessions *they* have made, ought to satisfy *all.*

That the *senate* may always be kept *full,* without the interference of Congress, it is provided that if vacancies happen by resignation or otherwise, during the recess of the legislature of any state, the executive thereof may make temporary appointments, until the next meeting of the legislature, which *shall* then fill up such vacancies.

As *to the house of representatives*, it is to consist of a number of persons, not exceeding one for every thirty thousand. Thus, *every* member of that house will be elected by a *majority of the electors of a whole state*; or, by a *majority of electors, among thirty thousand persons*. These electors will reside, widely dispersed, over an extensive country. Cabal and corruption will be as impracticable, as, on such occasions, human institutions can render them. *The will of freemen*, thus circumstanced, will give the *fiat*. The purity of election thus obtained, will amply compensate for the supposed defect of representation; and the members, thus chosen, will be most apt to harmonize in their proceedings, with the general interests, feelings, and sentiments of the people.

Allowing such an increase of population as, from experience and a variety of causes, may be expected, the *representatives*, in a short period, will amount to several hundreds, and most probably long before any change of manners for the worse, that might tempt or encourage our rulers to mal-administration, will take place on this continent.

That *this house* may *always* be kept *full*, without the interference of Congress, it is provided in the system, that when vacancies happen in any state, the executive authority thereof *shall* issue writs of election to fill such vacancies.

But, it seems, the number of the federal officers is not only too small: They are to hold their offices *too long*.

This objection surely applies not to *the house of representatives*, who are to be chosen *every two years*, especially if the extent of empire, and the vast variety and importance of their deliberations, be considered. In that view, *they* and *the senate* will actually be not only *legislative* but also *diplomatic* bodies, perpetually engaged in the arduous task of reconciling, in their determinations, the interests[4] of several *sovereign* states, not to insist on the necessity of a competent knowledge of *foreign* affairs, relative to the states.

They who desire the *representatives* to be chosen *every year*, should exceed *Newton* in calculations, if they attempt to evince, that the public business would, in that case, be better transacted, than when they are chosen *every two years*. The idea, however, should be excused for the zeal that prompted it.

Is monarchy or aristocracy to be produced, without the consent of the people, by a *house of representatives*, thus constituted?

It has been unanimously agreed by the friends of liberty, that[5] FREQUENT ELECTIONS OF THE REPRESENTATIVES OF THE PEOPLE, ARE THE

MOST SOVEREIGN REMEDY OF ALL GRIEVANCES IN A FREE GOVERNMENT. Let us pass on to the senate.

At the end of two years after the first election, *one third* is to be elected for *six* years. Of the remaining thirds, one will constantly have but *four* years, and the other but two years to continue in office. The whole number at first will amount but to *twenty-six*, must ever continue *very small*, will be regularly *renovated* by the *biennial* election of *one third*, and will be *overlooked, and overawed* by the house of *representatives*, nearly three times more numerous at the beginning, rapidly and vastly augmenting, and more enabled to overlook & overawe them, by holding *their* offices for *two* years, as thereby they will acquire better information, respecting national affairs. These *representatives* will also command the public purse, as *all* bills *for raising revenue*, must *originate* in their house.

As in the *Roman* armies, when the *Principes* and *Hastati* had failed, there were still the *Triarii*, who generally put things to rights, so we shall be supplied with another resource.

We are to have a *president*, to *superintend*, and if he thinks the public weal requires it, *to controul* any act of the *representatives* and *senate*.

This president is to be chosen, not by the people at large, because it may not be possible, that all the freemen of the empire should always have the necessary information, for directing their choice of such an officer; nor by Congress, lest it should disturb the national councils; nor BY ANY ONE BODY WHATEVER, for fear of undue influence.

He is to be chosen in the following manner. Each state shall appoint, as the legislature thereof may direct, a number of *electors*, equal to *the whole number of senators and representatives*, to which the state shall be entitled in Congress: but no *senator* or *representative*, or *person holding an office of trust* or profit under *the United States*, shall be appointed an elector. As these electors are to be appointed, as the legislature of each state may direct, of course they will be appointed by the people of the state, if *such be the pleasure of the people*. Thus, the fairest, freest opening is given, for each state to chuse such *electors* for this purpose, as shall be most signally qualified to fulfil the trust.

To guard against undue influence these electors, thus chosen, are to meet *in their respective states*, and vote *by ballot*; and still further to guard against it, Congress may determine the *time of chusing the electors, and the day on which they shall give their votes*—WHICH DAY SHALL BE THE SAME THROUGHOUT THE UNITED STATES. All the votes from the several states are to be transmitted to Congress, and therein counted. The president is to hold his office for *four* years.

When these electors meet in their respective states, utterly vain will be the unreasonable suggestions derived from *partiality*. The electors may throw away their votes, mark, with public disappointment, some person improperly favoured by them, or justly revering the duties of their office, dedicate their votes to the best interests of their country.

This president will be no *dictator*:[6] *two thirds of the representatives* and *the senate* may pass any law, *notwithstanding his dissent*; and he is *removable* and *punishable* for misbehaviour.

Can the limited, fluctuating *senate*, placed amidst such powers, if it should become willing, ever become able, to make *America* pass under its yoke? The senators will generally be inhabitants of places very distant one from another. They can scarcely be acquainted till they meet. Few of them can ever act together for any length of time, unless their good conduct recommends them to a re-election; and then there will be frequent changes in a body *dependent upon the choice of other bodies*, the legislatures of the several states, that are altering every year. *Machiavel* and *Cæsar Borgia* together could not form a conspiracy in such a senate, dangerous to any but themselves and their accomplices.

It is essential to every good government, that there should be *some council*, permanent enough to get a due knowledge of affairs internal and external; so constituted, that by some deaths or removals, the current of information should not be impeded or disturbed; and so regulated, as to be responsible to, and controulable *by the people*. Where can the authority for combining these advantages, be more *safely, beneficially* or *satisfactorily*, lodged, than in the senate, to be formed according to the plan proposed? Shall parts of the trust be committed to the president, with *counsellors* who shall subscribe their advices? If assaults upon liberty are to be guarded against, and surely they ought to be with sleepless vigilance, why should we depend more on *the commander in chief* of the army and navy of the United States, and of the militia of the several states, and on his counsellors, whom he may secretly influence, than on the *senate* to be appointed by the persons exercising, the *sovereign* authority of the several states? In truth, the objections against the powers of the senate originated from a desire to have them, or at least some of them, vested in a body, in which the several states should be represented, in proportion to the number of inhabitants, as in the house of representatives. This method is UNATTAINABLE, and the wish for it should be dismissed from every mind, that desires the existence of a confederation.

What assurance can be given, or what probability be assigned, that a board of councillors would continue honest, longer than the senate? Or, that they would possess more useful information, respecting all the states, then the senators of all the states? It appears needless to pursue this argument any further.

How varied, ballanced, concordant, and benign, is the system proposed to us? To secure the freedom, and promote the happiness of these and future states, by giving THE WILL OF THE PEOPLE a decisive influence over the whole, and over all the parts, with what a comprehensive arrangement does it embrace different modes of representation, from an election by a county to an election by an empire? What are the complicated ballot, and all the refined devices *of Venice* for maintaining her aristocracy, when compared *with* this plain dealing work for diffusing the blessings of *equal liberty and common prosperity* over myriads of the human race?

All the foundations before mentioned, of the federal government, are by the proposed system to be established, in the most clear, strong, positive, unequivocal expressions, of which our language is capable. *Magna charta*, or any other law, never contained clauses more decisive and emphatic. While the people of these states have sense, they will understand them; and while they have spirit, they will make them to be observed.

1. "Founded" substituted for "formed" in the errata in the *Pennsylvania Mercury*, 26 April.

2. The Articles of Confederation provided that delegates to Congress "shall be annually appointed in such manner as the legislature of each state shall direct" (CDR, 87), while the Constitution provided that U.S. senators were to be elected by the state legislatures.

3. "Fraternal" substituted for "paternal" in the *Mercury* errata.

4. "Interests" substituted for "interest" in the *Mercury* errata.

5. "That" inserted here in the *Mercury* errata.

6. The *Mercury* errata said that "a stop" should be put after the word "dictator." The *American Museum* inserted a semicolon.

## 685. Peter Prejudice: The New Breeches
## Philadelphia Federal Gazette, 15 April

The authorship of this allegorical essay is uncertain. The reprinting in the June issue of the Philadelphia *American Museum* revealed that "Peter Prejudice's complaint of the taylor, who, instead of mending his old Breeches, made him a new pair" was written by "John Mifflin, Esq." Mifflin (1759–1813) was a graduate of the College of Philadelphia (1775) and a prominent lawyer. He was elected a member of the American Philosophical Society in 1796 and was a trustee of the University of Pennsylvania from 1802 to 1813.

Postmaster General Ebenezer Hazard, writing from New York City where "Peter Prejudice" had been reprinted in the *New York Packet* on 22 April, thought that the prolific Federalist propagandist Francis Hopkinson was the author. In alluding to the breeches allegory, Hazard described the outcome of the New York election for convention delegates thusly: "I think it doubtful whether Feds. or Antis. will be most numerous in Convention, though I have little doubt that they will adopt the Constitution:—it is probable that some may propose to have the Breeches altered before they try them on; but I fancy the majority will be for wearing them as they are. I believe F.H. wrote the Piece about the Breeches" (to Jeremy Belknap, 10 May, CC:Vol. 4, p. 592. "Peter Prejudice" is not in the three volumes of Hopkinson's works published in 1792, *The Miscellaneous Essays and Occasional Writings of Francis Hopkinson, Esq.*).

Three weeks after reading "Peter Prejudice" in the Pittsfield, Mass., *Berkshire Chronicle* of 22 May, Antifederalist "Timothy Takeall" responded in the *Chronicle* of 12 June, urging his readers not to accept the new breeches because the tailor had not yet presented his bill. "Your taylor told you, when he made the old breeches, that they would last fifteen years without repairing; but after half of that time is expired, he informs you that they are past mending, and sends you a new pair, which he says are calculated for your benefit, but will not suffer you to try them on, and in case of their illy fitting you, to return them; but if you put them on, you must wear them, and pay the bill which he will then exhibit. Pride and ambition plead for the new breeches; prudence and œconomy for the old ones; and should the new breeches make you sore, as those which the sons of Jacob made for the Shechemites did them, you would as easily be overcome by your Taylor, as they were by the sons of Jacob" (Genesis 34). (Berkshire County was one of the centers of Shaysism and Antifederalism in Massachusetts, having in the state Convention voted 15 to 7 against ratification of the Constitution.)

In addition to the Philadelphia *American Museum*, "Peter Prejudice" was reprinted thirteen times by 2 July: Vt. (1), N.H. (1), Mass. (4), R.I. (1), Conn. (1), N.Y. (2), N.J. (1), Md. (1), Va. (1). Five of these reprints, starting with the *Massachusetts Spy*, 8 May, used the heading, "The NEW BREECHES." On 3 January 1789 the *Pittsburgh Gazette* reprinted "Peter Prejudice" by "particular desire" from the *American Museum*, although it dropped the identification of "John Mifflin, Esq.," as the author.

Mr. Editor, I some time since sent a pair of old breeches to a taylor, in order to have them patched; as the breaches, both in front and rear, were very numerous I was obliged to purchase a considerable quantity of cloth wherewith to mend them[1]—Well sir, what do you think the taylor has had the assurance to do? Why, after detaining my breeches upwards of four months, he has presumed to return them unpatched, and has also sent a new pair along with them, and a message, "That upon examining the old pair he had found them so rotten that they were not worth mending, nor could it be easily done, that he had also found that the cloth sent for that purpose was sufficient to make an entire new pair, much better than the old ones had ever been, which he had done accordingly, and hoped for my approbation of his conduct." He added moreover "that if upon trial they should happen to pinch me in any part, he had left a sufficient space for outlets at every seam."

Oh height of insult! said I on receiving this arrogant message, what has this fellow done! A conspiracy! A conspiracy! As sure as I'm alive the traitor, his journeymen, and apprentices have *meditated* the ruin of my old breeches, and *conspired* against the liberty of my thighs, knees, and loins, which they have insidiously attempted to confine and cramp by palming this "*gilded trap*" the new breeches on me, "*Curse on the villains!*" they have conspired to lay restraints upon my *free-born* members, which are utterly incompatible with our republican form of government! Here indignation choked my utterance—My dearly beloved spouse and my little children were all gather'd about me by this time, to know the cause of my anger. It was, however, a considerable while before the boiling madness of my rage was sufficiently calmed for me to give them the information they desired; but my heat being somewhat allayed, I at length deigned to answer their interrogatories.

Well my dear (said my sweet partner) I think you are under many obligations to our good neighbour the taylor, who has rendered you very important services on former occasions; and has certainly consulted your interest in this business; for my part, I highly approve of his conduct, and am well pleased that he has made you these pretty new *small clothes*, (for she does not like to say *breeches*) to hide your nakedness, and defend you from the inclemency of the weather. Sure you know how you have been laughed at, wherever you went, this long time past on account of your old pair, which the neighbours all say, are no better than an Indian's breech-clout; I protest my own modesty has been often put to the blush by the holes in that plaguy old pair— My lovely tormentor was about to proceed in her condemnation of the old pair, and her praises of the new—Hold! hold! said I, let us reason the matter fairly. In the first place, he has disobeyed my orders, which were only that he should repair the old breeches. But has he not made a new pair much preferable to the old? By no means, I replied, these cursed new breeches would utterly ruin me; they are calculated to enslave my thighs, to confine my waist, and totally to destroy the liberty of my knees, by buttoning tightly around them, they will also render a considerable part of my hose totally useless by buckling below my knees; nor is this all, they will imprison my femoral parts nor suffer them to enjoy fresh air as the old ones do; to be brief, they are *too long* and *too short*, *too strait* and *too wide*, they would *pinch me in all parts*, and *fit me in none*.

Methinks you reason very strangely, my love (replied my solicitous advocate for the new breeches, who was now joined by all the children,) your argument, against being under the restraint and confinement of clothes, is only calculated for a circle of savages, and can never have any weight among civilized and social beings; your objection to the want of breaches in the new pair, for admission of fresh air, is an excellent argument in their favour, and shews that they are well calculated to skreen you from the inclemency of the seasons; your concluding objections are so inconsistent and contradictory, that they fall to the ground without any comment. Further, continued she, if they have faults you know the taylor says they can be easily amended; would not you do well therefore to put them on, in order to ascertain their faults truly, and I shall have no objection to the necessary alterations being made in them.

No, no, said I, "*don't think to catch old birds with chaff.*" I'm determined never to draw them on, unless the amendments shall have been first made. Here again I was replied to—How in the name of goodness, said she, can you undertake to have amendments made, before you know that the parts you would wish to have amended are indeed faulty! By such preposterous doings you might spoil their best parts; but would have no tolerable chance of amending even one fault; therefore, I beg you may first try them on, that you may be enabled to discover their faults with precision. Do papa, do try on your new breeches, exclaimed the children with one voice.

Hush! hush! said I once more, I believe the woman and the children are all crazy! Do you think I am fool enough to be gulled thus! If I should put them on, how shall I be able to get them off again? I have no security that they will not cling to my skin, tear away my flesh, break my bones, and boil my marrow, like Hercules's poisoned shirt, which insidiously destroyed him. And all this must be born, without the liberty of even remonstrating against the tyranny of these accursed "*consolidating*" breeches. I say *consolidating*; for they are evidently calculated to supersede the use of every other garment; or at least to "melt them all down into one" general garment; and the taylor certainly intended this to be the case. Do they not already exhibit a specimen of their despotism, by being framed so as to "lord it over" a considerable part of my stockings and shirt? And is it not more than probable, that they would, very speedily, encroach upon the prerogative of *all* my clothes; nay, that they would even extend their sway to my head, and, by closing my mouth, prevent me from expostulating against my "cruel taskmasters?" With these over my face, for a mask, I should appear no less ridiculous, than a modern fine lady with her head in a calash, or in a fashionable bonnet.

Here the whole family burst into laughter, and the dispute ended for that time. I have reason to expect another attack on the same score shortly; for my wife is exceedingly fond of the new breeches, and is supported by all my neighbours in her controversies with me on this subject. As I am nearly exhausted, I will be much obliged to any of your correspondents who will be so condescending as to favour me with a fresh supply of arguments, sufficient to repel those of my spouse in our next rencountre.

1. As a note to his preface, the editor of the Philadelphia *American Museum* said that "For the information of European readers, it may be necessary to mention that the old breeches allude to the old articles of confederation—the quantity of cloth to the powers granted the late convention, &c. &c." When the *Pittsburgh Gazette*, 3 January 1789, reprinted this item from the *Museum* it changed the word "European" to "our."

## 686. Rufus King to John Langdon
### New York, 16 April[1]

I inclose under a Frank which General Knox has given me,[2] an address to the people of this State which may be of use in New Hampshire—if you should judge it a publication of value, I think the public Happiness will be advanced by circulating it in your State—Be assured that you ought not on any consideration to omit every Exertion which prudence and Virtue will authorise in favor of the constitution; very much will depend on your Decision[3]—Georgia has ceded upwards of Thirty millions of acres of land lying between the 31st & 33d degrees of lat. and between the Apalachicola & the Missisippi, to the United States, on condition that nine or more States ratify the new Constitution[4]—We have no News from So. or North Carolina—the former is said to be federal & the latter doubtful.

The Accounts of the Elections from Virginia indicate that the parties will be powerful & nearly equal. Our hopes are great that Maryland will be right Luther Martin notwithstanding; but we are not so confident of Maryland as we once were of New Hampshire—It is exquisitely problematical what the issue of the Business will be in this State—both parties are indifatigable and each seems confident of success—

New Hampshire must determine right and preserve our country—With great respect & Friendship Your obt. & very Hble Servt.

1. RC, King Papers, NHi.
2. Henry Knox was the Confederation Secretary at War and as such he had franking privileges.
3. King refers to John Jay's pamphlet *An Address to the People of the State of New-York . . .*, written under the pseudonym "A Citizen of New-York" and first offered for sale on 15 April (CC:683). On 6 May Langdon, a Portsmouth delegate to the New Hampshire Convention, replied to King: "I am honour'd with your kind favor of the

16th. ult. incloseg the Address to the people of New York, which is greatly Admired, here, I shall take great care to Circulate this and all other, peices that will give light to the Subject. You may depend every exertion, shall be made that is Possable to promote the Adoption, of the Constitution and I have no doubt notwithstanding our late Disappointments and Mortification we shall finally prevail, and thereby Make the people happy in Spight of their teeth as the Sayg. is" (King Papers, NHi. For the circulation of "A Citizen of New-York" in New Hampshire, see CC:683.).

4. On 20 October 1787 Congress requested that Georgia cede its western lands to Congress (as other states had done) so that Congress could sell these lands to pay off the federal debt. On 1 February 1788 the Georgia Assembly ceded a strip of land about 140 miles wide, but Congress rejected the cession in July (JCC, XXXIII, 692–93; XXXIV, 323–26; and RCS:Ga., 288, 292–93). King's information on Georgia appeared in the Portsmouth *New Hampshire Spy* on 6 May. See *Pennsylvania Packet*, 24 May, note 2 (CC:Vol. 6, Appendix I).

## 687. George Lee Turberville to James Madison
### Epping, Richmond County, Va., 16 April[1]

Yr. favor of ye. 1st. Ulto. reached me on the 7th. instant. The satisfactory information it contain'd deserves and receives my most Cordial & gratefull acknowledgements—altho I had satisfied myself in many respects touching ye arguments of the opponents to the new Constitution—yet I never before was so well acquainted with those powerfull reasons that may be urged agt. the adoption of a Bill of Rights—the favorite Topic of the ablest Antifœderal declamers—at the time I had ye honor of writing to you[2]—I had some expectation of being elected to the convention but it has pleased my County men to make choice of other Gentlemen, therefore my attention to this Subject for six months will be no other wise advantageous to me than that it has enabled me to form a judgement upon it from mature consideration for myself—Whereas had I not expected to have Voted upon it— I might have contented myself with the first opinion that reached me— What has not been done by ignorance—cunning—Interest—and Address to blast and blacken this Production? Misrepresentation—False reasoning—& wilful perversion have been made use of agt. ye. peice itself—Calumny and Falshood have Stamp'd ye *objects* of *those* who framed it with the most infamous colours—The design of Its artfull enemies whose interests are opposite to the operation of an efficient Government—have resorted to arts like those above enumerated—hoping to effectuate by the operation of Clamour upon ye. passions— (what Reason applied to ye senses wou'd for ever reprobate and condemn)—"*The rejection of the New Constitution*" The result of a very cool enquiry into the probable effects of the new Constitution in my mind— in a few Words, is that it is adequate to every beneficial consequence for which Governments are or ought to be instituted—whilst at the same time the Checks are so ingeniously interposed between ye Rulers and ye Citizens as to leave all power—in the hands of the people—and therefore it is impossible that it shou'd ever continue perverted to bad purposes untill it is dangerous—unless the great mass of the people shou'd become *Corrupt*! ignorant of their Birthright—and regardless of their posterity—shou'd such at any period be the unhappy Characteristick of My fellow Citizens—they will then deserve—& must inevitably wear the Yoke of slavery—it will not be in the power of Folios of Bills of rights to maintain their Liberties—The rights of Freemen are only to be maintain'd by Freemen—and when the Spirit of Freedom—(that has ever elevated those who felt its influence amongst Mankind—) becomes extinct in the bosoms of men—Liberty itself will be a curse to them—

Experience the parent of Wisdom has already taught us that unanimity amongst us can be successfull—& That an attempt to Tyrannize hath already given unanimity to America—Each state will still have a Legislature possessing its confidence as effectually as the old Assemblies did—as adequate to the purposes of calling forth the forces and resources of the States, and as free to commune with the assemblies of the sister states—have we any reason then to suppose that an Act of Oppression wou'd pass unnoticed when issued by the New Congress? that the states wou'd not be unanimous in their opposition? or that the general government which depends for support upon the individual states wou'd be enabled to triumph over the Liberties of America—when the Fleets and Armies of the British King supported by the Wealth of Britain were inadequate?

The sense of this State is it is to [be] feared but too much divided upon this weighty subject—indeed those who pretend to be acquainted with the opinions of the members elected do not hesitate to declare that the Members from Kentuckey will determine the question—and they admit that a Majority of 12 or 14 members are in favor of the adoption of the Gover[n]ment—from this Side of ye Cumberland Mountain—

I cou'd wish just for private gratification to be satisfied upon the subject of the Congress having the power to regulate the Time manner and place of holding Elections—the Clause is Ambiguous & Contradictory—First the States are to regulate—& then Congress are to alter—if they had declared that Congress might direct—in case of Neglect or refusal in the state—it wou'd have been clear—it is now as I have before said Ambiguous—and to Jealous minds it becomes an insurmountable objection—at the same time I am not apprehensive of Evil from that quarter, for was the Congress to attempt [the] Exercise of this power for party purposes—the intention wou'd be too apparent to pass by unnoticed—it wou'd create commotions that might prove fatal to the Congress itself—and therefore it is nugatory; for at the time when they may Venture upon the partial exercise of this power for *party purposes*—they may hold every constitutional check as dead letters—Suppose also that 2, 3 or 4 States shou'd reject the constitution—are they to form a separate confederation?—or are the nine to exercise coercion to bring them in?—or are they to be declared out of the Confederation?—This is by far the most exceptionable part of the Whole peice—

Pardon this long Letter replete with nothing that can be new or agreeable to you—remember when you are reading it that it is ye. want of matter not of inclination in ye writer to amuse you—Let me hope that as you may find yourself at Leizure you will be good enough to favor me with a line—remembring that in this retirement—a knowledge of what is passing in the world is doubly grateful—because it is so seldom that we ever become acquainted with it—

1. RC, Madison Collection, NN.
2. For Turberville's letter of 11 December 1787, which posed a number of questions about the Constitution, see CC:338; and RCS:Va., 231–35. Madison's reply of 1 March 1788 has not been located.

## 688. A Farmer
### Philadelphia Freeman's Journal, 16, 23 April[1]

*The* FALLACIES *of the* FREEMAN *detected by a* FARMER.

Some weeks since there was published in the Carlisle Gazette an Address to the Minority of the late Convention of this State, under the signature of a *Freeman*, which I then supposed had been written by some well-meaning person of that place,[2] who had not yet entered the porch of political knowledge, who was unacquainted with the nature of sovereignty, and incapable of distinguishing ministerial agency from the exercise of sovereignty; I therefore took no especial notice of it, until happening to see a Philadelphia Newspaper, I found the Address had originated there, and was ascribed to a gentleman who is far from being ignorant, as I had candidly supposed the author to be, but who hath habituated himself to presume much upon the supposed ignorance of the people, and whose expectations of future support and grandeur hath probably been very influential in framing and promoting the proposed system of government:—Upon this discovery, I read the Address again with more attention, and resolved to communicate, thro' your useful paper, the result of my observations thereon. I do not, however, design to answer the Address in detail, but to establish and explain such general principles as may assist people in judging for themselves, and have a tendency to detect the sophistry which characterises the performance. In order to do this, I shall explain,

*First*, The NATURE of SOVEREIGNTY.

*Second*, Of a FEDERAL REPUBLIC.

*Third*, Of a CONSOLIDATED GOVERNMENT.

*Fourth*, The NATURE of MINISTERIAL AGENCY.

*Fifth*, Examine the ADDRESS to the MINORITY (the occasion of these Enquiries.)

*Sixth*, Conclude with some GENERAL OBSERVATIONS on the TIMES.

I return to the *first* then: From the very design that induces men to form a society that has its common interests and to promote and secure which it ought to act in concert, it is necessary that there should be established a public authority, to order and direct what ought to be done by each individual as he stands in relation to the society itself, or to the individual members thereof; and this public authority consisting of that portion of natural liberty which each member surrenders to the society to be exercised for the common advantage, is the sovereignty which is often called political authority. If this sovereignty or political authority be vested in and exercised by the whole people, as in some of the ancient republics, or if it be delegated to representatives chosen by the people from among themselves, as in modern times, the government is called a democracy. If on the contrary the sovereignty be in a particular class of citizens who have not a common interest with the people at large, or body of the nation, it is called an aristocracy; and if in a single person, a monarchy or despotism; and these three kinds may be variously combined and modified as in the British government and others, but every nation that governs itself by its own laws let the form of government be what it may, is a sovereign state.

Sovereignty therefore consists in the understanding and will of the political society, and this understanding and will is originally and inherently in the people; the society having rested[3] it where and in what manner it pleases, he or they to whom it is delegated is the sovereign and is thus vested with the political understanding and will of the people for their good and advantage solely.

The power of making rules or laws to govern or protect the society is the essence of sovereignty, for by this the executive and judicial powers are directed and controuled, to this every ministerial agent is subservient, and to this all corporate or privileged bodies are subordinate: this power not only regulates the conduct, but disposes of the wealth and commands the force of the nation.. To keep this sovereign power therefore in due bounds hath fundamental laws, which we call constitutions and bills of rights, been made and declared. Scarcely hath the wisdom of man, matured by the experience of ages, been able with all the checks, negatives and balances either of ancient or modern invention to prevent abuses of this high sovereign authority.

Here I may possibly be misunderstood; it may perhaps be objected, that in Great Britain the *King* is called the Sovereign, and that he is an executive and not legislative officer. True, the King of Great Britain is the Supreme Executive of the nation, but it is not this alone that constitutes him a Sovereign; he hath a negative over the Legislative, the laws are made by and with his consent, and are called the King's Laws; he calls, prorogues and dissolves his Parliament when he pleases; the Parliament indeed so manage, that the necessity of the case obliges him to convene them frequently, but he is not obliged to do it by the Constitution; so that, properly speaking, it is the King and Parliament of Great Britain which is sovereign.—However, if the Legislative authority were to be distributed in various portions, that man, or body of men, who should be vested with the sole and uncontrouled power of taxation, would eventually become the sovereign, for whoever can command our whole property has the means in his power of ruling us as he pleases, because (as Montesquieu says) "sovereignty necessarily follows the power of taxation.["]

[23 April] *Secondly.* I shall proceed to define a FEDERAL REPUBLIC:— A Federal Republic is formed by two or more single or consolidated republics, uniting together by a perpetual confederacy, and without ceasing to be distinct states or sovereignties; they form together a federal republic or an empire of states. As individuals in a state of nature surrender a portion of their natural liberty to the society of which they become members, in order to receive in lieu thereof protection and conveniency; so in forming a federal republic the individual states surrender a part of their separate sovereignty to the general government or federal head, in order that, whilst they respectively enjoy internally the freedom and happiness peculiar to free republics, they may possess all that external protection, security, and weight by their confederated resources, that can possibly be obtained in the most extended, absolute monarchies.

The peculiar advantages and distinctive properties of a federal republic are, that each state or member of the confederation may be fully adequate for every local purpose, that it may subsist in a small territory, that the people may have a common interest, possess a competent knowledge of the resources and expenditures of their own particular government, that their immediate representatives in the state governments will know and be known by the citizens, will have a common interest with them, and must bear a part of all the burdens which they may lay upon the people, that they will be responsible to the people, and may be dismissed by them at pleasure; that therefore the government would be a government of confidence and possess sufficient energy without the aid of standing armies, that the collectors of the revenue would at least have the bowels of citizens, and not be the offscourings of Europe, or other states who have no interest in, or attachment to the people; that if one or more of the states should become the prey of internal despotism, or foreign foes, the other states may remain secure under the protection of their own state government; that if some popular and wealthy citizen should have influence enough to attempt the liberties of one state, he might be stopped in his career by the interposition of the others, for his influence could not be equally great in all the states; that if the general government should fail, or be revised or changed, yet the several state governments may remain entire to secure the happiness of the citizens; and that the members of a confederated republic may be encreased to any amount, and consequently its external strength without altering the nature of the government, or endangering the liberty of the citizens.

The perfection of a federal republic consists in drawing the proper line between those objects of sovereignty which are of a general nature, and which ought to be vested in the federal government, and those which are of a more local nature and ought to remain with the particular governments; any rule that can be laid down for this must vary according to the situation and circumstances of the confederating states; yet still this general rule will hold good, viz. that all that portion of sovereignty which involve the common interest of all the confederating states, and which cannot be exercised by the states in their individual capacity without endangering the liberty and welfare of the whole, ought to be vested in the general government, reserving such a proportion of sovereignty in the state governments as would enable them to exist alone, if the general government should fail either by violence or with the common consent of the confederates; the states should respectively have laws, courts, force, and revenues of their own sufficient for their own security; they ought to be fit to keep house alone if necessary; if this be not the case, or so far as it ceases to be so, it is a departure from a federal to a consolidated government; and this brings me to the next particular, which is to shew what is meant by a consolidated government.

*Thirdly.* The idea of a CONSOLIDATED GOVERNMENT is easily understood, where a single society or nation forms one entire separate government, and possess the whole sovereign power; this is a consolidated or national government. Whether a government be of a monarchical, aristocratical or democratical nature, it doth not alter the case, it is either a federal or a consolidated government, there being no medium as to kind.—The absoluteness of a despotic sovereignty is often restricted by corporate bodies, who are vested with peculiar privileges and franchises—and by a just distribution of the executive and ministerial powers; but although these may contribute to the happiness of the people, yet they do not change the nature of the government. Indeed, monarchies can never form a federal government; they may enter into alliances with each other; for monarchy cannot be divested of a competent proportion of sovereignty to form a general government without changing its nature. It is only free republics that can completely and safely form a federal republic; I say free republics, for there are republics who are not free, such as Venice, where a citizen carrying arms is punished with instant death, and where even the nobles dare not converse with strangers, and scarcely with their friends, and are liable by law to be put to death secretly without trial—or Poland which, in much the same words that are expressed in the new system, is by a league with the neighbouring powers guaranteed to be forever independent and of a republican form; yet a writer of their own says, that the body of the people are scarcely to be distinguished from brutes; and again he says, we have reduced the people of our kingdom by misery to a state of brutes; they drag out their days in stupidity, &c. Free republics are congenial to a federal republic. In order that a republic may preserve its liberty, it must not only have a good form of government, but it must be of small extent; for if it possess extensive territory, it would be ruined by internal imperfection. The authority of government in a large republic does not equally pervade all the parts; nor are the political advantages equally enjoyed by the citizens remote from the capital as by those in the vicinity; combinations consequently prevail among the members of the legislature, and this introduces corruption and is destructive of that confidence in government, without which a free republic cannot be supported; besides, the high influential trusts which must be vested in the great officers of state, would at particular times endanger the government, and are necessarily destructive of that equality among the citizens, which is the only permanent basis of a republic; in short, the diversity of the situation, habits, manners, and interests of the people in an extensive dominion, subjects the government to a thousand accidents, which would embarrass a republican government. The experience of nations and the nature of things, sufficiently prove, that the government of a single person, aided by armies and controuling influence, is necessary to govern a large consolidated empire.

And on the other hand, if the territory be small, the republic is liable to be destroyed by external force, therefore, reason and observation points out a confederation of republics, as the only method to preserve internal freedom, together with external strength and respectability.—Small republics forming a federal republic on these principles, may be resembled to divers small ropes plaited together to make a large and strong one, if the latter is untwisted, the small ropes are still useful as such, but if the former are untwisted, they are reduced to hemp, the original state.

To apply these principles to our present situation without respect to the proposed plan of government; in order to render the federal government adequate to the exigencies of the confederating states, it is necessary not only that the general government should be properly constructed in its forms, but that it should be vested with powers relative to all the federal objects of government, these objects are not only the powers of making peace and war, &c. but also with the power of making treaties respecting commerce, regulating and raising revenues therefrom, &c. to make requisitions of money when necessity requires it, from each of the states, and a certain well described power of compelling delinquent states to pay up their quota of such requisitions. Perhaps if each state had its own share of the domestic debt quotaed, so as they might each pay their own citizens, the general revenues would be sufficient for the other demands of the union in times of peace, if the government itself be not made too expensive by too great a number of officers being created. Congress ought, however, to have all powers which cannot be exercised by one state, without endangering the other states, such as the power of raising troops, treating with foreign nations, &c.—The power of levying imposts, will, by the particular states, be irregularly exercised, and the revenue in a great degree lost or misapplied, therefore, it ought not to be left with the states, but under proper checks, vested in the general government. All these the minority[4] were amongst the foremost willing to have vested in the federal head, and more than this, had never been asked by Congress, nor proposed by the greatest advocates for congressional power, nor is more than this consistent with the nature of a federal republic. When the existing confederation was adopted, powers were given with a sparing hand, and perhaps, not improperly at that period, until experience should point out the discriminating line with sufficient experience, well knowing that it is easy for a government to obtain an encrease of power when common utility points out the propriety, but that powers once vested in a government, however dangerous they may prove, are rarely recovered without bloodshed, and even that awful method of regaining lost liberty is seldom effectual. It is now however evident that the power of regulating commerce, being of a general nature, ought to belong to the general government, and the burthen of debt incurred by the revolution hath rendered a general revenue necessary, for this purpose imposts upon articles of importation present themselves, not only as a productive source of revenue, but as a revenue for which the governments of the particular states are for well known reasons, incompetent.—The danger of entrusting a government so far out of the people's reach as Congress must necessarily be, strongly impressed the public mind about four or five years since, but now a conviction of the advantage and probable safety of such a measure, pervades almost every mind, and none are more willing for putting it in operation, under proper guards, than the opposers of the new system; they are also willing to admit what the majority of the states may judge proper checks in the *form* of the general government, as far as those checks, or the distribution of powers and responsibility of those who be vested with those powers, may be consistent with the security of the essential sovereignty of the respective states. The minority of the convention (who I really believe, in their address, express the serious sentiments of the majority of this state) opposed vesting such powers in Congress as can be most effectually exercised by the state governments in a full consistency with the general interests of the confederating states, and which, not being of a general nature, are not upon federal principles, objects of the federal government, I mean the power of capitation, or poll tax, by which the head, or in other words, the existence of every person is put in their power by the new system as a property, subject to any price or tax that may be judged proper; I do not mean to say that this implies the power of life and death, although it certainly implies the power of selling the property, or if none is to be had, of imprisoning or selling the person for a servant, who doth not chuse, or is not able to pay the poll tax; the minority also objected to vesting Congress with power to tax the property, real and personal of the citizens of the several states, to what amount, and in what manner it may please, without any check or controul upon its discretion; also to the unlimitted power over the excise; if this could extend only to spirituous liquors as is usual with us, the danger would be less, but the power of excise extends to every thing we eat, drink, or wear, and in Europe it is thus extensively put in practice. Under the term duties, every species of indirect taxes is included, but it especially means the power of levying money upon printed books, and written instruments.

The Congress, by the proposed system, have the power of borrowing money to what amount they may judge proper, consequently to mortgage all our estates, and all our sources of revenue. The exclusive power of emmitting bills of credit is also reserved to Congress. They have, moreover, the power of instituting courts of justice without tryal by jury, except in criminal cases, and under such regulations as Congress may think proper to decide, not only in such cases as arise out of all the foregoing powers, but in the other cases which are enumerated in the system.

The absolute sovereignty in all the foregoing instances, as well as several others not here enumerated, are vested in the general government, without being subject to any constitutional check or controul from the state governments.[5]

It remains to examine the nature of the powers which are left with the states, and on this subject it is not necessary to follow *Freeman* through the numerous detail of particulars with which he confuses the reader. I shall examine only a few of the more considerable. The *Freeman* in his 2d Number, after mentioning in a very delusory manner divers powers which remain with the states, he says we shall find many other instances under the constitution which require or imply the existence or continuance of the sovereignty and severality of the states; he as well as all the advocates of the new system, take as their strong ground the election of senators by the state legislatures, and the special representation of the states in the federal senate, to prove that internal sovereignty still remains with the states; therefore they say that the new system is so far from annihilating the state governments, that it secures them, that it cannot exist without them, that the existence of the one is essential to the existence of the other. It is true that this particular partakes strongly of that mystery which is characteristic of the system itself; but if I demonstrate that this particular, so far from implying the continuance of the state sovereignties, proves in the clearest manner the want of it, I hope the other particular powers will not be necessary to dwell upon.

The state legislatures do not chuse senators by legislative or sovereign authority, but by a power of ministerial agency as mere electors or boards of appointment; they have no power to direct the senators how or what duties they shall perform; they have neither power to censure the senators, nor to supercede them for misconduct. It is not the power of chusing to office merely that designates sovereignty, or else corporations who appoint their own officers and make their own bye-laws, or the heads of department who chuse the officers under them, such as commanders of armies, &c. may be called sovereigns, because they can name men to office whom they cannot dismiss therefrom. The exercise of sovereignty does not consist in chusing masters, such as the senators would be, who, when chosen, would be beyond controul, but in the power of dismissing, impeaching, or the like, those to whom authority is delegated. The power of instructing or superceding of delegates to Congress under the existing confederation, hath never been complained of, altho' the necessary rotation of members of Congress hath often been censured for restraining the state sovereignties too much in the objects of their choice. As well may the electors who are to vote for the president under the new constitution, be said to be vested with the sovereignty, as the state legislatures in the act of chusing senators. The senators are not even dependent on the states for their wages, but in conjunction with the federal representatives establish their own wages. The senators do not vote by states, but as individuals. The representatives also vote as individuals, representing people in a consolidated or national government; they judge upon their own elections, and, with the senate, have the power of regulating elections in time, place and manner, which is in other words to say, that they have the power of elections absolutely vested in them.

That the state governments have certain ministerial and convenient powers continued to them is not denied, and in the exercise of which they may support, but cannot controul the general government, nor protect their own citizens from the exertions of civil or military tyranny, and this ministerial power will continue with the states as long as two thirds of Congress shall think their agency necessary; but even this will be no longer than two-thirds of Congress shall think proper to propose, and use the influence of which they would be so largely possessed to remove it.

But these powers, of which the *Freeman* gives us such a profuse detail, and in describing which he repeats the same powers with only varying the terms, such as the powers of officering and training the militia, appointing state officers, and governing in a number of internal cases, do not any of them separately, nor all taken together, amount to independent sovereignty; they are powers of mere ministerial agency, which may, and in many nations of Europe, are or have been vested, as before observed, in heads of departments, hereditary vassals of the crown, or in corporations; but not that kind of independent sovereignty which can constitute a member of a federal republic, which can enable a state to exist within itself if the general government should cease.

I have often wondered how any writer of sense could have the confidence to avow, or could suppose the people to be ignorant enough to believe, that, when a state is deprived of the power not only of standing armies (this the members of a confederacy ought to be) but of commanding its own militia, regulating its elections, directing or superceding its representatives or paying them their wages; who is, moreover, deprived of the command of any property, I mean source of revenue or taxation, or what amounts to the same thing, who may enact laws for raising revenue, but who may have these laws rendered nugatory, and the execution thereof superceded by the laws of Congress. This is not a strained construction, but the natural operation of the powers of Congress under the new constitution; for every object of revenue, every source of taxation, is vested in the general government. Even the power of making inspection laws, which, for obvious conveniency, is left with the several states, will be unproductive of the smallest revenue to the state governments; for, if any should arise, it is to be paid over to the coffers of Congress;—besides, the words "to make all laws necessary and proper for carrying into execution the foregoing powers, &c." give, without doubt, the power of repelling or forbidding the execution of any tax law whatever that may interfere with or impede the exercise of the general taxing power, and it would not be possible that two taxing powers should be exercised on the same sources of taxation without interfering with each other. May not the exercise of this power of Congress, when they think proper, operate not only to destroy those ministerial powers which are left with the states, but even the very forms? May they not forbid the state legislatures to levy a shilling to pay themselves, or those whom they employ, days wages? The state governments may contract for making roads (except post-roads) erecting bridges, cutting canals, or any other object of public importance; but when the contract is performed or the work done, may not Congress constitutionally prevent the payment? Certainly they may do all this and much more, and no man would have a right to charge them with breaking the law of their appointment. It is an established maxim, that wherever the whole power of the revenue or taxation is vested, there virtually is the whole effective, influential, sovereign power, let the forms be what they may: By this armies are procured, by this every other controuling guard is defeated. Every balance or check in government is only so far effective as it hath a controul over the revenue.

The state governments are not only destitute of all sovereign command of, or controul over, the revenue or any part of it, but they are divested of the power of commanding, or prescribing the duties, wages, or punishments of their own militia, or of protecting their life, property or characters from the rigours of martial law. The power of making treason laws is both a slower and an important defence of sovereignty; it is relative to and inseparable from it; to convince the states that they are consolidated into one national government, this power is wholly to be assumed by the general government. All the prerogatives, all the essential characteristics of sovereignty, both of the internal and external kind, are vested in the general government, and consequently the several states would not be possessed of any essential power, or effective guard of sovereignty.

Thus I apprehend, it is evident that the consolidation of the states, into one national government (in contradistinction from a confederacy) would be the necessary consequence of the establishment of the new constitution, and the intention of its framers—and that consequently the state sovereignties would be eventually annihilated, though the forms may long remain as expensive and burthensome remembrances, of what they were in the days when (although labouring under many disadvantages) they emancipated this country from foreign tyranny, humbled the pride, and tarnished the glory of royalty, and erected a triumphant standard to liberty and independence.

It is not my present object to decide, whether the government is a good or a bad one, it is only to prove in support of the minority, that the new system does not in reality, whatever its appearances may be, constitute a federal but a consolidated government.—From the distinguishing characteristics of these two kinds of government which I have stated, some assistance perhaps may be derived in judging which of them would be most suitable to our circumstances, and the best calculated to promote and secure the liberty and welfare of these United States.

A few general observations shall conclude this essay. It is commonly said by the friends of the system, that the dangers which we point out are imaginary, that we ought to depend more upon the virtue of those who shall exercise those powers; that we talk as if we supposed men would be possessed of a dæmon as soon as they should be vested with the proposed powers, &c. I shall in answer thereto join with a sensible reasoner in saying, that I will not abuse the new Congress until it exists, nor then until it misbehaves, nor then unless I dare; but it is a fact, that all governments that have ever been instituted amongst men, have degenerated and abused their power, and why we should conceive better of the proposed Congress than of all governments who have gone before us, I don't know; it is certainly incumbent on the supporters of this system, first to prove either that the uniform tes-

timony of history, and experience of society, is false, or else that the
new system will have the divine influence to inspire those who exercise
the powers which it provides, with wisdom and virtue in an infallible
degree. Surely the conduct of the framers and promoters of the new
constitution, do not present mankind as more worthy of confidence
now, than they have been in other periods of society. For proof of
this let us examine facts. The legislature of the various states, elected
members for a federal convention, without having authority for that
purpose from their constituents; this gave no alarm, as necessity perhaps justified the measure, but how dangerous is the smallest precedent
of usurped power, for the general convention when met, far out did
the example—they were strictly bound by the law of their appointment
to revise the confederation; the additional powers with which it ought
to have been vested were generally understood, and would have been
universally submitted to. This convention not only neglected the duty
of their appointment, but assumed a power of the most extraordinary
kind, they proceeded to destroy the very government which they were
solemnly enjoined to strengthen and improve, and framed a system
(to say no worse of it) that was destructive not only of the form, but
of the nature of the government whose foundations were laid in the
plighted faith and whose superstructure was cemented with the best
blood of the United States. The legislature of this state, whose leading
members were also self-chosen members of the general convention,
no sooner had it in their power, than notwithstanding the solemn trust
reposed in them, and still more solemn oath to preserve the constitution of this state inviolate, proceeded upon the expected last day of
their session to call a convention, in order to adopt the proposed
system of government before the people could be acquainted with it;
and to carry this into execution, they added violence to perfidy, and
by the aid of [a] mob compelled members, sanctified by their presence,
that usurped exertion of power, which their faith and trust obliged
them to discountenance. The consequence was, that about one-sixth
of the citizens only obeyed the irregular call of the assembly, and
elected members to the state convention: one-third of those members,
and who were chosen by nearly one-half of the voters who did elect,
voted against the adoption of the new constitution, and being refused
the right of entering their testimony on the minutes, laid their conduct
and their reasons before their constituents. About five out of six of
the people, whether disdaining to obey a call which neither the general
convention or assembly were authorised to make, or whether being
taken by surprise, they were not sufficiently informed to act with decision, and therefore did not choose to act at all: I cannot tell, but so

it is, that they have not yet publicly declared their sentiments for, nor have done any thing in favor of the proposed system: In this situation Pennsylvania hath adopted the system. It is a very serious question, whether supposing nine states had agreed to it in this manner, the system would be practicable, whether general confidence would not be necessary unless we had greater resources. In addition to Pennsylvania, Georgia, Delaware, New-Jersey, and Connecticut, have also adopted the system; these states are not only small, but in a high degree delinquent, and there is no provision made in the new constitution to compel delinquent states or persons to make up their deficiencies. The convention of Massachusetts have adopted the system with a solemn disapprobation, they have pointed out amendments on the same parchment with the act of ratification, and have solemnly enjoined those who may be the first deputies in the new Congress, to exert their every endeavours to have these amendments made part of the constitution, and to add weight to them, they have officially requested Pennsylvania and the other states to concur in their propositions of amendment.[6] The New-Hampshire convention have, on motion of the friends of the system, adjourned until June, in order to prevent an immediate rejection, which otherwise was unavoidable, the adjournment was carried by only three voices.[7] At present there is and will for some months be a solemn and serious pause, a time of deliberation, the result of which will fill an important page in the history of human society. For my own part I think the heaviest clouds are dispersed, and the gloomy darkness admits the chearing rays of hope, which promise meridian splendour to the sun of liberty. Most of those who were from the best motives friends to the system, have penetrated the shade of mystery in which it was wrapped, they see the snares, and discover the delusions with which it is replete, they see that every other system of government whether good or bad, is easy to be understood, but that this system excels all of the kind which hath come to their knowledge in darkness and ambiguity; they have been informed too, that this mysterious veil was the fruit of deliberation and design.

Whilst posts are prevented from carrying intelligence, whilst newspapers are made the vehicles of deception, and dark intrigue employs the avaricious office-hunters, who long to riot on the spoils of their country, the great body of the people are coolly watching the course of the times, and determining to preserve their liberties, and to judge for themselves by the principles of reason and common sense, and not by the weight of names.

1. The Philadelphia *Independent Gazetteer* printed "A Farmer" in two installments on 18 and 22 April, although it broke the essay differently. See note 5, below, for the break point. "A Farmer" responds to "A Freeman" I–III (Tench Coxe), *Pennsylvania Gazette*, 23, 30 January, and 6 February (CC:472, 488, 505).

2. On 13 February the *Carlisle Gazette* reprinted "A Freeman" I. The *Gazette* did not reprint the second and third "Freeman" essays.

3. "Vested" in the *Independent Gazetteer* printing of 18 April.

4. "A Farmer" defends the minority of the Pennsylvania Convention to whom "A Freeman" had directed his essays. For the "Dissent of the Minority of the Pennsylvania Convention," see CC:353.

5. The first installment of "A Farmer" in the *Independent Gazetteer*, 18 April, ends at this point. The *Gazetteer* printed the remainder of the essay on 22 April.

6. For the amendments proposed by the Massachusetts Convention, see CC:508.

7. For the adjournment of the New Hampshire Convention, see CC:554.

## 689. A Plebeian: An Address to the People of the State of New York, 17 April

On 17 April Thomas Greenleaf of the *New York Journal* announced that a pamphlet—entitled *An Address to the People of the State of New-York: Shewing the Necessity of Making Amendments to the Constitution, Proposed for the United States, Previous to Its Adoption* (Evans 21465)—was "Published this Day." It was available for sale at Greenleaf's New York City printing office and at the shop of Robert Hodge, a New York City printer and bookseller. The advertisement also indicated that the twenty-six-page pamphlet, by "A Plebeian," contained a postscript criticizing *An Address to the People of the State of New-York*, a pamphlet written by "A Citizen of New-York" (John Jay) which had been offered for sale two days earlier (CC:683).

Greenleaf ran the advertisement almost continuously until 26 July in his daily *New York Journal*. Between 11 June and 2 July, the pamphlet was also advertised for the price of two shillings in each issue of the weekly North Carolina *Wilmington Centinel*. In 1789 advertisements appeared in the *New York Journal* on 12 March, and in the Worcester *American Herald* on 19, 26 March, and 2, 9 April.

The entire pamphlet was reprinted in four installments in the Philadelphia *Independent Gazetteer* on 23, 24, 27, and 28 May. The editor of the Lansingburgh *Federal Herald* intended to reprint the entire pamphlet, but, after publishing thirteen pages (or about half of the pamphlet) in three installments on 28 April, and 5, 12 May, he discontinued the publication even though he indicated that it was "To be continued."

Paul Leicester Ford identified "A Plebeian" as New York Antifederalist leader Melancton Smith, but he provided no supporting evidence (*Pamphlets*, 89). Robin Brooks, Smith's biographer, was unable to verify Smith's authorship, but he indicated that the pamphlet's "forceful and unadorned style as well as the point of view closely resembled Smith's rhetoric expressed in speeches at the Poughkeepsie Convention." Brooks, however, warned his readers that the pseudonym "Plebeian" had been used before the Revolutionary War by John Lamb, another New York Antifederalist leader ("Melancton Smith: New York Anti-Federalist, 1744–1798" [Ph.D. diss., University of Rochester, 1964], 159, 173n, 181, 226n).

"A Plebeian" was commented upon in at least three articles. In the April issue of the New York *American Magazine*, a reviewer (probably editor Noah

Webster) challenged "A Plebeian's" assertions that Antifederalists were winning the propaganda war, that Federalists supported amendments to the Constitution, that Federalists believed that the Constitution endangered the rights
and liberties of the people, and that America was serene and prosperous. "A
Pennsylvanian" (Tench Coxe) also contradicted "A Plebeian" by painting a
dismal picture of public and private finances. He also chided him for using
that pseudonym "in a free and equal government, which rejects every preposterous distinction of blood or titles" (*Pennsylvania Gazette*, 11 June,
CC:780).

"Rusticus" defended "A Plebeian." He applauded the attack upon some
members of the Constitutional Convention and advised people not to vote
for the Constitution merely because great names were associated with its
framing. Since the Constitution had so many flaws, asserted "Rusticus," the
unanimity of the Constitutional Convention was not a virtue (*New York Journal*,
23 May).

FRIENDS AND FELLOW CITIZENS, The advocates for the proposed new constitution, having been beaten off the field of argument,
on its merits, have now taken new ground. They admit it is liable to
well-founded objections—that a number of its articles ought to be
amended; that if alterations do not take place, a door will be left open
for an undue administration, and encroachments on the liberties of
the people; and many of them go so far as to say, if it should continue
for any considerable period, in its present form, it will lead to a subversion of our equal republican forms of government.—But still, although they admit this, they urge that it ought to be adopted, and
that we should confide in procuring the necessary alterations after we
have received it. Most of the leading characters, who advocate its reception, now profess their readiness to concur with those who oppose
it, in bringing about the most material amendments contended for,
provided they will first agree to accept the proffered system as it is.
These concessions afford strong evidence, that the opposers of the
constitution have reason on their side, and that they have not been
influenced, in the part they have taken, by the mean and unworthy
motives of selfish and private interests with which they have been il-
liberally charged.—As the favourers of the constitution, seem, if their
professions are sincere, to be in a situation similar to that of Agrippa,
when he cried out upon Paul's preaching—"almost thou persuadest
me to be a christian," I cannot help indulging myself in expressing
the same wish which St. Paul uttered on that occasion, "Would to God
you were not only almost, but altogether such an one as I am."[1] But
alas, as we hear no more of Agrippa's christianity after this interview
with Paul, so it is much to be feared, that we shall hear nothing of
amendments from most of the warm advocates for adopting the new

government, after it gets into operation. When the government is once organized, and all the offices under it filled, the inducements which our great men will have to support it, will be much stronger than they are now to urge its reception. Many of them will then hold places of great honour and emolument, and others will be candidates for such places. It is much harder to relinquish honours or emoluments, which we have in possession, than to abandon the pursuit of them, while the attainment is held in a state of uncertainty.—The amendments contended for as necessary to be made, are of such a nature, as will tend to limit and abridge a number of the powers of the government. And is it probable, that those who enjoy these powers will be so likely to surrender them after they have them in possession, as to consent to have them restricted in the act of granting them? Common sense says— they will not.

When we consider the nature and operation of government, the idea of receiving a form radically defective, under the notion of making the necessary amendments, is evidently absurd.

Government is a compact entered into by mankind, in a state of society, for the promotion of their happiness. In forming this compact, common sense dictates, that no articles should be admitted that tend to defeat the end of its institution. If any such are proposed, they should be rejected. When the compact is once formed and put into operation, it is too late for individuals to object. The deed is executed— the conveyance is made—and the power of reassuming the right is gone, without the consent of the parties.—Besides, when a government is once in operation, it acquires strength by habit, and stability by exercise. If it is tolerably mild in its administration, the people sit down easy under it, be its principles and forms ever so repugnant to the maxims of liberty.—It steals, by insensible degrees, one right from the people after another, until it rivets its powers so as to put it beyond the ability of the community to restrict or limit it. The history of the world furnishes many instances of a people's increasing the powers of their rulers by persuasion, but I believe it would be difficult to produce one in which the rulers have been persuaded to relinquish their powers to the people. Wherever this has taken place, it has always been the effect of compulsion. These observations are so well-founded, that they are become a kind of axioms in politics; and the inference to be drawn from them is equally evident, which is this,—that, in forming a government, care should be taken not to confer powers which it will be necessary to take back; but if you err at all, let it be on the contrary side, because it is much easier, as well as safer, to enlarge the powers of your rulers, if they should prove not sufficiently extensive, than it is to abridge them if they should be too great.

It is agreed, the plan is defective—that some of the powers granted, are dangerous—others not well defined—and amendments are necessary. Why then not amend it? why not remove the cause of danger, and, if possible, even the apprehension of it? The instrument is yet in the hands of the people; it is not signed, sealed, and delivered, and they have power to give it any form they please.

But it is contended, adopt it first, and then amend it. I ask, why not amend, and then adopt it? Most certainly the latter mode of proceeding is more consistent with our ideas of prudence in the ordinary concerns of life. If men were about entering into a contract respecting their private concerns, it would be highly absurd in them to sign and seal an instrument containing stipulations which are contrary to their interests and wishes, under the expectation, that the parties, after its execution, would agree to make alterations agreeable to their desires.— They would insist upon the exceptionable clauses being altered before they would ratify the contract. And is a compact for the government of ourselves and our posterity of less moment than contracts between individuals? certainly not. But to this reasoning, which at first view would appear to admit of no reply, a variety of objections are made, and a number of reasons urged for adopting the system, and afterwards proposing amendments.—Such as have come under my observation, I shall state, and remark upon.

1. It is insisted, that the present situation of our country is such, as not to admit of a delay in forming a new government, or of time sufficient to deliberate and agree upon the amendments which are proper, without involving ourselves in a state of anarchy and confusion.

On this head, all the powers of rhetoric, and arts of description, are employed to paint the condition of this country, in the most hideous and frightful colours. We are told, that agriculture is without encouragement; trade is languishing; private faith and credit are disregarded, and public credit is prostrate; that the laws and magistrates are contemned and set at nought; that a spirit of licentiousness is rampant, and ready to break over every bound set to it by the government; that private embarrassments and distresses invade the house of every man of middling property, and insecurity threatens every man in affluent circumstances; in short, that we are in a state of the most grievous calamity at home, and that we are contemptible abroad, the scorn of foreign nations, and the ridicule of the world. From this high-wrought picture, one would suppose, that we were in a condition the most deplorable of any people upon earth. But suffer me, my countrymen, to call your attention to a serious and sober estimate of the situation in which you are placed, while I trace the embarrassments under which you labour, to their true sources. What is your condition? Does not every man sit under his own vine and under his own fig-tree, having none to make him afraid?[2] Does not every one follow his calling without impediments and receive the reward of his well-earned industry? The farmer cultivates his land, and reaps the fruit which the bounty of heaven bestows on his honest toil. The mechanic is exercised in his art, and receives the reward of his labour. The merchant drives his commerce, and none can deprive him of the gain he honestly acquires; all classes and callings of men amongst us are protected in their various pursuits, and secured by the laws in the possession and enjoyment of the property obtained in those pursuits. The laws are as well executed as they ever were, in this or any other country. Neither the hand of private violence, nor the more to be dreaded hand of legal oppression, are reached out to distress us.

It is true, many individuals labour under embarrassments, but these are to be imputed to the unavoidable circumstances of things, rather than to any defect in our governments. We have just emerged from a long and expensive war. During its existence few people were in a situation to encrease their fortunes, but many to diminish them. Debts contracted before the war were left unpaid while it existed, and these were left a burden too heavy to be borne at the commencement of peace. Add to these, that when the war was over, too many of us, instead of reassuming our old habits of frugality and industry, by which alone every country must be placed in a prosperous condition, took up the profuse use of foreign commodities. The country was deluged with articles imported from abroad, and the cash of the country has been sent out to pay for them, and still left us labouring under the weight of a huge debt to persons abroad. These are the true sources to which we are to trace all the private difficulties of individuals: But will a new government relieve you from these? The advocates for it have not yet told you how it will do it—And I will venture to pronounce, that there is but one way in which it can be effected, and that is by industry and œconomy; limit your expences within your earnings; sell more than you buy, and every thing will be well on this score. Your present condition is such as is common to take place after the con-clusion of a war. Those who can remember our situation after the termination of the war preceding the last, will recollect that our con-dition was similar to the present, but time and industry soon recovered us from it. Money was scarce, the produce of the country much lower than it has been since the peace, and many individuals were extremely embarrassed with debts; and this happened, although we did not experience the ravages, desolations, and loss of property, that were suffered during the late war.

With regard to our public and national concerns, what is there in our condition that threatens us with any immediate danger? We are at peace with all the world; no nation menaces us with war; Nor are we called upon by any cause of sufficient importance to attack any nation. The state governments answer the purposes of preserving the peace, and providing for present exigencies. Our condition as a nation is in no respect worse than it has been for several years past. Our public debt has been lessened in various ways, and the western territory, which has always been relied upon as a productive fund to discharge the national debt, has at length been brought to market, and a considerable part actually applied to its reduction.[3] I mention these things to shew, that there is nothing special, in our present situation, as it respects our national affairs, that should induce us to accept the proffered system, without taking sufficient time to consider and amend it. I do not mean by this, to insinuate, that our government does not stand in need of a reform. It is admitted by all parties, that alterations are necessary in our federal constitution, but the circumstances of our case do by no means oblige us to precipitate this business, or require that we should adopt a system materially defective. We may safely take time to deliberate and amend, without in the mean time hazarding a condition, in any considerable degree, worse than the present.

But it is said, that if we postpone the ratification of this system until the necessary amendments are first incorporated, the consequence will be a civil war among the states. On this head weak minds are alarmed with being told, that the militia of Connecticut and Massachusetts on the one side, and of New-Jersey and Pennsylvania on the other, will attack us with hostile fury; and either destroy us from off the face of the earth, or at best divide us between the two states adjoining us on either side. The apprehension of danger is one of the most powerful incentives to human action, and is therefore generally excited on political questions: But still, a prudent man, though he foreseeth the evil and avoideth it, yet he will not be terrified by imaginary dangers. We ought therefore to enquire what ground there is to fear such an event?—There can be no reason to apprehend, that the other states will make war with us for not receiving the constitution proposed, until it is amended, but from one of the following causes: either that they will have just cause to do it, or that they have a disposition to do it. We will examine each of these:—That they will have no just cause to quarrel with us for not acceding, is evident, because we are under no obligation to do it, arising from any existing compact or previous stipulation. The confederation is the only compact now existing between the states: By the terms of it, it cannot be changed without the consent of every one of the parties to it.[4] Nothing therefore can be more unreasonable than for part of the states to claim of the others, as matter of right, an accession to a system to which they have material objections. No war can therefore arise from this principle, but on the contrary, it is to be presumed, it will operate strongly the opposite way.—The states will reason on the subject in the following manner: On this momentous question, every state has an indubitable right to judge for itself: This is secured to it by solemn compact, and if any of our sister states disagree with us upon the question, we ought to attend to their objections, and accommodate ourselves as far as possible to the amendments they propose.

As to the inclination of the states to make war with us, for declining to accede, until it is amended, this is highly improbable, not only because such a procedure would be most unjust and unreasonable in itself, but for various other reasons.

The idea of a civil war amongst the states is abhorrent to the principles and feelings of almost every man of every rank in the union. It is so obvious to every one of the least reflection, that in such an event we should hazard the loss of all things, without the hope of gaining any thing, that the man who should entertain a thought of this kind, would be justly deemed more fit to be shut up in Bedlam,[5] than to be reasoned with. But the idea of one or more states attacking another, for insisting upon alterations in this system, before it is adopted, is more extravagant still; it is contradicting every principle of liberty which has been entertained by the states, violating the most solemn compact, and taking from the state the right of deliberation. Indeed to suppose, that a people, entertaining such refined ideas of the rights of human nature as to be induced to wage war with the most powerful nation on earth, upon a speculative point, and from the mere apprehension of danger only, should so far be lost to their own feelings and principles, as to deny to their brethren, who were associated with them in the arduous conflict, the right of free deliberation on a question of the first importance to their political happiness and safety, is equally an insult to the character of the people of America, and to common sense, and could only be suggested by a vicious heart and a corrupt mind.

The idea of being attacked by the other states, will appear visionary and chimerical, if we consider that tho' several of them have adopted the new constitution, yet the opposition to it has been numerous and formidable. The eastern states from whom we are told we have most to fear, should a civil war be blown up, would have full employ to keep in awe those who are opposed to it in their own governments. Massachusetts, after a long and dubious contest in their convention, has adopted it by an inconsiderable majority, and in the very act has marked it with a stigma in its present form.[6] No man of candour, judging from their public proceedings, will undertake to say, on which side the majority of the people are. Connecticut, it is true, have acceded to it, by a large majority of their convention; but it is a fact well known, that a large proportion of the yeomanry of the country are against it:—And it is equally true, that a considerable part of those who voted for it in the convention, wish to see it altered. In both these states the body of the common people, who always do the fighting of a country, would be more likely to fight against than for it: Can it then be presumed, that a country, divided among themselves, upon a question where even the advocates for it, admit the system they contend for needs amendments, would make war upon a sister state, who only insist that that should be done before they receive it, which it is granted ought to be done after, and where it is confessed no obligation lies upon them by compact to do it. Can it, I say, be imagined, that in such a case they would make war on a sister state? The idea is preposterous and chimerical.

It is farther urged, we must adopt this plan because we have no chance of getting a better. This idea is inconsistent with the principles of those who advance it. They say, it must be altered, but it should be left until after it is put in operation. But if this objection is valid, the proposal of altering, after it is received, is mere delusion.

It is granted, that amendments ought to be made; that the exceptions taken to the constitution, are grounded on just principles, but it is still insisted, that alterations are not to be attempted until after it is received: But why not? Because it is said, there is no probability of agreeing in amendments previous to the adoption, but they may be easily made after it. I wish to be informed what there is in our situation or circumstances that renders it more probable that we shall agree in amendments better after, than before submitting to it? No good reason has as yet been given; it is evident none can be given: On the contrary, there are several considerations which induce a belief, that alterations may be obtained with more ease before, than after its reception, and if so, every one must agree, it is much the safest. The importance of preserving an union, and of establishing a government equal to the purpose of maintaining that union, is a sentiment deeply impressed on the mind of every citizen of America. It is now no longer doubted, that the confederation, in its present form, is inadequate to that end: Some reform in our government must take place. In this, all parties agree: It is therefore to be presumed, that this object will be pursued with ardour and perseverance, until it is attained by all parties. But when a government is adopted that promises to effect this, we are to expect the ardour of many, yea, of most people, will be abated;—their exertions will cease, or be languid, and they will sit down easy, although they may see, that the constitution which provides for this, does not sufficiently guard the rights of the people, or secure them against the encroachments of their rulers. The great end they had in view, the security of the union, they will consider effected, and this will divert their attention from that which is equally interesting, safety to their liberties. Besides, the human mind cannot continue intensely engaged for any great length of time upon one object. As after a storm, a calm generally succeeds, so after the minds of a people have been ardently employed upon a subject, especially upon that of government, we commonly find that they become cool and inattentive: Add to this, that those in the community who urge the adoption of this system, because they hope by it to be raised above the common level of their fellow citizens; because they expect to be among the number of the few who will be benefitted by it, will more easily be induced to consent to the amendments before it is received than afterwards. Before its reception, they will be inclined to be pliant and condescending; if they cannot obtain all they wish, they will consent to take less. They will yield part to obtain the rest. But when the plan is once agreed to, they will be tenacious of every power, they will strenuously contend to retain all they have got; this is natural to human nature, and it is consonant to the experience of mankind. For history affords us no examples of persons once possessed of power, resigning it willingly.

The reasonings made use of to persuade us, that no alterations can be agreed upon previous to the adoption of the system, are as curious as they are futile. It is alledged, that there was great diversity of sentiments in forming the proposed constitution; that it was the effect of mutual concessions and a spirit of accommodation, and from hence it is inferred, that farther changes cannot be hoped for. I should suppose that the contrary inference was the fair one. If the convention, who framed this plan, were possessed of such a spirit of moderation and condescension, as to be induced to yield to each other certain points, and to accommodate themselves to each other's opinions, and even prejudices, there is reason to expect, that this same spirit will continue and prevail in a future convention, and produce an union of sentiments on the points objected to. There is the more reason to hope for this, because the subject has received a full discussion, and the minds of the people much better known than they were when the convention sat. Previous to the meeting of the convention, the subject of a new form of government had been little thought of, and scarcely written upon at all. It is true, it was the general opinion, that some alterations were requisite in the federal system. This subject had been contemplated by almost every thinking man in the union. It had been the subject of many well-written essays, and was the anxious wish of every true friend to America. But it never was in the contemplation of one in a thousand of those who had reflected on the matter, to have an entire change in the nature of our federal government—to alter it from a confederation of states, to that of one entire government, which will swallow up that of the individual states. I will venture to say, that the idea of a government similar to the one proposed, never entered the mind of the legislatures who appointed the convention, and of but very few of the members who composed it, until they had assembled and heard it proposed in that body: much less had the people any conception of such a plan until after it was promulgated. While it was agitated, the debates of the convention were kept an impenetrable secret, and no opportunity was given for well informed men to offer their sentiments upon the subject. The system was therefore never publicly discussed, nor indeed could be, because it was not known to the people until after it was proposed. Since that, it has been the object of universal attention—it has been thought of by every reflecting man—been discussed in a public and private manner, in conversation and in print; its defects have been pointed out, and every objection to it stated; able advocates have written in its favour, and able opponents have written against it. And what is the result? It cannot be denied but that the general opinion is, that it contains material errors, and requires important amendments. This then being the general sentiment, both of the friends and foes of the system, can it be doubted, that another convention would concur in such amendments as would quiet the fears of the opposers, and effect a great degree of union on the subject?—An event most devoutly to be wished. But it is farther said, that there can be no prospect of procuring alterations before it is acceded to, because those who oppose it do not agree among themselves with respect to the amendments that are necessary. To this I reply, that this may be urged against attempting alterations after it is received, with as much force as before; and therefore, if it concludes any thing, it is, that we must receive any system of government proposed to us, because those who object to it do not entirely concur in their objections. But the assertion is not true to any considerable extent. There is a remarkable uniformity in the objections made to the constitution, on the most important points. It is also worthy of notice, that very few of the matters found fault with in it, are of a local nature, or such as affect any particular state; on the contrary, they are such as concern the principles of general liberty, in which the people of New-Hampshire, New-York, and Georgia are equally interested.

It would be easy to shew, that in the leading and most important objections that have been made to the plan, there has been, and is an entire concurrence of opinion among writers, and in public bodies throughout the United States.

I have not time fully to illustrate this by a minute narration of particulars; but to prove that this is the case, I shall adduce a number of important instances.

It has been objected to the new system, that it is calculated to, and will effect such a consolidation of the States, as to supplant and overturn the state governments. In this the minority of Pennsylvania, the opposition in Massachusetts, and all the writers of any ability or note in Philadelphia, New-York, and Boston concur. It may be added, that this appears to have been the opinion of the Massachusetts convention, and gave rise to that article in the amendments proposed, which confines the general government to the exercise only of powers expressly given.[7]

It has been said, that the representation in the general legislature is too small to secure liberty, or to answer the intention of representation. In this there is an union of sentiments in the opposers.

The constitution has been opposed, because it gives to the legislature an unlimited power of taxation, both with respect to direct and indirect taxes, a right to lay and collect taxes, duties, imposts, and excises of every kind and description, and to any amount. In this, there has been as general a concurrence of opinion as in the former.

The opposers to the constitution have said that it is dangerous, because the judicial power may extend to many cases which ought to be reserved to the decision of the State courts, and because the right of trial by jury, is not secured in the judicial courts of the general government, in civil cases. All the opposers are agreed in this objection.

The power of the general legislature to alter and regulate the time, place, and manner of holding elections, has been stated as an argument against the adoption of the system. It has been urged, that this power will place in the hands of the general government, the authority, whenever they shall be disposed, and a favorable opportunity offers, to deprive the body of the people, in effect, of all share in the government. The opposers to the constitution universally agree in this objection, and of such force is it, that most of its ardent advocates admit its validity, and those who have made attempts to vindicate it, have been reduced to the necessity of using the most trifling arguments to justify it.

The mixture of legislative, judicial, and executive powers in the senate; the little degree of responsibility under which the great officers of government will be held; and the liberty granted by the system to establish and maintain a standing army, without any limitation or restriction, are also objected to the constitution; and in these, there is a great degree of unanimity of sentiment in the opposers.

From these remarks it appears, that the opponents to the system accord in the great and material points on which they wish amendments. For the truth of the assertion, I appeal to the protest of the minority of the convention of Pennsylvania, to all the publications against the constitution, and to the debates of the convention of Massachusetts.[8] As a higher authority than these, I appeal to the amendments proposed by the Massachusetts [Convention]; these are to be considered as the sense of that body upon the defects of the system. And it is a fact, which I will venture to assert, that a large majority of that convention were of opinion, that a number of additional alterations ought to be made. Upon reading the articles which they propose as amendments, it will appear, that they object to indefinite powers in the legislature—to the power of laying direct taxes—to the authority of regulating elections—to the extent of the judicial powers, both as it respects the inferior courts and the appellate jurisdiction—to the smallness of the representation, &c—It is admitted, that some writers have advanced objections that others have not noticed—that exceptions have been taken by some, that have not been insisted upon by others, and it is probable, that some of the opponents may approve what others will reject. But still these differences are on matters of small importance, and of such a nature as the persons who hold different opinions will not be tenacious of. Perfect uniformity of sentiment on so great a political subject is not to be expected. Every sensible man is impressed with this idea, and is therefore prepared to make concessions and accommodate on matters of small importance. It is sufficient that we agree in the great leading principles, which relate to the preservation of public liberty and private security. And on these I will venture to affirm we are as well agreed, as any people ever were on a question of this nature. I dare pronounce, that were the principal advocates for the proposed plan to write comments upon it, they would differ more in the sense they would give the constitution, than those

who oppose it do, in the amendments they would wish. I am justified
in this opinion, by the sentiments advanced by the different writers in
favour of the constitution.

It is farther insisted, that six states have already adopted the constitution; that probably nine will agree to it: in which case it will be
put in operation. That it is unreasonable to expect that those states
which have acceded to it, will reconsider the subject in compliance
with the wishes of a minority.

To perceive the force of this objection, it is proper to review the
conduct and circumstances of the states which have acceded to it. It
cannot be controverted, that Connecticut and New-Jersey were very
much influenced in their determinations on the question, by local considerations. The duty of impost laid by this state, has been a subject
of complaint by those states. The new constitution transfers the power
of imposing these duties from the state to the general government,
and carries the proceeds to the use of the union, instead of that of
those state[s]. This is a very popular matter with the people of those
states, and at the same time, is not advanced by the sensible opposers
to the system in this state as an objection to it.—To excite in the minds
of the people of these states an attachment to the new system, the
amount of the revenue arising from our impost has been magnified
to a much larger sum than it produces; it has been stated to amount
to from sixty to eighty thousand pounds lawful money: and a gentleman
of high eminence in Connecticut has lent the authority of his name
to support it. It has been said, that Connecticut pays a third of this
sum annually for impost,[9] and Jersey nearly as much. It has farther
been asserted, that the avails of the impost were applied to the separate
use of the state of New-York. By these assertions the people have been
grossly imposed upon, for neither of them are true.

The amount of the revenue from impost for two years past, has not
exceeded fifty thousand pounds currency, per annum, and a draw-back
of duties is allowed by law, upon all goods exported to either of the
beforementioned states, in casks or packages unbroken.[10]

The whole of this sum, and more, has been paid into the federal
treasury for the support of the government of the union.[11] All the
states therefore have actually derived equal benefit with the state of
New-York, from the impost. It may be said, I know, that this state has
obtained credit for the amount, upon the requisitions of Congress: It
is admitted; but still it is a fact, that other states, and especially those
who complain, have paid no part of the monies required of them, and
have scarcely made an effort to do it. The fact therefore is, that they
have received as much advantage from the impost of this state, as we

ourselves have. The proposed constitution directs to no mode, in which the deficiencies of states on former requisitions, are to be collected, but seems to hold out the idea, that we are to start anew, and all past payments be forgotten. It is natural to expect, that selfish motives will have too powerful an influence on mens minds, and that too often, they will shut the eyes of a people to their best and true interest. The people of those states have been persuaded to believe, that this new constitution will relieve them from the burden of taxes, by providing for all the exigencies of the union, by duties which can be raised only in the neighbouring states. When they come to be convinced, that this promise is a mere delusion, as they assuredly will, by finding the continental tax-gatherer knocking at their doors, if not before, they will be among the first to urge amendments, and perhaps the most violent to obtain them. But notwithstanding the local prejudices which operate upon the people of these states, a considerable part of them wish for amendments. It is not to be doubted, that a considerable majority of the people of Connecticut wish for them, and many in Jersey have the same desires, and their numbers are increasing. It cannot be disputed, that amendments would accord with the sentiments of a great majority in Massachusetts, or that they would be agreeable to the greater part of the people of Pennsylvania: There is no reason to doubt but that they would be agreeable to Delaware and Georgia—If then, the states who have already ratified the constitution, are desirous to have alterations made in it, what reason can be assigned why they should not cordially meet with overtures for that purpose from any state, and concur in appointing a convention to effect it? Mankind are easily induced to fall upon measures to obtain an object agreeable to them. In this case, the states would not only be moved by this universal principle of human nature, but by the strong and powerful motive of uniting all the states under a form of government agreeable to them.

I shall now dismiss the consideration of objections made to attempting alterations previous to the adoption of the plan, but before I close, I beg your indulgence, while I make some remarks on the splendid advantages, which the advocates for this system say are to be derived from it.—Hope and fear are two of the most active principles of our nature: We have considered how the latter is addressed on this occasion, and with how little reason: It will appear that the promises it makes, are as little to be relied upon, as its threatenings. We are amused with the fair prospects that are to open, when this government is put into operation—Agriculture is to flourish, and our fields to yield an hundred fold—Commerce is to expand her wings, and bear our productions to all the ports in the world—Money is to pour into our country through every channel—Arts and manufactures are to rear their heads, and every mec[h]anic find full employ—Those who are in debt, are to find easy means to procure money to pay them—Public burdens and taxes are to be lightened, and yet all our public debts are soon to be discharged.—With such vain and delusive hopes are the minds of many honest and well meaning people fed, and by these means are they led inconsiderately to contend for a government, which is made to promise what it cannot perform; while their minds are diverted from contemplating its true nature, or considering whether it will not endanger their liberties, and work oppression.

Far be it from me to object to granting the general government the power of regulating trade, and of laying imposts and duties for that purpose, as well as for raising a revenue: But it is as far from me to flatter people with hopes of benefits to be derived from such a change in our government, which can never be realized. Some advantages may accrue from vesting in one general government, the right to regulate commerce, but it is a vain delusion to expect any thing like what is promised. The truth is, this country buys more than it sells: It imports more than it exports. There are too many merchants in proportion to the farmers and manufacturers. Until these defects are remedied, no government can relieve us. Common sense dictates, that if a man buys more than he sells, he will remain in debt; the same is true of a country.—And as long as this country imports more goods than she exports—the overplus must be paid for in money or not paid at all. These few remarks may convince us, that the radical remedy for the scarcity of cash is frugality and industry. Earn much and spend little, and you will be enabled to pay your debts, and have money in your pockets; and if you do not follow this advice, no government that can be framed, will relieve you.

As to the idea of being relieved from taxes by this government, it is an affront to common sense, to advance it. There is no complaint made against the present confederation more justly founded than this, that it is incompetent to provide the means to discharge our national debt, and to support the national government. Its inefficacy to these purposes, which was early seen and felt, was the first thing that suggested the necessity of changing the government; other things, it is true, were afterwards found to require alterations; but this was the most important, and accordingly we find, that while in some other things the powers of this government seem to be in some measure limitted, on the subject of raising money, no bounds are set to it. It is authorised to raise money to any amount, and in any way it pleases. If then, the capital embarrassment in our present government arises from the want of money, and this constitution effectually authorises the raising of it, how are the taxes to be lessened by it? Certainly money can only be raised by taxes of some kind or other; it must be got either by additional impositions on trade, by excise, or by direct taxes, or what is more probable, by all together. In either way, it amounts to the same thing, and the position is clear, that as the necessities of the nation require more money than is now raised, the taxes must be enhanced. This you ought to know, and prepare yourselves to submit to.—Besides, how is it possible that the taxes can be decreased when the expences of your government will be greatly advanced? It does not require any great skill in politics, or ability at calculation to shew, that the new government will cost more money to administer it, than the present. I shall not descend to an estimate of the cost of a federal town, the salaries of the president, vice-president, judges, and other great officers of state, nor calculate the amount of the pay the legislature will vote themselves, or the salaries that will be paid the innumerable revenue and subordinate officers. The bare mention of these things is sufficient to convince you, that the new government will be vastly more expensive than the old: And how is the money to answer these purposes to be obtained? It is obvious, it must be taken out of the pockets of the people, by taxes, in some mode or other.

Having remarked upon the arguments which have been advanced, to induce you to accede to this government, without amendments, and I trust refuted them, suffer me to close with an address dedicated by the affection of a brother, and the honest zeal of a lover of his country.

*Friends, countrymen, and fellow citizens,*

The present is the most important crisis at which you ever have arrived. You have before you a question big with consequences, unutterably important to yourselves, to your children, to generations yet unborn, to the cause of liberty and of mankind; every motive of religion and virtue, of private happiness and public good, of honour and dignity, should urge you to consider cooly and determine wisely.

Almost all the governments that have arisen among mankind, have sprung from force and violence. The records of history inform us of none that have been the result of cool and dispassionate reason and reflection: It is reserved for this favoured country to exhibit to mankind the first example.—This opportunity is now given us, and we are to exercise our rights in the choice of persons to represent us in convention, to deliberate and determine upon the constitution proposed: It will be to our everlasting disgrace to be indifferent on such a subject, for it is impossible, we can contemplate any thing that relates to the affairs of this life of half the importance.

You have heard that both sides on this great question, agree, that there are in it great defects; yet the one side tell you, choose such men as will adopt it, and then amend it—while the other say, amend previous to its adoption.—I have stated to you my reasons for the latter, and I think they are unanswerable.—Consider you the common people, the yeomanry of the country, for to such I principally address myself, you are to be the principal losers, if the constitution should prove oppressive: When a tyranny is established, there are always masters as well as slaves; the great and the well-born are generally the former, and the middling class the latter—Attempts have been made, and will be repeated, to alarm you with the fear of consequences; but reflect, there are consequences on both sides, and none can be apprehended more dreadful, than entailing on ourselves and posterity a government which will raise a few to the height of human greatness and wealth, while it will depress the many to the extreme of poverty and wretchedness. Consequences are under the controul of that all-wise and all-powerful being, whose providence directs the affairs of men: Our part is to act right, and we may then have confidence that the consequences will be favourable. The path in which you should walk is plain and open before you; be united as one man, and direct your choice to such men as have been uniform in their opposition to the proposed system in its present form, or without proper alterations: In men of this description you have reason to place confidence, while on the other hand, you have just cause to distrust those who urge the adoption of a bad constitution, under the delusive expectation of making amendments after it is acceded to. Your jealousy of such characters should be the more excited, when you consider that the advocates for the constitution have shifted their ground. When men are uniform in their opinions, it affords evidence that they are sincere: When they are shifting, it gives reason to believe, they do not change from conviction. It must be recollected, that when this plan was first announced to the public, its supporters cried it up as the most perfect production of human wisdom: It was represented either as having no defects, or if it had, they were so trifling and inconsiderable, that they served only, as the shades in a fine picture, to set off the piece to the greater advantage. One gentleman in Philadelphia went so far, in the ardour of his enthusiasm in its favour, as to pronounce, that the men who formed it were as really under the guidance of Divine Revelation, as was Moses, the Jewish lawgiver.[12] Their language is now changed; the question has been discussed; the objections to the plan ably stated, and they are admitted to be unanswerable. The same men who held it almost perfect, now admit it is very imperfect; that it is necessary it should be amended. The only question between us, is simply this: Shall we accede to a bad constitution, under the uncertain prospect of getting it amended, after we have received it, or shall we amend it before we adopt it? Common sense will point out which is the most rational, which is the most secure line of conduct. May heaven inspire you with wisdom, union, moderation and firmness, and give you hearts to make a proper estimate of your invaluable privileges, and preserve them to you, to be transmitted to your posterity unimpaired, and may they be maintained in this our country, while Sun and Moon endure.

POSTSCRIPT.

Since the foregoing pages have been put to the press, a pamphlet has appeared, entitled, "An address to the people of the state of New-York, on the subject of the new constitution, &c."[13] Upon a cursory examination of this performance (for I have not had leisure to give it more than a cursory examination) it appears to contain little more than declamation and observations that have been often repeated by the advocates of the new constitution.

An attentive reader will readily perceive, that almost every thing deserving the name of an argument in this publication, has received consideration, and, I trust, a satisfactory answer in the preceding remarks, so far as they apply to prove the necessity of an immediate adoption of the plan, without amendments.

I shall therefore only beg the patience of my readers, while I make a few very brief remarks on this piece.

The author introduces his observations with a short history of the revolution, and of the establishment of the present existing federal government. He draws a frightful picture of our condition under the present confederation. The whole of what he says on that head, stripped of its artificial colouring, amounts to this, that the existing system is rather recommendatory than coercive, or that Congress have not, in most cases, the power of enforcing their own resolves. This he calls "a new and wonderful system." However "wonderful" it may seem, it certainly is not "new." For most of the *federal governments* that have been in the world, have been of the same nature.—The United Netherlands are governed on the same plan. There are other governments also now existing, which are in a similar condition with our's, with regard to several particulars, on account of which this author denominates it "new and wonderful."—The king of Great-Britain "may make war, but has not power to raise money to carry it on." He ["]may borrow money, but is without the means of repayment,"

&c. For these he is dependent on his parliament. But it is needless to add on this head, because it is admitted that the powers of the general government ought to be increased in several of the particulars this author instances. But these things are mentioned to shew, that the outcry made against the confederation, as being a system new, unheard of, and absurd, is really without foundation.

The author proceeds to depicture our present condition in the high-wrought strains common to his party.—I shall add nothing to what I have said on this subject in the former part of this pamphlet, but will only observe, that his imputing our being kept out of the possession of the western posts, and our want of peace with the Algerines, to the defects in our present government, is much easier said than proved. The British keep possession of these posts, because it subserves their interest, and probably will do so, until they perceive that we have gathered strength and resources sufficient to assert our rights with the sword. Let our government be what it will, this cannot be done without time and patience. In the present exhausted situation of the country, it would be madness in us, had we ever so perfect a government, to commence a war for the recovery of these posts.—With regard to the Algerines, there are but two ways in which their ravages can be prevented. The one is, by a successful war against them, and the other is by treaty.[14] The powers of Congress under the confederation are completely competent either to declare war against them, or to form treaties. Money, it is true, is necessary to do both these. This only brings us to this conclusion, that the great defect in our present government, is the want of powers to provide money for the public exigencies. I am willing to grant *reasonable* powers on this score, but not unlimited ones; commercial treaties may be made under the present powers of Congress. I am persuaded we flatter ourselves with advantages which will result from them, that will never be realized. I know of no benefits that we receive from any that have yet been formed.

This author tells us, "it is not his design to investigate the merits of the plan, nor of the objections made to it." It is well he did not undertake it, for if he had, from the specimen he has given, the cause he assumes would not have probably gained much strength by it.

He however takes notice of two or three of the many objections brought against the plan.

"We are told, (says he) among other strange things, that the liberty of the press is left insecure by the proposed constitution, and yet that constitution says neither more nor less about it, than the constitution of the state of New-York does. We are told it deprives us of trial by jury, whereas the fact is, that it expressly secures it in certain cases, and takes it away in none, &c. it is absurd to construe the silence of this, or of our own constitution relative to a great number of our rights into a total extinction of them; silence and a blank paper neither grant nor take away any thing."

It may be a strange thing to this author to hear the people of America anxious for the preservation of their rights, but those who understand the true principles of liberty, are no strangers to their importance. The man who supposes the constitution, in any part of it, is like a blank piece of paper, has very erroneous ideas of it. He may be assured every clause has a meaning, and many of them such extensive meaning, as would take a volume to unfold. The suggestion, that the liberty of the press is secure, because it is not in express words spoken of in the constitution, and that the trial by jury is not taken away, because it is not said in so many words and letters it is so, is puerile and unworthy of a man who pretends to reason. We contend, that by the indefinite powers granted to the general government, the liberty of the press may be restricted by duties, &c. and therefore the constitution ought to have stipulated for its freedom. The trial by jury, in all civil cases is left at the discretion of the general government, except in the supreme court on the appellate jurisdiction, and in this I affirm it is taken away, not by express words, but by fair and legitimate construction and inference; for the supreme court have expressly given them an appellate jurisdiction, in every case to which their powers extend (with two or three exceptions) both as to *law and fact*. The court are the judges; every man in the country, who has served as a juror, knows, that there is a distinction between the court and the jury, and that the lawyers in their pleading, make the distinction. If the court, upon appeals, are to determine both the law and the fact, there is no room for a jury, and the right of trial in this mode is taken away.

The author manifests equal levity in referring to the constitution of this state, to shew that it was useless to stipulate for the liberty of the press, or to insert a bill of rights in the constitution. With regard to the first, it is perhaps an imperfection in our constitution that the liberty of the press is not expressly reserved; but still there was not equal necessity of making this reservation in our State as in the general Constitution, for the common and statute law of England, and the laws of the colony are established, in which this privilege is fully defined and secured. It is true, a bill of rights is not prefixed to our consti-tution, as it is in that of some of the states; but still this author knows, that many essential rights are reserved in the body of it; and I will promise, that every opposer of this system will be satisfied, if the stipulations that they contend for are agreed to, whether they are prefixed, affixed, or inserted in the body of the constitution, and that they will not contend which way this is done, if it be but done. I shall add but one remark, and that is upon the hackneyed argument introduced by the author, drawn from the character and ability of the framers of the new constitution. The favourers of this system are not very prudent in bringing this forward. It provokes to an investigation of characters, which is an invidious task. I do not wish to detract from their merits, but I will venture to affirm, that twenty assemblies of equal number might be collected, equally respectable both in point of ability, integrity, and patriotism. Some of the characters which compose it I revere; others I consider as of small consequence, and a number are suspected of being great public defaulters, and to have been guilty of notorious peculation and fraud, with regard to public property in the hour of our distress. I will not descend to personalities, nor would I have said so much on the subject, had it not been in self defence. Let the constitution stand on its own merits. If it be good, it stands not in need of great men's names to support it. If it be bad, their names ought not to sanction it.

FINIS.

1. Acts 26:28–29.

2. Micah 4:4.

3. On the sale of western lands, see CC:692, notes 7–9.

4. See Article XIII of the Articles of Confederation (CDR, 93).

5. St. Mary of Bethlehem, a hospital for the mentally ill, in London.

6. On 6 February the Massachusetts Convention ratified the Constitution 187 to 168 and appended nine recommendatory amendments to its act of ratification. For the amendments, see CC:508.

7. The first Massachusetts amendment states: "That it be explicitly declared, that all powers, not expressly delegated by the aforesaid constitution, are reserved to the several states, to be by them exercised" (CC:508).

8. The "Dissent of the Minority of the Pennsylvania Convention" was printed in the *Pennsylvania Packet* on 18 December 1787 (CC:353) and the debates of the Massachusetts Convention were first offered for sale in the *Massachusetts Gazette* on 18 March.

9. On 4 January 1788 Oliver Ellsworth, a former delegate to the Constitutional Convention, told the Connecticut Convention: "The state of New-York raises 60 or 80,000 l. a year by impost. Connecticut consumes about one third of the goods upon which this impost is laid; and consequently pays one third of this sum to New-York" (*Connecticut Courant*, 7 January, CC:413. This speech was reprinted in the *New York Journal* on 16 January.).

10. A financial report made to the New York state legislature in January 1788 indicates that New York collected £32,852 in 1786 and £48,104 in 1787 from customs duties (Thomas C. Cochran, *New York in the Confederation: An Economic Study* [Philadelphia, 1932], 188).

11. Quarterly reports in the papers of the Confederation Congress reveal that, between 1 January 1786 and 31 December 1787, New York paid $103,381 (or £41,352)

in specie and almost $400,000 in indents to the Continental loan officer for New York (*ibid.*, 186).

12. "A Plebeian" refers to a speech that Benjamin Rush delivered in the Pennsylvania Convention on 12 December 1787. The *Pennsylvania Herald*, 15 December, reported: "Doctor Rush then proceeded to consider the origin of the proposed system, and fairly deduced it from heaven, asserting that he as much believed the hand of God was employed in this work, as that God had divided the Red Sea to give a passage to the children of Israel, or had fulminated the ten commandments from Mount Sinai!" Rush was widely criticized for this statement (CC:357).

13. See John Jay's pamphlet signed "A Citizen of New-York" which was first offered for sale on 15 April (CC:683).

14. During the 1780s the Barbary pirates preyed upon American commerce in the Mediterranean. Among the groups that protested these depredations was the New York Chamber of Commerce which in 1785 asked the state legislature to give Congress the power to establish a navy to protect American shipping from these pirates. Congress tried to negotiate treaties with the Barbary States, but it was successful only with Morocco (1787). No treaties were made with Algiers, Tunis, or Tripoli.

## 690. Fabius III
## Pennsylvania Mercury, 17 April

About the same time that "Fabius" I was published on 12 April (CC:677), John Vaughan received the manuscript for number III. After perusing it, Vaughan wrote the author John Dickinson that "I have read the 3d with Satisfaction—It has thrown a *new light* on generally admitted principle & made a happy application of them to the present question—The reasoning is perhaps too close to Catch the *Eye of the people*; but is very well adapted to *command the attention* of those who meet for the express purpose of deliberating upon the Subject—& will not fail of a good effect with those who make principle & not passion regulate their Conduct" ("N.W." to "Mr. Thomas," n.d., Dickinson Papers, PPL). On 17 April Vaughan informed Dickinson that numbers II and III were published and that IV was at the printer (see headnote to CC:684). And after the publication of number IV on 19 April, he sent newspaper copies of III and IV to Dickinson, declaring that "they are admired by all who wish to be *injoind to do right* & Strongly approved of by men of weight & reflection" (CC:693, 694).

"Fabius" III was reprinted in the Baltimore *Maryland Gazette*, 9 May; *Virginia Independent Chronicle*, 14 May; *New Hampshire Spy*, 27 May; *New Hampshire Gazette*, 5 June; *Providence Gazette*, 14 June; and the September issue of the Philadelphia *American Museum*.

OBSERVATIONS ON THE CONSTITUTION
proposed by the FEDERAL CONVENTION.

The Writer of this Address hopes, that he will now be thought so disengaged from the objections against the part of the principle assumed, concerning *the power of the people*, that he may be excused for recurring to his assertion, that—⟨*the power of the people* pervading the proposed system, together with *the strong confederation of the states*, will

form an adequate security against *every* danger that has been apprehended.)[1]

It is a mournful, but may be a useful truth, that the liberty of *single
republics* has generally been destroyed by *some of the citizens*, and of
*confederated republics*, by *some of the associated states*.

It is more pleasing, and may be more profitable to reflect, that, their
tranquility and prosperity have commonly been promoted, in proportion to the strength of their government for protecting *the worthy*
against *the licentious*.

As in forming a political society, each individual *contributes* some of
his rights, in order that he may, from *a common stock* of rights, derive
greater benefits, than he could from merely *his own*; so, in forming a
confederation, each political society should *contribute* such a share of
their rights, as will, from *a common stock* of rights, produce the largest
quantity of benefits for them.

But, *what is that share?* and, *how to be managed?* Momentous questions!
Here, flattery is treason; and error, destruction.

Are they unanswerable? No. Our most gracious Creator does not
*condemn* us to sigh for unattainable blessedness: But one thing he *demands*—that we should seek for it in *his* way, and not in *our own*.

*Humility* and *benevolence* must take place of *pride* and *overweening
selfishness*. Reason, then rising above these mists, will discover to us,
that we cannot be true to ourselves, without being true to others—
that to be solitary, is to be wretched—that to love our neighbours as
ourselves, is to love ourselves in the best manner—that is to give, is
to gain—and, that we never consult our own happiness more effectually, than when we most endeavour to correspond with the Divine
designs, by communicating happiness, as much as we can, to our fellow-
creatures. INESTIMABLE TRUTH! sufficient, if they do not barely ask what
it is, to melt tyrants into men, and sooth[e] the inflamed minds of a
multitude into mildness—(sufficient to overflow this earth with unknown felicity)[2]—INESTIMABLE TRUTH! which our Maker, in his providence, enables us, not only to talk and write about, but to adopt in
practice of vast extent, and of instructive example.

Let us now enquire, if there be not some *principle, simple* as the laws
of nature in other instances, from which, as from a source, the many
benefits of society are deduced.

We may with reverence say, that our Creator designed men for
society, because otherwise they could not be happy. They cannot be
happy without freedom; nor free without security; that is, without the
*absence of fear*; nor thus secure, without society. The conclusion is
strictly syllogistic—that men cannot be free without society. Of course,

they cannot be *equally free* without society, which freedom produces the greatest happiness.

As these premises are invincible, we have advanced a considerable way in our enquiry upon this deeply interesting subject. If we can determine, what share of his rights, every individual must contribute to the common stock of rights in forming a society, for obtaining *equal freedom*, we determine at the same time, what share of their rights each political society must contribute to the common stock of rights in forming a confederation, which is only a larger society, for obtaining *equal freedom:* For, if the deposit be not proportioned to the magnitude of the association in the latter case, it will generate the same mischief among the component parts of it, from their inequality, that would result from a defective contribution to association in the former case, among the component parts of it, from their inequality.

*Each* individual then must contribute such a share of his rights, as is necessary for attaining that SECURITY that is essential to freedom; and he is bound to make this contribution by the law of his nature; that is, by the command of his creator; therefore, *he must submit his will, in what concerns all, to the will of the whole society.* What does he lose by this submission? The power of doing injuries to others—the dread of suffering injuries from them—and, the incommodities of mental or bodily weakness.—What does he gain by it? The aid of those associated with him—protection against injuries from them or others— a capacity of enjoying his undelegated rights to the best advantage— a repeal of his fears—and tranquility of mind—or, in other words, that *perfect liberty* better described in the Holy Scriptures, than any where else, in these expressions—"When *every* man shall *sit* under his vine, and under his fig-tree, and NONE SHALL MAKE HIM AFRAID."[3]

The like submission, with a correspondent expansion and accommodation, must be made between states, for obtaining the like benefits in a confederation. Men are the materials of both. As the largest number is but a junction of units,—a confederation is but an assembly of *individuals*. The sanction of that *law* of his nature, upon which the happiness of a man depends in society, must attend him in confederation, or he becomes unhappy; for confederation should promote the happiness of *individuals*, or it does not answer the intended purpose. Herein there is a progression, not a contradiction. As man, he becomes a citizen; as a citizen, he becomes a *federalist.* The generation of one, is not the destruction of the other. He carries into society his naked rights: These thereby improved, he carries into confederation. If that sacred law before mentioned, is not here observed, the confederation would not be *real*, but *pretended*. He would confide, and be deceived.

The dilemma is inevitable. There must either be *one* will, or *several* wills. If but *one* will, *all* the people are concerned; if *several* wills, *few* comparatively are concerned. Surprizing! that this doctrine should be contended for by those, who declare, that the constitution is not founded on a *bottom broad enough*; and, though THE WHOLE PEOPLE of the United States are to be TREBLY represented in it in THREE DIFFERENT MODES of representation, and their servants will have the most advantageous situation and opportunities of acquiring all requisite information for the welfare of *the whole union*, yet insist for a privilege of *opposing, obstructing,* and *confounding* all their measures taken with common consent for the general weal, by the delays, negligences, rivalries, or other selfish views of *parts* of the union.

Thus, while one state should be relied upon by the union for giving aid, upon a recommendation of Congress, to another in distress, the latter might be ruined; and the state relied upon, might suppose, it would gain by such an event.

When any persons speak of a confederation, do they, or do they not acknowledge, that the *whole* is *interested* in the safety of *every* part—in the *agreement* of *parts*—in the *relation* of *parts* to *one another*—to the *whole*—or, to *other societies*? If they do—then, the *authority* of the *whole*, must be co-extensive with its *interests*—and if it is, the *will* of *the whole* must and *ought* in *such cases* to govern.

If they do not acknowledge, that *the whole* is *thus interested*, the conversation should cease. Such persons mean not a confederation, but something else.

As to the idea, that this superintending sovereign will must of consequence destroy the subordinate sovereignties of the several states, it is begging a concession of the question, by inferring that a manifest and great *usefulness* must necessarily end in *abuse*; and not only so, but it requires an extinction of *the principle of all society:* for, the subordinate sovereignties, or, in other words, the undelegated rights of the several states, in a confederation, stand upon the very same foundation with the undelegated rights of individuals in a society, the *federal sovereign will* being *composed* of the *subordinate sovereign wills* of the several confederated states. If as some persons seem to think, *a bill of rights* is *the best security* of rights, the sovereignties of the several states have *this* best security by the proposed constitution, & more than *this* best security, for they are not barely *declared* to be rights, but are taken into it as *component parts*, for *their* perpetual preservation by *themselves*. In short, the government of each State is, and is to be, *sovereign* and *supreme* in *all* matters that *relate* to each state *only*. It is to be *subordinate* barely in *those* matters that *relate* to *the whole*; and it will be their own faults, if the several states suffer the *federal sovereignty* to interfere in things of their respective jurisdictions. An instance of such interference with regard to *any single state*, will be a dangerous *precedent* as *to all*, and therefore will be guarded against *by all*, as the trustees or servants of the several states will not dare, if they retain their senses, so to violate the *independent sovereignty* of their respective states, that justly darling object of *American* affections, to which they are responsible, besides being endeared by all the charities of life.

The common sense of mankind agrees to the devolution of individual wills in society; and if it has not been as universally assented to in confederation, the reasons are evident, & worthy of being retained in remembrance by *Americans*. They were, want of opportunities, or the loss of them, through defects of knowledge and virtue. The principle however has been sufficiently vindicated in imperfect combinations, as their prosperity has generally been commensurate to its operation.

How beautifully and forcibly does the inspired Apostle Saint *Paul*, argue upon a sublimer subject, with a train of reasoning strictly applicable to the present ? His words are—"If the foot shall say, because I am not the hand, I am not of the body; is it therefore not of the body? and if the ear shall say, because I am not the eye, I am not of the body; is it therefore not of the body?"[4] As plainly inferring, as could be done in that allegorical manner, the strongest censure of such partial discontents and dissentions, especially, as his meaning is enforced by his description of the *benefits* of *union* in these expressions—"But, *now* they are *many members*, yet but *one body:* and the eye CANNOT say to the hand, *I have no need of thee*; nor again, the head to the feet, *I have no need of you*."[5]

When the commons of *Rome* upon a rupture with the senate, seceded in arms upon the *Mons sacer, Menenius Agrippa* used the like allusion to the human body, in his famous apologue of a quarrel among some of the members.[6] The unpolished but honest-hearted *Romans* of that day, understood him, and were appeased. They returned to the city, and—the world was conquered.

Another comparison has been made by statesmen and the learned, between a natural and a political *body*; and no wonder indeed, when the title of the latter was borrowed from the resemblance. It has therefore been justly observed, that if a mortification takes place in one or some of the limbs, and the rest of the body is sound, remedies may be applied, and not only the contagion prevented from spreading, but the diseased part or parts saved by the connection with the body, &

restored to former usefulness. When general putrefaction prevails, death is to be expected. History sacred and prophane tells us, that, CORRUPTION OF MANNERS IS THE VERY BASIS OF SLAVERY.

1. The text in angle brackets is from "Fabius" II (CC:684).
2. The text in angle brackets does not appear in the *American Museum*.
3. Micah 4:4.
4. 1 Corinthians 12:15–16.
5. 1 Corinthians 12:20–21.
6. According to Plutarch, Menenius Agrippa said: "It once happened that all the other members of a man mutinied against the stomach, which they accused as the only idle, uncontributing part in the whole body, while the rest were put to hardships and the expense of much labour to supply and minister to its appetites. The stomach, however, merely ridiculed the silliness of the members, who appeared not to be aware that the stomach certainly does receive the general nourishment, but only to return it again, and redistribute it amongst the rest. Such is the case ye citizens, between you and the senate. The counsels and plans that are there duly digested, convey and secure to all of you your proper benefit and support" (*The Lives of the Noble Grecians and Romans* [New York: Modern Library Edition, (1932)], 266. This edition of Plutarch was translated by John Dryden and revised by Arthur Hugh Clough.).

## 691. Elbridge Gerry Responds to the Maryland "Landholder" X Boston American Herald, 18 April

This essay is the concluding salvo in a newspaper debate among several members of the Constitutional Convention over what had transpired in that body. Between 26 November and 24 December 1787 Connecticut delegate Oliver Ellsworth published in the *Connecticut Courant* and Hartford *American Mercury* numbers IV, V, and VIII of the Connecticut "Landholder" criticizing Massachusetts delegate Elbridge Gerry for his activities in the Convention and for his objections to the Constitution (CC:295, 316, 371). Gerry answered in the *Massachusetts Centinel* on 5 January 1788 (CC:419), and Maryland delegate Luther Martin defended him in the *Maryland Journal* on the 18th (CC:460). On 29 February the Maryland "Landholder" X, possibly Maryland delegate Daniel of St. Thomas Jenifer, replied to Martin in the *Maryland Journal* (CC:580), and Martin responded in that newspaper on 7, 18, and 21 March (CC:604, 626, 636). The Maryland "Landholder" was reprinted in the *Massachusetts Centinel* on 5 April, and on the 18th Gerry replied in the Boston *American Herald*.

Elbridge Gerry's 18 April reply, printed at the request of "A Friend and Customer," was reprinted in the *New York Journal*, 30 April; Northampton *Hampshire Gazette*, 7 May; and *Salem Mercury*, 20 May. The printer of the *New York Journal* noted that "As the *Connecticut Landholder's* publications are dispersed through the state, it will be useful for the sake of truth to publish" the reply, while the printer of the *Salem Mercury* informed his readers that the reply was inserted at the request of a friend and a number of readers of the *Mercury*.

Unless otherwise noted, Gerry's quotes from "Landholder" are taken from the Maryland "Landholder" X (CC:580).

## To the PUBLIC.

An elegant writer, under the signature of "A LANDHOLDER," having, in a series of publications, with a modesty and delicacy *peculiar to himself*, undertaken to instruct members of legislatures, executives, and conventions, in their duty respecting the new constitution, is, in stating facts, *unfortunate*, in being repeatedly *detected in errors*; but his *perseverance therein* does honor "to his magnanimity," and reminds me of Doctor Sangerado (in Gil Blas) who being advised to *alter his practice*, as it was founded on false principles and destructive to his patients, firmly determined to pursue it, *because he had written a book in support of it.*[1] Had our learned author *the modern Sangerado*, confined himself to *facts* and to *reasoning* on the Constitution, he might have continued to write without interruption *from its opposers*, 'till *by instructing others*, he had obtained that instruction which *he* seems to need, or a temporary relief from that incurable malady, the *cacoethes scribendi*;[2] but his frequent misrepresentations having exposed him to suspicions that as a disciple of Mandeville,[3] he is an advocate for vice, or, that to correct his curiosity, some humourist has palmed on him a spurious history of the proceedings of the federal convention, and exhibited his credulity as a subject of ridicule, it is proper to set him right in facts, which, in almost every instance, he has mis[s]tated.

In a late address to the honorable Luther Martin, Esq. the Landholder has asserted, that Mr. Gerry "uniformly opposed Mr. Martin's principles;" but this is a circumstance *wholly unknown* to Mr. Gerry, until he was informed of it by the *Connecticut Landholder*; indeed Mr. Gerry, from his first acquaintance with Mr. Martin, has "uniformly" had a friendship for him.

This writer has also asserted, "that the day Mr. Martin took his seat in convention, without requesting information, or to be let into the reasons of the adoption of what he might not approve, he opened against them in a speech which held during two days."—But the facts are, *that* Mr. Martin had been a considerable time in convention before he spoke; *that* when he entered into the debates, he appeared not to need "information," as he was fully possessed of the subject; and *that* his speech, if published, would do him great honor.

Another assertion of this famous writer, is, that Mr. Gerry in "a sarcastical reply, admired the strength of Mr. Martin's lungs, and his profound knowledge in the first principles of government;" that "this reply" "left him a prey to the most humiliating reflections; but these did not teach him to bound his future speeches by the lines of moderation; for the very next day he exhibited, without a blush, another specimen of eternal volubility."—This is so *remote* from *truth*, that no such reply was made by Mr. Gerry to Mr. Martin, or to any member of the convention; on the contrary, Mr. Martin, on the first day he spoke, about the time of adjournment, signified to the convention that the heat of the season[4] and his indisposition prevented his proceeding, and the house adjourned without further debate, or a reply to Mr. Martin from any member whatever.

Again, the Landholder has asserted that Mr. Martin voted "an appeal should lay to the supreme judiciary of the United States for the correction of all errors both in *law* and *fact*," and "agreed to the clause that declares *nine States to be sufficient to put the government in motion;*" and in a note says, "Mr. Gerry agreed with Mr. Martin on these questions." Whether there is any truth in these assertions as they relate to Mr. Martin, he can best determine, but as they respect Mr. Gerry, *they reverse the facts*; for he not only voted against the first proposition (which is not stated by the Landholder, with the accuracy requisite for a *writer on government*) but contended for jury trials in civil cases, and declared his opinion, that a federal judiciary with the powers abovementioned, would be as oppressive and dangerous, as the establishment of a Star-Chamber.[5]—And as to the clause that "declares nine States to be sufficient to put the government in motion," Mr. Gerry was so much opposed to it, as to vote against it, in the first instance, and afterwards to move for a reconsideration of it.[6]

The Landholder having in a former publication asserted "that Mr. Gerry introduced a motion, respecting the redemption of old continental money," and the publick having been informed by a paragraph in the Massachusetts Centinel, No. 32 of vol. 8, as well as by the honorable Mr. Martin, that neither Mr. Gerry, or any other member had introduced such a proposition,[7] the Landholder now says, that "out of 126 days, Mr. Martin attended only 66," and then enquires "Whether it is to be presumed, that Mr. Martin could have been minutely informed, of all that happened in convention, and *committees of convention*, during the sixty days of his absence?" and "Why is it that we do not see Mr. M'Henry's verification of his assertion, who was of the *committee* for considering a provision for the debts of the Union?" But if these enquiries *were intended for subterfuges*, unfortunately for the Landholder, they will not avail him: for, had Mr. Martin not been present at the debates on this subject, the fact is, that Mr. Gerry was not on a committee with Mr. M'Henry,[8] or with any other person, for considering a provision for the debts of the union, or any provision that related to the subject of old continental money; neither did he make any proposition, in convention, committee, or on any occasion, to any member of convention or other person, respecting the redemption of such money; and the assertions of the Landholder to the contrary, are altogether destitute of the shadow of truth.

The Landholder, addressing Mr. Martin, further says, "Your reply to my second charge against Mr. Gerry, may be soon dismissed: compare his letter to the legislature of his state, with your defence, and you will find, that you have put into his mouth, *objections*[9] different from any thing it contains, so that if your representation be *true*, his must be *false*." The *objections* referred to, are those mentioned by Mr. Martin, as being made by Mr. Gerry, against the supreme power of Congress over the militia. Mr. Gerry, in his letter to the legislature, states as an objection, "That some of the powers of the federal legislature are ambiguous and *others*, (meaning the unlimited power of Congress, to keep up a standing army in time of peace, and their entire controul of the militia) are *indefinite* and *dangerous*."[10] Against both these did Mr. Gerry warmly contend, and why his representations must be *false*, if Mr. Martin's are *true*, which *particularized* what Mr. Gerry's stated *generally*, can only be discovered by such a *profound* reasoner, as the *Connecticut Landholder*.

The vanity of this writer, in supposing that *his* charges would be the subject of constitutional investigation, can only be equalled by his *impertinence*, in interferring with the politics of other States, or by his *ignorance*, in supposing a state convention could take cognizance of such *matters as he calls charges*, and that Mr. Gerry required a *formal defence*, or the *assistance* of his *colleagues*, to defeat the unprovoked and libellous attacks of the *Landholder*, or of any other *unprincipled reviler*.[11]

The Landholder says, "That Mr. Martin thought *the deputy attorney general of the United States, for the state of Maryland*, destined for a different character, and that inspired him with the hope, that he might derive from a desperate opposition, what he saw no prospect of gaining by a contrary conduct: but the Landholder ventures to predict, that though Mr. Martin was to double his efforts, he would fail in his object." By *this*, we may form some estimate of the *patriotism* of the Landholder, for, whilst he so readily resolves Mr. Martin's conduct into *a manœuvre for office*, he gives too much reason to suppose, that *he himself has no idea of any other motive in conducting politicks*. But how can the Landholder ascertain, that "Mr. Martin thought" the office mentioned "destined for a different character?" Was the Landholder *present* at the *distination?*" if so, it was natural for him, knowing there was a *combination* against Mr. Martin, (however remote this gentleman was from discovering it) to suppose his *accidental* opposition to the *complotters*, proceeded from *a discovery of the plot.*—Surely, the Landholder must have some reason for his conjecture respecting the motives of Mr. Martin's conduct, or be subject to the charge of publishing calumny, *knowing it to be such*. If then, this *great Statesman* was in a secret, which has been long impenetrable, he is now entitled to the honor of giving the public the most important information they have received, concerning, the *origin* of the new constitution: and having candidly informed them *who is not*, he ought to inform *who is to fill that office, and all others* of the new federal government.—It may then, in some measure be ascertained, what individuals have supported the constitution on *principles of patriotism*, and who under this *guise* have been only *squabbling for office*. Perhaps we shall find, that the *Landholder* is to have the *contract* for supplying the *standing army* under the new government, and that many others, who have recurred to *abuse* on this occasion, have *some such happy prospects*: indeed the Landholder puts it beyond doubt, *if we can believe him*, that it was determined in the *privy council* of the federal convention, that however Mr. Martin might advocate the new constitution, *he should not have the office mentioned:* for if this was not the case, how can the Landholder so roundly assert, that Mr. Martin could have *"no prospect by a contrary conduct* of gaining the office, and so remarkably sanguine is the Landholder, that the members of the privy council would be senators of the new Congress, in which case the elections, would undoubtedly be made according to the *conventional list of nominations*, as that he ventures to predict, tho' Mr. Martin was to *double his efforts*, he would *fail in his object."* Thus, whilst *this blazing star of federalism* is taking great pains to hold up Mr. Gerry and Mr. Mason, as having held private meetings, "to aggrandize Old Massachusetts, and the ancient Dominion," he has confessed enough to shew that *his private meetings were solely to aggrandize himself.*

1. Gerry refers to Alain René Le Sage's (1668–1747) picaresque novel *Histoire de Gil Blas de Santillane* (4 vols., Paris, 1715–1735).

2. "An itch for writing" or "scribbler's itch."

3. Gerry refers to Bernard Mandeville's (1670?–1733) two-part satire, *The Fable of the Bees: or, Private Vices, Publick Benefits*, a work that was produced over a period of about twenty-four years (1705–1729).

4. Martin made this speech on 27–28 June 1787. Connecticut delegate William Samuel Johnson noted in his diary that the 27th was hot, the 28th "Cool" (Farrand, III, 552). Since the Convention kept the windows closed to ensure secrecy, it was uncomfortable in the chamber.

5. For Martin's opinions on jury trials and the jurisdiction of the judiciary, see *Genuine Information* X, Baltimore *Maryland Gazette*, 1 February (CC:493).

6. On 31 August 1787 Massachusetts voted "yes" on the question of "nine." Gerry's individual vote was not recorded. In the debate on the next clause or article which was concerned with the submission of the Constitution to state conventions, Gerry "dwelt on the impropriety of destroying the existing Confederation, without the unanimous Consent of the parties to it," and he moved to postpone the discussion of this article.

His motion was defeated 8 states to 3. Massachusetts voted against postponement (Farrand, II, 477, 478, 479. For the text of the two clauses or articles [XXI and XXII] under consideration, see CDR, 269.).

7. See "Landholder" VIII, *Connecticut Courant*, 24 December 1787, note 3; *Massachusetts Centinel*, 5 January 1788; and *Maryland Journal*, 18 January (CC:371, 419, 460).

8. On 18 August 1787 the Convention appointed a grand committee "to consider the necessity and expediency of the debts of the several States being assumed by the United States." James McHenry represented Maryland and Rufus King, not Gerry, represented Massachusetts (Farrand, II, 322, 328).

9. The italics are Gerry's.

10. See Gerry's 18 October 1787 letter which was published in the *Massachusetts Centinel* on 3 November (CC:227-A). The italics in this quoted passage are not in the original. On 18 August 1787 Gerry "thought an army dangerous in time of peace & could never consent to a power to keep up an indefinite number." A motion by Luther Martin and Gerry to restrict the size of a peacetime army was defeated. On the same day, Gerry attacked the provision giving Congress the power to regulate and discipline the state militias. "If it be agreed to by the Convention," Gerry declared, "the plan will have as black a mark as was set on Cain. He had no such confidence in the Genl. Govt. as some Gentlemen possessed. . . ." On 23 August he stated that to place the militia under command of the federal government "would be regarded as a system of Despotism." And on 5 September Gerry opposed the two-year appropriation of money for the army (Farrand, II, 329, 330, 332, 385, 509).

11. The personal attacks upon him weighed heavily on Gerry as an excerpt from one of his letters demonstrates. Gerry noted that "The vigilant enemies of free government have been long in the execution of their plan to hunt down all who remain attached to revolution principles; they have attacked us in detail and have deprived you, Mr. S. Adams and myself in a great measure of that public confidence to which a faithful attachment to the public interest entitles us, and they are now aiming to throw Mr. Hancock out of the saddle, who, with all his foibles, is yet attached to the whig cause. There seems to be a disposition in the dominant party to establish a nobility of opinion, under whose control in a short time, will be placed the government of the union and the states, and whose insufferable arrogance marks out for degradation all who will not submit to their authority. It is beginning to be fashionable to consider the opponents of the constitution as embodying themselves with the lower classes of the people, and that one forfeits all title to the respect of a gentleman, unless he is one of the privileged order. Is this, my friend, to be the operation of the free government, which all our labours in the revolution have tended to produce?" (James T. Austin, *The Life of Elbridge Gerry, With Contemporary Letters to the Close of the American Revolution* [2 vols., Boston, 1828-1829], II, 85-86. Austin neglected to include the date of the letter, but he placed it after a letter of 28 June 1788 to James Warren [CC:791]. Since Gerry refers to the coming establishment of the new government under the Constitution, it seems likely that it was written after the Constitution was adopted by the necessary nine states.).

## 692. Charles Thomson to James McHenry
### New York, 19 April[1]

I am sorry I have not been able sooner to answer your letter of the 19 of last month. I happened to be in Philadelphia when it reached New York. It was transmitted to me and when I received it I was in hopes I should have finished my business & returned in a few days.

Therefore I immediately sent back the letter which was enclosed therein to be forwarded by the packet and deferred writing to you until I returned. My stay was longer than I expected, and after my return here I recd. your second letter of the 12 of this Month and at the same time an account of your election. I hope, notwithstanding the choice made by the counties of A[nne Arundel?] Baltimore and Harford,[2] that the elections [– – –] [– – –] are such as will ensure the adoption of the new constitution; for unless that takes place I confess to you my fears for the safety, tranquility and happiness of my country are greater than at any period of the late war. The present federal government is at the point of expiring.[3] It cannot I think survive the present year and if it could experience must have convinced every man of reflection that it is altogether inadequate to the end designed. What remedy then have we prepared for the train of disastrous events which must necessarily ensue from a dissolution of the Union or what security for our independence peace & happiness as a nation?

You ask me what is the amount of the foreign & domestic debt? With regard to the foreign debt I beg leave to refer you to the enclosed schedule of the french & dutch loans shewing the periods of their redemption, the annual interest payable thereon & the instalments stipulated for discharging the principal.[4] To this you must add about 150,000 dollars due to Spain & 186,427 dollars due to foreign Officers also a million of florins which from the failure of the states Congress were under the necessity of borrowing last year to defray the interest of the dutch loans & other demands in Europe.[5] As to the domestic debt I have to inform you that by the last estimate which the board of treasury laid before Congress, the amount thereof as far as then liquidated is 28,340,018 dollars[6] How much of this has been actually extinguished by the sale of western territory, I cannot certainly say. The tract which the Ohio company have in view to purchase is supposed to be between 5 & 6 millions of acres, but I believe they have only paid 500,000 dollars. The residue of the purchase money is to be paid by yearly instalments and the Company by their agreement are at liberty to confine their purchase within the compass of their abilities & to take no more land than they are able to pay for.[7] The tract which Symmes has agreed for is said to be 2 million acres & Flint Parker & Co. have applied for the purchase of 3 millions Acres; but I believe neither [– – –] have yet paid any money.[8] The quantity of land surveyed & laid out into townships agreeably to the Land Ordinance is upwards of 700,000 Acres but of this there is only about 100,000 sold.[9] As to the land unsurveyed the quantity is immense and in my opinion fully adequate to the extinguishment of the whole debt of the Union, provided we can have a firm stable federal government; but without this I am apprehensive the Union will derive little benefit from it. As to the amount of the duties on a 5 per cent impost & the expence of the civil list under the new government it is altogether conjectural, but of this I am confident that the new government if established will from prudential motives encrease the former and lessen the latter as much as possible and however proper it may have been judged to vest it with the power of direct taxation, it will not proceed to the exercise of that power except in the last necessity

Enclosed I send you the first volume of the fœderalist the second volume is in the press & will, it is expected be out in the course of a week or two. As soon as it is published I will forward it to you.[10]

1. RC, Miscellaneous Manuscripts Collection, PPAmP. Charles Thomson (1729–1824), a former teacher, distiller, manufacturer, and merchant, was a leader of the Philadelphia Sons of Liberty before the Revolution. He served as secretary of the Continental and Confederation congresses from 1774 to 1789. As secretary, he resided in New York City from 1784 to 1789. James McHenry represented the town of Baltimore in the Maryland Convention, where he voted to ratify the Constitution on 26 April.

2. On 7 April Jeremiah Townley Chase, Samuel Chase, John Francis Mercer, and Benjamin Harrison were elected from Anne Arundel County; Charles Ridgely, Charles Ridgely of William, Edward Cockey, and Nathan Cromwell from Baltimore County; and John Love, William Paca, William Pinkney, and Luther Martin from Harford County. The Maryland Convention ratified the Constitution 63 to 11 on 26 April, and all twelve men, except Paca, voted against ratification. Paca, an Antifederalist, submitted a list of amendments after the vote. (See CC:716 for Paca.)

3. Attendance in Congress was especially poor in April. Between 31 March and 1 May, there were never more than six state delegations in attendance (JCC, XXXIV, 116–19). Since seven states were needed for a quorum, Congress transacted no business. The President of Congress Cyrus Griffin wrote James Madison on 7 April that "it seems to me the period is fully arrived to close the Confederation." On 20 April Nathan Dane, a Massachusetts delegate, told George Thatcher that "Here we remain in an idle Situation. . . . Six States and as ma[n]y half States attend—The business of the union must be neglected, because one or two gentlemen, who are in the City, must attend to their private business" (LMCC, VIII, 714, 722).

4. Thomson probably sent McHenry a copy of the two-page broadside *Schedule of the French and Dutch Loans, Shewing the Periods of their Redemption, with the Annual Interest Payable thereon until their Final Extinction, for which Provision is Yet to be Made* [New York, 1786] (Evans 20082).

5. On 1 June 1787 John Adams, the American ambassador to Great Britain, signed an agreement for a Dutch loan of one million florins ($400,000), and on 11 October Congress ratified the loan (JCC, XXXIII, 412–15, 649; and LMCC, VIII, 668n).

6. See the 28 September 1787 report of the Board of Treasury (JCC, XXXIII, 579).

7. In July 1787 the Ohio Company purchased about 5,000,000 acres of land in southeastern Ohio from Congress. The company kept 1,500,000 for itself and the rest went to the Scioto Company. The Ohio Company agreed to pay $500,000 down when the contract was signed with Congress and another $500,000 when the survey was completed. The remainder of the $3,000,000 purchase price was to be paid in six equal annual installments (JCC, XXXIII, 399–401, 427–29; XXXIV, 565–66; and Benjamin

Hibbard, *A History of the Public Land Policies* [1924; reprint ed., New York, 1939], 45–50).

8. In August 1787 John Cleves Symmes of New Jersey petitioned Congress for about 2,000,000 acres in southwestern Ohio. A contract for 1,000,000 acres, at about sixty-seven cents an acre, was signed on 14 October 1788 (Hibbard, *Public Land Policies*, 50–51; and JCC, XXXIV, 565–66). In October 1787 Royal Flint, Joseph Parker, and associates petitioned Congress for a contract for the purchase of 2,000,000 acres on the Ohio River and another for 1,000,000 on the Mississippi River. In September 1788, Congress authorized the Board of Treasury to sell to Flint and Parker 1,000,000 acres in Ohio at the same price and on the same terms as Symmes. No contract, however, was ever signed (Hibbard, *Public Land Policies*, 44–45; and JCC, XXXIII, 695n, 697–98; XXXIV, 566).

9. By February 1787 geographer of the U.S. Thomas Hutchins and his staff had surveyed four of the seven ranges in eastern Ohio under the provisions of the Land Ordinance of 1785 (CDR, 156–63). After the four ranges were surveyed the sale of lands began, and between 21 September and 9 October 108,431 acres were sold for $176,000 (Hibbard, *Public Land Policies*, 41).

10. The first volume of *The Federalist* was offered for sale on 22 March and the second on 28 May (see CC:639; and Editors' Note, 28 May).

### 693. Fabius IV
### Pennsylvania Mercury, 19 April

After "Fabius" IV appeared in print, John Vaughan informed author John Dickinson that essays III and IV "are admired by all who wish to be *injoind to do right* & Strongly approved of by men of weight & reflection" (CC:694). Vaughan sent copies of number IV to Dickinson, John Langdon, and George Washington.

"Fabius" IV was reprinted in the Baltimore *Maryland Gazette*, 20 May; *Virginia Independent Chronicle*, 21 May; *New Hampshire Spy*, 31 May; *New Hampshire Gazette*, 12 June; *Providence Gazette*, 28 June; and the October issue of the Philadelphia *American Museum*.

OBSERVATIONS ON THE CONSTITUTION
proposed by the FEDERAL CONVENTION.

Another question remains. *How are the contributed rights to be managed?* The resolution has been in great measure anticipated, by what has been said concerning the system proposed. Some few reflections may perhaps finish it.

If it can be considered separately, [a] *Constitution* is the *organization* of *the contributed rights* in society. *Government* is certainly the *exercise* of them. It is intended for the benefit of *the governed*; of course can have no just powers but what conduce to *that end*: & the awefulness of the trust is demonstrated in this—that it is founded on the nature of man, that is, on the will of his MAKER, and is *therefore* sacred.

Let the reader be pleased to consider the writer, as treating of *equal liberty* with reference to the *people* and *states* of United *America*, and their meditated confederation.

If the organization of a constitution be defective, it may be amended.

A good constitution promotes, but not always produces a good administration.

The government must never be lodged in *a single body*. From such an one, with an unlucky composition of its parts, rash, partial, illegal, and when intoxicated with success, even cruel, insolent, & contemptible edicts, may at times be expected. By *these*, if other mischiefs do not follow, the national dignity may be impaired.

Several inconveniences might attend a division of the government into *two* bodies, that probably would be avoided in another arrangement.

The judgment of *the most enlightened* among mankind, confirmed by *multiplied experiments*, points out the propriety of government being committed to such a number of great departments, as can be introduced *without confusion, distinct in office, and yet connected in operation*. It seems to be agreed, that *three* or *four* of these departments are a competent number.

Such a repartition appears well calculated, to encrease the safety and repose of *the governed*, which, with the advancement of their happiness in other respects, are the objects of government; as thereby there will be more obstructions interposed, against errors, feuds, and frauds, in the administration, and the interference of the people need be less frequent. Thus, wars, tumults, and uneasinesses, are avoided. The departments so constituted, may *therefore* be said to be *balanced*.

But, notwithstanding, it must be granted, that a bad administration may take place. What is then to be done? The answer is instantly found—Let the *Fasces* be lowered before—not the *Majesty*, it is not a term fit for mortals—but, before the *supreme sovereignty* of the people. IT IS THEIR DUTY TO WATCH, AND THEIR RIGHT TO TAKE CARE, THAT THE CONSTITUTION BE PRESERVED; or in the *Roman* phrase on perilous occasions—TO PROVIDE, THAT THE REPUBLIC RECEIVE NO DAMAGE.

Political bodies are *properly* said to be *balanced*, with respect to this primary origination and ultimate destination, not to any intrinsic or constitutional properties. It is the power from which they *proceed*, and which they *serve*, that truly and of right *balances* them.

But, as a good constitution not always produces a good administration, a defective one not always excludes it. Thus, in governments very different from those of United *America*, general manners and customs, improvement in knowledge, and the education and disposition of princes, not unfrequently soften the features, and qualify the defects. Jewels of value are substituted, in the place of the rare and genuine orient of highest price and brightest lustre: and though the sovereigns *cannot* even in their ministers, be brought to account by the governed, yet there are instances of their conduct indicating a veneration for the rights of the people, and an internal conviction of the guilt that attends their violation. Some of them appear to be *fathers of their countries*. Revered princes! *Friends of mankind!* May peace be in their lives, and hope sit smiling[1] in their beds of death.

By this animating, presiding will of the people, is meant a reasonable, not a distracted will. When frensy seizes the mass, it would be madness to think of their happiness, that is, of their freedom. They will infallibly have a *Philip* or a *Cæsar*, to bleed them into soberness of mind. At present we are cool; and let us attend to our business.

Our government under the proposed confederation, will be guarded by a repetition of the strongest cautions against excesses. In the *senate* the *sovereignties* of the several states will be *equally* represented; in *the house of representatives*, the *people* of the whole union will be *equally represented*; and, in the *president*, and the federal independent *judges*, so much concerned in the execution of the laws, and in the determination of their constitutionality, the *sovereignties* of the several states and *the people* of the whole union, will be *conjointly* represented.

Where was there ever or where is there now upon the face of the earth, a government so diversified and attempered? If a work formed with so much deliberation, so respectful and affectionate an attention to the interests, feelings, and sentiments of all United *America*, will not satisfy, what would satisfy all United *America?*

It seems highly probable, that those who would reject this labour of public love, would also have rejected the Heaven-taught institution of trial by jury, had they been consulted upon its establishment. Would they not have cried out, that there never was framed so detestable, so paltry, and so tyrannical a device for extinguishing freedom, and throwing unbounded domination into the hands of the king and barons, under a contemptible pretence of preserving it? What! Can *freedom* be preserved by *imprisoning* its *guardians?* Can *freedom* be preserved, by keeping *twelve* men *closely confined* without *meat, drink, fire,* or *candle,* until they *unanimously agree,* and this to be infinitely repeated? Can *freedom* be preserved, by thus delivering up *a number of freemen* to a monarch and an aristocracy, fortified by dependant and obedient judges and officers, to be shut up, *until under duress they speak as they are ordered?* Why can't the twelve jurors *separate,* after hearing the evidence, return to their *respective homes,* and there *take time,* and *think* of the matter *at their ease?* Is there not *a variety of ways,* in which causes have been, and can be tried, without this tremendous, *unprecedented* inquisition? Why then is it insisted on; but because the fabricators of it *know* that it *will,* and *intend* that it *shall* reduce the people to slavery? Away with it—Freemen will never be enthralled by so insolent, so execrable, so pitiful a contrivance.

Happily for us our ancestors thought otherwise. They were not so over-nice & curious, as to refuse blessings, because, they might possibly be abused.

They perceived, that the *uses* included were great and manifest. Perhaps they did not foresee, that from this acorn, as it were, would grow up oaks, that changing their native soil for another element, would bound over raging mountains of waters, bestow and receive benefits around the globe, and *secure the just liberties of the nation for a long succession of ages.*[a] As to *abuses,* they trusted to their own spirit for preventing or correcting them: And worthy is it of deep consideration by every friend of freedom, that *abuses* that seem to be but *"trifles,"*[b] may be attended by fatal consequences. What can be *"trifling,"* that diminishes or detracts from the only defence, that ever was found against *"open attacks* and *secret machinations."*[c] It originates from a knowledge of human nature. With a superior force, wisdom, and benevolence united, it rives the difficulties that have distressed, or destroyed the rest of mankind. It reconciles contradictions, immensity of power, with safety of private station. It is ever new & always the same.

Trial by jury and the dependance of taxation upon representation, those corner stones of liberty, were not obtained by *a bill of rights,* or any other records, and have not been and cannot be preserved by them. They and all other rights must be preserved, by soundness of sense and honesty of heart. Compared with *these,* what are a bill of rights, or any characters drawn upon paper or parchment, those frail remembrancers? Do we want to be reminded, that the sun enlightens, warms, invigorates, and cheers? or how horrid it would be, to have his blessed beams intercepted, by our being thrust into mines or dungeons? Liberty is the sun of freemen, and the beams are their rights.

"It is the duty which every man owes to his country, his friends, his posterity, and himself, to maintain to the utmost of his power this valuable palladium in all its rights; to restore it to its antient dignity, if at all impaired by the different value of property, or otherwise deviated from its first institution; to *amend* it, wherever it is *defective;*[d] and above all, to guard with the most jealous circumspection against the new and arbitrary methods of trial, which, under a variety of plausible pretences, may in time imperceptibly undermine this best preservative of liberty."[e] Trial by jury is our birth-right; and tempted to his own ruin, by some seducing spirit, must be the man, who in opposition to the genius of United *America,* shall dare to attempt its subversion.

In the proposed confederation, it is preserved inviolable in criminal cases, and cannot be altered in other respects, but when the genius of[2] United *America* demands it.[3]

There seems to be a disposition in men to find fault, no difficult matter, rather than to do right. The works of creation itself have been objected to: and one learned prince declared, that if *he* had been consulted, they would have been improved. With what book has so much fault been found, as with the *Bible?* Perhaps, principally, because it *so clearly and strongly enjoins men to do right.* How many, how plausible objections have been made against it, with how much ardor, with how much pains? Yet, the book has done an immensity of good in the world; would do more, if duly regarded; and might lead the objectors themselves and their posterity to perpetual happiness, if they would value it as they ought.

When objections are made to a system of high import, should they not be weighed against the benefits? Are these great, positive, immediate? Is there a chance of endangering them by rejection or delay? May they not be attained without admitting the objections, supposing the objections to be well founded? If the objections are well founded, may they not be hereafter admitted, without danger disgust, or inconvenience? Is the system so formed, that they may be thus admitted? May they not be of less efficacy, than they are thought to be by their authors? Are they not designed to hinder evils, which are generally deemed to be sufficiently provided against? May not the admission of them prevent benefits, that might otherwise be obtained? In political affairs, is it not more safe and advantageous, for *all* to agree in measures that may not be best, than to quarrel *among themselves*, what are best?

When questions of this kind with regard to the plan proposed, are calmly considered, it seems reasonable to hope, that every faithful citizen of United *America*, will make up his mind, with much satisfaction to himself, and advantage to his country.

(a) Blackstone, III, 379.[4]
(b) Idem, IV, 350.[5]
(c) Idem, III, 381.[6]
(d) See an enumeration of *defects* in trials by jury, Blackstone, III, 381.[7]
(e) Idem, IIII, 350.[8]

1. The words "sit smiling" are not in the *American Museum* version.
2. The words "the genius of" are not in the *American Museum* version.
3. This paragraph was added by John Vaughan. Before Vaughan sent "Fabius" IV to the printer, he made some changes in John Dickinson's draft. On 17 April, Vaughan wrote Dickinson: "You will recollect that I hinted a possibility that part of the last

Sentiment, which So nobly winds up what relates to the *Jurys*, might not be So fully comprehended as you wished, you judged the observation to be without foundation & left the Subject as it Stood—Reading it to the friend mentioned by me before, he made the Same observation, '*I* feel what the author wishes, but he will be misunderstood, because immense pains have been taken to misrepresent upon this Subject & the opposition hinges in a great measure upon it'.—Reflecting upon it after he left me, I determined to consult you upon the Subject, but not finding an opportunity & the printer Calling for the paper I presumed to make an addition, which if you do not approve you must pardon for the Zeal which prompted it." Because the paragraph Vaughan inserted "in some measure" affected the "Sense" of some of the text of the preceding paragraph, Vaughan informed Dickinson that he had altered the last word in the preceding paragraph from "*Change*" to "*Subversion.*" He also told Dickinson "If you disapprove, & can let me know by tomorrow at 2 O'Clock it will not be too late to alter" (to "Mr. Thomas," Dickinson Papers, PPL).

4. *Commentaries*, Book III, chapter XXIII, 379. Describing the English Constitution in a chapter on trial by jury, Blackstone wrote: "A constitution, that I may venture to affirm has, under providence, secured the just liberties of this nation for a long succession of ages."

5. *Ibid.*, Book IV, chapter XXVII, 344. Blackstone said ". . . that these inroads upon this sacred bulwark of the nation [i.e., trial by jury] are fundamentally opposite to the spirit of our constitution; and that, though begun in trifles, the precedent may gradually increase and spread, to the utter disuse of juries in questions of the most momentous concern."

6. *Ibid.*, 343–44. The citation given by "Fabius" was incorrect. Blackstone stated: "So that the liberties of England cannot but subsist, so long as this *palladium* remains sacred and inviolate, not only from all open attacks, (which none will be so hardy as to make) but also from all secret machinations, which may sap and undermine it; by introducing new and arbitrary methods of trial, by justices of the peace, commissioners of the revenue, and courts of conscience."

7. *Ibid.*, Book III, chapter XXIII, 381–85. Blackstone enumerated and discussed four defects in the jury system.

8. *Ibid.*, 381. ("Book IIII, 350" was changed to "Book III, 381" in the *American Museum* version.) The italics in the quoted material were inserted by "Fabius." In Blackstone, the words "valuable palladium" read "valuable constitution."

## 694. John Vaughan to John Dickinson
## Philadelphia, c. 19 April[1]

I wrote you yesterday by post, I now send you 3;4 of Fabius.—they are admired by all who wish to be *injoind to do right* & Strongly approved of by men of weight & reflection—They are regularly forwarded as before mention'd, & I have Sent the whole 4—to Mr Langdon in N. Hampshire—*much* enquiry is made after the author, but he cannot be discovered—Another Number appears on Tuesday, & 6. on Thursday. I hope 7. will be ready on Fryday or before.[2]—The more I examine them the more I am persuaded of their Utility—

I have reason to be confirmed in my opinion that Maryland will decide favorably—& to lose my doubts respectg Virginia—Two anec-

dotes have been related on the Subject of the Election of this State—
Madisons County was against it—They had declared they would confide
in him on *any other* point—He arrived the day before the Election,
adressed them at the Election & convinced a Majority that he had *acted
as he ought* & that the Constitution ought to be Adopted.³—A con-
vincing proof that rational Means will not fail in their effect.—

Mr Grayson adressed in his County *against it* violently, & observed
that the example of the Paltry State of Pensylvania & Still more Paltry
Estate of Delaware, ought not to bind the Ancient dominion of Virginia—I mention this merely to *mark the Man*.⁴—In Carolina (from
whence we have late accounts) The Back Counties against, but Strong
expectations of Success in the Result—

In this days paper Some interesting news from N York State—A Riot
to punish the Young Surgeons for Stealing upon the Sacred Retiremt.
of the Grave, went Serious lengths—Jay, Steuben North & others dan-
gerously wounded by Stones, & the death of 4 & wound of 18. at last
dispersed them—The Governor was very ill-treated & abused & they
Say is now convinced of the necessity of an [efficient?] Governmt.⁵—
*if so* New York follows of course, *his* opposition is the only formidable
one.

P.S. I have Sent a *Conciliator* for your perusal⁶—

1. RC, Dickinson Papers, PPL. This letter is undated, unsigned, and the address page
reads "Mr Thomas—/with three papers." The letter is in the handwriting of John
Vaughan of Philadelphia, and "Mr Thomas" is John Dickinson whose "Fabius" essays
Vaughan was forwarding to the printer of the *Pennsylvania Mercury*. The date c. 19 April
has been assigned because the printed version of "Fabius" IV, enclosed in it with numbers II and III, was published in the *Mercury* on 19 April (CC:693), and the newspaper
article on the New York City doctors' riot (see note 5, below), described in it, was
printed in the same issue of the *Mercury*.

2. "Fabius" III–VII appeared in the *Pennsylvania Mercury* on 17, 19, 22, 24, and 26
April (CC:690, 693, 699, 705, 710). For John Langdon and the circulation of "Fabius"
in New Hampshire, see the headnote to CC:677.

3. Beginning in December 1787, James Madison's friends and family implored him
to return to Orange County from Congress and to stand for election to the Virginia
Convention. Convinced by these entreaties, Madison left New York City in early March
and reached home on 23 March, and the next day he and James Gordon, Jr., were
overwhelmingly elected. For the Orange County election, see RCS:Va., 595–606.

4. On 3 March William Grayson and Cuthbert Bullitt were elected to represent Prince
William County in the Virginia Convention, where they voted against ratification of the
Constitution. Hugh Williamson, a North Carolina delegate to Congress, described Gray-
son's performance thusly: "He harangued the People at the Court House having in his
Hand a snuff Box hardly so broad as a Moidore. The Point of finger and Thumb are
inserted with difficulty. Perhaps said he you may think it of Consequence that some
other States have accepted of the new Constitution, what are they? when compared to
Virginia they are no more than this snuff Box is to the Size of a Man. On being asked

afterwards by an intimate, why he had risqued such an assertion. There was not any short-Hand-man present said he" (to John Gray Blount, 3 June, RCS:Va., 608–9).

5. On 19 April the *Pennsylvania Mercury* and the Philadelphia *Federal Gazette* printed a long extract of a 16 April letter from New York City, describing a riot which took place there on 13–14 April. The riot began after people learned that several medical students from the hospital had disinterred bodies for the purposes of dissection. On several occasions, a mob threatened the city jail, where two students had been placed for their own protection. Governor George Clinton, Mayor James Duane, and many prominent citizens, including John Jay, William North, and Baron von Steuben, protected the students from a large and violent mob.

6. On 17 April Vaughan promised Dickinson that he would send "a paper Signed Conciliator, in which you will observe a *Consonance of Opinion*, relative *to the Spirit of america*" (to "Mr Thomas," 17 April, Dickinson Papers, PPL). Vaughan probably referred to an essay by "Conciliator," Philadelphia *Independent Gazetteer*, 20 February, which considered jury trials, the jurisdiction and tenure of the federal judiciary, and cases of treason (Mfm:Pa. 438).

## 695. George Washington and the Maryland Convention

The adjournment of the New Hampshire Convention in February 1788 without ratifying the Constitution had dashed Federalists' hopes that nine states would have ratified before the Virginia Convention met on 2 June. On 5 April George Nicholas warned James Madison (both delegates to the upcoming Virginia Convention) that "great efforts will be made to induce" the Maryland and South Carolina conventions to adjourn without ratifying the Constitution until after the Virginia Convention met. The division in the Virginia Convention was expected to be close, and if the Maryland and South Carolina conventions adjourned, Virginia ratification would become even more difficult. Consequently, Nicholas asked Madison to contact his friends in Maryland and South Carolina requesting that they try to prevent the adjournment of their conventions. On 9 April Nicholas wrote David Stuart, another Virginia Convention delegate and a friend and neighbor of George Washington, asking that he exert himself and "get Genl. Washington to do the same" in order to prevent the adjournment of the Maryland Convention (RCS:Va., 703, 712).

Madison promised Nicholas on 8 April that he would write friends in Maryland and South Carolina. Two days later Madison informed Washington that he had written to Daniel Carroll and James McHenry of Maryland, and he noted that "The difference between even a postponement and adoption in Maryland, may in the nice balance of parties here, possibly give a fatal advantage to that which opposes the Constitution" (RCS:Va., 707, 732–33).

On 20 April Washington wrote Thomas Johnson, a longtime friend, a former Maryland governor, and a delegate to the Maryland Convention, that the adjournment of the Convention "to a later period than the decision of the question in this State, will be tantamount to the rejection of the Constitution." Washington believed that the principal Antifederalists in Maryland and Virginia hoped for such an adjournment (below). James McHenry wrote Washington on 20 April and asked him whether an adjournment by the Maryland Convention "would operate with yours against its adoption. Our opposition intend to push for an adjournment under the pretext of a conference with yours respecting amendments. As I look upon such a step to amount to a rejection in both States I shall do every thing in my power to prevent it. Your Sentiments may be useful" (RCS:Va., 764n).

Washington replied to McHenry on 27 April declaring that "As you are pleased to ask my opinion of the consequences of an adjournment of your Convention until the meeting of ours, I shall tho' I have meddled very little in this political dispute (less perhaps than a man so thoroughly persuaded as I am of the evils and confusions which will result from the rejection of the proposed Constitution, ought to have done) give it as my sincere and decided opinion that the postponement of the question would be tantamount to the final rejection of it—that the adversaries of the new Constitution [in] Virginia and Maryland view it in this light—and the[y] will pass [i.e., press] for the accomplishment of this measure as the de[r]nier resort.—I have very good reason to believe [that] to adduce arguments in support of this opinion is as unnecessary as they would be prolex—They are obvious,—and will occur to you on a moments reflection" (RCS:Va., 763).

Because he was much concerned, Washington was pleased when he learned that on 26 April Maryland ratified the Constitution. On 2 May, he told Madison that Maryland's action was "A thorn" in the sides of Virginia's Antifederalist leaders (Rutland, *Madison*, XI, 33). Washington informed New York Federalist John Jay that, since the opponents of the Constitution in Virginia had failed to keep Federalists out of the state Convention and had been "baffled in their exertions to effect an adjournment in Maryland, they have become more passive *of late*" (15 May, RCS:Va., 804). In early June Baltimore merchants presented Washington with the *Federalist*, a miniature ship which had been part of the town's procession celebrating Maryland's ratification. Washington told the merchants that the action of the Maryland Convention "will not be without its due efficacy on the minds of their neighbours, who, in many instances, are intimately connected not only by the nature of their produce, but by the ties of blood and the habits of life. Under these circumstances, I cannot entertain an idea that the voice of the Convention of this State, which is now in session, will be dissonant from that of her nearly-allied sister, who is only seperated by the Potomac" (8 June, Fitzpatrick, XXIX, 516–17).

Washington's elation was dampened several weeks later when he received a copy of an extract of a 10 July letter that Dr. Lawrence Brooke of Fredericksburg had written to David Stuart. In this letter Brooke reported that James Mercer, an opponent of the Constitution and a judge of the Virginia General Court, had informed him that Colonel John Francis Mercer (James Mercer's brother), then visiting in Fredericksburg, "was furnished with documents to prove, that Genl. Washington had wrote a letter upon the present Constitution, to Governor Johnson of Maryland, and that Governor Johnson was so much displeased with the officiousness of Genl. Washington, as to induce him to take an active part in bringing about the amendments proposed by a Committee of the Convention of Maryland." Stuart made a copy of an excerpt of Dr. Brooke's letter and gave it to Washington (Washington Papers, DLC. Thomas Johnson and John Francis Mercer, who moved to Maryland in

1785, served on the committee of thirteen of the Maryland Convention that considered amendments to the Constitution. Both favored reporting amendments to the Convention, although Johnson voted to ratify the Constitution and Mercer voted not to ratify. See CC:716.).

On 31 August Washington wrote Johnson, quoting the excerpt and asking him "what foundation there is for so much" of the extract "as relates to the officious light in which my conduct was viewed for havg. written the letter alluded to." Washington insisted that he had not written Johnson in order "to make proselytes, or to obtrude my opinions with a view to influence the judgment of any one." He defied any Antifederalist "to say, with truth, that I ever wrote to, or exchanged a word with him on the subject of the New Constitution if (the latter) was not forced upon me in a manner not to be avoided." His sole purpose had been to warn Federalists in the Maryland Convention that the opponents of the Constitution in that body might try "to effect an adjournment." Washington asked whether or not he had interfered improperly in the activities of the Maryland Convention (Fitzpatrick, XXX, 77–79).

Johnson assured Washington that he had not acted improperly. In fact, Johnson said that he had shown Washington's letter and similar letters to some gentlemen in order "To strengthen the Friends of the new Constitution and expedite it's Adoption." Washington's letter had not influenced Johnson's position on amendments. Although not actively involved in initiating amendments, Johnson was distressed about the manner in which the Convention handled the amendments and he believed that the Constitution could be improved by some of them. Johnson further declared that, when showing Washington's letter to some gentlemen, he had also hinted that America would have need of Washington's "farther Services." "We cannot Sir," Johnson continued, "do without you and I and thousands more can explain to any Body but yourself why we cannot do without you." He concluded: "My Acquaintance with Colo. Mercer is not of long standing or very close—he will never find me acting on a great public Question from such unworthy Motives nor I hope displeased with any Letter I may have the Honor to receive from you" (10 October, Washington Papers, DLC). Nevertheless, Johnson's conciliatory attitude temporarily threw Federalists in the Maryland Convention into confusion. Federalist Daniel Carroll, who was not a member of the Convention, had been informed that Johnson's "accomodating disposition, and a respect to his character lead the Majority into a Situation, out of which they found some dificulty to extricat[e] themselves" (to James Madison, 28 May, Rutland, *Madison*, XI, 67).

## George Washington to Thomas Johnson, Mount Vernon, 20 April[1]

As well from report, as from the ideas expressed in your letter to me in December last,[2] I am led to conclude that you are disposed (circumstanced as our public affairs are at present) to ratify the Constitution which has been submitted by the general Convention to the People; and under this impression, I take the liberty of expressing a *single* sentiment on the occasion.—

It is, that an adjournment, (if attempted), of your Convention to a later period than the decision of the question in this State, will be tantamount to the rejection of the Constitution.—I have good ground for this opinion—and am told it is *the blow* which the leading characters of the opposition in [these two?] States[3] have meditated if it shall be found that a direct attack is not likely to succeed in yours.—If this be true, it cannot be too much deprecated, & guarded against.—

The postponement in New-Hampshire, altho' made without any reference to the Convention of this State, & altogether from the local circumstances of its own;[4] is ascribed by the opposition *here* to complaisance towards Virginia; and great use is made of it.—An event similar to this in Maryland, would have the worst tendency imaginable, for indecision there wld. have considerable influence upon South Carolina, the only other State which is to precede Virginia, and submits the question almost wholly to the determination of the latter.—The *pride* of the State is already touched upon this string, & will be strained much higher if there is an opening for it.[5]

The sentiments of Kentucky are not yet known here.—Independent of these, the parties with us, from the known, or presumed opinions of the members, are pretty equally balanced.—The one in favor of the Constitution p[r]eponderates at present—but a small matter cast into the opposite scale may make it the heaviest.

If in suggesting this matter, I have exceeded the proper limit, my motive must excuse me—I have but one public wish remaining—It is, that in *peace* and *retirement*, I may see this Country rescued from the danger which is pending, & rise into respectability maugre the Intrigues of its public & private enemies.—

1. RC, Miscellaneous Vertical File, #1118, Maryland Historical Society. Johnson (1732–1819), a Frederick County, Md., lawyer, had been a delegate to Congress, 1774–76, and Maryland's first governor, 1777–79. He served in the November–December 1787 session of the House of Delegates and voted to ratify the Constitution in the state Convention on 26 April. He was also a director of the Potowmack Navigation Company, of which Washington was president.

2. See Johnson to Washington, 11 December (CC:336).

3. The letterbook version reads: "in the next State" (Washington Papers, DLC).

4. See "The Adjournment of the New Hampshire Convention," 22 February (CC:554).

5. The letterbook version reads: "will be raised much higher if there is fresh cause" (Washington Papers, DLC).

### 696. Samuel Holden Parsons to George Washington
### Carlisle, Pa., 21 April[1]

I am now on my Road to the Settlements forming on the River Ohio, and take this only Method in my power to take leave of your Excellency & to assure you of my most cordial Wishes for your Happiness; should any Occurrances render my Services in that Country of Use to you, I shall never be more happy than in devoting myself to the execution of your Wishes—The State of our Country must give very sensible trouble to every good Citizen & to none more than to your Excellency who has acted so conspicuous a part in effecting our Independance—in the eastern States I think Opposition to the fœderal Government is nearly ended; we have our Eyes now turnd to Virginia, if there is Wisdom to adopt the propos'd plan in that State, I think we may hope to restore to our nation the Honor their folly has lost them;—I view the Adoption of the present plan with all its Imperfections as the only Means of preserving the Union of the States & securing the Happiness of all the parts of this extensive Country; I feel myself deeply interested in this Subject as it will affect the Country of which I am now commencing an Inhabitant, I am Sure it must ever be our Interest to continue connected with the Atlantic States, to them we must look up for protection, and from them we can receive such Supplies as we want with more facility than from our other Neighbours; but without an efficient Government, we can expect no Benefits of a Connection and I fear it will lead Us to improper Measures—the Navigation of the Potomac is very interesting to our Settlement, if it is perfected according to this proposd Scheme, we shall save a land transportation of five Hundred Miles the Rout we at present Pursue, our new Settlement progresses rapidly. Two Hundred Families will be within our City by July & I think we are sure of a thousand families from New England within One Year if we remain in peace

1. RC, Washington Papers, DLC. Washington endorsed this letter as received on 30 June. Major General Parsons (1737–1789) served in the Continental Army from 1776 to 1782 and was one of Washington's more effective commanders and one of his "old military friends" (Fitzpatrick, XXX, 14). In March 1787 Parsons, a Middletown, Conn., lawyer, was elected a director of the Ohio Company, and in October Congress appointed him the first judge of the Northwest Territory. He voted to ratify the Constitution in the Connecticut Convention in January 1788, and in April he left for Ohio, arriving at Marietta in late May.

### 697. Benjamin Franklin to Louis-Guillaume Le Veillard Philadelphia, 22 April (excerpt)[1]

My dear Friend

I received but a few Days since your Favour of Nov. 30. 1787. in which you continue to urge me to finish the Memoirs.[2] My three Years of Service will expire in October, when a new President[3] must be chosen, and I had the Project of retiring then to my Grandson's Villa[4] where I might be free from the Interruption of Visits, in order to compleat that Work for your Satisfaction; for in this City my Time is so cut to pieces by Friends and Strangers, that I have sometimes envied the Prisoners in the Bastille: But considering now the little Remnant of Life I have left, the Accidents that may happen between this and October, and your earnest Desire, I have come to a Resolution to proceed in that Work to-morrow, and continue at it daily till finished, which if my Health permits, may be in the Course of the ensuing Summer. As it goes on I will have a Copy made for you, and you may expect to receive a Part by the next Pacquet.

It is very possible as you suppose, that all the Articles of the propos'd new Government will not remain unchanged after the first Meeting of the new Congress. I am of Opinion with you that the two Chambers were not necessary, and I dislik'd some other Articles that are in, and wish'd for some that are not in the propos'd Plan; I nevertheless hope it may be adopted, tho' I shall have nothing to do with the Execution of it, being determined to quit all public Business with my present Employment. At 83 one certainly has a Right to ambition Repose.

We are not ignorant that the Duties paid at the Custom house on the Importation of Foreign Goods are finally reimburs'd by the Consumer, but we impose them as the easiest Way of levying a Tax from those Consumers. If our new Country were as closely inhabited as your old one, we might without much Difficulty collect a Land Tax that would be sufficient for all purposes: But where Farms are at 5 or 6 Miles distant from each other, as they are in a great part of our Country, the going of the Collectors from House to House to demand the Taxes, and being oblig'd to call more than once for the same Tax, makes the Trouble of Collecting in many Cases exceed the Value of the Sum collected. Things that are practicable in one Country, are not always so in another, where Circumstances differ.—Our Duties however are generally so small as to give little Temptation to smuggling. . . .

1. RC, Dreer Collection, PHi. This letter was addressed "A Monsieur Le Veillard à Passy pres de Paris." Le Veillard endorsed the letter as received on 30 May.

2. In 1771, while in England, Benjamin Franklin wrote part of his autobiography. He resumed writing in 1784, with the encouragement of friends. Franklin began again in August 1788, and in November 1789 he sent what was completed of his memoirs to Le Veillard. Between November 1789 and March 1790 Franklin added the last few pages (J. A. Leo Lemay and P. M. Zall, eds., *The Autobiography of Benjamin Franklin: A Genetic Text* [Knoxville, Tenn., 1981], xx–xxiii, xxxiii, xl–xlvi).

3. Franklin was president of the Supreme Executive Council of Pennsylvania from October 1785 to October 1788.

4. William Temple Franklin, Franklin's secretary in France from 1776 to 1785, lived on his grandfather's farm on Rancocas Creek, N.J., about sixteen miles from Philadelphia. In 1785 Franklin purchased the farm from William Temple's father William—the former Loyalist governor of New Jersey, then living in England (Claude-Anne Lopez

and Eugenia W. Herbert, *The Private Franklin: The Man and His Family* [New York, 1975], 285–86, 288, 291, 292, 312–13).

### 698. Don Diego de Gardoqui to Conde de Floridablanca
### New York, 22 April[1]

My Lord. The adverse winds which have detained the Perlador, to which some days ago I delivered the Packet of letters, give me the opportunity by which I add this one, in order to communicate to Your Excellency that the Information received this day from Virginia confirms very reliably the Suspicion that that State will not adopt the New Plan of Government.

With this News I have spoken in earnest with the President,[2] who is a Virginian and a sincere man, and he has Responded to me, that the likelihood is very much to the contrary, because the Representatives of Kentucky upon whom he was relying are very much opposed, from which he infers that the best that could possibly be expected is that it will be delayed much more than was believed.

To ground myself further, I have just spoken in earnest with General Knox, Minister of War who openly has made himself known a very vigorous and strong Supporter of the new Plan of Government.

This Individual, who promoted it with all his power, has told me countless times, that the organization would begin during the course of this year, but now he just confessed to me Discreetly, that the opposition is much greater than that which was believed, and he fears with good reason that the aforementioned Government will not be established before next year.[3]

This is the feeling of the day of the most partial Federalists, so that Your Excellency will infer that there is not the slightest probability of their being able to bring about a [commercial] Convention, as long as this Country is not established as a Nation.

In the meantime they scarcely find sufficient funds to Maintain the small expenditure of the President, and I believe the Employees moreover do not receive their Salaries.[4]

The discord is confirmed in [the State of] Franklin, whose Inhabitants are so involved in difficulties that [a number of?] encounters, and some Dead and wounded have resulted,[5] so, our Don Jaime[6] who should have left today, will arrive in good time.

It seems that it is going to set sail, for which reason I conclude, renewing my obedience, and praying God keep Your Excellency's Life for many years.

1. RC (Tr), Estado, Legajo 3894, Apartado 1, Letter 261, Archivo Histórico Nacional, Madrid, Spain.

2. For President of Congress Cyrus Griffin's pessimism about Virginia's ratification prospects, see RCS:Va., 737–38, 764.

3. By 24 April Secretary at War Henry Knox seems to have regained his optimism about the prospects of ratification. See CC:703, 707, 708, 712.

4. For the financial difficulties of Congress, see Nathan Dane to Samuel Holten, 15 March (CC:618) and Samuel A. Otis to James Warren, 6 February (LMCC, VIII, 696).

5. In 1785 the State of Franklin was created out of the western counties of North Carolina, and John Sevier became its governor. Early in 1788 a dispute erupted between the faction led by Sevier and another led by Colonel John Tipton, and in February the Sevier forces were defeated in a "battle" which signaled the beginning of the end of the self-proclaimed state. Gardoqui saw the turmoil in Franklin as an opportunity to extend Spanish influence into the territory. He believed that "the matter is ripe for trial because of the general debility of the country and because the District of Frankland lends itself to such a degree that I am informed that the government has *secret information* of that disposition." (See Arthur Preston Whitaker, *The Spanish-American Frontier: 1783–1795* [Boston and New York, 1927], 80, 86, 109–10; Gardoqui to Floridablanca, 18 April, in D. C. Corbitt and Roberta Corbitt, trans. and eds., "Papers from the Spanish Archives Relating to Tennessee and the Old Southwest, 1783–1800," East Tennessee Historical Society *Publications*, XVII (1945), 107, 108; and Gardoqui to Floridablanca, 24 October, Estado, Legajo 3894, Apartado 1, Letter 295, Archivo Histórico Nacional, Madrid, Spain.)

6. Gardoqui remembered some private conversations about the West that he had in 1786 with Dr. James White, a North Carolina delegate to Congress and the former Superintendent of Indian Affairs for the Southern District. Consequently, he hired White to "go to the state of Franklin to spread what seems convenient to me." He also wanted White to locate Sevier and to convince him to join forces with the Spanish. White left New York City on 1 May, and returned to Congress in October. A jubilant Gardoqui reported that White told him that "he had completed his mission perfectly." (See the sources cited in note 5, above.)

### 699. Fabius V
### Pennsylvania Mercury, 22 April[1]

OBSERVATIONS ON THE CONSTITUTION
proposed by the FEDERAL CONVENTION.

It has been considered, what are the rights to be contributed, and how they are to be managed; and it has been said, that republican tranquility and prosperity have commonly been promoted, in proportion to the strength of government for protecting *the worthy* against *the licentious.*

The protection herein mentioned, refers to cases *between* citizens and citizens, or states and states: But there is also a protection to be afforded to *all* the citizens, or states, against foreigners. It has been asserted, that *this* protection never can be afforded, but under an appropriation, collection, and application, of the general force, by the will of the whole combination. This protection is in a degree dependent on the former, as it may be weakened by internal discords and especially where the worst party prevails. Hence it is evident, that such establishments as tend most to protect *the worthy* against *the licentious*, tend most to protect *all* against foreigners. This position is found to be verified by indisputable facts, from which it appears, that when nations have been, as it were, *condemned* for their *crimes*, unless they first became *suicides*, foreigners have acted as *executioners*.

This is not all. As government is intended for the happiness of the people, the protection of the worthy against those of contrary characters, is calculated to promote the end of legitimate government, that is, the general welfare; for the government will partake of the qualities of those whose authority is prevalent. If it be asked, who are *the worthy*, we may be informed by a Heathen Poet—

> "Vir *bonus* est quis?
> Qui consulta patrum, qui leges juraque servat."[2]

The best foundations of this protection, that can be laid by men, are a constitution and government secured, as well as can be, from the undue influence of *passions* either in the people or their servants. Then in a contest between citizens and citizens, or states and states, the standard of *laws* may be displayed, explained and strengthened by the well-remembered sentiments and examples of our fore-fathers, which will give it a sanctity far superior to that of their eagles so venerated by the former masters of the world. This circumstance will carry powerful aids to the true friends of their country, and unless counteracted by the follies of *Pharsalia*, or the accidents of *Philippi*, may secure the blessings of freedom to succeeding ages.

It has been contended, that the plan proposed to us, adequately secures us against the influence of *passions* in the federal servants. Whether it as adequately secures us against the influence of *passions* in the people, or in particular states, *time will determine*, and may the determination be propitious.

Let us now consider the tragical play of the passions in similar cases; or, in other words, the consequences of their irregularities. Duly governed, they produce happiness.

Here the reader, is respectfully requested, to assist the intentions of the writer, by keeping in mind, the ideas of a single republic with *one* democratical branch in its government, and of a confederation of republics with *one* or *several* democratical branches in the government of the confederation, or in the government of its parts, so that as he proceeds, a comparison may easily run along, between any of these and the proposed plan.

History is entertaining and instructive; but, if it be admired chiefly for amusement, it may yield little profit. If read for improvement, it is apprehended, a slight attention only will be paid to the vast variety of particular incidents, unless it be such as may meliorate the heart. A knowle[d]ge of the distinguishing features of nations, the principles of their governments, the advantages and disadvantages of their situations, the methods employed to avail themselves of the first, and to alleviate the last, their manners, customs, and institutions, the sources of events, their progresses, and determining causes, may be eminently useful, tho' obscurity may rest upon a multitude of connecting circumstances. Thus, one nation may become prudent and happy, by the errors and misfortunes of another.

In *Carthage*, and *Rome*, there was a very numerous *senate*, strengthened by prodigious attachments, and in a great degree independent of the people. So there was in *Athens*, especially as the senate of that state was supported by the court of *Areopagus*. In each of these republics, their affairs at length became convulsed, and their liberty was subverted. What cause produced these effects? Encroachments of the *senate* upon the authority of the people? No! but directly the reverse, according to the unanimous voice of historians; that is, encroachments of the people upon the authority of the senate. The people of these republics absolutely laboured for their own destruction; and never thought themselves *so free*, as when they were promoting their subjugation. Though, even after these encroachments had been made, and ruin was spreading around, yet, the remnants of senatorial authority delayed the final catastrophe.

In more modern times, the *Florentines* exhibited a memorable example. They were divided into violent parties; and the prevailing one vested exorbitant powers in the house of *Medici*, then possessed, as it was judged, of more money, than any crowned head in Europe. Though that house engaged and perserved [i.e., persevered] in the attempt, yet the people were never despoiled of their liberty, until they were over-whelmed by the conjoined[3] armies of foreign princes, to whose enterprizes their situation exposed them.

Republics of later date and various form appeared. Their institutions consist of old errors tissued with hasty inventions, somewhat excusable, as the wills of the *Romans*, made with arms in their hands. Some of them were condensed by dangers. They are still compressed by them into a sort of solidity.[4] Their well-known transactions witness, that their connection is not enough compact and arranged. They have all suffered, or are suffering through that defect. Their existence seems to depend more upon others, than themselves.

The wretched mistake of the great men who were leaders in the long parliament of *England*, in attempting, by not filling up vacancies, to extend their power over a brave and sensible people accustomed to popular representation, and their downfall, when their victories and puis[s]ance by sea and land had thrown all Europe into astonishment and awe, shew, how difficult it is for rulers to usurp over a people who are not wanting to themselves.

Let the fortunes of confederated republics be now considered.

"*The Amphictionic council*," or "general court of *Greece*," claims the first regard. Its authority was very great: But, the parts were not sufficiently combined, to guard against the ambitious, avaricious, and selfish projects of some of them; or, if they had the power, they dared not to employ it, as the turbulent states were very sturdy, and made a sort of partial confederacies.

"*The Achæan league*" seems to be the next in dignity. It was at first, small, consisting of few states: afterwards, very extensive, consisting of many. In their Diet or Congress, they enacted laws, disposed of vacant employments, declared war, made peace, entered into alliances, compelled every state of the union to obey its ordinance, and managed other affairs. Not only their laws, but their magistrates, council, judges, money, weights and measures, were the same. So uniform were they, that all seemed to be but one state. Their chief officer called Strategos was chosen in the Congress by a majority of votes. He presided in the Congress and commanded the forces, and was vested with great power; especially in time of war: but was liable to be called to an account by the Congress, and punished, if convicted of misbehaviour.

These states had been domineered by the kings of *Macedon*, and insulted by tyrants. From their incorporation, says *Polybius*, may be dated the birth of that greatness, that by a constant augmentation, at length arrived to a marvellous height of prosperity. The fame of their wise laws and mild government reached the *Greek* colonies in *Italy*, where the *Crotoniates*, the *Sybarites*, and the *Cauloniates*, agreed to adopt them, and to govern their states conformably.

Did the delegates to the *Amphictionic council*, or to *the Congress of the Achæan league*, destroy the liberty of their country, by establishing a monarchy or an aristocracy among themselves? Quite the contrary. While the several states continued faithful to the union, they prospered. Their affairs were shattered by dissentions, emulations, and civil wars, artfully and diligently fomented by princes who thought it their interest; and in the case of *the Achæan league*, chiefly, by the folly and wickedness of *Greeks* not of the league, particularly the *Ætolians*, who repined at the glories, that constantly attended the banner of freedom, supported by virtue and conducted by prudence. Thus weakened, they all sunk together, the envied and the envying, under the domination, first of *Macedon*, and then of *Rome*.

Let any man of common sense peruse the mournful, but instructive pages of their stories, and he will be convinced, that if any nation could successfully have resisted those conquerers of the world, the illustrious deed[5] had been atchieved by *Greece*, that cradle of republics, if the several states had been cemented by some such league as the *Achæan*, and had honestly fulfilled its obligations.

It is not pretended, that *the Achæan league* was perfect, or that there were not monarchical and aristocratical factions among the people of it. Every concession of that sort, that can be asked, shall be made. It had many defects; every one of which, however, has been avoided in the plan proposed to us. It had also inveterately monarchical and aristocratical factions; from which, happily we are clear.

With all it defects, with all its disorders, yet such was the life and vigor communicated through *the whole*, by the *popular representation* of each part, and by the *close combination* of all, that the true spirit of republicanism *predominated*, and thereby advanced the happiness and glory of the people to so pre-eminent a state, that our ideas upon the pleasing theme cannot be too elevated. Here is the proof of this assertion. When the *Romans* had laid *Carthage* in ashes; had reduced the kingdom of *Macedon* to a province; had conquered *Antiochus* the great, and got the better of all their enemies in the East; these *Romans*, masters of so much of the then known world, determined to humble *the Achæan league*, because as history expressly informs us, *their great power* began to raise *no small jealousy* at *Rome*.

What an immense weight of argument do these circumstances and facts, add to the maintenance of the principle contended for by the writer of this address?

1. Reprinted: Baltimore *Maryland Gazette*, 23 May; *Virginia Independent Chronicle*, 28 May; *New Hampshire Spy*, 3 June; *New Hampshire Gazette*, 19 June; *Providence Gazette*, 5 July; Philadelphia *American Museum*, October.

2. Horace, *Epistles*, Book I, epistle 16, lines 40–41. "Whom call we good?/The man who keeps intact each law, each right, each statute, and each act."

3. "Conjoined" deleted in the *American Museum* version.

4. "A sort of union" substituted for "a sort of solidity" in the *American Museum* version.

5. "Work" substituted for "deed" in the *American Museum* version.

## 700. George Thatcher to Pierse Long
## Biddeford, Maine, 23 April[1]

Yours of the fifteenth inst. came to hand by the last Post, & would have been duly acknowledged, had not my ~~attention~~ time been taken up in some matters of Law that demanded immediate attention on my arrival home—

I assure you, Sir, I was very sorry in not finding you at home on my coming through Portsmouth; for tho' my hurry to get to York, the Court then seting at that place, would not have permited me to make a very long stay, yet I wanted to have enquired, of many things about your late Convention, the speakers, their debates, & the prospect of the Constitution being adopted on the adjournment—And possibly might in my turn given you some information upon the subject of your queries—

You enquire about the sale & settlement of the Western Country— To be particular upon this Question would involve answers to so many others, which would fall incidentally in the way as would be tedious for a Letter, & therefore for the present, I shall only observe generally—That the Companies of Cutler & Sergent—Flint & Parker— Symms & his associates have contracted for three several Tracts containing not more than eight or nine million of Acres—to be paid for in Continental Securities at certain periods by Installments upon which payments deeds are to be executed to the purchasers—but if not paid for no Title is to be given—And I believe I am justified in saying that all the payments by the three Companies do not exceed half a million of Dollars—& I am not certain that it does 270,000 Dollars—For my part I must acknowledge my faith of paying the Domestic Debt, by regular sails of the western Land, never was very great—There is Land eno' & that which is excellent—A few days before I left New-York, I was in company with the Geographer General[2] of the United States & he said, from a calculation he had made, he would warrant there was more than two hundred million of Acres of good Land on the northwest of the Ohio—But to me the Idea of runing this out, & by the neat proceeds of its sails discharging any considerable part of the Debt—is almost as chimerical as to count upon the number of Codfish, & whales in the ocean for that purpose—Not a great many purchasers have offered themselves, & few that have could give evidence of their ability, & of those that could, still a smaller number have, & probably ever will, fully comply with their contracts—Continental Securities have been for several years very low—perhaps lower than they ever will be hereafter should the proposed Constitution, or any other with energy enough to discharge the Interest, be adopted—Hence if purchasers have found it difficult to discharge their Contracts while public Securities have been sold from 6/- to 3/- on the pound—what probability is there of their being enabled after the adoption of a Constitution that shall secure their Redemption, & make them equal to silver & Gold—

As to the negotiation of public Treaties, it appears to me the *existing articles of Confederation* have exhibited to all Europe too evident marks of incompetency for any national purposes to induce foreign Powers to trust to Treaties made under them—The Queen of Portugal has shewn a disposition for negotiations of Friendship & Commerce—But here difficulties arise on the part of America—And perhaps if I were to say that Congress cannot command Cash or credit sufficient to support a negotiator at the Court of Lisbon, to promote & improve any overtures of this kind[3]—I should not be far from the truth—Money is universally acknowledged to be the Sinews of war—And I think it cannot be doubted to be equally necessary to the support of Civil Government, & the formation of foreign Treaties—

*The Importance of the Navigation of the Missisippie is a matter* I am not sufficiently informed to say much about—But from the general state of that Country there can be but little doubt, that if the navagation of the Missisippie should be benificial to the American Settlements, they will enjoy it—The idea of Spains interupting it is almost inadmissible—within 20 years—and upon the Settlement of a good Government the Danger will be on the side of Spains Loosing her possessions on the Western Waters—rather than the Americans loosing the navagation—But the navagation of that River will ever be attended with difficulty from its rapid Current From the mouth of the ohio to the mouth of the Messesipi as the River Runs, is one thousand miles—and on a right Line not more than five hundred a vessell or boat, may go down this River in less than three weeks, but three or four months are required in ascending the same distance

"Will all the southern States agree to the proposed Constitution?"

The Convention in Maryland meets this day for the purpose of considering the new plan of Government. When I came from New-York, which will be four week to morrow morning, it was the general opinion there that the Constitution would be adopted in Maryland by a large majority of the Convention—There being three fourths at least of the people warmly in favour of it—And that this was matter of fact I have no doubt, since both parties, antifederal as well as federal joined in this general opinion—

South-Carolina meets on the twelfth of May—from the best information we could get respecting the sentiments of that State upon the great Question the Federalists entertained no doubt—they were secure in the idea of its being adopted—But so we were last winter with regard to New-Hampshire—'tis almost impossible that disappointment should be greater than ours was on hearing the result of your Convention— However, I have faith—Can you strengthen it?—

There now remains Virginia & North-Carolina—The former meets in June, I think towards the last, And from many accounts from various parts of that State wherein the Federal & antifederal parties seemed to agree—there was at that time a decided & large majority in that State against It.

1. FC, Chamberlain Collection, MB. This unsigned draft of a letter is in the handwriting of George Thatcher. Editor William F. Goodwin identified the recipient as Pierse Long ("The Thatcher Papers," *The Historical Magazine*, VI [1869], 347). Internal evidence indicates that the recipient was a resident of Portsmouth, N.H., and perhaps a member of the New Hampshire Convention. Pierse Long (1739–1789), a Portsmouth merchant, attended both sessions (February and June 1788) of the New Hampshire Convention and voted to ratify the Constitution. Long was a delegate to Congress, 1785–86, and a member of the New Hampshire Senate, 1788–89.

2. Thomas Hutchins.

3. Negotiations with Portugal were commenced in early 1786 and were eventually dropped (RCS:Va., 1174, note 23).

### 701. Pennsylvania Gazette, 23 April[1]

The men who object to the new government, says another correspondent, because the mode of altering the old confœderation was not strictly *constitutional*, remind us of the conduct of the loyalists in the beginning of the late war, who objected to *associating, arming* and *fighting*, in defence of our liberties, because these measures were not *constitutional*. A free people should always be left in a condition competent to all their wants, and with every possible power to promote their own happiness. The people, as the sovereigns of a country, are above all constitutions, and a *majority* of them have a right to alter, or abolish, their constitutions at *any* time, and in *any* way they may think proper. The contrary opinion is the doctrine of Hobbes, and other advocates for passive obedience,[2] accommodated to the present state of government in the United States. While the royal parasites tell us that "kings give and grant liberty to their subjects," the officeholders under our state governments tell us, that we have no liberty but what is conferred upon us by our constitutions. To say that a government can be altered only in *one way*, or at *any one* time, when a majority of the people think otherwise, is to annihilate freedom, to check all improvements in government, and to prostrate unborn generations at the feet of that body of men who framed the government. Nature revolts at the idea as highly tyrannical, and the spirit of America, it is to be hoped, will reject it with abhorrence, by speedily adopting the new constitution.

1. Reprinted: *New York Packet*, 25 April; Hartford *American Mercury* and Lansingburgh *Federal Herald*, 5 May; *Massachusetts Gazette*, 6 May.

2. The concept of passive obedience to rulers, which became common in the 16th and 17th centuries, was related to the theory of the divine right of kings. Article IV of the Maryland Declaration of Rights (1776) provided that "The doctrine of non-resistance, against arbitrary power and oppression, is absurd, slavish, and destructive of the good and happiness of mankind." This article was copied in Article X of the New Hampshire Bill of Rights (1784), Article III of the proposed declaration of rights of the Virginia Convention (1788), and Article III of the proposed declaration of rights of the North Carolina Convention (1788) (Thorpe, III, 1687; IV, 2455; CC:790; and CC:821).

In the Virginia Convention, Antifederalist Patrick Henry charged that the arguments used by Federalists in favor of ratification were similar to arguments used in the past to justify "The doctrine of divine right and passive obedience, as said to be commanded by Heaven" (14 June 1788, RCS:Va., 1284–85).

## 702. None of the Well-Born Conspirators
## Philadelphia Freeman's Journal, 23 April

Even before the Constitutional Convention adjourned, the lines of battle were drawn for the contest over the ratification of the new Constitution. For example, on 12 September 1787, five days before the adoption of the Constitution, the Federalist *Pennsylvania Gazette* printed a short piece stating that "The former distinction of the citizens of America . . . into whigs and tories, should be lost in the more important distinction of *fœderal* and *antifœderal* men. The former are the friends of liberty and independence—the latter are the enemies of liberty, and the secret abettors of the interests of Great-Britain" (CC:73).

The terms federal and antifederal, however, were not new. According to Philadelphia Antifederalist Samuel Bryan, the use of the labels "Federalists" or "Federal Men" started in New York and New England prior to the calling of the Constitutional Convention in order to describe men who "were attached to the general Support of the United States, in Opposition to those who preferred local & particular Advantages" for their respective states (to Aedanus Burke, post-5 December 1789, Mfm:Pa. 700–D). For the most part, the terms federal and antifederal were used in the debate over whether or not Congress should be given additional powers to regulate commerce and to levy a federal impost that would provide it with an independent revenue. In February 1786 merchant Nathaniel Gorham hoped that his own state of Massachusetts would "send Men of good Federal ideas" to the Annapolis Convention to combat men "somewhat antifederal in their opinions" (to Caleb Davis, 23 February, Davis Papers, MHi, quoted in Robert A. East, "The Massachusetts Conservatives in the Critical Period," in Richard B. Morris, ed.,

*The Era of the American Revolution* [New York, 1939], 373). In May "Acirema," America spelled backwards, condemned the "few *designing wretches*" in the New York legislature, who obstructed "national measures." He believed that it was "high time for the other states to manifest their just indignation against this *anti-federal sister;* and if she will not *come in,* cast her *out, for ever.* It is better to *cut off a limb,* than to let the whole body perish" (New York *Daily Advertiser,* 11 May 1786). Sensing New York's anti-national conduct, David Humphreys of Connecticut told Thomas Jefferson in June that George Clinton, New York's governor, "is said to have become an Antifœderalist" (5 June 1786, Boyd, IX, 609).

By November 1786 the labels federal and antifederal had become fairly common in describing factions or parties in the politics of some states. Connecticut writer and grammarian Noah Webster disputed the negative attributes with which each group had labeled its opponents. Federal men, Webster maintained, were neither ambitious nor tyrannical, while antifederals were neither knaves nor "designing artful demagogues." Both groups, he said, supported the interests of their states and country, but, unfortunately, antifederals "think as they have been bred—their education has been rather indifferent—they have been accustomed to think on the small scale." Were antifederals "to travel, to sit in Congress, to converse with men who understand foreign policy," they would understand the need for a stronger central government (*Connecticut Courant,* 20 November, Mfm:Conn. 3). Another commentator was even less generous, referring to "the narrow-soul'd, antifederal politicians in the several States, who, by their influence, have hitherto damn'd us [as] a nation" (*Massachusetts Centinel,* 14 April 1787, CC:14).

Immediately after the Constitutional Convention, which many newspapers had been describing as the "Federal Convention," adjourned on 17 September 1787, supporters of the Constitution began calling themselves Federalists and their opponents Antifederalists. Federalists compared Antifederalists to the Tories of the American Revolution and the Shaysites of Massachusetts who had rebelled against their state government in 1786–87 ("Tar and Feathers," Philadelphia *Independent Gazetteer,* 2 October, RCS:Pa., 152). Antifederalists struck back, but, because of the prominence of such Federalists as George Washington and Benjamin Franklin, all Federalists could not be criticized, at least not directly. For example, according to "Fair Play," some leading Federalists were merely misled or duped by a conspiracy of "*downright Tories*" or "*lukewarm Whigs*"; while "Centinel" I said that Washington had been duped in the Convention and Franklin was too old to know what he was doing (Philadelphia *Independent Gazetteer,* 4 and 5 October, RCS:Pa., 154, and CC:133. "Centinel" did not refer to Washington and Franklin by name, but it was clear who he meant when he referred to "two illustrious personages.").

To combat the usurpation of the label Federalists by the proponents of the Constitution, the critics of the Constitution often argued that they were the true federalists. In December 1787 an anonymous newspaper writer stated that "A FEDERALIST is a Friend to a Federal Government—An ANTI-FEDERALIST is an Enemy to a Confederation—Therefore, the Friends to the New Plan of CONSOLIDATION, are Anti-Federal, and its Opposers are firm, Federal Patriots" (Boston *American Herald,* 10 December. See also "A Countryman" II [DeWitt Clinton], *New York Journal*, 13 December.). In January 1788 Luther Martin, a former Maryland delegate to the Constitutional Convention, revealed that in the Convention when the question was proposed " 'that a union of the States, merely federal, ought to be the sole object of the exercise of the powers vested in the convention'," it was rejected and a majority voted " 'that a *national* government ought to be formed'." Afterwards, " '*national*' was struck out by them, because they thought the *word* might tend to *alarm*." However, throughout the Convention, stated Martin, those delegates who supported amending the Articles of Confederation and opposed creating a new constitution were "stiled the *federal party*"; those who advocated abandoning the Articles and creating a new constitution that provided for a consolidated government were described as "*antifederal*" (Baltimore *Maryland Gazette*, 8 January, CC:425).

In March 1788 "A Farmer" suggested that there were only two kinds of government possible: those that operated directly on individuals, which were called national governments, and those where states combined together to form "a *league or confederacy*." Consequently, the friends of the Constitution had "improperly applied" the name Federalists to themselves. "This abuse of language does not help the cause,—every degree of imposition serves only to irritate, but can never convince.—They are *national men*, and their opponents, or at least a great majority of them, are *fœderal*, in the only true and strict sense of the word" (Baltimore *Maryland Gazette*, 7 March). In April "Horatio" explained that "The term *antifederal* is applied by the advocates of the *new* government for America, by way of reproach to all those who oppose it. Words are often misunderstood and as often misapplied. The government proposed is truly a *national*, and not a *federal* government. A *national* government is a supreme authority pervading and ruling over the *people* of a country: Its advocates therefore may, with propriety be called *nationals*; and its opponents *anti-nationals.*—A *federal* government is an union or league of independent States, for mutual protection and defence; and its advocates are truly *federal*" (*ibid.*, 22 April).

"The Impartial Examiner" II, writing in Virginia in May 1788, believed that most Americans favored the continuation of the Union. Antifederalists seemed "to act on the broader scale of true *fœderal principles*," while the supporters of "the new code wish all sovereignty to be lodged in the hands of Congress." If the new Constitution were adopted, the states would be compounded together into "one extended empire . . . thus destroying the sovereignty of each." Antifederalists, on the other hand, advocated the continued sovereignty of each state but were "anxious for such a degree of energy in the general government, as will cement the union in the strongest manner" (*Virginia Independent Chronicle*, 28 May, RCS:Va., 888–89. For another Antifederalist complaint about the misuse of the term federal, see *New York Journal*, 26 May, CC:Vol. 6, Appendix I.).

An Antifederalist correspondent, pleased with the "ingenious essay" of "None of the Well-Born Conspirators," predicted that Federalists "will soon change their name, since the term *federalism* has been so clearly proved . . . to mean a conspiracy. . . . It may be presumed that the bulk of the *federalists* would not be well pleased to have themselves called conspirators, in common

conversation, and yet this is a necessary consequence of their being denom-
inated *federalists*" (Philadelphia *Independent Gazetteer*, 25 April, Mfm:Pa. 659).

"None of the Well-Born Conspirators" was reprinted in two of America's
leading Antifederalist newspapers—the Philadelphia *Independent Gazetteer* of
24 April, and the *New York Journal* of 30 April.

In public disquisitions, especially political controversies, one of the
parties generally adopt some *cant word* or *phrase*, whereby they may be
distinguished from their opponents; and what renders the circumstance
remarkably curious, the *word* or *phrase* is nineteen times out of twenty
wrong applied. Thus in the party politics of Britain, under one administration *candor* was their *shibbolith*, when the most *abusive, uncandid,*
and *dirty mouthed* scoundrels in the kingdom were the favourites of
*court*; under another, *œconomy*, was the *watch-word*, yet *profuseness* and
*prodigality* in public concerns, was then at their *ne plus ultra*; again,
*national honor*, was buz[z]ed about, when not a fragment of *honor,*
*principle*, or even *national courage* could be traced at court; this was in
Lord North's ever memorable administration. Now in an exact agreement with this plan, one of our American political parties, are incessantly bellowing out, *federalism, federal measures, federal gentlemen, &c.*
*&c.*

If the words, Federal, Federalism, &c. are to be taken in their general
and common acceptation, as derived from Fœdus, a league, or cove-
nant, entered into for the mutual advantage of all; there cannot be
found a greater abuse of words than in this instance; for our modern
federalists, namely, the advocates of the new constitution, evidently
aim at nothing but the elevation and aggrandizement of a few over
the many. The *liberty, property*, and every social comfort in life of the
yeomanry in America, are to be sacrificed at the *altar* of tyranny.
*Federalism* then taken in this sense must imply something very remote
from its original natural import; it must, (and truly there is no help
for saying so) signify a league entered into against the sacred liberties
of the people; that is in plain terms a conspiracy; and this is the fifth
signification of the word Fœdus, given by Ainsworth in his excellent
Latin dictionary.[1] Perhaps the consciences of the conspirators in the
*dark conclave* urged them to assume a name which might be in some
measure a key to disclose their perfidy.[2] Conscience is a stern arbiter,
and often compels us to witness against ourselves. Accompanied by
such a faithful monitor the abettors of despotism adopted an epithet
that should, when perfectly understood, be the true index to their base
intentions. Take the word Federalism directly or indirectly, and it
amounts *neither* to more nor less in its modern acceptation[3] than a

conspiracy of the *Well-born few*, against the sacred rights and privileges of their fellow citizens.

1. The reference is to a Latin-English dictionary entitled *Thesaurus Linguae Latinae Compendiarius* which was published in 1736 by English lexicographer Robert Ainsworth (1660–1743).

2. The phrase "dark conclave," which described the Constitutional Convention, was employed earlier by such leading Philadelphia Antifederalists as "Centinel" and "Philadelphiensis" (CC:501, 507, 547). The related term, "secret conclave," was used by Antifederalist pamphleteer "A Columbian Patriot" (CC:581).

3. Both reprints substituted "exception" for "acceptation."

### 703. Henry Knox to John Doughty
### New York, 24 April (excerpt)[1]

. . . The check the new Constitution received by its postponement in New Hampshire produced at first some disagreable effects—But I beleive they will be surmo[u]nted and the constitution received at least by Nine states in the course of the Month of June—Virginia which has been much opposed appears to have elected a majority of federal members below the Mo[u]ntains—Should the Kentucky Members [imbibe?] no prejudices it is highly probable the new Constitution will be adopted in Virginia—Maryland will receive it by a large majority—as also will probably So Carolina—North Carolina will follow the example of Virginia—The Antifederalists in this state are extremely industrious in disseminating their opposition and it is at least problematical in the present moment whether they will not succeed—But let it be decided on which side it may it is most probable that the majority will be very small—It is very probable The Chances are in favor of New Hampshires accept[i]ng it in June—Rhode Island have rejected it by the majority of voices in the several Towns—but that little State have so sold themselves [to work?] iniquity that its acceptance would not have been a credit to the Thing

The ensuing year may be fairly deemed the crisis of the fate of this Country—If the New Constitution takes place, strong hopes may be entertained of our being a respectable nation—If it does not, we have no hope of being united & happy—It is to be apprehend[ed] in this case that we shall be torn by factions and possess no principle of securing for our lives or property—anarchy, horror and Misery are before us—

But I confess I have no doubt respecting the adoption of the constitution by nine States during the Course of the year—If nine adopt it is probable that New York Virginia and North Carolina will also accede to it—

Your friends are all well—

1. FC, Knox Papers, MHi. Major John Doughty of New Jersey (1754–1826), a graduate of Columbia College and an artillery officer, was aide-de-camp to Major General Philip Schuyler during the Revolution. In 1785 Doughty helped design and directed the construction of Fort Harmar on the Muskingum River, near what, in 1788, became Marietta, Ohio. He commanded the fort after its completion.

On 5 July 1788 Doughty, writing from Fort Pitt, replied to Knox: "I congratulate you on the Adoption of the new Constitution by the state of Virginia, as this makes the ninth state who have come into the Measure, I am in Hopes Health & Vigour will soon be restored to our Body politic—This happy Circumstance must cheer the Hearts of our Countrymen, particularly those of our military Brethren, who have been struggling through the late Revolution, & who to their immortal Honor appear to feel so much for the Honor & Dignity of their Country—for I flatter myself it will not be saying too much, to assert that our society are more generally Advocates for good Government, than perhaps any other Class of Citizens" (Knox Papers, MHi).

## 704. Samuel A. Otis to James Warren
### New York, 24 April (excerpts)[1]

... As to adjourning farther South it will not probably take place under the present Confederation.[2] What a new Year may effect, or the New System *you have so much at heart* may produce, depends upon various contingencies.

In regard to the accumulated & increasing debt of the Union, some people give broad hints that it will be paid with a sponge; Which I think under our present weak & *resourceless* circumstances, will be a natural Consequence. Under a new energetic Goverment, I hear some politicians say, our inability is an insuperable bar to payment. The same men say resources might be pointed to of importance sufficient to pay an interest of 3 p Ct; And I am of opinion could the debt be funded at 3 p Ct, the holders of securities left at their option to reloan at three or take their chance of unfunded securities at six, the bulk of the debt would be reloaned. To this it may be said the cry of injustice will be sett up; As it would indubitably at a sponge. Upon which I reply. In the first place that upon the whole, which will effect most extensive justice, to the greatest number of individuals, must be done. In the second place whats done by consent takes away error. And lastly. If it shall appear impracticable to effect more than three pr Cent, Will not necessity, which is paramount to all Law, justify the measure? You will reply let this necessity be made apparent prior to such proceeding; In which I am perfectly agreed. Before I go from the subject, I am induced to think that under our present impoverished circumstances, could any measures be devised to fund our debt, & make sacred appropriations for the interest at even less than three p Ct, it would reanimate a dead mass of useless paper, & instantly make it an efficient Capital, for the farmer, the Merchant, the man[u]-facturer, & every man in the Community.

Whether "regeneration" is necessary to induce N England, my honored Country, to adopt the New System or not, you who are in one of its largest states can form the best judgment; But am confident without that miraculous change, They will find the necessity of *that*, or one very like it. For as to the old wheel it wont budge an inch, & seems shattered to pieces. That some of the old spokes, & perhaps felloes, may do again I have no doubt, but that the nave must be taken out, & the whole worked over again appears to me indispensible—I do not form my judgment altogether upon what information I get from Boston, but compare it with that from my friends at Milton,[3] & other parts of the state. Puting all which together, the result seems to be that, N Hamshire are divided, & so is RI. The majority of *one*, I am convinced are against fœderal measures, & possibly of *both*. As to N Y one party are sure of adoption, another as positive it will be rejected. So no judgment can be formed. Some think Govr Clinton will be elected for the City, which I doubt. He will come in however by a handsome majority for Ulster County. Maryland by a very large majority will accede; So will So Carolina. N Carolina will probably operate as Virginia, which State I think will be nearly divided; But I rather think from the best information attainable, the majority will carry it for adopting, with amendments, upon the plan of Massachusetts. I have heard in the Circles here, you, or Sister W have written the Columbian patriot, I suspect you, but wish to have it ascertained;[4] for the purposes only of curiosity believe me.

To your demand, to know what we are doing in Congress I answer—Nothing—To your enquiry what have we done? I answer—almost nothing—Yet I dont know that those who have attended, which Massachusetts have incessantly, are to be blamed. The States have been in such a flutter about the New, that they have hardly paid attention to the old Government. One week we have nine States, then again we have only four or five. For to my surprise the Members are under no kind of control, & take themselves away whenever they think proper. The State of N York particularly altho there are sometimes two or three members in Town have for weeks together, had only a single member present. What is to be done? Massachusetts, & I presume others have written to their Legislatures upon the Subject. Is more in their power? Most of the members are either of the Convention, or just before election dance down to the Hustings, And whether they are successful candidates or not, their attendance upon Congress is withdrawn. We have a prospect however of a full House in May, when we shall soon finish the more important business, & if the States agree, follow our instructions in organizing the new Goverment, & *secede*. The doing *it* before is courting encroachment. And leaving the people to the mercy of any rude invader—And I am not ready for despotism.

Your refusal to christen "Parsons's bantling," and "an Eccho to the speech" shews a formidable combination is effected against the doings of convention.[5] . . .

[P.S.] . . . Upon perusal of the papers I am fully perswaded the ribaldry flung at you by your enimies will tend more to make you friends than anything else, And if their spleen had not blinded them they would see the natural consequence.[6] . . .

1. RC, Mercy Warren Papers, MHi. Printed: Massachusetts Historical Society *Proceedings*, XLV (1912), 333–36. The second digit in the day of the month of this letter is blotted out. Winslow Warren, a descendant of James Warren who read a portion of this letter to a meeting of the Massachusetts Historical Society, dated the letter as either 24 or 26 April.

2. Otis, a Massachusetts delegate to Congress, refers to moving Congress out of New York City. The location of the capital had not been an issue in Congress since the early months of 1787. On 6 February 1788 Otis wrote Warren that "Congress have it in Contemplation to adjourn in the Spring, And efforts will be made to get the place of adjournment to Philadelphia, but this will be opposed; I wish for the opinion of my judicious friends upon this subject; Possibly it might prevent a Seat more Southward" (LMCC, VIII, 696). On 19 April Otis wrote George Thatcher, also a Massachusetts delegate to Congress, that "The old influence is exerting to get to Phileda but presume it will hardly obtain" (*ibid.*, 717).

3. Warren was a resident of Milton, Mass.

4. "A Columbian Patriot" was written by Mercy Warren, Otis's sister and Warren's wife (CC:581).

5. It is not entirely clear what Otis had in mind. Theophilus Parsons, a prominent Federalist delegate to the Massachusetts Convention, was believed to have had a primary role in the drafting of the recommendatory amendments to the Constitution that John Hancock presented to the Convention on 31 January 1788. Hancock, the popular governor of the state and the president of the Convention, was acting in behalf of the Convention's leading Federalists who believed that ratification of the Constitution might not be possible without recommendatory amendments. Federalists had promised to support Hancock for reelection as governor and for vice president of the United States. (See CC:Vol. 3, pp. 562–63.) Samuel Adams, an Antifederalist leader, spoke in support of these amendments which, on 2 February, were turned over to a committee. The committee altered the amendments and on 6 February the Convention ratified the Constitution with nine recommendatory amendments. (See CC:508.)

The "bantling" (i.e., a young child or brat) apparently refers to the Massachusetts Convention's ratification of the Constitution with recommendatory amendments, or just to the amendments themselves. "An Eccho to the speech" is possibly an allusion to Samuel Adams's speech in support of the recommendatory amendments or to the failure of the legislature to agree to an adequate response to Governor Hancock's speech to it on 27 February (see note 6). (For the use of the term "bantling" by Mercy Warren to describe the government created by the Constitution, see "A Columbian Patriot," CC:581, p. 278.)

6. Otis probably refers to the newspaper attacks on Warren which were published in early March. Massachusetts Federalists criticized Warren, the speaker of the state House of Representatives, for assisting House Antifederalists in their attempt to censure the Massachusetts Convention for ratifying the Constitution. This criticism would have appeared in the legislature's reply to the governor's 27 February speech to that body. Federalists and Antifederalists in the legislature compromised and the Constitution was not mentioned in the legislature's reply (CC:566).

## 705. Fabius VI
## Pennsylvania Mercury, 24 April[1]

### OBSERVATIONS on the Constitution
### proposed by the FEDERAL CONVENTION.

Some of our fellow-citizens have ventured to predict the future fate of United *America*, if the system proposed to us, shall be adopted.

Though, every branch of the constitution and government is to be popular, and guarded by all the balances, that until this day have occurred to mankind, yet the system will end, they say, in the oppression of a monarchy or aristocracy by the fœderal servants or some of them.

Such a conclusion seems not in any manner suited to the premises. It startles, yet, not so much from its novelty, as from the respectability of the characters by which it is drawn.

We must not be too much influenced by our esteem for those characters: But, should recollect, that when the fancy is warmed, and the judgment inclined, by the proximity or pressure of particular objects, very extraordinary declarations are sometimes made. Such are the frailties of our nature, that genius and integrity sometimes[2] afford no protection against them.

Probably, there never was, and never will be, such an instance of dreadful denunciation, concerning the fate of a country, as was published while the union was in agitation between *England* and *Scotland*. The *English* were for a joint legislature, many of the *Scots* for separate legislatures, and urged, that they should be in a manner swallowed up and lost in the other, as then *they* would not possess *one eleventh* part in it.

Upon that occasion Lord *Belhaven*, one of the most distinguished orators of the age, made in the *Scottish* parliament a famous speech, of which the following extract is part.[3]

"My Lord Chancellor,

"When I consider this affair of an *union* between the two nations, as it is expressed in the several articles thereof, and now the subject of our deliberation at this time, I find my mind crowded with a variety of *very melancholy thoughts*, and I think it my duty to disburthen myself of some of them, by laying them before and exposing them to the serious consideration of this honorable house.

"I think, I SEE A FREE AND INDEPENDENT KINGDOM delivering up *that*, which all the world hath been fighting for since the days of *Nimrod*; yea, *that*, for which most of all the empires, kingdoms, states, principalities and dukedoms of *Europe*, are at this very time engaged in the most bloody and cruel wars that ever were; *to wit*, A POWER TO MANAGE THEIR OWN AFFAIRS BY THEMSELVES, WITHOUT THE ASSISTANCE AND COUNCIL OF ANY OTHER.

"I think, I see A NATIONAL CHURCH, founded upon a rock, secured by *a claim of right*, hedged and fenced about by the strictest and pointedest legal sanction that sovereignty could contrive, voluntarily descending into a plain, upon an equal level with *Jews, Papists, Socinians, Arminians, Anabaptists*, and other Sectaries, &c.

"I think, I see THE NOBLE AND HONORABLE PEERAGE OF SCOTLAND, whose valiant predecessors led armies against their enemies upon their own proper charges and expences, now divested of their followers and vassalages, and put upon such an equal foot with their vassals, that I think, I see a petty *English* Exciseman receive more homage and respect, than what was paid formerly to their *quondam Mackallamors*.

"I think, I see THE PRESENT PEERS OF SCOTLAND, whose noble ancestors conquered provinces, over-run countries, reduced and subjected towns and fortified places, exacted tribute through the greatest part of *England*, now walking in *the court of requests*, like so many *English* Attornies, laying aside their walking swords when in company with the *English* Peers, lest their self-defence should be found murder.

"I think, I see THE HONORABLE ESTATE OF BARONS, the bold assertors of the nation's rights and liberties in the worst of times, now setting A WATCH UPON THEIR LIPS and A GUARD UPON THEIR TONGUES, lest they be found guilty of SCANDALUM MAGNATUM.

"I think, I see THE ROYAL STATE OF BOROUGHS, walking their DESOLATE STREETS, hanging down their heads UNDER DISAPPOINTMENTS; wormed out of ALL THE BRANCHES OF THEIR OLD TRADE, uncertain WHAT HAND TO TURN TO, necessitated to become 'prentices to their unkind neighbours, and yet after all finding their TRADE SO FORTIFIED BY COMPANIES and secured by prescriptions, that they despair of any success therein.

"I think, I see OUR LEARNED JUDGES laying aside *their practiques & decisions*, studying the common law of *England*, gravelled with *certioraris, nisi priuses, writs of error, verdicts in dovar,*[4] *ejectiones firmæ, injunctions, demurrers*, &c. and frighted with APPEALS and AVOCATIONS, because of THE NEW REGULATIONS, and RECTIFICATIONS they meet with.

"I think, I see THE VALIANT AND GALLANT SOLDIERY, either sent to learn the plantation trade abroad, or at home petitioning for A SMALL SUBSISTANCE, as the reward of their honorable exploits, while their old corps are broken, the common soldiers left to beg, and the youngest *English* corps kept standing.

"I think, I see THE HONEST INDUSTRIOUS TRADESMAN loaded with NEW TAXES AND IMPOSITIONS, disappointed of the equivalents, drinking water in place of ale, eating his saltless pottage, petitioning for ENCOURAGEMENT TO HIS MANUFACTORIES, and answered by counter petitions.

"In short, I think I see THE LABORIOUS PLOUGHMAN, with his corn spoiling upon his hands FOR WANT OF SALE, cursing the day of his birth; dreading the expence of his burial, and uncertain whether to marry, or do worse.

"I think, I see the incurable difficulties of LANDED MEN, fettered under the golden chain of equivalents, their pretty daughters petitioning for want of husbands, and their sons for want of employments.

"I think, I see OUR MARINERS DELIVERING UP THEIR SHIPS to their *Dutch* partners, and what through PRESSES AND NECESSITY *earning their bread as underlings* in the *English* navy. But above all, my lord, I think, I see OUR ANTIENT MOTHER CALEDONIA, like *Cæsar*, sitting in the midst of our senate, *ruefully looking round about her*, covering herself with her royal garment, *attending the fatal blow*, and breathing out her last with a——*Et tu quoque, mi fili.*

"Are not these, my lord, *very afflicting thoughts?* And yet they are the least part suggested to me *by these dishonorable articles.* Should not the considerations of these things vivify these *dry bones* of ours? Should not the *memory of our noble predecessors valour and constancy* rouse up our drooping spirits? Are our noble predecessors souls got so far into the *English cabbage stocks and colliflowers*, that we should shew the least indignation[5] that way? Are our eyes *so blinded?* Are our ears *so deafened?* Are our hearts *so burdened?* Are our tongues *so faltered?* Are our hands *so fettered?* that in *this our day*, I say, my lord, *that in this our day, we should not mind the things that concern the very being and well being of our antient kingdom, before the day be hid from our eyes.*

"When I consider this treaty as it hath been explained, & spoke to, before us these three weeks by past; I see the ENGLISH constitution remaining firm, the same two houses of Parliament, the same taxes, the same customs, the same excises, the same TRADING COMPANIES, the same municipal laws and courts of judicature; and ALL OURS EITHER SUBJECT TO REGULATIONS OR ANNIHILATIONS, only *we* are to have THE HONOUR to pay THEIR OLD DEBTS, and to have *some few persons present for witnesses* to the validity of the deed, when they are pleased to contract more."

Let any candid *American* deliberately compare that transaction with the present, and laying his hand upon his heart, solemnly answer this question to himself—Whether, he does not verily believe the eloquent Peer before mentioned, had ten-fold more cause to apprehend evils from such an unequal match between the two kingdoms, than any citizen of these states has to apprehend them from the system proposed. Indeed not only that Peer, but other persons of distinction, and large numbers of the people of *Scotland* were filled with the utmost aversion to the union; and if the greatest diligence & prudence had not been employed by its friends in removing misapprehensions and refuting misrepresentations, and by the then subsisting government for preserving the public peace, there would certainly have been a rebellion.

Yet, what were the consequences to *Scotland* of that dreaded union with *England?*—The cultivation of her virtues and the correction of her errors—The emancipation of one class of her citizens from the yoke of their superiors—A relief of other classes from the injuries and insults of the great—Improvements in agriculture, science, arts, trade, and manufactures—The profits of industry and ingenuity enjoyed under the protection of laws, peace and security at home, and encrease of respectability abroad. Her *Church* is still *eminent*—Her *laws* and *courts of judicature* are safe—Her *boroughs* grown into cities—Her *mariners* and *soldiery* possessing *a larger subsistance*, than she could have afforded them, and her *tradesmen, ploughmen, landed men*, and her people of every rank, in a more flourishing condition, not only than they ever were, but in a more flourishing condition, than the clearest understanding could, at the time, have thought it possible for them to attain in so short a period, or even in many ages. *England* participated in the blessings. The *stock* of their union or ingraftment, as perhaps it may be called, being strong, and capable of drawing better nutriment and in greater abundance, than they could ever have done apart.

"Ere long, to Heaven the soaring branches shoot,
    and wonder at their *height*, and *more than native fruit*."

1. Reprinted: Baltimore *Maryland Gazette*, 6 June; *New Hampshire Spy*, 7 June; *Providence Gazette*, 12 July; Philadelphia *American Museum*, November.

2. "Not unfrequently" was substituted for "sometimes" in the *American Museum* version.

3. John Hamilton (1656–1708), 2nd Baron Belhaven and an opponent of union with England, made this speech on 2 November 1706. This and another of his speeches were printed as a broadside in Edinburgh and reprinted in a London pamphlet. Despite the

efforts of Lord Belhaven and others, the union between England and Scotland took place in 1707. He was imprisoned in 1708 for his opposition to union and died in prison the same year. The text of the speech was available to Dickinson in John Torbuck, *A Collection of Parliamentary Debates in England* . . . (21 vols., London, 1741–1742), V, 15–34; or, Daniel Defoe, *The History of the Union of Great Britain* (Edinburgh, 1709), "An Abstract of the Proceedings on the Treaty of Union Within the Parliament of Scotland . . .," Minute XIV. Saturday 2. November 1706.

4. "In dovar" was deleted from the *American Museum* version.

5. "Inclination" was substituted for "indignation" in the *American Museum* version.

### 706. George Washington to John Armstrong, Sr. Mount Vernon, 25 April[1]

From some cause or other which I do not know your favor of the 20th of February[2] did not reach me till very lately. This must apologize for its not being sooner acknowledged.—Altho Colo Blain forgot to call upon me for a letter before he left Philadelphia, yet I wrote a few lines to you previous to my departu[r]e from that place; whether they ever got to your hands or not you best know.[3]—

I well remember the observation you made in your letter to me of last year, "that my domestic retirement must suffer an interruption".[4]— This took place, notwithstanding it was utterly repugnant to my feelings, my interest and my wishes; I sacrificed every private consideration and personal enjoyment to the earnest and pressing solicitations of those who saw and knew the alarming situation of our public concerns, and had no other end in view but to promote the interest of their Country; and conceiving that under those circumstances, and at so critical a moment, an absolute refusal to act, might, on my part, be construed as a total dereliction of my Country, if imputed to no worse motives.—Altho' you say the same motives induce you to think that another tour of duty of this kind will fall to my lot, I cannot but hope that you will be disappointed, for I am so wedded to a state of retirement; and find the occupations of a rural life so congenial; with my feelings, that to be drawn unto public at the advanced age, would be a sacrifice that could admit of no compensation.

Your remarks on the impressions which will be made on the manners and sentiments of the people by the example of those who are first called to act under the proposed Government are very just; and I have no doubt but (if the proposed Constitution obtains) those persons who are chosen to administer it will have wisdom enough to discern the influence which their examples as rulers and legislators may have on the body of the people, and will have virtue enough to pursue that line of conduct which will most conduce to the happiness of their Country;—and as the first transactions of a nation, like those of an individual upon his enterance into life, make the deepest impression and are to form the leading traits in its character, they will undoubtedly pursue those measures which will best tend to the restoration of public and private faith and of consequence promote our national respectability and individual welfare.—

That the proposed Constitution will admit of amendments is acknowledged by its warmest advocates but to make such amendments as may be proposed by the several States the condition of its adoption would, in my opinion amount to a compleat rejection of it; for upon examination of the objections which are made by the opponents in different States and the amendments which have been proposed, it will be found that what would be a favourite object with one State is the very thing which is stren[u]ously opposed by another;—the truth is, men are too apt to be swayed by local prejudices, and those who are so fond of amendments which have the particular interest of their own State in view cannot extend their ideas to the general welfare of the Union—they do not consider that for every sacrifice which they make they receive an ample compensation by the sacrifices which are made by other States for their benefit—and that those very things which they give up will operate to their advantage through the medium of the general interest.—In addition to these considerations it should be remembered that a constitutional door is open for such amendments as shall be thought necessary by nine States.—When I reflect upon these circumstances I am surprized to find that any person who is acquainted with the critical state of our public affairs, and knows the veriety of views, inter[e]sts, feelings and prejudices which must be consulted and conciliated in framing a general Government for these States, and how little propositions in themselves so opposite to each other, will tend to promote that desireable an end, can wish to make amendments the ultimatum for adopting the offered system.

I am very glad to find that the opposition in your State, however formidable it has been represented, is, generally speaking, composed of such characters as cannot have an extensive influence; their fort[e], as well as that of those of the same class in other States seems to lie in misrepresentation, and a desire to inflame the passions and to alarm the fears by noisy declamation rather than to convince the understanding by some arguments or fair and impartial statements—Baffled in their attacks upon the constitution they have attempted to vilify and debase the Characters who formed it, but even here I trust they will not succeed.—Upon the whole I doubt whether the opposition to the Constitution will not ultimately be productive of more good than evil; it has called forth, in its defence, abilities (which would not perhaps have been otherwise exerted) that have thrown new lights upon the science of Government, they have given the rights of man a full and fair discussion, and have explained them in so clear and forcible a manner as cannot fail to make a lasting impression upon those who read the best publications on the subject, and particularly the pieces under the signiture of Publius.[5]—There will be a greater weight of abilities opposed to the system in the convention of this State than there has been in any other, but notwithstanding the unwearied pains which have been taken, and the vigorous efforts which will be made in the Convention to prevent its adoption, I have not the smallest doubt but it will obtain here.—

I am sorry to hear that the College in your neighbourhood is in so declining a state as you represent it, and that it is likely to suffer a farther injury by the loss of Dr. Nisbet whom you are afraid you shall not be able to support in a proper manner on account of the scarcity of Cash which prevents parents from sending their Children hither.[6] This is one of the numerous evils which arise from the want of a general regulating power, for in a Country like this where equal liberty is enjoyed, where every man may reap his own harvest, which by proper attention will afford him much more that [i.e., than] what is necessary for his own consumption, and where there is so ample a field for every mercantile and mechanical exertion, if there cannot be money found to answer the common purposes of education, not to mention the necessary commercial circulation, it is evident that there is something amiss in the ruling political power which requires a steady, regulating and energetic hand to connect and control. That money is not to be had, every mans experience tells him, and the great fall in the price of property is an unequivocal, and melancholy proof of it; when, if that property was well secured—faith and justice well preserved—a stable government well administered,—and confidence restored,—the tide of population and wealth would flow to us, from every part of the Globe, and, with a due sense of the blessing, make us the happiest people upon earth—

1. FC, Washington Papers, DLC. At the end of this letterbook copy, located after the letters for December 1788, Washington's secretary noted: "This preceding letter dated in April was not given to be recorded until after those for the year 1788 had been entered—which is the reason of it being in this place."

2. See CC:543.

3. The Constitutional Convention adjourned on 17 September 1787, and Washington left Philadelphia the next day. Colonel Ephraim Blaine, like Armstrong, lived in Carlisle, Pa.

4. Armstrong wrote Washington a six-page letter on 2 March 1787 outlining the defects of the Confederation, calling for the establishment of a strong central govern-

ment, and expressing approbation of Washington's appointment to the Constitutional Convention. Armstrong also reminded Washington that "In a former letter I ventured to say you were not likely to have altogether done with publick appointments" (Washington Papers, DLC). This "former letter" has not been located.

5. In November and December 1787, authors Alexander Hamilton and James Madison transmitted to Washington newspapers containing *The Federalist* I–XXII, and in March 1788 author John Jay sent him the just published Volume I of *The Federalist* which contained essays I–XXXVI (CC:201).

6. For Charles Nisbet's description of his difficulties as president of Dickinson College in Carlisle, see his letter of 25 December 1787 to the Earl of Buchan (CC:374).

## 707. Henry Knox to Marquis de Lafayette
## New York, 26 April (excerpt)[1]

. . . The Convention by you Mr. Jefferson and common Sense, judge wisely respecting the New Constitution requiring some amendments & of the time they should be effected.[2]

Most certainly if the amendments were made a condition of the adoption of the Constitution, neither amendments or constitution would ever be received—A more complex and difficult task cannot be imagined than to obtain the concurrence of a majority of all the States to a constitution, militating more or less with the prejudices, habits or interests of most of the States—The unanimity of the former convention may be regarded, as a rare evidence of the empire of reason and sound policy—Let another be assembled, and perhaps no four States would agree in any one System.

But I think my hopes are well founded that we shall not be under the necessity of having recourse to the miserable alternative of another Convention—For the prospects are very flattering that more than *nine* states will accept the Constitution in the course of two or three months—Six have already adopted it—New York Convention also sit in June—the issue problematical, but as eight states will have adopted it, and perhaps nine, before the session of this State, some allowance must be made for the influence of other States on the conduct of this.—In my opinion the result of the deliberations in this convention will be the adoption of the New Constitution—Maryland is now in session and will adopt it by a great Majority—The Elections in Virginia are just known to us, and notwithstanding all the falsehoods that have been propagated against the constitution it is now pretty well ascertained that it will be adopted in Virginia whose Convention meets the first Monday in June North Carolina the Convention of which meets in July will follow the Conduct of Virginia—South Carolina will meet the 12th. May and is said to be greatly in favor of the Constitution—

In short as the prospect now presents itself Hopes may be indulged of twelve states acceeding to the Constitution in the course of the Year.

As to Rhode-Island no little State of Greece ever exhibited greater turpitude than she does—paper money and tender laws engross her attention entirely—This is in other words plundering the Orphan & Widow by virtue of laws. . . .

1. FC, Knox Papers, MHi. Knox answers Lafayette's letters of November 1787 and February 1788, neither of which has been located. See note 2 for some idea about the contents of the February letter.

2. Lafayette's letter to Knox (see note 1) was probably similar to one that he had written to George Washington on 4 February. In that letter, Lafayette said that his views on amendments coincided with those of Thomas Jefferson (CC:Vol. 2, p. 501. For more on Lafayette's opinion on amendments, see *ibid.*, 492.). For more on Jefferson's views on amendments at this time, see his letters to William Stephens Smith, 2 February (*ibid.*, 500); and to James Madison, 6 February, and to Alexander Donald, 7 February (Boyd, XII, 569–70; and RCS:Va., 353–54). For earlier Jefferson letters, see CC:Vol. 2, pp. 480–81, 482–85.

### 708. Henry Knox to Jean-Baptiste Gouvion
### New York, 26 April (excerpt)[1]

. . . I have written the Marquis a concise statement,[2] respecting the prospects of our new Constitution—It will be adopted generally in the course of the year,—We hope much from its efficacy, more probably than it will realize But it became indispensably necessary to attempt something as the present Machine ~~was nearly stopped~~ is almost entirely worn out—

The necessary [measure?] of adopting the New Constitution, is perhaps as difficu[l]t and complex an operation as can be concievd—It is to undergo the discusion and opinion, not only of the convention which formed it—The Congress—The Legislatures of the respective states, The Counties towns and every individual freeman throughout the United States—In all its stages it is to be veiwed and decided upon by men [– – –] [– – –] [– – –] [– – –] of infinitely different education, & opinions and whose judgmts of course must be [– – –]—Abstractedly considered it is wonderful that there should be such a similar[it]y of veiws as to [– – –] a majority in its favor in any one of the states—It will however [certainly?] to my judgement be adopted by at least nine states immediately and probably by all the states excepting Rhode Island in the Course of the year—

1. FC, Knox Papers, MHi.
2. See CC:707.

## 709. Honestus
## New York Journal, 26 April

This Antifederalist satire by "Honestus" revived the debate begun by the Antifederalist "Cato" and the Federalist "Caesar" in September and October 1787 and continued by both Antifederalists and Federalists until the meeting of the New York Convention in June 1788. "Cato" I had encouraged all citizens of New York, who, like the citizens of other states, had "given to the world astonishing evidences of your greatness," to "Deliberate . . . on this new national government with coolness; analize it with criticism; and reflect on it with candour." Referring to George Washington, who signed the Constitution, "Cato" maintained that even "the wisest and best of men may err, and their errors, if adopted, may be fatal to the community" (*New York Journal*, 27 September, CC:103).

"Caesar" II, who was "not much attached to the *Majesty of the multitude*," argued that the people in general were "very ill qualified to *judge* for themselves what government will best suit their peculiar situations." They should maintain "a tractable and docile disposition . . . while others . . . with the advantages of genius and learning" consider the Constitution. Commenting on the work of the Constitutional Convention, "Caesar" I asked rhetorically: "Has not the wisdom of America been drawn, as it were, into a focus, and the proferred Constitution sent forth with an unanimity, that is unequalled in ancient or modern story?" (New York *Daily Advertiser*, 1, 17 October, CC:121, 169).

Entering into the spirit of satire displayed by "Honestus," Antifederalist printer Thomas Greenleaf explained why he published "Honestus": "Lest some illiberal Individual should superciliously, through his Ignorance of the important Subject of the FREEDOM OF THE PRESS, have the least Item, by which he might presume to stigmatise the Printer with the hateful Epithet of PARTIALITY, he has omitted several Pieces, Paragraphs, and Advertisements for the Purpose of giving Place to the *Performance* under the Signature of HONESTUS!!" (*New York Journal*, 26 April).

"Honestus" became an issue in the election for state ratifying convention delegates in the city and county of New York. It was "*Re-inserted by* particular *desire*" in the *New York Journal* on 28 April, the eve of the five-day election, and it drew an immediate Federalist response. "One and All," in a broadside dated 29 April, warned his fellow citizens to "Keep a good *Look-Out*. . . . The enemies of federalism know they can do nothing in this City by *fair play*. They are, therefore, trying to divide you, that they may, if possible, *smuggle in* a few of their friends, and they stick at nothing to effect this. Witness the publication in Greenleaf's paper, signed Honestus; who, under the mask of friendship to the proposed Constitution, insults the whole body of Mechanics, in order to raise their prejudices against it" (Evans 21500. The pseudonym "One and All" was probably taken from a Federalist nominating ticket drawn up three weeks earlier, with the words: "In Supporting the present Nomination let ONE AND ALL BE OUR MOTTO".). "Honestus" was unsuccessful as the city and county of New York elected nine Federalist delegates by at least a margin of twenty-to-one.

"Honestus" was reprinted in the *Massachusetts Centinel* on 14 May.

MR. GREENLEAF, I was led to the following reflections, by accidentally falling in company, some evenings since, with a number of characters (chiefly mechanics) at an ale-house, who were making absurd comments on the constitution proposed by the general convention; which convention was composed of the greatest and most enlightened characters in this country. It must be considered, that government is a very abstruse science, and political disquisition a very arduous task, far beyond the reach of common capacities; and that no men, but those who have had a liberal education, and have time to study, can possibly be competent to such an important matter, as the framing a government for such an extensive country, as is comprehended within the United States. Whenever men of neither abilities or education, presume to meddle, with such matters as are above the reach of their knowledge or abilities, they will find themselves out of their proper sphere.

The blacksmith will find that he had better attend to his hammer and anvil, and hammer out hob-nails, for country hoof, than concern himself with affairs of state, should he be weak enough to suppose that he has abilities equal to such an undertaking; he will find, that there is a material difference, between welding together two pieces of steel or iron, and that of uniting heterogeneous and jarring interests, so as to make them productive of the public good.

The mariner may very well understand, how to take an observation, and navigate his ship; but he cannot possibly be acquainted with every point of the political compass, or so to steer the ship of state, as to avoid the hidden and dangerous rocks, and shelves, that may lay in the way—and whenever he makes the attempt, he will undoubtedly find himself out of his latitude.

The distiller, brewer and baker, may be perfectly well acquainted with the principles of fermentation, and how to regulate and check the same, so as to answer their particular purposes; but they must be entirely ignorant of the laws and means that will be necessary to prevent a dangerous fermentation in the community, or what steps it may be necessary to take, to check such fermentation, when excited.

The farmer may have a sufficiency of knowledge to guide and govern the plough, and team; and understand the best method to thrash his grain—but he must be incompetent to the great purpose of guiding the machinery of the state, or to suggest the best and most effectual method, to thrash the enemies of his country.

The carpenter may be a perfect master of his trade, and understand the rules of architecture; he may frame an edifice, complete in all its parts, and sufficiently strong to secure the proprietor from the attempts of the midnight robber; but he will be totally ignorant, how to frame laws for the security of society, so as to prevent the artful and designing from preying upon the ignorant and innocent.

The miller may be a complete artist in his profession, and know how to regulate every thing appertaining to his mill; he may understand extremely well, how to separate the flour from the bran; but he cannot possibly be master of the address, that will be necessary, to distinguish the wheat from the chaff; in the choice of officers, to fill the different departments in the state.

The clock and watch-maker may know very well how to regulate the wheels, and other movements of a clock or watch; but he will be ignorant of the necessary art, how to regulate the complex machinery of government, so as to dispose the different wheels, as will prevent their interfering with, and bearing too hard on each other.

The mason may be an excellent workman, and understand how to lay the foundation of an house or a wall properly—but he will be at a loss how to determine what base will be necessary on which such a superstructure as government should be erected.

The sadler may be a proficient in his business, and may know what kind of curb is proper to restrain an unruly and restive horse—but he cannot possibly be a judge what laws or curbs will be proper and necessary to restrain the unruly passions of men, so as to prevent their injuring one another.

The turner may be a very expert artizan, but he cannot possibly be acquainted with all the turns and windings, that are used by bad men to evade the laws, and escape the punishment which they justly deserve.

The cooper may know extremely well, how to stop the flaws and worm holes in a cask, and make it so tight as to hold water, rum, or any other liquor; but he will be much puzzled to stop the flaws, and worm-holes in a law; so as to prevent its operating, either to the injury of individuals, or the government.

The barber may know very well how to make a wig, to suit either the priest, phisician or gentleman of the long-robe, or how to shave his customer with dexterity,—but whenever he attempts to meddle with affairs of state, he will find that his razors have lost their edge, and that he is himself compleatly in the suds.

If this production should operate in such a manner, as to prevent people's neglecting their business and meddling with public matters, beyond their capacities, it will be a sufficient compensation to the writer, who has no other object in view, than that of confining every man within his proper sphere.

## 710. Fabius VII
### Pennsylvania Mercury, 26 April[1]

OBSERVATIONS on the CONSTITUTION
Proposed by the FEDERAL CONVENTION.

Thus happily mistaken was the ingenious, learned, and patriotic Lord *Belhaven*, in his prediction concerning the fate of his country;[2] and thus happily mistaken, it is hoped, that some of our fellow-citizens will be, in their prediction concerning the fate of their country.

Had they taken larger scope, and assumed in their proposition the vicissitude of human affairs, and the passions that so often confound them, their prediction might have been a tolerably good guess. Amidst the mutabilities of terrestial things, the liberty of United *America* may be destroyed. As to that point, it is our duty, humbly, constantly, fervently, to implore the protection of our most gracious maker, "who doth not afflict willingly nor grieve the children of men,"[3] and incessantly to strive, as we are commanded, to recommend ourselves to that protection, by "doing his will," diligently exercising our reason in fulfilling the purposes for which that and our existence were given to us.

*How* the liberty of this country is to be destroyed, is another question. Here, the gentlemen assign a cause, in no manner proportioned, as it is apprehended, to the effect.

The uniform tenor of history is against them. That holds up the *licentiousness* of the people, and *turbulent temper* of some of the states, as the only causes to be dreaded, not the conspiracies of *federal officers*. Therefore, it is highly probable, that, if our liberty is ever subverted, it will be by one of the two causes first mentioned. Our tragedy will then have the same acts, with those of the nations that have gone before us; and we shall add one more example to the number already too great, of a people that would not take warning, not "know the things which belong to their peace."[4] But, we ought not to pass such a sentence against our country, & the interests of freedom: Though, no sentence whatever can be equal to the atrocity of our guilt, if through enormity of obstinacy or baseness, we betray the cause of our posterity and of mankind, by providence committed to our parental and fraternal care. "*Detur venia verbis*"[5]—The calamities of nations are the punishments of their sins.[6]

As to the first mentioned cause, it seems unnecessary to say any more upon it.

As to the second, we find, that the misbehaviour of the *constituent parts* acting separately, or in partial confederacies, debilitated the *Greeks* under "*the Amphictionic Council*," and under *the Achæan League*, and that this misbehaviour ruined *Greece*. As to the former, it was not entirely an assembly of strictly democratical republics. Besides, it wanted a sufficiently *close connection* of its parts. Tyrants and aristocracies sprung up. After these observations, we may call our attention from it.

'Tis true, *the Achæan League* was disturbed, by the misconduct of *some parts*, but, it is as true, that it surmounted these difficulties, and wonderfully prospered, until it was dissolved in the manner that has been described.

The glorious operations of its principles bear the clearest testimony to this distant age and people, that the wit of man never invented such an antidote against monarchical and aristocratical projects, as a *strong combination* of truly *democratical* republics. By strictly or truly democratical republics, the writer means republics, in which all the officers are from time to time chosen by the people.

The reason is plain. As *liberty* and *equality*, or as termed by *Polybius, benignity*, were the foundations of their institutions, and the *energy* of the government pervaded *all the parts* in things relating to the whole, it counteracted for the common welfare, the designs hatched by selfishness in separate councils.[7]

If folly or wickedness prevailed in any *parts*, friendly offices and salutary measures restored tranquility. Thus the public good was maintained. In its very formation, tyrannies and aristocracies submitted, by consent or compulsion. *Thus*, the *Ceraunians, Trezenians, Epidaurians, Megalopolitans, Argives, Hermionians*, and *Phlyarians*, were received into the league. A happy exchange! For history informs us, that so true were they to their noble and benevolent principles, that, in their diet, "no resolutions were taken, but what were equally advantageous to the whole confederacy, and the interest of each part so consulted, as to leave no room for complaints."[8]

How degrading would be the thought to a citizen of United *America*, that the people of these states, with institutions beyond comparison preferable to those of *the Achæan league*, and so vast a superiority in other respects, should not have wisdom & virtue enough, to manage their affairs, with as much prudence and affection of one for another, as these antients did.[9]

Would this be doing justice to our country? The composition of her temper is excellent, and seems to be acknowledged equal to that of any nation in the world. Her prudence will guard its warmth against two faults, to which it may be exposed—The one an imitation of foreign fashions, which from small things may lead to great. May her citizens aspire at a national dignity in every part of conduct, private as well as public. This will be influenced by the former. May *simplicity* be the characteristic feature of their manners, which inlaid in their other virtues and their forms of government, may then indeed be compared, in the eastern stile, to "apples of gold in pictures of silver."[10] Thus will they long, and may they, while their rivers run, escape the curse[11] of *luxury*—the issue of innocence debauched by folly, and the lineal predecessor of tyranny generated in rape and incest.[12] The other fault, of which, as yet, there are no symptoms among us, is the thirst of empire. This is a vice, that ever has been, and from the nature of things, ever must be, fatal to republican forms of government. Our wants, are sources of happiness: our desires, of misery. The abuse of prosperity, is rebellion against Heaven: and succeeds accordingly.

Do the propositions of gentlemen who object, offer to our view, any of the great points upon which, the fate, fame, or freedom of nations has turned, excepting what some of them have said about trial by jury, which has been frequently and fully answered? Is there one of them calculated to regulate, and if needful, to controul, those tempers and measures of constituent parts of an union, that have been so baneful to the weal of every confederacy that has existed? Do not some of them tend to enervate the authority evidently designed thus to regulate and controul? Do not others of them discover a bias in their advocates to particular connections, that if indulged to them, would enable persons of less understanding and virtue, to repeat the disorders, that have so often violated public peace and honor? Taking them altogether, would they afford as strong a security to our liberty, as the frequent election of the federal officers by the people, and the repartition of power among those officers, according to the proposed system?

It may be answered, that, they would be an additional security. In reply, let the writer be permitted at present to refer to what has been said.

The principal argument of gentlemen who object, involves a direct proof of the point contended for by the writer of this address, and as far as it may be supposed to be founded, a plain confirmation of Historic evidence.

They generally agree, that the great danger of a monarchy or aristocracy among us, will arise from the federal *senate*.

The members of this *senate*, are to be chosen by men exercising the sovereignty of their respective states. These men therefore, must be monarchically or aristocratically disposed, before they will chuse federal senators thus disposed; and what merits particular attention, is, that these men must have obtained an overbearing influence in their respective states, before they could with such disposition arrive at the exercise of the sovereignty in them: or else, the like disposition must be prevalent among the people of such states.

Taking the case either way, is not this a disorder in *parts* of the union, and ought it not to be rectified by *the rest*? Is it reasonable to expect, that the disease will seize *all* at the same time? If it is not, ought not the sound to possess a right and power, by which they may prevent the infection from spreading.

From the annals of mankind, these conclusions are deducible—that states together may act prudently and honestly, and a part foolishly and knavishly; but, that it is a defiance of all probability, to suppose, that states conjointly shall act with folly and wickedness, and yet separately with wisdom and virtue.

1. Reprinted: New Jersey *Brunswick Gazette*, 6 May; *New Hampshire Spy*, 10 June; Baltimore *Maryland Gazette*, 13 June; *Providence Gazette*, 19 July; Philadelphia *American Museum*, November.

2. See "Fabius" VI (CC:705), 24 April, at note 3.

3. Lamentations 3:33.

4. Luke 19:42.

5. "Detur venia verbis" was deleted in the *American Museum* version.

6. At the beginning of this sentence in the *American Museum* version, the following phrase was inserted: "There is reason to believe, that."

7. Polybius stated: "Nowhere could be found a more unalloyed and deliberately established system of equality and absolute freedom, and, in a word, of democracy, than among the Achaeans. This constitution found many of the Peloponnesians ready enough to adopt it of their own accord: many were brought to share in it by persuasion and argument: some, though acting under compulsion at first, were quickly brought to acquiesce in its benefits; for none of the original members had any special privilege reserved for them, but equal rights were given to all comers: the object aimed at was therefore quickly attained by the two most unfailing expedients of equality and fraternity. This then must be looked upon as the source and original cause of Peloponnesian unity and consequent prosperity" (F. Hultsch, Evelyn S. Schuckburgh, and F. W. Walbank, trans. and eds., *The Histories of Polybius* [2 vols., Bloomington, Ind., 1962], I, Book II, chapter 38, p. 134).

8. The quoted material, which has not been identified, is possibly from Polybius. At one point, Polybius wrote this about the Achaean League: ". . . not only is there in the Peloponnese a community of interests such as exists between allies or friends, but an absolute identity of laws, weights, measures, and currency. All the States have the same magistrates, senate, and judges. Nor is there any difference between the entire Peloponnese and a single city, except in the fact that its inhabitants are not included within the same wall; in other respects, both as a whole and in their individual cities, there is a nearly absolute assimilation of institutions" (*ibid.*, chapter 37, pp. 133–34).

9. An exclamation mark was substituted for the period at the end of this sentence in the *American Museum* version.

10. Proverbs 25:11.

11. "Contagion" was substituted for "curse" in the *American Museum* version.

12. "Generated in rape and incest" was deleted in the *American Museum* version.

### 711. Nathan Dane to Theodore Sedgwick
### New York, 27 April (excerpt)[1]

... Here we are in an idle and painful situation, no Congress for doing business more than one day in twelve or fifteen—public affairs neglected, and we kept here only as Spectators of a declining Government, and of those little wretched games of interest and self always played in times of disorders—and in the passage from one kind of Government to another—how long we shall remain in this situation is uncertain—however, I think not long—the Constitution must pretty soon take place in peace, or else the Scene become more turbulent, and consequently more active—should it be peaceably adopted our affairs will be, I believe, on a better footing, at least for some time— and as to the final consequences time and experience must determine— I have ever been as much discouraged about the administration of our Governments, as about the forms of our Constitutions—and I think we may depend on this—that we may make and alter Constitutions eternally on paper, it will answer little or no purpose—if we be not more Steady and attentive in the administration of public affairs—Sir Wm. Temple[2] observes, and I think Justly, that the Dutch had neither parts, genius or wit, and that they had but very indifferent Constitutions, and yet, that they were the best Statesmen in the world, and enjoyed an exceeding good Government; that by their industry, application, and uniform perseverance, and by their frugality, &c. they made compensation for all the defects of their Constitutions, and for their defficiencies in point of genius, and quickness of discernment— In fact the Dutch merely by the force of system and application in the administration of their affairs, have long been respectable in a miserable Country, in a mixture of sand, mud, and water, where any other people on Earth would have perished—they see the ship as well ballast'd, and the first requisite in their magistrates is a capacity for applying Systematically to business—are we not in this Country often deceived with a brilliant imagination, when there is no depth of Judgment, or any talents for business?—have not the States often, in delegating men to Congress, chosen their most Showy and, yet in fact, their most triffling characters; men who never come forward with a view Steadily to pursue and support Systems, and to shew their abilities in that line; but only with a view to overturn all measures adopted by others, and to introduce new ones of their own, and thereby perpetuate change and instability?—

We have done no business of any importance in Congress this year— nor is there much to be done—we have eight States and three half

States—Just money received into the Treasury to keep the Government in motion—no foreign Communications of any importance—the present calm in Europe is thought generally to be but temporary—the affairs of the Dutch [are?] unsettled—punishments and confiscations carried with a pretty high hand—Mr. Adams returns to Boston soon, probably by the middle of May[3]—and Colo. Smith to New York[4]— Brother Thatcher returned to Massa. about the last of March—and proposes to be again in Congress about the first of August[5]—I wish you to attend if you can find it convenient early in the Summer—my affairs then will require that I should, for a short time, be in Massa., and I will be very much obliged to you to let me know, as soon as you conveniently can, your determinations respecting your attendance in Congress[6]—It is probable by the first of August that nine States will have agreed to the Constitution—and it is my wish to attend to my private affairs in Massa. and be returned to Congress by that time— Maryland Convention is now in Session, and I believe will adopt the Constitution, without any doubt—South Carolina Convention will, probably, adopt it by the first of June—Virginia and New Hampshire will probably decide by the first of July—& there is pretty clearly more than an equal chance that one or the other of these states will adopt— I am rather disposed to believe that all the States except R.I. will adopt; but, at present, little can be said with certainty as to New Hampshire N.Y. Virga. or N. Carolina—Be kind enough, Sir, to give my respects to Brother Strong and to our friend Bacon when you see them, and let my best regards always be remembred for your family—

with Sentiments of esteem and friendship I am, Dear Sir, your affecta. Hum Servant—

P.S. Let me know when you shall have a leisure hour how elections and politics stand in your part of the State—as to several of the Counties from which we have had information, as Essex Suffolk &c. I think the elections have a favourable appearance—

1. RC, Sedgwick Papers, MHi. This letter, addressed to Sedgwick's Stockbridge home, was "Forwarded from Springfield/by your humble/Servt/Thomas Dwight."

2. In 1673 Sir William Temple (1628–1699) published in London *Observations Upon the United Provinces of the Netherlands,* a popular work that went to several editions.

3. John Adams, the American minister to Great Britain, and his wife Abigail arrived in Boston on 17 June.

4. William Stephens Smith, Adams's son-in-law and the secretary of the American legation in London, and his wife arrived in New York City in May and settled in Jamaica, N.Y.

5. George Thatcher served in Congress from 21 January to 25 March; was reelected on 6 June; and returned on 6 August.

6. Theodore Sedgwick arrived in Congress on 31 July. Dane served in Congress continuously from 21 February to at least 13 September.

## 712. Henry Knox to Jeremiah Wadsworth
### New York, 27 April (excerpts)[1]

... The recent information from Virginia is highly flattering—By a statement which I have seen of all the Counties excepting eight, the result is thus,

| | |
|---|---|
| Federals. | 88 |
| Neutrals | 3 |
| Against | 66 |
| | 157[2] |

One of the neutrals is Colo Carringtons Brother the Cheif Justice who will certainly be for it as will his colleauge who is another neutral in the statement[3]—

The eight Counties (Kentucky) not returned are supposed to be mostly for it—at any rate they will be equall which will give a very decisive majority—This is *more than was expected*—Mr Mad–n writes that, the weight of ability and character on the federal side far outweigh those of the Antis—this however as it respects him to be a secret[4]—

Maryland will be nearly as Colonel Howard stated to you sometime ago[5]—They are now in session—South Carolina Virginia and Maryland will probably decide favorably before the convention of this state have proceeded to any determin[ation] North Carolina will follow Virginia, but independently of this circumstance the accounts are favorable—

On tuesday next the elections will be made throughout this state— The issue quite problematical—the majority be it on which side it may will be very small—The weight of abilities and personal character will be greatly on the side of the Feds—If the parties be nearly balanced on the conventions first assembling, most probably the influence of the other states who have and will adopt it will be such as to turn the scale on the side of the constitution—I flatter myself that New Hampshire will accept it—

The elections in Massachusetts of federal men for Govr, Lt Govr, and the great majority of the senate will have the happiest effect on the general politics, and at the same time [evince?] that the conduct of the convention is approved by the great majority of the people—

In short my dear friend I am deeply impressed with the beleif that the Constitution will be adopted generally in the course of the present year—probably by 12 States—Rhode Island—let her alone We shall have the opportunity of making all the experiments the new form will admit—The highest wisdom and policy will be required to set it agoing so as to produce the blessings that we have been taught to expect from it—God grant that we be not disapointed. ...

[P.S.] No Congress yet since your departure—One will probably be formed of seven states this week—a Gentleman from Maryland having just arrived—

1. RC, Wadsworth Papers, CtHi. This letter was sent to Wadsworth in Hartford, Conn. A similar letter was printed on 7 May in the Boston *Massachusetts Centinel* as excerpts of "A letter from a gentleman of the first distinction and information in New-York, dated the 27th ult." (RCS:Va., 762). Knox responds to four letters, mostly about business, that Wadsworth had written him between 17 and 23 April. Wadsworth had speculated on 17 April that neither George Mason nor William Grayson would be "very influential in Virginia." He hoped that New York Federalists "will continue to be industrious" because "the Anti s had been busy and too Sucessfull." Lastly, he feared that New Hampshire would reject the Constitution (Knox Papers, MHi).

2. Knox probably refers to a statement that was received from Virginia by Colonel David Henley a commissioner for settling Virginia's claims concerning the western lands it had ceded to the United States. Henley copied the statement and mailed it to his father Samuel in Charlestown, Mass. The statement consists of a rough alphabetical listing of the Virginia counties, the names of the delegates, and how each delegate was expected to vote. Henley's totals were 85 Federalists, 66 Antifederalists, and 3 Doubtful. A note indicates that there were no returns for eight counties, but that "they are mostly in favor of the constitution" (Henley to Henley, 28 April, RCS:Va., 629, 630n; and Mfm:Va. 189).

3. Paul Carrington, chief justice of the General Court of Virginia and brother of Edward Carrington, and Thomas Read, clerk of Charlotte County, were elected to represent that county in the Virginia Convention in June. Carrington voted for ratification of the Constitution; Read against it.

4. On 9 April James Madison wrote to John Brown, a Virginia delegate to Congress in New York City, that "It seems pretty clear now that in point of characters the advantage will be on the federal side" (RCS:Va., 711).

5. Around 24 March, John Eager Howard, a Maryland delegate to Congress, wrote Wadsworth: "I am happy to inform you that upon my arrival in Maryland I found the prospect of the Constitution being adopted was fully equal to my expectations. . . . You need not be under uneasiness on account of us for a Majority is certain, and it is not improbable but we shall be almost unanimous" (Wadsworth Papers, CtHi).

## 713. Aristocrotis: The Government of Nature Delineated; or An Exact Picture of the New Federal Constitution, Carlisle, Pa., c. 27 April

The western county of Cumberland in Pennsylvania was a hotbed of opposition to the Constitution and remained so even after the Pennsylvania Convention ratified on 12 December 1787. One of the leaders of this opposition was William Petrikin, a Scottish immigrant and Carlisle tailor. He was one of twenty-one men called before the county magistrates on 25 February 1788 for their part in breaking up a Federalist celebration of ratification in Carlisle on 26 December 1787. Petrikin and six others went to jail rather than accept bail while their cases were pending. On 1 March 1788 hundreds of militiamen from Cumberland and the neighboring counties descended on Carlisle to free the prisoners forcibly. However, some Carlisle Federalists prevented such an action by agreeing to petition the state Supreme Executive Council to end the prosecution against all twenty-one defendants. Petrikin and his fellow prisoners consented to leave the jail and the militiamen left town. On 20 March the Council instructed the state attorney general to drop the prosecution (CC:407; and RCS:Pa., 670–708).

On 24 February 1788, the day before Petrikin appeared before the magistrates, he informed Philadelphia Antifederalist John Nicholson, the state comptroller general and the organizer of a petition campaign requesting that the state legislature not "confirm" the state's ratification of the Constitution, that "The Pamphlet for which we sent you the Subscription paper is in the Press and will be out emediatly." Fourteen hundred copies were ordered for which the printers would be paid £15. Petrikin was "persuaded 3 times that number of them would befor the 1t of may when you see it I think you will say that it is both good Satir and good reasoning." He wanted to know if anyone in Philadelphia had subscribed because the printers' bill had to "be paid in hand before the Books is taken away" (RCS:Pa., 695).

This subscription paper had been sent to Nicholson more than a month earlier by John Jordan, one of the twenty-one defendants and a judge of the Court of Common Pleas. On 26 January Jordan had written Nicholson that it would be a pity if the pamphlet, already in manuscript, were not published. The author of the pamphlet, stated Jordan, was the same person who had just published two Antifederalist newspaper pieces—"One of the People" and "The Scourge," *Carlisle Gazette*, 9, 23 January (RCS:Pa., 674–78, 685–92). "It will cost a good deal to have it printed," continued Jordan, "and our friends here is not of the richest sort I realy think the piece might be of use however exercise your own Judgement but please to write me emediatly whether you think proper to apply for subscribers or not I would have sent the manuscript but it could not be spared" (RCS:Pa., 693).

On 9 April Kline and Reynolds, the printers of the *Carlisle Gazette*, announced that *The Government of Nature Delineated; or An Exact Picture of the New Federal Constitution* (Evans 21117) was "Now in the PRESS, and speedily will be Published." This thirty-two-page pamphlet, signed by "Aristocrotis," appeared by 27 April, the day that Federalist John Montgomery of Carlisle, a former delegate to Congress, wrote that "petrikens Pamphlet has made its apearence [in Carlisle.] it is [a] foolish thing" (to William Irvine, Mfm:Pa. 662). If Petrikin was the author, someone must have edited it for spelling, capitalization, and punctuation because the pamphlet is far more literate than Petrikin's letter.

In biting sarcasm, "Aristocrotis" praised the Constitution as designed to allow the few to control the many. The pamphlet was dedicated to the "most honourable highly renowned" James Wilson, the "principal fabricator of the New Constitution" and "political hackney writer" in the employ of Robert Morris. "Aristocrotis" suggested that Wilson would restore his fortune and enrich himself if the Constitution were ratified. In the text of the pamphlet, "Aristocrotis" predicted that the new Congress would be dominated by the wellborn, rich, and powerful who would eventually make membership in it hereditary. A standing army and the congressionally controlled militia would crush popular opposition to arbitrary government and compel the payment of taxes. The guarantees of the freedom of the press and trial by jury were deliberately omitted from the Constitution in order to remove those traditional impediments to absolute government. The Constitution destroyed the restraint that religion provided against the abuse of power by government. In short, "The congress having thus disentangled themselves from all popular checks and choices; and being supported by a well disciplined army and active militia, will certainly command dread and respect abroad, obedience and submission at home; they will then look down with awful dignity and tremendous majesty from the pinnacle of glory, to which fortune has raised them upon the insignificant creatures, their subjects, whom they have reduced to that state of vassallage and servile submission, for which they were primar[i]ly destined by nature."

"Aristocrotis" ended his pamphlet with an attack on Federalists for acting precipitately in obtaining ratification, relying on the influence of great names, unjustly stigmatizing Antifederalists as selfish men who threatened the Union, lying to the people, blocking the dissemination of Antifederalist material, disarming the militia while plotting to establish a standing army, and exaggerating the distress of the people and the ability of the Constitution to solve the problems of the Confederation. He concluded with an "Appendix" in which he praised Luther Martin's *Genuine Information* (CC:389) and "Centinel" XVI (CC:565) for their revelations about the Constitutional Convention. He supported the effort to amend the Constitution.

[A photographic facsimile of this pamphlet appears as Mfm:Pa. 661.]

### 714. Richard Henry Lee to Samuel Adams
### Chantilly, 28 April[1]

Your favour of December 3d, in the last year,[2] reached me the last of January following, and it should have been answered with my thanks long since, if the uncommon badness of the winter, stopping all communication, had not prevented.[3] Your sentiments on the new political structure, are, in my mind, strong and just. Both reason and experience prove, that so extensive a territory as that of the United States, including such a variety of climates, productions, interests; and so great difference of manners, habits, and customs; cannot be governed in freedom—until formed into states, sovereign, *sub modo*, and confederated for the common good. In the latter case, opinion founded on the knowledge of those who govern, procures obedience without force. But remove the opinion, which must fall with a knowledge of characters in so widely extended a country, and force then becomes necessary to secure the purposes of civil government; hence the military array at Kamtschatka, at Petersburg, and through every part of the widely extended Russian empire. Thus force, the parent and the support of tyranny, is demanded for good purposes, although for ever abused to bad ones—that a consolidated, and not a federal government, was the design of *some*, who formed this new project, I have no doubt about. The dazzling ideas of glory, wealth, and power uncontrolled, unfettered by popular opinions, are powerful to captivate the ambitious and the avaricious. With such people, obedience resulting from fear, the offspring of force, is preferable to obedience flowing from esteem and confidence, the legitimate offspring of the knowledge that men have of wisdom and virtue in their governors; and, above all, from the conviction that abuses may be rectified by the substantial checks that political freedom furnish. Massachusetts, I see, has adopted the plan; but proposes to insist perseveringly on amendments.[4] If it were permitted an individual to question so enlightened an assembly, I would ask, why submit to a system requiring such amendments, and trust to creatures of our own creation, for the correcting of evils in it that threaten the destruction of those ends for which the system was formed? The fear of greater evils has been stated: but I cannot help considering such fears as being generated by design upon weakness. The objections to the present system, if accurately considered, will, I believe, be found to grow out of those temporary pressures, created by a long and expensive war, which time and prudence may remove. But, though it were admitted that some amendments to the present confederation would better promote the ends designed by it, why, for that reason, exterminate the present plan, and establish on its ruins another, so replete with power, danger, and hydra-headed mischief? The Massachusetts amendments are good, so far as they go. The first, third, and fourth amendments are well contrived to keep in existence the state sovereignties; and the first particularly proper for securing liberty from the abuse of construction, which the new plan most amply admits of. But why, my dear friend, was the provision in your seventh proposition of amendment, confined to causes between citizens of different states, since the reason applies to suitors of every country, and foreigners will be more apt than our own citizens to abuse, in the way, which, that part of the proffered plan permits, and which this amendment of Massachusetts is designed to prevent? England and Scotland are united for every good purpose of defence and offence, yet a foreigner cannot sue a resident Scotsman in England for debt contracted in Scotland: nor will any foreign nation upon earth grant a similar privilege to our citizens over theirs, of calling their people from their own countries to answer demands against them—the fixt idea of all the European nations being, that strangers are not to have privileges in their own country superior to what their own subjects enjoy.

1. Printed: Richard H. Lee, *Memoir of the Life of Richard Henry Lee, and His Correspondence* ... (2 vols., Philadelphia, 1825), II, 86–87. "Chantilly" was the name of Lee's estate in Westmoreland County, Va. The name of the recipient does not appear, but

Samuel Adams had written Lee on 3 December 1787 and the text reveals that the letter was written to Adams.

2. See Adams to Lee, 3 December (CC:315).

3. For the severity of the winter in Virginia and its impact upon the mails, see CC:Vol. 4, pp. 28, 101, 580n. For more on the severity of the Virginia winter, see RCS:Va., 322, 387, 477n, 479, 610, 745.

4. For the recommendatory amendments of the Massachusetts Convention and the role that Convention delegate Adams played in their adoption in February, see CC:508.

## 715. George Washington to Marquis de Lafayette
## Mount Vernon, 28 April, 1 May (excerpts)[1]

I have now before me, my dear Marqs. your favor of the 3d of August in the last year; together with those of the 1st. of January, the 2d. of January and the 4th. of February in the present[2]—Though the first is of so antient a date, they all came to hand lately, and nearly at the same moment. The frequency of your kind remembrance of me, and the endearing expressions of attachment, are by so much the more satisfactory, as I recognise them to be a counterpart of my own feelings for you. In truth, you know I speak the language of sincerity and not of flattery, when I tell you, that your letters are ever most wellcome and dear to me.

This I lay out to be a letter of Politics. We are looking anxiously across the atlantic for news and you are looking anxiously back again for the same purpose. It is an interesting subject, to contemplate how far the war, kindled in the north of Europe, may extend it[s] conflagrations, and what m[a]y be the result before its extinction. The Turke appears to have lost his old and acquired a new connection.—Whether England has not, in the hour of her pride, overacted her part and pushed matters too far [for] her own interest, time will discover: but, in my opinion (though from my distance and want of minute information I should form it with diffidence) the affairs of that nation cannot long go on in the same prosperous train: in spite of expedients and in spite of resources, the Paper bubble will one day burst. And it will whelm many in the ruins. I hope the affairs of France are gradually sliding into a better state. Good effects may, and I trust will ensue, without any public convulsion. France, were he[r] resources properly managed and her administrations wisely conducted, is (as you justly observe) much more potent in the scale of empire, than her rivals at present seem inclined to believe.

I notice with pleasure the additional immunities and facilities in trade, which France has granted by the late Royal Arret to the United States.[3] I flatter myself it will have the desired effect, in some measure, of augmenting the commercial intercourse. From the productions and

wants of the two countries, their trade with each other is certainly
capable of great amelioration, to be actuated by a spirit of unwise
policy. For so surely as ever we shall have an efficient government
established, so surely will that government impose retaliating restrictions, to a certain degree, upon the trade of Britain, at present, or
under our existing form of Confederations, it would be idle to think
of making com[m]ercial regulations on our part. One State passes a
prohibitory law respecting some article—another State opens wide the
avenue for its admission. One Assembly makes a system—another Assembly unmakes it. Virginia, in the very last session of her Legislature,
was about to have passed some of the most extravigant and preposterous Edicts on the subject of trade, that ever Stained the leaves of
a Legislative Code.[4] It is in vain to hope for a remedy of these and
innumerable other evils, untill a general Government shall be adopted.

The Convention[s] of Six States only have as yet accepted the new
Constitution. No one has rejected it. It is believed that the Convention
of Maryland, which is now in session; and that of South Carolina, which
is to assemble on the 12th of May, will certainly adopt it. It is, also,
since the elections of Members for the Convention have taken place
in this State, more general[ly] believed that it will be adopted here
than it was before those elections were made. There will, however, be
powerful and elequent speeches on both sides of the question in the
Virginia Convention, but as Pendleton, Wythe, Blair, Madison, Jones,
Nicholas, Innis and many other of our first characters will be advocates
for its adoption, you may suppose the weight of abilities will rest on
that side. Henry and Masson are its great adversaries—The Governor,[5]
if he opposes it at all will do it feebly.—

On the General Merits of this proposed Constitution, I wrote to
you, some time ago, my sentiments pretty freely.[6] That letter had not
been received by you, when you addressed to me the last of yours
which has come to my hands. I had never supposed that perfection
could be the result of accomodation and mutual concession. The opinion of Mr. Jefferson & yourself is certainly a wise one, that the Constitution ought by all means to be accepted by nine States before any
attempt should be made to procure amendments.[7] For, if that acceptance shall not previously take place, men's minds will be so much
agitated and soured, that the danger will be greater than ever of our
becoming a disunited People. Whereas, on the other hand, with prudence in temper and a spirit of moderation, every essential alteration,
may in the process of time, be expected.

You will doubtless, have seen, that it was owing to this conciliatory
and patriotic principle that the Convention of Massachusetts adopted

the Constitution in toto;—but recommended a number of specific alterations and quieting explanations, as an early, serious and unremitting subject of attention. Now, although it is not to [be] expected that every individual, in Society, will or can ever be brought to agree upon what is, exactly, the best form of government; yet, there are many things in the Constitution which only need to be explained, in order to prove equally satisfactory to all parties. For example: there was not a member of the convention, I believe, who had the least objection to what is contended for by the Advocates for a *Bill of Rights* and *Tryal by Jury*. The first, where the people evidently retained every thing which they did not in express terms give up, was considered nugatory as you will find to have been more fully explained by Mr. Wilson[8] and others:—And as to the second, it was only the difficulty of establishing a mode which should not interfere with the fixed modes of any of the States, that induced the Convention to leave it, as a matter of future adjustment.

There are other points on which opinions would be more likely to vary. As for instance, on the ineligibility of the same person for President, after he should have served a certain course of years. Guarded so effectually as the proposed Constitution is, in respect to the prevention of bribery and undue influence in the choice of President: I confess, I differ widely myself from Mr Jefferson and you, as to the necessity or expediency of rotation in that appointment.[9] The matter was fairly discussed in the Convention, & to my full convictions; though I cannot have time or room to sum up the arguments in this letter. There cannot, in my Judgment, be the least danger that the President will by any practicable intriegue ever be able to continue himself one moment in office, much less perpetuate himself in it—but in the last stage of corrupted morals and political depravity: and even then there is as much danger that any other species of domination would prevail. Though, when a people shall have become incapable of governing themselves and fit for a master, it is of little consequence from what quarter he comes.

Under an extended view of this part of the subject, I can see no propriety in precluding ourselves from the services of any man, who on some great emergency, shall be deemed, universally, most capable of serving the Public.—

In answer to the observations you make on the probability of my election to the Presidency[10] (knowing me as you do) I need only say, that it has no enticing charms, and no fascinating allurements for me. However, it might not be decent for me to say I would refuse to accept or even to speak much about an appointment, which may never take place: for in so doing, one might possibly incur the application of the moral resulting from that Fable, in which the Fox is represented as inveighing against the sourness of the grapes, because he could not reach them. All that it will be necessary to add, my dear Marquis, in order to shew my decided predelection, is, that, (at my time of life and under my circumstances) [t]he encreasing infirmities of nature and the growing love of retirement do not permit me to entertain a wish, beyond that of living and dying an honest man on my own farm. Let those follow the pursuits of ambition and fame, who have a keener relish for them; or who may have more years, in store, for the enjoyment! . . .

P.S. May 1st.—

Since writing the foregoing letter, I have received Authentic Accounts that the Convention of Maryland have ratified the new Constitution by a Majority of 63 to 11.—

1. FC, Washington Papers, DLC. Printed: Fitzpatrick, XXIX, 475–80.

2. For Lafayette's letters of 1 January and 4 February, see CC:Vol. 2, pp. 492, 501.

3. Lafayette sent Washington a copy of the arrêt of the French Council of State on 1 January 1788 and a duplicate of it on 2 January. In the latter letter, Lafayette said that he hoped that the arrêt would increase commerce between France and the United States. For the text of the arrêt, adopted on 29 December 1787, see Boyd, XII, 468–71. On 31 December American minister to France Thomas Jefferson sent a copy of the arrêt to Secretary for Foreign Affairs John Jay (ibid., 479–83).

4. Washington probably refers to resolutions that Patrick Henry presented to the Virginia House of Delegates on 5 November 1787 "to prohibit entirely the importation of rum, brandy, cordage, and many other articles." After some debate, Henry's resolutions were dropped from further consideration on 27 December (Rutland, Madison, X, 248, 248n–49n, 294; and RCS:Va., 171, 172n–73n, 176). On 9 December James Madison told Thomas Jefferson that "A project of this sort without the concurrence of the other States, is little short of madness" (Rutland, Madison, X, 313). Jefferson replied on 6 February 1788 that if these resolutions had been adopted the French arrêt (note 3, above) would have been repealed (ibid., 474–75).

5. Edmund Randolph.

6. See Washington to Lafayette, 7 February 1788 (CC:509).

7. For Lafayette's opinion, see CC:Vol. 2, p. 501; and for Jefferson's, see four letters that he wrote between 20 December 1787 and 7 February 1788 (CC:Vol. 2, pp. 482–83, 500; RCS:Va., 353–54; and Boyd, XII, 569–70).

8. See James Wilson's speech of 6 October 1787 before a Philadelphia public meeting (CC:134).

9. See CC:Vol. 2, pp. 492, 501. For Jefferson's views concerning the reeligibility of the President, see ibid., 463–64, 480, 483–84, 489–90, 500; and RCS:Va., 354.

10. See CC:Vol. 2, p. 492.

## 716 A–B. Amendments of the Minority of the Maryland Convention, 29 April

The Maryland Convention met in Annapolis on 21 April. After electing officers and adopting rules, the delegates rejected an Antifederalist attempt to have the Constitution discussed clause-by-clause. The majority resolved on 23 April to take only one vote, on whether "this Convention do assent to and ratify" the Constitution. On the 24th former governor William Paca, a Harford County delegate, indicated "that he had great objections to the constitution proposed, in its present form, and meant to propose a variety of amendments, not to prevent, but to accompany, the ratification." Because Paca, who had only arrived that day, was not ready to present his amendments, the Convention adjourned until the next morning. When Paca attempted to present his amendments on 25 April, Federalists prevented their introduction. Federalists insisted that they "were under an obligation to vote for the government" and that they had no authority to propose or consider amendments on behalf of their constituents who had not given them any instructions concerning amendments. For the rest of the day and until the afternoon of the next day, Antifederalists continued to object to the Constitution. Federalists remained silent and finally called the question, at which point the Convention ratified the Constitution 63 to 11. Paca, who had voted to ratify, was finally permitted to read his amendments. The Convention voted "66 for, and not more than 7 against," to create a committee of thirteen, consisting of nine Federalists, three Antifederalists, and Paca himself, to consider amendments. Paca's amendments were referred to the committee. (For the text of Paca's amendments, see CC:716–A.)

On Monday, 28 April, the sixty-three ratifying delegates signed the Form of Ratification, and the next day the Convention instructed the governor to transmit the Form to Congress. After considerable wrangling among the members of the committee of thirteen, committee chairman Paca informed the Convention on 29 April that the committee "could come to no Agreement to make any Report" (*Maryland Journal*, 2 May). Whereupon, the Convention thanked its president and adjourned.

Believing that the form of government proposed by the Constitution was "very defective" and "the liberty and happiness of the people" were endangered if the Constitution was not amended, Paca and the eleven non-ratifying delegates prepared an address to the people of Maryland. They laid before the people the thirteen amendments agreed upon by the committee of thirteen and the fifteen amendments that the Federalist majority on the committee rejected. The Antifederalists indicated that they had offered "not only [to] cease to oppose the government, but [to] give all their assistance to carry it into execution so amended" if the committee would only submit the first three rejected amendments to the Convention for a vote. The minority related how their offer was rejected 8 to 5, one Federalist voting with them. When the committee refused to make a report, all amendments were lost. In the address the Antifederalist minority presented the amendments to the public "for your consideration, that you may express your sense as to such alterations as you may think proper to be made in the new constitution." (For an excerpt from the address, transcribed from the Annapolis *Maryland Gazette*, 1 May, see CC:716–B.)

Paca's amendments were printed in Maryland and reprinted throughout America. On 29 April both the Baltimore *Maryland Gazette* and the *Maryland Journal* printed the amendments "proposed by a Member," with a brief account of the proceedings of 26 April, including the vote totals on ratification and a reference to the committee of thirteen. Both newspapers "hoped that the great and essential Rights of the People will be declared and secured." The *Maryland Journal's* printing of the "Proposed Amendments" was headed: "*Late last Night the following Particulars were delivered to the Editor, for Publication in this Day's Paper.*"

Paca's proposed amendments, transcribed from the *Maryland Journal* of 29 April, were reprinted forty-four times by 9 June: N.H. (3), Mass. (8), R.I. (3), Conn. (6), N.Y. (8), N.J. (2), Pa. (8), Va. (4), S.C. (1), Ga. (1). Many of these newspapers also reprinted the brief account of the proceedings of 26 April.

The address of the Antifederalist minority, signed by Paca and the eleven non-ratifying delegates, first appeared in Annapolis either in the *Maryland Gazette* of 1 May, or as a broadside published by the *Gazette's* printers, Frederick and Samuel Green (Evans 45288). On 2 May the Baltimore *Maryland Gazette* and *Maryland Journal* announced that they would print the address in their next issues, which they did on the 6th. The address was also reprinted in the *Pennsylvania Packet*, 8 May; Philadelphia *Independent Gazetteer*, 8 May; *New York Journal*, 12 May; Philadelphia *Freeman's Journal*, 14 May; Boston *American Herald*, 22, 26 May; Charleston *City Gazette*, 2 June; *Providence Gazette*, 7 June; and in the May issue of the Philadelphia *American Museum*.

The Antifederalist *New York Journal* prefaced its reprinting: "As the Citizens of New-York have yet had no regular Accounts of the *Proceedings* of the *Maryland Convention*, the Editor embraces this earliest Opportunity to lay before them the following Particulars, for which he is indebted to the MARY-LAND GAZETTE, printed at *Annapolis*, May the 1st." The Antifederalist Boston *American Herald* prefaced its reprinting: "The Editor hereof conceiving it of the first importance to the publick, to have [even?] the most minute circumstance relative to the Federal Constitution, laid before them, embraces this his earliest opportunity of presenting his readers with the following particulars on that great subject, which occurred in the Convention of the State of Maryland, on the consideration thereof."

Both Antifederalists and Federalists in Maryland recognized the impact that the Maryland amendments might have on the convention of neighboring Virginia, scheduled to meet on 2 June. Daniel Carroll told James Madison that "It is thought the [minority] address will be of little consequence" in Maryland but might "be of some with you to hear both sides" (28 May, Rutland, *Madison*, XI, 66–67). An anonymous Federalist member of the committee of thirteen (probably Alexander Contee Hanson) promised to publish "another narrative" of the committee's proceedings to correct the misstatements and omissions in the address of the Antifederalist minority ("One of the Committee," Annapolis *Maryland Gazette*, 8 May). An Antifederalist Convention delegate defended the minority and reviewed what had transpired in the Convention. He added that the majority refused to agree to amendments because their publication "might produce bad consequences in Virginia, and the other States, who had not ratified, where the opponents of the Government might be equal, or nearly equal, in number to it's friends" ("A Member of Convention," Baltimore *Maryland Gazette*, 13 May). James McHenry, a Federalist member of the committee of thirteen, informed George Washington on 18 May that "The amendments were intended to injure the cause of federalism in your

State, and had we agreed to them they were well calculated to effect it" (Washington Papers, DLC).

On 28 May Daniel Carroll sent James Madison a copy of the address of the minority of the Maryland Convention and an address that some Federalist members of the committee of thirteen had wanted to affix to any amendments the Convention might recommend. According to Carroll, "This alone serves, to give a different cast to the proceedings of the Committee than appears without it." Carroll also told Madison that Alexander Contee Hanson (a committee member) was in the process of preparing a report "which will disclose some matters not mention'd in the Address, & may give a different cast to those proceedings." Carroll had asked Hanson for a copy of the address when completed which he would forward to Madison in Virginia. Hanson had hoped to get four fellow-Federalist committeemen (who were then in Annapolis attending the general assembly and the general court) to sign his address. These potential co-signers "were indeed doubtful as to the propriety of answering a narrative, which, they conceived, had made little impression on the people, either injurious to the common cause, or unfavorable to the convention and committee." They were also too busy "to spare the necessary time" to assist in drafting the address. Hanson, however, "was determined to complete" his draft and have it sent to Richmond in time for the meeting of the Virginia Convention, even if it was not possible to get it printed in a timely fashion. An illness delayed Hanson's writing and Daniel Carroll left Annapolis before the draft was finished.

Hanson completed his draft on 2 June and on that day sent it directly to Madison. The address—written from minutes taken by three Federalist committee members—had not been submitted to Hanson's colleagues, only two of whom were still in Annapolis. Because of the "dispersion" of the Federalist committee members and "so considerable a lapse of time," Hanson felt that "no address would be published by them." But Hanson's "anxiety for the common cause" convinced him to send the draft to Virginia—"a step, which perhaps cold prudence may condemn." In forwarding the draft, Hanson hoped that Madison would use it in any way "which your own judgment may prescribe." Hanson preferred that the address not be printed in Virginia newspapers unless Madison thought "the cause likely to be thereby promoted." He hoped that his address would encourage Virginia Federalists and discourage those Antifederalists "who may look for countenance and support from the people of Maryland" (Rutland, *Madison*, XI, 66–67, 69–71).

In the Virginia Convention some Antifederalists made passing references to the Maryland amendments. Patrick Henry contended on 9 June that sixty members of the Maryland Convention had supported amendments and that the Convention had "instituted a committee to propose amendments" (RSC:Va., 1053, 1056). On 25 June Benjamin Harrison asserted that "in Maryland there is a considerable number who wish amendments to be had" (RCS:Va., 1517). In a letter written midway through the Virginia Convention, Theodorick Bland, another Antifederalist delegate, suggested that a majority favored previous amendments similar to those recommended by the Massachusetts and South Carolina conventions and to "the main points of the committee of Maryland" (to Arthur Lee, 13 June, RCS:Va., 1617).

*716–A. Amendments Proposed by William Paca in the Maryland
Convention, Maryland Journal, 29 April*

That it be declared that all Persons entrusted with the Legislative
or Executive Powers of Government, are the Trustees and Servants of
the Public, and as such accountable for their Conduct:

WHEREFORE, whenever the Ends of Government are perverted, and
public Liberty manifestly endangered, and all other Means of Redress
are ineffectual, the People may, and of right ought, to object to, reform
the old, or establish a new Government—That the Doctrine of Non-
resistance against arbitrary Power and Oppression is absurd, slavish,
and destructive of the Good and Happiness of Mankind—That it be
declared, That every Man hath a Right to petition the Legislature, for
the Redress of Grievances, in a peaceable and orderly Manner—That
in all criminal Prosecutions every Man hath a Right to be informed
of the Accusation against him, to have a Copy of the Indictment or
Charge in due Time (if required) to prepare for his Defence, to be
allowed Council, to be confronted with the Witnesses against him, to
have Process for his Witnesses, to examine the Witnesses for and
against him, on Oath, and to a speedy Trial, by an impartial Jury.

That no Freeman ought to be taken, or imprisoned, or deprived of
his Freehold, Liberties or Privileges, or outlawed or exiled, or in any
manner destroyed, or deprived of his Life, Liberty or Property, but
by the lawful Judgment of his Peers, or by the Law of the Land.

That no Power of suspending Laws, or the Execution of Laws, unless
derived from the Legislature, ought to be exercised or allowed.

That all Warrants, without Oath, or Affirmation of a Person conscientiously scrupulous of taking an Oath, to search suspected Places,
or to seize any Person, or his Property, are grievous and oppressive;
and all General Warrants, to search suspected Places, or to apprehend
any Person suspected, without naming or describing the Place or Person in special, are dangerous and ought not to be granted.

That there be no Appeal to the Supreme Court of Congress in a
Criminal Case.

Congress shall have no Power to alter or change the Regulations
respecting the Times, Places, or Manner of holding Elections for Senators or Representatives.

All Imposts and Duties laid by Congress, shall be placed to the Credit
of the State in which the same be collected, and shall be deducted out
of such State's Quota of the common or general Expences of Government.

No Member of Congress shall be eligible to any Office of Trust, or
Profit, under Congress, during the time for which he shall be chosen.

That there be no National Religion established by Law; but that all Persons be equally entitled to Protection in their religious Liberty.

That Congress shall not lay direct Taxes on Land, or other Property, without a previous Requisition of the respective Quotas of the States, and a failing, within a Limited Time, to comply therewith.

In all Cases of Trespasses, Torts, Abuses of Power, personal Wrongs and Injuries done on Land, or within the Body of a County, the Party injured shall be entitled to Trial by Jury, in the State where the Offence shall be committed; and the State Courts, in such Cases, shall have concurrent Jurisdiction with the Federal Courts; and there shall be no Appeal, excepting on Matter of Law.

That the Supreme Federal Court shall not admit of Fictions, to extend its Jurisdiction; nor shall Citizens of the same State, having Controversies with each other, be suffered to make collusive Assignments of their Rights, to Citizens of another State, for the Purpose of defeating the Jurisdiction of the State Courts; nor shall any Matter, or Question, already determined in the State Courts, be revived or agitated in the Federal Courts; that there be no Appeal from Law, or Fact, to the Supreme Court, where the Claim, or demand, does not exceed Three Hundred Pounds Sterling.

That no standing Army shall be kept up in Time of Peace, unless with the Consent of Three Fourths of the Members of each Branch of Congress: Nor shall Soldiers, in Time of Peace, be quartered upon private Houses, without the Consent of the Owners.

No Law of Congress, or Treaties, shall be effectual to repeal or abrogate the Constitutions, or Bill of Rights, of the States, or any of them, or any Part of the said Constitutions or Bills of Rights.

Militia not to be subject to the Rules of Congress, nor marched out of the State, without Consent of the Legislature of such State.

That Congress have no Power to lay a Poll-Tax.

That the People have a Right to Freedom of Speech, of writing and publishing their Sentiments, and therefore that the Freedom of the Press ought not to be restrained, and the Printing Presses ought to be free to examine the Proceedings of Government, and the Conduct of its Officers.

That Congress shall exercise no Power, but what is expressly delegated by this Constitution.

That the President shall not command the Army, in Person, without the Consent of Congress.

    True Extract from the Minutes of the Convention, of the State of Maryland,

                        WILLIAM HARWOOD, Clk. Con.

Done in Convention, April 26, 1788.

*716–B. Address of the Minority of the Maryland Convention*
*Annapolis Maryland Gazette, 1 May (excerpt)*

... The following amendments to the proposed constitution were separately agreed to by the committee, most of them by an *unanimous* vote, and all of them by a *great majority:*

1. That congress shall exercise no power but what is expressly delegated by this constitution.

By this amendment, the general powers given to congress by the first and last paragraphs of the 8th sect. of art. 1, and the second paragraph of the 6th article, would be in a great measure restrained: those dangerous expressions by which the bills of rights and constitutions of the several states may be repealed by the laws of congress, in some degree moderated, and the exercise of *constructive* powers wholly prevented.

2. That there shall be a trial by jury in all criminal cases, according to the course of proceeding in the state where the offence is committed; and that there be no appeal from matter of fact, or second trial after acquittal; but this provision shall not extend to such cases as may rise in the government of the land or naval forces.

3. That in all actions on debts or contracts, and in all other controversies respecting property, of which the inferior federal courts have jurisdiction, the trial of facts shall be by jury, if required by either party; and that it be expressly declared, that the state courts, in such cases, have a concurrent jurisdiction with the federal courts, with an appeal from either, only as to matter of law, to the supreme federal court, if the matter in dispute be of the value of _____ dollars.

4. That the inferior federal courts shall not have jurisdiction of less than _____ dollars; and there may be an appeal in all cases of revenue, as well to matter of fact as law, and congress may give the state courts jurisdiction of revenue cases, for such sums, and in such manner, as they may think proper.

5. That in all cases of trespasses done within the body of a county, and within the inferior federal jurisdiction, the party injured shall be entitled to trial by jury in the state where the injury shall be committed; and that it be expressly declared, that the state courts, in such cases, shall have concurrent jurisdiction with the federal courts; and there shall be no appeal from either, except on matter of law; and that no person be exempt from such jurisdiction and trial but ambassadors and ministers privileged by the law of nations.

6. That the federal courts shall not be entitled to jurisdiction by fictions or collusion.

7. That the federal judges do not hold any other office of profit,

or receive the profits of any other office under congress, during the time they hold their commission.

The great objects of these amendments were, 1st. To secure the trial by jury in all cases, the boasted birth-right of Englishmen, and their descendants, and the palladium of civil liberty; and to prevent the *appeal from fact*, which not only destroys that trial in civil cases, but by *construction*, may also elude it in criminal cases: a mode of proceeding both expensive and burthensome, and also by blending law with fact, will destroy all check on the judiciary authority, render it almost impossible to convict judges of corruption, and may lay the foundation of that gradual and silent attack on individuals, by which the approaches of tyranny become irresistable. 2d. To give a concurrent jurisdiction to the state courts, in order that congress may not be compelled, as they will be under the present form, to establish inferior federal courts, which if not numerous will be inconvenient, and if numerous very expensive; the circumstances of the people being unequal to the increased expence of double courts, and double officers; an arrangement that will render the law so complicated and confused, that few men can know how to conduct themselves with safety to their persons or property, the great and only security of freemen. 3dly, To give such jurisdiction to the state courts, that transient foreigners, and persons from other states, committing injuries in this state, may be amenable to the state, whose laws they violate, and whose citizens they injure. 4thly, To prevent an extension of the federal jurisdiction, which may, and in all probability will, swallow up the state jurisdictions, and consequently sap those rules of descent and regulations of personal property, by which men now hold their estates; and lastly, To secure the independence of the federal judges, to whom the happiness of the people of this great continent will be so greatly committed by the extensive powers assigned them.

8. That all warrants without oath, or affirmation of a person conscientiously scrupulous of taking an oath, to search suspected places, or to seize any person or his property, are grievous and oppressive; and all general warrants to search suspected places, or to apprehend any person suspected, without naming or describing the place or person in special, are dangerous, and ought not to be granted.

This amendment was considered indispensable by many of the committee, for congress having the power of laying excises, the horror of a free people, by which our dwelling-houses, those castles considered so sacred by the English law will be laid open to the insolence and oppression of office, there could be no constitutional check provided, that would prove so effectual a safeguard to our citizens. General warrants too, the great engine by which power may destroy those individuals who resist usurpation, are also hereby forbid to those magistrates who are to administer the general government.

9. That no soldier be enlisted for a longer time than four years except in time of war, and then only during the war.

10. That soldiers be not quartered in time of peace upon private houses, without the consent of the owners.

11. That no mutiny bill continue in force longer than two years.

These were the only checks that could be obtained against the unlimitted power of raising and regulating standing armies, the natural enemies to freedom, and even with these restrictions, the new congress will not be under such constitutional restraints as the parliament of Great-Britain; restraints which our ancestors have bled to establish, and which have hitherto preserved the liberty of their posterity.

12. That the freedom of the press be inviolably preserved.

In prosecutions in the federal courts for libels, the constitutional preservation of this great and fundamental right, may prove invaluable.

13. That the militia shall not be subject to martial law, except in time of war, invasion or rebellion.

This provision to restrain the powers of congress over the militia, although, by no means so ample as that provided by magna charta, and the other fundamental and constitutional laws of Great Britain, (it being contrary to magna charta to punish a freeman by martial law in time of peace, and murder to execute him,) yet it may prove an inestimable check; for all other provisions in favour of the rights of men, would be vain and nugatory, if the power of subjecting all men able to bear arms to martial law at any moment, should remain vested in congress.

Thus far the amendments were agreed to.

The following amendments were laid before the committee, and negatived by a majority.

1. That the militia, unless selected by lot or voluntarily enlisted, shall not be marched beyond the limits of an adjoining state, without the consent of their legislature or executive.

2. That congress shall have no power to alter or change the time, place or manner, of holding elections for senators or representatives, unless a state shall neglect to make regulations, or to execute its regulations, or shall be prevented by invasion or rebellion; in which cases only congress may interfere, until the cause be removed.

3. That, in every law of congress imposing *direct* taxes, the collection thereof shall be *suspended* for a certain reasonable time therein limited,

and on payment of the sum by any state, by the time appointed, such taxes shall not be collected.

4. That no standing army shall be kept up *in time of peace*, unless with the consent of two thirds of the members present of each branch of congress.

5. That the president shall not command the army in person, without the consent of congress.

6. That no treaty shall be effectual to repeal or abrogate the *constitutions* or *bills of rights* of the states, or any part of them.

7. That no regulation of commerce, or navigation act, shall be made, unless with the consent of two thirds of the members of each branch of congress.

8. That no member of congress shall be eligible to any office of profit under congress during the time for which he shall be appointed.

9. That congress shall have no power to lay a *poll tax*.

10. That no person, conscientiously scrupulous of bearing arms in any case, shall be compelled *personally* to serve as a soldier.

11. That there be a responsible council to the president.

12. That there be no national religion established by law, but that all persons be equally entitled to protection in their religious liberty.

13. That all imposts and duties laid by congress shall be placed to the credit of the state in which the same be collected, and shall be deducted out of such state's quota of the common or general expences of government.

14. That every man hath a right to petition the legislature for the redress of grievances in a peaceable and orderly manner.

15. That it be declared, that all persons intrusted with the legislative or executive powers of government are the trustees and servants of the public, and as such accountable for their conduct. Wherefore, whenever the ends of government are perverted, and public liberty manifestly endangered, and all other means of redress are ineffectual, the people may, and of right ought, to reform the old, or establish a new government; the doctrine of non-resistance against arbitrary power and oppression, is absurd, slavish, and destructive of the good and happiness of mankind.

The committee having proceeded thus far, all the members who voted for the ratification declared, that they would engage themselves under every tie of honour to support the amendments they had agreed to, both in their public and private characters, until they should become a part of the general government; but a great majority of them insisted on this express condition, that none of the propositions rejected, or any others, should be laid before the convention for their consideration, except those the committee had so agreed to.

The gentlemen of the minority, who had made the propositions which had been rejected, reduced to the necessity of accommodating their sentiments to the majority, through fear of obtaining no security whatever for the people—notwithstanding they considered *all* the amendments as highly important to the welfare and happiness of the citizens of the states, yet to conciliate, they agreed to confine themselves to the first three of those propositions, and solemnly declared and pledged themselves, that if these were added, and supported by the other gentlemen, they would not only cease to oppose the government, but give all their assistance to carry it into execution so amended. Finally, they only required liberty to take the sense of the convention on the three first propositions, agreeing that they would hold themselves bound by the decision of a majority of that body.

The first of these objections concerning the militia they considered as essential, for to march beyond the limits of a neighbouring state, the general militia, who consist of so many poor people that can illy be spared from their families and domestic concerns, by power of congress, who could know nothing of their circumstances, without consent of their own legislature or executive, ought to be restrained.

The second objection respecting the power of congress to alter elections, they thought indispensable. Montesquieu says, that the rights of election should be established unalterably by fundamental laws in a free government.

The third objection concerning previous requisition, they conceived highly important; they thought if money required by direct taxation could be paid with certainty and in due time to congress, that every good consequence would be secured to the union, and the people of the state thereby relieved from the great inconvenience and expence of a double collection and a double set of tax-gatherers, and they might also get rid of those odious taxes by excise and poll, without injury to the general government.

They were, however, again proposed and rejected. . . .

### 717. Fabius VIII
### Pennsylvania Mercury, 29 April[1]

OBSERVATIONS on the Constitution
proposed by the Federal Convention.

The proposed confederation offers to us a system of diversified representation in the legislative, executive, and judicial departments, as essentially necessary to the good government of an extensive republican empire. Every argument to recommend it, receives new force, by contemplating events, that must take place. The number of states in *America* will encrease. If not united to the present, the consequences are evident. If united, it must be by a plan that will communicate *equal liberty* and assure *just protection* to them. These ends can never be attained, but by *a close combination* of the several states.

It has been asserted, that a very extensive territory cannot be ruled by a government of republican form. What is meant by this proposition?[2] Is it intended to abolish all ideas of connection, and to precipitate us into the miseries of division, either as single states, or partial confederacies? To stupify us into despondence, that destruction may certainly seize us? The fancy of poets never feign'd so dire a *Metamorphosis*, as is now held up to us. The *Ægis* of their *Minerva* was only said to turn men into stones. This spell is to turn "a band of brethren,"[3] into a monster, preying upon itself, and prey'd upon by all its enemies.

If hope is not to be abandoned, common sense teaches us to attempt the best means of preservation. This is all that men can do, and this they ought to do. Will it be said, that any kind of disunion, or a connection tending to it, is preferable to a firm union? Or, is there any charm in that despotism, which is said, to be alone competent to the rule of such an empire? There is no evidence of fact, nor any deduction of reason, that justifies the assertion. It is true, that extensive territory has in general been arbitrarily governed; and it is as true, that a number of republics, in such territory, *loosely connected*, must inevitably rot into despotism. Such territory has never been governed by a confederacy of republics. Granted. But, where was there ever a confederacy of republics, in such territory, united, as these states are to be by the proposed constitution? Where was there ever a confederacy, in which, the sovereignty of each state was *equally represented* in one legislative body, the people of each state *equally represented* in another, and the sovereignties & people of all the states *conjointly represented* in a third branch? Or, in which, no law could be made, but by the agreement of three such branches? Or, in which, the appointment to federal offices was vested in a chief magistrate chosen as our president is to be, with the concurrence of a senate elected by the sovereignties of each state? Or, in which, the other acts of the executive department were regulated, as they are to be with us? Or, in which, the fœderal judges were to hold their offices independently and *during good behaviour*? Or, in which, the authority over the militia and troops was so distributed and controuled, as it is to be with us? Or, in which, the people were so drawn together by religion, blood, language, manners and customs, undisturbed by former feuds or prejudices? Or, in which, the affairs relating to the whole union, were to be managed by an assembly of several representative bodies, invested with different powers that became efficient only in concert, without their being embarrassed by attention to other business? Or, in which, a provision was made for the fœderal revenue, without recurring to coertion, the miserable expedient of every other confederacy that has existed, an expedient always attended with odium, & often with a delay productive of irreparable damage? Where was there ever a confederacy, that thus adhered to *the first principle of society*, obliging by its direct authority every individual, to contribute, when the public good necessarily required it, a just proportion of aid to the support of the commonwealth protecting him—without disturbing him in the discharge of the duties owing by him to the state of which he is an inhabitant; and at the same time so amply, so anxiously provided, for bringing the interests, and even the wishes of *every sovereignty* and of *every person* of the union, under all their various modifications and impressions, into their full operation and efficacy in the national councils? The instance never existed. The conclusion ought not to be made. It is without premises.

It has been said, that the varied representation of sovereignties and people in the legislature, was a mere compromise.

This is a great and dangerous mistake. The equal representation of each state in one branch of the legislature, was an original substantive proposition, as the writer is instructed, made in Convention, very soon after the draft offered by *Virginia*,[4] to which state United *America* is much indebted not only in other respects, but for her merit in the origination and prosecution of this momentous business.

The proposition was expressly made upon this principle, that a territory of such extent as that of United *America*, could not *be safely and advantageously governed*, but by a combination of republics, each retaining all the rights of supreme sovereignty, excepting such as ought to be contributed to the union; that for the securer preservation of these sovereignties, they ought to be represented in a body by themselves, and with equal suffrage; and that they would be annihilated, if both branches of the legislature were to be formed of representatives of the people, in proportion to the number of inhabitants in each state.

The principle appears to be well founded in reason. Why cannot a very extensive territory be ruled by a government of republican form? Because, its power must languish through distance of parts. Granted, if it be not a "body by joints and bands having nourishment ministered and knit together." If it be such a body, the objection is removed. Instead of such a perfect body, framed upon the principle that commands men to associate, and societies to confederate; that which by communicating and extending happiness, corresponds with the gracious intentions of our maker towards us his creatures; what is proposed? Truly, that the natural legs and arms of this body should be cut off, because they are too weak, and their places supplied by stronger limbs of wood and iron.

Arbitrary princes rule extensive territories, by sending viceroys to govern certain districts.

*America* is, and will be, divided into several sovereign states, each possessing every power proper for governing within its own limits for its own purposes, and also for acting as a member of the union.

They will be civil and military stations, conveniently planted throughout the empire, with lively and regular communications. A stroke, a touch upon any part, will be immediately felt by the whole. *Rome* famed for imperial arts, had a glimpse of this great truth; and endeavoured, as well as her hard hearted policy would permit, to realize it in her COLONIES. They were miniatures of the capital: But wanted the vital principle of sovereignty, and were too small. They were melted down into, or overwhelmed by the nations around them. Were they now existing, they might be called, little statues[5]—something like to our living originals. *These* will bear a remarkable resemblance to the mild features of patriarchal government, in which each son ruled his own houshold, and in other matters the whole family was directed by the common ancestor.

Will a people thus happily situated, and attached as they will naturally be, with an ardor of affection to their own state, ever desire to exchange their condition, for subjection to an absolute ruler, or can they ever look but with veneration, or act but with deference to that union, that alone can, under providence, preserve them from such subjection?

Can any government be devised, that will be more suited to citizens, who wish for equal freedom and common prosperity? better calculated for preventing corruption of manners? for advancing the improvements that endear or adorn life? or that can be more conformed to the nature and understanding, to the best and the last end of man? What harvests of happiness may grow from the seeds of liberty that are now sowing? The cultivation will indeed demand continual care, unceasing diligence, and frequent conflicts with difficulties. This too is consonant to the laws of our nature. As we pass through night into day, so we do through trouble into joy. Generally, the higher the prize, the deeper the suffering. We die into immortality. To object against the benefits offered to us by our Creator, by excepting to the terms annexed, is a crime to be equalled only by its folly.

Delightful are the prospects that will open to the view of United *America*—her sons well prepared to defend their own happiness, and ready to relieve the misery of others—her fleets formidable, but only to the unjust—her revenue sufficient, yet unoppressive—her commerce affluent, without debasing—peace and plenty within her borders—and the glory that arises from a proper use of power, encircling them.

Whatever regions may be destined for servitude, let us hope, that some portions of this land may be blessed with liberty; let us be convinced, that nothing short of such an union as has been proposed, can preserve the blessing; and therefore let us be resolved to adopt it.

As to alterations, a little experience will cast more light upon the subject, than a multitude of debates. Whatever qualities are possessed by those who object, they will have the candor to confess, that they will be encountered by opponents, not in any respect inferior, and yet differing from them in judgment, upon every point they have mentioned.

Such untired industry to serve their country, did the delegates to the federal convention exert, that they not only laboured to form the best plan they could, but, provided for making at any time amendments on the authority of the people, without shaking the stability of the government. For this end, the Congress, whenever two thirds of both houses shall deem it necessary, shall propose amendments to the constitution, or, on the application of the legislatures of two thirds of the several states, SHALL call a convention for proposing amendments, which, in either case, shall be valid to all intents and purposes, as part of the constitution, when ratified by the legislatures of three-fourths of the several states, or by conventions in three-fourths thereof, as one or the other mode of ratification may be proposed by Congress.

Thus, by a gradual progress, as has been done in *England*, we may from time to time introduce every improvement in our constitution, that shall be suitable to our situation. For this purpose, it may perhaps be adviseable, for every state, as it sees occasion, to form with the utmost deliberation, drafts of alterations respectively required by them, and to enjoin their representatives, to employ every proper method to obtain a ratification.

In this way of proceeding the undoubted sense of every state, collected in the coolest manner, not the sense of individuals, will be laid before the whole union in Congress, and that body will be enabled with the clearest light that can be afforded by every part of it, and with the least occasion of irritation, to compare and weigh the sentiments of all United *America*; forthwith to adopt such alterations as are recommended by general unanimity; by degrees to devise modes of conciliation upon contradictory propositions; and to give the revered advice of our common country, upon those, if any such there should be, that in her judgment are inadmissible, because they are incompatible with the happiness of these states.

It cannot be with reason apprehended, that Congress will refuse to act upon any articles calculated to promote the *common welfare*, tho' they may be unwilling to act upon such as are designed to advance PARTIAL *interests:* but, whatever their sentiments may be, they MUST call a Convention for proposing amendments, on applications of two-thirds of the legislatures of the several states.

May those good citizens, who have sometimes turned their thoughts towards a second Convention, be pleased to consider, that there are men who speak as they do, yet do not mean as they do. These borrow the sanction of their respected names, to conceal desperate designs. May they also consider, whether persisting in the suggested plan, in preference to the constitutional provision, may not kindle flames of jealousy and discord, which all their abilities and virtues can never extinguish.

1. Reprinted: *New Hampshire Spy*, 17 June; Baltimore *Maryland Gazette*, 20 June; *Providence Gazette*, 26 July; Philadelphia *American Museum*, December.

2. "Position" was substituted for "proposition" in the *American Museum* version.

3. William Shakespeare, *King Henry V*, Act IV, scene 3, line 60. "We few, we happy few, we band of brothers."

4. The Virginia Resolutions were presented to the Constitutional Convention on 29 May 1787 (CDR, 243–45). On 2 June Dickinson himself expressed the hope that "each State would retain an equal voice at least in one branch of the National Legislature." A motion stating that each state was to have one vote in the second branch of the legislature was defeated on 11 June and 2 July. Finally, on 16 July the Convention agreed that each state should have an equal vote in the Senate (Farrand, I, 87, 193, 201–2, 460, 468–70, 509, 510–16; II, 13–14).

5. "Curious *automata*" was substituted for "little statues" in the *American Museum* version.

## 718. Philadelphia Independent Gazetteer, 30 April[1]

Extract of a letter from Franklin county, 24th April, 1788.

"The necessary arrangements," as they are termed here, have taken place in these counties; committees of observation and correspondence are appointed in every township, who correspond with the militia officers and leading men in every county in the state; the counties of Cumberland, Dauphine, and Franklin, appear to take the lead, and have been long since repairing and cleaning their arms, and every young fellow who is able to do it, is providing himself with a *rifle* or musket, and amunition: They have also nominated a commanding officer, it is said to be General ——, and say that they can turn out, at ten days warning, TWENTY THOUSAND expert woodsmen, completely armed; this is I believe very true, as all the counties, this side the Susquehanna, are nearly unanimous, and near three fourths of the other counties. They say the strength of their opponents are in the city, and give out that it will be in vain for them to make any resistance; they mean to make * * *[2] and are promised assistance from a neighbouring state, who, I find, are as warmly opposed as this state to the system. The *lawyers*, &c. when they precipitated with such fraud and deception the new system upon us, it seems to me, did not recollect, that the militia had arms; however, it will be an awful lesson to tyrants, if they should feel the resentment of an enraged people; I can assure Mr. Wilson that the people are now as *determined* to secure their liberties as he is *anxious* for power and offices;[3] and let the worst come to the worst, the opposition have the constitution of the state, the established law of the land, on their side; this yet remains good and firm, any doings, *or acts of a faction, or illegal mob convention,*[4] *to the contrary notwithstanding. A civil war* is dreadful, but a little blood spilt now, will perhaps prevent much more hereafter. However, another general convention being called, will prevent any thing like it happening; the people appear anxious for farther powers being granted to Congress; and are generally agreed, that those offered by the minority of the convention of this state[5] would be quite sufficient, and all their rights and privileges would be then secured by the proposed bill of rights, consequently unity and harmony would follow: on the other hand, if the votaries of power and offices do not agree to peaceable measures, by having another general convention called, I dread the consequences to themselves.

"N. B. I hear no more of the attempt to execute the order of Council to disarm the militia,[6] I believe the *sub-lieutenants* in most of the counties refused to deliver up the arms, it was well enough, for the people were determined not to part with them. It is hinted that since the western members went down, they cancelled the order."

1. Reprinted: *New York Journal,* 6 May; *New York Morning Post,* 6 May; *Providence Gazette,* 17 May; *Norwich Packet,* 22 May; *New Hampshire Recorder,* 3 June. This newspaper item reflects the continuing turmoil over the Constitution in western Pennsylvania. In March 1788 Antifederalists in at least eight counties submitted petitions to the state legislature signed by more than 6,000 people requesting that the state's ratification of the Constitution "not be confirmed" (RCS:Pa., 709–25). Moreover, Cumberland County had only recently become pacified in the aftermath of the Carlisle riot of 26 December 1787. (See headnote to CC:713.)

2. At this point the *Independent Gazetteer* printed two lines of asterisks, indicating that material perhaps too sensitive to print was omitted. The reprints contain as many as two lines of asterisks to as few as three asterisks.

3. For example, "Cincinnatus" accused James Wilson of wanting to be either attorney general or chief justice of the Supreme Court under the new government ("Cincinnatus" VI, *New York Journal*, 6 December 1787, CC:324).

4. Probably a reference to the call of the state Convention by a mob-assisted legislature on 28–29 September 1787 (CC:125; and RCS:Pa., 54–126).

5. See the "Dissent of the Minority of the Pennsylvania Convention," *Pennsylvania Packet*, 18 December 1787 (CC:353).

6. On 4 December 1787 the Supreme Executive Council resolved "That the Lieutenants of the city and several counties within this state, be directed to collect all the public arms within their respective counties, have them repaired, and make return to Council, with the accounts and vouchers necessary for payment." Some Antifederalists charged that this was part of a Federalist plot to force the Constitution upon the people. The Council denied the charge, and it published some of its earlier resolves concerning the militia to demonstrate that it was actually arming the militia in order to protect the people, especially on the frontier. As a further demonstration of its goodwill, the Council resolved on 12 January 1788 "That the Lieutenants of the city and counties throughout the state, be directed, as soon as the public arms are repaired, to deliver them to the battalions under their command, apportioning them to the number of men in each, take receipts for them, and make report to Council." (For this issue, see "The Militia and the Supreme Executive Council," 19 December 1787–5 February 1788," Mfm:Pa. 273.)

## 719. Pennsylvania Gazette, 30 April[1]

The late controversy, says a correspondent, respecting the constitution of the United States, has exhibited the talents of the Americans in a most exalted point of view. Never did any subject produce a greater display of ingenuity, knowledge, wit, and powerful eloquence. The writings under the signatures of Publius, Aristides, Fabius, and the Landholder, are full of profound political wisdom.[2] The speeches of Mr. Wilson and Mr. M'Kean contain a complete system of republican government.[3] Mr. Hopkinson's inimitable allegories are as full of argument, as they are of humor, in favor of the government.[4] To these performances nothing has been opposed but impudent assertions, and calumnies against General Washington,[5] and the framers of the constitution[6]—extracts of letters from Maryland, &c. composed in Philadelphia—ribaldry—scurrility—seditious falshoods—⟨or, to use a word which includes them all, and every thing else that is base and wicked— nothing but BRIANISM.⟩[7]

1. Reprinted: *Pennsylvania Mercury*, 3 May; New York *Independent Journal*, 3 May; *Massachusetts Gazette*, 9 May; Baltimore *Maryland Gazette*, 13 May; Charleston *City Gazette*, 17 May; *Newport Mercury*, 26 May. See also note 7, below. For a parody of this item, see the Philadelphia *Independent Gazetteer*, 9 May (CC:737).

2. For editorial notes about Federalist writers "Publius," "Landholder," "Aristides," and "Fabius," see CC:201, 230, 490, 677.

3. The speeches of James Wilson and Thomas McKean, delivered in the Pennsylvania Convention, were transcribed by Thomas Lloyd and first offered for sale as a volume on 7 February (CC:511).

4. See, for example, "The New Roof," *Pennsylvania Packet*, 29 December (CC:395), and "A.B.," "The Raising: A New Song for Federal Mechanics," *Pennsylvania Gazette*, 6 February (CC:504).

5. For examples of attacks on George Washington, see "Centinel" XI and XVII, Philadelphia *Independent Gazetteer*, 16 January and 24 March (CC:453, 642); and "An American," Boston *American Herald*, 28 January (CC:386–F).

6. The "Centinel" and "Philadelphiensis" essays were particularly critical of the members of the Constitutional Convention.

7. The text in angle brackets was not reprinted in the *Pennsylvania Mercury*, the Baltimore *Maryland Gazette*, and the Charleston *City Gazette*.

## 720. The Society of Western Gentlemen Revises the Constitution
## Virginia Independent Chronicle, 30 April, 7 May (Extra)

On 8 March Arthur Campbell, the county lieutenant of Washington County and a member of the Virginia House of Delegates, wrote Francis Bailey, the rabidly Antifederalist editor of the Philadelphia *Freeman's Journal*, that he was forwarding to him (via Adam Orth of Lancaster County, Pa.) "a revised Copy" of the Constitution. Campbell said that this revision was "the work of a Society of Western Gentlemen, who took this method to investigate and understand the piece & to some of them it has lately been hinted, that the most of the pieces wrote for and against the Constitution, were rather declamatory, and bewildered common readers in the perusal; but by our mode it may be shewn at one view, what is deamed right or what is wrong." Campbell, on behalf of the Society, asked Bailey to edit the revised Constitution and to insert it on the first page of his newspaper, where it would probably have to be published in two installments. The Society also wanted Bailey to ask the editor of the Philadelphia *American Museum* to publish the revised Constitution (CC:606–A. For a newspaper article that Campbell, a fierce opponent of the Constitution, published attacking that document, see "Many," *Virginia Independent Chronicle*, 18 June, RCS:Va., 1638–40.).

On 9 March Campbell wrote Adam Orth, the owner of an iron forge, and sent him a copy of the revised Constitution (including a declaration of rights), which Campbell now believed should be printed as a pamphlet so that it could be circulated "especially in Pensylvania, N. York and Virginia." (Pennsylvania Antifederalists were actively engaged in a petition campaign requesting that the state legislature not "confirm" the state's ratification of the Constitution; the New York and Virginia conventions, where ratification would be difficult, were scheduled to convene in June.) Campbell hoped that either two or three printers, or Pennsylvania's Antifederalists, might assume the cost of publication. In particular, he thought that if 500 copies of the pamphlet were forwarded "to a trusty correspondent" in Petersburg, Va., they "would sell fast." Campbell asked Orth to discuss the matter of publishing a pamphlet with such prominent western Pennsylvania Antifederalists as William Findley, Robert Whitehill, John Smilie, and James McLene. He also hoped that Dr. John Ewing, a Philadelphia Presbyterian minister and provost of the University of Pennsylvania, might revise the Society's work. Campbell further believed that the proposed declaration of rights "will please most" people (CC:606–B).

Orth apparently did inform Philadelphia's Antifederalist leaders because the letter that he had received from Campbell is in the papers of George Bryan, one of the city's principal Antifederalists. Evidently, neither Francis Bailey nor the city's leading Antifederalists thought the revised Constitution or the declaration of rights should be printed because neither ever appeared in the *Freeman's Journal* or any other city newspaper. Instead, they were printed in two installments in the *Virginia Independent Chronicle* on 30 April and 7 May (extraordinary) (RCS:Va., 769–79).

Among the Society of Western Gentlemen's major changes to the Constitution were the inclusion of a declaration of rights; the establishment of annual and triennial elections for representatives and senators, respectively; the elimination of the "three-fifths clause" in apportioning representatives; the requirement that all bills originate in the House of Representatives; the protection of the freedom of the press; the elimination of the ban on the power of Congress to prohibit the foreign slave trade before 1808; the elimination of the power of Congress to levy direct taxes; the elimination of the presidential veto power; a prohibition of consecutive terms for the president; the limitation of federal judicial appointments to seven-year terms, with the possibility for reeligibility; a provision for jury trials in civil cases; the requirement that Congress call a constitutional convention on application of a majority of states; and the requirement of religious tests for officeholding. Campbell believed that such changes or amendments to the Constitution "will make it a more mild & we hope a more just plan of government." The Constitution simply had "too many of the features of despotism," making it a danger to the liberties of Americans (CC:606 A–B).

The Society's declaration of rights appears to have been taken largely from the Virginia Declaration of Rights (1776), which, even though it omitted some important rights, was an encompassing expression of the rights of English and American freemen. The Virginia Declaration also influenced the Virginia Convention in June 1788 in recommending a declaration of rights to the Constitution. (For the texts of the Virginia Declaration of Rights [1776] and the declaration of rights of the Virginia Convention, see RCS:Va., 530–31; and CC:790.)

[The complete text of the declaration of rights of the Society of Western Gentlemen and the Society's revised portions of the Constitution are printed in RCS:Va., 769–79. A photographic reproduction of the declaration of rights and the revised Constitution, as printed in the *Virginia Independent Chronicle* on 30 April and 7 May (extraordinary), appears as Mfm:Va. 190.]

## 721. Address to the Members of the New York and Virginia Conventions, Post–30 April

This address was drafted after the Maryland Convention ratified the Constitution and after efforts to present recommendatory amendments failed on 26 and 29 April, respectively. The draft refers to "the late conduct" of the

Federalists in the state Convention which was designed to create the impression that there was little or no support in Maryland for amendments. Directed at the members of the New York and Virginia conventions which were scheduled to meet in June, the address attempted to demonstrate that there was considerable support in Maryland for amendments safeguarding "THE NATURAL & UNALIENABLE RIGHTS OF MEN." (For more on amendments in the Maryland Convention, see CC:716.) The manuscript of this address, which is in two parts, is located in the Etting Collection (Old Congress) at the Historical Society of Pennsylvania. The address has not been located in any newspaper.

The authorship of the address is not clear. At a later date someone wrote "James Mercer?" on the manuscript of the first part of the essay. The second part bears two later-day attributions: "John Fenton Mercer" and "Mercer, Jno Francis"; the former appears at the top of the first page, the latter at the bottom of the last page. John Francis Mercer (1759–1821), who is the most likely choice to be the author, was a native of Virginia who had represented that state in the Confederation Congress in 1783 and 1784 before moving to Maryland in 1785. He attended the Constitutional Convention but left before it adjourned *sine die*. He opposed the Constitution; and in the Maryland Convention, he voted against ratification and was a member of the committee of thirteen to consider amendments. His half brother, James Mercer (1736–1793), a judge of the Virginia General Court, also opposed ratification of the Constitution. John Fenton Mercer, another half brother, was killed in 1756 during the French and Indian War.

Herbert J. Storing, who believes that John Francis Mercer was the author of the address, writes that some of the arguments used in the address are similar to those employed by Mercer in a 14 August 1787 speech in the Constitutional Convention; by "A Farmer," who published seven lengthy essays in the Baltimore *Maryland Gazette* between 15 February and 25 April; and by Mercer in an 1804 letter to Thomas Jefferson. Storing also thinks that Mercer was probably the author of "A Farmer" (*The Complete Anti-Federalist* [7 vols., Chicago, 1981], V, 5–73, 101–6). Although similarities can be found in Mercer's Constitutional Convention speech and the essays by "A Farmer," the speech seems to be unconnected—and at times even contradictory—to the address.

## Gentlemen

The galling Chains of Despotizm under the oppressive weight of which nine tenths of our Fellow mortals groan—the Tortures which unfeeling Tyranny has invented and fearlessly practiced in every Age and every Clime, are melancholy and terrifying proofs of the Incapacity of the *many* to defend those rights, which God and Nature gave them, from the artful and unceasing usurpations of the *Few*:—and they are frightful Lessons to teach us a watchful Jealousy of great and unnecessary Grants of Power and of changes in a State of Society which we know to be mild and free—Still there are moments of national Languor & Lethargy which the ambitious ever enterprizing mark with alacrity and use with Success.—The People long unaccustom'd in a good and guarded Government, to bold and selfish Designs in their Rulers, look up with an unsuspicious Confidence, to any alteration, which those entrusted with Power may propose—however unconstitutional the changes, if recommended by Men used to govern them, they seem to come forward under the Sanction of legal authority—if prepared in Secrecy—the public mind taken by surprize, and every Engine previously set in Motion—the unconcerted & unconnected Defence of Individuals is branded with the opprobrious Epithet of *Opposition* and overwhelmed in the directed Tide of popular Clamour—a clamour which a Number of wealthy men may at all Times command at a small Expence from the most indigent of the [*Mob?*] Populace.—

We forbear to remark on the manner in which the Constitution proposed for the united States came forward—as the circumstances are known to you, your own Feelings will render any observations unnecessary.

The object of our present Address is to prevent your forming unjust Conclusions from the Adoption of the Constitution in the State of Maryland by so large a Majority of the Convention and the subsequent dissolution of that Body, without proposing any amendments.—

Permit us to assure You that the Torrent which burst forth at the Birth of the Constitution had but little Effect on the Minds of many of us—and altho' it might prevent our having that weight with our Countrymen, in the first Paroxisms of Phrenzy which for ever accompany great and sudden Revolutions in Government—we were yet determined not to be wanting in our Duty to the Republic, at that Moment when Reason should resume her Empire over the unagitated Minds of our fellow Citizens—from many Circumstances we despaired of this in Maryland untill the adoption of the Constitution—At that Period, when our Efforts could not be subjected to Calumniating Misrepresentation,—we expected that an Appeal to the reflection of our Countrymen, would be listened to with attention and produce those Effects which unanswered and unanswerable Reasons ought to command—All opposition being thus postponed & every necessary Step to inform the minds of our Citizens on one Side neglected—while unremitting Exertions by a Number of wealthy & respectable Characters were continued on the other—it cannot be surprizing that the Elections were generally favorable to the Constitution—In a very few of the Counties did any Candidates propose themselves against it—very few voted & even in those Counties where the Opposition succeeded by such a decided Majority—those Gentlemen's offering was merely accidental. They had refused every Solicitation of the People & had actually determin'd not to serve in Convention until within 6 Days before the Election—

That the People of the State would have made alterations & amendments a Condition of Adoption, is a Question which from the above Circumstances it is impossible to decide—but that four fifths of the people of Maryland are now in favor of considerable alterations and amendments, and will insist on them,—we dont hesitate to declare (as our Opinion) to you and the world.—The difference between Amending *before* or *after* Adoption, (provided it is amended) is certainly not worth a Distinction.—

We are persuaded that the People of so large a Continent, so different in Interests, so distinct in Habits, cannot in all cases legislate in one Body by themselves or their Representatives—By themselves it is obviously impracticable—By their Representatives it will be found on Investigation equally so—for if these representatives are to pursue the general Interest without Constitutional checks & restraints—it must be done by a mutual Sacrifice of the Interests, wishes and prejudices of the parts they represent—and then they cannot be said to represent those Parts, but to misrepresent them—Besides as their Constituents cannot judge of their Conduct by their own Sense of what is right and proper—and as a representative can always in this view screen his abuse of Trust under the Cloak of Compromize, we do not see what check can remain in the Hands of the Constituents—for they cannot Know how far the Compromise was necessary, and the representative wrong— and to turn out and disgrace a Man when they cannot prove him wrong, and when he will have of Course the voice of the Body he is a Member of in his Favor, would in the Event be found subversive of the Principles of good Government.—

Thus then the pursuit of the general Interest produces an unchecked misrepresentation—but if Representatives are to pursue the partial Interests of the Districts they represent (which to recommend themselves to their Constituents it is most probable they will do) then the majority must ruin the Minority, for the majority will be found interested to throw the Burthens of Government upon that minority which in these States present a fair Opening by difference of *Cultivation—Importation* and *property*—In such extensive Territories governed by one Legislature, the Experience of Mankind tells us that if not by Preference the People will at least be led gradually to confide the legislative Power to the Hands of one man and his Family—who alone can represent the whole, without partial Interests and this is or leads to unlimited Despotizm[1]—

We have not that permanent & fixed distinction of ranks or orders of Men among us, which unalterably seperating the interests & views, produces that division in pursuits, which is the great security of the mixed Government we seperated from, & which we now seem so anxiously to copy:—if the new Senate of the United States will be really opposite in their pursuits & views from the Representatives, have they not a most dangerous power of interesting foreign Nations by Treaty [to?] support *their* views?—for instance the relinquishment of the navigation of Missisippi—and yet these Treaties are expressly declared paramount to the Constitutions of the several States & being the *supreme Law*, must of course control the national legislature, if not supersede the Constitution of the United States itself—the check of the President over a Body, with which he must act in concert, or his influence & power be almost annihilated, can prove no great constitutional security; And even the Representative body itself—& much more the Senate—are not sufficiently numerous to secure them from corruption—for all Governments tend to corruption, in proportion as power concentrating in the hands of the *few*, renders them objects of corruption to Foreign Nations & among themselves—

For these & many other reasons we are for preserving the Rights of the State Governments, where they must not be necessarily relinquished for the welfare of the Union—& where so relinquished the line shoud be definitely drawn if under the proposed Constitution the States exercise any Power, it woud seem to be at the mercy of the General Government—for it is remarkable that the clause securing to them those rights not expressly relinquished in the old Confœderation, is left out in the new Constitution;[2] And we conceive that there is no Power which Congress may *think* necessary to exercise for the *general Welfare*, which they may not assume under this Constitution—& this *Constitution* & the Laws made under it are declared paramount even to the unalienable rights, which have heretofore been secured to the Citizens of these States by their Constitutional compacts.—

Altho' this new Constitution can boast indeed of a Bill of Rights of seven Articles—yet of what nature is that Bill of Rights? to hold out such a security to the rights of property as might lead very wealthy & influential Men & Families into a blind compliance & adoption—whilst the Rights that are essential to the great body of Yeomanry of America are entirely disregarded.—

Moreover those very powers, which are to be expressly vested in the new Congress, are of a nature most liable to abuse—They are those which tempt the avarice & ambition of Men to a violation of the rights of their fellow Citizens, & they will be screen'd under the sanction of an undefined & unlimited authority—Against the *abuse* & *improper* exercise of these special powers, the People have a right to be secured by a sacred Declaration, defining the rights of the Individual & limiting by them, the extent of the exercise—The People were secured against the abuse of those Powers by fundamental Laws & a Bill of Rights, under the Government of Britain & under their own Constitutions— That Government which permits the abuse of Power, recommends it; & will deservedly experience the tyrany which it authorizes; for the history of Mankind establishes the truth of this political adage—*that in Government what may be done will be done*

The most blind admirer of this Constitution must in his heart confess that it is as far inferior to the British Constitution, of which it is an imperfect imitation as darkness is to light—In the British Constitution, the rights of men, the primary objects of the social Compact—are fixed on an immoveable foundation & clearly defined & ascertained by their Magna Charta, their Petition of Rights & Bill of Rights & their Effective administration by Ostensible Ministers, secures Responsability—In this new Constitution—a complicated System sets responsability at defiance & the Rights of Men neglected & undefined are left at the mercy of events; we vainly plume ourselves on the safeguard alone of Representation, forgetting that it will be a Representation on principles inconsistent with true & just Representation—that it is but a delusive shadow of Representation proffering in theory what can never be fairly reduced to practice—And after all Government by Representation (unless confirm'd in its views & conduct by the constant inspection, immediate superintendance, & frequent interference & control of the People themselves on one side, or an hœreditary nobility on the other, both of which orders have fixed & permanent views) is [really?] only a scene of perpetual rapine & confusion—& even with the best checks it has failed in all the Governments of Europe, of which it was once the basis, except that of England.—

When We turn our Eyes back to the scenes of blood & desolation which we have waded through to seperate from Great Britain—we behold with manly indignation that our blood & treasure have been wasted to establish a Government in which the Interest of *the few* is preferrd to the Rights *of the many*—When we see a Government so every way inferior to that we were born under, proposed as the reward of our sufferings in an eight years calamitous war—our astonishment is only equall'd by our resentment—On the conduct of Virginia & New York, two important States the preservation of Liberty in a great measure depends—the chief security of a Confœderacy of Republics was boldly disregarded & the old Confœderation violated by requiring Nine States instead of 13. voices to alter the Constitution.—but still the resistance of either of these States in the present temper of America (for the late conduct of the Party here must open the eyes of the People in Massachusetts with respect to the fate of their amendments)[3] will secure all that We mean to contend for—THE NATURAL & UNALIENABLE RIGHTS OF MEN in a Constitutional manner—At the distant appearance of danger to these, We took up Arms in the late Revolution—& may we never have cause to look back with regret on that period when connected with the Empire of Great Britain, We were *happy, secure & free.—*

1. The first part of the address ends here.

2. Article II of the Articles of Confederation states: "Each state retains its sovereignty, freedom and independence, and every Power, Jurisdicition and right, which is not by this confederation expressly delegated to the United States, in Congress assembled" (CDR, 86).

3. For the actions of Maryland Federalists on amendments in the Maryland Convention, see CC:716. As of 30 April, the Massachusetts Convention had been the only convention to recommend amendments (CC:508).

## 722. Fabius IX
## Pennsylvania Mercury, 1 May[1]

OBSERVATIONS ON THE CONSTITUTION
proposed by the FEDERAL CONVENTION.

When the sentiments of some objectors, concerning the *British* constitution, are considered, it is surprizing, that they should apprehend so much danger to United *America*, as they say, will attend the ratification of the plan proposed to us, by the late fœderal convention.

These gentlemen will acknowledge, that *Britain* has sustained many internal convulsions, and many foreign wars, with a gradual advancement in freedom, power and prosperity. They will acknowledge, that no nation that has existed, ever so perfectly united those distant extremes, *private security* of life, liberty and property, with exertion of *public force*; so advantageously combined the various powers of militia, troops, and fleets; or so happily blended together arms, arts, commerce, and agriculture. From what spring has flowed this stream of happiness? The gentlemen will acknowledge, that these advantages are derived from *a single* democratical branch in her legislature. They will also acknowledge, that in this branch, called the house of commons, only 131 are members for counties, that nearly one half of the whole house is chosen by about 5700 persons mostly of no property, that 56 members are elected by about 370 persons,[2] and the[(a)] rest in an enormous disproportion to the numbers of inhabitants who ought to vote.[(b)]

Thus are all the millions of people in that kingdom, said to be represented in the house of commons.

Let the gentlemen be so good, on a subject so familiar to them, as to make a comparison between the *British* constitution, and that proposed to us. Questions like these will then probably present themselves. Is there more danger to our liberty, from such a president as we are to have, than to that of *Britons*, from an hereditary monarch, with a vast revenue; *absolute* in the erection and disposal of offices, and in the exercise of the whole executive power; in the command of the militia, fleets, and armies, and the direction of their operations; in the establishment of fairs and markets, the regulation of weights and measures, and coining of money; who can call parliaments with a breath, and dissolve them with a nod; who can at his will, make war, peace, and treaties irrevocably binding the nation; and who can grant pardons or titles of nobility, as it pleases him? Is there more danger to us, from 26 senators, or double the number, than to *Britons*, from an hereditary aristocratic body, consisting of many hundreds, possessed of immense wealth in lands and money, strengthened by a host of dependents, and who availing themselves of defects in the constitution, send many of these into the house of commons; who hold a third part of the legislative power in their own hands; and, who form the highest court of judicature in the nation? Is there more danger to us, from a house of representatives to be chosen by ALL THE FREEMEN OF THE UNION EVERY TWO YEARS, than to *Britons*, from such a sort of representation as they have in the house of commons, the members of which, too, are chosen but every *seven* years? Is there more danger to us from the intended fœderal officers, than to *Britons*, from such a monarch, aristocracy, and house of commons together? What bodies are there in *Britain*, vested with such capacities for enquiring into, checking, and regulating the conduct of national affairs, as our sovereignty states? What proportion does the number of freeholders in *Britain* bear to the number of people? And what is the proportion in United *America*?

If any person, after considering such questions, shall say, there will be more danger to our freedom under the proposed plan, than to that of *Britons* under their constitution, he must mean, that *Americans* are, or will be, beyond all comparison inferior to *Britons* in understanding and virtue; otherwise with a constitution and government, every branch of which is so extremely popular, they certainly might guard their rights, at least as well, as *Britons* can guard their rights, under such political institutions as they have; unless, the person has some inclination to an opinion, that monarchy and aristocracy are favourable to the preservation of their rights. If he has, he cannot too soon recover himself. If ever monarchy or aristocracy appear in this country, it must be in the hideous forms of despotism.

What an infatuated, depraved people must *Americans* become, if with such unequalled advantages, committed to their trust in a manner almost miraculous, they lose their liberty? Through a single diseased organ of representation, *in the legislature only*, of the kingdom just mentioned,[3] such portions of popular sense and integrity, have been conveyed into the national councils, as have purified other parts, and preserved the whole in its present state of healthfulness. To their own vigor and attention, therefore, is that people, under providence, indebted for the blessings they enjoy. They have held, and now hold *the true balance* in their government. While they retain their enlightened spirit, they will continue to hold it, and, if they regard what they owe to others *as well* as what they owe to themselves, most probably, to be happy.[4]

They know, that there are powers that cannot be expressly limitted, without injury to themselves, and their magnanimity scorns any fear of such powers. This magnanimity taught *Charles* the first, that he was but a royal servant; and this magnanimity caused *James* the second's army, raised, paid and kept up by himself, to counfound him with huzzas for liberty.

They ask not for compacts, of which the national welfare, and in some cases its existence, may demand violations. They despise such dangerous provisions against danger.

They know, that *all powers* whatever, even those that according to the forms of the constitution are irresistable and absolute, of which there are very many, *ought to be exercised for the public good; and that when they are used to the public detriment, they are unconstitutionally exerted.*

This plain text, commented upon by their experienced intelligence, has led them safe through hazards of every kind, and they now are, what we see them. Upon the review, one is almost tempted to believe, that their insular situation, soil, climate, and some other circumstances, have compounded a peculiarity of temperature—uncommonly favourable to the union of reason and passion.

Certainly, 'tis very memorable with what life, impartiality, and prudence, they have interposed on great occasions; have by their patriotism communicated temporary soundness to their disordered representation; and have bid public confusions to cease. Two instances out of many may suffice. The excellent *William* the third, was distressed by a house of commons. He dissolved the parliament, and appealed to the people. They relieved him. His successor, the present king, in the like distress, made the same appeal; and received equal relief.

Thus *they* have acted: but, *Americans*, who have the same blood in their veins, have, it seems, very different heads and hearts. We shall be enslaved by a president senators and representatives, chosen by ourselves, and continually rotating within the period of time assigned for the continuance in office of members, in the house of commons? 'Tis strange. But, we are told, 'tis true. It may be so. As we have our *all* at stake, let us enquire, in what way this event is to be brought about. Is it to be before or after a general corruption of manners? If after, it is not worth attention. The loss of happiness then following of course. If before, how is it to be accomplished? Will a virtuous and sensible people chuse villains or fools for their officers? Or, if they should chuse men of wisdom and integrity, will these lose both or either, by taking their seats? If they should, will not their places be quickly supplied by another choice? Is the like derangment again, and again, and again, to be expected? Can any man believe, that such astonishing phœnomena are to be looked for? Was there ever an instance, where rulers thus selected by the people from their own body, have in the manner apprehended, outraged their own tender connections, and the interests, feelings, and sentiments of their affectionate and confiding countrymen? Is such a conduct more likely to prevail in this age of mankind, than in the darker periods that have preceded? Are men more disposed now than formerly, to prefer uncertainties to certainties, things perilous and infamous, to those that are safe and honourable? Can all the misteries of such iniquity, be so wonderfully managed by treacherous rulers, that none of their enlightened constituents, nor any of their honest associates acting with them in public bodies, shall ever be able to discover the conspiracy, till at last it shall burst with destruction to the whole federal constitution? Is it not ten thousand times less probable, that such transactions will happen, than it is, that we shall be exposed to innumerable calamities, by rejecting the plan proposed, or even by delaying to accept it?

Let us consider our affairs in another light, and take council from those who cannot love us, any farther than as we may be subservient to their views.

Not a monarch or sovereignty in *Europe*, can desire to see these states formed into one flourishing empire. Difference of government, participation in commerce, improvement in policy, and magnitude of power, can be no favourite objects of their attention. Our loss will be their gain—Our fall, their rise—Our shame, their triumph. Divided, they may distract, dictate, and destroy. United, their efforts will be waves dashing themselves into foam against a rock. May our national character be—an animated moderation, that seeks only its own, and will not be satisfied with less.

To his beloved fellow-citizens of United *America*, the writer dedicates this imperfect testimony of his affection, with fervent prayers, for a perpetuity of freedom, virtue, piety and felicity, to them and their posterity.

> (a) No member of parliament ought to be elected by fewer than the majority of 800, upon the most moderate calculation, according to Doctor Price.[5]
>
> (b) By the constitution proposed to us, *a majority* of the house of representatives, and of the senate, makes a quorum to do business: But, if the writer is not mistaken, about *a fourteenth* part of the members of the house of commons, makes a quorum to do business.[6]

1. Reprinted: *New Hampshire Spy*, 21 June; Baltimore *Maryland Gazette*, 24 June; *Providence Gazette*, 2 August; Philadelphia *American Museum*, December. See notes 3, 4, and 6 (below) for significant differences between the *Pennsylvania Mercury* and *American Museum* printings.

2. These figures, some of which "Fabius" rounded off, are probably from Burgh, *Political Disquisitions*, I, Book II, chapter IV, 45–48.

3. In the *American Museum*, this portion of the sentence was rephrased to read: "Through a single organ of representation, in the legislature only, of the kingdom just mentioned, though that organ is diseased."

4. The *American Museum* added this note here: "If to the union of England, Wales and Scotland, one more generous nation be added, the representation in the house of commons be improved, and the prerogative of creating peers be regulated, there seems to be the highest probability, that the empire will be much strengthened and aggrandized."

5. James Burgh cited Dr. Richard Price as the source for this statement (*Political Disquisitions*, I, Book II, chapter IV, 48).

6. The *American Museum* changed "to do business" to "for that purpose."

## 723. Federal Farmer: An Additional Number of Letters to the Republican, New York, 2 May

On 2 May nearly identical advertisements in the *New York Journal* and the *New York Packet* announced as "Just Published" a pamphlet entitled *An Additional Number of Letters from the Federal Farmer to the Republican; Leading to a Fair Examination of the System of Government, Proposed by the Late Convention; and to Several Essential and Necessary Alterations in It; and Calculated to Illustrate and Support the Principles and Positions Laid Down in the Preceding Letters* (Evans 21197). The pamphlet could be purchased from Thomas Greenleaf of the *Journal* and Samuel and John Loudon of the *Packet* and from booksellers Robert Hodge, Thomas Allen, Samuel Campbell, and John Reid, all of New York City.

The advertisement, run in the daily *Journal* until 26 July and in the sem-iweekly *Packet* until 13 June, added that "The former letters, published under the signature of the Federal Farmer [CC:242], have undergone several impressions in the different states, and several thousands of them have been sold. They are admitted, by candid men of both parties, to be written with a spirit of moderation and candour.

"A number of principles are laid down in them, highly interesting to the people of America, which ought to be more fully illustrated, than the bounds which the author set to himself, in the former letters, would permit.

"The design of these additional letters, is, more fully to explain and enforce the positions laid down in the former. The author does not aim to foment the passions; his appeal is to the reason of his readers. He wishes every man to examine for himself, and form his own opinion on the merits of the question.

"There are very few dispassionate men, who do not wish to see amendments made to this system. The great drift of these additional letters, is, to point out what these amendments ought to be, and to adduce arguments to support them.

"It is a matter of small importance, whether these amendments precede or succeed the adoption of the constitution, so that they be made.

"It is hoped, therefore, that gentlemen who are sincere in declaring that they wish for amendments, will unite in turning their attention to the subject, that they may be prepared to accede to such as are proper.—To those who are thus disposed, this publication is recommended."

The title page indicates only that the pamphlet was printed in the year 1788. Neither the place of publication nor the name of the printer appears. The first two pages of the *Additional Letters* (43 and 44 in roman numerals) consist of an "Advertisement," dated "UNITED STATES, *Jan.* 30, 1788," which reads: "Four editions, (and several thousands) of the pamphlets entitled the FEDERAL FARMER, being in a few months printed and sold in the several states; and as they appear to be much esteemed by one party, on the great question, and, by the other, generally allowed to possess merit; and as they contain positions highly interesting, which ought to be fully illustrated, an additional number of letters have been written.

"The subject before the public is interesting, and ought to receive a candid and full investigation. These letters are not calculated to foment the passions; they appeal to reason; they are written in a plain stile, with all the perspicuity and brevity that can be expected in writing on a subject so new, so intricate and extensive; and they have this peculiar excellency, that they lead people to examine and think for themselves, in an affair of the last importance to them.

"As to any attempts to injure the members of the convention, or any other characters whatever, the writer has no disposition to do it. Whoever will examine his letters, will perceive he is well acquainted with the members of the convention, the characters, parties, and politics of the country; and, on the whole, says, the convention was as respectable a body of men as America, probably, ever will see assembled: at the same time they will perceive, that he saw unwarrantable attempts, among designing ardent men without doors, to impose upon a free people, by a parade of names, that in the hurry of affairs defects in the system might escape their observation. Whoever reflects coolly upon the conduct of many individuals, when the constitution first appeared, will perceive, that it was the duty of men, who saw the pernicious tendency of such conduct, in a decent manner, to disapprove it, and to endeavour to induce the people to decide upon the all-important subject before them, by its own intrinsic merits and faults."

Letters I–V in the "Federal Farmer" are dated between 8 and 13 October 1787 (CC:242) and end on page 40. Letters VI–XVIII of the *Additional Letters*, dated between 25 December 1787 and 25 January 1788, begin on page 45 and end on page 181. The author of "Federal Farmer" has not been identified. For speculation about his identity, see the headnote to CC:242.

The Antifederalist New York Federal Republican Committee distributed the *Additional Letters* widely. In mid-May John Lamb, the chairman of the committee, wrote letters to prominent Antifederalists in New Hampshire, New York, Pennsylvania, Maryland, Virginia, North and South Carolina, and possibly Rhode Island calling for cooperation in obtaining amendments before nine states ratified the Constitution. In his letters, Lamb noted that he was transmitting "a series of Letters from the Federal Farmer to the Republican." It is possible that Lamb meant both the *Letters* and the *Additional Letters*. Virginia Antifederalist Richard Henry Lee, one of the men who received pamphlets, told Lamb that he would read them "with great pleasure" (27 June, CC:750–O). Antifederalist Joshua Atherton, a delegate to the New Hampshire Convention, informed Lamb that he "had not Time to avail myself of the federal Farmer's Sentiments, and have yet had only Time to gallop through that candid Performance." Atherton then complained: "Is it not surprising" that pamphlets like those by the "Federal Farmer" "have been kept back?" (23 June, CC:750–L).

Some Federalists were disturbed by the distribution of the second set of "Federal Farmer" letters and other pamphlets by New York's Antifederalists. William R. Davie, a delegate to the North Carolina Convention, declared that it was "astonishing the pains" that John Lamb had taken to disseminate "a large Packet of Antifederal pamphlets" to several prominent North Carolina Antifederalists (to James Iredell, 9 July, Iredell Papers, NcD). The *Newport Herald*, 29 May, criticized the "placeman, pensioner, and noted antifederalist" John Lamb for sending to the governor of Rhode Island "a large ⟨and fresh⟩ packet of pamphlets against the proposed constitution of the United States, accompanied with an anonymous letter, insidiously calculated to excite jealousies,—to disturb the peace of the union, and subvert the rising fabric of order, justice and liberty." The reprint in the *Massachusetts Centinel*, 7 June, added the two words in angle brackets and this introductory statement: "It is but justice to be inexorably severe towards the eminently guilty—we will, therefore, continue to delineate the characters of such with the point of the diamond—and thus *blazoned in the face of the day*, the abhorrence and execrations of mankind will consign them to infamous immortality." ("A Rhode-Islander," *Newport Herald*, 12 June, also attacked Lamb for sending pamphlets to the governor of Rhode Island. No letter from Lamb to Governor John Collins of Rhode Island has been located.)

The ideas expressed by "Federal Farmer" produced little Federalist response. Edward Carrington informed Thomas Jefferson that the two "Federal
Farmer" pamphlets "are reputed the best of any thing that has been written
in the opposition" (9 June, RCS:Va., 1591). A reviewer in the May issue of
the New York *American Magazine*, probably Noah Webster, complimented
"Federal Farmer" for his "many judicious remarks on the proposed federal
government" even though "the arguments want method, and the reader is
consequently fatigued with numberless repetitions." The reviewer agreed with
"Federal Farmer" that the general government might abuse its powers,
thereby endangering the liberties of the people, but he believed that it was
impossible to frame "a system of government which shall not be liable to the
same objection." "The only question then," the reviewer continued, "is,
whether the new constitution is as good as it may or can be. The political
wisdom of neither party can solve this question—the decision of it *must* be
left to *experiment*." He also challenged "Federal Farmer's" positions on representation in Congress and on rotation in office. (See notes 5 and 24, below.)
The reviewer concluded that "Several passages in the work before us are
equally exceptionable; but on the whole, it is conducted with more candor
and good sense, than most of the publications against the new constitution."
In a speech to the New York Convention on 21 June, Alexander Hamilton
attacked the description of what "Federal Farmer" called the "natural aristocracy." (See note 10, below.)

On 12 March 1789, a week after the first federal Congress was scheduled
to convene, the *New York Journal* advertised the sale of the two "Federal
Farmer" pamphlets, along with three other Antifederalist pamphlets by "A
Columbian Patriot," Luther Martin, and "A Plebeian" (CC:581, 678, 689),
John Adams's *Defence of the Constitutions* (CC:16), and copies of the new Con-
stitution. From 19 March to 9 April 1789, Antifederalist printer Edward E.
Powars advertised the sale of "A Few Copies" of the *Letters* and *Additional
Letters* in his weekly Worcester *American Herald*.

### LETTER VI.

DECEMBER 25, 1787.

DEAR SIR, My former letters to you, respecting the constitution proposed, were calculated merely to lead to a fuller investigation of the
subject; having more extensively considered it, and the opinions of
others relative to it, I shall, in a few letters, more particularly endeavour to point out the defects, and propose amendments. I shall in this
make only a few general and introductory observations, which, in the
present state of the momentous question, may not be improper; and
I leave you, in all cases, to decide by a careful examination of my
works, upon the weight of my arguments, the propriety of my remarks,
the uprightness of my intentions, and the extent of my candor—I
presume I am writing to a man of candor and reflection, and not to
an ardent, peevish, or impatient man.

When the constitution was first published, there appeared to prevail

a misguided zeal to prevent a fair unbiassed examination of a subject
of infinite importance to this people and their posterity—to the cause
of liberty and the rights of mankind—and it was the duty of those who
saw a restless ardor, or design, attempting to mislead the people by a
parade of names and misrepresentations, to endeavour to prevent their
having their intended effects. The only way to stop the passions of
men in their career is, coolly to state facts, and deliberately to avow
the truth—and to do this we are frequently forced into a painful view
of men and measures.

Since I wrote to you in October, I have heard much said, and seen
many pieces written, upon the subject in question; and on carefully
examining them on both sides, I find much less reason for changing
my sentiments, respecting the good and defective parts of the system
proposed than I expected—The opposers, as well as the advocates of
it, confirm me in my opinion, that this system affords, all circumstances
considered, a better basis to build upon than the confederation. And
as to the principal defects, as the smallness of the representation, the
insecurity of elections, the undue mixture of powers in the senate, the
insecurity of some essential rights, &c. the opposition appears, generally, to agree respecting them, and many of the ablest advocates
virtually to admit them—Clear it is, the latter do not attempt manfully
to defend these defective parts, but to cover them with a mysterious
veil; they concede, they retract; they say we could do no better; and
some of them, when a little out of temper, and hard pushed, use
arguments that do more honor to their ingenuity, than to their candor
and firmness.

Three states have now adopted the constitution without amendments; these, and other circumstances, ought to have their weight in
deciding the question, whether we will put the system into operation,
adopt it, enumerate and recommend the necessary amendments, which
afterwards, by three-fourths of the states, may be ingrafted into the
system, or whether we will make the amendments prior to the adoption—I only undertake to shew amendments are essential and necessary—how far it is practicable to ingraft them into the plan, prior to
the adoption, the state conventions must determine. Our situation is
critical, and we have but our choice of evils—We may hazard much by
adopting the constitution in its present form—we may hazard more by
rejecting it wholly—we may hazard much by long contending about
amendments prior to the adoption. The greatest political evils that can
befal us, are discords and civil wars—the greatest blessings we can wish
for, are peace, union, and industry, under a mild, free, and steady
government. Amendments recommended will tend to guard and direct

the administration—but there will be danger that the people, after the system shall be adopted, will become inattentive to amendments—Their attention is now awake—the discussion of the subject, which has already taken place, has had a happy effect—it has called forth the able advocates of liberty, and tends to renew, in the minds of the people, their true republican jealousy and vigilance, the strongest guard against the abuses of power; but the vigilance of the people is not sufficiently constant to be depended on—Fortunate it is for the body of a people, if they can continue attentive to their liberties, long enough to erect for them a temple, and constitutional barriers for their permanent security: when they are well fixed between the powers of the rulers and the rights of the people, they become visible boundaries, constantly seen by all, and any transgression of them is immediately discovered: they serve as centinels for the people at all times, and especially in those unavoidable intervals of inattention.

Some of the advocates, I believe, will agree to recommend *good* amendments; but some of them will only consent to recommend indefinite, specious, but unimportant ones; and this only with a view to keep the door open for obtaining in some favourable moment, their main object, a complete consolidation of the states, and a government much higher toned, less republican and free than the one proposed. If necessity, therefore, should ever oblige us to adopt the system, and recommend amendments, the true friends of a federal republic must see they are well defined, and well calculated, not only to prevent our system of government moving further from republican principles and equality, but to bring it back nearer to them—they must be constantly on their guard against the address, flattery, and manœuvres of their adversaries.

The gentlemen who oppose the constitution, or contend for amendments in it, are frequently, and with much bitterness, charged with wantonly attacking the men who framed it. The unjustness of this charge leads me to make one observation upon the conduct of parties, &c. Some of the advocates are only pretended federalists; in fact they wish for an abolition of the state governments. Some of them I believe to be honest federalists, who wish to preserve *substantially* the state governments united under an efficient federal head; and many of them are blind tools without any object. Some of the opposers also are only pretended federalists, who want no federal government, or one merely advisory. Some of them are the true federalists, their object, perhaps, more clearly seen, is the same with that of the honest federalists; and some of them, probably, have no distinct object. We might as well call the advocates and opposers tories and whigs, or any thing else, as federalists and anti-federalists. To be for or against the constitution, as it stands, is not much evidence of a federal disposition; if any names are applicable to the parties, on account of their general politics, they are those of republicans and anti-republicans. The opposers are generally men who support the rights of the body of the people, and are properly republicans. The advocates are generally men not very friendly to those rights, and properly anti-republicans.

Had the advocates left the constitution, as they ought to have done, to be adopted or rejected on account of its own merits or imperfections, I do not believe the gentlemen who framed it would ever have been even alluded to in the contest by the opposers. Instead of this, the ardent advocates begun by quoting names as incontestible authorities for the implicit adoption of the system, without any examination—treated all who opposed it as friends of anarchy; and with an indecent virulence addressed M—n G—y, L—e,[1] and almost every man of weight they could find in the opposition by name. If they had been candid men they would have applauded the moderation of the opposers for not retaliating in this pointed manner, when so fair an opportunity was given them; but the opposers generally saw that it was no time to heat the passions; but, at the same time, they saw there was something more than mere zeal in many of their adversaries; they saw them attempting to mislead the people, and to precipitate their divisions, by the sound of names, and forced to do it, the opposers, in general terms, alledged those names were not of sufficient authority to justify the hasty adoption of the system contended for. The convention, as a body, was undoubtedly respectable; it was, generally, composed of members of the then and preceding Congresses: as a body of respectable men we ought to view it. To select individual names, is an invitation to personal attacks, and the advocates, for their own sake, ought to have known the abilities, politics, and situation of some of their favourite characters better, before they held them up to view in the manner they did, as men entitled to our implicit political belief: they ought to have known, whether all the men they so held up to view could, for their past conduct in public offices, be approved or not by the public records, and the honest part of the community. These ardent advocates seem now to be peevish and angry, because, by their own folly, they have led to an investigation of facts and of political characters, unfavourable to them, which they had not the discernment to foresee. They may well apprehend they have opened a door to some Junius,[2] or to some man, after his manner, with his polite addresses to men by name, to state serious facts, and unfold the truth; but these advocates may rest assured, that cool men in the opposition, best acquainted with the affairs of the country, will not, in the critical passage of a people from one constitution to another, pursue inquiries, which, in other circumstances, will be deserving of the highest praise. I will say nothing further about political characters, but examine the constitution; and as a necessary and previous measure to a particular examination, I shall state a few general positions and principles, which receive a general assent, and briefly notice the leading features of the confederation, and several state conventions [i.e., constitutions], to which, through the whole investigation, we must frequently have recourse, to aid the mind in its determinations.

We can put but little dependance on the partial and vague information transmitted to us respecting antient governments; our situation as a people is peculiar: our people in general have a high sense of freedom; they are high spirited, though capable of deliberate measures; they are intelligent, discerning, and well informed; and it is to their condition we must mould the constitution and laws. We have no royal or noble families, and all things concur in favour of a government entirely elective. We have tried our abilities as freemen in a most arduous contest, and have succeeded; but we now find the main spring of our movements were the love of liberty, and a temporary ardor, and not any energetic principle in the federal system.

Our territories are far too extensive for a limited monarchy, in which the representatives must frequently assemble, and the laws operate mildly and systematically. The most elligible system is a federal republic, that is, a system in which national concerns may be transacted in the centre, and local affairs in state or district governments.

The powers of the union ought to be extended to commerce, the coin, and national objects; and a division of powers, and a deposit of them in different hands, is safest.

Good government is generally the result of experience and gradual improvements, and a punctual execution of the laws is essential to the preservation of life, liberty, and property. Taxes are always necessary, and the power to raise them can never be safely lodged without checks and limitation, but in a full and substantial representation of the body of the people; the quantity of power delegated ought to be compensated by the brevity of the time of holding it, in order to prevent the possessors increasing it. The supreme power is in the people, and rulers possess only that portion which is expressly given them; yet the wisest people have often declared this is the case on proper occasions, and have carefully formed stipulations to fix the extent, and limit the exercise of the power given.

The people by Magna Charta, &c. did not acquire powers, or receive privileges from the king, they only ascertained and fixed those they were entitled to as Englishmen; the title used by the king "we grant," was mere form. Representation, and the jury trial, are the best features of a free government ever as yet discovered, and the only means by which the body of the people can have their proper influence in the affairs of government.

In a federal system we must not only balance the parts of the same government, as that of the state, or that of the union; but we must find a balancing influence between the general and local governments— the latter is what men or writers have but very little or imperfectly considered.

A free and mild government is that in which no laws can be made without the formal and free consent of the people, or of their constitutional representatives; that is, of a substantial representative branch. Liberty, in its genuine sense, is security to enjoy the effects of our honest industry and labours, in a free and mild government, and personal security from all illegal restraints.

Of rights, some are natural and unalienable, of which even the people cannot deprive individuals: Some are constitutional or fundamental; these cannot be altered or abolished by the ordinary laws; but the people, by express acts, may alter or abolish them—These, such as the trial by jury, the benefits of the writ of habeas corpus, &c. individuals claim under the solemn compacts of the people, as constitutions, or at least under laws so strengthened by long usuage as not to be repealable by the ordinary legislature—and some are common or mere legal rights, that is, such as individuals claim under laws which the ordinary legislature may alter or abolish at pleasure.

The confederation is a league of friendship among the states or sovereignties for the common defence and mutual welfare—Each state expressly retains its sovereignty, and all powers not expressly given to congress—All federal powers are lodged in a congress of delegates annually elected by the state legislatures, except in Connecticut and Rhode-Island, where they are chosen by the people—Each state has a vote in congress, pays its delegates, and may instruct or recall them; no delegate can hold any office of profit, or serve more than three years in any six years—Each state may be represented by not less than two, or more than seven delegates.[3]

Congress (nine states agreeing) may make peace and war, treaties and alliances, grant letters of marque and reprisal, coin money, regulate the alloy and value of the coin, require men and monies of the states by fixed proportions, and appropriate monies, form armies and navies, emit bills of credit, and borrow monies.

Congress (seven states agreeing) may send and receive ambassadors, regulate captures, make rules for governing the army and navy, institute courts for the trial of piracies and felonies committed on the high seas, and for settling territorial disputes between the individual states, regulate weight and measures, post offices, and Indian affairs.

No state, without the consent of congress, can send or receive embassies, make any agreement with any other state, or a foreign state, keep up any vessels of war or bodies of forces in time of peace, or engage in war, or lay any duties which may interfere with the treaties of congress—Each state must appoint regimental officers, and keep up a well regulated militia—Each state may prohibit the importation or exportation of any species of goods.

The free inhabitants of one state are intitled to the privileges and immunities of the free citizens of the other states—Credit in each state shall be given to the records and judicial proceedings in the others.

Canada, acceding, may be admitted, and any other colony may be admitted by the consent of nine states.

Alterations may be made by the agreement of congress, and confirmation of all the state legislatures.

The following, I think, will be allowed to be unalienable or fundamental rights in the United States:—

No man, demeaning himself peaceably, shall be molested on account of his religion or mode of worship—The people have a right to hold and enjoy their property according to known standing laws, and which cannot be taken from them without their consent, or the consent of their representatives; and whenever taken in the pressing urgencies of government, they are to receive a reasonable compensation for it—Individual security consists in having free recourse to the laws—The people are subject to no laws or taxes not assented to by their representatives constitutionally assembled—They are at all times intitled to the benefits of the writ of habeas corpus, the trial by jury in criminal and civil causes—They have a right, when charged, to a speedy trial in the vicinage; to be heard by themselves or counsel, not to be compelled to furnish evidence against themselves, to have witnesses face to face, and to confront their adversaries before the judge—No man is held to answer a crime charged upon him till it be substantially described to him; and he is subject to no unreasonable searches or seizures of his person, papers or effects—The people have a right to assemble in an orderly manner, and petition the government for a redress of wrongs—The freedom of the press ought not to be restrained—No emoluments, except for actual service—No hereditary honors, or orders of nobility, ought to be allowed—The military ought to be subordinate to the civil authority, and no soldier be quartered on the citizens without their consent—The militia ought always to be armed and disciplined, and the usual defence of the country—The supreme power is in the people, and power delegated ought to return to them at stated periods, and frequently—The legislative, executive, and judicial powers, ought always to be kept distinct—others perhaps might be added.

The organization of the state governments—Each state has a legislature, an executive, and a judicial branch—In general legislators are excluded from the important executive and judicial offices—Except in the Carolinas there is no constitutional distinction among Christian sects—The constitutions of New York, Delaware, and Virginia, exclude the clergy from offices civil and military—the other states do nearly the same in practice.

Each state has a democratic branch elected twice a-year in Rhode-Island and Connecticut, biennially in South-Carolina, and annually in the other states—There are about 1500 representatives in all the states, or one to each 1700 inhabitants, reckoning five blacks for three whites—The states do not differ as to the age or moral characters of the electors or elected, nor materially as to their property.

Pennsylvania has lodged all her legislative powers in a single branch, and Georgia has done the same; the other eleven states have each in their legislatures a second or senatorial branch. In forming this they have combined various principles, and aimed at several checks and balances. It is amazing to see how ingenuity has worked in the several states to fix a barrier against popular instability. In Massachusetts the senators are apportioned on districts according to the taxes they pay, nearly according to property. In Connecticut the freemen, in September, vote for twenty counsellors, and return the names of those voted for in the several towns; the legislature takes the twenty who have the most votes, and gives them to the people, who, in April, chuse twelve of them, who, with the governor and deputy governor, form the senatorial branch. In Maryland the senators are chosen by two electors from each county; these electors are chosen by the freemen, and qualified as the members in the democratic branch are: In these two cases checks are aimed at in the mode of election. Several states have taken into view the periods of service, age, property, &c. In South-Carolina a senator is elected for two years, in Delaware three, and in New-York and Virginia four, in Maryland five, and in the other states for one. In New-York and Virginia one-fourth part go out yearly. In Virginia a senator must be twenty-five years old, in South-Carolina thirty. In New-York the electors must each have a freehold worth 250 dollars, in North-Carolina a freehold of fifty acres of land; in the other states the electors of senators are qualified as electors of representatives are. In Massachusetts a senator must have a freehold in his own right worth 1000 dollars, or any estate worth 2000, in New-Jersey any estate worth 2666, in South-Carolina worth 1300 dollars, in North-Carolina 300 acres of land in fee, &c. The numbers of senators in each state are from ten to thirty-one, about 160 in the eleven states, about one to 14000 inhabitants.

Two states, Massachusetts and New-York, have each introduced into their legislatures a third, but incomplete branch. In the former, the governor may negative any law not supported by two-thirds of the senators, and two-thirds of the representatives: in the latter, the governor, chancellor, and judges of the supreme court may do the same.

Each state has a single executive branch. In the five eastern states the people at large elect their governors; in the other states the legislatures elect them. In South Carolina the governor is elected once in two years; in New-York and Delaware once in three, and in the other states annually. The governor of New-York has no executive council, the other governors have. In several states the governor has a vote in the senatorial branch—the governors have similar powers in some instances, and quite dissimilar ones in others. The number of executive counsellers in the states are from five to twelve. In the four eastern states, New-Jersey, Pennsylvania, and Georgia, they are of the men returned legislators by the people. In Pennsylvania the counsellers are chosen triennially, in Delaware every fourth year, in Virginia every three years, in South-Carolina biennially, and in the other states yearly.

Each state has a judicial branch; each common law courts, superior and inferior; some chancery and admiralty courts: The courts in general sit in different places, in order to accommodate the citizens. The trial by jury is had in all the common law courts, and in some of the admiralty courts. The democratic freemen principally form the juries; men destitute of property, of character, or under age, are excluded as in elections. Some of the judges are during good behaviour, and some appointed for a year, and some for years; and all are dependant on the legislatures for their salaries—Particulars respecting this department are too many to be noticed here.

## LETTER VII.

### DECEMBER 31, 1787.

DEAR SIR, In viewing the various governments instituted by mankind, we see their whole force reducible to two principles—the important springs which alone move the machines, and give them their intended influence and controul, are force and persuasion: by the former men are compelled, by the latter they are drawn. We denominate a government despotic or free, as the one or other principle prevails in it. Perhaps it is not possible for a government to be so despotic, as not to operate persuasively on some of its subjects; nor is it, in the nature of things, I conceive, for a government to be so free, or so supported by voluntary consent, as never to want force to compel obedience to the laws. In despotic governments one man, or a few men, independant of the people, generally make the laws, command obedience, and inforce it by the sword: one-fourth part of the people are armed, and obliged to endure the fatigues of soldiers, to oppress the others and keep them subject to the laws. In free governments the people, or their representatives, make the laws; their execution is principally the effect of voluntary consent and aid; the people respect the magistrate, follow their private pursuits, and enjoy the fruits of their labour with very small deductions for the public use. The body of the people must evidently prefer the latter species of government; and it can be only those few, who may be well paid for the part they take in enforcing despotism, that can, for a moment, prefer the former. Our true object is to give full efficacy to one principle, to arm persuasion on every side, and to render force as little necessary as possible. Persuasion is never dangerous not even in despotic governments; but military force, if often applied internally, can never fail to destroy the love and confidence, and break the spirits, of the people; and to render it totally impracticable and unnatural for him or them who govern, and yield to this force against the people, to hold their places by the peoples' elections.

I repeat my observation, that the plan proposed will have a doubtful operation between the two principles; and whether it will preponderate towards persuasion or force is uncertain.

Government must exist—If the persuasive principle be feeble, force is infallibly the next resort—The moment the laws of congress shall be disregarded they must languish, and the whole system be convulsed— that moment we must have recourse to this next resort, and all freedom vanish.

It being impracticable for the people to assemble to make laws, they must elect legislators, and assign men to the different departments of the government. In the representative branch we must expect chiefly to collect the confidence of the people, and in it to find almost entirely the force of persuasion. In forming this branch, therefore, several important considerations must be attended to. It must possess abilities to discern the situation of the people and of public affairs, a disposition to sympathize with the people, and a capacity and inclination to make laws congenial to their circumstances and condition: it must afford security against interested combinations, corruption and influence; it must possess the confidence, and have the voluntary support of the people.

I think these positions will not be controverted, nor the one I formerly advanced, that a fair and equal representation is that in which the interests, feelings, opinions and views of the people are collected, in such manner as they would be were the people all assembled.[4] Having made these general observations, I shall proceed to consider further my principal position, viz. that there is no substantial representation of the people provided for in a government, in which the most essential powers, even as to the internal police of the country, are proposed to be lodged; and to propose certain amendments as to the representative branch: 1st, That there ought to be *an increase of the numbers of representatives:* And, 2dly, That the elections of them ought to be better secured.[5]

1. The representation is unsubstantial and ought to be increased. In matters where there is much room for opinion, you will not expect me to establish my positions with mathematical certainty; you must only expect my observations to be candid, and such as are well founded in the mind of the writer. I am in a field where doctors disagree; and as to genuine representation, though no feature in government can be more important, perhaps, no one has been less understood, and no one that has received so imperfect a consideration by political writers. The ephori in Sparta, and the tribunes in Rome, were but the shadow; the representation in Great-Britain is unequal and insecure. In America we have done more in establishing this important branch on its true principles, than, perhaps, all the world besides: yet even here, I conceive, that very great improvements in representation may be made. In fixing this branch, the situation of the people must be surveyed, and the number of representatives and forms of election apportioned to that situation. When we find a numerous people settled in a fertile and extensive country, possessing equality, and few or none of them oppressed with riches or wants, it ought to be the anxious care of the constitution and laws, to arrest them from national depravity, and to preserve them in their happy condition. A virtuous people make just laws, and good laws tend to preserve unchanged a virtuous people. A virtuous and happy people by laws uncongenial to their characters, may easily be gradually changed into servile and depraved creatures. Where the people, or their representatives, make the laws, it is probable they will generally be fitted to the national character

and circumstances, unless the representation be partial, and the imperfect substitute of the people. However, the people may be electors, if the representation be so formed as to give one or more of the natural classes of men in the society an undue ascendency over the others, it is imperfect; the former will gradually become masters, and the latter slaves. It is the first of all among the political balances, to preserve in its proper station each of these classes. We talk of balances in the legislature, and among the departments of government; we ought to carry them to the body of the people. Since I advanced the idea of balancing the several orders of men in a community, in forming a genuine representation,[6] and seen that idea considered as chemerical, I have been sensibly struck with a sentence in the marquis Beccaria's treatise: this sentence was quoted by congress in 1774, and is as follows:—"In every society there is an effort continually tending to confer on one part the height of power and happiness, and to reduce the others to the extreme of weakness and misery; the intent of good laws is to oppose this effort, and to diffuse their influence universally and equally."[7] Add to this Montesquieu's opinion, that "in a free state every man, who is supposed to be a free agent, ought to be concerned in his own government: therefore, the legislative should reside in the whole body of the people, or their representatives."[8] It is extremely clear that these writers had in view the several orders of men in society, which we call aristocratical, democratical, merchantile, mechanic, &c. and perceived the efforts they are constantly, from interested and ambitious views, disposed to make to elevate themselves and oppress others. Each order must have a share in the business of legislation actually and efficiently. It is deceiving a people to tell them they are electors, and can chuse their legislators, if they cannot, in the nature of things, chuse men from among themselves, and genuinely like themselves. I wish you to take another idea along with you; we are not only to balance these natural efforts, but we are also to guard against accidental combinations; combinations founded in the connections of offices and private interests, both evils which are increased in proportion as the number of men, among which the elected must be, are decreased. To set this matter in a proper point of view, we must form some general ideas and descriptions of the different classes of men, as they may be divided by occupations and politically: the first class is the aristocratical. There are three kinds of aristocracy spoken of in this country—the first is a constitutional one, which does not exist in the United States in our common acceptation of the word. Montesquieu, it is true, observes, that where a part of the persons in a society, for want of property, age, or moral character, are excluded any share

in the government, the others, who alone are the constitutional electors
and elected, form this aristocracy;[9] this according to him, exists in each
of the United States, where a considerable number of persons, as all
convicted of crimes, under age, or not possessed of certain property,
are excluded any share in the government; the second is an aristocratic
faction, a junto of unprincipled men, often distinguished for their
wealth or abilities, who combine together and make their object their
private interests and aggrandizement; the existence of this description
is merely accidental, but particularly to be guarded against. The third
is the natural aristocracy; this term we use to designate a respectable
order of men, the line between whom and the natural democracy is
in some degree arbitrary; we may place men on one side of this line,
which others may place on the other, and in all disputes between the
few and the many, a considerable number are wavering and uncertain
themselves on which side they are, or ought to be. In my idea of our
natural aristocracy in the United States, I include about four or five
thousand men; and among these I reckon those who have been placed
in the offices of governors, of members of Congress, and state senators
generally, in the principal officers of Congress, of the army and militia,
the superior judges, the most eminent professional men, &c. and men
of large property[10]—the other persons and orders in the community
form the natural democracy; this includes in general the yeomanry,
the subordinate officers, civil and military, the fishermen, mechanics
and traders, many of the merchants and professional men. It is easy
to perceive that men of these two classes, the aristocratical, and democratical, with views equally honest, have sentiments widely different,
especially respecting public and private expences, salaries, taxes, &c.
Men of the first class associate more extensively, have a high sense of
honor, possess abilities, ambition, and general knowledge: men of the
second class are not so much used to combining great objects; they
possess less ambition, and a larger share of honesty: their dependence
is principally on middling and small estates, industrious pursuits, and
hard labour, while that of the former is principally on the emoluments
of large estates, and of the chief offices of government. Not only the
efforts of these two great parties are to be balanced, but other interests
and parties also, which do not always oppress each other merely for
want of power, and for fear of the consequences; though they, in fact,
mutually depend on each other; yet such are their general views, that
the merchants alone would never fail to make laws favourable to themselves and oppressive to the farmers, &c. the farmers alone would act
on like principles; the former would tax the land, the latter the trade.
The manufacturers are often disposed to contend for monopolies,

buyers make every exertion to lower prices, and sellers to raise them; men who live by fees and salaries endeavour to raise them, and the part of the people who pay them, endeavour to lower them; the public creditors to augment the taxes, and the people at large to lessen them. Thus, in every period of society, and in all the transactions of men, we see parties verifying the observation made by the Marquis; and those classes which have not their centinels in the government, in proportion to what they have to gain or lose, must infallibly be ruined.

Efforts among parties are not merely confined to property; they contend for rank and distinctions; all their passions in turn are enlisted in political controversies—Men, elevated in society, are often disgusted with the changeableness of the democracy, and the latter are often agitated with the passions of jealousy and envy: the yeomanry possess a large share of property and strength, are nervous and firm in their opinions and habits—the mechanics of towns are ardent and changeable, honest and credulous, they are inconsiderable for numbers, weight and strength, not always sufficiently stable for the supporting free governments; the fishing interest partakes partly of the strength and stability of the landed, and partly of the changeableness of the mechanic interest. As to merchants and traders, they are our agents in almost all money transactions; give activity to government, and possess a considerable share of influence in it. It has been observed by an able writer, that frugal industrious merchants are generally advocates for liberty. It is an observation, I believe, well founded, that the schools produce but few advocates for republican forms of government; gentlemen of the law, divinity, physic, &c. probably form about a fourth part of the people; yet their political influence, perhaps, is equal to that of all the other descriptions of men; if we may judge from the appointments to Congress, the legal characters will often, in a small representation, be the majority; but the more the representatives are encreased, the more of the farmers, merchants, &c. will be found to be brought into the government.

These general observations will enable you to discern what I intend by different classes, and the general scope of my ideas, when I contend for uniting and balancing their interests, feelings, opinions, and views in the legislature; we may not only so unite and balance these as to prevent a change in the government by the gradual exaltation of one part to the depression of others, but we may derive many other advantages from the combination and full representation; a small representation can never be well informed as to the circumstances of the people, the members of it must be too far removed from the people, in general, to sympathize with them, and too few to communicate with them: a representation must be extremely imperfect where the representatives are not circumstanced to make the proper communications to their constituents, and where the constituents in turn cannot, with tolerable convenience, make known their wants, circumstances, and opinions, to their representatives; where there is but one representative to 30,000, or 40,000 inhabitants, it appears to me, he can only mix, and be acquainted with a few respectable characters among his constituents, even double the federal representation, and then there must be a very great distance between the representatives and the people in general represented. On the proposed plan, the state of Delaware, the city of Philadelphia, the state of Rhode Island, the province of Main[e], the county of Suffolk in Massachusetts, will have one representative each; there can be but little personal knowledge, or but few communications, between him and the people at large of either of those districts. It has been observed, that mixing only with the respectable men, he will get the best information and ideas from them; he will also receive impressions favourable to their purposes particularly. Many plausible shifts have been made to divert the mind from dwelling on this defective representation, these I shall consider in another place.[11]

Could we get over all our difficulties respecting a balance of interests and party efforts, to raise some and oppress others, the want of sympathy, information and intercourse between the representatives and the people, an insuperable difficulty will still remain, I mean the constant liability of a small number of representatives to private combinations; the tyranny of the one, or the licentiousness of the multitude, are, in my mind, but small evils, compared with the factions of the few. It is a consideration well worth pursuing, how far this house of representatives will be liable to be formed into private juntos, how far influenced by expectations of appointments and offices, how far liable to be managed by the president and senate, and how far the people will have confidence in them. To obviate difficulties on this head, as well as objections to the representative branch, generally, several observations have been made—these I will now examine, and if they shall appear to be unfounded, the objections must stand unanswered.

That the people are the electors, must elect good men, and attend to the administration.

It is said that the members of Congress, at stated periods, must return home, and that they must be subject to the laws they may make, and to a share of the burdens they may impose.

That the people possess the strong arm to overawe their rulers, and the best checks in their national character against the abuses of power, that the supreme power will remain in them.

That the state governments will form a part of, and a balance in the system.

That Congress will have only a few national objects to attend to, and the state governments many and local ones.

That the new Congress will be more numerous than the present, and that any numerous body is unwieldy and mobbish.

That the states only are represented in the present Congress, and that the people will require a representation in the new one; that in fifty or an hundred years the representation will be numerous.

That congress will have no temptation to do wrong; and that no system to enslave the people is practicable.

That as long as the people are free they will preserve free governments; and that when they shall become tired of freedom, arbitrary government must take place.

These observations I shall examine in the course of my letters; and, I think, not only shew that they are not well founded, but point out the fallacy of some of them; and shew, that others do not very well comport with the dignified and manly sentiments of a free and enlightened people.

### LETTER VIII.

JANUARY 3, 1788.

DEAR SIR, Before I proceed to examine the objections, I beg leave to add a valuable idea respecting representation, to be collected from De Lome,[12] and other able writers, which essentially tends to confirm my positions: They very justly impute the establishment of general and equal liberty in England to a balance of interests and powers among the different orders of men; aided by a series of fortunate events, that never before, and possibly never again will happen.

Before the Norman conquest the people of England enjoyed much of this liberty. The first of the Norman kings, aided by foreign mercenaries and foreign attendants, obnoxious to the English, immediately laid arbitrary taxes, and established arbitrary courts, and severely oppress[ed] all orders of people: The barons and people, who recollected their former liberties, were induced, by those oppressions, to unite their efforts in their common defence: Here it became necessary for the great men, instead of deceiving and depressing the people, to enlighten and court them; the royal power was too strongly fixed to be annihilated, and rational means were, therefore directed to limiting it within proper bounds. In this long and arduous task, in this new species of contests, the barons and people succeeded, because they had been freemen, and knew the value of the object they were contending for; because they were the people of a small island—one people who found it practicable to meet and deliberate in one assembly, and act under one system of resolves, and who were not obliged to meet in different provincial assemblies, as is the case in large countries, as was the case in France, Spain, &c. where their determinations were inconsistent with each other, and where the king could play off one assembly against another.

It was in this united situation the people of England were for several centuries, enabled to combine their exertions, and by compacts, as Magna Charta, a bill of rights, &c. were able to limit, by degrees, the royal prerogatives, and establish their own liberties. The first combination was, probably, the accidental effect of pre-existing circumstances; but there was an admirable balance of interests in it, which has been the parent of English liberty, and excellent regulations enjoyed since that time. The executive power having been uniformly in the king, and he the visible head of the nation, it was chimerical for the greatest lord or most popular leader, consistent with the state of the government, and opinion of the people, to seriously think of becoming the king's rival, or to aim at even a share of the executive power; the greatest subject's prospect was only in acquiring a respectable influence in the house of commons, house of lords, or in the ministry; circumstances at once made it the interests of the leaders of the people to stand by them. Far otherwise was it with the ephori in Sparta, and tribunes in Rome. The leaders in England have led the people to freedom, in almost all other countries to servitude. The people in England have made use of deliberate exertions, their safest and most efficient weapons. In other countries they have often acted like mobs, and been enslaved by their enemies, or by their own leaders. In England, the people have been led uniformly, and systematically by their representatives to secure their rights by compact, and to abolish innovations upon the government: they successively obtained Magna Charta, the powers of taxation, the power to propose laws, the habeas corpus act, bill of rights, &c. they, in short, secured general and equal liberty, security to their persons and property; and, as an everlasting security and bulwark of their liberties, they fixed the democratic branch in the legislature, and jury trial in the execution of the laws, the freedom of the press, &c.

In Rome, and most other countries, the reverse of all this is true. In Greece, Rome, and wherever the civil law has been adopted, torture has been admitted. In Rome the people were subject to arbitrary confiscations, and even their lives would be arbitrarily disposed of by consuls, tribunes, dictators, masters, &c. half of the inhabitants were slaves, and the other half never knew what equal liberty was; yet in England the people have had king, lords, and commons; in Rome they had consuls, senators and tribunes: why then was the government of England so mild and favourable to the body of the people, and that of Rome an ambitious and oppressive aristocracy? Why in England have the revolutions always ended in stipulations in favour of general liberty, equal laws, and the common rights of the people, and in most other countries in favour only of a few influential men? The reasons, in my mind, are obvious: In England the people have been substantially represented in many respects; in the other countries it has not been so. Perhaps a small degree of attention to a few simple facts will illustrate this.—In England, from the oppressions of the Norman kings to the revolution in 1688, during which period of two or three hundred years, the English liberties were ascertained and established, the aristocratic part of that nation was substantially represented by a very large number of nobles, possessing similar interests and feelings with those they represented. The body of the people, about four or five millions, then mostly a frugal landed people, were represented by about five hundred representatives, taken not from the order of men which formed the aristocracy, but from the body of the people, and possessed of the same interests and feelings. De Lome, speaking of the British representation, expressly founds all his reasons on this union; this similitude of interests, feelings, views and circumstances. He observes, the English have preserved their liberties, because they and their leaders or representatives have been strictly united in interests, and in contending for general liberty.[13] Here we see a genuine balance founded in the actual state of things. The whole community, probably, not more than two-fifths more numerous than we now are, were represented by seven or eight hundred men; the barons stipulated with the common people, and the king with the whole. Had the legal distinction between lords and commons been broken down, and the people of that island been called upon to elect forty-five senators, and one hundred and twenty representatives, about the proportion we propose to establish, their whole legislature evidently would have been of the natural aristocracy, and the body of the people would not have had scarcely a single sincere advocate; their interests would have been neglected, general and equal liberty forgot, and the balance lost; contests and conciliations, as in most other countries, would have been merely among the few, and as it might have been necessary to serve their purposes, the people at large would have been flattered or threatened, and probably not a single stipulation made in their favour.

In Rome the people were miserable, though they had three orders, the consuls, senators and tribunes, and approved the laws, and all for want of a genuine representation. The people were too numerous to assemble, and do any thing properly themselves; the voice of a few, the dupes of artifice, was called the voice of the people. It is difficult for the people to defend themselves against the arts and intrigues of the great, but by selecting a suitable number of men fixed to their interests to represent them, and to oppose ministers and senators. And the people's all depends on the number of the men selected, and the manner of doing it. To be convinced of this, we need only attend to the reason of the case, the conduct of the British commons, and of the Roman tribunes: equal liberty prevails in England, because there was a representation of the people, in fact and reality, to establish it; equal liberty never prevailed in Rome, because there was but the shadow of a representation. There were consuls in Rome annually elected to execute the laws, several hundred senators represented the great families; the body of the people annually chose tribunes from among themselves to defend them and to secure their rights; I think the number of tribunes annually chosen never exceeded ten. This representation, perhaps, was not proportionally so numerous as the representation proposed in the new plan; but the difference will not appear to be so great, when it shall be recollected, that these tribunes were chosen annually; that the great patrician families were not admitted to these offices of tribunes, and that the people of Italy who elected the tribunes were a long while, if not always, a small people compared with the people of the United States. What was the consequence of this triffling representation? The people of Rome always elected for their tribunes men conspicuous for their riches, military commands, professional popularity, &c. great commoners, between whom and the noble families there was only the shadowy difference of legal distinction. Among all the tribunes the people chose for several centuries, they had scarcely five real friends to their interests. These tribunes lived, felt and saw, not like the people, but like the great patrician families, like senators and great officers of state, to get into which it was evident, by their conduct, was their sole object. These tribunes often talked about the rights and prerogatives of the people, and that was all; for they never even attempted to establish equal liberty: so far from establishing the rights of the people, they suffered the senate, to the exclusion of the people, to engross the powers of taxation; those excellent and almost only real weapons of defence even the people of England possess. The tribunes obtained that the people should be eligible to some of the great offices of state, and marry, if they pleased, into the noble families; these were advantages in their nature, confined to a few elevated commoners, and of triffling importance to the people at large. Nearly the same observations may be made as to the ephori of Sparta.

We may amuse ourselves with names; but the fact is, men will be governed by the motives and temptations that surround their situation. Political evils to be guarded against are in the human character, and not in the name of patrician or plebian. Had the people of Italy, in the early period of the republic, selected yearly, or biennially, four or five hundred of their best informed men, emphatically from among themselves, these representatives would have formed an honest respectable assembly, capable of combining in them the views and exertions of the people, and their respectability would have procured them honest and able leaders, and we should have seen equal liberty established. True liberty stands in need of a fostering hand; from the days of Adam she has found but one temple to dwell in securely; she has laid the foundation of one, perhaps her last, in America; whether this is to be compleated and have duration, is yet a question. Equal liberty never yet found many advocates among the great: it is a disagreeable truth, that power perverts mens views in a greater degree, than public employments inform their understandings—they become hardened in certain maxims, and more lost to fellow feelings. Men may always be too cautious to commit alarming and glaring iniquities: but they, as well as systems, are liable to be corrupted by slow degrees. Junius well observes, we are not only to guard against what men will do, but even against what they may do.[14] Men in high public offices are in stations where they gradually lose sight of the people, and do not often think of attending to them, except when necessary to answer private purposes.

The body of the people must have this true representative security placed some where in the nation; and in the United States, or in any extended empire, I am fully persuaded can be placed no where, but in the forms of a federal republic, where we can divide and place it in several state or district legislatures, giving the people in these the means of opposing heavy internal taxes and oppressive measures in the proper stages. A great empire contains the amities and animosities of a world within itself. We are not like the people of England, one people compactly settled on a small island, with a great city filled with frugal merchants, serving as a common centre of liberty and union: we are dispersed, and it is impracticable for any but the few to assemble in one place: the few must be watched, checked, and often resisted—tyranny has ever shewn a prediliction to be in close amity with them, or the one man. Drive it from kings and it flies to senators, to dicemvirs, to dictators, to tribunes, to popular leaders, to military chiefs, &c.

De Lome well observes, that in societies, laws which were to be equal to all are soon warped to the private interests of the administrators, and made to defend the usurpations of a few.[15] The English, who had tasted the sweets of equal laws, were aware of this, and though they restored their king, they carefully delegated to parliament the advocates of freedom.

I have often lately heard it observed, that it will do very well for a people to make a constitution, and ordain, that at stated periods they will chuse, in a certain manner, a first magistrate, a given number of senators and representatives, and let them have all power to do as they please. This doctrine, however it may do for a small republic, as Connecticut, for instance, where the people may chuse so many senators and representatives to assemble in the legislature, in an eminent degree, the interests, the views, feelings, and genuine sentiments of the people themselves, can never be admitted in an extensive country; and when this power is lodged in the hands of a few, not to limit the few, is but one step short of giving absolute power to one man—in a numerous representation the abuse of power is a common injury, and has no temptation—among the few, the abuse of power may often operate to the private emolument of those who abuse it.

## LETTER IX.

January 4, 1788.

Dear Sir, The advocates of the constitution say we must trust to the administration, and elect good men for representatives. I admit, that in forming the social compact, we can fix only general principles, and, of necessity, must trust something to the wisdom and integrity of the administration. But the question is, do we not trust too much, and to men also placed in the vortex of temptation, to lay hold of proffered advantages for themselves and their connections, and to oppress the body of the people.

It is one thing to authorise a well organized legislature to make laws, under the restraints of a well guarded constitution, and another to assemble a few men, and to tell them to do what they please. I am not the more shaken in my principles, or disposed to despair of the cause of liberty, because some of our able men have adopted the yielding language of non-resistance, and writers dare insult the people with the signatures of Cæsar, Mark Antony, and of other tyrants; because I see even moderate and amiable men, forced to let go of monarchy in 1775, still in love with it, to use the simile of our countrymen, when the political pot boils, the skum will often get uppermost and make its appearance. I believe the people of America, when they shall fully understand any political subject brought before them, will talk in a very different stile, and use the manly language of freedom.

But "the people must elect good men:"—Examine the system, Is it practicable for them to elect fit and proper representatives where the number is so small? "But the people may chuse whom they please." This is an observation, I believe, made without due attention to facts and the state of the community. To explain my meaning, I will consider the descriptions of men commonly presented to the people as candidates for the offices of representatives—we may rank them in three classes. 1. The men who form the natural aristocracy, as before defined. 2. Popular demagogues: these men also are often politically elevated, so as to be seen by the people through the extent of large districts; they often have some abilities, without principle, and rise into notice by their noise and arts. 3. The substantial and respectable part of the democracy; they are a numerous and valuable set of men, who discern and judge well, but from being generally silent in public assemblies are often overlooked; they are the most substantial and best informed men in the several towns, who occasionally fill the middle grades of offices, &c. who hold not a splendid, but a respectable rank in private concerns: these men are extensively diffused through all the counties, towns, and small districts in the union; even they, and their immediate connections, are raised above the majority of the people, and as representatives are only brought to a level with a more numerous part of the community, the middle orders, and a degree nearer the mass of the people. Hence it is, that the best practical representation, even in a small state, must be several degrees more aristocratical than the body of the people. A representation so formed as to admit but few or none of the third class, is, in my opinion, not deserving of the name—even in armies, courts-martial are so formed as to admit subaltern officers into them. The true idea is, so to open and enlarge the representation as to let in a due proportion of the third class with those of the first. Now, my opinion is, that the representation proposed is so small, as that ordinarily very few or none of them can be elected; and, therefore, after all the parade of words and forms, the government must possess the soul of aristocracy, or something worse, the spirit of popular leaders.

I observed in a former letter, that the state of Delaware, of Rhode-

Island, the Province of Main[e], and each of the great counties in Massachusetts, &c. would have one member,[16] and rather more than one when the representatives shall be increased to one for each 30,000 inhabitants. In some districts the people are more dispersed and unequal than in others: In Delaware they are compact, in the Province of Main dispersed; how can the elections in either of those districts be regulated so as that a man of the third class can be elected?— Exactly the same principles and motives, the same uncontroulable circumstances, must govern the elections as in the choice of the governors. Call upon the people of either of those districts to chuse a governor, and it will, probably, never happen that they will not bestow a major part, or the greatest number, of their votes on some very conspicuous or very popular character. A man that is known among a few thousands of people, may be quite unknown among thirty or forty thousand. On the whole, it appears to me to be almost a self-evident position, that when we call on thirty or forty thousand inhabitants to unite in giving their votes for one man, it will be uniformly impracticable for them to unite in any men, except those few who have become eminent for their civil or military rank, or their popular legal abilities: it will be found totally impracticable for men in the private walks of life, except in the profession of the law, to become conspicuous enough to attract the notice of so many electors and have their suffrages.

But if I am right, it is asked why so many respectable men advocate the adoption of the proposed system. Several reasons may be given— many of our gentlemen are attached to the principles of monarchy and aristocracy; they have an aversion to democratic republics. The body of the people have acquired large powers and substantial influence by the revolution. In the unsettled state of things, their numerous representatives, in some instances, misused their powers, and have induced many good men suddenly to adopt ideas unfavourable to such republics, and which ideas they will discard on reflection. Without scrutinizing into the particulars of the proposed system, we immediately perceive that its general tendency is to collect the powers of government, now in the body of the people in reality, and to place them in the higher orders and fewer hands; no wonder then that all those of and about these orders are attached to it: they feel there is something in this system advantageous to them. On the other hand, the body of the people evidently feel there is something wrong and disadvantageous to them; both descriptions perceive there is something tending to bestow on the former the height of power and happiness, and to reduce the latter to weakness, insignificance, and misery. The people evidently feel all this though they want expressions to convey their ideas. Further, even the respectable part of the democracy, have never yet been able to distinguish clearly where the fallacy lies; they find there are defects in the confederation; they see a system presented, they think something must be done, and, while their minds are in suspence, the zealous advocates force a reluctant consent. Nothing can be a stronger evidence of the nature of this system, than the general sense of the several orders in the community respecting its tendency; the parts taken generally by them proves my position, that notwithstanding the parade of words and forms, the government must possess the soul of aristocracy.

Congress, heretofore, have asked for moderate additional powers, the cry was give them—be federal: but the proper distinction between the cases that produce this disposition, and the system proposed, has not been fairly made and seen in all its consequences. We have seen some of our state representations too numerous, and without examining a medium we run into the opposite extreme. It is true, the proper number of federal representatives, is matter of opinion in some degree; but there are extremes which we immediately perceive, and others which we clearly discover on examination. We should readily pronounce a representative branch of 15 members small in a federal government, having complete powers as to taxes, military matters, commerce, the coin, &c. &c. On the other hand, we should readily pronounce a federal representation as numerous as those of the several states, consisting of about 1500 representatives, unwieldly and totally improper. It is asked, has not the wisdom of the convention found the medium? perhaps not: The convention was divided on this point of numbers: at least some of its ablest members urged, that instead of 65 representatives there ought to be 130 in the first instance: They fixed one representative for each 40,000 inhabitants, and at the close of the work, the president suggested, that the representation appeared to be too small and without debate, it was put at, not exceeding one for each 30,000.[17] I mention these facts to shew, that the convention went on no fixed data. In this extensive country it is difficult to get a representation sufficiently numerous: Necessity, I believe, will oblige us to sacrifice in some degree the true genuine principles of representation: But this sacrifice ought to be as little as possible: How far we ought to increase the representation I will not pretend to say; but that we ought to increase it very considerably, is clear—to double it at least, making full allowances for the state representations: and this we may evidently do, and approach accordingly towards safety and perfection, without encountering any inconveniences. It is with great difficulty the people can unite these different interests and views even tolerably, in the state senators, who are more than twice as numerous as the federal representatives, as proposed by the convention; even these senators are considered as so far removed from the people, that they are not allowed immediately to hold their purse strings.

The principle objections made to the increase of the representation are, the expence and difficulty in getting the members to attend. The first cannot be important; the last, if founded, is against any federal government. As to the expence, I presume, the house of representatives will not be in sessions more than four months in the year. We find by experience, that about two-thirds of the members of representative assemblies usually attend; therefore, of the representation proposed by the convention, about forty-five members probably will attend, doubling their number, about 90 will probably attend: their pay, in one case, at four dollars a day each (which is putting it high enough) will amount to, yearly, 21,600 dollars; in the other case, 43,200 dollars difference 21,600 dollars;—reduce the state representatives from 1500 down to 1000, and thereby save the attendance of two-thirds of the 500, say three months in a year, at one dollar and a quarter a day each 37,125 dollars. Thus we may leave the state representations sufficient large, and yet save enough by the reduction nearly to support exceeding well the whole federal representation I propose. Surely we never can be so unwise as to sacrifice, essentially, the all-important principles of representation for so small a sum as 21,600 dollars a year for the United States; a single company of soldiers would cost this sum. It is a fact that can easily be shewn, that we expend three times this sum every year upon useless inferior offices and very triffling concerns. It is also a fact which can be shewn, that the United States in the late war suffered more by a faction in the federal government, than the pay of the federal representation will amount to for twenty years.

As to the attendance—Can we be so unwise as to establish an unsafe and inadequate representative branch, and give it as a reason, that we believe only a few members will be induced to attend; we ought certainly to establish an adequate representative branch, and adopt measures to induce an attendance; I believe that a due proportion of 130 or 140 members may be induced to attend: there are various reasons for the non-attendance of the members of the present congress; it is to be presumed that these will not exist under the new system.

To compensate for the want of a genuine representation in a government, where the purse and sword, and all important powers, are proposed to be lodged, a variety of unimportant things are enumerated by the advocates of it.

In the second place, it is said the members of congress must return home, and share in the burdens they may impose; and, therefore, private motives will induce them to make mild laws, to support liberty, and ease the burdens of the people: this brings us to a mere question of interest under this head. I think these observations will appear, on examination, altogether fallacious; because this individual interest, which may coincide with the rights and interests of the people, will be far more than balanced by opposite motives and opposite interests. If, on a fair calculation, a man will gain more by measures oppressive to others than he will lose by them, he is interested in their adoption. It is true, that those who govern, generally, by increasing the public burdens increase their own share of them; but by this increase they may, and often do, increase their salaries, fees, and emoluments, in a ten-fold proportion, by increasing salaries, forming armies and navies, and by making offices—If it shall appear the members of congress will have these temptations before them, the argument is on my side—they will view the account, and be induced continually to make efforts advantageous to themselves and connections, and oppressive to others.

We must examine facts—Congress, in its present form, have but few offices to dispose of worth the attention of the members, or of men of the aristocracy; yet, from 1774 to this time, we find a large proportion of those offices assigned to those who were or had been members of congress, and though the states chuse annually sixty or seventy members, many of them have been provided for; but few men are known to congress in this extensive country, and, probably, but few will be to the president and senate, except those who have or shall appear as members of congress, or those whom the members may bring forward. The states may now chuse yearly ninety-one members of congress;[18] under the new constitution they will have it in their power to chuse exactly the same number, perhaps afterwards, one hundred and fifteen, but these must be chosen once in two and six years; so that, in the course of ten years together, not more than two-thirds so many members of congress will be elected and brought into view, as there now are under the confederation in the same term of time: but at least there will be five, if not ten times, as many offices and places worthy the attention of the members, under the new constitution, as there are under the confederation: therefore, we may fairly presume, that a very great proportion of the members of congress, especially the influential ones, instead of returning to private life, will be provided for with lucrative offices, in the civil or military department, and not only the members, but many of their sons, friends, and connection. These offices will be in the constitutional disposition of the president and senate, and, corruption out of the question, what kind of security can we expect in a representation, so many of the members of which may rationally feel themselves candidates for these offices?—let common sense decide. It is true, that members chosen to offices must leave their seats in congress, and to some few offices they cannot be elected till the time shall be expired for which they were elected members; but this scarcely will effect the biass arising from the hopes and expectations of office.

It is not only in this point of view, the members of congress, by their efforts, may make themselves and friends powerful and happy, while the people may be oppressed: but there is another way in which they may soon warp laws, which ought to be equal, to their own advantages, by those imperceptible means, and on those doubtful principles which may not alarm. No society can do without taxes; they are the efficient means of safety and defence, and they too have often been the weapons by which the blessings of society have been destroyed. Congress will have power to lay taxes at pleasure for the general welfare; and if they mis-judge of the general welfare, and lay unnecessary oppressive taxes, the constitution will provide, as I shall hereafter shew, no remedy for the people or states—the people must bear them, or have recourse, not to any constitutional checks or remedies, but to that resistence which is the last resort, and founded in self-defence.[19]

It is well stipulated, that all duties, imposts, and excises shall be equal; and that direct taxes shall be apportioned on the several states by a fixed rule, but nothing further. Here commences a dangerous power in matters of taxation, lodged without any regard to the balance of interests of the different orders of men, and without any regard to the internal policy of the states. Congress having assigned to any state its quota, say to New-Jersey, 80,000 dollars in a given tax, congress will be entirely at liberty to apportion that sum on the counties and towns, polls, lands, houses, labour, &c. and appoint the assessors and collectors in that state in what manner they please; there will be nothing to prevent a system of tax laws being made, unduly to ease some descriptions of men and burden others; though such a system may be unjust and injudicious, though we may complain, the answer will be, congress have the power delegated by the people, and, probably, congress has done what it thought best.

By the confederation taxes must be quotaed on the several states by fixed rules, as before mentioned: but then each state's quota is apportioned on the several numbers and classes of citizens in the state by the state legislature, assessed and collected by state laws. Great pains have been taken to confound the two cases, which are as distinct as light and darkness; this I shall endeavour to illustrate, when I come to the amendment respecting internal taxes. I shall only observe, at present, that in the state legislatures the body of the people will be genuinely represented, and in congress not; that the right of resisting oppressive measures is inherent in the people, and that a constitutional barrier should be so formed, that their genuine representatives may stop an oppressive ruinous measure in its early progress, before it shall come to maturity, and the evils of it become in a degree fixed.

It has lately been often observed, that the power or body of men intrusted with the national defence and tranquility, must necessarily possess the purse unlimitedly, that the purse and sword must go to-gether—this is new doctrine in a free country, and by no means tenable. In the British government the king is particularly intrusted with the national honor and defence, but the commons solely hold the purse. I think I have amply shewn that the representation in congress will be totally inadequate in matters of taxation, &c. and, therefore, that the ultimate controul over the purse must be lodged elsewhere.

We are not to expect even honest men rigidly to adhere to the line of strict impartiality, where the interest of themselves or friends is particularly concerned; if we do expect it, we shall deceive ourselves, and make a wrong estimate of human nature.

But it is asked how shall we remedy the evil, so as to complete and perpetuate the temple of equal laws and equal liberty? Perhaps we never can do it. Possibly we never may be able to do it, in this immense country, under any one system of laws however modified; nevertheless, at present, I think the experiment worth a making. I feel an aversion to the disunion of the states, and to separate confederacies; the states have fought and bled in a common cause, and great dangers too may attend these confederacies. I think the system proposed capable of very considerable degrees of perfection, if we pursue first principles. I do not think that De Lome, or any writer I have seen, has sufficiently pursued the proper inquiries and efficient means for making repre-sentation and balances in government more perfect; it is our task to do this in America. Our object is equal liberty, and equal laws diffusing their influence among all orders of men; to obtain this we must guard against the biass of interest and passions, against interested combi-nations, secret or open; we must aim at a balance of efforts and strength.

Clear it is, by increasing the representation we lessen the prospects of each member of congress being provided for in public offices; we proportionably lessen official influence, and strengthen his prospects of becoming a private citizen, subject to the common burdens, without the compensation of the emoluments of office. By increasing the representation we make it more difficult to corrupt and influence the members; we diffuse them more extensively among the body of the people, perfect the balance, multiply information, strengthen the confidence of the people, and consequently support the laws on equal and free principles. There are two other ways, I think, of obtaining in some degree the security we want; the one is, by excluding more extensively the members from being appointed to offices; the other is, by limiting some of their powers; but these two I shall examine hereafter.

## LETTER X.

JANUARY 7, 1788.

DEAR SIR, It is said that our people have a high sense of freedom, possess power, property, and the strong arm; meaning, I presume, that the body of the people can take care of themselves, and awe their rulers; and, therefore, particular provision in the constitution for their security may not be essential. When I come to examine these observations, they appear to me too triffling and loose to deserve a serious answer.

To palliate for the smallness of the representation, it is observed, that the state governments in which the people are fully represented, necessarily form a part of the system. This idea ought to be fully examined. We ought to enquire if the convention have made the proper use of these essential parts; the state governments then we are told will stand between the arbitrary exercise of power and the people: true they may, but armless and helpless, perhaps, with the privilege of making a noise when hurt—this is no more than individuals may do. Does the constitution provide a single check for a single measure, by which the state governments can constitutionally and regularly check the arbitrary measures of congress? Congress may raise immediately fifty thousand men, and twenty millions of dollars in taxes, build a navy, model the militia, &c. and all this constitutionally. Congress may arm on every point, and the state governments can do no more than an individual, by petition to congress, suggest their measures are alarming and not right.

I conceive the position to be undeniable, that the federal government will be principally in the hands of the natural aristocracy, and the state governments principally in the hands of the democracy, the representatives of the body of the people. These representatives in Great-Britain hold the purse, and have a negative upon all laws. We must yield to circumstances, and depart something from this plan, and strike out a new medium, so as to give efficacy to the whole system, supply the wants of the union, and leave the several states, or the people assembled in the state legislatures, the means of defence.

It has been often mentioned, that the objects of congress will be few and national, and require a small representation; that the objects of each state will be many and local, and require a numerous representation. This circumstance has not the weight of a feather in my mind. It is certainly unadvisable to lodge in 65 representatives, and 26 senators, unlimited power to establish systems of taxation, armies, navies, model the militia, and to do every thing that may essentially tend soon to change, totally, the affairs of the community; and to assemble 1500 state representatives, and 160 senators, to make fence laws, and laws to regulate the descent and conveyance of property, the administration of justice between man and man, to appoint militia officers, &c.

It is not merely the quantity of information I contend for. Two taxing powers may be inconvenient; but the point is, congress, like the senate of Rome, will have taxing powers, and the people no check— when the power is abused, the people may complain and grow angry, so may the state governments; they may remonstrate and counteract, by passing laws to prohibit the collection of congressional taxes; but these will be acts of the people, acts of sovereign power, the dernier resort unknown to the constitution; acts operating in terrorum, acts of resistence, and not the exercise of any constitutional power to stop or check a measure before matured: a check properly is the stopping, by one branch in the same legislature, a measure proposed by the other in it. In fact the constitution provides for the states no check, properly speaking, upon the measures of congress—Congress can immediately enlist soldiers, and apply to the pockets of the people.

These few considerations bring us to the very strong distinction between the plan that operates on federal principles, and the plan that operates on consolidated principles. A plan may be federal or not as to its organization; each state may retain its vote or not; the sovereignty of the state may be represented, or the people of it. A plan may be federal or not as to its operations—federal when it requires men and monies of the states, and the states as such make the laws for raising the men and monies—Not federal, when it leaves the states governments out of the question, and operates immediately upon the persons and property of the citizens. The first is the case with the confederation, the second with the new plan: in the first the state governments may be [a] check, in the last none at all. This distinction I shall pursue further hereafter, under the head before mentioned, of amendments as to internal taxes.[20] And here I shall pursue a species of checks which writers have not often noticed.

To excuse the smallness of the representation, it is said the new congress will be more numerous than the old one. This is not true; and for the facts I refer you to my letter of the 4th instant, to the plan and confederation;[21] besides there is no kind of similitude between the two plans. The confederation is a mere league of the states, and congress is formed with the particular checks, and possess the united powers, enumerated in my letter of the 25th ult.[22] The new plan is totally a different thing: a national government to many purposes administered, by men chosen for two, four, and six years, not recallable, and among whom there will be no rotation; operating immediately in all money and military matters, &c. on the persons and property of the citizens—I think, therefore, that no part of the confederation ought to be adduced for supporting or injuring the new constitution. It is also said that the constitution gives no more power to congress than the confederation, respecting money and military matters; that congress, under the confederation, may require men and monies to any amount, and the states are bound to comply. This is generally true; but, I think, I shall in a subsequent letter satisfactorily prove, that the states have well founded checks for securing their liberties.[23]

I admit the force of the observation, that all the federal powers, by the confederation, are lodged in a single assembly; however, I think much more may be said in defence of the leading principles of the confederation. I do not object to the qualifications of the electors of representatives, and I fully agree that the people ought to elect one branch.

Further, it may be observed, that the present congress is principally an executive body, which ought not to be numerous; that the house of representatives will be a mere legislative branch, and being the democratic one, ought to be numerous. It is one of the greatest advantages of a government of different branches, that each branch may be conveniently made conformable to the nature of the business assigned it, and all be made conformable to the condition of the several orders of the people. After all the possible checks and limitations we can devise, the powers of the union must be very extensive; the sovereignty of the nation cannot produce the object in view, the defence and tranquility of the whole, without such powers, executive and judicial. I dislike the present congress a single, assembly, because it is impossible to fit it to receive those powers: the executive and judicial powers, in the nature of things, ought to be lodged in a few hands, the legislature in many hands; therefore, want of safety, and unavoidable hasty measures, out of the question, they never can all be lodged in one assembly properly—it, in its very formation, must imply a contradiction.

In objection to increasing the representation, it has also been observed, that it is difficult to assemble a hundred men or more without making them tumultuous and a mere mob; reason and experience do not support this observation. The most respectable assemblies we have any knowledge of and the wisest, have been those, each of which consisted of several hundred members; as the senate of Rome, of Carthage, of Venice, the British Parliament, &c. &c. I think I may without hazarding much, affirm, that our more numerous state assemblies and conventions have universally discovered more wisdom, and as much order, as the less numerous ones: There must be also a very great difference between the characters of two or three hundred men assembled from a single state, and the characters of the number or half the number assembled from all the united states.

It is added, that on the proposed plan the house of representatives in fifty or a hundred years, will consist of several hundred members: The plan will begin with sixty-five, and we have no certainty that the number ever will be encreased, for this plain reason—that all that combination of interests and influence which has produced this plan, and supported so far, will constantly oppose the increase of the representation, knowing that thereby the government will become more free and democratic: But admitting, after a few years, there will be a member for each 30,000 inhabitants, the observation is trifling, the government is in a considerable measure to take its tone from its early movements, and by means of a small representation it may in half of 50 or 100 years, get moved from its basis, or at least so far as to be incapable of ever being recovered. We ought, therefore, on every principle now to fix the government on proper principles, and fit to our present condition—when the representation shall become too numerous, alter it; or we may now make provision, that when the representation shall be increased to a given number, that then there shall be one for each given number of inhabitants, &c.

Another observation is, that congress will have no temptations to do wrong—the men that make it must be very uninformed, or suppose they are talking to children. In the first place, the members will be governed by all those motives which govern the conduct of men, and have before them all the allurements of offices and temptations, to establish unequal burdens, before described. In the second place, they and their friends, probably, will find it for their interests to keep up large armies, navies, salaries, &c. and in laying adequate taxes. In the third place, we have no good grounds to presume, from reason or experience, that it will be agreeable to their characters or views, that the body of the people should continue to have power effectually to interfere in the affairs of government. But it is confidently added, that congress will not have it in their power to oppress or enslave the people, that the people will not bear it. It is not supposed that congress will act the tyrant immediately, and in the face of day light. It is not supposed congress will adopt important measures, without plausible pretences, especially those which may tend to alarm or produce opposition. We are to consider the natural progress of things: that men unfriendly to republican equality will go systematically to work, gradually to exclude the body of the people from any share in the government, first of the substance, and then of the forms. The men who will have these views will not be without their agents and supporters. When we reflect, that a few years ago we established democratic republics, and fixed the state governments as the barriers between congress and the pockets of the people; what great progress has been made in less than seven years to break down those barriers, and essentially to change the principles of our governments, even by the armless few: is it chimerical to suppose that in fifteen or twenty years to come, that much more can be performed, especially after the adoption of the constitution, when the few will be so much better armed with power and influence, to continue the struggle? probably, they will be wise enough never to alarm, but gradually prepare the minds of the people for one specious change after another, till the final object shall be obtained. Say the advocates, these are only possibilities—they are probabilities, a wise people ought to guard against; and the address made use of to keep the evils out of sight, and the means to prevent them, confirm my opinion.

But to obviate all objections to the proposed plan in the last resort: it is said our people will be free, so long as they possess the habits of freemen, and when they lose them, they must receive some other forms of government. To this I shall only observe, that this is very humiliating language, and can, I trust, never suit a manly people, who have contended nobly for liberty, and declared to the world they will be free.

I have dwelt much longer than I expected upon the increasing the representation, the democratic interest in the federal system; but I hope the importance of the subject will justify my dwelling upon it. I have pursued it in a manner new, and I have found it necessary to be somewhat prolix, to illustrate the point I had in view. My idea has ever been, when the democratic branch is weak and small, the body of the people have no defence, and every thing to fear; if they expect to find genuine political friends in kings and nobles, in great and powerful men, they deceive themselves. On the other hand, fix a genuine democratic branch in the government, solely to hold the purse, and with the power of impeachment, and to propose and negative laws, cautiously limit the king and nobles, or the executive and the senate, as the case may be, and the people, I conceive, have but little to fear, and their liberties will be always secure.

I think we are now arrived to a new æra in the affairs of men, when the true principles of government will be more fully unfolded than heretofore, and a new world, as it were, grow up in America. In contemplating representation, the next thing is the security of elections. Before I proceed to this, I beg leave to observe, that the pay of the representatives of the people is essentially connected with their interests.

Congress may put the pay of the members unreasonably high, or so low as that none but the rich and opulent can attend; there are very strong reasons for supposing the latter, probably, will be the case, and a part of the same policy, which uniformly and constantly exerts itself to transfer power from the many to the few. Should the pay be well fixed, and made alterable by congress, with the consent of a majority of the state legislatures, perhaps, all the evils to be feared on this head might, in the best practicable manner, be guarded against, and proper security introduced. It is said the state legislatures fix their own pay— the answer is, that congress is not, nor can it ever be well formed on those equal principles the state legislatures are. I shall not dwell on this point, but conclude this letter with one general observation, that the check[s] I contend for in the system proposed, do not, in the least, any of them tend to lessen the energy of it; but giving grounds for the confidence of the people, greatly to increase its real energy, by insuring their constant and hearty support.

## LETTER XI.

JANUARY 10, 1788.

DEAR SIR, I shall now add a few observations respecting the organization of the senate, the manner of appointing it, and its powers.

The senate is an assembly of 26 members, two from each state, though the senators are apportioned on the federal plan, they will vote individually; they represent the states, as bodies politic, sovereign to certain purposes; the states being sovereign and independent, are all considered equal, each with the other in the senate. In this we are governed solely by the ideal equalities of sovereignties; the federal and state governments forming one whole, and the state governments an essential part, which ought always to be kept distinctly in view, and preserved: I feel more disposed, on reflection, to acquiesce in making them the basis of the senate, and thereby to make it the interest and duty of the senators to preserve distinct, and to perpetuate the respective sovereignties they shall represent.

As to the appointments of senators, I have already observed, that they must be appointed by the legislatures, by concurrent acts, and each branch have an equal share of power, as I do not see any probability of amendments, if advisable, in these points, I shall not dwell upon them.

The senate, as a legislative branch, is not large, but as an executive branch quite too numerous. It is not to be presumed that we can form a genuine senatorial branch in the United States, a real representation of the aristocracy and balance in the legislature, any more than we can form a genuine representation of the people. Could we separate the aristocratical and democratical interests; compose the senate of the former, and the house of assembly of the latter, they are too unequal in the United States to produce a balance. Form them on pure principles, and leave each to be supported by its real weight and connections, the senate would be feeble, and the house powerful:—I say, on pure principles; because I make a distinction between a senate that derives its weight and influence from a pure source, its numbers and wisdom, its extensive property, its extensive and permanent connections; and a senate composed of a few men, possessing small property, small and unstable connections, that derives its weight and influence from a corrupt or pernicious source; that is, merely from the power given it by the constitution and laws, to dispose of the public offices, and the annexed emoluments, and by those means to interest officers, and the hungry expectants of offices, in support of its measures. I wish the proposed senate may not partake too much of the latter description.

To produce a balance and checks, the constitution proposes two branches in the legislature; but they are so formed, that the members of both must generally be the same kind of men—men having similar interests and views, feelings and connections—men of the same grade in society, and who associate on all occasions (probably, if there by any difference, the senators will be the most democratic.) Senators and representatives thus circumstanced, as men, though convened in two rooms, to make laws, must be governed generally by the same motives and views, and therefore pursue the same system of politics; the partitions between the two branches will be merely those of the building in which they sit: there will not be found in them any of those genuine balances and checks, among the real different interests, and efforts of the several classes of men in the community we aim at; nor can any such balances and checks be formed in the present condition of the United States in any considerable degree of perfection: but to give them the greatest degree of perfection practicable, we ought to make the senate respectable as to numbers, the qualifications of the electors and of the elected; to increase the numbers of the representatives, and so to model the elections of them, as always to draw a majority of them substantially from the body of the people. Though I conclude the senators and representatives will not form in the legislature those balances and checks which correspond with the actual state of the people; yet I approve of two branches, because we may notwithstanding derive several advantages from them. The senate, from the mode of its appointment, will probably be influenced to support the state governments, and, from its periods of service will produce stability in legislation, while frequent elections may take place in the other branch. There is generally a degree of competition between two assemblies even composed of the same kind of men; and by this, and by means of every law's passing a revision in the second branch, caution, coolness, and deliberation are produced in the business of making laws. By means of a democratic branch we may particularly secure personal liberty; and by means of a senatorial branch we may particularly protect property. By the division, the house becomes the proper body to impeach all officers for misconduct in office, and the senate the proper court to try them; and in a country where limited powers must be lodged in the first magistrate, the senate, perhaps, may be the most proper body to be found to have a negative upon him in making treaties, and in managing foreign affairs.

Though I agree the federal senate, in the form proposed, may be useful to many purposes, and that it is not very necessary to alter the organization, modes of appointment, and powers of it in several respects; yet, without alterations in others, I sincerely believe it will, in a very few years, become the source of the greatest evils. Some of these alterations, I conceive, to be absolutely necessary, and some of them at least advisable.

1. By the confederation the members of congress are chosen annually. By art. 1. sect. 2. of the constitution, the senators shall be chosen for six years. As the period of service must be, in a considerable degree, matter of opinion on this head, I shall only make a few ob-

servations, to explain why I think it more advisable to limit it to three or four years.

The people of this country have not been accustomed to so long appointments in their state governments, they have generally adopted annual elections. The members of the present congress are chosen yearly, who, from the nature and multip[l]icity of their business, ought to be chosen for longer periods than the federal senators—Men six years in office absolutely contract callous habits, and cease, in too great a degree, to feel their dependance, and for the condition of their constituents. Senators continued in offices three or four years, will be in them longer than any popular erroneous opinions will probably continue to actuate their electors—men appointed for three or four years, will generally be long enough in office to give stability, and amply to acquire political information. By a change of legislators, as often as circumstances will permit, political knowledge is diffused more extensively among the people, and the attention of the electors and elected more constantly kept alive; circumstances of infinite importance in a free country. Other reasons might be added, but my subject is too extensive to admit of my dwelling upon less material points.

2. When the confederation was formed, it was considered essentially necessary that the members of congress should at any time be recalled by their respective states, when the states should see fit, and others be sent in their room. I do not think it less necessary that this principle should be extended to the members of congress under the new constitution, and especially to the senators. I have had occasion several times to observe, that let us form a federal constitution as extensively, and on the best principles in our power, we must, after all, trust a vast deal to a few men, who, far removed from their constituents, will administer the federal government; there is but little danger these men will feel too great a degree of dependance: the necessary and important object to be attended to, is to make them feel dependant enough. Men elected for several years, several hundred miles distant from their states, possessed of very extensive powers, and the means of paying themselves, will not, probably, be oppressed with a sense of dependance and responsibility.

The senators will represent sovereignties, which generally have, and always ought to retain, the power of recalling their agents; the principle of responsibility is strongly felt in men who are liable to be recalled and censured for their misconduct; and, if we may judge from experience, the latter will not abuse the power of recalling their members; to possess it, will, at least be a valuable check. It is in the nature of all delegated power, that the constituents should retain the right to judge concerning the conduct of their representatives; they must exercise the power, and their decision itself, their approving or disapproving that conduct implies a right, a power to continue in office, or to remove from it. But whenever the substitute acts under a constitution, then it becomes necessary that the power of recalling him be expressed. The reasons for lodging a power to recall are stronger, as they respect the senate, than as they respect the representatives; the latter will be more frequently elected, and changed of course, and being chosen by the people at large, it would be more difficult for the people than for the legislatures to take the necessary measures for recalling: but even the people, if the powers will be more beneficial to them than injurious, ought to possess it. The people are not apt to wrong a man who is steady and true to their interests; they may for a while be misled by party representations, and leave a good man out of office unheard; but every recall supposes a deliberate decision, and a fair hearing; and no man who believes his conduct proper, and the result of honest views, will be the less useful in his public character, on account of the examination his actions may be liable to; and a man conscious of the contrary conduct, ought clearly to be restrained by the apprehensions of a trial. I repeat it, it is interested combinations and factions we are particularly to guard against in the federal government, and all the rational means that can be put into the hands of the people to prevent them, ought to be provided and furnished for them. Where there is a power to recall, trusty centinels among the people, or in the state legislatures, will have a fair opportunity to become useful. If the members in congress from the states join in such combinations, or favour them, or pursue a pernicious line of conduct, the most attentive among the people, or in the state legislatures, may formally charge them before their constituents; the very apprehensions of such constitutional charges may prevent many of the evils mentioned, and the recalling the members of a single state, a single senator, or representative, may often prevent many more; nor do I, at present, discover any danger in such proceedings, as every man who shall move for a recall will put his reputation at stake, to shew he has reasonable grounds for his motion; and it is not probable such motions will be made unless there be good apparent grounds for succeeding; nor can the charge or motion be any thing more than the attack of an individual or individuals, unless a majority of the constituents shall see cause to go into the enquiry. Further, the circumstance of such a power being lodged in the constituents, will tend continually to keep up their watchfulness, as well as the attention and dependance of the federal senators and representatives.

3. By the confederation it is provided, that no delegate shall serve more than three years in any term of six years, and thus, by the forms of the government, a rotation of members is produced: a like principle has been adopted in some of the state governments, and also in some antient and modern republics. Whether this exclusion of a man for a given period, after he shall have served a given time, ought to be ingraf[t]ed into a constitution or not, is a question, the proper decision materially depends upon the leading features of the government: some governments are so formed as to produce a sufficient fluctuation and change of members of course, in the ordinary course of elections, proper numbers of new members are, from time to time, brought into the legislature, and a proportionate number of old ones go out, mix, and become diffused among the people. This is the case with all numerous representative legislatures, the members of which are frequently elected, and constantly within the view of their constituents. This is the case with our state governments, and in them a constitutional rotation is unimportant. But in a government consisting of but a few members, elected for long periods, and far removed from the observation of the people, but few changes in the ordinary course of elections take place among the members; they become in some measure a fixed body, and often inattentive to the public good, callous, selfish, and the fountain of corruption. To prevent these evils, and to force a principle of pure animation into the federal government, which will be formed much in this last manner mentioned, and to produce attention, activity, and a diffusion of knowledge in the community, we ought to establish among others the principle of rotation. Even good men in office, in time, imperceptibly lose sight of the people, and gradually fall into measures prejudicial to them. It is only a rotation among the members of the federal legislature I shall contend for: judges and officers at the heads of the judicial and executive departments, are in a very different situation, their offices and duties require the information and studies of many years for performing them in a manner advantageous to the people. These judges and officers must apply their whole time to the detail business of their offices, and depend on them for their support; then they always act under masters or superiors, and may be removed from office for misconduct; they pursue a certain round of executive business: their offices must be in all societies confined to a few men, because but few can become qualified to fill them: and were they, by annual appointments, open to the people at large, they are offices of such a nature as to be of no service to them; they must leave these offices in the possession of the few individuals qualified to fill them, or have them badly filled. In the

judicial and executive departments also, the body of the people possess
a large share of power and influence, as jurors and subordinate officers, among whom there are many and frequent rotations. But in every
free country the legislatures are all on a level, and legislation becomes
partial whenever, in practice, it rests for any considerable time in a
few hands. It is the true republican principle to diffuse the power of
making the laws among the people, and so to modify the forms of the
government as to draw in turn the well informed of every class into
the legislature.

To determine the propriety or impropriety of this rotation, we must
take the inconveniencies as well as the advantages attending it into
view: on the one hand, by this rotation, we may sometimes exclude
good men from being elected. On the other hand, we guard against
those pernicious connections, which usually grow up among men left
to continue long periods in office, we increase the number of those
who make the laws and return to their constituents; and thereby spread
information, and preserve a spirit of activity and investigation among
the people: hence a balance of interests and exertions are preserved,
and the ruinous measures of factions rendered more impracticable. I
would not urge the principle of rotation, if I believed the consequence
would be an uninformed federal legislature; but I have no apprehension of this in this enlightened country. The members of congress, at
any one time, must be but very few, compared with the respectable
well informed men in the United States; and I have no idea there will
be any want of such men for members of congress, though by a principle of rotation the constitution should exclude from being elected
for two years those federal legislators, who may have served the four
years immediately preceding, or any four years in the six preceding
years. If we may judge from experience and fair calculations, this
principle will never operate to exclude at any one period a fifteenth
part, even of those men who have been members of congress. Though
no man can sit in congress, by the confederation, more than three
years in any term of six years, yet not more than three, four, or five
men in any one state, have been made ineligible at any one period;
and if a good man happen to be excluded by this rotation, it is only
for a short time. All things considered, the inconveniencies of the
principle must be very inconsiderable compared with the many advantages of it. It will generally be expedient for a man who has served
four years in congress to return home, mix with the people, and reside
some time with them: this will tend to reinstate him in the interests,
feelings, and views similar to theirs, and thereby confirm in him the
essential qualifications of a legislator. Even in point of information, it

may be observed, the useful information of legislators is not acquired merely in studies in offices, and in meeting to make laws from day to day; they must learn the actual situation of the people, by being among them, and when they have made laws, return home, and observe how they operate. Thus occasionally to be among the people, is not only necessary to prevent or banish the callous habits and self-interested views of office in legislators, but to afford them necessary information, and to render them useful: another valuable end is answered by it, sympathy, and the means of communication between them and their constituents, is substantially promoted; so that on every principle legislators, at certain periods, ought to live among their constituents.

Some men of science are undoubtedly necessary in every legislature; but the knowledge, generally, necessary for men who make laws, is a knowledge of the common concerns, and particular circumstances of the people. In a republican government seats in the legislature are highly honorable; I believe but few do, and surely none ought to consider them as places of profit and permanent support. Were the people always properly attentive, they would, at proper periods, call their law-makers home, by sending others in their room: but this is not often the case, and therefore, in making constitutions, when the people are attentive, they ought cautiously to provide for those benefits, those advantageous changes in the administration of their affairs, which they are often apt to be inattentive to in practice. On the whole, to guard against the evils, and to secure the advantages I have mentioned, with the greatest degree of certainty, we ought clearly, in my opinion, to increase the federal representation, to secure elections on proper principles, to establish a right to recall members, and a rotation among them.[24]

4. By the art. 2. sect. 2. treaties must be made with the advice and consent of the senate, and two-thirds of those present must concur: also, with consent of the senate, almost all federal officers, civil and military, must be appointed. As to treaties I have my doubts; but as to the appointments of officers, I think we may clearly shew the senate to be a very improper body indeed to have any thing to do with them. I am not perfectly satisfied, that the senate, a branch of the legislature, and court for trying impeachments, ought to have a controuling power in making all treaties; yet, I confess, I do not discern how a restraint upon the president in this important business, can be better or more safely lodged: a power to make and conclude all treaties is too important to be vested in him alone, or in him and an executive council, only sufficiently numerous for other purpose[s], and the house of representatives is too numerous to be concerned in treaties of peace and

of alliance. This power is now lodged in congress, to be exercised by the consent of nine states. The federal senate, like the delegations in the present congress, will represent the states, and the consent of two-thirds of that senate will bear some similitude to the consent of nine states. It is probable the United States will not make more than one treaty, on an average, in two or three years, and this power may always be exercised with great deliberation: perhaps the senate is sufficiently numerous to be trusted with this power, sufficiently small to proceed with secrecy, and sufficiently permanent to exercise this power with proper consistency and due deliberation. To lodge this power in a less respectable and less numerous body might not be safe; we must place great confidence in the hands that hold it, and we deceive ourselves if we give it under an idea, that we can impeach, to any valuable purpose, the man or men who may abuse it.

On a fair construction of the constitution, I think the legislature has a proper controul over the president and senate in settling commercial treaties. By art. 1. sect. 2. the legislature will have power to regulate commerce with foreign nations, &c. By art. 2. sect. 2. the president, with the advice and consent of two-thirds of the senate, may make treaties. These clauses must be considered together, and we ought never to make one part of the same instrument contradict another, if it can be avoided by any reasonable construction. By the first recited clause, the legislature has the power, that is, as I understand it, the sole power to regulate commerce with foreign nations, or to make all the rules and regulations respecting trade and commerce between our citizens and foreigners: by the second recited clause, the president and senate have power generally to make treaties.—There are several kinds of treaties—as treaties of commerce, of peace, of alliance, &c. I think the words to "make treaties," may be consistently construed, and yet so as it shall be left to the legislature to confirm commercial treaties; they are in their nature and operation very distinct from treaties of peace and of alliance; the latter generally require secrecy, it is but very seldom they interfere with the laws and internal police of the country; to make them is properly the exercise of executive powers, and the constitution authorises the president and senate to make treaties, and gives the legislature no power, directly or indirectly, respecting these treaties of peace and alliance. As to treaties of commerce, they do not generally require secrecy, they almost always involve in them legislative powers, interfere with the laws and internal police of the country, and operate immediately on persons and property, especially in the commercial towns: (they have in Great-Britain usually been confirmed by parliament;) they consist of rules and regulations respecting commerce; and to regulate commerce, or to make regulations respecting commerce, the federal legislature, by the constitution, has the power. I do not see that any commercial regulations can be made in treaties, that will not infringe upon this power in the legislature; therefore, I infer, that the true construction is, that the president and senate shall make treaties; but all commercial treaties shall be subject to be confirmed by the legislature. This construction will render the clauses consistent, and make the powers of the president and senate, respecting treaties, much less exceptionable.

### LETTER XII.

JANUARY 12, 1788.

DEAR SIR, On carefully examining the parts of the proposed system, respecting the elections of senators, and especially of the representatives, they appear to me to be both ambiguous and very defective. I shall endeavour to pursue a course of reasoning, which shall fairly lead to establishing the impartiality and security of elections, and then to point out an amendment in this respect.

It is well observed by Montesquieu, that in republican governments, the forms of elections are fundamental; and that it is an essential part of the social compact, to ascertain by whom, to whom, when, and in what manner suffrages are to be given.[25]

Wherever we find the regulation of elections have not been carefully fixed by the constitution, or the principles of them, we constantly see the legislatures new modifying its own form, and changing the spirit of the government to answer partial purposes.

By the proposed plan it is fixed, that the qualifications of the electors of the federal representatives shall be the same as those of the electors of state representatives; though these vary some in the several states the electors are fixed and designated.

The qualifications of the representatives are also fixed and designated, and no person under 25 years of age, not an inhabitant of the state, and not having been seven years a citizen of the United States, can be elected; the clear inference is, that all persons 25 years of age, and upwards, inhabitants of the state, and having been, at any period or periods, seven years citizens of the United States, may be elected representatives. They have a right to be elected by the constitution, and the electors have a right to chuse them. This is fixing the federal representation, as to the elected, on a very broad basis: it can be no objection to the elected, that they are Christians, Pagans, Mahometans, or Jews; that they are of any colour, rich or poor, convict or not: Hence many men may be elected, who cannot be electors. Gentlemen who have commented so largely upon the wisdom of the constitution, for excluding from being elected young men under a certain age, would have done well to have recollected, that it positively makes pagans, convicts, &c. eligible. The people make the constitution; they exclude a few persons, by certain descriptions, from being elected, and all not thus excluded are clearly admitted. Now a man 25 years old, an inhabitant of the state, and having been a citizen of the the states seven years, though afterwards convicted, may be elected, because not within any of the excluding clauses, the same of a beggar, an absentee, &c.

The right of the electors, and eligibility of the elected being fixed by the people, they cannot be narrowed by the state legislatures, or congress: it is established, that a man being (among other qualifications) an inhabitant of the state, shall be eligible. Now it would be narrowing the right of the people to confine them in their choice to a man, an inhabitant of a particular county or district in the state. Hence it follows, that neither the state legislatures or congress can establish district elections; that is, divide the state into districts, and confine the electors of each district to the choice of a man resident in it. If the electors could be thus limited in one respect, they might in another be confined to chuse a man of a particular religion, of certain property, &c. and thereby half of the persons made eligible by the constitution be excluded. All laws, therefore, for regulating elections must be made on the broad basis of the constitution.

Next, we may observe, that representatives are to be chosen by the people of the state. What is a choice by the people of the state? If each given district in it choose one, will that be a choice within the meaning of the constitution? Must the choice be by plurality of votes, or a majority? In connection with these questions, we must take the 4th sect. art. 1. where it is said the state legislatures shall prescribe the times, places, and manner of holding elections; but congress may make or alter such regulations. By this clause, I suppose, the electors of different towns and districts in the state may be assembled in different places, to give their votes; but when so assembled, by another clause they cannot, by congress or the state legislatures, be restrained from giving their votes for any man an inhabitant of the state, and qualified as to age, and having been a citizen the time required. But I see nothing in the constitution by which to decide, whether the choice shall be by a plurality or a majority of votes: this, in my mind, is by far the most important question in the business of elections. When we say a representative shall be chosen by the people, it seems to imply that he shall be chosen by a majority of them; but states which use the same phraseology in this respect, practice both ways. I believe a majority of the states, chuse by pluralities, and, I think it probable, that the federal house of representatives will decide that a choice of its members by pluralities is constitutional. A man who has the most votes is chosen in Great-Britain. It is this, among other things, that gives every man fair play in the game of influence and corruption. I believe that not much stress was laid upon the objection that congress may assemble the electors at some out of the way place. However, the advocates seem to think they obtain a victory of no small glory and importance, when they can shew, with some degree of colour, that the evils is rather a possibility than a probability.

When I observed that the elections were not secured on proper principles,[26] I had an idea of far more probable and extensive evils, secret mischiefs, and not so glaring transgressions, the exclusions of proper district elections, and of the choice by a majority.

It is easy to perceive that there is an essential difference between elections by pluralities and by majorities, between choosing a man in a small or limited district, and choosing a number of men promiscuously by the people of a large state; and while we are almost secure of judicious unbiassed elections by majorities in such districts, we have no security against deceptions, influence and corruption in states or large districts in electing by pluralities. When a choice is made by a plurality of votes, it is often made by a very small part of the electors, who attend and give their votes, when by a majority, never by so few as one half of them. The partialities and improprieties attending the former mode may be illustrated by a case that lately happened in one of the middle states.—Several representatives were to be chosen by a large number of inhabitants compactly settled, among whom there were four or five thousand voters. Previous to the time of election a number of lists of candidates were published, to divide and distract the voters in general—about half a dozen men of some influence, who had a favourite list to carry, met several times, fixed their list, and agreed to hand it about among all who could probably be induced to adopt it, and to circulate the other lists among their opponents, to divide them. The poll was opened, and several hundred electors, suspecting nothing, attended and put in their votes; the list of the half dozen was carried, and men were found to be chosen, some of whom were very disagreeable to a large majority of the electors: though several hundred electors voted, men on that list were chosen who had only 45, 43, 44, &c. votes each; they had a plurality, that is, more than any other persons: the votes generally were scattered, and those who made even a feeble combination succeeded in placing highest upon the list several very unthought of and very unpopular men. This evil never could have happened in a town where all the voters meet in one place, and consider no man as elected unless he have a majority, or more than half of all the votes; clear it is, that the men on whom thus but a small part of the votes are bestowed, cannot possess the confidence of the people, or have any considerable degree of influence over them.

But as partial, as liable to secret influence, and corruption as the choice by pluralities may be, I think, we cannot avoid it, without essentially increasing the federal representation, and adopting the principles of district elections. There is but one case in which the choice by the majority is practicable, and that is, where districts are formed of such moderate extent that the electors in each can conveniently meet in one place, and at one time, and proceed to the choice of a representative; when, if no man have a majority, or more than half of all the votes the first time, the voters may examine the characters of those brought forward, accommodate, and proceed to repeat their votes till some one shall have that majority. This, I believe, cannot be a case under the constitution proposed in its present form. To explain my ideas, take Massachusetts, for instance, she is entitled to eight representatives, she has 370,000 inhabitants, about 46,000 to one representative; if the elections be so held that the electors throughout the state meet in their several towns or places, and each elector puts in his vote for eight representatives, the votes of the electors will ninety-nine times in a hundred, be so scattered that on collecting the votes from the several towns or places, no men will be found, each of whom have a majority of the votes, and therefore the election will not be made. On the other hand, there may be such a combination of votes, that in thus attempting to chuse eight representatives, the electors may chuse even fifteen. Suppose 10,000 voters to attend and give their votes, each voter will give eight votes, one for each of eight representatives; in the whole 80,000 votes will be given—eight men, each having 5001 votes, in the whole 40,008 will have each a majority, and be chosen—39,092 votes will be bestowed on other men, and if they all be bestowed on seven men, they may have each a considerable majority, and also be chosen. This indeed is a very rare combination; but the bestowing all the votes pretty equally upon nine, ten, or eleven men, and chusing them all, is an event too probable not to be guarded against.

If Massachusetts be divided into eight districts, each having about 46,000 inhabitants, and each district directed to chuse one representative, it will be found totally impracticable for the electors of it to meet in one place; and, when they meet in several towns and places in the district, they will vote for different men, and nineteen times in twenty, so scatter their votes, that no one man will have a majority of the whole and be chosen: we must, therefore, take the man who has the most votes, whether he has three quarters, one quarter, or one tenth part of the whole; the inconveniencies of scattering votes will be increased, as men not of the district, as well as those that are in it, may be voted for.[27]

I might add many other observations to evince the superiority and solid advantages of proper district elections, and a choice by a majority, and to prove, that many evils attend the contrary practice: these evils we must encounter as the constitution now stands.

I see no way to fix elections on a proper footing, and to render tolerably equal and secure the federal representation, but by increasing the representation, so as to have one representative for each district in which the electors may conveniently meet in one place, and at one time, and chuse by a majority. Perhaps this might be effected pretty generally, by fixing one representative for each twelve thousand in- habitants; dividing, or fixing the principles for dividing the states into proper districts; and directing the electors of each district to the choice, by a majority, of some men having a permanent interest and residence in it. I speak of a representation tolerably equal, &c. because I am still of opinion, that it is impracticable in this extensive country to have a federal representation sufficiently democratic, or substantially drawn from the body of the people: the principles just mentioned may be the best practical ones we can expect to establish. By thus increasing the representation, we not only make it more democratical and secure, strengthen the confidence of the people in it, and thereby render it more nervous[28] and energetic; but it will also enable the people es- sentially to change, for the better, the principles and forms of elections. To provide for the people's wandering throughout the state for a representative, may sometimes enable them to elect a more brilliant or an abler man, than by confining them to districts, but generally this latitude will be used to pernicious purposes, especially connected with the choice by plurality; when a man in the remote part of the state, perhaps, obnoxious at home, but ambitious and intriguing, may be chosen to represent the people in another part of the state far distant, and by a small part of them, or by a faction, or by a combination of some particular description of men among them. This has been long the case in Great-Britain, it is the case in several of the states, nor do I think that such pernicious practices will be merely possible in our federal concerns, but highly probable. By establishing district elections, we exclude none of the best men from being elected; and we fix what, in my mind, is of far more importance than brilliant talents, I mean a sameness, as to residence and interests, between the representative and his constituents; and by the election by a majority, he is sure to be the man, the choice of more than half of them.

Though it is impossible to put elections on a proper footing as the constitution stands, yet I think regulations respecting them may be introduced of considerable service: it is not only, therefore, important to enquire how they may be made, but also what body has the controuling power over them. An intelligent, free and unbiassed choice of representatives by the people is of the last importance: we must then carefully guard against all combinations, secret arts, and influence to the contrary. Various expedients have been adopted in different countries and states to effect genuine elections; as the constitution now stands, I confess, I do not discover any better than those adopted in Connecticut, in the choice of counsellers, before mentioned.[29]

The federal representatives are to be chosen every second year (an odd mode of expression). In all the states, except South-Carolina, the people, the same electors, meet twice in that time to elect state representatives. For instance, let the electors in Massachusetts, when they meet to chuse state representatives, put in their votes for eight federal representatives, the number that state may chuse, (merely for distinction sake, we may call these the votes of nomination), and return a list of the men voted for, in the several towns and places, to the legislature, or some proper body; let this list be immediately examined and published, and some proper number, say 15 or 20, who shall have the most votes upon the list, be sent out to the people; and when the electors shall meet the next year to chuse state representatives, let them put in their votes for the eight federal representatives, confining their votes to the proper number so sent out; and let the eight highest of those thus voted for in the two votes (which we may call, by way of distinction, votes of election), be the federal representatives: thus a choice may be made by the people, once in two years, without much trouble and expence, and, I believe, with some degree of security. As soon as the votes of nomination shall be collected and made known, the people will know who are voted for, and who are candidates for their votes the succeeding year; the electors will have near a year to enquire into their characters and politics, and also into any undue means, if any were taken, to bring any of them forward; and such as they find to be the best men, and agreeable to the people, they may vote for in giving the votes of election. By these means the men chosen will ultimately always have a majority, or near a majority, of the votes of the electors, who shall attend and give their votes. The mode itself will lead to the discovery of truth and of political characters, and to prevent private combinations, by rendering them in a great measure of no effect. As the choice is to be made by the people, all combinations and checks must be confined to their votes. No supplying the want of a majority by the legislatures, as in Massachusetts in the choice of senators,[30] &c. can be admitted: the people generally judge right when informed, and, in giving their votes the second time, they may always correct their former errors.

I think we are all sufficiently acquainted with the progress of elections to see, that the regulations, as to times, places, and the manner merely of holding elections, may, under the constitution, easily be made useful or injurious. It is important then to enquire, who has the power to make regulations, and who ought to have it. By the constitution, the state legislatures shall prescribe the times, places, and manner of holding elections, but congress may make or alter such regulations. Power in congress merely to alter those regulations, made by the states, could answer no valuable purposes; the states might make, and congress alter them *ad infinitum:* and when the state should cease to make, or should annihilate its regulations, congress would have nothing to alter. But the states shall make regulations, and congress may make such regulations as the clause stands: the true construction is, that when congress shall see fit to regulate the times, places, and manner of holding elections, congress may do it, and state regulations, on this head, must cease: for if state regulations could exist, after congress should make a system of regulations, there would, or might, be two incompatible systems of regulations relative to the same subject.

It has been often urged, that congress ought to have power to make these regulations, otherwise the state legislatures, by neglecting to make provision for elections, or by making improper regulations, may destroy the general government. It is very improbable that any state legislature will adopt measures to destroy the representation of its own constituents in congress, especially when the state must, represented in congress or not, pay its proportion of the expence of keeping up the government, and even of the representatives of the other states, and be subject to their laws. Should the state legislatures be disposed to be negligent, or to combine to break up congress, they have a very simple way to do it, as the constitution now stands—they have only to neglect to chuse senators, or to appoint the electors of the president, and vice-president: there is no remedy provided against these last evils: nor is it to be presumed, that if a sufficient number of state legislatures to break up congress, should, by neglect or otherwise, attempt to do it, that the people, who yearly elect those legislatures, would elect under the regulations of congress. These and many other reasons must evince, that it was not merely to prevent an annihilation of the federal government that congress has power to regulate elections.

It has been urged also, that the state legislatures chuse the federal senators, one branch, and may injure the people, who chuse the other, by improper regulations; that therefore congress, in which the people will immediately have one, the representative branch, ought to have power to interfere in behalf of the people, and rectify such improper regulations. The advocates have said much about the opponents dwelling upon possibilities: but to suppose the people will find it necessary to appeal to congress to restrain the oppressions of the state legislatures, is supposing a possibility indeed. Can any man in his senses suppose that the state legislatures, which are so numerous as almost to be the people themselves, all branches of them depending yearly, for the most part, on the elections of the people, will abuse them in regulating federal elections, and make it proper to transfer the power to congress, a body, one branch of which is chosen once in six years by these very legislatures, and the other biennially, and not half so numerous as even the senatorial branches in those legislatures?

Senators are to be chosen by the state legislatures, where there are two branches the appointment must be, I presume, by a concurrent resolution, in passing which, as in passing all other legislative acts, each branch will have a negative; this will give the senatorial branch just as much weight in the appointment as the democratic: the two branches form a legislature only when acting separately, and therefore, whenever the members of the two branches meet, mix and vote individually in one room, for making an election, it is expressly so directed by the constitutions. If the constitution, by fixing the choice to be made by the legislatures, has given each branch an equal vote, as I think it has, it cannot be altered by any regulations.

On the whole, I think, all general principles respecting electors ought to be carefully established by the constitution, as the qualifications of the electors and of elected: the number of the representatives, and the inhabitants of each given district, called on to chuse a man from among themselves by a majority of votes; leaving it to the legislature only so to regulate, from time to time, the extent of the districts so as to keep the representatives proportionate to the number of inhabitants in the several parts of the country; and so far as regulations as to elections cannot be fixed by the constitution, they ought to be left to the state legislatures, they coming far nearest to the people themselves; at most, congress ought to have power to regulate elections only where a state shall neglect to make them.

## LETTER XIII.

JANUARY 14, 1788.

DEAR SIR, In this letter I shall further examine two clauses in the proposed constitution respecting appointments to office.—By art. 2. sect. 2. the president shall nominate, and by and with the advice and consent of the senate, shall appoint ambassadors, other public ministers and consuls, judges of the supreme court, and all other officers of the United States, whose appointments, &c. By art. 1, sect. 6. No senator or representative shall, during the term for which he was elected, be appointed to any civil office under the authority of the United States, which shall have been created, or the emoluments whereof shall have been increased during such time.

Thus the president must nominate, and the senate concur in the appointment of all federal officers, civil and military, and the senators and representatives are made ineligible only to the few civil offices abovementioned. To preserve the federal government pure and uncorrupt, peculiar precautions relative to appointments to office will be found highly necessary from the very forms and character of the government itself. The honours and emoluments of public offices are the objects in all communities, that ambitious and necessitous men never lose sight of. The honest, the modest, and the industrious part of the community content themselves, generally, with their private concerns; they do not solicit those offices which are the perpetual source of cabals, intrigues, and contests among men of the former description, men embarrassed, intriguing, and destitute of modesty. Even in the most happy country and virtuous government, corrupt influence in appointments cannot always be avoided; perhaps we may boast of our share of virtue as a people, and if we are only sufficiently aware of the influence, biasses, and prejudices, common to the affairs of men, we may go far towards guarding against the effects of them.

We all agree, that a large standing army has a strong tendency to depress and inslave the people; it is equally true that a large body of selfish, unfeeling, unprincipled civil officers has a like, or a more pernicious tendency to the same point. Military, and especially civil establishments, are the necessary appendages of society; they are deductions from productive labour, and substantial wealth, in proportion to the number of men employed in them; they are oppressive where unnecessarily extended and supported by men unfriendly to the people; they are injurious when too small, and supported by men too timid and dependant. It is of the last importance to decide well upon the necessary number of offices, to fill them with proper characters, and to establish efficiently the means of punctually punishing those officers who may do wrong.

To discern the nature and extent of this power of appointments, we need only to consider the vast number of officers necessary to execute a national system in this extensive country, the prodigious biasses the hopes and expectations of offices have on their conduct, and the influence public officers have among the people—these necessary officers, as judges, state's attornies, clerks, sheriffs, &c. in the federal supreme and inferior courts, admirals and generals, and subordinate officers in the army and navy, ministers, consuls, &c. sent to foreign countries; officers in the federal city, in the revenue, post office departments, &c. &c. must, probably, amount to several thousands, without taking into view the very inferior ones. There can be no doubt but that the most active men in politics, in and out of congress, will be the foremost candidates for the best of these offices; the man or men who shall have the disposal of them, beyond dispute, will have by far the greatest share of active influence in the government; but appointments must be made, and who shall make them? what modes of appointments will be attended with the fewest inconveniencies? is the question. The senators and representatives are the law makers, create all offices, and whenever they see fit, they impeach and try officers for misconduct; they ought to be in session but part of the year, and as legislators, they must be too numerous to make appointments, perhaps, a few very important ones excepted. In contemplating the necessary officers of the union, there appear to be six different modes in which, in whole or in part, the appointments may be made, 1. By the legislature; 2. by the president and senate—3. by the president and an executive council—4. by the president alone—5. by the heads of the departments—and 6. by the state governments—Among all these, in my opinion, there may be an advantageous distribution of the power of appointments. In considering the legislators, in relation to the subject before us, two interesting questions particularly arise—1. Whether they ought to be eligible to any offices whatever during the period for which they shall be elected to serve, and even for some time afterwards—and 2. How far they ought to participate in the power of appointments. As to the first, it is true that legislators in foreign countries, or in our state governments, are not generally made ineligible to office: there are good reasons for it; in many countries the people have gone on without ever examining the principles of government. There have been but few countries in which the legislators have been a particular set of men periodically chosen: but the principal reason is, that which operates in the several states, viz. the legislators are so frequently chosen, and so numerous, compared with the number of offices for which they can reasonably consider themselves as candidates, that the chance of any individual member's being chosen, is too small to raise his hopes or expectations, or to have any considerable influence upon his conduct. Among the state legislators, one man in twenty may be appointed in some committee business, &c. for a month or two; but on a fair computation, not one man in a hundred sent to the state legislatures is appointed to any permanent office of profit: directly the reverse of this will evidently be found true in the federal administration. Throughout the United States, about four federal senators, and thirty-three representatives, averaging the elections, will be chosen in a year; these few men may rationally consider themselves as the fairest candidates for a very great number of lucrative offices, which must become vacant in the year, and pretty clearly a majority of the federal legislators, if not excluded, will be mere expectants for public offices. I need not adduce further arguments to establish a position so clear; I need only call to your recollection my observations in a former letter, wherein I endeavoured to shew the fallacy of the argument, that the members must return home and mix with the people.[31] It is said, that men are governed by interested motives, and will not attend as legislators, unless they can, in common with others, be eligible to offices of honor and profit. This will undoubtedly be the case with some men, but I presume only with such men as never ought to be chosen legislators in a free country; an opposite principle will influence good men; virtuous patriots, and generous minds, will esteem it a higher honor to be selected as the guardians of a free people; they will be satisfied with a reasonable compensation for their time and service; nor will they wish to be within the vortex of influence. The valuable effects of this principle of making legislators ineligible to offices for a given time, has never yet been sufficiently attended to or considered: I am assured, that it was established by the convention after long debate, and afterwards, on an unfortunate change of a few members, altered.[32] Could the federal legislators be excluded in the manner proposed, I think it would be an important point gained; as to themselves, they would be left to act much more from motives consistent with the public good.

In considering the principle of rotation I had occasion to distinguish the condition of a legislator from that of mere official man[33]—We acquire certain habits, feelings, and opinions, as men and citizens—others, and very different ones, from a long continuance in office: It is, therefore, a valuable observation in many bills of rights, that rulers ought frequently to return and mix with the people. A legislature, in a free country, must be numerous; it is in some degree a periodical assemblage of the people, frequently formed—the principal officers in the executive and judicial departments, must have more permanency in office. Hence it may be inferred, that the legislature will remain longer uncorrupted and virtuous; longer congenial to the people, than the officers of those departments. If it is not, therefore, in our power to preserve republican principles, for a series of ages, in all the departments of government, we may a long while preserve them in a well formed legislature. To this end we ought to take every precaution to prevent legislators becoming mere office-men; chuse them frequently, make them recallable, establish rotation among them, make them ineligible to offices, and give them as small a share as possible in the disposal of them. Add to this, a legislature, in the nature of things, is not formed for the detail business of appointing officers; there is also generally an impropriety in the same men's making offices and filling them, and a still greater impropriety in their impeaching and trying the officers they appoint. For these, and other reasons, I conclude, the legislature is not a proper body for the appointment of officers in general. But having gone through with the different modes of appointment, I shall endeavour to shew what share in the distribution of the power of appointments the legislature must, from necessity, rather than from propriety, take. 2. Officers may be appointed by the president and senate—this mode, for general purposes, is clearly not defensible. All the reasoning touching the legislature will apply to the senate; the senate is a branch of the legislature, which ought to be kept pure and unbiassed; it has a part in trying officers for misconduct, and in creating offices, it is too numerous for a council of appointment, or to feel any degree of responsibility: if it has an advantage of the legislature, in being the least numerous, it has a disadvantage in being more unsafe: add to this, the senate is to have a share in the important branch of power respecting treaties. Further, this sexennial senate of 26 members, representing 13 sovereign states, will not, in practice, be found to be a body to advise, but to order and dictate in fact; and the president will be a mere *primus inter pares*. The consequence will be, that the senate, with these efficient means of influence, will not only dictate, probably, to the president, but manage the house, as the constitution now stands; and under appearances of a balanced system, in reality, govern alone. There may also, by this undue connection, be particular periods when a very popular president may have a very improper influence upon the senate and upon the legislature. A council of appointment must very probably sit all, or near all, the year—the senate will be too important and too expensive a body for this. By giving the senate, directly or indirectly, an undue influence over the representatives, and the improper means of fettering, embarrassing, or controuling the president or executive, we give the government, in the very out set, a fatal and pernicious tendency to that middle undesirable point—aristocracy. When we, as a circumstance not well to be avoided, admit the senate to a share of power in making treaties, and in managing foreign concerns, we certainly progress full far enough towards this most undesirable point in government. For with this power, also, I believe, we must join that of appointing ambassadors, other foreign ministers, and consuls, being powers necessarily connected.—In every point of view, in which I can contemplate this subject, it appears extremely clear to me, that the senate ought not generally to be a council of appointment. The legislature, after the people, is the great fountain of power, and ought to be kept as pure and uncorrupt as possible, from the hankerings, biasses, and contagion of offices—then the streams issuing from it, will be less tainted with those evils. It is not merely the number of impeachments, that are to be expected to make public officers honest and attentive in their business. A general opinion must pervade the community, that the house, the body to impeach them for misconduct, is disinterested, and ever watchful for the public good; and that the judges who shall try impeachments, will not feel a shadow of biass. Under such circumstances, men will not dare transgress, who, not deterred by such accusers and judges, would repeatedly misbehave. We have already suffered many and extensive evils, owing to the defects of the confederation, in not providing against the misconduct of public officers. When we expect the law to be punctually executed, not one man in ten thousand will disobey it: it is the probable chance of escaping punishment that induces men to transgress. It is one important mean to make the government just and honest, rigidly and constantly to hold, before the eyes of those who execute it, punishment, and dismission from office, for misconduct. These are principles no candid man, who has just ideas of the essential features of a free government, will controvert. They are, to be sure, at this period, called visionary, speculative and anti-governmental—but in the true stile of courtiers, selfish politicians, and flatterers of despotism—discerning republican men of both parties see their value. They are said to be of no value, by empty boasting advocates for the constitution, who, by their weakness and conduct, in fact, injure its cause much more than most of its opponents. From their high sounding promises, men are led to expect a defence of it, and to have their doubts removed. When a number of long pieces appear, they, instead of the defence, &c. they expected, see nothing but a parade of names—volumes written without ever coming to the point—cases quoted between which and ours there is not the least similitude—and partial extracts made from histories and governments, merely to serve a purpose. Some of them, like the true admirers of royal and senatorial robes, would fain prove, that nations who have thought like freemen and philosophers about government, and endeavoured to be free, have often been the most miserable: if a single riot, in the course of five hundred years happened in a free country, if a salary, or the interest of a public or private debt was not paid at the moment, they seem to lay more stress upon these triffles (for triffles they are in a free and happy country) than upon the oppressions of despotic government for ages together. ⟨As to the lengthy writer in New-York you mention, I have attentively examined his pieces; he appears to be a candid good-hearted man, to have a good stile, and some plausible ideas; but when we carefully examine his pieces, to see where the strength of them lies; when the mind endeavours to fix on those material parts, which ought to be the essence of all voluminous productions, we do not find them: the writer appears constantly to move on a smooth surface, the part of his work, like the parts of a cob-house, are all equally strong and all equally weak, and all like those works of the boys, without an object; his pieces appear to have but little relation to the great question, whether the constitution is fitted to the condition and character of this people or not.⟩[34] But to return—

3. Officers may be appointed by the president and an executive council—when we have assigned to the legislature the appointment of a few important officers—to the president and senate the appointment of those concerned in managing foreign affairs—to the state governments the appointment of militia officers, and authorise the legislature, by legislative acts, to assign to the president alone, to the heads of the departments, and courts of law respectively, the appointment of many inferior officers; we shall then want to lodge some where a residuum of power, a power to appoint all other necessary officers, as established by law. The fittest receptacle for this residuary power is clearly, in my opinion, the first executive magistrate, advised and directed by an executive council of seven or nine members, periodically chosen from such proportional districts as the union may for the purpose be divided into. The people may give their votes for twice the number of counsellers wanted, and the federal legislature take twice the number also from the highest candidates, and from among them chuse the seven or nine, or number wanted. Such a council may be rationally formed

for the business of appointments; whereas the senate, created for other purposes, never can be—Such councils form a feature in some of the best executives in the union—they appear to be essential to every first magistrate, who may frequently want advice.

To authorise the president to appoint his own council would be unsafe: to give the sole appointment of it to the legislature, would confer an undue and unnecessary influence upon that branch. Such a council for a year would be less expensive than the senate for four months. The president may nominate, and the counsellers always be made responsible for their advice and opinions, by recording and signing whatever they advise to be done. They and the president, to many purposes, will properly form an independent executive branch; have an influence unmixed with the legislative, which the executive never can have while connected with a powerful branch of the legislature. And yet the influence arising from the power of appointments be less dangerous, because in less dangerous hands—hands properly adequate to possess it. Whereas the senate, from its character and situation will add a dangerous weight to the power itself, and be far less capable of responsibility, than the council proposed. There is another advantage; the residuum of power, as to appointments, which the president and council need possess, is less than that the president and senate must have. And as such a council would render the sessions of the senate unnecessary many months in the year, the expences of the government would not be increased, if they would not be lessened by the institution of such a council. I think I need not dwell upon this article, as the fitness of this mode of appointment will perhaps amply appear by the evident unfitness of the others.

4. Officers may be appointed by the president alone. It has been almost universally found, when a man has been authorized to exercise power alone, he has never done it alone; but, generally, aided his determinations by, and rested on the advice and opinions of others. And it often happens when advice is wanted, the worst men, the most interested creatures, the worst advice is at hand, obtrude themselves, and misdirect the mind of him who would be informed and advised. It is very seldom we see a single executive depend on accidental advice and assistance; but each single executive has, almost always, formed to itself a regular council, to be assembled and consulted on important occasions; this proves that a select council, of some kind, is, by experience, generally found necessary and useful. But in a free country, the exercise of any considerable branch of power ought to be under some checks and controuls. As to this point, I think the constitution stands well, the legislature may, when it shall deem it expedient, from

time to time, authorise the president alone to appoint particular inferior officers, and when necessary to take back the power. His power,
therefore, in this respect, may always be increased or decreased by the
legislature, as experience, the best instructor, shall direct: always keeping him, by the constitution, within certain bounds.

## LETTER XIV.

JANUARY 17, 1788.

DEAR SIR, To continue the subject of appointments:—Officers, in
the fifth place, may be appointed by the heads of departments or courts
of law. Art. 2. sect. 2. respecting appointments, goes on—"But congress
may by law vest the appointment of such inferior officers as they think
proper in the president alone, in the courts of law, or in the heads
of departments." The probability is, as the constitution now stands,
that the senate, a branch of the legislature, will be tenacious of the
power of appointment, and much too sparingly part with a share of
it to the courts of law, and heads of departments. Here again the
impropriety appears of the senate's having, generally, a share in the
appointment of officers. We may fairly presume, that the judges, and
principal officers in the departments, will be able well informed men
in their respective branches of business; that they will, from experience,
be best informed as to proper persons to fill inferior offices in them;
that they will feel themselves responsible for the execution of their
several branches of business, and for the conduct of the officers they
may appoint therein.—From these, and other considerations, I think
we may infer, that impartial and judicious appointments of subordinate
officers will, generally, be made by the courts of law, and the heads
of departments. This power of distributing appointments, as circumstances may require, into several hands, in a well formed disinterested
legislature, might be of essential service, not only in promoting beneficial appointments, but, also, in preserving the balance in government: a feeble executive may be strengthened and supported by placing
in its hands more numerous appointments; an executive too influential
may be reduced within proper bounds, by placing many of the inferior
appointments in the courts of law, and heads of departments; nor is
there much danger that the executive will be wantonly weakened or
strengthened by the legislature, by thus shifting the appointments of
inferior officers, since all must be done by legislative acts, which cannot
be passed without the consent of the executive, or the consent of two
thirds of both branches—a good legislature will use this power to preserve the balance and perpetuate the government. Here again we are

brought to our ultimatum:—is the legislature so constructed as to deserve our confidence?

6. Officers may be appointed by the state governments. By art. 1. sect. 8. the respective states are authorised exclusively to appoint the militia-officers. This not only lodges the appointments in proper places, but it also tends to distribute and lodge in different executive hands the powers of appointing to offices, so dangerous when collected into the hands of one or a few men.

It is a good general rule, that the legislative, executive, and judicial powers, ought to be kept distinct; but this, like other general rules, has its exceptions; and without these exceptions we cannot form a good government, and properly balance its parts: and we can determine only from reason, experience, and a critical inspection of the parts of the government, how far it is proper to intermix those powers. Appointments, I believe, in all mixed governments, have been assigned to different hands—some are made by the executive, some by the legislature, some by the judges, and some by the people. It has been thought adviseable by the wisest nations, that the legislature should so far exercise executive and judicial powers as to appoint some officers, judge of the elections of its members, and impeach and try officers for misconduct—that the executive should have a partial share in legislation—that judges should appoint some subordinate officers, and regulate so far as to establish rules for their own proceedings. Where the members of the government, as the house, the senate, the executive, and judiciary, are strong and complete, each in itself, the balance is naturally produced, each party may take the powers congenial to it, and we have less need to be anxious about checks, and the subdivision of powers.

If after making the deductions, already alluded to, from the general power to appoint federal officers the residuum shall be thought to be too large and unsafe, and to place an undue influence in the hands of the president and council, a further deduction may be made, with many advantages, and, perhaps, with but a few inconveniencies; and that is, by giving the appointment of a few great officers to the legislature—as of the commissioners of the treasury—of the comptroller, treasurer, master coiner, and some of the principal officers in the money department—of the sheriffs or marshalls of the United States—of states attornies, secretary of the home department, and secretary at war, perhaps, of the judges of the supreme court—of major-generals and admirals. The appointments of these officers, who may be at the heads of the great departments of business, in carrying into execution the national system, involve in them a variety of considerations; they will not often occur and the power to make them ought to remain in safe hands. Officers of the above description are appointed by the legislatures in some of the states, and in some not. We may, I believe, presume that the federal legislature will possess sufficient knowledge and discernment to make judicious appointments: however, as these appointments by the legislature tend to increase a mixture of power, to lessen the advantages of impeachments and responsibility, I would by no means contend for them any further than it may be necessary for reducing the power of the executive within the bounds of safety. To determine, with propriety, how extensive power the executive ought to possess relative to appointments, we must also examine the forms of it, and its other powers; and these forms and other powers I shall now proceed briefly to examine.

By art. 2. sect. 1. the executive power shall be vested in a president elected for four years, by electors to be appointed from time to time, in such manner as the state legislatures shall direct—the electors to be equal in numbers to the federal senators and representatives: but congress may determine the time of chusing senators [i.e. electors], and the day on which they shall give their votes; and if no president be chosen by the electors, by a majority of votes, the states, as states in congress, shall elect one of the five highest on the list for president. It is to be observed, that in chusing the president, the principle of electing by a majority of votes is adopted; in chusing the vice president, that of electing by a plurality. Viewing the principles and checks established in the election of the president, and especially considering the several states may guard the appointment of the electors as they shall judge best, I confess there appears to be a judicious combination of principles and precautions. Were the electors more numerous than they will be, in case the representation be not increased, I think, the system would be improved; not that I consider the democratic character so important in the choice of the electors as in the choice of representatives: be the electors more or less democratic, the president will be one of the very few of the most elevated characters. But there is danger, that a majority of a small number of electors may be corrupted and influenced, after appointed electors, and before they give their votes, especially if a considerable space of time elapse between the appointment and voting. I have already considered the advisory council in the executive branch: there are two things further in the organization of the executive, to which I would particularly draw your attention; the first, which, is a single executive. I confess, I approve; the second, by which any person from period to period may be re-elected president, I think very exceptionable.

Each state in the union has uniformly shewn its preference for a single executive, and generally directed the first executive magistrate to act in certain cases by the advice of an executive council. Reason, and the experience of enlightened nations, seem justly to assign the business of making laws to numerous assemblies; and the execution of them, principally, to the direction and care of one man. Independent of practice a single man seems to be peculiarly well circumstanced to superintend the execution of laws with discernment and decision, with promptitude and un[i]formity: the people usually point out a first man—he is to be seen in civilized as well as uncivilized nations—in republics as well as in other governments. In every large collection of people there must be a visible point serving as a common centre in the government, towards which to draw their eyes and attachments. The constitution must fix a man, or a congress of men, superior in the opinion of the people, to the most popular men in the different parts of the community, else the people will be apt to divide and follow their respective leaders. Aspiring men, armies and navies, have not often been kept in tolerable order by the decrees of a senate or an executive council. The advocates for lodging the executive power in the hands of a number of equals, as an executive council, say, that much wisdom may be collected in such a council, and that it will be safe; but they agree, that it cannot be so prompt and responsible as a single man—they admit that such a council will generally consist of the aristocracy, and not stand so indifferent between it and the people as a first magistrate. But the principal objection made to a single man is, that when possessed of power he will be constantly struggling for more, disturbing the government, and encroaching on the rights of others. It must be admitted, that men, from the monarch down to the porter, are constantly aiming at power and importance and this propensity must be as constantly guarded against in the forms of the government. Adequate powers must be delegated to those who govern, and our security must be in limiting, defining, and guarding the exercise of them, so that those given shall not be abused, or made use of for openly or secretly seizing more. Why do we believe this abuse of power peculiar to a first magistrate? Is it because in the wars and contests of men, one man has often established his power over the rest? Or are men naturally fond of accumulating powers in the hands of one man? I do not see any similitude between the cases of those tyrants, who have sprung up in the midst of wars and tumults, and the cases of limited executives in established governments; nor shall we, on a careful examination, discover much likeness between the executives in Sweden, Denmark, Holland, &c. which have, from time to time, increased their powers, and become more absolute, and the executives, whose powers are well ascertained and defined, and which remain, by the constitution, only for a short and limited period in the hands of any one man or family. A single man, or family, can long and effectually direct its exertions to one point. There may be many favourable opportunities in the course of a man's life to seize on additional powers, and many more where powers are hereditary; and there are many circumstances favourable to usurpations, where the powers of the man or family are undefined, and such as often may be unduly extended before the people discover it. If we examine history attentively, we shall find that such exertions, such opportunities, and such circumstances as these have attended all the executives which have usurped upon the rights of the people, and which appear originally to have been, in some degree, limited. Admitting that moderate and even well defined powers, long in the hands of the same man or family, will, probably, be unreasonably increased, it will not follow that even extensive powers placed in the hands of a man only for a few years will be abused. The Roman consuls and Carthagenian suffetes possessed extensive powers while in office; but being annually appointed, they but seldom, if ever, abused them. The Roman dictators often possessed absolute power while in office; but usually being elected for short periods of time, no one of them for ages usurped upon the rights of the people. The kings of France, Spain, Sweden, Denmark, &c. have become absolute merely from the encroachments and abuse of power made by the nobles. As to kings, and limited monarchs, generally, history furnishes many more instances in which their powers have been abridged or annihilated by the nobles or people, or both, than in which they have been increased or made absolute; and in almost all the latter cases, we find the people were inattentive and fickle, and evidently were not born to be free. I am the more particular respecting this subject, because I have heard many mistaken observations relative to it. Men of property, and even men who hold powers for themselves and posterity, have too much to lose, wantonly to hazard a shock of the political system; the game must be large, and the chance of winning great, to induce them to risque what they have, for the uncertain prospect of gaining more. Our executive may be altogether elective, and possess no power, but as the substitute of the people, and that well limited, and only for a limited time. The great object is, in a republican government, to guard effectually against perpetuating any portion of power, great or small, in the same man or family; this perpetuation of power is totally uncongenial to the true spirit of republican governments: on the one hand the first executive magistrate ought to remain in office so long as to avoid instability in the execution of the laws; on the other, not so long as to enable him to take any measures to establish himself. The convention, it seems, first agreed that the president should be chosen for seven years, and never after to be eligible.[35] Whether seven years is a period too long or not, is rather matter of opinion; but clear it is, that this mode is infinitely preferable to the one finally adopted. When a man shall get the chair, who may be re-elected, from time to time, for life, his greatest object will be to keep it; to gain friends and votes, at any rate; to associate some favourite son with himself, to take the office after him: whenever he shall have any prospect of continuing the office in himself and family, he will spare no artifice, no address, and no exertions, to increase the powers and importance of it; the servile supporters of his wishes will be placed in all offices, and tools constantly employed to aid his views and sound his praise. A man so situated will have no permanent interest in the government to lose, by contests and convulsions in the state, but always much to gain, and frequently the seducing and flattering hope of succeeding. If we reason at all on the subject, we must irresistably conclude, that this will be the case with nine tenths of the presidents; we may have, for the first president, and, perhaps, one in a century or two afterwards (if the government should withstand the attacks of others) a great and good man,[36] governed by superior motives; but these are not events to be calculated upon in the present state of human nature.

A man chosen to this important office for a limited period, and always afterwards rendered, by the constitution, ineligible, will be governed by very different considerations: he can have no rational hopes or expectations of retaining his office after the expiration of a known limited time, or of continuing the office in his family, as by the constitution there must be a constant transfer of it from one man to another, and consequently from one family to another. No man will wish to be a mere cypher at the head of the government: the great object of each president then will be, to render his government a glorious period in the annals of his country. When a man constitutionally retires from office, he retires without pain; he is sensible he retires because the laws direct it, and not from the success of his rivals, nor with that public disapprobation which being left out, when eligible, implies. It is said, that a man knowing that at a given period he must quit his office, will unjustly attempt to take from the public, and lay in store the means of support and splendour in his retirement; there can, I think, be but very little in this observation. The same constitution that makes a man eligible for a given period only, ought to make no man eligible till he arrive to the age of forty or forty-five years: if he be a man of fortune, he will retire with dignity to his estate; if not, he may, like the Roman consuls, and other eminent characters in republics, find an honorable support and employment in some respectable office. A man who must, at all events, thus leave his office, will have but few or no temptations to fill its dependant offices with his tools, or any particular set of men; whereas the man constantly looking forward to his future elections, and, perhaps, to the aggrandizement of his family, will have every inducement before him to fill all places with his own props and dependants. As to public monies, the president need handle none of them, and he may always rigidly be made [to] account for every shilling he shall receive.

On the whole, it would be, in my opinion, almost as well to create a limited monarchy at once, and give some family permanent power and interest in the community, and let it have something valuable to itself to lose in convulsions in the state, and in attempts of usurpation, as to make a first magistrate eligible for life, and to create hopes and expectations in him and his family, of obtaining what they have not. In the latter case, we actually tempt them to disturb the state, to foment struggles and contests, by laying before them the flattering prospect of gaining much in them without risking any thing.

The constitution provides only that the president shall hold his office during the term of four years; that, at most, only implies, that one shall be chosen every fourth year; it also provides, that in case of the removal, death, resignation, or inability, both of the president and vice-president, congress may declare what officer shall act as president; and that such officers shall act accordingly, until the disability be removed, *or a president shall be elected*: it also provides that congress may determine the time of chusing electors, and the day on which they shall give their votes. Considering these clauses together, I submit this question—whether in case of a vacancy in the office of president, by the removal, death, resignation, or inability of the president and vice-president, and congress should declare, that a certain officer, as secretary for foreign affairs, for instance, shall act as president, and suffer such officer to continue several years, or even for his life, to act as president, by omitting to appoint the time for chusing electors of another president, it would be any breach of the constitution? This appears to me to be an intended provision for supplying the office of president, not only for any remaining portion of the four years, but in cases of emergency, until another president shall be elected; and that at a period beyond the expiration of the four years: we do not know that it is impossible; we do not know that it is improbable, in case a popular officer should thus be declared the acting president, but that he might continue for life, and without any violent act, but merely by neglects and delays on the part of congress.

I shall conclude my observations on the organization of the legislature and executive, with making some remarks, rather as a matter of amusement, on the branch, or partial negative, in the legislation:— The third branch in the legislature may answer three valuable purposes, to impede in their passage hasty and intemperate laws, occasionally to assist the senate or people, and to prevent the legislature from encroaching upon the executive or judiciary. In Great Britain the king has a complete negative upon all laws, but he very seldom exercises it. This may be well lodged in him, who possesses strength to support it, and whose family has independent and hereditary interests and powers, rights and prerogatives, in the government, to defend: but in a country where the first executive officer is elective, and has no rights, but in common with the people, a partial negative in legislation, as in Massachusetts and New-York, is, in my opinion, clearly best: in the former state, as before observed, it is lodged in the governor alone; in the latter, in the governor, chancellor, and judges of the supreme court—the new constitution lodges it in the president. This is simply a branch of legislative power, and has in itself no relation to executive or judicial powers. The question is, in what hands ought it to be lodged, to answer the three purposes mentioned the most advantageously? The prevailing opinion seems to be in favour of vesting it in the hands of the first executive magistrate. I will not say this opinion is ill founded. The negative, in one case, is intended to prevent hasty laws, not supported and revised by two-thirds of each of the two branches; in the second, it is to aid the weaker branch; and in the third, to defend the executive and judiciary. To answer these ends, there ought, therefore, to be collected in the hands which hold this negative, firmness, wisdom, and strength; the very object of the negative is occasional opposition to the two branches. By lodging it in the executive magistrate, we give him a share in making the laws, which he must execute; by associating the judges with him, as in New-York, we give them a share in making the laws, upon which they must decide as judicial magistrates; this may be a reason for excluding the judges: however, the negative in New-York is certainly well calculated to answer its great purposes: the governor and judges united must possess more firmness and strength, more wisdom and information, than either alone, and also more of the confidence of the people; and as to the balance among the departments, why should the executive alone hold the scales, and the judicial be left defenceless? I think the negative in New-York is found

best in practice; we see it there frequently and wisely put upon the
measures of the two branches; whereas in Massachusetts it is hardly
ever exercised, and the governor, I believe, has often permitted laws
to pass to which he had substantial objections, but did not make them;
he, however, it is to be observed, is annually elected.

LETTER XV.

JANUARY 18, 1788.

DEAR SIR, Before I proceed to examine particularly the powers
vested, or which ought to be, vested in each branch of the proposed
government, I shall briefly examine the organization of the remaining
branch, the judicial, referring the particular examining of its powers
to some future letters.[37]

In forming this branch, our objects are—a fair and open, a wise and
impartial interpretation of the laws—a prompt and impartial administration of justice, between the public and individuals, and between
man and man. I believe, there is no feature in a free government more
difficult to be well formed than this, especially in an extensive country,
where the courts must be numerous, or the citizens travel to obtain
justice.

The confederation impowers congress to institute judicial courts in
four cases. 1. For settling disputes between individual states. 2. For
determining, finally, appeals in all cases of captures. 3. For the trial
of piracies and felonies committed on the high seas: And, 4. For the
administration of martial law in the army and navy. The state courts
in all other cases possess the judicial powers, in all questions arising
on the laws of nations, of the union, and of the states individually—
nor does congress appear to have any controul over state courts, judges
or officers. The business of the judicial department is, properly speaking, judicial in part, in part executive, done by judges and juries, by
certain recording and executive officers, as clerks, sheriffs, &c. they
are all properly limbs, or parts, of the judicial courts, and have it in
charge, faithfully to decide upon, and execute the laws, in judicial
cases, between the public and individuals, between man and man. The
recording and executive officers, in this department, may well enough
be formed by legislative acts, from time to time: but the offices, the
situation, the powers and duties of judges and juries, are too important, as they respect the political system, as well as the administration
of justice, not to be fixed on general principles by the constitution.
It is true, the laws are made by the legislature; but the judges and
juries, in their interpretations, and in directing the execution of them,
have a very extensive influence for preserving or destroying liberty,

and for changing the nature of the government. It is an observation
of an approved writer, that judicial power is of such a nature, that
when we have ascertained and fixed its limits, with all the caution and
precision we can, it will yet be formidable, somewhat arbitrary and
despotic—that is, after all our cares, we must leave a vast deal to the
discretion and interpretation—to the wisdom, integrity, and politics of
the judges[38]—These men, such is the state even of the best laws, may
do wrong, perhaps, in a thousand cases, sometimes with, and sometimes without design, yet it may be impracticable to convict them of
misconduct. These considerations shew, how cautious a free people
ought to be in forming this, as well as the other branches of their
government, especially when connected with other considerations
equally deserving of notice and attention. When the legislature makes
a bad law, or the first executive magistrate usurps upon the rights of
the people, they discover the evil much sooner, than the abuses of
power in the judicial department; the proceedings of which are far
more intricate, complex, and out of their immediate view. A bad law
immediately excites a general alarm; a bad judicial determination,
though not less pernicious in its consequences, is immediately felt,
probably, by a single individual only, and noticed only by his neighbours, and a few spectators in the court. In this country, we have been
always jealous of the legislature, and especially the executive; but not
always of the judiciary: but very few men attentively consider the essential parts of it, and its proceedings, as they tend to support or to
destroy free government: only a few professional men are in a situation
properly to do this; and it is often alledged, that instances have not
frequently occurred, in which they have been found very alert watch-
men in the cause of liberty, or in the cause of democratic republics.
Add to these considerations, that particular circumstances exist at this
time to increase our inattention to limiting properly the judicial powers, we may fairly conclude, we are more in danger of sowing the seeds
of arbitrary government in this department than in any other. In the
unsettled state of things in this country, for several years past, it has
been thought, that our popular legislatures have, sometimes, departed
from the line of strict justice, while the law courts have shewn a disposition more punctually to keep to it. We are not sufficiently attentive
to the circumstances, that the measures of popular legislatures naturally settle down in time, and gradually approach a mild and just medium; while the rigid systems of the law courts naturally become more
severe and arbitrary, if not carefully tempered and guarded by the
constitution, and by laws, from time to time. It is true, much has been
written and said about some of these courts lately, in some of the

states; but all has been about their fees, &c. and but very little to the purposes, as to their influence upon the freedom of the government.

By art. 3. sect. 1. the judicial power of the United States shall be vested in one supreme court, and in such inferior courts, as congress may, from time to time, ordain and establish—the judges of them to hold their offices during good behaviour, and to receive, at stated times, a compensation for their services, which shall not be diminished during their continuance in office; but which, I conceive, may be increased. By the same art. sect. 2. the supreme court shall have original jurisdiction, "in all cases affecting ambassadors, and other public ministers, and consuls, and those in which a state shall be a party, and appellate jurisdiction, *both as to law and fact,* in all other federal causes, with such exceptions, and under such regulations, as the congress shall make." By the same section, the judicial power shall extend in law and equity to all the federal cases therein enumerated. By the same section the jury trial, in criminal causes, except in cases of impeachment, is established; but not in civil causes, and the whole state may be considered as the vicinage in cases of crimes. These clauses present to view the constitutional features of the federal judiciary: this has been called a monster by some of the opponents, and some, even of the able advocates, have confessed they do not comprehend it. For myself, I confess, I see some good things in it, and some very extraordinary ones. "There shall be one supreme court." There ought in every government to be one court, in which all great questions in law shall finally meet and be determined: in Great-Britain, this is the house of lords, aided by all the superior judges; in Massachusetts, it is, at present, the supreme judicial court, consisting of five judges; in New-York, by the constitution, it is a court consisting of the president of the senate, the senators, chancellor and judges of the supreme court; and in the United States the federal supreme court, or this court in the last resort, may, by the legislature, be made to consist of three, five, fifty, or any other number of judges. The inferior federal courts are left by the constitution to be instituted and regulated altogether as the legislature shall judge best; and it is well provided, that the judges shall hold their offices during good behaviour. I shall not object to the line drawn between the original and appellate jurisdiction of the supreme court; though should we for safety, &c. be obliged to form a numerous supreme court, and place in it a considerable number of respectable characters, it will be found inconvenient for such a court, originally, to try all the causes affecting ambassadors, consuls, &c. Appeals may be carried up to the supreme court, under such regulations as congress shall make. Thus far the legislature does not appear to be limited to improper rules or principles in instituting judicial courts: indeed the legislature will have full power to form and arrange judicial courts in the federal cases enumerated, at pleasure, with these eight exceptions only. 1. There can be but one supreme federal judicial court. 2. This must have jurisdiction as to law and fact in the appellate causes. 3. Original jurisdiction, when foreign ministers and the states are concerned. 4. The judges of the judicial courts must continue in office during good behaviour—and, 5. Their salaries cannot be diminished while in office. 6. There must be a jury trial in criminal causes. 7. The trial of crimes must be in the state where committed—and, 8. There must be two witnesses to convict of treason.

In all other respects Congress may organize the judicial department according to their discretion; the importance of this power, among others proposed by the legislature (perhaps necessarily) I shall consider hereafter. Though there must, by the constitution, be but one judicial court, in which all the rays of judicial powers as to law, equity, and fact, in the cases enumerated must meet; yet this may be made by the legislature, a special court, consisting of any number of respectable characters or officers, the federal legislators excepted, to superintend the judicial department, to try the few causes in which foreign ministers and the states may be concerned, and to correct errors, as to law and fact, in certain important causes on appeals. Next below this judicial head, there may be several courts, such as are usually called superior courts, as a court of chancery, a court of criminal jurisdiction, a court of civil jurisdiction, a court of admiralty jurisdiction, a court of exchequer, &c. giving an appeal from these respectively to the supreme judicial court. These superior courts may be considered as so many points to which appeals may be brought up, from the various inferior courts, in the several branches of judicial causes. In all these superior and inferior courts, the trial by jury may be established in all cases, and the law and equity properly separated. In this organization, only a few very important causes, probably, would be carried up to the supreme court.—The superior courts would, finally, settle almost all causes. This organization, so far as it would respect questions of law, inferior, superior, and a special supreme court, would resemble that of New-York in a considerable degree, and those of several other states. This, I imagine, we must adopt, or else the Massachusetts plan; that is, a number of inferior courts, and one superior or supreme court, consisting of three, or five, or seven judges, in which one supreme court all the business shall be immediately collected from the inferior ones. The decision of the inferior courts, on either plan, probably will not much be relied on; and on the latter plan, there must be a prodigious accumulation of powers and business in all cases touching law, equity and facts, and all kinds of causes in a few hands, for whose errors of ignorance or design, there will be no possible remedy. As the legislature may adopt either of these, or any other plan, I shall not dwell longer on this subject.

In examining the federal judiciary, there appears to be some things very extraordinary and very peculiar. The judges or their friends may seize every opportunity to raise the judges salaries; but by the constitution they cannot be diminished. I am sensible how important it is that judges shall always have adequate and certain support; I am against their depending upon annual or periodical grants, because these may be withheld, or rendered too small by the dissent or narrowness of any one branch of the legislature; but there is a material distinction between periodical grants, and salaries held under permanent and standing laws: the former at stated periods cease, and must be renewed by the consent of all and every part of the legislature; the latter continue of course, and never will cease or be lowered, unless all parts of the legislature agree to do it. A man has as permanent an interest in his salary fixed by a standing law, so long as he may remain in office, as in any property he may possess; for the laws regulating the tenure of all property, are always liable to be altered by the legislature. The same judge may frequently be in office thirty or forty years; there may often be times, as in cases of war, or very high prices, when his salary may reasonably be increased one half or more; in a few years money may become scarce again, and prices fall, and his salary, with equal reason and propriety be decreased and lowered: not to suffer this to be done by consent of all the branches of the legislature, is, I believe, quite a novelty in the affairs of government. It is true, by a very forced and unnatural construction, the constitution of Massachusetts, by the governor and minority in the legislature, was made to speak this kind of language. Another circumstance ought to be considered; the mines which have been discovered are gradually exhausted, and the precious metals are continually wasting: hence the probability is, that money, the nominal representative of property, will gradually grow scarcer hereafter, and afford just reasons for gradually lowering salaries. The value of money depends altogether upon the quantity of it in circulation, which may be also decreased, as well as encreased, from a great variety of causes.

The supreme court, in cases of appeals, shall have jurisdiction both as to law and fact: that is, in all civil causes carried up [to] the supreme court by appeals, the court, or judges, shall try the fact and decide the law. Here an essential principle of the civil law is established, and the most noble and important principle of the common law exploded. To dwell a few minutes on this material point: the supreme court shall have jurisdiction both as to law and fact. What is meant by court? Is the jury included in the term, or is it not? I conceive it is not included: and so the members of convention, I am very sure, understand it. Court, or curia, was a term well understood long before juries existed; the people, and the best writers, in countries where there are no juries, uniformly use the word court, and can only mean by it the judge or judges who determine causes: also, in countries where there are juries we express ourselves in the same manner; we speak of the court of probate, court of chancery, justices court, alderman's court, &c. in which there is no jury. In our supreme courts, common pleas, &c. in which there are jury trials, we uniformly speak of the court and jury, and consider them as distinct. Were it necessary I might site a multitude of cases from law books to confirm, beyond controversy, this position, that the jury is not included, or a part of the court.

But the supreme court is to have jurisdiction as to law and fact, under such regulations as congress shall make. I confess it is impossible to say how far congress may, with propriety, extend their regulations in this respect. I conceive, however, they cannot by any reasonable construction go so far as to admit the jury, on true common law principles, to try the fact, and give a general verdict. I have repeatedly examined this article: I think the meaning of it is, that the judges in all final questions, as to property and damages, shall have complete jurisdiction, to consider the whole cause, to examine the facts, and on a general view of them, and on principles of equity, as well as law, to give judgment.

As the trial by jury is provided for in criminal causes, I shall confine my observations to civil causes—and in these, I hold it is the established right of the jury by the common law, and the fundamental laws of this country, to give a general verdict in all cases when they chuse to do it, to decide both as to law and fact, whenever blended together in the issue put to them. Their right to determine as to facts will not be disputed, and their right to give a general verdict has never been disputed, except by a few judges and lawyers, governed by despotic principles. Coke, Hale, Holt, Blackstone, De Lome, and almost every other legal or political writer, who has written on the subject, has uniformly asserted this essential and important right of the jury. Juries in Great-Britain and America have universally practised accordingly. Even Mansfield, with all his wishes about him, dare not directly avow the contrary. What fully confirms this point is, that there is no instance to be found, where a jury was ever punished for finding a general verdict, when a special one might, with propriety, have been found. The jury trial, especially politically considered, is by far the most important feature in the judicial department in a free country, and the right in question is far the most valuable part, and the last that ought to be yielded, of this trial. Juries are constantly and frequently drawn from the body of the people, and freemen of the country; and by holding the jury's right to return a general verdict in all cases sacred, we secure to the people at large, their just and rightful controul in the judicial department. If the conduct of judges shall be severe and arbitrary, and tend to subvert the laws, and change the forms of government, the jury may check them, by deciding against their opinions and determinations, in similar cases. It is true, the freemen of a country are not always minutely skilled in the laws, but they have common sense in its purity, which seldom or never errs in making and applying laws to the condition of the people, or in determining judicial causes, when stated to them by the parties. The body of the people, principally, bear the burdens of the community; they of right ought to have a controul in its important concerns, both in making and executing the laws, otherwise they may, in a short time, be ruined. Nor is it merely this controul alone we are to attend to; the jury trial brings with it an open and public discussion of all causes, and excludes secret and arbitrary proceedings. This, and the democratic branch in the legislature, as was formerly observed, are the means by which the people are let into the knowledge of public affairs—are enabled to stand as the guardians of each others rights, and to restrain, by regular and legal measures, those who otherwise might infringe upon them. I am not unsupported in my opinion of the value of the trial by jury; not only British and American writers, but De Lome, and the most approved foreign writers, hold it to be the most valuable part of the British constitution, and indisputably the best mode of trial ever invented.[39]

It was merely by the intrigues of the popish clergy, and of the Norman lawyers, that this mode of trial was not used in maritime, ecclesiastical, and military courts, and the civil law proceedings were introduced; and, I believe, it is more from custom and prejudice, than for any substantial reasons, that we do not in all the states establish the jury in our maritime as well as other courts.

In the civil law process the trial by jury is unknown; the consequence is, that a few judges and dependant officers, possess all the power in the judicial department. Instead of the open fair proceedings of the common law, where witnesses are examined in open court, and may be cross examined by the parties concerned—where council is allowed, &c. we see in the civil law process judges alone, who always, long previous to the trial, are known and often corrupted by ministerial influence, or by parties. Judges once influenced, soon become inclined to yield to temptations, and to decree for him who will pay the most for their partiality. It is, therefore, we find in the Roman, and almost all governments, where judges alone possess the judicial powers and try all cases, that bribery has prevailed. This, as well as the forms of the courts, naturally lead to secret and arbitrary proceedings—to taking evidence secretly—exparte, &c. to perplexing the cause—and to hasty decisions:—but, as to jurors, it is quite impracticable to bribe or influence them by any corrupt means; not only because they are untaught in such affairs, and possess the honest characters of the common freemen of a country; but because it is not, generally, known till the hour the cause comes on for trial, what persons are to form the jury.

But it is said, that no words could be found by which the states could agree to establish the jury-trial in civil causes. I can hardly believe men to be serious, who make observations to this effect. The states have all derived judicial proceedings principally from one source, the British system; from the same common source the American lawyers have almost universally drawn their legal information. All the states have agreed to establish the trial by jury, in civil as well as in criminal causes. The several states, in congress, found no difficulty in establishing it in the Western Territory, in the ordinance passed in July 1787.[40] We find, that the several states in congress, in establishing government in that territory, agreed, that the inhabitants of it, should always be entitled to the benefit of the trial by jury. Thus, in a few words, the jury trial is established in its full extent; and the convention with as much ease, have established the jury trial in criminal cases. In making a constitution, we are substantially to fix principles.—If in one state, damages on default are assessed by a jury, and in another by the judges—if in one state jurors are drawn out of a box, and in another not—if there be other trifling variations, they can be of no importance in the great question. Further, when we examine the particular practices of the states, in little matters in judicial proceedings, I believe we shall find they differ near as much in criminal processes as in civil ones. Another thing worthy of notice in this place—the convention have used the word equity, and agreed to establish a chancery jurisdiction; about the meaning and extent of which, we all know, the several states disagree much more than about jury trials—in adopting the latter, they have very generally pursued the British plan; but as to the former, we see the states have varied, as their fears and opinions dictated.

By the common law, in Great Britain and America, there is no appeal from the verdict of the jury, as to facts, to any judges whatever—the jurisdiction of the jury is complete and final in this; and only errors in law are carried up to the house of lords, the special supreme court in Great Britain; or to the special supreme courts in Connecticut, New-York, New-Jersey, &c. Thus the juries are left masters as to facts: but, by the proposed constitution, directly the opposite principles is established. An appeal will lay in all appellate causes from the verdict of the jury, even as to mere facts, to the judges of the supreme court. Thus, in effect, we establish the civil law in this point; for if the jurisdiction of the jury be not final, as to facts, it is of little or no importance.

By art. 3. sect. 2. "the judicial power shall extend to all cases in law and equity, arising under this constitution, the laws of the United States," &c. What is here meant by equity? what is equity in a case arising under the constitution? possibly the clause might have the same meaning, were the words "in law and equity," omitted. Cases in law must differ widely from cases in law and equity. At first view, by thus joining the word equity with the word law, if we mean any thing, we seem to mean to give the judge a discretionary power. The word equity, in Great Britain, has in time acquired a precise meaning—chancery proceedings there are now reduced to system—but this is not the case in the United States. In New-England, the judicial courts have no powers in cases in equity, except those dealt out to them by the legislature, in certain limited portions, by legislative acts. In New-York, Maryland, Virginia, and South Carolina, powers to decide, in cases of equity, are vested in judges distinct from those who decide in matters of law: and the states generally seem to have carefully avoided giving unlimitedly, to the same judges, powers to decide in cases in law and equity. Perhaps, the clause would have the same meaning were the words, "this constitution," omitted: there is in it either a careless complex misuse of words, in themselves of extensive signification, or there is some meaning not easy to be comprehended. Suppose a case arising under the constitution—suppose the question judicially moved, whether, by the constitution, congress can suppress a state tax laid on polls, lands, or as an excise duty, which may be supposed to interfere with a federal tax. By the letter of the constitution, congress will appear to have no power to do it: but then the judges may decide the question on principles of equity as well as law. Now, omitting the words, "in law and equity," they may decide according to the spirit and true meaning of the constitution, as collected from what must appear to have been the intentions of the people when they made it. Therefore, it would seem, that if these words mean any thing, they must have a further meaning: yet I will not suppose it intended to lodge an arbitrary power or discretion in the judges, to decide as their conscience, their opinions, their caprice, or their politics might dictate. Without dwelling on this obscure clause, I will leave it to the examination of others.

## LETTER XVI.

JANUARY 20, 1788.

DEAR SIR, Having gone through with the organization of the government, I shall now proceed to examine more particularly those clauses which respect its powers. I shall begin with those articles and stipulations which are necessary for accurately ascertaining the extent of powers, and what is given, and for guarding, limiting, and restraining them in their exercise. We often find, these articles and stipulations placed in bills of rights; but they may as well be incorporated in the body of the constitution, as selected and placed by themselves. The constitution, or whole social compact, is but one instrument, no more or less, than a certain number of articles or stipulations agreed to by the people, whether it consists of articles, sections, chapters, bills of rights, or parts of any other denomination, cannot be material. Many needless observations, and idle distinctions, in my opinion, have been made respecting a bill of rights. On the one hand, it seems to be considered as a necessary distinct limb of the constitution, and as containing a certain number of very valuable articles, which are applicable to all societies; and, on the other, as useless, especially in a federal government, possessing only enumerated power—nay, dangerous, as individual rights are numerous, and not easy to be enumerated in a bill of rights, and from articles, or stipulations, securing some of them, it may be inferred, that others not mentioned are surrendered. There appears to me to be general indefinite propositions without much meaning—and the man who first advanced those of the latter description, in the present case, signed the federal constitution, which directly contradicts him.[41] The supreme power is undoubtedly in the people, and it is a principle well established in my mind, that they reserve all powers not expressly delegated by them to those who govern; this is as true in forming a state as in forming a federal government. There is no possible distinction but this founded merely in the different modes of proceeding which take place in some cases. In forming a state constitution, under which to manage not only the great but the little concerns of a community: the powers to be possessed by the government are often too numerous to be enumerated; the people to adopt the shortest way often give general powers, indeed all powers, to the government, in some general words, and then, by a particular enumeration, take back, or rather say they however reserve certain rights as sacred, and which no laws shall be made to violate: hence the idea that all powers are given which are not reserved; but in forming a federal constitution, which *ex vi termine*, supposes state governments existing, and which is only to manage a few great national concerns, we often find it easier to enumerate particularly the powers to be delegated to the federal head, than to enumerate particularly the individual rights to be reserved; and the principle will operate in its full force, when we carefully adhere to it. When we particularly enumerate the powers given, we ought either carefully to enumerate the rights reserved, or be totally silent about them; we must either particularly enumerate both, or else suppose the particular enumeration of the powers given adequately draws the line between them and the rights reserved, particularly to enumerate the former and not the latter, I think most advisable: however, as men appear generally to have their doubts about these silent reservations, we might advantageously enumerate the powers given, and then in general words, according to the mode adopted in the 2d art. of the confederation, declare all powers, rights and privileges, are reserved, which are not explicitly and expressly given up. People, and very wisely too, like to be express and explicit about their essential rights, and not to be forced to claim them on the precarious and unascertained tenure of inferences and general principles, knowing that in any controversy between them and their rulers, concerning those rights, disputes may be endless, and nothing certain:—But admitting, on the general principle, that all rights are reserved of course, which are not expressly surrendered, the people could with sufficient certainty assert their rights on all occasions, and establish them with ease, still there are infinite advantages in particularly enumerating many of the most essential rights reserved in all cases; and as to the less important ones, we may declare in general terms, that all not expressly surrendered are reserved. We do not by declarations change the nature of things, or create new truths, but we give existence, or at least establish in the minds of the people truths and principles which they might never otherwise have thought of, or soon forgot. If a nation means its systems, religious or political, shall have duration, it ought to recognize the leading principles of them in the front page of every family book. What is the usefulness of a truth in theory, unless it exists constantly in the minds of the people, and has their assent:—we discern certain rights, as the freedom of the press, and the trial by jury, &c. which the people of England and of America of course believe to be sacred, and essential to their political happiness, and this belief in them is the result of ideas at first suggested to them by a few able men, and of subsequent experience; while the people of some other countries hear these rights mentioned with the utmost indifference; they think the privilege of existing at the will of a despot much preferable to them. Why this difference amongst beings every way formed alike. The reason of the difference is obvious—it is the effect of education, a series of notions impressed upon the minds of the people by examples, precepts and declarations. When the people of England got together, at the time they formed Magna Charta, they did not consider it sufficient, that they were indisputably entitled to certain natural and unalienable rights, not depending on silent titles, they, by a declaratory act, expressly recognized them, and explicitly declared to all the world, that they were entitled to enjoy those rights; they made an instrument in writing, and enumerated those they then thought essential, or in danger, and this wise men saw was not sufficient; and therefore, that the people might not forget these rights, and gradually become prepared for arbitrary government, their discerning and honest leaders caused this instrument to be confirmed near forty times, and to be read twice a year in public places, not that it would lose its validity without such confirmations, but to fix the contents of it in the minds of the people, as they successively come upon the stage.—Men, in some countries do not remain free, merely because they are entitled to natural and unalienable rights; men in all countries are entitled to them, not because their ancestors once got together and enumerated them on paper, but because, by repeated negociations and declarations, all parties are brought to realize them, and of course to believe them to be sacred. Were it necessary, I might shew the wisdom of our past conduct, as a people in not merely comforting ourselves that we were entitled to freedom, but in constantly keeping in view, in addresses, bills of rights, in news-papers, &c. the particular principles on which our freedom must always depend.

It is not merely in this point of view, that I urge the engrafting in the constitution additional declaratory articles. The distinction, in itself just, that all powers not given are reserved, is in effect destroyed by this very constitution, as I shall particularly demonstrate—and even independent of this, the people, by adopting the constitution, give many general undefined powers to congress, in the constitutional exercise of which, the rights in question may be effected. Gentlemen who oppose a federal bill of rights, or further declaratory articles, seem to view the subject in a very narrow imperfect manner. These have for their objects, not only the enumeration of the rights reserved, but principally to explain the general powers delegated in certain material points, and to restrain those who exercise them by fixed known boundaries. Many explanations and restrictions necessary and useful, would be much less so, were the people at large all well and fully acquainted with the principles and affairs of government. There appears to be in the constitution, a studied brevity, and it may also be probable, that several explanatory articles were omitted from a circumstance very common. What we have long and early understood ourselves in the common concerns of the community, we are apt to suppose is understood by others, and need not be expressed; and it is not unnatural or uncommon for the ablest men most frequently to make this mistake. To make declaratory articles unnecessary in an instrument of government, two circumstances must exist; the rights reserved must be indisputably so, and in their nature defined; the powers delegated to the government, must be precisely defined by the words that convey them, and clearly be of such extent and nature as that, by no reasonable construction, they can be made to invade the rights and prerogatives intended to be left in the people.

The first point urged, is, that all power is reserved not expressly given, that particular enumerated powers only are given, that all others are not given, but reserved, and that it is needless to attempt to restrain congress in the exercise of powers they possess not. This reasoning is logical, but of very little importance in the common affairs of men; but the constitution does not appear to respect it even in any view. To prove this, I might cite several clauses in it. I shall only remark on two or three. By article 1, section 9, "No title of nobility shall be granted by congress." Was this clause omitted, what power would congress have to make titles of nobility? in what part of the constitution would they find it? The answer must be, that congress would have no such power—that the people, by adopting the constitution, will not part with it. Why then by a negative clause, restrain congress from doing what it would have no power to do? This clause, then, must have no meaning, or imply, that were it omitted, congress would have the power in question, either upon the principle that some general words in the constitution may be so construed as to give it, or on the principle that congress possess the powers not expressly reserved. But this clause was in the confederation, and is said to be introduced into the constitution from very great caution. Even a cautionary provision implies a doubt, at least, that it is necessary; and if so in this case, clearly it is also alike necessary in all similar ones. The fact appears to be, that the people in forming the confederation, and the convention, in this instance, acted, naturally, they did not leave the point to be settled by general principles and logical inferences; but they settle the point in a few words, and all who read them at once understand them.

The trial by jury in criminal as well as in civil causes, has long been considered as one of our fundamental rights, and has been repeatedly recognized and confirmed by most of the state conventions. But the constitution expressly establishes this trial in criminal, and wholly omits it in civil causes. The jury trial in criminal causes, and the benefit of the writ of habeas corpus, are already as effectually established as any of the fundamental or essential rights of the people in the United States. This being the case, why in adopting a federal constitution do we now establish these, and omit all others, or all others, at least, with a few exceptions, such as again agreeing there shall be no ex post facto laws, no titles of nobility, &c. We must consider this constitution when adopted as the supreme act of the people, and in construing it hereafter, we and our posterity must strictly adhere to the letter and spirit of it, and in no instance depart from them: in construing the federal constitution, it will be not only impracticable, but improper to refer to the state constitutions. They are entirely distinct instruments and inferior acts: besides, by the people's now establishing certain fundamental rights, it is strongly implied, that they are of opinion, that they would not otherwise be secured as a part of the federal system, or be regarded in the federal administration as fundamental. Further, these same rights, being established by the state constitutions, and secured to the people, our recognizing them now, implies, that the people thought them insecure by the state establishments, and extinguished or put afloat by the new arrangement of the social system, unless re-established.—Further, the people, thus establishing some few rights, and remaining totally silent about others similarly circumstanced, the implication indubitably is, that they mean to relinquish the latter, or at least feel indifferent about them. Rights, therefore, inferred from general principles of reason, being precarious and hardly ascertainable in the common affairs of society, and the people, in forming a federal constitution, explicitly shewing they conceive these rights to be thus circumstanced, and accordingly proceed to enumerate and establish some of them, the conclusion will be, that they have established all which they esteem valuable and sacred. On every principle, then, the people especially having began, ought to go through enumerating, and establish particularly all the rights of individuals, which can by any possibility come in question in making and executing federal laws. I have already observed upon the excellency and importance of the jury trial in civil as well as in criminal causes, instead of establishing it in criminal causes only; we ought to establish it generally;—instead of the clause of forty or fifty words relative to this subject, why not use the language that has always been used in this country, and say, "the people of the United States shall always be entitled to the trial by jury." This would shew the people still hold the right sacred, and enjoin it upon congress substantially to preserve the jury trial in all cases, according to the usage and custom of the country. I have observed before, that it is *the jury trial* we want; the little different appendages and modifications tacked to it in the different states, are no more than a drop in the ocean: the jury trial is a solid uniform feature in a free government; it is the substance we would save, not the little articles of form.

Security against expost facto laws, the trial by jury, and the benefits of the writ of habeas corpus, are but a part of those inestimable rights the people of the United States are entitled to, even in judicial proceedings, by the course of the common law. These may be secured in general words, as in New-York, the Western Territory, &c. by declaring the people of the United States shall always be entitled to judicial proceedings according to the course of the common law, as used and established in the said states. Perhaps it would be better to enumerate the particular essential rights the people are entitled to in these proceedings, as has been done in many of the states, and as has been done in England. In this case, the people may proceed to declare, that no man shall be held to answer to any offence, till the same be fully described to him; nor to furnish evidence against himself: that, except in the government of the army and navy, no person shall be tried for any offence, whereby he may incur loss of life, or an infamous punishment, until he be first indicted by a grand jury: that every person shall have a right to produce all proofs that may be favourable to him, and to meet the witnesses against him face to face: that every person shall be entitled to obtain right and justice freely and without delay: that all persons shall have a right to be secure from all unreasonable searches and seizures of their persons, houses, papers, or possessions; and that all warrants shall be deemed contrary to this right, if the foundation of them be not previously supported by oath, and there be not in them a special designation of persons or objects of search, arrest, or seizure: and that no person shall be exiled or molested in his person or effects, otherwise than by the judgment of his peers, or according to the law of the land. A celebrated writer observes upon this last article, that in itself it may be said to comprehend the whole end of political society.[42] These rights are not necessarily reserved, they are established, or enjoyed but in few countries: they are stipulated rights, almost peculiar to British and American laws. In the execution of those laws, individuals, by long custom, by magna charta, bills of rights &c. have become entitled to them. A man, at first, by act of parliament, became entitled to the benefits of the writ of habeas corpus—men are entitled to these rights and benefits in the judicial proceedings of our state courts generally: but it will by no means follow, that they will be entitled to them in the federal courts, and have a right to assert them, unless secured and established by the constitution or federal laws. We certainly, in federal processes, might as well claim the benefits of the writ of habeas corpus, as to claim trial by a jury—the right to have council—to have witnesses face to face— to be secure against unreasonable search warrants, &c. was the constitution silent as to the whole of them:—but the establishment of the former, will evince that we could not claim them without it; and the omission of the latter, implies they are relinquished, or deemed of no importance. These are rights and benefits individuals acquire by compact; they must claim them under compacts, or immemorial usage—it is doubtful, at least, whether they can be claimed under immemorial usage in this country; and it is, therefore, we generally claim them under compacts, as charters and constitutions.

The people by adopting the federal constitution, give congress general powers to institute a distinct and new judiciary, new courts, and to regulate all proceedings in them, under the eight limitations mentioned in a former letter;[43] and the further one, that the benefits of the habeas corpus act shall be enjoyed by individuals. Thus general powers being given to institute courts, and regulate their proceedings, with no provision for securing the rights principally in question, may not congress so exercise those powers, and constitutionally too, as to destroy those rights? clearly, in my opinion, they are not in any degree secured. But, admitting the case is only doubtful, would it not be prudent and wise to secure them and remove all doubts, since all agree the people ought to enjoy these valuable rights, a very few men excepted, who seem to be rather of opinion that there is little or nothing in them? Were it necessary I might add many observations to shew their value and political importance.

The constitution will give congress general powers to raise and support armies. General powers carry with them incidental ones, and the means necessary to the end. In the exercise of these powers, is there any provision in the constitution to prevent the quartering of soldiers on the inhabitants? you will answer, there is not. This may sometimes be deemed a necessary measure in the support of armies; on what principle can the people claim the right to be exempt from this burden? they will urge, perhaps, the practice of the country, and the provisions made in some of the state constitutions—they will be answered, that their claim thus to be exempt, is not founded in nature, but only in custom and opinion, or at best, in stipulations in some of the state constitutions, which are local, and inferior in their operation, and can have no controul over the general government—that they had adopted a federal constitution—had noticed several rights, but had been totally silent about this exemption—that they had given general powers relative to the subject, which, in their operation, regularly destroyed the claim. Though it is not to be presumed, that we are in any immediate danger from this quarter, yet it is fit and proper to establish, beyond dispute, those rights which are particularly valuable to individuals, and essential to the permanency and duration of free government. An excellent writer observes, that the English, always in possession of their freedom, are frequently unmindful of the value of it:[44] we, at this period, do not seem to be so well off, having, in some instances abused ours; many of us are quite disposed to barter it away for what we call energy, coercion, and some other terms we use as vaguely as that of liberty—There is often as great a rage for change and novelty in politics, as in amusements and fashions.

All parties apparently agree, that the freedom of the press is a fundamental right, and ought not to be restrained by any taxes, duties, or in any manner whatever. Why should not the people, in adopting a federal constitution, declare this, even if there are only doubts about it. But, say the advocates, all powers not given are reserved.—true; but the great question is, are not powers given, in the excercise of which this right may be destroyed? The people's or the printers claim to a free press, is founded on the fundamental laws, that is, compacts, and state constitutions, made by the people. The people, who can annihilate or alter those constitutions, can annihilate or limit this right. This may be done by giving general powers, as well as by using particular words. No right claimed under a state constitution, will avail against a law of the union, made in pursuance of the federal constitution: therefore the question is, what laws will congress have a right to make by the constitution of the union, and particularly touching the press? By art. 1. sect. 8. congress will have power to lay and collect taxes, duties, imposts and excise. By this congress will clearly have power to lay and collect all kind of taxes whatever—taxes on houses, lands, polls, industry, merchandize, &c.—taxes on deeds, bonds, and all written instruments—on writs, pleas, and all judicial proceedings, on licences, naval officers papers, &c. on newspapers, advertisements, &c. and to require bonds of the naval officers, clerks, printers, &c. to account for the taxes that may become due on papers that go through their hands. Printing, like all other business, must cease when taxed beyond its profits; and it appears to me, that a power to tax the press at discretion, is a power to destroy or restrain the freedom of it. There may be other powers given, in the exercise of which this freedom may be effected; and certainly it is of too much importance to be left thus liable to be taxed, and constantly to constructions and inferences. A free press is the channel of communication as to mercantile and public affairs; by means of it the people in large countries ascertain each others sentiments; are enabled to unite, and become formidable to those rulers who adopt improper measures. Newspapers may sometimes be the vehicles of abuse, and of many things not true; but these are but small inconveniencies, in my mind, among many advantages. A celebrated writer, I have several times quoted, speaking in high terms of the English liberties, says, "lastly the key stone was put to the arch, by the final establishment of the freedom of the press."[45] I shall not dwell longer upon the fundamental rights, to some of which I have attended in this letter, for the same reasons that these I have mentioned, ought to be expressly secured, lest in the exercise of general powers given they may be invaded: it is pretty clear, that some other of less importance, or less in danger, might with propriety also be secured.

I shall now proceed to examine briefly the powers proposed to be vested in the several branches of the government, and especially the mode of laying and collecting internal taxes.

### LETTER XVII.

January 23, 1788.

Dear Sir, I believe the people of the United States are full in the opinion, that a free and mild government can be preserved in their extensive territories, only under the substantial forms of a federal republic. As several of the ablest advocates for the system proposed, have acknowledged this (and I hope the confessions they have published will be preserved and remembered) I shall not take up time to establish this point. A question then arises, how far that system partakes of a federal republic.—I observed in a former letter, that it appears to be the first important step to a consolidation of the states; that its strong tendency is to that point.[46]

But what do we mean by a federal republic? and what by a consolidated government? To erect a federal republic, we must first make a number of states on republican principles; each state with a government organized for the internal management of its affairs: The states, as such, must unite under a federal head, and delegate to it powers to make and execute laws in certain enumerated cases, under certain restrictions; this head may be a single assembly, like the present congress, or the Amphictionic council; or it may consist of a legislature, with one or more branches; of an executive, and of a judiciary. To form a consolidated, or one entire government, there must be no state, or local governments, but all things, persons and property, must be subject to the laws of one legislature alone; to one executive, and one judiciary. Each state government, as the government of New Jersey, &c. is a consolidated, or one entire government, as it respects the counties, towns, citizens and property within the limits of the state.— The state governments are the basis, the pillar on which the federal head is placed, and the whole together, when formed on elective principles, constitute a federal republic. A federal republic in itself supposes state or local governments to exist, as the body or props, on which the federal head rests, and that it cannot remain a moment after they cease. In erecting the federal government, and always in its councils, each state must be known as a sovereign body; but in erecting this government, I conceive, the legislature of the state, by the expressed or implied assent of the people, or the people of the state, under the direction of the government of it, may accede to the federal compact: Nor do I conceive it to be necessarily a part of a confederacy of states, that each have an equal voice in the general councils. A confederated republic being organized, each state must retain powers for managing its internal police, and all delegate to the union power to manage general concerns: The quantity of power the union must possess is one thing, the mode of exercising the powers given, is quite a different consideration; and it is the mode of exercising them, that makes one of the essential distinctions between one entire or consolidated government, and a federal republic; that is, however the government may be organized, if the laws of the union, in most important concerns, as in levying and collecting taxes, raising troops, &c. operate immediately upon the persons and property of individuals, and not on states, extend to organizing the militia, &c. the government, as to its administration, as to making and executing laws, is not federal, but consolidated. To illustrate my idea—the union makes a requisition, and assigns to each state its quota of men or monies wanted; each state, by its own laws and officers, in its own way, furnishes its quota: here the state governments stand between the union and individuals; the laws of the union operate only on states, as such, and federally: Here nothing can be done without the meetings of the state legislatures— but in the other case the union, though the state legislatures should not meet for years together, proceeds immediately, by its own laws and officers, to levy and collect monies of individuals, to inlist men, form armies, &c. here the laws of the union operate immediately on the body of the people, on persons and property; in the same manner the laws of one entire consolidated government operate.—These two modes are very distinct, and in their operation and consequences have directly opposite tendencies: The first makes the existence of the state governments indispensable, and throws all the detail business of levying and collecting the taxes, &c. into the hands of those governments, and into the hands, of course, of many thousand officers solely created by, and dependent on the state. The last entirely excludes the agency of the respective states, and throws the whole business of levying and collecting taxes, &c. into the hands of many thousand officers solely created by, and dependent upon the union, and makes the existence of the state government of no consequence in the case. It is true, congress in raising any given sum in direct taxes, must by the constitution, raise so much of it in one state, and so much in another, by a fixed rule, which most of the states some time since agreed to: But this does not effect the principle in question, it only secures each state against any arbitrary proportions. The federal mode is perfectly safe and eligible, founded in the true spirit of a confederated republic there could be no possible exception to it, did we not find by experience, that the states will sometimes neglect to comply with the reasonable requisitions of the union. It being according to the fundamental principles of federal republics, to raise men and monies by requisitions, and for the states individually to organize and train the militia, I conceive, there can be no reason whatever for departing from them, except this, that the states sometimes neglect to comply with reasonable requisitions, and that it is dangerous to attempt to compel a delinquent state by force, as it may often produce a war. We ought, therefore, to enquire attentively, how extensive the evils to be guarded against are, and cautiously limit the remedies to the extent of the evils. I am not about to defend the confederation, or to charge the proposed constitution with imperfections not in it; but we ought to examine facts, and strip them of the false colourings often given them by incautious observations, by unthinking or designing men. We ought to premise, that laws for raising men and monies, even in consolidated governments, are not often punctually complied with. Historians, except in extraordinary cases, but very seldom take notice of the detail collection of taxes; but these facts we have fully proved, and well attested; that the most energetic governments have relinquished taxes frequently, which were of many years standing. These facts amply prove, that taxes assessed, have remained many years uncollected. I agree there have been instances in the republics of Greece, Holland, &c. in the course of several centuries, of states neglecting to pay their quotas of requisitions; but it is a circumstance certainly deserving of attention, whether these nations which have depended on requisitions principally for their defence, have not raised men and monies nearly as punctually as entire governments, which have taxed directly; whether we have not found the latter as often distressed for the want of troops and monies, as the former. It has been said, that the Amphictionic council, and the Germanic head, have not possessed sufficient powers to controul the members of the republic in a proper manner. Is this, if true, to be imputed to requisitions? Is it not principally to be imputed to the unequal powers of those members, connected with this important circumstance, that each member possessed power to league itself with foreign powers, and powerful neighbours, without the consent of the head. After all, has not the Germanic body a government as good as its neighbours in general? and did not the Grecian republic remain united several centuries, and form the theatre of human greatness? No government in Europe has commanded monies more plentifully than the government of Holland. As to the United States, the separate states lay taxes directly, and the union calls for taxes by way of requisitions; and is it a fact, that more monies are due in proportion on requisitions in the United States, than on the state taxes directly laid?— It is but about ten years since congress begun to make requisitions, and in that time, the monies, &c. required, and the bounties given for men required of the states, have amounted, specie value, to about 36 millions dollars, about 24 millions of dollars of which have been actually paid; and a very considerable part of the 12 millions not paid, remains so not so much from the neglect of the states, as from the sudden changes in paper money, &c. which in a great measure rendered payments of no service, and which often induced the union indirectly to relinquish one demand, by making another in a different form. Before we totally condemn requisitions, we ought to consider what immense bounties the states gave, and what prodigious exertions they made in the war, in order to comply with the requisitions of congress; and if since the peace they have been delinquent, ought we not carefully to enquire, whether that delinquency is to be imputed solely to the nature of requisitions? ought it not in part to be imputed to two other causes? I mean first, an opinion, that has extensively prevailed, that the requisitions for domestic interest have not been founded on just principles; and secondly, the circumstance, that the government itself, by proposing imposts, &c. has departed virtually from the constitutional system; which proposed changes, like all changes proposed in government, produce an inattention and negligence in the execution of the government in being.

I am not for depending wholly on requisitions; but I mention these

few facts to shew they are not so totally futile as many pretend. For
the truth of many of these facts I appeal to the public records; and
for the truth of the others, I appeal to many republican characters,
who are best informed in the affairs of the United States. Since the
peace, and till the convention reported, the wisest men in the United
States generally supposed, that certain limited funds would answer the
purposes of the union: and though the states are by no means in so
good a condition as I wish they were, yet, I think, I may very safely
affirm, they are in a better condition than they would be had congress
always possessed the powers of taxation now contended for. The fact
is admitted, that our federal government does not possess sufficient
powers to give life and vigor to the political system; and that we experience disappointments, and several inconveniencies; but we ought
carefully to distinguish those which are merely the consequences of a
severe and tedious war, from those which arise from defects in the
federal system. There has been an entire revolution in the United States
within thirteen years, and the least we can compute the waste of labour
and property at, during that period, by the war, is three hundred
million of dollars. Our people are like a man just recovering from a
severe fit of sickness. It was the war that disturbed the course of
commerce, introduced floods of paper money, the stagnation of credit,
and threw many valuable men out of steady business. From these
sources our greatest evils arise; men of knowledge and reflection must
perceive it;—but then, have we not done more in three or four years
past, in repairing the injuries of the war, by repairing houses and
estates, restoring industry, frugality, the fisheries, manufactures, &c.
and thereby laying the foundation of good government, and of individual and political happiness, than any people ever did in a like time;
we must judge from a view of the country and facts, and not from
foreign newspapers, or our own, which are printed chiefly in the commercial towns, where imprudent living, imprudent importations, and
many unexpected disappointments, have produced a despondency, and
a disposition to view every thing on the dark side. Some of the evils
we feel, all will agree, ought to be imputed to the defective administration of the governments. From these and various considerations, I
am very clearly of opinion, that the evils we sustain, merely on account
of the defects of the confederation, are but as a feather in the balance
against a mountain, compared with those which would, infallibly, be
the result of the loss of general liberty, and that happiness men enjoy
under a frugal, free, and mild government.

Heretofore we do not seem to have seen danger any where, but in
giving power to congress, and now no where but in congress wanting

powers; and, without examining the extent of the evils to be remedied, by one step, we are for giving up to congress almost all powers of any importance without limitation. The defects of the confederation are extravagantly magnified, and every species of pain we feel imputed to them: and hence it is inferred, there must be a total change of the principles, as well as forms of government: and in the main point, touching the federal powers, we rest all on a logical inference, totally inconsistent with experience and sound political reasoning.

It is said, that as the federal head must make peace and war, and provide for the common defence, it ought to possess all powers necessary to that end: that powers unlimited, as to the purse and sword, to raise men and monies, and form the militia, are necessary to that end; and, therefore, the federal head ought to possess them. This reasoning is far more specious than solid: it is necessary that these powers so exist in the body politic, as to be called into exercise whenever necessary for the public safety; but it is by no means true, that the man, or congress of men, whose duty it more immediately is to provide for the common defence, ought to possess them without limitation. But clear it is, that if such men, or congress, be not in a situation to hold them without danger to liberty, he or they ought not to possess them. It has long been thought to be a well founded position, that the purse and sword ought not to be placed in the same hands in a free government. Our wise ancestors have carefully separated them—placed the sword in the hands of their king, even under considerable limitations, and the purse in the hands of the commons alone: yet the king makes peace and war, and it is his duty to provide for the common defence of the nation. This authority at least goes thus far—that a nation, well versed in the science of government, does not conceive it to be necessary or expedient for the man entrusted with the common defence and general tranquility, to possess unlimitedly the powers in question, or even in any considerable degree. Could he, whose duty it is to defend the public, possess in himself independently, all the means of doing it consistent with the public good, it might be convenient: but the people of England know that their liberties and happiness would be in infinitely greater danger from the king's unlimited possession of these powers, than from all external enemies and internal commotions to which they might be exposed: therefore, though they have made it his duty to guard the empire, yet they have wisely placed in other hands, the hands of their representatives, the power to deal out and controul the means. In Holland their high mightinesses must provide for the common defence, but for the means they depend, in a considerable degree, upon requisitions made on the state or local assemblies. Reason and facts evince, that however convenient it might be for an executive magistrate, or federal head, more immediately charged with the national defence and safety, solely, directly, and independently to possess all the means; yet such magistrate, or head, never ought to possess them, if thereby the public liberties shall be endangered. The powers in question never have been, by nations wise and free, deposited, nor can they ever be, with safety, any where, but in the principal members of the national system:—where these form one entire government, as in Great-Britain, they are separated and lodged in the principal members of it. But in a federal republic, there is quite a different organization; the people form this kind of government, generally, because their territories are too extensive to admit of their assembling in one legislature, or of executing the laws on free principles under one entire government. They convene in their local assemblies, for local purposes, and for managing their internal concerns, and unite their states under a federal head for general purposes. It is the essential characteristic of a confederated republic, that this head be dependant on, and kept within limited bounds by, the local governments; and it is because, in these alone, in fact, the people can be substantially assembled or represented. It is, therefore, we very universally see, in this kind of government, the congressional powers placed in a few hands, and accordingly limited, and specifically enumerated: and the local assemblies strong and well guarded, and composed of numerous members. Wise men will always place the controuling power where the people are substantially collected by their representatives. By the proposed system, the federal head will possess, without limitation, almost every species of power that can, in its exercise, tend to change the government, or to endanger liberty; while in it, I think it has been fully shewn, the people will have but the shadow of representation, and but the shadow of security for their rights and liberties. In a confederated republic, the division of representation, &c. in its nature, requires a correspondent division and deposit of powers, relative to taxes and military concerns: and I think the plan offered stands quite alone, in confounding the principles of governments in themselves totally distinct. I wish not to exculpate the states for their improper neglects in not paying their quotas of requisitions; but, in applying the remedy, we must be governed by reason and facts. It will not be denied, that the people have a right to change the government when the majority chuse it, if not restrained by some existing compact—that they have a right to displace their rulers, and consequently to determine when their measures are reasonable or not—and that they have a right, at any time, to put a stop to those measures they may deem prejudicial to them, by such forms and negatives as they may see fit to provide. From all these, and many other well founded considerations, I need not mention, a question arises, what powers shall there be delegated to the federal head, to insure safety, as well as energy, in the government? I think there is a safe and proper medium pointed out by experience, by reason, and facts. When we have organized the government, we ought to give power to the union, so far only as experience and present circumstances shall direct, with a reasonable regard to time to come. Should future circumstances, contrary to our expectations, require that further powers be transferred to the union, we can do it far more easily, than get back those we may now imprudently give. The system proposed is untried: candid advocates and opposers admit, that it is, in a degree, a mere experiment, and that its organization is weak and imperfect; surely then, the safe ground is cautiously to vest power in it, and when we are sure we have given enough for ordinary exigencies, to be extremely careful how we delegate powers, which, in common cases, must necessarily be useless or abused, and of very uncertain effect in uncommon ones.

By giving the union power to regulate commerce, and to levy and collect taxes by imposts, we give it an extensive authority, and permanent productive funds, I believe quite as adequate to the present demands of the union, as excises and direct taxes can be made to the present demands of the separate states. The state governments are now about four times as expensive as that of the union; and their several state debts added together, are nearly as large as that of the union—Our impost duties since the peace have been almost as productive as the other sources of taxation, and when under one general system of regulations, the probability is, that those duties will be very considerably increased: Indeed the representation proposed will hardly justify giving to congress unlimited powers to raise taxes by imposts, in addition to the other powers the union must necessarily have. It is said, that if congress possess only authority to raise taxes by imposts, trade probably will be overburdened with taxes, and the taxes of the union be found inadequate to any uncommon exigencies: To this we may observe, that trade generally finds its own level, and will naturally and necessarily heave off any undue burdens laid upon it: further, if congress alone possess the impost, and also unlimited power to raise monies by excises and direct taxes, there must be much more danger that two taxing powers, the union and states, will carry excises and direct taxes to an unreasonable extent, especially as these have not the natural boundaries taxes on trade have. However, it is not my object to propose to exclude congress from raising monies by internal taxes, as by duties, excises, and direct taxes; but my opinion is, that congress, especially in its proposed organization, ought not to raise monies by internal taxes, except in strict conformity to the federal plan; that is, by the agency of the state governments in all cases, except where a state shall neglect, for an unreasonable time, to pay its quota of a requisition; and never where so many of the state legislatures as represent a majority of the people, shall formally determine an excise law or requisition is improper, in their next session after the same be laid before them. We ought always to recollect that the evil to be guarded against is found by our own experience, and the experience of others, to be mere neglect in the states to pay their quotas; and power in the union to levy and collect the neglecting states' quotas with interest, is fully adequate to the evil. By this federal plan, with this exception mentioned, we secure the means of collecting the taxes by the usual process of law, and avoid the evil of attempting to compel or coerce a state; and we avoid also a circumstance, which never yet could be, and I am fully confident never can be, admitted in a free federal republic; I mean a permanent and continued system of tax laws of the union, executed in the bowels of the states by many thousand officers, dependent as to the assessing and collecting federal taxes, solely upon the union. On every principle then, we ought to provide, that the union render an exact account of all monies raised by imposts and other taxes; and that whenever monies shall be wanted for the purposes of the union, beyond the proceeds of the impost duties, requisitions shall be made on the states for the monies so wanted; and that the power of laying and collecting shall never be exercised, except in cases where a state shall neglect, a given time, to pay its quota. This mode seems to be strongly pointed out by the reason of the case, and spirit of the government; and I believe, there is no instance to be found in a federal republic, where the congressional powers ever extended generally to collecting monies by direct taxes or excises. Creating all these restrictions, still the powers of the union in matters of taxation, will be too unlimited; further checks, in my mind, are indispensably necessary. Nor do I conceive, that as full a representation as is practicable in the federal government, will afford sufficient security: the strength of the government, and the confidence of the people, must be collected principally in the local assemblies; every part or branch of the federal head must be feeble, and unsafely trusted with large powers. A government possessed of more power than its constituent parts will justify, will not only probably abuse it, but be unequal to bear its own burden; it may as soon be destroyed by the pressure of power, as languish and perish for want of it.

There are two ways further of raising checks, and guarding against undue combinations and influence in a federal system. The first is, in levying taxes, raising and keeping up armies, in building navies, in forming plans for the militia, and in appropriating monies for the support of the military, to require the attendance of a large proportion of the federal representatives, as two-thirds or three-fourths of them; and in passing laws, in these important cases, to require the consent of two-thirds or three-fourths of the members present. The second is, by requiring that certain important laws of the federal head, as a requisition or a law for raising monies by excise shall be laid before the state legislatures, and if disapproved of by a given number of them, say by as many of them as represent a majority of the people, the law shall have no effect. Whether it would be adviseable to adopt both, or either of these checks, I will not undertake to determine. We have seen them both exist in confederated republics. The first exists substantially in the confederation, and will exist in some measure in the plan proposed, as in chusing a president by the house, in expelling members; in the senate, in making treaties, and in deciding on impeachments, and in the whole in altering the constitution. The last exists in the United Netherlands, but in a much greater extent. The first is founded on this principle, that these important measures may, sometimes, be adopted by a bare quorum of members, perhaps, from a few states, and that a bare majority of the federal representatives may frequently be of the aristocracy, or some particular interests, connections, or parties in the community, and governed by motives, views, and inclinations not compatible with the general interest.—The last is founded on this principle, that the people will be substantially represented, only in their state or local assemblies; that their principal security must be found in them; and that, therefore, they ought to have ultimately a constitutional controul over such interesting measures.

I have often heard it observed, that our people are well informed, and will not submit to oppressive governments; that the state governments will be their ready advocates, and possess their confidence, mix with them, and enter into all their wants and feelings. This is all true; but of what avail will these circumstances be, if the state governments, thus allowed to be the guardians of the people, possess no kind of power by the forms of the social compact, to stop, in their passage, the laws of congress injurious to the people. State governments must stand and see the law take place; they may complain and petition—so may individuals; the members of them, in extreme cases, may resist, on the principles of self-defence—so may the people and individuals.

It has been observed, that the people, in extensive territories, have more power, compared with that of their rulers, than in small states. Is not directly the opposite true? The people in a small state can unite and act in concert, and with vigour; but in large territories, the men who govern find it more easy to unite, while people cannot; while they cannot collect the opinions of each part, while they move to different points, and one part is often played off against the other.

It has been asserted, that the confederate head of a republic at best, is in general weak and dependent;—that the people will attach themselves to, and support their local governments, in all disputes with the union. Admit the fact: is it any way to remove the inconvenience by accumulating powers upon a weak organization? The fact is, that the detail administration of affairs, in this mixed republic, depends principally on the local governments; and the people would be wretched without them: and a great proportion of social happiness depends on the internal administration of justice, and on internal police. The splendor of the monarch, and the power of the government are one thing. The happiness of the subject depends on very different causes: but it is to the latter, that the best men, the greatest ornaments of human nature, have most carefully attended: it is to the former tyrants and oppressors have always aimed.

## LETTER XVIII.

JANUARY 25, 1788.

DEAR SIR, I am persuaded, a federal head never was formed, that possessed half the powers which it could carry into full effect, altogether independently of the state or local governments, as the one, the convention has proposed, will possess. Should the state legislatures never meet, except merely for chusing federal senators and appointing electors, once in four and six years, the federal head may go on for ages to make all laws relative to the following subjects, and by its own courts, officers, and provisions, carry them into full effect, and to any extent it may deem for the general welfare; that is, for *raising taxes*, borrowing and coining monies, and for applying them—for forming and governing *armies* and *navies*, and for directing their operations— for regulating commerce with foreign nations, and among the several states, and with the Indian tribes—for regulating *bankruptcies*, weights and measures, post-offices and post-roads, and captures on land and water—for establishing a uniform rule of naturalization, and for promoting the progress of science and useful arts—for defining and punishing piracies and felonies committed on the high seas, the offences of counterfeiting the securities and current coin of the United States, and offences against the law of nations, and for regulating all maritime concerns—for *organizing, arming* and *disciplining* the militia (the respective states training them, and appointing the officers)—for *calling them forth* when wanted, and for governing them when in the service of the union—for the *sole and exclusive government* of a federal city or town, not exceeding ten miles square, and of places ceded for forts, magazines, arsenals, dock-yards, and other needful buildings—for granting letters of marque and reprisal, and making war—for regulating the *times, places,* and *manner of holding elections* for senators and representatives—for making and concluding all treaties, and carrying them into execution—for judicially deciding all questions arising on the constitution, laws, and treaties of the union, in law and equity, and questions arising on state laws also, where ambassadors, other public ministers, and consuls, where the United States, individual states, or a state, where *citizens of different states,* and where foreign states, or a *foreign subject,* are parties or party—for impeaching and trying federal officers—for deciding on elections, and for expelling members, &c. All these enumerated powers we must examine and contemplate in all their extent and various branches, and then reflect, that the federal head will have full power to make all laws whatever respecting them; and for carrying into full effect all powers vested in the union, in any department, or officers of it, by the constitution, in order to see the full extent of the federal powers, which will be supreme, and exercised by that head at pleasure, conforming to the few limitations mentioned in the constitution. Indeed, I conceive, it is impossible to see them in their full extent at present: we see vast undefined powers lodged in a weak organization, but cannot, by the enquiries of months and years, clearly discern them in all their numerous branches. These powers in feeble hands, must be tempting objects for ambition and a love of power and fame.

But, say the advocates, they are all necessary for forming an energetic federal government; all necessary in the hands of the union, for the common defence and general welfare. In these great points they appear to me to go from the end to the means, and from the means to the end, perpetually begging the question. I think in the course of these letters, I shall sufficiently prove, that some of these powers need not be lodged in the hands of the union—that others ought to be exercised under better checks, and in part, by the agency of the states—some I have already considered, some in my mind, are not liable to objections, and the others, I shall briefly notice in this closing letter.

The power to controul the military forces of the country, as well as the revenues of it, requires serious attention. Here again, I must premise, that a federal republic is a compound system, made up of constituent parts, each essential to the whole: we must then expect the real friends of such a system will always be very anxious for the security and preservation of each part, and to this end, that each constitutionally possess its natural portion of power and influence—and that it will constantly be an object of concern to them, to see one part armed at all points by the constitution, and in a manner destructive in the end, even of its own existence, and the others left constitutionally defenceless.

The military forces of a free country may be considered under three general descriptions—1. The militia. 2. the navy—and 3. the regular troops—and the whole ought ever to be, and understood to be, in strict subordination to the civil authority; and that regular troops, and select corps, ought not to be kept up without evident necessity. Stipulations in the constitution to this effect, are perhaps, too general to be of much service, except merely to impress on the minds of the people and soldiery, that the military ought ever to be subject to the civil authority, &c. But particular attention, and many more definite stipulations, are highly necessary to render the military safe, and yet useful in a free government; and in a federal republic, where the people meet in distinct assemblies, many stipulations are necessary to keep a part from transgressing, which would be unnecessary checks against the whole met in one legislature, in one entire government.— A militia, when properly formed, are in fact the people themselves, and render regular troops in a great measure unnecessary. The powers to form and arm the militia, to appoint their officers, and to command their services, are very important; nor ought they in a confederated republic to be lodged, solely, in any one member of the government. First, the constitution ought to secure a genuine and guard against a select militia, by providing that the militia shall always be kept well organized, armed, and disciplined, and include, according to the past and general usuage of the states, all men capable of bearing arms; and that all regulations tending to render this general militia useless and defenceless, by establishing select corps of militia, or distinct bodies of military men, not having permanent interests and attachments in the community to be avoided. I am persuaded, I need not multiply words to convince you of the value and solidity of this principle, as it respects general liberty, and the duration of a free and mild government: having this principle well fixed by the constitution, then the federal head may prescribe a general uniform plan, on which the respective states shall form and train the militia, appoint their officers and solely manage them, except when called into the service of the union, and when called into that service, they may be commanded and governed by the union. This arrangement combines energy and safety in it; it places the sword in the hands of the solid interest of the community, and not in the hands of men destitute of property, of principle, or of attachment to the society and government, who often form the select corps of peace or ordinary establishments: by it, the militia are the people, immediately under the management of the state governments, but on a uniform federal plan, and called into the service, command, and government of the union, when necessary for the common defence and general tranquility. But, say gentlemen, the general militia are for the most part employed at home in their private concerns, cannot well be called out, or be depended upon; that we must have a select militia; that is, as I understand it, particular corps or bodies of young men, and of men who have but little to do at home, particularly armed and disciplined in some measure, at the public expence, and always ready to take the field. These corps, not much unlike regular troops, will ever produce an inattention to the general militia; and the consequence has ever been, and always must be, that the substantial men, having families and property, will generally be without arms, without knowing the use of them, and defenceless; whereas, to preserve liberty, it is essential that the whole body of the people always possess arms, and be taught alike, especially when young, how to use them; nor does it follow from this, that all promiscuously must go into actual service on every occasion. The mind that aims at a select militia, must be influenced by a truly anti-republican principle; and when we see many men disposed to practice upon it, whenever they can prevail, no wonder true republicans are for carefully guarding against it. As a farther check, it may be proper to add, that the militia of any state shall not remain in the service of the union, beyond a given period, without the express consent of the state legislature.

As to the navy, I do not see that it can have any connection with the local governments. The want of employment for it, and the want of monies in the hands of the union, must be its proper limitation. The laws for building or increasing it, as all the important laws mentioned in a former letter,[47] touching military and money matters, may be checked by requiring the attendance of a large proportion of the representatives, and the consent of a large proportion of those present, to pass them as before mentioned.

By art. 1. sect. 8. "Congress shall have *power to provide for* organizing, arming, and disciplining the militia": *power to provide for*—does this imply any more than power to prescribe a general uniform plan? And must not the respective states pass laws (but in conformity to the plan) for forming and training the militia.

In the present state of mankind, and of conducting war, the government of every nation must have power to raise and keep up regular troops: the question is, how shall this power be lodged? In an entire government, as in Great-Britain, where the people assemble by their representatives in one legislature, there is no difficulty, it is of course properly lodged in that legislature: But in a confederated republic, where the organization consists of a federal head, and local governments, there is no one part in which it can be solely, and safely lodged. By art. 1. sect. 8. "congress shall have power to raise and support armies," &c. By art. 1. sect. 10. "no state, without the consent of congress, shall keep troops, or ships of war, in time of peace." It seems fit the union should direct the raising of troops, and the union may do it in two ways; by requisitions on the states, or by direct taxes— the first is most conformable to the federal plan, and safest; and it may be improved, by giving the union power, by its own laws and officers, to raise the states quota that may neglect, and to charge it with the expence; and by giving a fixed quorum of the state legislatures power to disapprove the requisition. There would be less danger in this power to raise troops, could the state governments keep a proper controul over the purse and over the militia; but after all the precautions we can take, without evidently fettering the union too much, we must give a large accumulation of powers to it, in these and other respects. There is one check, which, I think, may be added with great propriety—that is, no land forces shall be kept up, but by legislative acts annually passed by congress, and no appropriation of monies for their support shall be for a longer term than one year. This is the constitutional practice in Great-Britain, and the reasons for such checks in the United States appear to be much stronger. We may also require that these acts be passed by a special majority, as before mentioned. There is another mode still more guarded, and which seems to be founded in the true spirit of a federal system: it seems proper to divide those powers we can with safety, lodge them in no one member of the government alone; yet substantially to preserve their use, and to ensure duration to the government, by modifying the exercise of them—it is to empower congress to raise troops by direct levies, not exceeding a given number, say 2000 in time of peace, and 12,000 in a time of war, and for such further troops as may be wanted, to raise them by requisitions qualified as before mentioned. By the above recited clause no state shall keep troops, &c. in time of peace—this clearly implies, it may do it in time of war: this must be on the principle, that the union cannot defend all parts of the republic, and suggests an idea very repugnant to the general tendency of the system proposed, which is to disarm the state governments: a state in a long war may collect forces sufficient to take the field against the neighbouring states. This clause was copied from the confederation, in which it was of more importance than in the plan proposed, because under this the separate states, probably, will have but small revenues.

By article 1. section 8. congress shall have power to establish uniform laws on the subject of bankruptcies, throughout the United States. It is to be observed, that the separate states have ever been in possession of the power, and in the use of it, of making bankrupt laws, militia laws, and laws in some other cases, respecting which, the new constitution, when adopted, will give the union power to legislate, &c.—but no words are used by the constitution to exclude the jurisdiction of the several states, and whether they will be excluded or not, or whether they and the union will have concurrent jurisdiction or not, must be determined by inference; and from the nature of the subject; if the power, for instance, to make uniform laws on the subject of bankruptcies, is in its nature indivisible, or incapable of being exercised by two legislatures independently, or by one in aid of the other, then the states are excluded, and cannot legislate at all on the subject, even though the union should neglect or find it impracticable to establish uniform bankrupt laws. How far the union will find it practicable to do this, time only can fully determine. When we consider the extent of the country, and the very different ideas of the different parts in it, respecting credit, and the mode of making men's property liable for paying their debts, we may, I think, with some degree of certainty, conclude that the union never will be able to establish such laws; but if practicable, it does not appear to me, on further reflection, that the union ought to have the power; it does not appear to me to be a power properly incidental to a federal head, and, I believe, no one ever possessed it; it is a power that will immediately and extensively interfere with the internal police of the separate states, especially with their administering justice among their own citizens. By giving this power to the union, we greatly extend the jurisdiction of the federal judiciary, as all questions arising on bankrupt laws, being laws of the union, even between citizens of the same state, may be tried in the federal courts; and I think it may be shewn, that by the help of these laws, actions between citizens of different states, and the laws of the federal city, aided by no overstrained judicial fictions, almost all civil causes may be drawn into those courts. We must be sensible how cautious we ought to be in extending unnecessarily the jurisdiction of those courts for reasons I need not repeat. This article of power too, will considerably increase, in the hands of the union, an accumulation of powers, some of a federal and some of a unfederal nature, too large without it.

The constitution provides, that congress shall have the sole and exclusive government of what is called the federal city, a place not exceeding ten miles square, and of all places ceded for forts, dock-yards, &c. I believe this is a novel kind of provision in a federal republic; it is repugnant to the spirit of such a government, and must be founded in an apprehension of a hostile disposition between the federal head and the state governments; and it is not improbable, that the sudden retreat of congress from Philadelphia, first gave rise to it.[48]—With this apprehension, we provide, the government of the union shall have secluded places, cities, and castles of defence, which no state laws whatever shall invade. When we attentively examine this provision in all its consequences, it opens to view scenes almost without bounds. A federal, or rather a national city, ten miles square, containing a hundred square miles, is about four times as large as London; and for forts, magazines, arsenals, dock-yards, and other needful buildings, congress may possess a number of places or towns in each state. It is true, congress cannot have them unless the state legislatures cede them; but when once ceded, they never can be recovered, and though the general temper of the legislatures may be averse to such cessions, yet many opportunities and advantages may be taken of particular times and circumstances of complying assemblies, and of particular parties, to obtain them. It is not improbable, that some considerable towns or places, in some intemperate moments, or influenced by anti-republican principles, will petition to be ceded for the purposes mentioned in the provision. There are men, and even towns, in the best republics, which are often fond of withdrawing from the government of them, whenever occasion shall present. The case is still stronger; if the provision in question holds out allurements to attempt to withdraw, the people of a state must ever be subject to state as well as federal taxes; but the federal city and places will be subject only to the latter, and to them by no fixed proportion; nor of the taxes raised in them, can the separate states demand any account of congress.—These doors opened for withdrawing from the state governments entirely, may, on other accounts, be very alluring and pleasing to those anti-republican men who prefer a place under the wings of courts.

If a federal town be necessary for the residence of congress and the public officers, it ought to be a small one, and the government of it fixed on republican and common law principles, carefully enumerated and established by the constitution. It is true, the states, when they shall cede places, may stipulate, that the laws and government of congress in them, shall always be formed on such principles; but it is easy to discern, that the stipulations of a state, or of the inhabitants of the place ceded, can be of but little avail against the power and gradual encroachments of the union. The principles ought to be established by the federal constitution, to which all the states are parties; but in no event can there be any need of so large a city and places for forts, &c. totally exempted from the laws and jurisdictions of the state governments. If I understand the constitution, the laws of congress, constitutionally made, will have complete and supreme jurisdiction to all federal purposes, on every inch of ground in the United States, and exclusive jurisdiction on the high seas, and this by the highest authority, the consent of the people. Suppose ten acres at West-Point shall be used as a fort of the union, or a sea port town as a dock-yard, the laws of the union in those places respecting the navy, forces of the union, and all federal objects, must prevail, be noticed by all judges and officers, and executed accordingly: and I can discern no one reason for excluding from these places, the operation of state laws, as to mere state purposes; for instance, for the collection of state taxes in them, recovering debts, deciding questions of property arising within them on state laws, punishing, by state laws, theft, trespasses, and offences committed in them by mere citizens against the state laws.

The city, and all the places in which the union shall have this exclusive jurisdiction, will be immediately under one entire government, that of the federal head; and be no part of any state, and consequently no part of the United States. The inhabitants of the federal city and places, will be as much exempt from the laws and controul of the state governments, as the people of Canada or Nova Scotia will be. Neither the laws of the states respecting taxes, the militia, crimes or property, will extend to them; nor is there a single stipulation in the constitution, that the inhabitants of this city, and these places, shall be governed by laws founded on principles of freedom. All questions, civil and criminal, arising on the laws of these places, which must be the laws of congress, must be decided in the federal courts; and also, all questions that may, by such judicial fictions as these courts may consider reasonable, be supposed to arise within this city, or any of these places, may be brought into these courts; and by a very common legal fiction, any personal contract may be supposed to have been made in any place. A contract made in Georgia may be supposed to have been made in the federal city, in Pennsylvania; the courts will admit the fiction, and not in these cases, make it a serious question, where it was in fact made. Every suit in which an inhabitant of a federal district may be a party, of course may be instituted in the federal courts—also, every suit in which it may be alledged, and not denied, that a party in it is an inhabitant of such a district—also, every suit to which a foreign state or subject, the union, a state, citizens of different states, in fact, or by reasonable legal fictions, may be a party or parties: And thus, by means of bankrupt laws, federal districts, &c. almost all judicial business, I apprehend may be carried into the federal courts, without essentially departing from the usual course of judicial proceedings. The courts in Great Britain have acquired their powers, and extended, very greatly, their jurisdictions by such fictions and suppositions as I have mentioned. The constitution, in these points, certainly involves in it principles, and almost hidden cases, which may unfold, and in time exhibit consequences we hardly think of. The power of naturalization, when viewed in connection with the judicial powers and cases, is, in my mind, of very doubtful extent. By the constitution itself, the citizens of each state will be naturalized citizens of every state, to the general purposes of instituting suits, claiming the benefits of the laws, &c. And in order to give the federal courts jurisdiction of an action, between citizens of the same state, in common acceptation, may not a court allow the plaintiff to say, he is a citizen of one state, and the defendant a citizen of another, without carrying legal fictions so far, by any means, as they have been carried by the courts of King's Bench and Exchequer, in order to bring causes within their cognizance—Further, the federal city and districts, will be totally distinct from any state, and a citizen of a state will not of course be a subject of any of them; and to avail himself of the privileges and immunities of them, must he not be naturalized by congress in them? and may not congress make any proportion of the citizens of the states naturalized subjects of the federal city and districts, and thereby entitle them to sue or defend, in all cases, in the federal courts? I have my doubts, and many sensible men, I find, have their doubts, on these points; and we ought to observe, they must be settled in the courts of law, by their rules, distinctions, and fictions. To avoid many of these intricacies and difficulties, and to avoid the undue and unnecessary extension of the federal judicial powers, it appears to me, that no federal districts ought to be allowed, and no federal city or town, except perhaps a small town, in which the government shall be republican, but in which congress shall have no jurisdiction over the inhabitants, but in common with the other inhabitants of the states. Can the union want, in such a town, any thing more than a right to the soil on which it may set its buildings, and extensive jurisdiction over the federal buildings, and property, its own members, officers, and servants in it? As to all federal objects, the union will have complete jurisdiction over them, of course any where, and every where. I still think, that no actions ought to be allowed to be brought in the federal courts, between citizens of different states, at least, unless the cause be of very considerable importance: that no action against a state government, by any citizen or foreigner, ought to be allowed, and no action, in which a foreign subject is party, at least, unless it be of very considerable importance, ought to be instituted in the federal courts—I confess, I can see no reason whatever, for a foreigner, or for citizens of different states, carrying sixpenny causes into the federal courts; I think the state courts will be found by experience, to be bottomed on better principles, and to administer justice better than the federal courts.

The difficulties and dangers I have supposed, will result from so large a federal city, and federal districts, from the extension of the federal judicial powers, &c. are not, I conceive, merely possible, but probable. I think, pernicious political consequences will follow from them, and from the federal city especially, for very obvious reasons, a few of which I will mention.

We must observe, that the citizens of a state will be subject to state as well as federal taxes, and the inhabitants of the federal city and districts, only to such taxes as congress may lay—We are not to suppose all our people are attached to free government, and the principles of the common law, but that many thousands of them will prefer a city governed, not on republican principles—This city, and the government of it, must indubitably take their tone from the characters of the men, who from the nature of its situation and institution, must collect there. This city will not be established for productive labour, for mercantile, or mechanic industry; but for the residence of government, its officers and attendants. If hereafter it should ever become a place of trade and industry, in the early periods of its existence, when its laws and government must receive their fixed tone, it must be a mere court, with its appendages, the executive, congress, the law courts, gentlemen of fortune and pleasure, with all the officers, attendants, suitors, expectants and dependants on the whole, however brilliant and honourable this collection may be, if we expect it will have any sincere attachments to simple and frugal republicanism, to that liberty and mild government, which is dear to the laborious part of a free people, we most assuredly deceive ourselves. This early collection will draw to it men from all parts of the country, of a like political description: we see them looking towards the place already.

Such a city, or town, containing a hundred square miles, must soon be the great, the visible, and dazzling centre, the mistress of fashions, and the fountain of politics. There may be a free or shackled press in this city, and the streams which may issue from it may overflow the country, and they will be poisonous or pure, as the fountain may be corrupt or not. But not to dwell on a subject that must give pain to the virtuous friends of freedom, I will only add, can a free and enlightened people create a common head so extensive, so prone to corruption and slavery, as this city probably will be, when they have it in their power to form one pure and chaste, frugal and republican.

Under the confederation congress has no power whereby to govern its own officers and servant[s]; a federal town, in which congress might have special jurisdiction, might be expedient; but under the new constitution, without a federal town, congress will have all necessary powers of course over its officers and servants; indeed it will have a complete system of powers to all the federal purposes mentioned in the constitution; so that the reason for a federal town under the confederation, will by no means exist under the constitution.—Even if a trial by jury should be admitted in the federal city, what man, with any state attachments or republican virtue about him, will submit to be tried by a jury of it.

I might observe more particularly upon several other parts of the constitution proposed; but it has been uniformly my object in examining a subject so extensive, and difficult in many parts to be illustrated, to avoid unimportant things, and not to dwell upon points not very material. The rule for apportioning requisitions on the states, having some time since been agreed to by eleven states,[49] I have viewed as settled. The stipulation that congress, after twenty one years may prohibit the importation of slaves, is a point gained, if not so favourable as could be wished for. As monopolies in trade perhaps, can in no case be useful, it might not be amiss to provide expressly against them. I wish the power to repri[e]ve and pardon was more cautiously lodged, and under some limitations. I do not see why congress should be allowed to consent that a person may accept a present, office, or title of a foreign prince, &c. As to the state governments, as well as the federal, are essential parts of the system, why should not the oath taken by the officers be expressly to support the whole? As to debts due to and from the union, I think the constitution intends, on examining art. 4. sect. 8. and art. 6. that they shall stand on the same ground under the constitution as under the confederation. In the article respecting amendments, it is stipulated that no state shall ever be deprived of its equal vote in the senate without its consent; and that alterations may be made by the consent of three-fourths of the states. Stipulations to bind the majority of the people may serve one purpose, to prevent frequent motions for change; but these attempts to bind the majority, generally give occasion for breach of contract. The states all agreed about seven years ago, that the confederation should remain unaltered, unless every state should agree to alterations:[50] but we now see it agreed by the convention, and four states,[51] that the old confederacy shall be destroyed, and a new one, of nine states, be erected, if nine only shall come in. Had we agreed, that a majority should alter the confederation, a majority's agreeing would have bound the rest: but now we must break the old league, unless all the states agree to alter, or not proceed with adopting the constitution. Whether the adoption by nine states will not produce a nearly equal and dangerous division of the people for and against the constitution—whether the circumstances of the country were such as to justify the hazarding a probability of such a situation, I shall not undertake to determine. I shall leave it to be determined hereafter, whether nine states, under a new federal compact, can claim the benefits of any treaties made with a confederation of thirteen, under a distinct compact and form of existence—whether the new confederacy can recover debts due to the old confederacy, or the arrears of taxes due from the states excluded.

It has been well observed, that our country is extensive, and has no external enemies to press the parts together: that, therefore, their union must depend on strong internal ties. I differ with the gentlemen who make these observations only in this, they hold the ties ought to be strengthened by a considerable degree of internal consolidation; and my object is to form them and strengthen them, on pure federal principles. Whatever may be the fate of many valuable and necessary amendments in the constitution proposed, the ample discussion and respectable opposition it will receive, will have a good effect—they will operate to produce a mild and prudent administration, and to put the wheels of the whole system in motion on proper principles—they will evince, that true republican principles and attachments are still alive and formidable in this country. These, in view, I believe, even men quite disposed to make a bad use of the system, will long hesitate before they will resolve to do it. A majority from a view of our situation, and influenced by many considerations, may acquiese in the adoption of this constitution; but, it is evident, that a very great majority of the people of the United States think it, in many parts, an unnecessary and unadviseable departure from true republican and federal principles.

1. A reference to George Mason, Elbridge Gerry, and Richard Henry Lee. For examples of attacks on their published writings criticizing the Constitution, see CC:227, 276, 325; and for attacks on Mason and Gerry for not signing the Constitution, see CC:171.

2. "Junius" was most likely the pseudonym of Philip Francis (1740–1818), the first clerk of the British War Office, who in late 1768 launched (under that signature) a series of more than sixty newspaper articles in the London *Public Advertiser* attacking the Duke of Grafton's ministry for maladministration and violating the constitution, thereby endangering the rights and liberties of Englishmen. He continued these attacks against the succeeding administration of Lord North. In 1772 the publisher of the *Public Advertiser*, printed these essays in two volumes as *The Letters of Junius* which were prepared for press by the author himself.

3. This paragraph and the following six paragraphs summarize the Articles of Confederation (CDR, 86–94).

4. See Letters II and III (CC:242), 25–26, 30–31.

5. In commenting upon the discussion of representation and suffrage which follows, the reviewer of the *Additional Letters* in the May issue of the New York *American Magazine* (probably Noah Webster) states that "The author maintains that the federal representation will be too small, and that all orders of men, merchants, farmers, mechanics, &c. should be represented by some of their own professions. In these positions, especially in the latter, we do not agree with the Federal Farmer. The suffrages of the people must be left free. To restrict them to particular classes of men would be an abridgement of that liberty for which our author contends. But the principle that each order of men should be separately represented in the national Legislature, is not well founded. However it may be useful or necessary to represent each profession in the state assemblies, yet the principle will not apply to the federal legislature; for in the latter, *States* are represented, and not particular orders or districts. The people at large, it is true, choose the delegates of one branch; but the men chosen represent the *collective interest* of all orders—the State. Delegates, therefore, should understand, not merely the interest of *one order* of men, but the *combined interest* of the community. He should be a man of *general information.*"

6. See note 4 (above).

7. Cesare Bonesana, Marchese di Beccaria, *An Essay on Crimes and Punishments* (3rd ed., London, 1770), 1. (This work was first published in Livorno [Leghorn] in 1764.) The passage quoted here represents the first two sentences of Beccaria's "Introduction." It was quoted in "An Address to the Inhabitants of the Province of Quebec," adopted by the First Continental Congress on 26 October 1774 (JCC, I, 106). Thomas Cushing, Richard Henry Lee, and John Dickinson composed the committee that drafted this address, which was printed in Philadelphia in both English and French by order of Congress. A German edition, for which Congress had made Pennsylvania's delegates responsible, was also printed in Philadelphia. The address was then reprinted in several other towns and cities (Evans 13726–36, 13740).

8. *Spirit of Laws*, I, Book XI, chapter VI, 226.

9. *Ibid.*, I, Book II, chapter II, 11–18. This chapter is entitled: "Of the Republican Government, and the Laws in relation to Democracy."

10. Commenting on this passage while addressing the New York Convention on 21 June 1788, Alexander Hamilton stated that "The author reckons in the aristocracy, all governors of states, members of Congress, chief magistrates, and all officers of the militia.—This description, I presume to say, is ridiculous.—The image is a phantom. Does the new government render a rich man more eligible than a poor one? No. It requires no such qualification. It is bottomed on the broad and equal principle of your state

constitution" (*The Debates and Proceedings of the Convention of the State of New-York . . .* [New York, 1788], 39 [Evans 21310]).

11. See Letters VIII–X (below).

12. A reference to Jean Louis De Lolme, *The Constitution of England . . .* , which was first published in French in 1771. Between 1775 and 1788, more than ten English-language editions appeared, none of them in America.

13. See De Lolme, *The Constitution of England . . .* (London, 1816), Book II, chapter VI, 256–59. "Federal Farmer" refers to a footnote at the end of the chapter entitled "Advantages that accrue to the People from appointing Representatives." The footnote reads: "All the above reasoning essentially requires that the representatives of the people should be united in interests with the people. We shall soon see that this union really prevails in the English constitution, and may be called the master-piece of it."

14. "Junius's" Letter XVIII, dated 29 July 1769 and addressed to Sir William Blackstone, solicitor general to Her Majesty, states that "laws you know are intended to guard against what men *may* do, not to trust to what they *will* do" (John Cannon, ed., *The Letters of Junius* [Oxford, Eng., 1978], 97).

15. *The Constitution of England*, Book II, chapter V, 240–55. The chapter is entitled: "In which an Inquiry is made, whether it would be an Advantage to public Liberty, that the Laws should be enacted by the Votes of the People at large."

16. See Letter VII (above).

17. On 10 July 1787, James Madison moved in the Constitutional Convention that the proposed number of representatives in the first branch of the legislature, sixty-five, be doubled. Supported by Elbridge Gerry, George Mason, and George Read, the motion was defeated, nine states to two. The ratio of 1:40,000, first proposed on 5 July by a committee appointed to resolve the question of representation in the two houses of Congress, was incorporated into the Committee of Detail report of 6 August and adopted by the Convention on 8 August. The question of the ratio of representation arose several more times, for the last time on 17 September, when the Convention unanimously adopted Nathaniel Gorham's motion (supported by George Washington in his only recorded speech) that the ratio be changed to 1:30,000 (Farrand, I, 527, 568–70; II, 178, 223, 643–44). For more on Washington's role, see CC:233.

18. According to Article V of the Articles of Confederation, no state could "be represented in Congress by less than two, nor by more than seven Members" (CDR, 87). Most states elected fewer than seven delegates annually. It is true that the thirteen states could appoint as many as ninety-one delegates (seven each) to Congress, but for the federal year beginning November 1786 the thirteen states appointed fewer than sixty delegates.

19. See Letter X (below).

20. See Letter XVII (below).

21. See Letter IX (above).

22. See Letter VI (above).

23. See Letter XVII (below).

24. Commenting on this section dealing with rotation in office, the reviewer (probably Noah Webster) in the May issue of the New York *American Magazine* stated: "We likewise differ from our author in respect to the principle of *rotation*. It is a favorite maxim in some of the States, that when a man has served as an officer a year or a number of years, he should be rendered ineligible, at least for a time. The maxim deserves ridicule; but I will treat it with more respect. It is objectionable in two points of view. In the first place, it is a reflection on the integrity and understanding of the freemen who are to be future electors; and in the second place, it is an usurpation of power by the State that adopts the principle. For a freeman to say that he dares not trust himself with the

full power of election, three years hence is a gross insult to his own understanding; and for the freemen of a State, this year, to declare that the freeman of the State, three years hence, shall not exercise the same unlimited power of choosing legislators, as they themselves exercise, is a flagrant violation of the *first* and *best* privilege in government. That there may be a propriety in a rotation of offices, at certain times, is certain; but there may be also a great impropriety in it at other times; and of this propriety or impropriety, the free men have at *all times* the unlimited right of judging."

25. *Spirit of Laws*, I, Book II, chapter II, 12.

26. See Letter III (CC:242), 31–32, 33.

27. In the first federal elections of members to the U.S. House of Representatives, the Massachusetts legislature divided the state into eight districts and required a majority vote to win each election. Four districts needed at least a second election, while one district (Hampshire-Berkshire) needed five elections. See DHFFE, I, chapter 5, *passim*.

28. In the eighteenth century, "nervous" was defined as strong, vigorous, or robust.

29. See Letter VI (above).

30. In those districts that failed to elect state senators by a majority vote, the members of the House of Representatives and the duly elected senators would vote by ballot from a slate of candidates not exceeding double the number of vacancies to be filled (Thorpe, III, 1897).

31. See Letter IX (above).

32. Under the Virginia Resolutions of 29 May 1787 members of Congress were "to be ineligible to any office established by a particular State, or under the authority of the United States, except those peculiarly belonging to the functions of the first [or second] branch, during the term of service, and for the space of ___ after its expiration." On 12 June the Convention inserted "one year" in the blank space after defeating a motion that would have made it three years. On 22 and 23 June and 14 August the Convention defeated attempts to make the prohibition milder, although on 23 June it agreed to strike out the words "by a particular State." Finally, on 3 September those who wanted a milder prohibition were successful and the clause was changed to read: "The members of each House shall be ineligible to any Civil office under the authority of the U. States, created, or the emoluments whereof shall have been increased during the time for which they shall respectively be elected—And no person holding any office under the U.S. shall be a member of either House during his continuance in office" (Farrand, I, 20–21, 210, 217, 370, 375–77, 383, 386–90; II, 282, 283–91, 483, 484, 486–87, 489–92). For Convention delegate Luther Martin's discussion of this provision, see *Genuine Information*, V, Baltimore *Maryland Gazette*, 11 January 1788 (CC:441).

33. See Letter XI (above).

34. The text in angle brackets was reprinted in the *New York Journal* on 27 May at the request of "A Customer." The reference that "Federal Farmer" made "to the lengthy writer in New-York" refers to "Publius," the author of *The Federalist*. "A Customer" footnoted the reprinted text between the words "he" and "appears," stating that "*There is a great difference between* appearance *and* reality."

35. The Virginia Resolutions of 29 May 1787 did not stipulate the length of the President's term, only that he would be ineligible for a second term. On 1 June the President's term was set at seven years; it remained so in the 6 August report of the Committee of Detail. On 4 September the Committee of Eleven (David Brearley, chairman) changed the term to four years. Two days later the Convention defeated a motion to restore the seven-year term and another motion setting it at six years (Farrand, I, 21, 68–69; II, 185, 497, 525).

36. The phrase "a great and good man" was often used to describe George Wash-

ington. (See John P. Kaminski and Jill Adair McCaughan, eds., *A Great and Good Man: George Washington in the Eyes of His Contemporaries* [Madison, Wis., 1989].)

37. The judiciary is also discussed briefly in Letter XVIII (below).

38. De Lolme, *The Constitution of England*, Book I, chapter XII, 167–68.

39. In concluding a chapter on trial by jury in criminal cases, De Lolme stated: "All these circumstances have combined to introduce such a mildness into the exercise of criminal justice, that the trial by jury is that point of their liberty to which the people of England are most thoroughly and universally wedded; and the only complaint I have ever heard uttered against it, has been by men who, more sensible of the necessity of public order than alive to the feelings of humanity, think that too many offenders escape with impunity" (*The Constitution of England*, Book I, chapter XIII, 187). De Lolme also called trial by jury "an admirable institution" (p. 182), and in another place he said "In fine, such is the happy nature of this institution, that the judicial power, a power so formidable in itself, which is to dispose, without finding any resistance, of the property, honour, and life of individuals, and which, whatever precautions may be taken to restrain it, must in a great degree remain arbitrary, may be said, in England, to exist,—to accomplish every intended purpose,—and to be in the hands of nobody" (p. 184). For Sir William Blackstone's opinion of the English jury, see note 42 (below).

40. Article II of the Northwest Ordinance, adopted by Congress on 13 July 1787, states that "The inhabitants of the said territory shall always be entitled to the benefits of the writ of habeas corpus, and of the trial by jury; . . . and of judicial proceedings according to the course of the common law; . . . no man shall be deprived of his liberty or property but by the judgment of his peers, or the law of the land. . . ." (CDR, 172).

41. On 6 October 1787 James Wilson, a Pennsylvania signer of the Constitution, stated at a public meeting in Philadelphia that "in delegating fœderal powers, another criterion was necessarily introduced, and the congressional authority is to be collected, not from tacit implication, but from the positive grant expressed in the instrument of union. Hence it is evident, that in the former case [state constitutions] every thing which is not reserved is given, but in the latter the reverse of the proposition prevails, and every thing which is not given, is reserved. This distinction being recognized, will furnish an answer to those who think the omission of a bill of rights, a defect in the proposed constitution: for it would have been superfluous and absurd to have stipulated with a fœderal body of our own creation, that we should enjoy those privileges, of which we are not divested either by the intention or the act, that has brought that body into existence" (CC:134).

42. Blackstone, *Commentaries*, Book III, chapter XXIII, 379. Sir William Blackstone states that "The impartial administration of justice, which secures both our persons and our properties, is the great end of civil society." Chapter XXIII deals with trial by jury which Blackstone considered "the glory of the English law." It was "the most transcendent privilege which any subject can enjoy, or wish for, that he cannot be affected either in his property, his liberty, or his person, but by the unanimous consent of twelve of his neighbours and equals" (*ibid.*).

43. See Letter XV (above).

44. De Lolme, in his introduction to *The Constitution of England* (p. 4), stated that "The English themselves (the observation cannot give them any offence) having their eyes open, as I may say, upon their liberty, from their first entrance into life, are perhaps too much familiarised with its enjoyment, to enquire, with real concern, into its causes. Having acquired practical notions of their government long before they have meditated on it, and these notions being slowly and gradually imbibed, they at length behold it without any high degree of sensibility; and they seem to me, in this respect, to be like

... a man who, having always had a beautiful and extensive scene before his eyes, continues for ever to view it with indifference."

45. De Lolme, *The Constitution of England*, Book I, chapter III, 59.

46. See Letter I (CC:242), 18.

47. See Letter III (CC:242), 39.

48. In June 1783, soldiers of the Pennsylvania Line of the Continental Army demonstrated outside the meeting place of Congress in Philadelphia because Congress had furloughed them without settling their financial accounts. Congress asked the Supreme Executive Council of Pennsylvania to call out the militia, but the Council was reluctant. Congress discussed the matter for several days, and then, for safety's sake, adjourned to Princeton, N.J.

49. In April 1783 Congress proposed an amendment to the Articles of Confederation specifying that requisitions should be raised among the states according to population, not on land as provided for under the Articles (CDR, 148–50). By 1787 every state, except New Hampshire and Rhode Island, had ratified the amendment.

50. The Articles of Confederation, adopted on 1 March 1781, provided that "the union shall be perpetual" and that alterations in them should be made only after the change was agreed to in Congress and "confirmed by the legislatures of every state" (CDR, 93).

51. By 25 January 1788, the date of this letter, the Constitution had been ratified by five states—Delaware, Pennsylvania, New Jersey, Georgia, and Connecticut, in that order. Connecticut adopted the Constitution on 9 January.

### 724. Nicholas Gilman to John Langdon
### New York, 3 May[1]

I am honored with your obliging favor of the 14th Ultimo and most heartily Sympathize with the good Citizens of your place in their present depressed situation;—but at the same time rejoice with you in the hope of relief under the new System of government.—

The flame of opposition enkindled by the adjournment of our Convention is daily decreasing and the prospect of a general adoption begins to brighten.[2]—The enclosed paper announces the ratification by a large Majority of the Convention of Maryland; which is confirmed by authentic letters from a number of Gentlemen.—The federal ticket for members to represent this City in Convention is carryed by a very large majority; and accounts of several elections in the neighbouring Counties (that have come to hand) are much more favourable than was generally expected.—The latest accounts from Virginia are favourable.—Pennsylvania is in a State of tranquility and the general opposition—seems to be once more on the decline.

The State of Georgia has made a large Cession of Western lands to the United States on Conditions that the new System is adopted and that they be allowed thirty thousand dollars for expences in defending that Country.—In haste

P. S. All the bells in this City are now ringing to Celebrate the news from Maryland.

1. RC, John G. M. Stone Collection of Revolutionary and Early National Period Documents, Annapolis, Md. Gilman was a New Hampshire delegate to Congress.

2. For the impact of the adjournment of the New Hampshire Convention without taking a vote on the Constitution, see CC:554. On 22 February Langdon himself, a Federalist Convention delegate from Portsmouth, had moved for adjournment because Antifederalists had the votes to defeat the Constitution.

## 725. Caleb Wallace to William Fleming
### Locust Groves, Ky., 3 May (excerpt)[1]

We have received your sympathetic letter of March the 8th. by Miss M'Bride and one from Mrs. Fleming of the 6th. of April which gave us much consolation, especially as they came from friends whom we are persuaded do realy bear a part of our Affliction.[2] This bereavement and the ill state of health I have been in for some months past have greatly indisposed my mind to political investigations; for which reasons I omitted returning you my sentiments on the proposed form of Continental Government to which you called my attention last fall. But hearing that you have accepted an appointment to our State Convention[3] I shall now attempt a few observations on the interesting subject

As by a Federal Union the independence of the American States was obtained, I have always considered the continuing and perfecting that Confederation equally essential to its permanency and rising glory; therefore the calling a continental Convention was my anxious desire, and I confess on the first perusal the government they have devised seemed in the main to answer my expectations. Wishing Congress to be invested with ample powers to accomplish all federal purposes, the new System pleased me in this which I thought the most important article; in some other instances my feelings were hurt and my fears alarmed, but being much distressed for our National Faith and security I did not then so fully realize, as I have since done, the danger of introducing greater evils than those from which we had been delivered at the expence of much blood and treasure. How common, how natural is it for narrow minded man by avoiding *Scylla* to fall into *Charybdis*! To say no more in this way our American sages have erred. The complication of powers and prerogatives they have heaped on their Senate President and Vice President are intolerable. Their Judicial Courts in various respects are equally so. Their omitting a Declaration of Rights almost induces me to suspect the virtue of their intentions. And their want of precision in defining the limits of the several departments of their intended Government gives suspicion an ascendency I wish my charity to possess. I have lately perused Masons Randolph's and Gerry's reasons for dissent[4] with some other writings on the same side of the question, and find myself constrained to embrace their sentiments; only I cannot join in opinion with some of them that by the constitution of gover[n]ment a man should be excluded from office as soon as by experience he is qualified to fill it.

But as a repetition of the remarks that have been made by others cannot be entertaining I shall principally attend to two or three objections that I think deserve consideration and that have not been taken notice of in any of the publications I have seen. (1) Congress are to exercise exclusive legislation over ten miles square; that is to say, they are to exercise absolute dominion over the inhabitants, as by the System this district cannot have the shadow of representation in the government to which they are to be subjected. This from a combination of circumstances will be the most successful nursery of slaves that ever was devised by man: the money, the amusements, and the elegance if not splendor that will centre here must make it very populous. It will be a market where liberty may be sold for a valuable consideration: if these advantages will not be thought an equivolent by some, the honours and emoluments that may be solicited and obtained from government, will, in addition, come up to the price of the bulk of mankind. The sum of the whole is, that these numerous and wealthy slaves will infallibly be devoted to the views of their masters; and having surrendered their own, will always be ready to trample on the rights of free men. This suggests another objection. (2) Numerous offices of profit and honour will be in the gift of the continental Executive; And on whom will these be generally conferred? No doubt on courtiers. By these officers, or rather creatures of state, the supreme government will be administered and Congressional purposes accomplished without regard to the State governments or feeling for individuals. With the assistance of these two powerful Armies what may not be effected by Congress even though they had not the continental sword and purse at their command. As to the ten Miles square the idea should be execrated as it is dictated by vanity and not by necessity; and the Officers should be recommended by and be actual inhabitants of the respective States in which they are severally to officiate; at least they should be elected by the representatives of the people assembled in Congress; which would in a great measure guard against the evils I have stated, and give the meritorious in the most distant parts of the union some chance for preferment. (3) The third objection more immediately relates to this and the other western parts of the Union. Under this New Government Imports and Exports cannot be taxed nor prohibited without the consent of Congress. This is a restriction that the general good does not absolutely require, but must be ruinous to those whose local situation makes it necessary to discourage foreign superfluities and to encourage home Manufactures. To say that Congress will give every reasonable indulgence; and that individuals will not be restrained from industry nor compelled to purchase gewgaws is little to the purpose, as it is evidently unsafe to depend on one or the other in this Case. If the State Governments are to have an existence, their end must be to guard their communities from evils that may not effect the union in general; and if in any instance these communities are deprived of the power to restrain individuals from doing that which will be injurious to their common interest, so far their Gover[n]ments will be a burthen without an advantage; or I might rather say, they will evidently and materially fall short of their end.[5]

I also wish to say something on the danger of giving Congress an unlimited power of internal taxation. The more I consider it the more I am alarmed. If the circumstances of the union requires the measure I am willing to submit to it as a necessary evil; but if it can in any way be restrained or guarded from abuse, nothing can be more advisable.

You will gather from what I have written that I think the calling another continental Convention should not be delayed, to which I can foresee no impediment but obstinacy. Indeed I am decided in my opinion that the proposed plan of Government should be subjected to a reconsideration for ye. single reason, if no other, that it was done by men who exceeded their Commission, and whatever may be pleaded in excuse from the necessity of the case, something should certainly be done to disclaim the dangerous president [i.e., precedent] which will otherwise be established. I still hope that an attachment to the independence of America and that love of equal liberty which first gave it existence will silence party heats and cabals and lead to a system that will promise lasting internal security and tranquility to all the members of the union, which ought to be the first object; as external respectability will be an inseperable concomitant. If the event should be otherwise, it will be obvious that the late struggle with Great Britain was excited by ambition and not by virtue, and we may yet have much cause to lament the immence sacrifices we have made in vain. In this case I indulge the hope that Virginia will have spirit to oppose a System of domination though she should be the only dissenting State. By doing this she may be the happy instrument of obliging the others to return to their duty as she was the first that dared to counteract British oppression. If she cannot immediately stop the current of despotism, she may check its rapidity, and keep alive an enquiry that will increase the wisdom and establish the virtue of her own people without sub-

jecting them to greater evils than must attend a willing subjection to
a burthensome newfangled Aristocracy. . . .

1. RC, Hugh Blair Grigsby Papers, ViHi. Wallace (1742–1814), a graduate of the
College of New Jersey (Princeton), a former clergyman, and a lawyer, was an associate
judge of the District Court of Kentucky. He represented Lincoln County in the Virginia
House of Delegates, 1783–84, and was an active supporter of Kentucky statehood. When
Kentucky became a state in 1792, Wallace helped to write its constitution and seven
years later he was a delegate to that state's second constitutional convention.

2. Wallace's young son had died in an accident earlier in the year (Wallace to Fleming,
22 March, RCS:Va., 515, note 2).

3. Fleming represented Botetourt County in the Virginia Convention, where he voted
to ratify the Constitution in June 1788.

4. For Mason's, Randolph's, and Gerry's objections, see CC:138–B, CC:385, and
CC:227–A, respectively.

5. For more on the opposition to the Constitution in the western parts of the United
States, see the petition that some members of Kentucky's "court party" (including Wallace) presented to the Court of Fayette County (Ky.) in late February (CC:578).

### 726. Paine Wingate to John Sullivan
### New York, 3 May[1]

By the last post I received a letter from a friend of mine dated
Baltimore April 26, informing me that the convention of Maryland
had that day ratifyed the new constitution—yeas 63, nays 11 only—
This intelligence, so agreeable to your Excellency's wishes, I have taken
the first opportunity of communicating.—The state of New York have
this week had their elections for delegates to their convention. In this
city the votes are generally in favor of federalists, and it is said that
they are so in other counties beyond expectation. It is now the opinion
of those who are well acquainted with the sentiments of the people
thrô the state that the probability is in favor of adopting the constitution here. The latest accounts from Virginia are, that from the returns of the delegates which are now generally made, a majority will
be for the new government.—South carolina does not seem to be
doubted.—Upon the whole the encouragement of having a peaceable
& good government soon established is dayly encreasing. I hope we
shall not be disappointed.—Georgia have made a considerable cession
to the United states of their Western lands upon condition that the
new constitution shall be adopted & that they be allowed thirty thousand dollars for their expences, in defending that territory during the
late war.—

We have not had a congress until yesterday for some time past,
owing to two or three members going out of Town. Other members

are expected on dayly. There have been no very material dispatches to Congress since I wrote to your Excellency last.—

PS. Mr. Gilman desires his most respectful compliments—

1. RC, State Papers Relating to the Revolution, Vol. II (1785–1789), Nh-Ar. Wingate was a New Hampshire delegate to Congress.

### 727. Rufus King to John Langdon
New York, 4 May[1]

Maryland has adopted the constitution on a division of Sixty three affirmatives and Eleven negatives: the convention sat but one week, and that we are told was mostly spent in hearing Mr. Mercer and one or two other Antifederalists—the convention meets in South Carolina on the 12th instant, and we have the highest confidence of their assent—the accounts from Virginia are more and more favorable, and it seems agreed by every one that the great unanimity of Maryland will have a very favorable Effect on that state—The Elections were made in this State during the last week, but the result is as yet unknown except in this City. Of three thousand votes given in this City, it is supposed that not more than two hundred were in favor of the Antifederal Ticket, which was headed by Governor Clinton—Mr. Jay, Mr. Duane, Chancellor Livingston, Col. Hamilton, Judge Morris, Judge Hobart, Mr. Harrison Mr. Rosevelt & Mr. Nicholas Low, who composed the federal Ticket had the other Votes and are elected—from the information which I have obtained concerning this State, I am rather inclined to think they will adopt the Constitution; I hope and believe that New Hampshire will be in better company than that of R. Island—I shall be mortified if I am disappointed—Mrs. King will accompany me to Boston in about a Fortnight, and we do not intend denying ourselves the pleasure of visiting Portsmouth, although we shall be disappointed in the pleasure of seeing you there—Concord is a long distance from the Metropolis—

1. RC, King Papers, NHi.

### 728. Pierce Butler to Weeden Butler
Mary-Ville, 5 May (excerpt)[1]

... I am not only much obliged, but much flattered by Your opinion of the result of Our Deliberations last Summer, because I had a small hand in the formation[2]—It is a subject that, fortunately for me, I have for some Years past turnd my thoughts to; yet still I am sensible I am unequal to the Magnitude of it—I therefore, previous to the Election, declined serving; but as I was Elected, I woud not refuse going—It is truly an Important Æra to the United States; And they now seem sensible of it—The Constitution I think will be agreed to; and be adopted thõ it has some few opponents—Where is that work of Man that pleases every body! Pains and attention were not spared to form such a Constitution, as woud preserve to the individual as large a share of natural right as coud be left consistent with the good of the whole—to balance the powers of the three Branches, so that no one shoud too greatly preponderate—We had before Us all the Antient and modern Constitutions on record, And none of them was more influential on Our Judgements than the British, in Its *Original* purity—Let You and I compare the two for a moment—yet if I begin I shall tire You—I will be as concise as possible—indeed I am ill able to write at present, and much less to think—

You have a King, House of Lords and House of Commons—We have a President, Senate and House of Representatives—their powers in some general points are Similar; but when we attentively compare the total of the two Governments, we shall find, I think, a material difference—In One, the People at large have little to say, and less to do; the other is much more of a popular Government—the whole is Elective—In the King of G–B. not only all Executive power is lodged, but He is himself, also a very important and essential Branch of the Legislature—Without him there can be no Parliament—And in him is the sole power of Dissolving it—No Law can be passd without His Consent—He can put a Negative upon any Bill, thõ it may previously have met with the Unanimous approbation of the people—He can Alone form Treaties, which shall bind the Nation—He has the sole Right of declaring War or making Peace, So that the lives of thousands of His Subjects are at His Will—He has the Sole power of Confering honors and Titles—It is truly observed by one of Your Law Writers that "the House of Lords seems politicaly constituted for the support of the rights of the Crown" He is the head of the Church, All Your Dignities flow from Him—He may by a Ne Exeat Regnum,[3] prevent any person from leaving the Kingdom—He alone has the right of Erecting Courts of Judicature—the Court of King's Bench, I mean the Officers of it, are Created by letters Patent from Him—The Crown is Hereditary—A weak Man, or a Madman may, as Heir Ascend to it—He is not responsible—["]*the King can do no wrong*["][4] His person is Sacred, even thõ the measure pursued in His Reign be Arbitrary; for no Earthly Jurisdiction has power to try Him in a Criminal way—The President of the United States is the Supreme Executive Officer—He has no separate Legislative power whatever—He cañt prevent a Bill from passing into a Law—In making Treaties two thirds of the Senate must Concur—In the Appointment of Ambassadors, Judges of the Supreme Court &ca. He must have the Concurrence of the Senate—He is responsible to His Constituents for the Use of His power—He is Impeachable—His Election, the mode of which I had the honor of proposing in the Comm͠ee, in my weak judgement, precludes Corruption and tumult[5]—Yet after all my Dear Sir, I am free to acknowledge that His powers are full great; and greater than I was disposed to make them—Nor, Entre Nous, do I believe they woud have been so great had not many of the Members cast their eyes towards General Washington as President; and Shaped their Ideas of the Powers to be given to a President, by their opinions of His Virtue—So that the Man who, by His Patriotism & Virtue, Contributed largely to the Emancipation of His Country, may, be the Innocent means of its being, when He is lay'd low, oppressd—

I am free to confess, that after all Our Endeavours, our System is little better than matter of Experiment; and that much must depend on the Morals and manners of the People at large—It is a large and wide Extended Empire, let then the System be ever so perfect, good Order and Obedience must greatly depend on the Patriotism of the Citizen—I am not insensible that the Constitution We have Ventured to recommend to the States has its faults; but the Circumstances under which It was framed are some alleviation of them—It is probable there were Abilities in the Convention to bring forward a more perfect System of Government for a Country better adapted to the reception of it than America ever can be—Was America, or rather the States, more Compact It is possible Our System woud have been more perfect— Besides, Our Labours required the Unanimous Consent of the States in Convention, to Insure success from abroad—We were therefore, in prudence, obliged to Accommodate Ourselves to Interests, not only opposite, but, in some measure as You observe, Clashing—I will just mention One Object, and that an Important One, in which there appeared a Clashing of Interests—I mean Commerce—When We withdrew from G Britain the Eastern States were deprived of a benefit they long enjoyd in a large participation of the Carrying Trade; with many other benefits that they had in Common with the British, under Your Navigation Laws and wise Commercial System—that lucrative Branch of Trade the fishing on the Banks, was neither Enlarged nor better secured by withdrawing from Britain—What then did Our Brethern of the Eastern States gain by a long & bloody Contest? Why nothing but the honor of Calling themselves Independent States—Let Us turn Our Eyes for a moment to the Southern or Staple States, And We

Shall see how they stood before the War, and wherein they have benefited by Independence—While they were Colonies they were in a great measure confined to One market for a Sale of their Produce—They were restricted to Ship in British Bottoms—By Independence a Variety of Markets were thrown open to them—the Ships of every Nation may come into their Ports—thus an Emulation is Created in the Carrying Trade, which of Course lowers Freights and raises the price of Staple Articles—thus Circumstanced We were obliged to Accommodate Ourselves to the Interests of the Whole; And Our System shoud be Considered as the result of a Spirit of Accommodation, And not as the most perfect System, that under other Circumstances, coud be devised by the Convention—When You consider my Dear Sir, the Great Extent of Territory, the Various Climates & products, the differing manners and, as I before observed, the Contending Commercial Interests, You will agree with me, that it required a pretty General Spirit of Accommodation in the Members of Convention to bring forward such a system as woud be agreed to and approved of by all—In this light then are You to View the product of Our Joint Endeavours—The Convention saw, I think justly, the Critical Situation of the United States—Slighted from abroad, and totering on the brink of Confusion at home; they therefore thought it wise to bring forward such a System as bid fairest for General approbation And Adoption so as to be brought soon into operation—

I think by this time You must be heartily tired of me and Our Constitution I will therefore Close My letter with requesting You to present the best wishes of me and my family to Mrs Butler for a Continuance of Her health And the many blessings She enjoys—

Believe me to be in truth & Sincerity My Dear Sir Yr Affectionate friend

[P.S.] As the Ship is on the wing I have not time to run my Eye over this long Epistle—take it then as it is meant, and Excuse its wants and imperfections—It is wrote in the spirit of friendship without attending to anything else. . . .

1. RC, Additional Manuscripts, 16603, Letters of Major Pierce Butler of South Carolina, Department of Manuscripts, British Library, London. Endorsed: "Ansd. 2 Sepr 88." In the omitted part of this letter, Pierce Butler discussed the prospects for his son who was in England under the care of the Reverend Weeden Butler. "Mary-Ville" was Butler's plantation on the Ashley River in South Carolina.

2. On 8 October 1787 Butler, a South Carolina delegate to the Constitutional Convention, had written the Reverend Butler describing the proceedings of that body (CC:139). Reverend Butler had replied to that letter on 24 December (not found).

3. See Blackstone, *Commentaries*, Book I, chapter VII, 265–66.

4. See *ibid.*, Book I, chapter VII, 244–45, 246; Book III, chapter XVII, 254–55.

5. On 25 July 1787 Pierce Butler asserted in the Constitutional Convention that "The two great evils to be avoided are cabal at home, & influence from abroad. It will be difficult to avoid either if the Election be made by the Natl Legislature. On the other hand, the Govt. should not be made so complex & unwieldy as to disgust the States. This would be the case, if the election shd. be referred to the people. He liked best an election by Electors chosen by the Legislatures of the States. He was agst. a re-eligibility at all events. He was also agst. a ratio of votes in the States. An equality should prevail in this case. The reasons for departing from it do not hold in the case of the Executive as in that of the Legislature" (Farrand, II, 112).

## 729. Philadelphia Independent Gazetteer, 5 May[1]

The opposition to the new constitution in Maryland, says a correspondent, labored under many disadvantages, and the little exertion they made, early evinced that the others had stolen to the windward of them. In the first place, the press was not free till the people were generally prejudiced in favor of this mysterious system, by the artful management of its advocates; and when *Mr. Martin's* information was published, it was only in one newspaper at Baltimore[2] (the extremity of the state); which could be seen by few in the country. (We find it had effect in the town and in the counties adjacent.) In the next place, the *aristocratic* party in that state is considerable, and devoted to the nod of its leaders. And the very idea of *Mr. Martin's* being connected with the *opposition*, was sufficient to prejudice the *tories* (who are another considerable part of the state) in favor of the system; Mr. Martin being very unpopular among that class of citizens owing to the office he holds.[3] Thus the *tories* and *aristocratics* united, together with the wish of *all* to grant farther powers to Congress, the example of the other states in adopting the system, the industry of the advocates of it in circulating sophistical publications, and delusive and electioneering falsehoods among the people, and promising to recommend the necessary amendments with the adoption of it, procured the great majority they had in convention. And here again, they excluded all debate, fearing it would open the eyes of the deluded members; (does not this shew the badness of their cause?) And being thus deluded we find that this body of men as implicit to the direction of their leader (McHenry)[4] as the majority of our packed convention was to *Mr. Wilson*; and does not the conduct of these leaders fully shew the *designs* of the junto on the continent, who are endeavoring to take from us our liberties? Have they not been amusing us with an idea of procuring amendments, and that, like Massachusetts, the states should recommend amendments with the adoption? But has the convention of Maryland (alias McHenry and his sticklers) recommended any amendments? No, they have not![5] This should teach those who have been annoyed with such fallacious hopes, that such ideas were only held out by the junto for the moment to carry their point; and that, like the Maryland convention, our new Congress once vested with unbounded sway, will never relinquish a single item, will never listen to the calls for amendments or the least security of our rights and privileges, which are intended to be laid at their feet! No, while they have a military force to back their despotic decrees, they may laugh at the people? But it is to be hoped this treachery in Maryland will be a lesson to the *six* remaining states, and teach them to *reject* and *then amend*. Secure your invaluable rights and liberties, and be not swayed by the insidious arts and practices of the designing or the mercenary cries of the deluded: Ye sons of Virginia, of the Carolinas, ye honest sons of New-Hampshire and New-York; the blood of thousands of your virtuous brethren who fell in the late glorious cause of liberty, cry aloud to you, to preserve and hand down to your posterity those rights and privileges in defence of which they fell martyrs!

A correspondent says, that there is now a fair opportunity of settling the prosperity and happiness of the United States, upon a permanent foundation. The state of Rhode Island is now willing to accede to the five per cent impost, demanded by Congress, and will also give the power of regulating commerce, with whatever shall be thought reasonable for the general interest of the country, provided there is no consolidation of the several states into one national government.[6] If, therefore, the Congress will be content with what was at first demanded, we may be an united and flourishing people; we may pay off, before long, our foreign debt, establish our national credit at home, build a navy, raise and pay troops, whenever they shall be found necessary, for the land service, encourage emigration, promote agriculture, manufactures, arts and sciences, and rival the greatest powers of the globe. Whereas, if a spirit of pride and obstinacy should induce to force down the new constitution upon the people, Rhode Island perhaps will be supported in her opposition to it, by the greater part of the state of Massachusetts, by the people of New-Hampshire, by half of the people of New-York; nor will the people in the back part of the state of Pennsylvania, be very ready to march to dragoon the Rhode Island men into compliance, whom they begin more and more to esteem. It is an eternal truth, which should be indelibly impressed upon our minds, that, "a kingdom divided against itself, cannot stand."[7]

1. Both paragraphs were reprinted in the *New York Journal*, 14 May, and the *Newport Mercury*, 19 May; the second paragraph was also reprinted in the Providence *United States Chronicle*, 5 June.

2. Luther Martin's *Genuine Information* appeared only in the Baltimore *Maryland Gazette*. (See CC:389.)

3. Martin had been Maryland's attorney general since 1778.

4. James McHenry.

5. For the failure of the Maryland Convention to recommend amendments, see CC:716. James McHenry was a member of the Convention's committee of thirteen which considered whether or not amendments should be recommended.

6. In March and October 1785 and March 1786, the Rhode Island legislature passed the 1784 grant of commercial power to Congress and the Impost of 1783. (For the Impost and the grant of power, see CDR, 146–48, 153–54.)

7. From Mark 3:24 which states "And if a kingdom be divided against itself, that kingdom cannot stand." See also Matthew 12:25.

## 730. A Steady and Open Republican
## State Gazette of South Carolina, 5 May[1]

MRS. TIMOTHY, *The enclosed,*[2] *copied from a paper sent me by a friend, seems so peculiarly adapted to our present situation, that I cannot forbear selecting it from the croud of publications since the appearance of the proposed federal constitution, and recommending it thro' your paper, to the most serious attention of all our fellow-citizens, but previously a few HINTS, by way of introduction, will not, I hope, be impertinent.*

New-Hampshire and Georgia are the two extreme barriers of the United States, if the latter can with any propriety be called a barrier without this state in conjunction; and both together, we know, are not in point of force, ready for any sudden emergency, to be compared to New Hampshire.

It cannot be doubted that Great-Britain has her busy emissaries throughout the states, and not a few amongst us, and should the constitution be rejected, how long can we flatter ourselves to be free from Indian cruelties and depredations, some time since begun in Georgia, and if at this moment warded off from us, 'tis principally owing to the dread of an efficacious union of the states by the adoption of the federal constitution.—The three southern states particularly, we have had for several years past, good grounds to think Great Britain wishes to separate from the rest, and to have reverted to her if possible.

Mr. Martin's long mischievous detail of the opinions and proceedings of the late general convention, (already occupying a large space in six of your gazettes, and still unfinished,)[3] with all his colourings and uncandid insinuations, in regard to general Washington and Doct. Franklin, may suit the short sighted selfish wishes of *an individual* of a state, situated almost in the centre of the rest, and much safer by that means from sudden alarms. But the generous, manly *and truly federal sentiments of Maryland* are well known, and 'tis not doubted will be unequivocally shewn at her convention very shortly to be held—and that New-Hampshire, early in her first meeting on that important subject, has only by consent taken farther time to consider of it, and will at her next meeting adopt it, is the general opinion.

What pity the salutary caution of Doct. Franklin, just previous to his signing the constitution recommended by the convention, had not been strictly attended to.—If we split, it will in all probability happen in running head-long on the dangerous rock he so prophetically (as it were) warned us from, "That the opinions of the errors of the constitution born within the walls of the convention, should die there, and not a syllable be whispered abroad."[4]—This Hint is full of that foresight and penetration the Doctor has always been remarkable for.

When the general convention met, no citizen of the United States could expect less from it than I did, so many jarring interests and prejudices to reconcile! The variety of pressing dangers at our doors, even during the war, were barely sufficient to force us to act in concert, and necessarily give way at times to each other.—But when the great work was done and published, I was not only most agreeably disappointed, but struck with amazement.—Nothing less than that superintending hand of providence, that so miraculously carried us through the war, (in my humble opinion,) could have brought it about so compleat, upon the whole.

The constitution recommended, in all respects, takes its rise, where it ought, from the people; its president, senate, and house of representatives, are sufficient and wholsome checks on each other, and at proper periods are dissolved again into the common mass of the people; longer periods would probably have produced danger, shorter, tumult, instability, and inefficacy, every article of these and other essentials to a republican government, are, in my opinion, well secured; were it otherwise, not a citizen of the United States would have been more alarmed, or more early in opposition to it, than

A Steady and Open Republican.

*Charleston, May 2, 1788.*

1. Reprinted: *New York Morning Post*, 31 May; *Massachusetts Gazette*, 13 June; Exeter, N.H., *Freeman's Oracle*, 27 June. "A Steady and Open Republican" was probably Christopher Gadsden, a Charleston merchant-planter, who had used the pseudonym before. (For Gadsden's authorship, see Richard Walsh, ed., *The Writings of Christopher Gadsden, 1746–1805* [Columbia, S.C., 1966], 248n. Walsh rejects Paul Leicester Ford's identification of Charles Pinckney as "A Steady and Open Republican.") The essay was addressed to Mrs. Ann Timothy, publisher of the *State Gazette of State Carolina*. Gadsden was a delegate to the South Carolina Convention, where he voted to ratify the Constitution on 23 May.

2. Probably a reference to Oliver Ellsworth's "The Landholder" X, *Connecticut Cour-*

*ant*, 3 March (CC:588), which the *State Gazette of South Carolina* reprinted immediately after "A Steady and Open Republican."

3. Between 10 April and 22 May, the *State Gazette of South Carolina* printed, in whole or in part, nine of the twelve installments of Luther Martin's *Genuine Information*. (For this series, see CC:389.)

4. Benjamin Franklin's 17 September 1787 speech, which was reprinted in the Charleston *City Gazette* on 27 December, actually reads: "The opinions I have had of its error I sacrifice to the public good. I have never whispered a syllable of them abroad. Within these walls they were born, and here they shall die." The material quoted in the *City Gazette* originally appeared in the *Virginia Independent Chronicle*, 5 December, the first Southern printing of the speech. The first Northern printing in the *Boston Gazette* on 3 December does not contain the quoted material. For the text of the manuscript version of the entire speech, see CC:77–A.

## 731. Peter Allaire: Journal of Occurrences
## New York, 6 May–5 June (excerpts)[1]

. . . Our present Situation is, Seven States have already Confirmed the New Constitution, Delaware, Philadelphia, Jersey, Connecticut, Massachusets, Georgia and Maryland. South Carolina, meet the 14th May, and Virginia the 28th May: South Carolina are Federalists three to one, and by the best information from Virginia they will have a Majority of upwards of forty, those two States, adopting the Constitution, forms the federal Union. New York meets the 17th June but it is doubtfull w[h]ether it will be adopted, (however, the Southern Counties, by far the most numerous & Richest have determined, to Join the Confederation, and leave the back Country to shift for themselves). New Hampshire also meets the 17th June & North Carolina the 4th July: as for Rhode Island they have not Complyed with the Order of Congress in ordering their Counties to nominate Members for the Convention, but have desired the people to meet in Each County and give their Votes, for or against the New Constitution; and their appears, Seven to one against it.

My Opinion is, that when South Carolina & Virginia have adopted it, the other States must comply, or form another Republick on their own plan, and those States, not being near each other, but on the Contrary, the most distant apart, and surrounded by Federal Governments, have no Alternative. I make not the least doubt but the New Federal Constitution will be finally adjusted, and will Act in their Legislative Capacity in the course of this Year. . . .

May [i.e., June] 3d Accounts from Maryland, that the Convention of that State had Adopted the federal Constitution 63 to 11 Majority 52—Virginia are become federalist & South Carolina: Virginia we expect will Adopt it this Month: & S: Carolina Early in June, which will form the Confederacy: Seven having Ratified & Confirmed it.

Congress are become a mere Cypher, they do verry little business, not making a house above once a fortnight, they waite with Impatiency the Adoption of the Federal Constitution.

1. RC, Foreign Office, Class 4, America, Vol. 6, ff. 155–64, Public Record Office, London. This unsigned journal, largely concerned with commercial matters, was endorsed "Intelligence/from New York./R. 25th. June 1788./From Sr. George Yonge." Entitled "Occurrences from 6th May to 5th June, 1788" and dated "New York 6 May [June] 1788," this journal was written by Peter Allaire (1740–1820), a New York City merchant and a secret agent in the employ of the British Foreign Office. It was turned over to the Foreign Office by Allaire's friend, British Secretary for War Sir George Yonge, through whose influence Allaire had been hired to report on "Intelligence" from America. Allaire, whose family had settled in New Rochelle, N.Y., in the late 17th century, had worked for British intelligence in Paris during the Revolution. After the war, he was a merchant in New York City, where he sometimes boarded members of Congress. For more on Allaire and his activities as the writer of "Occurrences," see Boyd, XVII, 91n.

### 732. Tench Coxe to Henry Bromfield
### Philadelphia, 6 May (excerpt)[1]

. . . I presume our Countrymen in England are not a little anxious about the depending plan of general Government in which all may Participate & in which every man has a Voice, desire to see it adopted. The Want of efficiency in our late Confederation, The Relaxation of government in general, legal tenders & suspension of Laws with various other Evils have extreemly deranged this Country—and I fear have rendered it as disrespected abroad as uncomfortable at home[.] Maryland has just adopted the Plan & South Carolina will probably be but a Short time about it. Next comes Virginia in which we confidently expect a Majority tho not a large one, of New York there is not any doubt tho there also the Majority will not exceed ⅔ds.—I have no doubts of ten or eleven States being in before the 1st. August, so that the Government will be in effect, nor have I any apprehensions that one State will finally refuse. Rhode Island will be the latest, but after her infamous Game of Depreciation is completely played she also must come in. . . .

1. FC, Coxe Papers, Series I, Volumes and Printed Material, Tench Coxe Letterbook, vol. 4, PHi. Bromfield (1751–1837), a merchant, moved from Boston to London in October 1787.

### 733. Benjamin Rush to Jeremy Belknap
### Philadelphia, 6 May[1]

I beg your acceptance of my thanks for the volume of the debates of your convention.[2] They do great honor to your State, and will remain I hope as a lasting monument of the good Sense—virtue—and knowledge that characterised the year 1788 in the United states of America.—

The commerce in African slaves has breathed its last in Pennsylvania. I shall send you a copy of our late law respecting that trade as soon as it is published.[3]—I am encouraged by the Success that has finally attended the exertions of the friends of universal freedom & justice, to go on in my romantic Schemes (as they have often been called) of serving my Countrymen.—My next Object shall be the extirpation of the *Abuse* of Spirituous liquors. For this purpose I have every year for several years past republished the enclosed tract two or three weeks before harvest.[4] The effects of this *perseverance* begin already to shew themselves in our State. A family—or a township—is hit with the publication one year that neglected, or perhaps rediculed it the year before. Associations are forming in many places to give no Spirits at the ensuing harvest. The Quakers & methodists take the lead in these Associations, as they have often done in all enterprizes that have morality, or the happiness of Society for thier Objects. many Store keepers among the Quakers now refuse to buy or sell spirituous liquors.—In a short time, I expect there will be an Act of the Quaker Society to forbid the Sale or even use of them altogether, except as a medicine.—

As my opinions Upon the subject of the fœderal government have been often misrepresented, by our antifœderal Scriblers, I have to beg the favor of you to republish the enclosed extract of one of my letters to my friend Dr Ramsay of Charleston in some of your papers.[5]—It contains my principles fairly stated. I beleive I gave *a part* of them in my last letter to you.[6]

The minority of Pennsylvania have nearly exhausted their malice. There will be no Opposition by arms in any County in this State to the goverment, when it is set in motion.—Mr Bryan[7] like his brother Shays will soon be left a solitary example of political insanity & wickedness. All will end well.—The last thing that I can beleive is, that providence has brought us over the red Sea of the late war, to perish in the present wilderness of Anarchy & Vice.—What has been, will be, & there is nothing new under the sun.—we are advancing thro' *Suffering* (the usual road) to peace & happiness. night, preceeded day, & Chaos,—Order, in the creation of the world.—

PS: Dr Clarkson[8] & his amiable family are all well.

1. RC, Belknap Papers, MHi. Belknap replied to Rush on 22 June (Rush Papers, PPL).

2. On 7 April Belknap sent Rush a copy of the Massachusetts Convention's *Debates* (Evans 21242).

3. On 29 March the Pennsylvania Assembly passed "An Act to explain and amend

an act, entituled, 'An Act for the gradual abolition of slavery.' " (Excerpts from this act appear in W. E. B. Du Bois, *The Suppression of the African Slave-Trade to the United States of America, 1638–1870* [1896; Baton Rouge, La., 1969], 231–32.)

4. Rush refers to his pamphlet entitled *An Enquiry into the Effects of Spirituous Liquors upon the Human Body, and Their Influence upon the Happiness of Society*, the first printing of which had appeared by July 1784 (Butterfield, *Rush*, I, 272n). The proposed 1788 reprinting has not been located. For the 1787 reprint, see Evans 20690.

5. Rush's letter to David Ramsay, which first appeared in the Charleston *Columbian Herald*, 14 April (CC:680), was reprinted in the *Massachusetts Centinel*, 7 May, and Boston *Independent Chronicle*, 8 May. On 22 June Belknap wrote Rush that "The piece which you desired me to reprint in our Papers had appeared & was much approved before your Letter came to hand" (Rush Papers, PPL).

6. Probably Rush to Belknap, 28 February (CC:573).

7. Rush refers to George Bryan, one of Pennsylvania's most prominent Antifederalist leaders.

8. Dr. Gerardus Clarkson was a physician and the treasurer of the Philadelphia College of Physicians.

## 734. Robert R. Livingston to Marquis de la Luzerne
### Clermont, 7 May[1]

I have delayed replying to your obliging favor by the Ct De Mou[s]tiers in hope that I might be able to give you some satisfactory information relative to the important events that are now taking place here but having lately heard of those in which your happiness is immediately interested your marriage[2] & your appointment as ambassadour to G B: I can not defer my congratulations. The first of these will I dare say render you as happy as the prudence & propriety of the choice you have made gave your friends reason to hope[.] The pleasure I receive from the second I confess is not unmixed with regret [that] had it been consistent with your personal interests & the views of [Friends?] to have send you here with the same rank I am satisfied that you wd have rendered essential services to both countries—The present moment is very interesting I cannot but believe that America is going to undergo a change in her political constitution which may add to her importance in the scale of nations—The present disturbed State of Europe & seeds of Jealousy which are sown between france & G britain will if I mistake not soon involve them in new quarells in which case America if her government is established may not be unimportant to either[.] The British interest is by no means inconsiderable among us nor can it be prevented from acquiring an undue influence but by the attention of a minister acquainted with the character of the inhabitants solicitous to conciliate their affections & ready to accomodate himself to their prejudices—Without intending the smallest reflection upon the Ct. De Moustiers (who has not *yet* formed so intimate a connection with any of us as to permit us to judge of his character) I can not but think that a reciprocal connection between both nations would have been greatly strengthened by your residence in a country where you have so many friends—But having lost all ~~hope~~ prospect of this we must console ourselves in your absence by the interest we take in your advancement to a more agreeable & more important mission—

You Have doubtless seen the proposed federal constitution[.] it has met with many antagonists but the great bulk of the people & [– – –] particularly those who have most experience & information are warmly attatched to it[.] seven States Georgia Maryland Delaware P. NJ C: & Mast: have acceeded to it—Rhode Island is the only one that has as yet rejected it nor do I imagine it runs any other risk but from New York where parties are very equally balanced[.] the popular demagogues being fearful that it may lessen their importance are warmly opposed to it—Tho this constitution is by no means free from faults yet if well administered it may tend to unite us more firmly than we are & will certainly be much more vigorous in its operation than that we now have[3]—You are in a country where you will hear of nothing but our poverty disstress & convultions yet be assured that nothing can be more groundless—The people of this country are the happyest in the world[.] poverty is hardly known in it[.] our population is more rapid than you can have any Idea of[.] such is the improved State of our agriculture that notwithstanding the inconveniences our trade labours under the general ballance will this year be in our favor—and will daily be more so—I speak of this State particularly—Many articles heretofore furnished from Europe are now made cheaper in the Northern States than they can be imported as nails, oil, coarse linnens glass—This is one of the good consequences which results from discouraging our foreign commerce & it will daily extend itself to a variety of other articles[.] Thus in this as in most human affairs good arises out of the evils our political enemies intended us—You will excuse the length of this & charge it to the desire I have of giving you a political ske[t]ch of a country in whose happiness I know you interest yourself with the further hope that it may be useful to you in your present situation—Be assured Sir of the Sincerity of the attattchment with which I have the honor to be Your Excellencys Most Ob Hum: Servt:

1. FC, Livingston Papers, NHi. Livingston (1746–1813), a 1765 graduate of King's College (Columbia) and a lawyer, was a delegate to Congress, 1775–76, 1779–80, 1784–85; a member of the committee of Congress which drafted the Declaration of Independence, 1776; a member of the committee of the New York provincial convention which drafted the state constitution of 1777; chancellor of the state of New York, 1777–

1801; the Continental Secretary for Foreign Affairs, 1781–83; and a delegate to the New York Convention, where he voted to ratify the U.S. Constitution in July 1788. "Clermont" was his estate in Columbia County.

Anne-César, Marquis de la Luzerne (1741–1791), was French minister plenipotentiary to the U.S., 1779–84; French ambassador to Great Britain, 1788–91; and a member of the Society of the Cincinnati in France. In 1785 he lost the title of Chevalier of the Order of Malta when he announced that he was secretly married. The Order bound its members to celibacy and military service. As compensation, Louis XVI gave him the title of marquis. (The Marquis is sometimes confused with his brother, César-Henri, Comte de la Luzerne, who was French Minister of Marine and Colonies, 1787–90.) Livingston and Luzerne had developed a close relationship when the former was a delegate to Congress and Secretary for Foreign Affairs. The two men corresponded after Luzerne returned to France in 1784.

2. Livingston was unaware that Luzerne's wife had died in March.

3. In the spring of 1787 Livingston had been uncertain about the prospects of the Constitutional Convention. On 24 April he had written Luzerne "That we have suffered in reputation abroad can not be disputed—That we are happy at home is equaly true . . . so that upon the whole I may venture to say that we are among the happiest people in the world—notwithstanding those defects in our government which render us contemptible abroad—Whether this evill will be corrected by the convention that meet at Philadelphia I know not tho' I confess to you I do not expect much from their endeavours & for this obvious reason that the people finding themselves happy will not wish for a change tho those who think public reputation & public credit of importance may" (Robert R. Livingston Papers, NHi).

## 735. Samuel A. Otis to Benjamin Lincoln
### New York, 8 May (excerpt)[1]

I have been pretty much taken up with [a] variety of attentions, & nothing of importance having taken place except what was in the papers, I have much against my inclination, defered replying to your last of        But I assure you nothing on my part shall be wanting to cultivate a correspondence which at once gratifies my vanity, & promises me improvement. Congress have not been idle, altho they have been so interrupted by the appointment of its members to Convention, in one place & another that much less has been effected than could be wished. It was however the general, & invariable opinion that it would be more expedient that Congress should continue in sessions, during this uncertain & agitated year, even if nothing very important was effected, Than to leave the States without any bond of Union, or even the semblance of a fœderal Goverment. Indeed the frequent returns of the states who have been wise enough to adopt the new Constitution, renders it amongst other things expedient that Congress should continue in sessions. Maryland ratification is now reading,[2] And I have no doubt we shall soon have that of So Carolina—I presume from what intelligence is stiring that No Carolina will follow the lead of Virginia *where* the opposition has gained no ground of late, & will be weakened by the unanimity of Maryland. Virginia remains doubtful however—yet I can hardly suppose She will refuse to adopt, as, I am informed, upon the plan of Massachusetts.

N York are nearly equally divided. The fœderalists are very positive, so are the opposition. Govr Clinton is pitted at all events against it, & indeed it is with him a very great stake; for if he is in the minority upon this question I think he must lose his election. The supporters of the measure are however powerful. The City almost unanimously, & all the commercial interest. The Schylers, & great proprietors, with a large number of farmers &c. Clintons friends pushed him very injudiciously for the City. What is an omen of success in my view is, that the most steady opposers in this quarter begin to dispair, and say it must be adopted with amendments. I hear a suggestion that N York opposers have no hope of rejection, but only hold up a good countenance, in order to effect amendments, upon the Massachusetts plan— Upon the whole I recollect no period at which the prospect looked more bright than the present—I can form no judgment of N Hamshr, their adjournment into the Wilderness augurs ill, but Langdon & Sullivan, the great leaders are both agreed in fœderal measures, altho I presume their cordiality is not very perfect in other points. R Island will be overwhelmed with argument & influence, and their own minority exerting, I think may be brot to their senses.

I exceedingly rejoice at the unanimity of Massachusetts & congratulate her upon the honor she is about to acquire in her elections. The people who are united in electing a Governor, Lieut Governour, & senate, who have evinced steady measures & good policy, can hardly fail of makg a good election of Representatives. . . .

1. RC, J. S. H. Fogg Autograph Collection, Maine Historical Society.

2. Governor William Smallwood's 1 May letter to the President of Congress transmitting Maryland's ratification was read in Congress on 8 May (JCC, XXXIV, 149n).

## 736. An Attempt at Cooperation between Virginia and New York Antifederalists, 8 May–15 October

Between 12 and 15 September 1787, delegates in the Constitutional Convention defeated efforts to add a bill of rights to the draft Constitution and to have a second constitutional convention called to consider amendments that might be proposed by state ratifying conventions. Later in September, advocates of the Constitution derailed an effort in the Confederation Congress to propose amendments (including a declaration or bill of rights). (See CC:75, 95.) Opponents of the Constitution in several states, especially Virginia and New York, attempted to cooperate with one another in order to agree upon a bill of rights and other amendments which they hoped would be considered by a second constitutional convention.

In early December Virginia Antifederalists tried to formalize such cooperation. The opportunity to do so was provided when the Virginia legislature
considered an act to provide for payment and privileges of state Convention
delegates. During the debate in the Virginia House of Delegates on the bill
for paying the delegates, Antifederalists—led by Patrick Henry and George
Mason—tried but failed to obtain provisions specifically giving the state Convention the power to propose amendments to the Constitution and to appoint
delegates to a second constitutional convention. Henry even wanted the speakers of the House of Delegates and the Senate to "form a Committee of
Correspondence to communicate" with the other states about a second constitutional convention. As finally adopted on 12 December, the act for paying
state Convention delegates, though not mentioning either amendments or a
second convention, provided for "such reasonable expences as may be incurred," if the state Convention "should deem it necessary to hold any communications with any of the sister states or the Conventions thereof which
may be then met." On 27 December the legislature requested that Governor
Edmund Randolph transmit this act to the executives and legislatures of the
other states. On the same day, Randolph wrote the state executives, sending
each two broadsides of the act, one for the executive and the other for the
legislature (RCS:Va., 183–93).

By the time Governor Randolph forwarded the act to the other states, ten
state legislatures had called ratifying conventions and three of these conventions had already adopted the Constitution. In November, the Rhode Island
legislature had refused to call a convention, while the South Carolina and
New York legislatures called conventions on 19 January and 1 February 1788,
respectively. In New York, Antifederalists in the Assembly proposed a resolution giving the state Convention the right to recommend amendments, but
Federalists narrowly defeated the measure. (The resolution was similar to one
adopted by the Virginia legislature on 31 October 1787.)

Governor Randolph's letter of 27 December probably was sent to New
York Governor George Clinton at his residence in New York City. It was then
forwarded to Poughkeepsie, where the legislature had convened on 1 January
1788, and where, except for about two weeks, Clinton resided from 3 January
to 23 March. (From 12 to 24 January, Clinton was probably in New York
City.) On 10 March Governor Clinton delivered Governor Randolph's letter
and its enclosures to the Assembly, indicating that "it may not be improper
to mention that it was not received by me before last Friday evening" (7
March). (Other state executives received Randolph's letter by late January or
early February.)

Both houses of New York's legislature read Randolph's letter and its enclosures and ordered that they be turned over to committees of the whole
house. The legislature, however, adjourned on 22 March before either house
took notice of Virginia's suggestion that the state conventions might want to
communicate with each other.

On 8 May, Clinton wrote Randolph complaining about the delay in receiving his letter. Clinton expressed the wish that, on such a matter of "vast
Importance" as the Constitution, the people of the several states should communicate with each other. Because Virginia's convention was scheduled to

meet before New York's, Governor Clinton expected that Virginians would take the lead in corresponding with New Yorkers. Since he had received "no Direction" from his legislature, Clinton's remarks were "expressive" of his own feelings, which he believed were supported by a majority of New Yorkers (RCS:Va., 790–91).

Clinton's 8 May letter apparently set the stage for a subsequent invitation to cooperate from the Federal Republican Committee, a group of Antifederalists in and around New York City. Addressed primarily to prominent Antifederalists in states where the Constitution had not yet been ratified, the Federal Republican Committee's circular letter of 18 May requested that a correspondence be opened among supporters of amendments to the Constitution. (See "The New York Federal Republican Committee Seeks Interstate Cooperation in Obtaining Amendments to the Constitution," 18 May–6 August, CC:750.)

The exact date that Governor Randolph received Governor Clinton's 8 May letter is unknown. "Immediately on receiving" it, however, Randolph laid it before the Virginia Council of State, requesting an opinion "whether it was of a public or private nature." The Council believed that it was a public letter. Therefore, Randolph felt justified in withholding the letter from the Virginia Convention, which met from 2 to 27 June, because he was obligated to submit it at the earliest opportunity only to the legislature (RCS:Va., 792).

On 23 June the Virginia legislature met in special session. The House of Delegates attained a quorum the next day, and the speaker laid before it a letter from Randolph, dated 23 June, enclosing five public documents, the last of which was Clinton's letter of 8 May. Randolph's letter and the enclosures "were partly read" and then ordered to lie on the table. On 26 June, the House "resumed the reading" of the letter and its enclosures. Presumably, Clinton's letter was first read by the House at this time—too late to be submitted to the Convention, which had ratified the Constitution the previous day.

State Convention delegate George Mason (who was not a member of the legislature) drafted resolutions that were apparently designed for presentation to the House of Delegates, although they do not appear on the Journals. One resolution affirms that Clinton's letter should have been laid before the Convention at its first meeting so that the delegates could have considered a communication with the New York Convention. Another resolution calls for the appointment of a committee to ask Randolph (1) why he did not lay Clinton's letter before the Convention; (2) why he delayed laying the letter before the House until the day after the Convention ratified the Constitution; and (3) why his letter of 27 December 1787 and its enclosures took so long to reach Clinton (RCS:Va., 792). (With respect to the second question, Mason appears to have confused the date that Clinton's letter was read with the date that it was laid before the House.)

On 6 August Randolph wrote to Clinton asking him to check the postmark on the 27 December 1787 letter and whether or not Clinton's absence from New York City might have delayed the delivery of the letter (Mfm:Va. 340). Clinton replied on 4 October that the letter had a Richmond postmark, but that neither the day nor the month was legible. Although he spent most of

January through March in Poughkeepsie, Clinton declared that this should not have delayed the reception of the letter for more than two or three days, because the mail was delivered regularly between New York City and Albany twice a week and Poughkeepsie was on that route. Clinton added that, since the Constitution was in "agitation," some letters to him had been delayed or not delivered (Mfm:Va. 347).

On 15 October Richmond postmaster Augustine Davis, at Randolph's request, certified that his records revealed that "a Mail was made up for the Northward" on 27 December, but Davis could not be certain whether or not Randolph's letter to Clinton had been included. However, Davis continued, the letters brought to the post office on 27 December were sent to the stage office that night. On 18 October Randolph filed Davis' certificate and other papers with Archibald Blair, the Keeper of the Public Seal and the clerk of the Council of State, requesting that Blair "keep [them] in the archives, without putting them on record" (Mfm:Va. 349).

### 737. Philadelphia Independent Gazetteer, 9 May[1]

The present controversy, says a correspondent, respecting the *new leviathan* or proposed constitution for the United States, has exhibited the talents of the Americans in a most exalted point of view. Never did any subject produce a greater display of ingenuity, knowledge, wit, and powerful eloquence. The writings under the signatures of Centinel, Philadelphiensis, Brutus, a Countryman, and Farmer, are full of political wisdom—The information of Mr. Martin, and the dissent of the minority of Pennsylvania, contain a complete system of republican government. To these performances nothing has been opposed but the sophistry of Mr. Wilson, the low similies of Mr. M'Kean, such as— "if the sky should fall, we should catch larks, and if the rivers should run mud, we should catch eels"[2]—the dry trash of *Publius* in 150 numbers—the *divine* allegories of Galen,[3] the triffling railleries of the little Admiralty Judge,[4] impudent assertions and calumnies against those who have had resolution and independency of spirit to animadvert on the new constitution, and on the conduct of its framers— Extracts of letters from Maryland, Virginia, Boston, &c. composed in Philadelphia—ribaldry—scurrility—seditious falsehoods—or, to use a word which includes them all, and every thing else that is infamous, base and wicked—nothing but *Rushisms*.[5]

1. Reprinted: *New York Journal*, 16 May; Baltimore *Maryland Gazette*, 16 May; *Newport Mercury*, 26 May. This item satirizes a piece printed in the *Pennsylvania Gazette* on 30 April (CC:719).

2. Quoted from Federalist Thomas McKean's lengthy 10 December 1787 speech in the Pennsylvania Convention (RCS:Pa., 542).

3. A reference to Benjamin Rush, a Philadelphia physician and Federalist propagandist.

4. A reference to Federalist propagandist Francis Hopkinson who had been a judge of the Admiralty Court of Pennsylvania since 1779.

5. On 30 January "Centinel" XIII had described Benjamin Rush as "Doctor Puff the paragraphist," through whose "creative pen thousands of correspondents rise into view" (CC:487).

# APPENDIX I

The documents printed in Appendix I are, for the most part, widely circulated squibs or fillers. Most of the squibs are either reports on the prospects of ratification in the various states or speculations about the attitudes of one or more persons on the Constitution. Others are reports of events, followed by some partisan commentary about them. Since Federalists controlled most newspapers, the majority of the squibs favor the Constitution or attack its opponents.

### Pennsylvania Packet, 3 April[1]

The legislators of America in convention assembled, without royalty and without nobility, are endeavouring to imitate the British constitution, and out of one estate to create three. What success will attend their labours, it seems not very difficult to predict. An elective chief magistrate, without prerogative, and without influence; a senate without hereditary dignity or privilege; and a representative body, of which every individual may aspire to the office of first magistrate, can bear little resemblance to a constitution, the foundation of which is laid in three several and distinct bodies, possessing each hereditary, indefeasible and independent powers. The democracy must evidently preponderate, or rather the whole constitution will be one demonstracy.[2]

1. Reprints by 26 May (10): Mass. (2), Conn. (2), N.Y. (1), Pa. (1), Md. (2), Va. (1), S.C. (1). The *Pennsylvania Packet*, 3 April, and the Baltimore *Maryland Gazette*, 8 April, printed this item under a dateline of Kingston, Jamaica, 16 February. On 8 April the *Maryland Journal* placed it within quotation marks and described it as a *"Paragraph from an Edinburgh News-Paper."* All other newspapers which reprinted this item also noted that it was from an Edinburgh newspaper, although one said that it was from a Scottish newspaper. Beginning with the *Massachusetts Gazette*, 25 April, five newspapers reprinted the article under the heading "Scotch Prediction." The *State Gazette of South Carolina*, 24 April, which provided the most detailed information on the source of the piece, noted that it was an *"Extract from an Edinburgh paper, dated in November last."*
2. The reprint in the Baltimore *Maryland Gazette*, 8 April, changed the word to "demonocracy." All other reprints substituted "democracy."

### Massachusetts Centinel, 9 April[1]

The Assembly of Rhode-Island, we are informed by a gentleman from Providence, at their session last week, at East-Greenwich, REFUSED TO COMPLY with the requests of a number of towns, to call a CONVENTION for taking the federal Constitution under consideration.—*Laus Deo!*

1. Reprints by 24 May (10): N.H. (2), Mass. (3), Conn. (3), Pa. (2). Four newspapers omitted the closing "*Laus Deo*," which translates "Praise be to God." On 24 March the Constitution was rejected in a statewide referendum by a margin of more than eleven to one (see CC:664). Whereupon, the Federalist towns of Bristol, Newport, and Providence issued instructions to their delegates to the General Assembly requiring them to do their utmost to obtain a state convention. The towns also petitioned the March session of the Assembly. Shortly after the Assembly attained a quorum on 2 April, Newport deputy Henry Marchant's motion calling for a state convention was defeated by a majority of twenty-seven.

## Pennsylvania Gazette, 9 April[1]

We learn that the Honorable Mr. Blount, of North-Carolina,[2] writes, as his opinion, that a great majority of the people of that state are in favor of the proposed constitution for the United States. So many reports, paragraphs and assertions have been circulated to the contrary, that it is a particular satisfaction to have this fact ascertained on such respectable authority.[3]

*Extract of a letter from Baltimore, dated April 3, 1788.*

"The best information from Virginia says, it will be a close poll; but the fœderalists will *certainly* carry, but by no great majority. Maryland is a hollow matter. We are fœderal in convention: I mean they will be as five to three, or fifty to thirty. Out of convention, we are three to one all over the state."[4]

*Extract of a letter from a gentleman of note in Charleston,
South-Carolina, to a gentleman in this city.*

"The new constitution is acceptable to nine tenths of the people of this state. I am sorry there is so much opposition to it in yours—I think their fears are groundless, and that much good will result from its adoption."[5]

1. Two newspapers, the Middletown, Conn., *Middlesex Gazette*, 21 April, and the *Newport Herald*, 1 May, reprinted all three paragraphs; while eight newspapers reprinted only the first two paragraphs by 1 May: Mass. (1), R.I. (1), Conn. (3), N.Y. (1), Pa. (1), S.C. (1). See also notes 3–5 (below).

2. William Blount, a signer of the Constitution, was defeated for a seat in the North Carolina Convention which met in Hillsborough in July and August 1788. He voted to ratify the Constitution in the North Carolina Convention which met in Fayetteville in November 1789.

3. This paragraph was reprinted twelve times by 1 May: Mass. (1), R.I. (2), Conn. (4), N.Y. (1), Pa. (2), S.C. (2). On 11 April the *New York Packet* reprinted only the first sentence, and by 8 May six newspapers followed the *Packet's* lead: Mass. (3), R.I. (1), Md. (1), Va. (1).

4. This paragraph was reprinted eleven times by 17 May: Mass. (1), R.I. (2), Conn. (3), N.Y. (1), Pa. (1), S.C. (2), Ga. (1).

5. This paragraph was reprinted in the Middletown, Conn., *Middlesex Gazette*, 21 April; Richmond *Virginia Gazette and Weekly Advertiser*, 24 April; *Newport Herald*, 1 May; and Winchester *Virginia Gazette*, 7 May.

### Annapolis Maryland Gazette, 10 April[1]

*Extract of a letter from a gentleman in Alexandria, of the
8th instant, to a gentleman of this city.*

"I have the pleasure to inform you, that, on the close of the elections in this state for delegates to convention, there is a considerable majority of federal members, and among these, characters of the first influence, both in point of popularity and abilities, such as Madison, Pendleton, Wythe, Innes, Marshall, Nicholas, &c. &c. so that there is little doubt of the adoption of the constitution."

1. Reprints by 10 May (11): Mass. (1), Conn. (1), N.Y. (3), N.J. (1), Pa. (3), Md. (1), S.C. (1). Each man named in this extract voted to ratify the Constitution in the Virginia Convention in June.

### New York Morning Post, 11 April[1]

By the new system of government, proposed by the late American Convention, the poor Africans (as if the States, in their bustle about liberty, had discovered a right to enslave them) are doomed to endure a continuance of depredation, rapine, and murder, for 21 years to come. The Congress being, for that time, absolutely precluded from interference with that most flagrant violation of natural justice.

1. This item, printed under a dateline of London, 6 February, was reprinted six times by 2 May: Mass. (1), Pa. (1), Md. (1), Va. (3). The reprinting newspapers also printed this paragraph under a London dateline, but under such dates as 2 and 28 January and 4 and 6 February.

### Massachusetts Centinel, 12 April[1]

The experience of every revolving day, more and more speaks the necessity of the establishment of such a government, as will enable us to convince the world that we will not suffer any nation to insult us with impunity. Under our present government our enemies act with us as they please—and while it exists will continue so to do.—A recent instance of this truth we have in an extract of a letter received by a gentleman in this town yesterday, dated,

*"Lake Champlain, March* 18, 1788.

"Lord Dorchester[2] has ordered the people *ten miles on this side the lines*, to be enrolled with the militia of Canada—they are to chuse their officers next week, are to be governed by the laws of that province, and protected by the same. As soon as the ice on the lake breaks up, the Ship Maria is to come up the lake, 10 miles, to keep up order and regulation, if necessary."

1. Reprints by 21 May (19): Vt. (1), N.H. (2), Mass. (2), R.I. (2), Conn. (3), N.Y. (1), Pa. (3), Md. (2), Va. (2), S.C. (1). Excerpts appeared in two South Carolina newspapers.
2. Guy Carleton, the first Baron Dorchester, was governor of Quebec from 1786 to 1791.

## Philadelphia Federal Gazette, 12 April[1]

We are favoured with the following extract from a letter, written by a gentleman in Richmond, and received by this day's mail:

"All the returns for delegates to the convention are now received from every part of the state; and it is with pleasure I inform you, that the list is such as will ensure the adoption of the constitution in this state, by a decided majority. From the apparent sentiments of the different members, at present, a majority of about 18 or 19 are avowedly federal. The governor[2] is not reckoned as one of this number, though I have many reasons for believing that the constitution will have his firm support. When we reflect on the advantages that have resulted to the federal cause, in the conventions of other states, from free investigation, which has uniformly tended to dispel the mists of ignorance and prejudice, I think we may very reasonably expect, that a similar conviction will take place in the minds of many in our convention, when they shall have heard the merits of the constitution and the objections to it candidly examined; and that Virginia will shortly become one of the brightest pillars of the federal edifice."

As several other letters, lately received from the same quarter, corroborate the truth of the above intelligence, we may venture to pronounce it unquestionable, and founded on the best information.

1. Five newspapers reprinted this item in toto; ten omitted the last paragraph; and two newspapers printed excerpts by 12 May (17): Vt. (1), Mass. (4), R.I. (2), Conn. (3), N.Y. (5), N.J. (1), Pa. (1).
2. Governor Edmund Randolph refused to sign the Constitution in September 1787, but he voted to ratify in the Virginia Convention in June 1788.

## New Hampshire Spy, 15, 22 April

*The Federal Hat, 15 April*[1]

It is recommended to the Ladies who lead the fashions, that instead of the *Wind-mill-Hats*, they introduce one under the name of the "*Federal Hat*." The form of this Hat may be pretty, neat and genteel; the thirteen States may be represented by thirteen rings; these may be constructed in such a manner as will answer for the ream; the poll and crown may represent the GRAND FEDERAL EDIFICE—while the ribbons and wavers, with stars interspersed, which decorate it, might be so disposed as to represent the United States and the several Kingdoms with whom they are in alliance. A hat of this form would certainly command respect—it would discover that the fair are patrons of the *federal cause*, and that the federal Patriot will ever meet with their genuine approbation.

### Variety Store, 22 April[2]

Mr. OSBORNE, *We expect to receive, in a very short time, a great variety of new invented CAPS, BONNETS, and HATS, previous to which it will be necessary to inform the public of their different qualities.*

—If suitable encouragement offers, in a short time will be opened, *the Variety Store*, where will be sold the following new invented *Caps, Bonnets* and *Hats*, viz.

1st. *A Cap with a Conductor*—to prevent the ladies from being *thunder struck* in August; the conductor appears in the front several inches above the surface, and lays horizontal from the brim to the back of the cap, from whence it descends behind the lady's back.

2d. *The Weather Cock Bonnet*. A bonnet, with a variety of weather-cocks very elegantly coloured with sea-green. These bonnets are much used by those ladies whose husbands are navigators—as they will discover, at any hour of the day, *how the wind is*—they are also very necessary for seamen *under sailing orders*, &c.

3d. *Chapeau de Bataille*—is made in the form of a battery, (agreeable to the newest mode of fortification) with two flanks, very necessary for *some* gentlemen, who, for want of modesty to the ladies, find themselves unexpect[ed]ly engaged in a warm *action* from the *head*, where no *quarter* is given, but where the *broadside* makes the finishing stroke.

4th. *The Flambeau Cap*, illuminated with light. This cap serves only for evening visits. It is a capital invention, for it shews *light* where *darkness* prevailed. It is of great use in a seaport, where *light actions* are much practiced.

5th. *The electrical mock-night Cap*—designed only for *old maids*—the *electricity* is chiefly in that part of the border which lies next to the cheek. The vulgar term this cap—*"touch me not!"*

6th. *The Enchanting Hat*, for unmarried ladies. This hat breaks many a lover's *what you call it*—It gives him a fine prospect—the eye beholds surprizing charms in favour of the wearer; the enchantment consists in the view of *houses, farms, lands*, &c. scattered on the brim; the ribbons are *public securities*, and notes *payable on demand*, all tied together with a string of *ready cash*. This enchantment lasts as long as the hat is on the lady's head, for after a while it turns out against the owner's interest.

7th. *The Modest Hat.* This hat is made of a rich black silk, trimmed with fine black gauze and ribbons, very neat and elegant, and always fashionable—*but very unsaleable.* It is presumed this hat will sell well, Anno Domini, 9871.

8th. *The Antifederal Hat.* This hat is designed for those who are *delicate* in matters of *conscience*—fearful—under continual apprehensions of being cheated, &c. The foundation of this hat is a *hard Stone*, the trimmings are a representation of *canker-worms, rattle-snakes, crocodiles, adders*, &c. the brim is covered with *cobwebs* and *spiders* sucking *little insects* and *flies*: the poll is made of *blood-suckers*, tied with the *string* of *discord*:—the whole decorated with a variety of gems from the land of *annihilation*—this hat met with a rapid sale in *Rogue-Island*— and was much admired by the *Wrongheads* in Connecticut.[3]

9th. *Federal Caps, Bonnets, and Hats*, for young misses. These are made by Madam *Federalist*, in Concord, at her shop, at the sign of the *Horn of Abundance.* The materials are of American manufacture, and are composed of *snow white lawn*—the ribbons are striped with thirteen different colours—the garland of flowers are made in imitation of virgin modesty—Jack in the green—Sweet William—lillies and little roses.

*Jean Francois Frizeur,*  
    *Coeffeur,*  
    *Beuveur,*  
    *Trompeur,*  
    *Moqueur,*      }    *en Compainie.*  
    *Turlipineur,*  
    *Chasseur, et*  
    *Crevecoeur,*

1. Reprinted in the Exeter, N.H., *Freeman's Oracle*, 25 April, and *Massachusetts Centinel*, 7 May. A slightly altered version was reprinted ten times by 2 July: Mass. (1), R.I. (2), N.Y. (2), N.J. (1), Pa. (3), S.C. (1).

2. This item was printed in an extra issue of the *Spy*.

3. Hugh Ledlie, an Antifederalist from Hartford, complained that Connecticut's Federalists ("those mighty men of Moab") referred to the state's Antifederalists "by the opprobrious Name of Wrongheads" (to John Lamb, 15 January 1788, RCS:Conn., 577). For other references to "Wrongheads" in Connecticut, see RCS:Conn., 455, 465, 473– 76, 501, 507, 580.

## Salem Mercury, 15 April[1]

The brig *Lydia*, Captain *John Murphy*, arrived in this port, on Saturday last, from Alicant, in Spain, after a passage of 68 days.—March 26th, in lat. 24, long. 46,30, he spoke the brig Agnes, Capt. Dennie, belonging to Col. Sargent of Boston, from Boston bound to Martinico, who, in a heavy gale, two days after he sailed, lost every thing off deck, except his boats—all well on board.

So seldom do the vessels of the United States venture so far up the Mediterranean, that the American flag was viewed at Alicant as a novelty.

While Capt. Murphy was at Alicant, he had opportunity of noticing several instances of that meanness and implacable hatred to the Americans, which uniformly operates in the breasts of some individuals of the British nation, from whose exalted stations we should expect a more honourable conduct:—He had authentick information, thro' the friendship of the Swedish Consul, that immediately on his arrival at that port, the British Consul (Pat. Wilkie) sent intelligence thereof to Algiers, with a description of the vessel, &c. and that she was an object worth their pursuit. Captain Murphy, therefore, to frustrate the inimical intention of Mr. Wilkie, took the precaution, just before he sailed, to alter the complexion of his vessel.—An English Nobleman, who was at Alicant, discovered equal animosity towards our nation: Mr. Montgomery, merchant at that place, offered him our New Constitution for perusal, contained in a newspaper he had received of Capt. Murphy; but he could not condescend to read an *American* paper, saying, he should soon have an opportunity of seeing it in the *English* papers. This NOBLE-man was very angry at the enterprising genius of our citizens, and with some warmth observed to Mr. Montgomery, that he seemed to be the Protector of the Americans—*No*, replied the latter, *General WASHINGTON is their Protector*. The mention of this revered name was more ungrateful to my lord, than a peal of thunder.

1. Reprints in whole or in part by 8 May (14): N.H. (2), Mass. (4), Conn. (3), N.Y. (1), N.J. (2), Pa. (2).

### Philadelphia Freeman's Journal, 16 April[1]

The General Court, (or House of Representatives) of Massachusetts Bay have lately reprobated in the most express and pointed terms the proceedings of the General Convention and the Convention of their own state.[2] The consequences of this will be fatal to the new Constitution in all the New-England states in particular, and must be a great stab to it every where in the Union, as Massachusetts is one of the most powerful and respectable in the thirteen. We see by this in what light that state views the childish parade and flummery of the town of Boston.[3]

1. Reprints by 7 May (6): Md. (3), Va. (3).

2. In Massachusetts, the General Court was composed of the House of Representatives and the Senate. For an attempt in the House to censure the Constitutional Convention and the Massachusetts Convention, see CC:566.

3. The "childish parade" refers to the procession held in Boston on 8 February to celebrate the ratification of the Constitution by the Massachusetts Convention. This procession, in which about 4,500 people took part, was the first of the huge state celebrations commemorating ratification. On 20 February the *Freeman's Journal* itself had reprinted a lengthy account of the procession from the *Massachusetts Centinel* of 9 February.

## Philadelphia Independent Gazetteer, 16 April[1]

Extract of a letter from a gentleman of character in the state of Virginia, to his friend in this city, dated 30th March, 1788.

"You will no doubt be astonished when I inform you that the election of members to serve in the approaching convention, have generally been decided in favor of the opponents to the new constitution. Indeed I do not hear of a single instance where an exertion has been made in the opposition to the system, that has not succeeded. Colonel Mason is returned for Stafford county—Colonel Grayson for Prince William— Mr. Patrick Henry for Prince Edward, and Mr. E. Randolph for Henrico;[2] there remains not a doubt but the exertions of those able and truly patriotic characters, will be crowned with success; and that Virginia will, by a very decided majority, reject a measure which I am candid to own at first met with my approbation; but which, I am, on an investigation, convinced will endanger those liberties for which America gloriously contended, during an eight years war."

The fate of the new constitution, observes a correspondent, is now determined; its warmest advocates scarcely squeak; the patriotic writings have awakened the people of this state to a proper sense of the danger they were in, and they are determined to assert their liberties like men: The *Centinel*, in particular, has been of infinite service in explaining the latent mischiefs of this system of tyranny, and the conduct of its promoters. This publication has acquired the approbation of every good man, for its ability and candour, elegance of composition, and for its spirited and patriotic ardour, while it is dreaded by the *junto*, their sycophants and tools, as the key to all their juggling and dark politics.

1. These two paragraphs were reprinted in the *New York Journal*, 19 and 21 April, and Boston *American Herald*, 28 April; while the first paragraph alone was reprinted in the Poughkeepsie *Country Journal*, 29 April, and Providence *United States Chronicle*, 1 May.

2. George Mason, William Grayson, and Patrick Henry voted against ratification of the Constitution in the Virginia Convention in June, while Edmund Randolph voted for ratification.

## Philadelphia Federal Gazette, 17 April[1]

By a gentleman who left Baltimore last Monday afternoon, we are informed that Mr. Martin declares he will make no further opposition to the new plan of government, seeing so great a majority of the people of Maryland are in favour of it;[2] that Mr. Martin's writings, like Centinel and Philadelphiensis in this state, have made no impressions on the minds of the people, tho' in the language of antifederalism, they are ranked with the Bible[a]; that he is despised in every county except one, and in all probability will not be suffered to continue in the office of Attorney General another year.

(a) *See an advertisement in the Freeman's Journal and Independent Gazetteer.*[3]

1. Reprints in whole or in part by 8 May (7): N.H. (1), Mass. (3), R.I. (1), N.Y. (2). Only four of these newspapers reprinted the reference to the Bible.
2. On 26 April Luther Martin voted against ratification of the Constitution in the Maryland Convention.
3. For this advertisement, see the headnote to CC:678.

## Pennsylvania Mercury, 17 April[1]

*Extract of a letter from Richmond, Virginia, dated April 4.*

"The election for Delegates to our state convention is now over, and on enquiry, we are able to count a respectable majority, in favour of the new constitution—amongst this number, is the virtuous MADISON.[2]—I am informed, that some counties are so convinced of the necessity of the adoption of the Constitution, that they are about to instruct their members so to do—Thus, my friend, your fears for Virginia are ill founded."

1. This item, also printed in the Philadelphia *Federal Gazette* on 17 April, was reprinted six times by 7 May: N.H. (1), Mass. (2), R.I. (1), Conn. (1), N.Y. (1).
2. For the election of James Madison as an Orange County delegate to the Virginia Convention, see RCS:Va., 595–606.

## Philadelphia Independent Gazetteer, 17 April[1]

Time, that discoverer of all solid truths, will shew that the new constitution will never be received by the union as a government. The state of New-Hampshire are becoming more averse to it; the Massachusetts House of Representatives in their answer to *President Hancock's* speech, have reprobated it in the strongest terms,[2] so it is probable it will be *reconsidered* by that state; Rhode Island have rejected it; New-York will crush it at least by two-thirds; five-sixths of the people of Pennsylvania are determined not to receive a system of tyranny adopted illegally by the other *sixth*, under the influence of a mob; Maryland will, if they do not reject it immediately, adjourn the decision to June or July; Virginia rejects it, and so of North-Carolina; South-Carolina is doubtful, but it is probable they will not differ with her sister states to the southward. Notwithstanding the people have been so much deceived and kept in the dark by the mock federalists, still providence will enable them to rise superior to all the wicked arts practised to ensnare their liberties.

1. Reprinted: *New York Journal*, 23 April; Boston *American Herald*, 5 May; Portland *Cumberland Gazette*, 15 May.

2. At this point, the *American Herald* and *Cumberland Gazette* inserted: "*(this is a mistake, for the House did not return his Excellency any answer at all).*" For Governor John Hancock's speech of 27 February opening the session of the Massachusetts legislature and the proposed response of the House of Representatives, see CC:566.

### Pennsylvania Gazette, 23 April[1]

By the last vessels from Charleston was received the ticket for that place, containing the names of 32 gentlemen proposed to be elected members of the State Convention. Among them are members of the Fœderal Convention, members of the Assembly, several of their Governors, Speakers of Assembly, and private gentlemen of much worth, and friendly to the proposed Constitution. Things wear the most promising appearance in that patriotic and important state.

1. Reprints by 15 May (10): Mass. (4), R.I. (1), N.Y. (1), Pa. (1), Md. (1), Va. (2). The *Pennsylvania Gazette* probably refers to the list of thirty-two numbered delegates elected for the parish of St. Philip and St. Michael's which was printed in the Charleston *Columbian Herald* on 17 April. This list was also printed by the Charleston *City Gazette* and the *State Gazette of South Carolina* on the same day, but neither of these two newspapers numbered the delegates. On 22 April the *Pennsylvania Mercury* published the names of the thirty-two delegates and identified only four of them as Antifederalists. Two of the thirty-two delegates—Edward Rutledge and Charles Cotesworth Pinckney—had signed the Constitution.

### New York Journal, 24 April[1]

MR. GREENLEAF, *You will be pleased to insert in your paper, the following extract of a letter from a gentleman of character, in one of the towns, in Montgomery county, in the state of Pennsylvania, to his friend in this city; dated March 6, 1788.*

"I have set myself down at this place, and intend to become a farmer—the prospect of domestic happiness, for a long time before public business would permit me to remain at home with my family, were very flattering; but I now find myself much disappointed. A constitution has been formed for the government of the United States; and by the *cunning, deception, and address,* of its advocates, has been precipitately adopted, by this state; since which, the fears of the people throughout the country are much alarmed. The address of the minority of our convention, has carried conviction through the state; communities are forming in every county, with a determination to prevent its taking place, in its present form; and I can assure you, that the opposition has become very general; in many counties it has scarce a man in its favor."[2]

(The printer can vouch for the authenticity of the above extract, having seen the original.)

1. This item was reprinted in the Philadelphia *Independent Gazetteer,* 28 April; Boston *American Herald,* 5 May; and Portland *Cumberland Gazette,* 15 May. All three reprints omitted the editorial statement following the extract of the letter.

2. For the "Dissent of the Minority of the Pennsylvania Convention," first printed in the *Pennsylvania Packet* on 18 December, see CC:353; and for the Antifederalist petition campaign requesting that the state legislature not "confirm" the state's ratification of the Constitution, see RCS:Pa., 709–25.

## New York Morning Post, 28 April[1]

A *new* PRETENDER *of the line of Stuart* hath arisen up like the Demetrius's in Russia, to the astonishment of Europe: In consequence of which the Jacobites in England have made serious overtures to the Antifederalists in the United States to elevate him to a throne in America.—If the Antifederalists will accede to this proposal, by rejecting the new constitution, the Jacobites stipulate the subjugation of Great Britain to this kingdom, and that they will remove here with the Papal See.

1. This item was reprinted in the *Newport Herald,* 1 May; Newburyport *Essex Journal,* 7 May; *Boston Gazette,* 12 May; *New Hampshire Gazette,* 15 May; and Boston *American Herald,* 19 May. It has been transcribed from the 1 May issue of the *Newport Herald,* the first newspaper to reprint it. The *Boston Gazette* reprinted the item under a dateline of New York, 28 April, indicating that it was probably reprinted from the no longer extant *New York Morning Post* of 28 April. (The piece has not been located in any other New York City newspaper printed on or around 28 April.)

## Charleston City Gazette, 29 April[1]

*Extract of a letter from a gentleman*
*in Beaufort to his friend in this city.*
"Our people this way are well inclined towards the new government.

I enclose you a copy of an address from the grand jury to the court on the subject."[2]

*To the honorable the Court of General Sessions.*

After discharging our duty as grand jurors with attention, and we flatter ourselves with fidelity, we avail ourselves of being thus convened to declare our sentiments upon a subject of the greatest magnitude to our state particularly, and to our country generally. To preserve the union of the states we hold to be an indispensable duty incumbent on every citizen of America. With grateful acknowledgements to the supreme being and heart felt satisfaction, we view a form of federal government, calculated to answer this salutary purpose, now submitted for their adoption. On this momentous occasion, impelled by zeal for the prosperity of our country, we think it our duty to bear this public testimony of our approbation of a measure which appears to us to have been dictated by the same spirit of liberty which brought about the revolution, and which, in our opinion, has every safeguard which human foresight can suggest for perpetuating the blessings of freedom, tranquility, union, and the prosperity of the whole.[3]

1. Reprints by 4 June (11): Mass. (4), N.Y. (2), Pa. (2), Md. (2), Va. (1). The *New Hampshire Spy*, 24 May, reprinted only the introductory paragraph and the following description of the address: "This address breath[e]s the purest principles of federalism, and a desire of the states being united under an efficient government." A copy of the Charleston *City Gazette*, 29 April, was carried to New York City by a Captain Freneau; while another copy was brought to Boston by a Captain Hichborn of the Sloop *Industry* (New York *Daily Advertiser*, 14 May; and *Massachusetts Centinel*, 21 May).

2. This address, signed by the grand jurors, was printed in South Carolina's newspapers by order of the Court of General Sessions. Between 19 May and 12 June, it appeared six times in the Charleston *Columbian Herald*, and between 19 May and 2 June three times in the *State Gazette of South Carolina*.

3. Immediately below the address, the *Massachusetts Centinel*, 21 May, stated that "Capt. Hichborn was assured by the gentlemen of knowledge and intelligence in Charleston, that their Convention would ratify the Constitution by a very large majority." The *New Hampshire Spy*, 24 May, and Portland *Cumberland Gazette*, 29 May, reprinted this statement.

### Pennsylvania Gazette, 30 April[1]

The accounts from Maryland and South-Carolina, says a correspondent, are so favorable to the adoption of the proposed fœderal constitution, that the question now only is, which member of the old confederacy will put the key-stone to the arch of the new. There seems little or no reason to apprehend a rejection by any state, Rhode-Island excepted; for every day adds more solid reasons in favor of the measure. A curious instance now exists in Georgia. They have a paper money *a legal tender*, though at four or five for one; and yet the shame, that would attend the wicked conduct of cancelling a debt on such terms, prevents any tenders from being made. How happy would it be, where government is so remiss as not to repeal a law tempting the people to fraud, if the existence of the new constitution had been early enough to prevent the emission. We learn, however, that paper money has deeply injured their commerce, both foreign and internal.

By advice received yesterday afternoon from MARYLAND, we find that the CONVENTION of that state have adopted THE NEW FEDERAL CONSTITUTION, by a majority of 63 in favor and 11 against it, which is near six to one. Such are the effects of FULL DISCUSSION, and such their determination at the distance of seven months from the time of promulgation.

1. Both paragraphs were reprinted in whole or in part six times by 15 May: Mass. (3), N.Y. (1), N.J. (1), Pa. (1). The first paragraph was reprinted eight times by 14 May: Mass. (3), N.Y. (2), N.J. (1), Pa. (1), Md. (1). The Portland *Cumberland Gazette*, 15 May, reprinted only the first two sentences. The second paragraph was reprinted fifteen times by 29 May: N.H. (2), Mass. (7), N.Y. (2), N.J. (1), Pa. (1), S.C. (1), Ga. (1). The *State Gazette of South Carolina*, 19 May, and *Gazette of the State of Georgia*, 29 May, added this sentence at the end of the paragraph: "No amendments were recommended by the convention."

### Providence United States Chronicle, 1 May[1]

"A Correspondent remarks, That the Re-election of the present worthy Chief Magistrate of Massachusetts, his Excellency Governor HANCOCK—the Election of General LINCOLN for Lieutenant-Governor—and the Certainty of there being a Majority of the new Senators, *federal Men*, and of Course Friends to good Government,—all which is now beyond a Doubt, must give every Friend to America great Satisfaction, and excite the most pleasing Sensations.—It must convince every candid Mind, that *Antifederalism* is on the Decline; and that a Majority of that respectable State, in Numbers, as well as in Wealth, are Friends to good Government; and that they will *support* the Federal Constitution—*any Suggestions of* OUR ANTI's *to the contrary notwithstanding.*"

1. Reprinted: *New York Morning Post*, 20 May; Philadelphia *Independent Gazetteer*, 21 May; Charleston *City Gazette*, 17 June.

### New York Daily Advertiser, 1 May[1]

*Extract of a letter from a gentleman of information, on the Frontiers of Virginia, to his friend in this city, dated* 19th March, 1788.

"I have lately been informed, that favorable proposals have been made to the Kentuckians, by Great-Britain, in order to induce them to quit our Confederacy.—With respect to the new Constitution, it will be adopted by Virginia, fully, in the first instance; and some amendments may probably afterwards be proposed."

1. Reprints by 7 June (23): N.H. (1), Mass. (5), R.I. (2), N.Y. (4), Pa. (5), Md. (2), Va. (2), N.C. (1), S.C. (1). On 2 August the *Kentucky Gazette* also reprinted this item.

## Pennsylvania Mercury, 1 May[1]

*Extract of a letter from Baltimore, April* 24.

"By my last accounts from Virginia, there will be a majority of more than twenty in their convention. In South-Carolina we have a clear majority of three to one."

1. Reprints by 19 May (13): N.H. (1), Mass. (4), R.I. (3), Conn. (1), N.Y. (3), N.J. (1). The *State Gazette of South Carolina*, 19 May, Charleston *City Gazette*, 21 May, and Charleston *Columbian Herald*, 22 May, reprinted only the first sentence.

## Pennsylvania Packet, 2 May[1]

"⟨By the best and latest information from Virginia, there is a majority of forty voices in favor of adopting the Federal Constitution⟩; and by letters from Charleston we are assured it will be received in South-Carolina without much opposition. Thus will America be a second time rescued from desolation and confusion, by the united exertions of her heroes, philosophers, and patriots—And it will not be in vain that the best blood of America has been immolated at the altar of freedom."

1. This paragraph was originally printed as the second paragraph of an "Extract of a letter from Annapolis, dated 28th April," in the *Pennsylvania Packet* on 2 May. The lengthy first paragraph (not printed here) described the events that took place in the Maryland Convention on 26 April, the day that body ratified the Constitution. (For this paragraph, see RCS:Md.) The complete extract of the Annapolis letter was reprinted thirteen times by 22 May: Mass. (1), R.I. (3), Conn. (1), N.Y. (4), Pa. (3), S.C. (1). The second paragraph only was reprinted by the *Massachusetts Centinel*, 14 May, and by 23 May it was reprinted eight more times: N.H. (2), Mass. (4), N.Y. (1), N.J. (1). The Newburyport *Essex Journal*, 21 May, reprinted only the text in angle brackets.

## Philadelphia Independent Gazetteer, 6 May[1]

A CAUTION.

Whereas, in the year 1787, some vessels were fitted out at the port of Philadelphia, for the iniquitous purpose of stealing the inhabitants of Africa, from all the endearments of domestic life;[2] one of which vessels has succeeded in obtaining a number of poor blacks, and has taken them to a port in the West Indies, where they are under the iron hand of oppression. From this shameful traffic, this horrid source, the proprietors of the vessel have purchased some West India produce, which, after landing at Wilmington, they have brought up to this city, and offered for sale.

It is a grateful circumstance to the supporters of the common rights of mankind, that the virtuous inhabitants of the city, reprobate the horrid idea.—A correspondent hopes, that the citizens will further testify their disapprobation of the practice, by turning with indignation from the purchase of any property, thus basely procured by men so lost to the common feelings of humanity; notwithstanding the *patriotic* convention, at which a *Washington* presided, have declared that this abominable traffic shall be continued for TWENTY years by the people of America!

1. Reprinted: Philadelphia *Freeman's Journal*, 14 May; *New York Journal*, 16 May; *Boston Gazette*, 19 May; Winchester *Virginia Gazette*, 21 May.

2. In March 1788 the Pennsylvania legislature passed an act prohibiting the fitting out of vessels in any of the state's ports for the purpose of engaging in the slave trade.

### Pennsylvania Gazette, 7 May[1]

Every day, says a correspondent, adds to the weighty arguments in favor of the proposed fœderal constitution. The friends of the American union in Europe and in Kentucke have certainly a belief, that overtures have been made by Great Britain to leading characters on the western waters, to induce the inhabitants of that country to dissever themselves from their brethren on the Atlantic.[2] This idea has been suggested, no doubt, by the late divisions and distracted politics of our country; and nothing can prevent its being carried into execution but a firm union, a constitution of general government with sufficient powers, and a wise and honest administration. Were we to lose the government now proposed to the people of America, and fall into single and separate states, and the people of the western country were to be seduced into the schemes of Great Britain, miserable would be the situation of Virginia, the Carolinas, and Georgia, on the south, and of New Hampshire and New York on the north. Some of them would be seized by Britain as their outlet to the Atlantic; for they would rather risque a quarrel with a single detached American state, from which they could fear nothing, than hazard a quarrel with the house of Bourbon.[3]

*Extract of a letter from Charleston, April* 21.

"This day three weeks our convention meets, to deliberate on the constitution. I am pretty confident that it will be ratified. Some opposition is expected from the framers of the instalment, pine-barren, valuation and legal tender laws. Excepting from this quarter, our convention has little to apprehend. I hope in my next to congratulate you upon South-Carolina becoming the seventh pillar of the new government. God grant it, and a speedy and general ratification and operation."

It is impossible (says a correspondent) to tell the influence which the American revolution will have upon the happiness of mankind. The spirit of liberty which has of late appeared in France was transplanted from the United States. It was first excited by the translation and republication of the *Farmer's Letters*,[4] and since by the *Declaration of Independence*, and many other American productions, which were pregnant with just ideas of liberty. This noble spirit has been encreased and still further diffused among all ranks of people by the French officers and soldiers, who served in America during the late war, and who caught it from the American citizens and soldiers. The just ideas which have at last pervaded the English nation upon the subject of the commerce and slavery of the Africans, originated in Philadelphia. From the effects of our conduct upon the opinions and actions of two of the first nations in the world, what may we not expect, when we shall have made greater improvements and progress in political knowledge and happiness?—The praises of our fœderal constitution have been echoed back from every civilized and enlightened part of Europe. Philosophers and the friends of mankind have suspended all other enquiries, and now fix their eyes solely on the conduct of the United States, as if all the happiness and dignity of human nature was to be determined by it. The oppressed and distressed every where wait only for the news of the general adoption of the government, to quit their chains; while the tyrants of Europe, and their mercenary dependents, *only*, view the whole system of our fœderal republic as visionary and impracticable and insist upon it that man was made (through the medium of anarchy) only for SLAVERY and for KINGS.

1. These three paragraphs were all reprinted in the *Pennsylvania Mercury*, 10 May; Baltimore *Maryland Gazette*, 13 May; and Pittsfield *Berkshire Chronicle*, 5 June. The first paragraph was reprinted in whole or in part in nineteen newspapers by 16 August: Vt. (1), Mass. (4), R.I. (1), Conn. (1), N.Y. (2), N.J. (1), Pa. (1), Md. (2), Va. (2), N.C. (2), S.C. (1), Ga. (1). Two of these nineteen newspapers—the *Pennsylvania Mercury* and Baltimore *Maryland Gazette*—reprinted this paragraph a second time from the no longer extant 12 June issue of the Newbern *State Gazette of North Carolina*. The second paragraph was reprinted eleven times by 3 June: N.H. (1), Mass. (1), R.I. (1), N.Y. (2), Pa. (3), Md. (2), Va. (1). The third paragraph was reprinted seven times by 12 June: N.H. (1), Mass. (4), Pa. (1), Md. (1).
2. See the New York *Daily Advertiser*, 1 May (above).
3. Spain.

4. In 1769 *Letters from a Farmer in Pennsylvania*, which had first appeared in 1767 and 1768 in Philadelphia, was translated and edited by Jean Barbeu Dubourg and printed in Paris, although the title page gives Amsterdam as the place of publication.

## Delaware Gazette, 7 May[1]

WONDERFUL INTELLIGENCE, copied from a St. Kitts Paper—*Rosseau*[2] *(Dominico) Feb.* 3. By the latest advices from America we learn, that the whole State of Rhode-Island is to be sold to a private citizen of Georgia by private contract; and that Congress have resolved to apply the purchase money to pay off their national debt.

1. Reprints by 26 June (9): Mass. (2), N.Y. (2), Pa. (2), Md. (1), Va. (1), S.C. (1). It was reprinted in the *Pennsylvania Journal*, 14 May, under a dateline of Wilmington, 7 May. Because the Wilmington *Delaware Gazette*, 7 May, is not extant, this item has been transcribed from the *Pennsylvania Packet*, 10 May, the earliest known reprint.
2. Roseau is the port city and capital of Dominica.

## Maryland Journal, 9 May[1]

*Extract of a Letter from a Gentleman in London, to his*
*Friend in Maryland, dated Jan.* 31, 1788.

"People here talk much of the Distractions on your Side [of] the Water; but, I believe, they are magnified. Men are more easily governed than is generally thought, at least while they continue poor and virtuous; the former being the best Security of the latter. Anarchy has always ended in absolute Monarchy; but that is only in old States, where Wealth has accumulated in the Hands of Individuals, whose Vices, co-operating with the Profligacy of the lower Order of People, have overbalanced the middle Rank, which is the most, or only, virtuous one in all Countries. The Equality in America, one would think, would, for a long Time, preserve Order without any Government at all.

"The Trade of Great-Britain was never in so flourishing a State. The Excess in the Customs, and, indeed, all other Taxes, is immense, and People, who look no farther than Revenue, think the Loss of America to be a Gain.—Few lament Losses they do not feel."

1. Reprints by 3 June (7): Mass. (1), N.Y. (2), N.J. (1), Pa. (2), Va. (1).

# APPENDIX II

This table illustrates the circulation of all items in Volume 5 of *Commentaries on the Constitution* that were published in newspapers or as broadsides or pamphlets. The total figure for each item includes the original publication and all reprints, including the reprints of significant excerpts. An asterisk (*) indicates publication in the Philadelphia *American Museum*, which had a national circulation. A plus sign (+) indicates publication as a broadside, pamphlet, or book.

This table is included in *Commentaries* as an aid in comparing reprint data. Headnotes and footnotes of documents often contain additional information about circulation and should also be consulted.

| | | New Hampshire | Massachusetts | Rhode Island | Connecticut | New York | New Jersey | Pennsylvania | Delaware | Maryland | Virginia | North Carolina | South Carolina | Georgia | Vermont | Total |
|---|---|---|---|---|---|---|---|---|---|---|---|---|---|---|---|---|
| 656. | Publius The Federalist 76 | | | | | 3+ | | | | | | | | | | 3 |
| 657. | Publius The Federalist 77 | | | | | 3+ | | | | | | | | | | 3 |
| 658. | Pa. Gazette | | | | | 2 | 1 | 2 | | 1 | 1 | | 1 | | | 8 |
| 659. | A Native of Virginia | | | | | | | | | | 1+ | | | | | 1 |
| 662. | Luther Martin Address No. IV | | 1 | | | 1 | | 1 | 1 | | | | | | | 4 |
| 666. | Observations on Constitution | | | | | 1+ | | | | | | | | | | 1 |
| 668. | "K" | | | | | | | 5* | 1 | 1 | | | | | | 7 |
| 670. | Arms, Maynard, and Field: Dissent | | 1 | | | | | | | | | | | | | 1 |
| 671. | Centinel XVIII | | | | | 1 | | 2 | | | | | | | | 3 |
| 672. | Philadelphiensis XII | | | | | | | 2 | | | | | | | | 2 |
| 674. | Brutus XVI | | 1 | | | 1 | | | | | | | | | | 2 |
| 675. | Spurious Luther Martin V | | | | | | | 1 | | | | | | | | 1 |
| 677. | Fabius I | 2 | 1 | | | | | 3* | 1 | 1 | | 1 | | | | 9 |
| 678A–D. | Luther Martin Genuine Information | | | | | | | 1+ | | | | | | | | 1 |
| 680. | Rush to Ramsay | | 3 | 1 | | | 2 | 2* | 1 | | | | 1 | | | 10 |
| 683. | A Citizen of New-York | 3 | 4+ | 1 | | 1+ | 1 | 3* | | | | 1 | | | | 14 |
| 684. | Fabius II | 2 | 1 | | | | | 2* | 1 | 1 | | | | | | 7 |
| 685. | Peter Prejudice | 1 | 4 | 1 | 1 | 2 | 1 | 2* | 1 | 1 | | | | | 1 | 15 |
| 688. | A Farmer | | | | | | | 2 | | | | | | | | 2 |
| 689. | A Plebeian | | | | | 2+ | | 1 | | | | | | | | 3 |

| | | New Hampshire | Massachusetts | Rhode Island | Connecticut | New York | New Jersey | Pennsylvania | Delaware | Maryland | Virginia | North Carolina | South Carolina | Georgia | Vermont | Total |
|---|---|---|---|---|---|---|---|---|---|---|---|---|---|---|---|---|
| 690. | Fabius III | 2 | 1 | | | | | 2* | | 1 | 1 | | | | | 7 |
| 691. | Gerry Responds to Md. "Landholder" X | | 3 | | | 1 | | | | | | | | | | 4 |
| 693. | Fabius IV | 2 | 1 | | | | | 2* | | 1 | 1 | | | | | 7 |
| 699. | Fabius V | 2 | 1 | | | | | 2* | | 1 | 1 | | | | | 7 |
| 701. | Pa. Gazette | | 1 | | | 1 | 2 | 1 | | | | | | | | 5 |
| 702. | None of Well-Born Conspirators | | | | | | 1 | 2 | | | | | | | | 3 |
| 705. | Fabius VI | 1 | 1 | | | | | 2* | | 1 | | | | | | 5 |
| 709. | Honestus | | 1 | | | 1 | | | | | | | | | | 2 |
| 710. | Fabius VII | 1 | 1 | | | | 1 | 2* | | 1 | | | | | | 6 |
| 713. | Aristocrotis | | | | | | | 1+ | | | | | | | | 1 |
| 716. | Md. Convention | | | | | | | | | | | | | | | |
| 716A. | Paca Amendments | 3 | 8 | 3 | 6 | 8 | 2 | 8 | | 2 | 4 | | 1 | 1 | | 46 |
| 716B. | Address of Md. Minority | | 1 | 1 | | 1 | | 4* | | 2+ | | | 1 | | | 10 |
| 717. | Fabius VIII | 1 | 1 | | | | | 2* | | 1 | | | | | | 5 |
| 718. | Phila. Independent Gazetteer | 1 | | | 1 | 1 | 2 | 1 | | | | | | | | 6 |
| 719. | Pa. Gazette | | 1 | 1 | | 1 | | 2 | | 1 | | | 1 | | | 7 |
| 720. | Soc. of Western Gentlemen Revises Constitution | | | | | | | | | | | 1 | | | | 1 |
| 722. | Fabius IX | 1 | 1 | | | | | 2* | | 1 | | | | | | 5 |
| 723. | Federal Farmer | | | | | 1+ | | | | | | | | | | 1 |
| 729. | Phila. Independent Gazetteer | | 2 | | | 1 | | 1 | | | | | | | | 4 |
| 730. | A Steady and Open Republican | 1 | 1 | | | 1 | | | | | | | 1 | | | 4 |
| 737. | Phila. Independent Gazetteer | | 1 | | | 1 | | 1 | | 1 | | | | | | 4 |

APPENDIX I: SQUIBS

| | New Hampshire | Massachusetts | Rhode Island | Connecticut | New York | New Jersey | Pennsylvania | Delaware | Maryland | Virginia | North Carolina | South Carolina | Georgia | Vermont | Total |
|---|---|---|---|---|---|---|---|---|---|---|---|---|---|---|---|
| Pa. Packet 3 April | | 2 | | | 2 | 1 | 2 | | 2 | 1 | | 1 | | | 11 |
| Mass. Centinel 9 April | 2 | 4 | | | 3 | | 2 | | | | | | | | 11 |
| Pa. Gazette 9 April (all) | | | 1 | 1 | | | 1 | | | | | | | | 3 |
| (1st paragraph) | | 4 | 3 | 4 | 2 | | 3 | | 1 | 1 | | 2 | | | 20 |
| (2nd paragraph) | | 1 | 2 | 3 | 1 | | 2 | | | | | 2 | 1 | | 12 |
| (3rd paragraph) | | 1 | 1 | | | | 1 | | | 2 | | | | | 5 |
| Annapolis Md. Gazette 10 April | | 1 | | 1 | 3 | 1 | 3 | | 2 | | | 1 | | | 12 |
| N.Y. Morning Post 11 April | | 1 | | | 1 | | 1 | | 1 | 3 | | | | | 7 |

| | New Hampshire | Massachusetts | Rhode Island | Connecticut | New York | New Jersey | Pennsylvania | Delaware | Maryland | Virginia | North Carolina | South Carolina | Georgia | Vermont | Total |
|---|---|---|---|---|---|---|---|---|---|---|---|---|---|---|---|
| **Mass. Centinel** | | | | | | | | | | | | | | | |
| 12 April | 2 | 3 | 2 | 3 | 1 | | 3 | | 2 | 2 | | 3 | | 1 | 22 |
| **Federal Gazette** | | | | | | | | | | | | | | | |
| 12 April | | 4 | 2 | 3 | 5 | 1 | 2 | | | | | | | 1 | 18 |
| **N.H. Spy** | | | | | | | | | | | | | | | |
| 15, 22 April | | | | | | | | | | | | | | | |
| The Federal Hat | 2 | 2 | 2 | | 2 | 1 | 3 | | | | | 1 | | | 13 |
| Variety Store | 1 | | | | | | | | | | | | | | 1 |
| **Salem Mercury** | | | | | | | | | | | | | | | |
| 15 April | 2 | 5 | | 3 | 1 | 2 | 2 | | | | | | | | 15 |
| **Freeman's Journal** | | | | | | | | | | | | | | | |
| 16 April | | | | | | | 1 | | 3 | 3 | | | | | 7 |
| **Independent Gazetteer** | | | | | | | | | | | | | | | |
| 16 April | | 1 | | | 1 | | 1 | | | | | | | | 3 |
| (1st paragraph alone) | | 1 | 1 | | 2 | | 1 | | | | | | | | 5 |
| **Federal Gazette** | | | | | | | | | | | | | | | |
| 17 April | 1 | 3 | 1 | | 2 | | 1 | | | | | | | | 8 |
| **Pa. Mercury** | | | | | | | | | | | | | | | |
| 17 April | 1 | 2 | 1 | 1 | 1 | | 2 | | | | | | | | 8 |
| **Independent Gazetteer** | | | | | | | | | | | | | | | |
| 17 April | | 2 | | | 1 | | 1 | | | | | | | | 4 |
| **Pa. Gazette** | | | | | | | | | | | | | | | |
| 23 April | | 4 | 1 | | 1 | | 2 | | 1 | 2 | | | | | 11 |
| **N.Y. Journal** | | | | | | | | | | | | | | | |
| 24 April | | 2 | | | 1 | | 1 | | | | | | | | 4 |
| **N.Y. Morning Post** | | | | | | | | | | | | | | | |
| 28 April | 1 | 3 | 1 | | 1 | | | | | | | | | | 6 |
| **City Gazette** | | | | | | | | | | | | | | | |
| 29 April | 1 | 4 | | | 2 | | 2 | | 2 | 1 | | 1 | | | 13 |
| **Pa. Gazette** | | | | | | | | | | | | | | | |
| 30 April (both) | | 3 | | | 1 | 1 | 2 | | | | | | | | 7 |
| (1st paragraph) | | 4 | | | 2 | 1 | 2 | | 1 | | | | | | 10 |
| (2nd paragraph) | 2 | 7 | | | 2 | 1 | 2 | | | | | | 1 | 1 | 16 |
| **U.S. Chronicle** | | | | | | | | | | | | | | | |
| 1 May | | | 1 | | 1 | | 1 | | | | | 1 | | | 4 |
| **N.Y. Daily Advertiser** | | | | | | | | | | | | | | | |
| 1 May | 1 | 5 | 2 | | 5 | | 5 | | 2 | 2 | 1 | 1 | | | 24 |
| **Pa. Mercury** | | | | | | | | | | | | | | | |
| 1 May | 1 | 4 | 3 | 1 | 3 | 1 | 1 | | | | | 3 | | | 17 |
| **Pa. Packet** | | | | | | | | | | | | | | | |
| 2 May | 2 | 7 | 3 | 1 | 5 | 1 | 4 | | | | | 1 | | | 24 |
| **Independent Gazetteer** | | | | | | | | | | | | | | | |
| 6 May | | 1 | | | 1 | | 2 | | | 1 | | | | | 5 |

| | New Hampshire | Massachusetts | Rhode Island | Connecticut | New York | New Jersey | Pennsylvania | Delaware | Maryland | Virginia | North Carolina | South Carolina | Georgia | Vermont | Total |
|---|---|---|---|---|---|---|---|---|---|---|---|---|---|---|---|
| **Pa. Gazette** | | | | | | | | | | | | | | | |
| 7 May (all) | | 1 | | | | | 2 | | 1 | | | | | | 4 |
| (1st paragraph) | | 4 | 1 | 1 | 2 | 1 | 3 | | 3 | 2 | 2 | 1 | 1 | 1 | 22 |
| (2nd paragraph) | 1 | 1 | 1 | | 2 | | 4 | | 2 | 1 | | | | | 12 |
| (3rd paragraph) | 1 | 4 | | | | | 2 | | 1 | | | | | | 8 |
| **Del. Gazette** | | | | | | | | | | | | | | | |
| 7 May | | 2 | | | 2 | | 2 | 1 | 1 | 1 | | | 1 | | 10 |
| **Md. Journal** | | | | | | | | | | | | | | | |
| 9 May | | 1 | | | 2 | 1 | 2 | | 1 | 1 | | | | | 8 |

# Index

An asterisk denotes a signer of the Constitution. Several main entries are compilations of similar items: Biblical References; Broadsides, Pamphlets, and Books; Classical Antiquity; Governments, Ancient and Modern; Newspapers; Political and Legal Writers and Writings; Printers and Booksellers; and Pseudonyms. The pseudonymous items printed in this volume and in earlier volumes of *Commentaries on the Constitution* are also indexed separately. When a pseudonym has been identified, the name of the author has been placed in parentheses. Biographical information in earlier volumes of *Commentaries* is indicated by a volume and page reference placed in parentheses immediately after the name of the person. Sketches of newspapers printed in Volume 1 of *Commentaries* have been placed in parentheses immediately following the name of the newspaper.

ACCUSATION, CAUSE AND NATURE OF, 240, 274, 347

ADAMS, ABIGAIL (Mass.; CC:Vol. 2, 462n), 227n

ADAMS, JOHN (Mass.; CC:Vol. 1, 81n), 179n, 227, 268
— letter from: quoted, 97n

ADAMS, SAMUEL (Mass.; CC:Vol. 1, 325n), 52, 53n; opposes dual officeholding by federal officials, 63, 64n; Federalists attempt to discredit, 177n; role in Mass. ratification, 209n
— letter to, 231–33n

ADMIRALTY JURISDICTION, 274, 276. *See also* Judiciary, U.S.

ADMIRALTY LAW, 333–34, 339

AGRICULTURE: distress of, 109, 110; under Constitution, 159; under Confederation, 386, 393. *See also* Farmers

ALBANY, N.Y., 31

ALBANY ANTIFEDERAL COMMITTEE
— letter from: quoted, 83–84

ALLAIRE, PETER (N.Y.): id., 390n
— journal of, 389–90

ALLEN, THOMAS (N.Y.), 265

AMBASSADORS: appointment of, 4, 322; President to receive, 12, 13; proposed amendment concerning, 242; under Articles of Confederation, 274

AMENDMENTS TO ARTICLES OF CONFEDERATION: need for, 232; procedure for, 274; method of apportioning federal expenses, 370. *See also* Articles of Confederation; Constitutional Convention; Impost of 1781; Impost of 1783

AMENDMENTS TO CONSTITUTION: opposition to proposal for council of appointment, 12; could be obtained after ratification if needed, 14, 119, 120, 147–48, 184, 192, 215, 234, 250; need for, 32, 92, 149–66, 218n, 231, 232, 258,

266, 268–69, 269–70, 371, 395–98; opposition to, 33, 63, 80, 103, 217; difference of opinion among Antifederalists on, 33, 215, 250; Harrisburg Convention called to consider, 60n; states that have not yet ratified will probably adopt, 94; several states ratify without recommending, 116; praise of constitutional provision for, 127–28, 129, 250–51; denial that Federalists favor, 147; Federalists admit some are needed, 147; Federalists differ over those they would support, 157–58; nine states should ratify Constitution and then amend, 234; some Antifederalists have ulterior motives for supporting, 251; criticism of constitutional provision for, 255, 370–71; will not be adopted after ratification of Constitution, 386; expected from N.Y. Convention, 395
— in Maryland, 258; proposed in Convention of, 188–89, 236–46, 255–56, 385–86
— in Massachusetts: proposed by Convention of, 26n, 42, 63, 64n, 83, 145, 153, 156, 157, 166n, 209, 209n, 232, 235; will be ignored, 261, 385; method of ratification will be adopted by Va. and N.Y., 395
— in Virginia: sought before ratification in, 23; will ratify with recommendatory, 208, 395; revisions by gentlemen in western Va., 254–55; will be proposed by, 413
*See also* Antifederalists; Bill of Rights; Civil liberties; Convention, second constitutional

AMERICA: has opportunity to prove republican government can work, 14–15; must show that men can govern themselves through reason, 120; as an example,

421

expenses, 370; state representation in Congress, 373n; as a perpetual union, 376n
See also Amendments to Articles of Confederation; Congress under Articles of Confederation; Economic conditions under the Confederation; Political conditions under the Confederation
ARTICLES OF WAR (1775), 89, 93n
ARTISANS: See Mechanics
ARTS, 159
ASSEMBLY, RIGHT OF, 274
ATHERTON, JOSHUA (N.H.)
— letters from: quoted, 85, 267
ATTORNEYS: See Lawyers

BACON, JOHN (Mass.), 227
BAILEY, FRANCIS (Pa.; CC:Vol. 1, xxxiv–xxxv), 57, 60n
— letters to: quoted, 254, 255
See also Newspapers, Pennsylvania Freeman's Journal
BALANCED GOVERNMENT, 181; lack of under Constitution, 321–22. See also Mixed government
BALTIMORE, 188, 385
BANKRUPTCY, 365–66, 368
BARRELL, JOSEPH (Mass.; CC:Vol. 3, 51n)
— letter from: quoted, 105
— letter to: quoted, 103
BEDFORD COUNTY, PA., 58
BELHAVEN, LORD: See Hamilton, John
BELKNAP, JEREMY (Mass.; CC:Vol. 2, 529n)
— letters from: quoted, 53n, 95, 392n
— letters to, 390–92n; quoted, 95, 126–27
BERKS COUNTY, PA., 58
BIBLICAL REFERENCES: Aaron, 37–38, 40; Acts, 147, 166n; Adam, 287; (Herod) Agrippa II, 147; Bible, 84, 85, 184, 408; Cain, mark of, 177n; Canaanites, 39; Chronicles, 120n; 1 Corinthians, 171, 172n; Creation, 391; Deuteronomy, 84; Egypt, 21, 23n, 38–39, 39; Esau's birthright, 93; Exodus, 21, 23n, 40, 47, 53n; Garden of Paradise, 108; Genesis, 94n, 127; golden calf, 38; Haggai, 120n; Israel, 118; Israelites, 21, 23n, 36, 37–39; Jacob's sons, 127; Jesus, 39; Job, 19, 22n, 52, 54n; Joel, 20, 23n, 73n; 1 Kings, 120n; Korah, 36, 38; Lamentations, 222, 225n; Luke, 47, 53n, 222, 225n; Mark, 386, 387n; Matthew, 47, 53n, 116, 120n, 386, 387n; Messiah, 39;

Micah, 120n, 150, 166n, 169, 172n; Moses, 36, 37–39, 40, 162, 167n; Mount Sinai, 167n; Nimrod, 18; Numbers, 40; Paul, 147, 171; Pharaoh, 38; Proverbs, 120n, 224, 225n; Red Sea, 167n, 391; 2 Samuel, 120n; Scriptures, 37; Shechemites, 127; Supreme Being, 37; Ten Commandments, 162, 167n; vine and fig tree, 108, 150, 169; wilderness, 391, 395; Zechariah, 120n. See also God; Religion
BICAMERALISM: praise of, 69, 96, 303; opposition to, 192; in eleven state legislatures, 275. See also Checks and balances; Unicameralism
BILL OF RIGHTS: in England, 16, 89, 96, 260, 284, 347; unnecessary in U.S., 16, 96, 131, 170, 235, 375n; need for, 84, 91–93, 93, 106, 252, 255, 259–60, 268–69, 270, 343, 344–45, 346, 377, 395; and N.Y. constitution, 112, 164, 165; needed in monarchy, 112–13; unnecessary in republican government, 112–13; not sufficient to preserve liberty, 132, 183; as limit on abuse of sovereign power, 135; Constitutional Convention not opposed to principles of, 235; of states should not be violated by federal laws or treaties, 241, 242, 245; some rights guaranteed in Constitution, 259; nature of, 342; important in confirming rights, 344. See also Amendments to Constitution; Civil liberties; Convention, second constitutional; Habeas corpus, writ of; Religion, freedom of
BINGHAM, WILLIAM (Pa.; CC:Vol. 1, 134n)
— letters from: quoted, 103, 105
BLACKSTONE, SIR WILLIAM (England; CC:Vol. 1, 54n), 184, 185n, 338, 347, 373n, 375n, 382, 385n
BLAINE, EPHRAIM (Pa.; CC:Vol. 4, 151n), 214, 216n
BLAIR, ARCHIBALD (Va.), 398
BLAIR, JOHN* (Va.; CC:Vol. 1, 285n), 234
BLAND, THEODORICK (Va.; CC:Vol. 2, 398n)
— letter from: quoted, 239
BLOUNT, JOHN GRAY (N.C.)
— letter to: quoted, 186n–87n
BLOUNT, WILLIAM* (N.C.; CC:Vol. 1, 472n): id., 401n; 401
BOOKS: See Broadsides, pamphlets, and books

tend, 26, 28; criticism of, 29, 58, 62, 82n, 83, 145, 147, 166, 175, 377n, 406, 407n; occasionally near dissolution, 33, 81; spirit of accommodation in, 33, 154, 217, 234, 383, 384, 388; was not divinely inspired, 39–40; described as dark conclave, 61, 82n, 205, 206n; Luther Martin's activities in, 70, 73n, 93n, 173–76, 204; and contempt for Luther Martin, 72; praise of compromises of, 81, 111–12, 114, 115; N.Y. delegates leave, 84, 86; secrecy of, 88, 145, 155, 176n, 257, 388; refuses to publish journals, 88; unanimity of praised, 110, 112, 114, 217, 219; not authorized by people, 144; violates Articles of Confederation, 144, 201–2, 260, 371; violated its instructions only to revise Articles of Confederation, 144, 370; delegates to did not initially favor a major change, 155; hot weather during, 173; Elbridge Gerry's activities in, 173–76, 373n; favors national government, 204; Centinel and Luther Martin praised for revelations about, 231; criticism of Antifederalists who attack, 253; defense of Antifederalists who criticize, 270; Virginia Resolutions in, 374n; criticized for omitting bill of rights, 377; intellectual influences on, 382; prediction that it will not succeed in changing government, 394n; difficulty facing, 400; criticism of for continuing slave trade, 413–14
— debates in over: no delegates in objected to principles of a bill of rights, 235; no delegates in objected to principles of trial by jury, 235; ineligibility of President, 235; representation, 248, 251n; representation in the House of Representatives, 291, 373n; restrictions on members of Congress holding other appointments, 320, 374n; term of President, 330, 374n; establishment of jury trial in criminal but not civil cases, 340; dual officeholding, 374n; election of President, 385n
CONSTITUTIONALIST PARTY (in Pa.), 29
CONSTITUTIONS: as limits on abuse of sovereign power, 135
CONSTITUTIONS, STATE: restrict standing armies, 89; opposition to Pa.'s, 97, 98n; more care taken in creating than in drafting Articles of Confederation, 109; N.Y.'s does not protect freedom of press, 112; N.Y.'s fails to recognize certain rights, 164, 165; liberties conferred by, 201; forms of are less important than proper administration, 226; should not be violated by congressional laws or treaties (proposed amendment concerning), 241, 245; will not protect against federal Constitution, 242, 259, 346, 348–49, 349; Pa.'s still exists to preserve liberty, 252; rights of people secured under, 260; descriptions of, 275; judiciaries of, 276; number of state senators in, 276; rotation in office in, 306; veto power over legislature in, 332; and reserved powers theory, 342–43. See also individual states
CONTINENTAL ASSOCIATION, 52, 54n
CONVENTION, SECOND CONSTITUTIONAL: opposition to, 24, 33, 63–64, 81, 103, 115–18, 217, 251; only way to avoid a civil war, 61, 252; support for, 62, 82n, 379, 395–98; accommodating spirit will prevail in, 154–55; should be called by request of a majority of states, 255; and N.Y. Federal Republican Committee, 397–98. See also Amendments to Constitution
CONVENTIONS, STATE: state legislatures favored over, 101. See also Ratification, procedure for; individual states
CORRUPTION: in British House of Commons, 8; unlikely that President always will be able to influence Senate, 8; power corrupts because of human nature, 18–19, 19, 287, 299–300; human nature is corrupt, 20, 171, 287; Moses and Aaron charged with, 38–39; not likely in electing U.S. Representatives, 123; more likely in large republics, 137; no form of government will protect people if they become corrupt, 235; danger of in Congress under Constitution, 259, 293, 295–96; as cause of despotism in government, 264; House of Representatives is subject to, 282; is result of lack of rotation in office, 306; in appointments to office happens in all countries, 318; and bribery in civil law systems, 340; and federal capital, 370, 378
COUNCIL OF APPOINTMENT: opposition to creation of, 11–12
COUNSEL, RIGHT TO: needs protecting in federal Constitution, 240, 274, 348

erred, 219; explanation of why they favor Constitution, 289

GREENLEAF, THOMAS (N.Y.; CC:Vol. 1, xxxvii–xxxviii): as publisher of Antifederalist literature, 30, 31; as printer of *New York Journal*, 146, 219; sells A Plebeian, 146; sells Federal Farmer pamphlet, 265. *See also* Newspapers, New York, *New York Journal*

GRIFFIN, CYRUS (Va.; CC:Vol. 4, 139n), 35, 36n, 193
— letter from: quoted, 179n

HABEAS CORPUS, WRIT OF: as a fundamental right, 273, 274, 346; protected in Great Britain, 284, 347–48; protection for in Constitution proves that reserved power theory is wrong, 347; protected in Northwest Ordinance, 347, 375n; needs protecting in Constitution, 348. *See also* Bill of rights

HAMILTON, ALEXANDER* (N.Y.; CC:Vol. 1, 141n): as author of *The Federalist*, 4–8, 9–13, 17; and distribution of *The Federalist*, 26n, 217n; as candidate for N.Y. Convention, 381
— letter from, 16–17
— speech of in N.Y. Convention quoted, 268, 372n–73n

HAMILTON, JOHN, LORD BELHAVEN (Scotland): id., 213n–14n
— speech of criticizing union of England and Scotland, 210–13, 222

HANCOCK, JOHN (Mass.; CC:Vol. 1, 410n), 412; Federalists attempt to discredit, 177n; role in Mass. ratification, 209n; Mass. House of Representatives responds to speech of, 408–9

HANSON, ALEXANDER CONTEE (Md.; CC:Vol. 3, 517n): as Aristides, 22, 253; and Md. Convention's proposed amendments, 238, 239
— letter from: quoted, 239

HAPPINESS: Constitution does not endanger, 14; Antifederalists hope to promote, 61; Constitution endangers, 61, 237, 354; Constitution will encourage, 79, 81, 97, 126, 191, 249, 250, 264, 391, 415; Constitutional Convention called to promote by establishing a permanent government, 88; promoted by federal republics, 136; as end of government, 148, 169, 181, 195, 360; giving to others provides for ourselves, 168; not possible without freedom, 168; society necessary for, 168, 249, 249–50; endangered under Articles of Confederation, 178, 179n; wants as sources of, 224; passive obedience to arbitrary power destroys, 240, 245; God wishes men to form societies to promote their own, 249, 249–50; postwar strides to reestablish, 354; likely if impost is adopted for Confederation Congress, 386; and reform movements, 391; people experience under Articles of Confederation, 393, 394n; American Revolution will contribute to mankind's, 415

HARISON, RICHARD (N.Y.), 381

HARRISBURG CONVENTION, 60n

HARRISON, BENJAMIN (Md.), 179n

HARRISON, BENJAMIN (Va.; CC:Vol. 1, 223n)
— speech in Va. Convention quoted, 239

HAZARD, EBENEZER (N.Y.; CC:Vol. 1, 384n): id., 95n
— letters from, 94–95n; quoted, 94n–95n, 126–27

HAZARD, JONATHAN J. (R.I.), 27

HELME, ROWSE J. (R.I.), 27

HENLEY, DAVID (Va.): id., 229n
— letter from: quoted, 229n

HENLEY, SAMUEL (Mass.)
— letter to: quoted, 229n

HENRY, PATRICK (Va.; CC:Vol. 1, 223n): supposed to favor separate confederacies, 3, 24; in Va. legislature, 25, 236n, 396; criticism of Antifederalism of, 64, 64n; as prominent Antifederalist in Va. Convention, 234, 407
— speech in Va. Convention, 202n; quoted, 239

HISTORY: proves man is corrupt, 20; proves depravity of human nature, 44, 45; full of examples of vices of people and kings, 96; experience is best teacher, 108; teaches importance of unanimity among Americans, 132; demonstrates that a large area must be ruled by one person, 137–38; demonstrates that all governments abuse their power, 143–44, 329; demonstrates that governments increase their powers, 148, 154; teaches that most governments formed by force and violence, 161; teaches that corruption of manners is basis of slavery, 171; is entertaining and instructive, 196;

shows licentiousness of people is great danger to liberty, 222; shows that republican confederation is antidote to aristocracy and monarchy, 223; demonstrates that states together act prudently and honestly, 225; misuse of by Federalist polemicists, 323; shows that nobles or people seize power from kings, 329. *See also* Biblical references; Classical antiquity; Governments, ancient and modern; Political and legal writers and writings

Hobart, John Sloss (N.Y.), 381
Hodge, Robert (N.Y.), 146, 265
Hogeboom, Catherine (N.Y.)
— letter to: quoted, 103
"Honestus," 219–21
Hopkinson, Francis (Pa.; CC:Vol. 3, 180n): as author of New Roof, 29, 30n; as author of "A.B.," 30n; as possible author of Peter Prejudice, 126–27; praise of allegorical writings of, 253; criticism of writings of, 398, 399n
— letter to, 28–30
House of Representatives, U.S.: first federal elections to, 60n, 374n; compared to British House of Commons, 262, 400; subject to corruption, 282
— organization of: restrictions on members of being appointed to federal office, 8; opposition to proportional representation in, 71; election of criticized, 71, 72–73, 310–15; two-year term of defended, 122, 123, 388; defense of method of filling vacancies in, 123–24; objection to per capita voting in, 141; annual elections of favored, 255, 315–16; majority is a quorum of, 265; and salaries of, 292; election of by people is acceptable, 298; and qualifications of electors of, 298; need for recall provision for, 305; constitutional qualifications for, 310–11
— representation in: too small, 61, 156, 157, 259, 268–69, 278–79, 289–96, 296–301, 308, 314, 321, 356; Mass. amendments propose to increase size of, 63; as democratic branch, 67, 182, 298, 339; opposition to proportional representation in, 71; size of defended, 122, 123, 299; debate in Constitutional Convention over, 251n, 373n; lawyers will predominate in, 290; democracy cannot be properly represented in, 302

— powers of: opposition to appointment power for, 12; agrees that President may remove officeholders without approval of, 13n; and money bills, 68, 124; will not be overawed by Senate, 124; will be controlled by President and Senate, 282, 321–22; and impeachment power, 301, 303; as check on Senate, 302–3, 388; too large for treaty-making power, 308–9; and election of President, 327; as check on President, 388; Senate as check on, 388
*See also* Bicameralism; Congress under Constitution, debate over powers of; Elections, U.S.; Impeachment; Senate, U.S.
Howard, John Eager (Md.; CC:Vol. 4, 569n), 228
— letter from: quoted, 229n
Hubley, John (Pa.)
— letter from: quoted, 105
Human Nature: wrong to consider mankind universally bad or good, 8; power corrupts, 18–19, 19, 287, 299–300; avarice of, 19, 48–49, 232, 259; ambition of, 19, 232, 259, 361; lust for power and domination, 19, 328, 330, 361; corruptibility of, 20, 171, 287; depravity of, 44, 45; danger of long term of office, 67, 304, 306, 308; tends to go against natural justice, 73; the "governed" are not always virtuous, 96; man can be safely entrusted with power, 96; praise of open-mindedness of, 106; personal gain more important than patriotism after Revolution, 107; majority of men do not follow advice given by best of men, 108; man is error prone, 108, 113; zeal for public good can carry men to unreasonable actions, 110; men will honestly differ on difficult subjects, 114; man is subject to partisanship, 115–16; apprehension of danger is powerful incentive for action, 151; prudent men will not be terrified by imaginary dangers, 151; human mind cannot continue intensely engaged for a long time, 154; persons possessed of power will not voluntarily give it away, 154; hope and fear are elements of, 159; self-interest followed, 159, 287, 295, 320; uniformity of opinion indicates sincerity, 162; humility and benevolence takes precedence over pride and selfishness, 168; jury

83, 400; praise of as single executive, 327, 328–31; debate over in Constitutional Convention, 374n, 385n
— election, tenure, etc.: praise of election of, 13, 124–25, 327; criticism of election of, 71, 72–73; not necessary for rotation in office, 235; criticism of reeligibility of, 255, 327, 330–31, 385n; elected by majority in House of Representatives, 327; term of, 330, 374n, 388; age qualification for, 330–31; uncertainty of in determining line of succession for, 331–32
— powers of: defense of appointment power of, 4–8, 9–12, 247; danger of appointment power of, 9, 323–24, 324, 378; to call special sessions of and to adjourn Congress, 12; to deliver State of the Union address, 12; power to receive ambassadors, 12, 13; praise of, 12, 13, 125, 247; too powerful, 61–62, 303, 377; as commander in chief, 62; and veto, 124, 125, 255, 259, 332; should not command army in person without consent of Congress, 241, 245; and treaty-making, 309–10; as check on House of Representatives, 388
*See also* Electors, presidential; Impeachment
PRESS, FREEDOM OF THE: endangered by Constitution, 19–20, 164–65, 231, 349–50; criticism of Federalists shackling of access to, 55; post office endangers, 57; importance of, 57, 274, 343–44, 349–50; not protected in N.Y. constitution, 112; not endangered by Constitution, 112, 122; impartiality of *New York Journal*, 219; should be protected in Constitution, 241, 244, 255. *See also* Bill of rights
PRICE, RICHARD (England; CC:Vol. 1, 101n), 265
PRINCETON, N.J., 376n
PRINTERS AND BOOKSELLERS:
— Massachusetts: Edward E. Powars, 268
— New York: Thomas Allen, 265; Samuel Campbell, 265; Robert Hodge, 146, 265; Samuel and John Loudon, 101–2, 265; John Reid, 265
— Pennsylvania: Alexander J. Dallas, 59n; Daniel Humphreys, 76; Thomas Lloyd, 18n, 77
*See also* Bailey, Francis; Carey, Mathew; Greenleaf, Thomas; Newspapers; Oswald, Eleazer

PRIVATE INTEREST, 39, 110; personal gain more important than patriotism after Revolution, 107; self-interest followed, 159, 287, 295, 320; men are too apt to be swayed by local prejudices, 215; mankind tries to elevate his own class in society and lower others, 279. *See also* Interest groups
PRIVILEGES AND IMMUNITIES, 274, 368
PRIVY COUNCIL: need for, 62, 245, 323–24; opposition to, 125–26; in state constitutions, 276; method of selection of, 324
PROFESSIONAL MEN, 280–81. *See also* Lawyers; Merchants
PROPERTY, PRIVATE: Constitution does not endanger, 14; as unalienable right, 43, 274; argument that slaves are not legitimate property, 49; Constitution endangers, 61, 62, 92, 139; defense of lack of property qualifications for holding federal office, 63; unsafe under Confederation, 90; Constitution will protect, 94, 150, 216, 259, 303; government should protect from licentious and from foreigners, 194–95; has fallen in value because of lack of money, 216; state laws concerning endangered by federal judiciaries, 243; punctual execution of laws is required for preservation of, 272; as qualifications of for officeholding and voting in state constitutions, 275–76; to be protected by Senate, 303. *See also* Eminent domain
PROVIDENCE, R.I., 401n
PSEUDONYMS: reasons for using, 59, 76; prominent men should not use, 78, 102; attack on writers who use, 288–89; "A.B." (Francis Hopkinson), 30n; Acirema (America spelled backwards), 203; An American Citizen (Tench Coxe), 61–62; Aristides (Alexander Contee Hanson), 22; Aristocrotis (William Petrikin), 229–31; Brutus, 64–69, 398; Cæsar (Alexander Hamilton?), 219, 289; Cato (George Clinton?), 219; Centinel (Samuel Bryan), 30, 30n, 59, 60n, 83, 398, 399n, 407, 408; A Citizen of New-York (John Jay), 101–20, 146; A Citizen of the State of Maryland, 84, 89–93; A Columbian Patriot (Mercy Warren), 22n, 30–31, 208, 268; Conciliator, 186, 187n; A Countryman (N.Y.), 398; Doctor Puff (Benjamin Rush), 399n; Fabius

50, 383; danger to in America, 270; best suited for America, 272; people make laws in, 307; importance of elections in, 310; must keep perpetual power from one man or family, 329; description of a federal republic, 350–51, 362; a select militia is anti-republican, 362–63; and jurisdiction of federal capital, 366–70; endangered by nature of life in a federal capital, 370; Constitution provides, 388. *See also* Government, debate over nature of

REQUISITIONS: states do not abide by after Revolution, 107, 158–59, 352–54, 356, 357; central government in America needs power to make, 138; adopting states described as delinquent, 145; N.Y. pays, 158–59, 166n; requisition system should be used before direct taxation, 240, 241, 244–45, 245, 246, 358; Confederation Congress has power to request states to provide men and money, 273; praise of system of under Articles of Confederation, 294–95, 298; total required by Congress and amount actually paid, 353–54. *See also* Taxation

RESERVED POWERS: debate over, 17, 17n; denial that Constitution leaves to states, 92–93, 94n, 232, 342, 344–45, 349–50; Mass. proposed amendment concerning, 166n; principle of enunciated by James Wilson, 92, 94n, 235, 342, 375n, 398; should have been explicitly guaranteed to states in Constitution, 259, 342–43. *See also* Enumerated powers; General welfare clause; Necessary and proper clause; States, impact of Constitution upon

REVOLUTION, RIGHT OF: inherent in people, 45–46, 295; description of, 50; proposed in amendments considered by Md. Convention, 240, 245. *See also* Despotism; Natural rights; Passive obedience; Social compact; Tyranny

RHODE ISLAND: defeats Constitution in statewide referendum, 26–28, 30, 35, 36n, 83, 99, 206, 381, 389, 393, 401n, 409; unrepresented in Confederation Congress, 27, 28; Federalists in, 27, 35; adopts grant of power over commerce, 28n, 386, 387n; adopts Impost of 1783, 28n, 386, 387n; paper money policies of, 35, 41, 72, 206, 218, 390; Antifederalists in, 35, 386; representation of in

House of Representatives, 71; encourages Antifederalists in other states, 99; legislature of rejects calling state convention, 99, 400, 401n; called Rogue Island, 405; satire says it is to be sold to private citizen, 416
— constitution of: people elect delegates to Confederation Congress, 273; assembly of elected twice a year, 275
— prospects for ratification in: uncertain, 208; will eventually ratify, 395; will reject, 41, 218, 227, 228; will be only state not to ratify, 390, 411

RIDGELY, CHARLES (Md.), 179n
RIDGELY, CHARLES, OF WILLIAM (Md.), 179n
RITTENHOUSE, DAVID (Pa.), 30
RODNEY, THOMAS (Del.): id., 101
— letter from, 100–101
ROMAN CATHOLICS, 410
ROME: *See* Governments, ancient and modern
ROOSEVELT, ISAAC (N.Y.), 381
ROTATION IN OFFICE: should be required for U.S. Senate, 67–68; in Confederation Congress, 141, 273, 306, 307; not necessary for President, 235; not in Constitution, 298; failure to have makes men callous, 304, 306; in some state constitutions, 306; failure to have leads to corruption, 306; should be required in Congress under Constitution, 306–8; benefits of, 307–8, 320–21; opposition to, 307–8, 373n–74n, 378; criticism of reeligibility of President, 327
RUSH, BENJAMIN (Pa.; CC:Vol. 1, 45n–46n): as Federalist essayist, 80; in Pa. Convention, 162, 167n; criticism of writings of, 398, 398n, 399n
— letters from, 95–98n, 390–92n; quoted, 60n, 76, 80, 95
— letters to: quoted, 53n, 76, 95, 105, 392n

SAILORS, 109, 220
SALARIES: objections to Senators and Representatives setting their own, 141; objections to Senators and Representatives receiving from central government, 142; will raise cost of federal government, 161; no emoluments except for service as an unalienable right in America, 274; of state judiciaries, 276; danger they will

be raised by Congress, 293; should be well fixed to avoid too high and too low, 301; of federal judges, 337. *See also* Expenses of government

Schuyler, Philip (N.Y.), 395

Scioto Company, 179n

Searches and Seizures: general warrants should be prohibited, 240, 243–44; search warrants should be properly limited, 243, 347, 348; unreasonable searches violate natural rights, 274. *See also* Bill of rights

Sectionalism: and admission of new states, 34

Sedgwick, Theodore (Mass.; CC:Vol. 3, 91n), 54n, 227, 227n
— letter to, 226–27

Self-Incrimination, 274, 347

Senate, U.S.: critical analysis of, 66–69; debate over aristocratic nature of, 67, 224–25, 302; connection of with President, 68, 125, 157, 259, 268–69, 282, 321–22, 324, 388; criticism of lack of power of states to instruct, 140; represents interests of states, 140–41, 182, 301–2, 303; compared to House of Lords, 262, 400
— organization of: restrictions on members of being appointed to federal office, 8; size of, 61, 122, 259, 296–301, 302; age and residency qualifications of, 66; election of, 66, 122, 124, 125, 302, 303, 310, 317; filling vacancies in, 66, 122–23; equal representation of states in, 66, 125, 248, 251n; and term of office, 66–68, 255, 303, 303–4, 321, 388; rotation in office should be required, 67–68; need for recall of, 68, 304–5; salary of from federal treasury, 141; per capita voting in, 141; quorum of, 265
— powers of, 68–69, 122, 377; and appointments, 4–8, 9, 13n, 68, 247, 302, 308, 321–22, 324, 325; and treaty-making, 12, 67, 68, 259, 303, 308–9, 309–10, 321, 322; and impeachment, 66, 68, 157, 303; and money bills, 68; no danger from, 125; as check on House of Representatives, 302–3, 388; and election of Vice President, 327
*See also* Appointment power; Bicameralism; Congress under Constitution, debate over powers of; House of Representatives, U.S.; Impeachment; Recall; Separation of powers; Treaties

Separate Confederacies: criticism of, 3, 81, 116, 247, 295, 414; would non-ratifying states form, 133. *See also* Henry, Patrick; Union

Separation of Powers: Constitution praised for, 13n, 96, 182, 210, 247, 248, 382; necessity of, 65, 111, 181; criticism of Senate's power as violating, 68–69, 268–69; some co-mingling is necessary, 68–69, 326; favored for Pa. constitution, 98n; criticism of Constitution for failure to maintain, 157, 377; as an unalienable right in America, 275; as usual format of state governments, 275; in Great Britain, 356. *See also* Balanced government; Checks and balances; Division of powers; House of Representatives, U.S.; Judiciary, U.S.; Mixed government; President, U.S.; Senate, U.S.

Sevier, John (N.C.), 194n

Shays, Daniel (Mass.), 391

Shays's Rebellion, 42, 57

Shipbuilding, 109. *See also* Sailors

Short, William (Va.; CC:Vol. 1, 455n), 106
— letter to, 3–4

Slave Trade: defense of prohibition on Congress' power to ban, 43; criticism of prohibition on Congress to ban, 46–50, 255, 370, 402, 413–14; argument that it will continue and expand under Constitution, 50; not prohibited by Articles of Confederation, 54n; prohibited in Pa., 391, 391n–92n

Slavery: of Israelites, 38; criticism of, 47–48, 50, 402; idea of is illegitimate, 49; slaves confiscated by British during Revolution, 49; argument that Constitution will lead to abolition of, 50, 53n–54n; and runaways during Revolution, 50; criticism of Constitution for requiring aid to states to quell slave revolts, 51; declared unconstitutional in Mass., 54n; importance of Philadelphia in leading opposition to, 415

Smilie, John (Pa.; CC:Vol. 4, 354n), 254

Smith, John (N.Y.)
— letter from: quoted, 103

Smith, Melancton (N.Y.), 146. *See also* A Plebeian

Smith, William Stephens (N.Y.; CC:Vol. 2, 465n), 227

Social Compact: description of, 50, 134, 135, 168; rights of man are main pro-

— in Confederation Congress: legislatures of have power to recall delegates to Congress, 68, 304; representation of in, 122, 126, 273, 373n; have not elected best men to, 226; have right to instruct delegates to, 273

— governments of: constitutions of do not define treason, 16; legislatures of misuse powers, 73, 99, 290–91, 291; are too democratic, 97; effectiveness of, 151; legislatures of ratify amendments to Articles of Confederation, 152, 274; restrictions on under Articles of Confederation, 274, 364–65; size of legislatures of, 275; have separation of powers, 275; bicameralism versus unicameralism, 275; state senators in, 275–76, 291, 373n; election of executive councils in, 276; election of governors in, 276; large legislatures are as orderly as small ones, 299; as buffer between people and Congress concerning taxation, 300; described as democratic republics, 300; most have annual elections, 304; rotation in office in constitutions of, 306; high expenses of, 357

See also Articles of Confederation; Commerce; Congress under Articles of Confederation; Constitutional Convention; Conventions, state; Economic conditions under the Confederation; Political conditions under the Confederation; Ratification, procedure for

STAY LAWS, 390, 414–15. See also Tender laws

"A STEADY AND OPEN REPUBLICAN" (Christopher Gadsden), 387–89n

STEUBEN, FRIEDRICH WILLIAM AUGUSTUS, BARON VON (N.Y.), 186, 187n

STRONG, CALEB (Mass.; CC:Vol. 1, 357n), 54n, 227

STUART, DAVID (Va.; CC:Vol. 1, 386n)

— letter to: quoted, 187

SUFFRAGE, 275–76, 372n. See also Elections, U.S.

SULLIVAN, JOHN (N.H.; CC:Vol. 1, 516n), 41, 42n, 104, 395

— letters to, 40–42n, 380–81; quoted, 104

SUPREMACY CLAUSE: opposition to treaties as supreme law of land, 41, 259; Congress will be supreme, 46; endangers rights guaranteed in state constitutions, 241, 242, 259, 346, 349, 361; and fed-

eral jurisdiction over federal capital, 367. See also Judiciary, U.S.

SUPREME COURT, U.S.: See Judiciary, U.S.

SYMMES, JOHN CLEVES (N.J.), 178, 179n–80n, 199–201

THE TALMUD, 38

TAXATION: denial of danger of from Constitution, 122; power over determines sovereignty, 135; central government for America needs power of, 138; objection that states are deprived of sources of, 142; danger from under Constitution, 156, 159, 231, 246, 294, 297, 298, 349–50, 354, 358, 379; Constitution will raise, 161; should always be based on representation, 183; praise of Constitution's provision for, 248, 250; is necessary, but should be guarded in representatives, 272, 274, 301; is required in society, 294

— under Articles of Confederation: Congress should be given power to levy excise taxes, 28; states do not pay, 107, 145, 356, 357; defective in, 160–61; need to augment Congress' power over, 164; amount paid by states, 166n, 353–54; power of praised, 298

— direct: opposition to three-fifths clause apportionment for, 43–44; criticism of Congress' power to levy, 157, 255, 294, 357–58; will only be used under Constitution when absolutely necessary, 179; Congress should have power over only after requisitions on states are not paid, 240, 241, 244–45, 245, 246, 358

— excises: Confederation Congress should be given power to levy, 28; opposition to Congress' power to levy, 139, 156, 246, 357–58

— imposts: opposition to Congress' power to levy, 139–40, 357–58; import duties easiest to collect in U.S., 192

— land tax: opposition to Congress' power to levy, 139; too difficult to collect in U.S., 192

— poll tax: under Israelites, 38, 39; opposition to Congress' power to levy, 139, 241, 245, 246

— purse and sword: objection to coupling of, 46, 295, 355

See also Debt, U.S.; Duties; Expenses of government; House of Representatives,